Dictionary of the Vietnam War

Dictionary of the Vietnam War

EDITED BY

James S. Olson

GREENWOOD PRESS

NEW YORK · WESTPORT, CONNECTICUT · LONDON

Library of Congress Cataloging-in-Publication Data

Dictionary of the Vietnam War.

  Bibliography: p.
  Includes index.
    1. Vietnamese Conflict, 1961–1975—Dictionaries.
I. Olson, James Stuart, 1946–   .
DS557.7.D53   1988   959.704′3′0321   87-12023
ISBN 0-313-24943-1 (lib. bdg. : alk. paper)

British Library Cataloguing in Publication Data is available.

Library of Congress Catalog Card Number: 87-12023
ISBN: 0-313-24943-1

First published in 1988

Greenwood Press, Inc.
88 Post Road West, Westport, Connecticut 06881

Printed in the United States of America

The paper used in this book complies with the
Permanent Paper Standard issued by the National
Information Standards Organization (Z39.48-1984).

    8   7   6   5   4   3

Contents

Preface

Only now, fifteen years after the last U.S. combat troops left Southeast Asia, are Americans finally coming to terms with the Vietnam War, recognizing the complex political and ideological forces at work there, realizing the tremendous cost of the conflict, but at the same time coming to appreciate the individual sacrifices of millions of men and women who served there under the most difficult of circumstances. Historians will, no doubt, continue to debate the origins of the conflict and, with "twenty-twenty hindsight," suggest what might have been. No one, however, will question that the Vietnam War was a seminal event in modern American history—a watershed against which the past will be measured for generations. In a sense, the war ended "the American century," that period of unrivaled power and virtue the United States enjoyed between 1918 and 1965. During the Vietnam years, liberalism gave way to cynicism, internationalism to isolationism, and naive innocence to cold reality. Quite simply, America was a different place in 1975 than it had been in 1964; life would never be the same again, and the Vietnam War was responsible.

This *Dictionary of the Vietnam War* is designed to provide a ready reference tool for students and scholars. Its major focus is the thirty years between 1945 and 1975, although critically important individuals and events from earlier years are also discussed. The *Dictionary* provides brief descriptive essays on most of the people, legislation, military operations, and controversies important to American participation in the Vietnam War. References at the end of each entry provide sources of additional information for those wishing to pursue the subject further. Entries are arranged in alphabetical order. Cross-references within the text of most entries, designated by an asterisk, will help the reader to find related items. Five appendixes provide a description of the population of South Vietnam, the minority groups of South Vietnam, a glossary of acronyms and slang expressions, a selected bibliography of the Vietnam War, and a chronology of the Vietnam War.

I wish to express my thanks to the scholars who contributed essays to the

Dictionary. Their names appear at the end of the entries they wrote. All unsigned entries were written by me. I would also like to thank the librarians who assisted me in locating hard-to-find material. I am especially grateful to J. Larry Murdock, Ann Holder, Paul Culp, and Bill Bailey, all of the Newton Gresham Library at Sam Houston State University. Finally, I am indebted to my wife, Judy, for her patience in tolerating what has seemed an endless task in producing this volume.

—James S. Olson

Dictionary
of the
Vietnam War

·A·

A-1 SKYRAIDER

During the Vietnam War, fighter-bombers (*see* Fighters) played a critical role in providing close air support to American and South Vietnamese soldiers. The propeller-driven A-1 Skyraider was frequently the battlefield choice of commanders who needed fighter-bomber support. Nicknamed the "Spad," the A-1 had been operational since 1946, and could deliver up to 8,000 pounds of explosives, including napalm,* phosphorus, and cluster bomb* units. The A-1 could fire rockets and carry four 20mm cannons that together could fire over 2,000 rounds a minute. Although its maximum air speed was only 318 mph, the A-1 could remain airborne over targets much longer than jet aircraft, and it was also highly accurate delivering its bomb loads. During the Korean War the A-1 had been widely used on naval aircraft carriers, but by the early 1960s the navy was replacing the A-1 with the A-4 Skyhawk* jet. The A-1s were transferred to the United States Air Force* and the Vietnamese Air Force,* where they were first employed in Operation Farmgate.* By 1968 the A-1 Skyraider was the backbone of close air support operations in the Vietnamese Air Force.

Source: Steve Birdsall, *The A-1 Skyraider*, 1970.

A-4 SKYHAWK

The A-4 Skyhawk flew more missions in Vietnam than any other naval aircraft. Developed in the mid-1950s by Douglas, the A-4 could carry a maximum payload of 8,200 pounds and a functional payload of 5,000 pounds. Its maximum speed was 685 mph and it had a range of 700 miles. Its built-in armament consisted of two 20mm cannons. The A-4 Skyhawk was propelled by either a 7,700-pound thrust Wright J65 engine or a 8,500-pound thrust Pratt and Whitney J52 engine.

Source: Ray Wagner, *American Combat Planes*, 1982.

A–6 INTRUDER

Manufactured by Grumman, the A–6 Intruder was equipped with two 9,300-pound Pratt and Whitney J52 turbojets and had a maximum speed of 640 mph. The A–6 could carry up to 15,000 pounds of ordnance and had a range of 1,077 miles (3,100 miles when equipped with external fuel tanks). Its advanced navigation system, known as DIANE (Digital Integrated Attack Navigation Equipment), had a terrain avoidance radar capability and allowed the A–6 to fly long distances at low altitudes, regardless of weather conditions. Its forte was pinpoint attacks at night or in poor weather conditions.

Sources: John Morrocco, *The Vietnam Experience. Thunder from Above: Air War 1941–1968*, 1985; Ray Wagner, *American Combat Planes*, 1982.

A–7 CORSAIR II

The Vought A–7 Corsair II first deployed to Vietnam aboard the USS *Ranger* in December 1967. It was powered by an 11,350-pound thrust TF30 turbofan and had a maximum speed of 679 mph, a range of 700 miles, and an ordnance capacity of 20,000 pounds. A later version, the A–7E, which entered combat in 1970, had a 15,000-pound thrust Allison TF41 engine and a 20mm M61 Vulcan rapid-fire cannon. Its weapons delivery system was highly accurate, and the A–7 was especially useful in attacking the Ho Chi Minh Trail* and making night assaults on Hanoi* and Haiphong.

Sources: Ray Wagner, *American Combat Planes*, 1982; Anthony Robinson, "Air Forces in Vietnam," in John S. Bowman, ed., *The Vietnam War: An Almanac*, 1985.

ABRAMS, CREIGHTON

Creighton Abrams was born in Springfield, Massachusetts, on September 16, 1914. Described as "tough," "crusty," and "gruff," Abrams graduated from West Point in 1936. Considered one of the great combat officers of World War II, Abrams served in General George Patton's Third Army and took part in the relief of Bastogne. Upon assuming command of Military Assistance Command, Vietnam* (MACV) in July 1968, when General William Westmoreland* left, Abrams shifted American tactics in the direction of small-unit operations in an attempt to keep pressure on Vietcong* and North Vietnamese Army* (NVA) forces while avoiding the heavy American casualties that often resulted from Westmoreland's large-scale "search and destroy"* sweeps. Also, in the latter half of 1968, Abrams launched the Accelerated Pacification Campaign,* in which the United States and South Vietnam committed a major share of their military resources to controlling the Vietnamese countryside. The campaign enjoyed only short-term success.

As MACV commander, Abrams was responsible for implementing the Vietnamization* program, which had originated in the Johnson* administration and which was announced with much public fanfare in 1969 by President Richard M. Nixon.* Abrams viewed the Cambodian incursion of 1970 (*see* Operation Binh Tay) as a means of keeping Vietcong and NVA pressure off the gradual

American withdrawal mandated by Vietnamization. Although Abrams privately doubted the ability of the South Vietnamese army to replace U.S. troops effectively, he was successful in carrying out the American troop withdrawal called for by Vietnamization. During his tenure as MACV commander, Abrams saw American strength reach its peak (543,482) in April 1969, and also witnessed the departure of the last United States Army* combat unit (3rd Battalion, 21st Infantry) from Vietnam in August 1972. Abrams was promoted to chief of staff of the United States Army in 1972, a post he held until his death on September 4, 1974.

Sources: R. E. Dupuy, *The Compact History of the U.S. Army*, 1973; David Halberstam, *The Best and the Brightest*, 1972; George C. Herring, *America's Longest War: The United States in Vietnam, 1950–1975*, 1986; *New York Times*, September 5, 1974.

Sean A. Kelleher

AC–47 GUNSHIP

Technological developments have always been the result of war. The era of American involvement in Vietnam was no exception. One of the most exciting was the development of fixed-wing gunships.* The theory behind the development of gunships was simple; it involved the placement of rapid-fire weapons on one side of a large aircraft to fire at ground targets as the firing platform circled an area at a constant altitude and speed. The development of this idea in Vietnam stemmed directly from unique battlefield situations in the theater of operations and eventually evolved into an effective and impressive weapon system.

The selection of the C–47 as the first gunship during the early years of the Vietnam War married the new 7.62mm minigun to one of the air force's oldest operational aircraft. The first flight of a Douglas DC–3, the civilian version of the C–47, took place on December 18, 1935, but the aircraft earned a reputation as a versatile performer during World War II when the armed forces had nearly 10,000 in service. Although most of the C–47s had been retired by 1960, air force personnel realized that it was the ideal platform for the mounting of weapons with which to attack ground targets.

The formation of the first AC–47 gunship squadron began in May 1965 when Headquarters United States Air Force* (USAF) directed the Air Force Logistics Command (AFLC) to prepare a feasibility study on installation of 7.62mm guns on twenty C–47s. This study demonstrated the practicality of such a modification and during the summer of 1965 the Warner-Robins Air Materiel Area, Robins Air Force Base (AFB), Georgia, undertook the work, adding not only three miniguns to the port side but also attaching flare launchers to make the aircraft capable of night operations.

Even as these modifications were underway at Robins AFB, crews for these aircraft were being trained at Forbes AFB, Kansas, by the Tactical Air Command (TAC). Early in November 1965 the USAF activated the 4th Air Commando Squadron as the operational unit for these crews and aircraft and began deployment to Vietnam. During the remainder of 1965 this squadron flew 1,441 hours and 277 combat missions. It expended 137,136 rounds of ammunition and 2,548 flares and received credit for 105 Vietcong* killed. Most of its operations were conducted during the hours of darkness in support of fort and village defense.

These operations demonstrated the effectiveness of the AC–47 gunship not only as a powerful destructive force but also as an instrument of terror. Its capability to strike quickly in far-flung parts of Southeast Asia and the tremendous firepower it possessed was thought by American commanders a valuable tool in deterring Vietcong activity. It could be used both for air defense and air interdiction. The AC–47 gunship also flew reconnaissance and forward air control missions at night. So successful were combat operations that the USAF increased the number of AC–47s operated by the 4th Air Commando Squadron to twenty-two, and on October 25, 1967, it activated the 14th Air Commando Squadron with a complement of sixteen additional AC–47s. Later a third squadron operating AC–47 aircraft was activated, and the three units were redesignated Special Operations Squadrons.

During 1969 the AC–47 gunships flew their last operational missions in Vietnam. They were being replaced by AC–130 gunships* and helicopter gunships* that were more versatile, speedy, and less aged. For four years the AC–47 had been an integral part of the Vietnam War, recognized as both an offensive and defensive weapon. A total of fifty-three AC–47s had been built at a cost of about $6.7 million, many of which had been in operation for three or more years. As the gunship pioneer, the AC–47 was the progenitor of a second generation of improved gunships and tactics that followed between 1970 and 1973.

Source: Jack S. Ballard, *The United States Air Force in Southeast Asia: Development and Employment of Fixed-Wing Gunships, 1962–1972*, 1982.

Roger D. Launius

AC–130 GUNSHIP

The AC–130s were fixed-wing gunships introduced to the Vietnam War in 1968. They were C–130* transport ships converted to AC–130s by equipping them with two multibarreled machine guns, four 20mm Vulcan multibarreled guns and 40mm Bofors cannon, along with infrared sensors, radar, low-light television, and laser target designators. The AC–130s were used both to provide ground support and to interdict supplies being shipped along the Ho Chi Minh Trail.*

Sources: Jack Ballard, *The United States Air Force in Southeast Asia: Development and Employment of Fixed-Wing Gunships, 1962–1972*, 1982; William W. Momyer, *Airpower in Three Wars*, 1978.

Robert S. Browning III

ACCELERATED PACIFICATION CAMPAIGN

After the Tet Offensive* of February 1968, the United States renewed its commitment to a stronger military and political position in the Republic of Vietnam,* and that became especially important later in the year when Vietcong* representatives at the Paris peace talks* began hinting at their willingness to accept a "cease-fire in place." If that really was a possibility, it was important for the United States to gain control of the countryside through more aggressive pacification programs. On November 1, 1968, the United States launched the Accelerated Pacification Campaign, with an objective of expanding government control over 1,200 villages currently controlled by the Vietcong. The Accelerated Pacification Campaign was put under the control of William Colby*, and he was given a ninety-day time frame for the program. The United States had high hopes for the program because the Vietcong had been badly drained by the Tet Offensive and had essentially adopted a defensive strategy. The Phoenix Program* was launched simultaneously.

The Accelerated Pacification Campaign was basically a "clear and hold"* strategy using Regional Forces* (RF) and Popular Forces* (PF). Operating in or near their home villages, the RF and PF were familiar with the countryside as well as the people, knew how to differentiate between Vietcong and non-political families, and built some confidence because villagers knew they would remain in the area. After destroying or at least expelling the Vietcong infrastructure, Accelerated Pacification then turned its attention to economic development, and included clearing roads, repairing bridges, building schools, and increasing farm production. The Americans also tried to train villagers in free elections and then trained elected officials in village administration. Finally, Accelerated Pacification tried to bring about land reform by distributing land to peasant farmers.

The results of Accelerated Pacification were mixed at best. By March 1970 more than one million hectares of land had been redistributed, and the number of RF and PF engaged in pacification had increased to 500,000 men. They were armed with M–16 rifles* and had received improved training. But destruction of the Vietcong infrastructure was never achieved, nor did Accelerated Pacification really change the way most South Vietnamese looked upon the government of Nguyen Van Thieu.* Nor could Accelerated Pacification really survive the withdrawal of American troops which President Richard Nixon* began implementing in the summer of 1969. As the U.S. military presence declined, the South Vietnamese were unable to fill the vacuum.

Sources: Robert W. Komer, "Pacification: A Look Back," *Army* (June 1970), 20–29; James Walker Trullinger, *Village at War: An Account of Revolution in Vietnam*, 1980; Samuel L. Popkin, "Pacification: Politics and the Village," *Asian Survey* (August 1970).

ACHESON, DEAN GOODERHAM

Dean Acheson was born on April 11, 1893, in Middletown, Connecticut. Coming from a prosperous New England family, he graduated from Yale in 1915 and the Harvard Law School in 1918. Acheson served as private secretary to Supreme Court Justice Louis Brandeis until 1921, practiced law privately in Washington, D.C., until 1933, and then joined the New Deal as under secretary of state. Acheson resigned that post in opposition to the gold buying program of 1933, practiced law again, but then returned to the Franklin D. Roosevelt* administration in 1941 as an assistant secretary of state. He became under secretary of state in August 1946 and secretary of state under Harry S. Truman* in July 1949. Acheson left the State Department in 1953 and returned to his law practice. During the 1960s he advised both the Kennedy* and Johnson* administrations on foreign policy, and became part of the informal policy group known as the "Wise Old Men"* in 1965. By 1966 Acheson began expressing serious reservations about the American presence in South Vietnam, and by 1967 he was urging Lyndon B. Johnson to de-escalate the conflict. Acheson was present at the March 1968 meeting in which the Wise Old Men told Johnson that the war was lost. Dean Acheson died on October 12, 1971.

Sources: Dean Acheson, *Present at the Creation*, 1969; *New York Times*, October 13, 1971; Walter Isaacson and Evan Thomas, *The Wise Men: Six Friends and the World They Made*, 1986.

ADAMS-WESTMORELAND CONTROVERSY

In 1965 Sam Adams was an intelligence officer with the Central Intelligence Agency* (CIA) working on Vietnam. Using captured enemy documents and interrogations of enemy personnel, Adams found support for Pentagon estimates of enemy killed, wounded, captured, and deserted—figures that the news media believed were inflated. Adams also found support for a far higher estimate of the number of enemy in South Vietnam, for the infiltration* rate of regular troops from North Vietnam to the South, and a higher capability for supplying those larger numbers than the U.S. Army intelligence estimates coming out of Military Assistance Command, Vietnam* headquarters in Saigon.*

Adams gradually became the center of a growing controversy. He was unable to gain upper-level support within the CIA for his revisions of the size of the enemy; meetings between intelligence officials of the CIA and various military commands could not reach a compromise figure. General William Westmoreland* was unwilling to change enemy totals, although he was willing to reallocate figures within various categories. With the Tet Offensive* of 1968, Adams felt the battle weakened the enemy less than army officers claimed, since he believed the enemy was originally stronger.

In 1975 Adams made his charges public in *Harper's* magazine, and in January 1982 in a CBS News documentary. The documentary charged General Westmoreland with a conspiracy to report low figures for the enemy. After Westmoreland sued, the resulting court trial in 1985 seemingly found support for Adams's original contention and vindication for his lonely vigil. Westmoreland and CBS settled their suit out of court.

Source: Bob Brewin and Sydney Shaw, *Vietnam on Trial: Westmoreland vs. CBS*, 1986.

AD HOC TASK FORCE ON VIETNAM

The Tet Offensive* of 1968 dealt a deathblow to the American war effort in Vietnam by undermining the political atmosphere at home. Doubtful congressmen began evaluating their positions while the military was requesting greater investment of resources in the conflict. Late in February 1968, General William C. Westmoreland* asked President Lyndon B. Johnson* for the deployment of 200,000 more troops to Southeast Asia, and the president convened the Ad Hoc Task Force on Vietnam to evaluate Westmoreland's request. The debate was also taking place in the midst of the presidential primary campaign of 1968, where Lyndon Johnson was facing considerable pressure from Senators Eugene McCarthy* of Minnesota and Robert F. Kennedy* of New York. Clark Clifford,* the new secretary of defense, chaired the group. The debate was wide-ranging, dealing with the Vietnam War in particular and American commitments abroad in general. General Maxwell Taylor* and Walt W. Rostow,* both presidential advisers, supported the commitment, as did General Earle Wheeler,* chairman of the Joint Chiefs of Staff (*see* Chairman, JCS), but the escalation was opposed by other prominent people, including Paul Nitze,* deputy under secretary of defense, and Paul Warnke,* assistant secretary of defense. Although Clifford took no formal position in the debate, his own doubts about the nature of the war were confirmed. Those opposing the escalation prevailed, and Westmoreland received only 25,000 of the 200,000 troops he requested. Later in March, President Lyndon Johnson announced his decision not to run for reelection and to de-escalate the war effort.

Sources: Harry G. Summers, Jr., *Vietnam War Alamanac*, 1985; Clark M. Clifford, "A Viet Nam Reappraisal," *Foreign Affairs* (July 1969), 601–22; Clark Dougan and Steven Weiss, *The Vietnam Experience: Nineteen Sixty-Eight*, 1983.

AEROMEDICAL EVACUATION　　*See* Medevac

AGENT BLUE　　*See* Defoliation

AGENT ORANGE

To counter the natural advantage that dense jungles offered Vietnamese guerrillas, the U.S. Defense Department developed a strategy of using herbicides (*see* Operation Ranch Hand) and incendiary bombs to defoliate the countryside and disrupt the food supply of the Vietcong* and North Vietnamese Army.* Herbicides were used on a wide scale and had a devastating ecological impact. The most common chemicals used in South Vietnam were Agent Orange, Agent White (*see* defoliation) and Agent Blue (*see* defoliation), the color designations coinciding with the markings on shipping containers. Agents Orange and White were used to defoliate forestlands, while Agent Blue was used primarily for crop destruction. The defoliation campaign lasted from 1962 until the first half of 1969 in Vietnam, and in Cambodia (*see* Kampuchea) until 1971. More than 46 percent of South Vietnam's forest area was sprayed at least once, and 500,000 of the more than 5 million acres sprayed were cropland.

Although the effect of defoliation on controlling guerrilla forces has been hotly debated, the North Vietnamese began claiming in April 1966 that herbicides were causing permanent ocular lesions, chromosome alterations, and congenital deformities in infants, as well as long-term damage to crops, trees, and entire ecosystems. The Defense Department denied those claims, but crop destruction was disastrous for civilians, since mobile military groups were able to find other sources of supply. One result of defoliation was that the United States had to supply food for the Vietnamese people. Tens of thousands of tons of wheat and rice and soybean seeds were shipped to South Vietnam. With the destruction of rice crops, the United States had to import billions of tons of the grain to keep prices stabilized and prevent the economic base from collapsing. A study of the health effects of phenoxy herbicides by Bionetics Research Laboratories completed in 1969 indicated that the tetracholoridbenzo-para-dioxin in Agent Orange caused birth defects. Also, Agent Orange contained dioxin, which is extremely hazardous to health and maintains its toxicity levels up to thirty years. Some symptoms connected with Agent Orange are frequent mood changes, nervousness, severe headaches, chloracne (a chronic rash), loss of sex drive, ringing in the ears, chest pains, miscarriages, stillbirths, cancer, and severe birth defects. In 1970, pending review, Military Assistance Command, Vietnam* stopped the spraying of Agent Orange. Crop destruction and defoliation were finally terminated in 1971.

Vietnam veterans exposed to Agent Orange began complaining of health problems in the mid–1970s, and they filed a class-action suit in 1979 against the Veterans Administration, the Department of Defense, and several manufacturers of the chemical. In response the Pentagon argued that Agent Orange did not cause those symptoms and that it might actually have helped the Vietnamese economy by giving the lumber industry easier access routes to haul wood and small farmers by giving them new space to plant gardens near roads, which provided them with new markets. In an out-of-court settlement, the chemical companies involved established a $180 million fund to compensate veterans with "legitimate" claims. The fund was administered by a federal court; veterans with total disabilities and the families of veterans who died from Agent Orange exposure have access to the fund for damages.

Sources: J. B. Neilands, *Harvest of Death: Chemical Warfare in Vietnam and Cambodia*, 1972; Carol Van Strum, *A Bitter Fog: Herbicides and Human Rights*, 1983; Clifford Linedecker, *Kerry: Agent Orange and an American Family*, 1982; Fred A. Wilcox, *Waiting for an Army to Die: Tragedy of Agent Orange*, 1983.

John E. Wilson and Kim Younghaus

AGENT WHITE   *See* Defoliation

AGNEW, SPIRO THEODORE

Spiro Agnew was born on November 9, 1918, in Baltimore, Maryland. Before World War II he attended Johns Hopkins University and the Baltimore Law School, and after serving in an army armor unit during the war, he graduated from the Baltimore Law School in 1947. Agnew began practicing law and working in local Republican politics, and in 1957 he was appointed to the Baltimore County Zoning Board of Appeals. He won election to the position of county executive in 1962, and in 1966 he won the governorship of Maryland, defeating a segregationist Democrat and earning liberal credentials. During his two terms as governor Agnew became increasingly conservative and strident in his rhetoric. In 1968 he supported Richard Nixon's* candidacy for president, and Nixon rewarded him with the spot of running mate. They won the election over Democrat Hubert Humphrey,* and Agnew became vice president of the United States in 1969.

As vice president, Agnew carried the battle to the opponents and critics of the Nixon administration. Critics of the Vietnam War, whether in Congress* or on campus, were the special targets of Agnew's alliterative verbal assaults. The baiting and buzzwords of the 1950s were dusted off for reuse, together with many new ones of Agnew's invention. But while Agnew carried the cudgels for the administration, his excesses often inflamed an already overheated national debate, and Agnew himself was severely criticized for exacerbating the situation.

Thus, when Agnew's past caught up with him, those who had been the victims of his denunciation could hardly conceal their delight. Faced with the threat of prosecution and impeachment for violation of bribery, conspiracy, and tax laws, on October 10, 1973, Agnew entered into a plea bargaining agreement, pleading no contest (nolo contendere) to one count of income tax invasion, and resigned from the vice presidency.

Sources: *Current Biography*, 1968, pp. 9–12; *Facts on File*, October 7–13, 1973, pp. 840–50.

Joseph M. Rowe, Jr.

AGRICULTURAL REFORM TRIBUNALS

By 1954, after the defeat of the French at the Battle of Dien Bien Phu,* Ho Chi Minh* was firmly in control of Vietnam, especially in the north. Although he faced no real political problems, the economy was in a state of disaster, which he proceeded to make worse through the imposition of awkward ideological controls. Determined to wipe out "landlord" elements as a symbol of his devout Marxism, Ho unleashed cadre teams to search out the landlord class, which he estimated at 2 percent of the rural population. It was a preposterous assumption, since few Vietnamese peasants in the north had more than three to four acres. Nevertheless, by 1955 the cadres had established Agricultural Reform Tribunals in each village to identify the landlords. Accusations, lies, informants, and a vicious neighbor-against-neighbor mentality filled rural villages. Thousands of so-called landlords were killed and thousands more were sent to labor camps. The rural economy was disrupted. The tribunals had quotas of landlords to find and kill, and their justice was quick and capricious. Concerned about the random killings and economic disruption, Ho Chi Minh repudiated the campaigns in August 1956.

Sources: Stanley Karnow, *Vietnam: A History*, 1983; Jean Lacouture, *Ho Chi Minh: A Political Biography*, 1968; Charles Fenn, *Ho Chi Minh: A Biographical Introduction*, 1973.

AGROVILLE PROGRAM

Because of increasing instability and Vietcong* insurgency in rural areas, President Ngo Dinh Diem* launched the Agroville Program in 1959. Its main purpose was to protect Vietnamese peasants from Vietcong terrorism by relocating them to secure areas controlled by the Army of the Republic of Vietnam* (ARVN). The government of South Vietnam built several new communities as part of the Agroville Program, complete with schools, medical clinics, and electricity, but financial incentives for peasants were meager and peasants had no desire to leave ancestral homelands. In many instances ARVN had to forcibly remove peasants to the new agroville communities, and the program inspired bitter resentment against the Diem regime. The Agroville Program was abandoned in 1961 when the government committed its resources to the Strategic Hamlet Program.*

Sources: Denis Warner, *The Last Confucian*, 1963; Douglas S. Blaufarb, *The Counterinsurgency Era: U.S. Doctrine and Performance 1950 to Present*, 1977; William A. Nighswonger, *Rural Pacification in Vietnam*, 1966.

AH–1G HELICOPTER

The AH–1G helicopter, also known as the "Cobra," was first delivered to South Vietnam in 1967 but not deployed in large numbers until 1968. The AH–1G had a length of 52 feet, 11 inches; a weight of 5,783 pounds; and a payload of 1,993 pounds. Its primary purpose was escort reconnaissance and direct fire support. The AH–1G was an attack vehicle firing grenades, machine guns, and rockets in support of American and South Vietnamese infantry.

Sources: John J. Tolson, *Airmobility, 1961–1971*, 1973; Shelby L. Stanton, *Vietnam Order of Battle*, 1981.

AIKEN, GEORGE DAVID

George D. Aiken was born at Dummerston, Vermont, on August 20, 1892. In keeping with family tradition, he was a farmer and a politician. Running as a Republican, Aiken was elected to the Vermont legislature in 1930, lieutenant governor in 1935, and governor in 1937. During two terms in the governor's mansion, Aiken established a record as a progressive maverick, and in 1940 he was elected to the U.S. Senate and became one of the country's most prominent liberal Republicans. In 1954, Aiken gave up thirteen years of seniority on the Labor and Public Welfare Committee to take a seat on the Foreign Relations Committee.* Had he not exercised his option to do so, the seat would have gone to Senator Joseph McCarthy of Wisconsin, whom Aiken thoroughly disliked. During the next twenty years Aiken became one of the most respected members of the committee.

In the 1960s, when President Lyndon B. Johnson* escalated the Vietnam conflict, Aiken at first supported him. But by 1966, he joined the ranks of the doves. In that year, he gave some widely quoted advice to Johnson. He said that the president should pull American troops out of the fighting, and to save face simply "declare the United States the winner and begin de-escalation." Aiken would later point out that President Nixon* had essentially followed that course in extricating American ground forces from Vietnam. In 1975 Aiken retired from the Senate and returned to his beloved farm in Vermont. He died on November 19, 1984.

Sources: George G. Aiken, *The Aiken Senate Diary*, 1976; *New York Times*, November 20, 1984.

Joseph M. Rowe, Jr.

AIR AMERICA

One of the many civilian airlines operating in Southeast Asia, Air America was a Central Intelligence Agency* (CIA) "proprietary." A proprietary is an entity that appears to be a normal, legitimate enterprise but actually is operated and controlled by the CIA. To maintain its appearance as an independent business, Air America engaged in activities common to air carriers, especially cargo transportation. In Southeast Asia, even during the war, businesses continued to operate normally, and so civilian air transport was a necessary and lucrative venture. Approximately 75 percent of Air America's flights were not related to the war or to the CIA's involvement in the war, so Air America employees may even have been unaware of its connection to the agency. However, the company primarily was used by the CIA for its numerous war-related activities.

The pilots and crews that were involved in the clandestine activities of Air America were often military veterans, many of whom had served previous tours of duty in Southeast Asia. While some of the CIA-related Air America flights were undramatic, such as commonplace transportation of personnel, materiel, and payrolls, often the flights were extremely dangerous. They frequently involved trips to remote areas dominated by the enemy, and for security reasons, they were usually flown at night and/or under cover of clouds or fog. Also, they were not confined to Vietnam, since the CIA operated extensively in Cambodia (*see* Kampuchea) and especially Laos* throughout the war. Most of the flights did not involve combat action by the Air America planes, although the aircraft available to Air America did include combat-capable types.

Sources: John Morrocco, *The Vietnam Experience. Rain of Fire; Air War 1969–1973*, 1984; Christopher Robbins, *Air America*, 1979.

Stafford T. Thomas

AIR BASE DEFENSE

In the early morning of November 1, 1964, Communist Vietnamese forces attacked Bien Hoa* Air Base, outside of Saigon.* Positioning six 81mm mortars about 400 meters north of the base, these forces fired some eighty rounds onto parked aircraft and troop billets. These forces then withdrew undetected and unmolested, after killing four American military advisers, wounding thirty others, and hitting twenty B–57 bombers. Of these, five aircraft were completely destroyed. Increasingly after this time American aerial defense forces became attractive targets for Communist forces. Through 1973 there were 475 enemy attacks on American air bases in Vietnam, resulting in 898 American aircraft damaged and 155 service personnel killed in action. An additional 305 aircraft and 154 personnel assigned to the Republic of Vietnam* armed forces were also lost in these attacks.

To counter these attacks the U.S. military directed that forces be deployed to Vietnam to secure these airfields. The first force, the 9th Marine Expeditionary Brigade,* landed at Da Nang* in March 1965. United States Army* and Air Force* air base defense units followed soon thereafter. These units combated several threats present to aircraft in Vietnam: sabotage, sapper infiltration, ground attack, and shelling by standoff weapons. Sabotage was little used. Ground attacks by battalion-sized forces took place on only two occasions. Sapper raids posed a more serious threat, but in terms of numbers and damage, standoff rocket and mortar fire presented the greatest hazard. The air base defense forces were partially successful in countering these threats. From 1969 on attacks decreased every year until the American withdrawal. The casualties and aircraft losses registered similar declines. At the same time, the U.S. air bases in Vietnam were always vulnerable to Communist attack.

Source: Roger P. Fox, *Air Base Defense in the Republic of Vietnam, 1961–1973*, 1979.

Roger D. Launius

AIRBORNE FORCES

The term "airborne" refers to soldiers who parachute into battle. During the Vietnam War, several airborne units—the 101st Airborne Division,* the Third Brigade of the 82nd Airborne Division,* and the 173rd Airborne Brigade*—were deployed to Southeast Asia, but they were used as infantry helicoptered into battle. Except for isolated exceptions, airborne tactics did not play a significant role in the Vietnam War.

Sources: Harry G. Summers, Jr., *Vietnam War Almanac*, 1985; Shelby L. Stanton, *Vietnam Order of Battle*, 1981, and *The Rise and Fall of an American Army: U.S. Ground Troops in Vietnam, 1965–1973*, 1985.

AIR CAVALRY

During the nineteenth century American cavalry units were horse-mounted troops designed to survey enemy positions and provide screens for incoming infantry units. The horse-mounted cavalry gave way during the twentieth century to armored personnel carriers* and tanks. A major innovation of the Vietnam War was the use of air cavalry units where troops are moved into battlefield positions by helicopters. The 1st Cavalry Division* was one of the main air cavalry units in Southeast Asia.

Sources: John J. Tolson, *Airmobility, 1961–1971*, 1973; Shelby L. Stanton, *The Rise and Fall of an American Army: U.S. Ground Troops in Vietnam, 1965–1973*, 1985; Andrew F. Krepinevich, Jr., *The Army and Vietnam*, 1986.

AIRCRAFT CARRIERS

Between 1964 and 1975, the Seventh Fleet's* Task Force 77 operated off the coast of Vietnam in the South China Sea. Until the summer of 1966, there were usually two to three carriers in Task Force 77, but beginning in mid–1966 three to four carriers were usually deployed there. Each carrier wing consisted of between 65 and 100 aircraft—A–4 Skyhawks,* A–1 Skyraiders,* A–7 Corsairs II's,* A–6 Intruders,* F–4 Phantom II's,* and F–8 Crusaders. The aircraft were used over North Vietnam, South Vietnam, Laos,* and Cambodia (*see* Kampuchea) to disrupt enemy supply lines and for close air support of American and South Vietnamese ground operations. Nineteen aircraft carriers served separate missions off the coast of Vietnam between 1964 and 1975: the *America, Constellation, Ticonderoga,** *Yorktown, Franklin D. Roosevelt, Enterprise, Bon Homme Richard, Coral Sea, Forrestal, Hancock, Hornet, Intrepid, Kitty Hawk, Midway, Oriskany, Ranger, Saratoga,* and *Shangri-La.*

Sources: Peter Mersky and Norman Polmar, *The Naval Air War in Vietnam: 1965–1975*, 1981; Edward J. Marolda and G. Wesley Pryce III, *A Short History of the United States Navy and the Southeast Asian Conflict, 1950–1975*, 1984.

AIR-CUSHION VEHICLES

Because of the extensive marshlands of South Vietnam, and the frequent difficulty of moving propeller-driven craft through water thick with grass, the United States and South Vietnam had to develop a river craft giving its own troops the mobility enjoyed by Vietcong* using sampans. What they turned to was the air-cushion vehicle, a modified Bell Aerosystem craft which moved on a base of air about four feet thick. Its speed was up to 75 knots. United States Navy* and Army Special Forces* personnel used air-cushion vehicles to patrol extensive areas of the Mekong Delta.* Generally, the air-cushion vehicles were plagued with problems, including heavy fuel consumption, noise, and frequent breakdowns.

Sources: Edward J. Marolda and G. Wesley Pryce III, *A Short History of the United States Navy and the Southeast Asian Conflict, 1950–1975*, 1984; Shelby L. Stanton, *Green Berets at War*, 1985; Edgar C. Doleman, Jr., *The Vietnam Experience: Tools of War*, 1984.

AIR DEFENSE, NORTH VIETNAM

The North Vietnamese constructed the most elaborate air defense system in the world during the 1960s and 1970s. Beginning in 1965 North Vietnam began installing Soviet SA–2 surface-to-air missiles, or SAM.* They also employed MiG–17s and MiG–21s to attack American bombers. Finally, North Vietnam used a variety of antiaircraft weapons against American planes: 37mm guns which fired eighty 1.6-pound shells a minute to an altitude of 9,000 feet; 57mm

S–60s which fired seventy 6-pound shells a minute to 15,000 feet; 8mm M1944s which fired twenty 20-pound shells a minute to 30,000 feet; 100mm guns which fired fifteen 35-pound shells a minute to 45,000 feet; and 130mm guns which fired twelve 74-pound shells a minute to 45,000 feet.

Sources: Paul Burbage, et al., *The Battle for the Skies Over North Vietnam, 1964–1972*, 1976; Anthony Robinson, ''Air Forces in Vietnam,'' in John S. Bowman, ed., *The Vietnam War: An Almanac*, 1985.

AIR FORCE, UNITED STATES

The United States Air Force played a major role in the American military effort during the Vietnam War, providing close air support, tactical airlift,* and high-altitude bombing strikes by B–52* bombers. The Seventh Air Force* directed all close air support, tactical air-lift, and the Military Air Command, while the Strategic Air Command directed the B–52 strikes. During the war the air force had 1,737 personnel killed-in-action, nearly 3,500 wounded, and lost 2,257 aircraft.

Sources: Carl Berger, ed., *The United States Air Force in Southeast Asia, 1961–1973*, 1977; John Morrocco, *The Vietnam Experience: Thunder from Above*, 1985, and *The Vietnam Experience: Rain of Fire*, 1984; Harry G. Summers, Jr., *Vietnam War Almanac*, 1985.

AIR FORCE, VIETNAMESE   *See* Vietnamese Air Force

AIRMOBILE OPERATIONS

Airmobile operations involved the use of helicopters to transport troops into battle and to provide fire support at battle sites. Instead of transporting troops into battle while artillery barrages prepared the way, airmobile operations had transport helicopters move troops simultaneously with artillery and gunship fire, keeping the enemy off guard. During the Vietnam War, airmobile operations were used extensively by the United States Army* and Marine Corps,* but the major airmobile unit was the 101st Airborne Division.* Since airmobile operations had not even been tested until the 1950s when reliable helicopters were functioning, Vietnam became the combat breakthrough for airmobile tactics. They proved to be the major tactical innovation of the Vietnam War.

Sources: John J. Tolson, *Airmobility, 1961–1971*, 1973; John H. Hay, Jr., *Tactical and Materiel Innovations*, 1975.

AIRMUNITIONS SUPPLY

Beginning in 1965 the United States Air Force* in Southeast Asia began extensive combat operations, requiring the acquisition and shipment to the theater of a vast quantity of conventional bombs, rockets, ammunition, and associated ordnance. The Air Force Logistics Command (AFLC), charged with support of operational weapons used by the air force, procured these airmunitions, while the Military Air Transport Service, later renamed the Military Airlift Command,*

and the Navy's Military Sealift* Transport System transported the necessary materiel to Southeast Asia. As operations increased in the combat theater during the latter 1960s, these organizations created a pipeline for airmunition movement from American bases to theater dispersal sites. Based on a requirement to maintain a 30-day supply at the forward Southeast Asian bases and a 120-day supply in the Philippines,* the AFLC was forced to plan for airmunitions resupply seven to eight months ahead of estimated operational usage.

To reduce these excessively long lead times in 1965 and 1966, the Department of Defense approved a plan for dedicated transport of munitions to Southeast Asia. The navy made available five cargo ships with a combined capacity of 35,300 tons, and the air force developed the Southeast Asia Airlift system, designated by the acronym SEAIR, to move all types of munitions used in Vietnam. In all, more than one million tons of airmunitions were moved to Southeast Asia between 1965 and 1973. The system worked effectively from 1966 on as bombs, airmunitions, flares, rockets, missiles, and assorted ordnance were moved to combat areas on a timely basis.

Source: Bernard J. Termena, "Logistics in War and Peace," in *Logistics: An Illustrated History of AFLC and Its Antecedents, 1921–1981* (Wright-Patterson AFB, Ohio: AFLC Office of History, n.d.)

Roger D. Launius

AIR POWER

Throughout the more than a decade of American involvement in Vietnam, one critical factor allowed the United States to maintain a military superiority: air power. Air power is a concept, a philosophy developed over several generations by thoughtful flyers and seemingly validated by the conduct of World War II. At its fundamental level it is the ability of an air force to take and maintain control of the skies over its armies; to strike at enemy resources such as combat forces, transportation facilities, and industrial complexes; and to support ground units through the projection of force over long distances.

A certain tension between United States Air Force* resources allocated to the tactical mission of ground support and air interdiction of enemy forces behind the battle lines and those allocated to the strategic bombing of enemy industrial and transportation resources has been present since the 1930s. The ideal of strategic bombing, developed between the wars and validated during World War II, became the dominant air force goal thereafter. The primacy of strategic thinking was reflected in the first postwar division of the nation's air resources into three commands in the late 1940s: Strategic Air Command, Air Defense Command, and Tactical Air Command. The first was given more than 100,000 people, the second 26,000, and the third 7,000.

The use of air power in Southeast Asia followed patterns established early in American strategic thinking. Believing that air power alone might succeed in containing the insurgents in South Vietnam, early in the 1960s the United States Air Force and Navy* adopted a contingency plan which called for a holding action in South Vietnam using air strike squadrons positioned around the periphery of China. By relying on technology rather than manpower, planners contended, this approach would avoid getting the United States bogged down on the ground in Asia. But air power without ground commitment was insufficient, and in April 1965 President Lyndon B. Johnson* sent American ground forces to Vietnam. Other steps followed in rapid succession and before long the air force was fighting four air wars: North Vietnam, South Vietnam, northern Laos,* and southern Laos. The bombing* campaign against North Vietnam never succeeded as intended, in part because of political decisions to halt operations and in part because of fragmented control by service representatives. The second air war in Southeast Asia, the one fought in South Vietnam, was also less than effective because it was pursued simultaneously by at least six air forces. The tactical air force, the navy, the United States Marines* and Army,* the Vietnamese Air Force,* and the Strategic Air Force of fifty or so B–52s* each pursued a fragmented strategy of operations. The two air wars in Laos were attempts to interrupt the flow of men and supplies coming out of North Vietnam, westward toward the Plain of Jars, and along the Ho Chi Minh Trail* toward South Vietnam. Once again, politics at both the international and interservice levels hampered effective operations. Indeed, air power in the Vietnam War suffered from the traditional drawbacks of coalition warfare.

Sources: John Schlight, "The Impact of the Orient on Air Power," in Joe C. Dixon, ed., *The American Military and the Far East: Proceedings of the Ninth Military History Symposium USAF Academy, 1980*, 1980; Robert Frank Futrell, *Aces and Aerial Victories: The United States Air Force in Southeast Asia, 1965–1973*, 1976.

Roger D. Launius

AK–47

The AK–47 was the basic infantry weapon of the North Vietnamese Army* (NVA) and the Vietcong* (VC). Originally manufactured by the Soviet Union,* most of these "assault rifles" used in the war were made in the People's Republic of China,* which was the major supplier of armaments to NVA and VC forces. Also known as the Kalishnikov, after its Russian inventor, this weapon was sturdy, reliable, compact, and relatively lightweight. It fired a 7.62mm bullet in a fully automatic mode (continuous firing, like a machine gun, as long as the trigger was squeezed). The high muzzle velocity (speed of the bullet after firing) and the tumbling action of the bullet at the point of impact contributed to its effectiveness since the results were large entry and exit wounds, severe tissue damage, and extensive trauma in body areas near the wound. The combination of these effects plus its rapid-fire capability meant that accuracy was not a major requirement, thus reducing the training time before a soldier could be sent into combat.

Most armaments analysts judge the AK–47, which normally holds thirty bullets, to be superior to the U.S. M–16,* which became the standard weapon of American, Korean, and South Vietnamese troops. It was more durable and less adversely affected by the climate* and conditions of Vietnam. There are a number of accounts of cases in which American troops preferred to use the AK–47 and in fact did use it when combat conditions permitted. The continuing popularity of this weapon is illustrated by its use in many military hostilities since the Vietnam War.

Sources: Ray Bonds, ed., *The Vietnam War*, 1983; Edgar C. Doleman, Jr., *The Vietnam Experience: Tools of War*, 1984; Edward Clinton Ezell, *The Great Rifle Controversy*, 1984.

Stafford T. Thomas

ALI, MUHAMMAD

Muhammad Ali was born as Cassius Clay on January 18, 1942, in Louisville, Kentucky. He began boxing at the age of twelve, won two Golden Gloves championships, and in 1960 took the gold medal at the Olympic Games in Rome. Patterning himself after the wrestler Gorgeous George, he developed into a showman, and in 1964 he won the heavyweight championship by defeating Sonny Liston. Immediately after becoming champion he joined the Black Muslims and took the name Muhammad Ali. Two years later his draft* board revoked his 1-Y deferment, which he had received for failing the IQ test, and reclassified him 1-A. Ali appealed for deferment as a conscientious objector on religious principles. "I ain't got no quarrel with those Vietcong,* anyway," he said. "They never called me nigger." His appeal was denied and he was drafted on April 18, 1967. Ali refused to go, the World Boxing Association stripped him of the championship, and in June 1967 he was convicted of violating the Selective Service Act, fined $10,000, and sentenced to five years in prison. Ali became a hero of the antiwar movement,* as well as for poor people and blacks. In June 1970 the Supreme Court reversed his conviction, and in October 1974 Ali regained the heavyweight championship. He retired from the ring in 1980. Later that year President Jimmy Carter appointed him a special envoy to Africa to urge an African boycott of the 1980 Moscow Olympic games.

Source: Muhammad Ali, *The Greatest*, 1975.

John Ricks

ALVAREZ, EVERETT, JR.

A native of San Jose, California, Lieutenant Everett Alvarez, Jr., was stationed on the USS *Constellation* in the South China Sea at the time of the Gulf of Tonkin Resolution* in 1964. Piloting an A–4 Skyhawk,* Alvarez was shot down over North Vietnam on August 5, 1964. He was transferred to the "Hanoi Hilton"* prison and spent the next eight years as a prisoner of war. Alvarez was the first American pilot taken prisoner by the North Vietnamese.

Source: Terrence Maitland and Steven Weiss, *The Vietnam Experience: Raising the Stakes*, 1982.

AMERICAL DIVISION   *See* 23rd Infantry Division

AMERICAN FRIENDS OF VIETNAM

Formed in the fall of 1955, the American Friends of Vietnam (also known as the Vietnam Lobby) had its origins in 1950 after a meeting between Wesley Fishel of Michigan State University and Ngo Dinh Diem,* then living in self-imposed exile. At Fishel's urging, Diem came to the United States where he met Cardinal Spellman, Senators Mike Mansfield* and John Kennedy,* and Supreme Court Justice William Douglas, all of whom became Lobby supporters. Friends of Vietnam was an odd aggregation of former leftist intellectuals, conservative generals, and liberal politicians. Their search for a "third way" or "independent nationalist alternative" to "communist totalitarianism" grew out of the Cold War and McCarthyism as many liberals fought to prove their anti-communism rather than attack red-baiting witch-hunts. To prove his Americanism, Senator Kennedy gave a major speech in April 1954 in which he opposed any negotiated settlement allowing Ho Chi Minh* participation in Vietnamese governance.

Lobby members convinced officials in the Eisenhower* administration that Diem, an anti-Communist untainted by French or Japanese association, was right for premier. Eisenhower, however, was never really sold on Diem. In 1955 Diem's regime tottered, but he successfully confronted the Binh Xuyen* and the Hoa Hao* and Cao Dai* religious sects, enabling the Friends of Vietnam to use their political power and press contacts to maneuver Eisenhower into reaffirming and increasing support for "Free Vietnam" against Communist aggression. This required selling Diem to Americans as an Asian democrat, no easy job given Diem's often antidemocratic remarks. The Vietnam Lobby eventually created a number of myths to bolster American support for Diem: (1) the "miracle myth" of political stability, economic development, land reform, and refugee resettlement; (2) the "democratic myth" justifying refusal to hold reunification elections mandated by the Geneva Accords* because Communists would win by subverting the election process; (3) the myth that refugees* moving south were portrayed as peasants "voting with their feet" against "Communist oppression"; and (4) the myth that North Vietnamese aggression necessitated Diem's totalitarian measures and substantial increases in American military assistance.

While possessing grains of truth, these myths created false images. "Stability" resulted from brutal oppression. The local economy was disintegrating, thanks partially to American aid. Land reform was a failure, and Diem's favoritism toward northern refugees created animosity among native southerners. Ho Chi Minh was a hero even in the south and would have defeated Diem in both northern and southern Vietnam in a fair election. Rather than common peasants, northern refugees were almost exclusively Catholics having served either in the French colonial government or the French Union Forces* and were urged to migrate by U.S. General Edward Lansdale's* propaganda campaign. The Vietcong* organized resistance to Diem over the North Vietnamese government's opposition at first. The Lobby's fealty to Diem was short-lived. After his murder, the Lobby sent a congratulatory telegram to the generals.

Sources: Frances FitzGerald, *Fire in the Lake: The Vietnamese and the Americans in Vietnam*, 1972; Robert Sheer and Warren Hinckle, "The Vietnam Lobby," *Ramparts*, January 25, 1969, pp. 31–36; Denis Warner, *The Last Confucian*, 1963; Hillaire Du Berrier, *Background to Betrayal: The Tragedy of Vietnam*, 1965.

Samuel Freeman

AMPHIBIOUS FORCES

Task Force 76 of the Seventh Fleet* was responsible for amphibious action during the Vietnam War. Using transport and cargo ships, helicopters, tank landing ships, and dock landing ships, Task Force 76 carried out large numbers of amphibious assaults, especially in I Corps* where the Marine Amphibious Force was operating. Amphibious forces, including Task Force 76 and Task Force 76.8, assisted in the removal of refugees* from Cambodia (*see* Kampuchea) and South Vietnam, as well as American personnel, during the evacuations of 1975.

Sources: Peter L. Hilgartner, *The Marines in Vietnam, 1954–1973*, 1974; Edward J. Marolda and G. Wesley Pryce III, *A Short History of the United States Navy and the Southeast Asia Conflict, 1950–1975*, 1984; Harry G. Summers, Jr., *Vietnam War Almanac*, 1985.

AN LOC, BATTLE OF (1972)

Between April 13 and July 11, 1972, the siege of An Loc was a major part of the North Vietnamese Eastertide Offensive.* An Loc was the capital of Binh Long Province, an area approximately 65 miles north of Saigon.* Combined Vietcong* and North Vietnamese Army* (NVA) forces left their Cambodian bases and captured Loc Ninh, a town 15 miles north of An Loc. The ARVN 5th Division (*see* Army of the Republic of Vietnam) went up to defend An Loc, and the NVA then surrounded the town and cut off reinforcements. Through more than three months of intense fighting, the South Vietnamese held their ground, enjoying massive support from American B–52* bombing sorties.* On July 11, 1972, the North Vietnamese and Vietcong ended the battle and withdrew from Binh Long Province.

Sources: Tom Carhart, *Battles and Campaigns in Vietnam, 1954–1984*, 1984; Ngo Quang Truong, *The Easter Offensive of 1972*, 1980; G. H. Turley, *The Easter Offensive: Vietnam 1972*, 1985.

ANNAM

Along with Tonkin* and Cochin China,* Annam was the name applied by the French to one of the three major regions of Vietnam. Annam was composed of nearly 57,000 square miles of land joining Cambodia (*see* Kampuchea) and Laos* on the west and the South China Sea on the east, north, and south of the seventeenth parallel (*see* Geneva Accords). Its former capital was Hue* and other principal cities were Binh Dinh, Da Nang,* Quang Tri, and Vinh. Anciently inhabited by the Cham* people, Annam was conquered by the Chinese in the third century B.C. and remained a colony until the revolution of 986. The Chinese were expelled by invading Annamites, retook the area in 1407, and were expelled again in 1428, after which Annam remained an independent monarchy until 1802, when the French brought it under their control.

Annam was south of the Red River Delta and at several points was only 30 miles wide. Except for the Montagnard* people in the highlands, most of the people of Annam lived along the coast and, in addition to rice cultivation, engaged in a vigorous coastal trade because of the abundance of sheltered bays along the coast.

Sources: Virginia Thompson, *French Indochina*, 1937; Joseph Buttinger, *The Smaller Dragon*, 1958; Henry McAleavy, *Black Flags in Vietnam: The Story of the Chinese Intervention*, 1968.

ANTICOLONIALISM

Anticolonialism is opposition to a nation's acquisition of colonies or holding of colonies or a particular colony. It may arise in the home country itself, as in American opposition to acquiring the Philippines* in 1898–99 and in later American desire to grant the islands their independence. There was such anticolonialism in Europe as well, especially during the second half of the nineteenth century, the era of rapid colonization.

Anticolonialism also arose in Western nations' colonies, expressed by the National Congress in India, Sarekat Islam and the Indonesian Nationalist party in Indonesia, and Katipunan in the Philippines. Vietnamese anticolonialism first appeared in 1859 when the French captured Saigon* and guerrillas operated in Cochin China* thereafter. In the 1885 rebellion of young Emperor Han Nghi and his chief adviser, Ton That Thuyet, the two were defeated at Hue* and fled to Laos,* where Thuyet organized a resistance movement. Various nationalists and groups existed early in the twentieth century, using Vietnamese reactions to having to recite in school "Our ancestors the Gauls formerly inhabited Gaul." From French schooling Vietnamese also learned of political and civil liberties and realized that they were denied these by colonialism.

Violence reappeared with the Viet Nam Quoc Dan Dang* (Vietnamese Nationalist party), organized by the Chinese Nationalists and never quite eradicated by the French. Ho Chi Minh* created the Indochinese Communist party (see Lao Dong party) in 1929, in Hong Kong, and eventually it helped to create the Vietnam Independence League, the Vietminh,* which later defeated France. Vietnamese anticolonialism, combined with guerrilla war, won victory in the First Indochina War (1946–54) and was crucial to American failure in the second war when the Saigon government was unable to rally its adherents.

The Communist government of unified Vietnam shares another form of anticolonialism with peoples in many former colonies. Expressed in what has come to be called "neutralism," it is the view that economic and cultural colonialism continued after independence and must also be overcome.

Sources: Selig S. Harrison, *The Widening Gulf: Asian Nationalism and American Policy*, 1978; David G. Marr, *Vietnamese Anticolonialism, 1885–1925*, 1971; William J. Duiker, *The Rise of Nationalism in Vietnam, 1900–1941*, 1975.

Robert W. Sellen

ANTIWAR MOVEMENT

The United States has often experienced antiwar movements, but never did the opposition become as influential, divisive, and widespread as during the Vietnam War. From 1961 to 1963, American troop levels in South Vietnam increased from 685 to 16,000. At first, Americans paid scant attention to U.S. involvement. Beginning in 1965, troop levels increased rapidly, reaching a peak of 543,000 in 1969. The increase, with concomitant increases in casualties, piqued public interest and became a formative factor in the development of the antiwar movement. As the war intensified, the antiwar movement—in reality many movements with diverse goals—emerged, and the National Mobilization to End the War in Vietnam became the most well-known group.

The antiwar movement owed much to the civil rights movement, borrowing heavily from its direct action techniques based on civil disobedience. College students became deeply involved, especially those who saw civil rights and the war in Vietnam as directly related. After the Vietcong* attack on Pleiku in 1965, the United States responded with massive air strikes against North Vietnam, and teach-ins occurred on many campuses. Protest marches, speeches, and congressional hearings followed.

Even though very small, the antiwar movement disagreed over methods and goals. Activists divided over whether to protest the war or the system producing it. Increasingly, a generation gap developed. Alienated young Americans developed a counterculture to demonstrate their anger—long hair, bizarre dress, communal living, and drug use. Older, more affluent Americans began to develop questions about the war when troop levels and casualties increased and draft* calls began reaching their children. Some people believed the war was morally wrong, some thought it unwinnable, and some criticized it for diverting attention and resources from more important domestic problems. Some hoped to use the antiwar movement as a vehicle for altering America's economic and political system. Many divergent groups constituted the antiwar movement—students, the New Left, the Old Left, pacifists, Communists, church groups, liberals, conservatives, intellectuals, anarchists, utopians, and idealists. When protests failed to alter policies in 1967 and 1968, the movement increasingly split between those advocating militant, nonviolent civil disobedience and those calling for violent confrontation and the use of force. Groups like the Southern Christian Leadership Conference advocated nonviolence while others like the Students for a Democratic Society* and the Weather Underground became increasingly militant and prone to violent protests. Militant demonstrators attempted to close Selective Service offices, burned or turned in draft cards, destroyed Selective

Service files, boycotted and demonstrated against weapons manufacturers, held massive rallies, bombed ROTC buildings, and practiced self-immolation.

In 1968, the antiwar movement rallied behind the political campaigns of Senator Robert Kennedy* of New York and Senator Eugene McCarthy* of Minnesota. The Tet Offensive* in February 1968 energized the antiwar movement, toppled Lyndon B. Johnson's* political hopes, and convinced increasingly large numbers of "middle-Americans" that the Vietnam War was a losing effort. After the assassinations of Robert Kennedy and Martin Luther King, Jr.,* in the spring of 1968, the antiwar movement temporarily lost some of its momentum, and its frustrations exploded with tempestuous demonstrations at the Democratic National Convention in Chicago.

After Richard Nixon's* election in 1968, the war and protests continued. Nixon began reducing U.S. troop levels but intensified the bombing* of North Vietnam, Laos,* and Cambodia (see Kampuchea). A nationwide moratorium, involving more than a million demonstrators, occurred in October 1969, and widespread protests followed the U.S. invasion of Cambodia and the Kent State University* incident in 1970. By 1971 polls showed that 71 percent of Americans believed the war had been a mistake. The antiwar minority had become the majority. Because of Nixon's Vietnamization policy and the Watergate* controversy, the war consumed less and less political energy in 1972 and 1973, and the antiwar movement gradually dissipated. Activists either devoted their time to other counterculture issues, joined the radical underground, or returned to mainstream society.

Sources: Thomas Powers, *Vietnam, The War at Home*, 1984; Clark Dougan and Samuel Lipsman, *The Vietnam Experience: A Nation Divided*, 1984; Nancy Zaroulis and Gerald Sullivan, *Who Spoke Up? American Protest Against the War in Vietnam 1963–1975*, 1984.

James Hindman

AP BAC, BATTLE OF (1963)

The Battle of Ap Bac began to develop in December 1962. Ap Bac was a village in the Mekong Delta,* approximately 40 miles southwest of Saigon.* Three Vietcong* companies built defensive positions along a mile-long canal connecting Ap Bac with the village of Ap Tan Thoi. The Vietcong dug in behind trees, grass, and shrubs with clear view of the surrounding rice fields. The Army of the Republic of Vietnam* (ARVN) Seventh Division attacked the position, and although they outnumbered the Vietcong by ten to one, they were defeated. ARVN was characterized by incompetent officers and terrible morale. At the end of the battle on January 2, 1963, the ARVN had lost five helicopters and sixty dead, while the Vietcong suffered only three casualties. Although American military advisers in South Vietnam tried to claim the battle a victory because the Vietcong abandoned their position, the engagement showed how difficult a guerrilla war would be and how much learning the United States would have to do about the nature of warfare in Southeast Asia.

Sources: Stanley Karnow, *Vietnam: A History*, 1983; Joseph Buttinger, *Vietnam: A Dragon Embattled*. Vol. 2, *Vietnam at War*, 1967.

AP BIA   *See* Hamburger Hill

APC   *See* Armored Personnel Carrier

APOCALYPSE NOW

Apocalypse Now, a United Artists film directed by Francis Ford Coppola and starring Marlon Brando and Martin Sheen, was released in August 1979 after consuming more than $30 million in four years of production. Based on Joseph Conrad's novella *Heart of Darkness*, the film focuses on a search by Captain Willard (Sheen) for Colonel Walter Kurtz (Brando), a mysterious and insane Special Forces* soldier who has abandoned the war and established an "Angkor Wat-like" kingdom upriver in Cambodia (*see* Kampuchea). Along the way, Willard encounters absurdity after absurdity, from American go-go dancers and Playboy bunnies airlifted into the war zone to Lieutenant Colonel Kilgore (Robert Duval), who slaughters Vietnamese to music and instructs his men in the art of surfing in the middle of battle. Despite defects in the narrative, *Apocalypse Now* is a powerful exposé of the "dementia" of the war and the explosive firepower of the American military machine.

Source: *Magill's Survey of Cinema. English Language Films*, 1981.

Terry Martin

ARC LIGHT OPERATIONS

Code name for the devastating aerial raids of B–52* Stratofortresses against enemy positions in Southeast Asia, the first B–52 Arc Light raid took place on June 18, 1965, on a suspected Vietcong* base north of Saigon.* For this raid elements of the 2nd and 320th Bombardment Wings, of the Strategic Air Command, had deployed from the United States to Anderson Air Force Base, Guam. Shortly after this strike, the results of which were inconclusive, several Americans began to question the advisability of "swatting flies with sledgehammers." During the eight years of Arc Light operations, such criticism became increasingly common.

The B–52s assigned to the Arc Light mission were involved in several types of operations; air interdiction, strategic bombing, and raids on such important targets as Hanoi* and Haiphong were only a few such episodes. For instance, in November 1965, B–52s directly supported American ground forces for the first time, and were used regularly for that purpose thereafter. Perhaps the most important such action involved support of incursions into Cambodia (*see* Kampuchea; Operation Binh Tay) and Laos (*see* Lam Son 719) in 1970 and 1971, operations designed to check flows of North Vietnamese personnel and assets from safe havens on South Vietnam's border into the country.

Between June 18, 1965, and August 18, 1973, the effective dates of Arc Light operations, the Strategic Air Command scheduled 126,663 combat sorties* for B–52s, of which 126,615 were actually launched. Of this total, 125,479 sorties actually reached their target areas and 124,532 successfully released their bombs on target. Geographically, 27 percent of the missions were flown in Laos, 12 percent in Cambodia, and 6 percent in North Vietnam. The remainder attacked targets in South Vietnam. These missions expended more than 3.5 million tons of conventional ordnance. Altogether, the Air Force lost thirty-one B–52s during Arc Light operations—eighteen from hostile fire over North Vietnam and thirteen from other operational causes.

Source: Robert R. Kritt, "B–52 Arc Light Operations," in Carl Berger, ed., *The United States Air Force in Southeast Asia, 1961–1973, An Illustrated Account*, 1977.

Robert D. Launius

ARMORED PERSONNEL CARRIERS

Highly adaptable vehicles running on tanklike tracks, the armored personnel carriers, or APCs, proved to be the backbone of armored cavalry formations during the Vietnam War. The M113 was the most important APC, and it could be adapted for use as a carrier for mortars, machine guns, flamethrowers, troops, and command posts. When properly armed and protected with heavy machine guns and hatch, they could also be used as assault vehicles. The M113 was lightly armored with aluminum and equipped with a .50 caliber Browning heavy machine gun on its roof. In addition to its driver, the M113 APC carried eleven infantry troops and a machine gunner. It had a speed of 40 mph on land and nearly 4 mph in water. By January 1968 there were more than 2,100 M113 APCs in Vietnam. By that time the APC had even evolved into an ACAV— armored cavalry assault vehicle. Armored cavalry units were reequipped with M113s upon arrival in Vietnam, and they modified the vehicle by building armored shields around the .50 caliber machine gun and adding two 7.62mm M60 machine guns.

Sources: Ian Vhoog, "Land Forces in Vietnam and Their Weapons," in John S. Bowman, ed., *The Vietnam War: An Almanac*, 1985; Shelby L. Stanton, *Vietnam Order of Battle*, 1981; Edgar C. Doleman, Jr., *The Vietnam Experience: Tools of War*, 1984.

ARMORED WARFARE

Although jungle fighting has traditionally not been a hospitable environment for armored battle, the Vietnam War provided an exception, with both sides using tanks and armored personnel carriers* (APCs). Before 1965 the United States and the Army of the Republic of Vietnam* (ARVN) had only some M113 APCs, M8 armored cars, and Gage V–100 Commando armored cars. But beginning in 1965 the United States Marines* had a tank battalion* of M48 A3 Patton tanks with each of its two divisions. Early in 1966 the army's 1st Infantry Division* also brought a squadron of M48s to Vietnam. In 1969 the M551 Sheridan tanks were deployed to Vietnam, but they suffered from constant elec-

tronic, engine, and transmission problems in the wet South Vietnamese climate.*
The M48 remained the backbone of American armor. The M113 APCs were
important, especially after they were reequipped with new armored shields around
the .50 caliber machine gun and new 7.62mm M60 machine guns. Eventually,
the United States had three tank battalions in Vietnam, as well as ten battalions
of APC mounted infantry, one armored regiment, and five armored cavalry
squadrons. By the end of the war ARVN had three tank battalions and eighteen
armored cavalry units.

North Vietnam did not employ tanks until later in the conflict. Their tanks
first appeared in 1968 with the use of Soviet PT–76 amphibious tanks to attack
a Special Forces* camp near Khe Sanh.* Eventually they added Soviet T–34,
T–54, and T–59 tanks until their armor totaled 700 vehicles by 1975. Because
of inferior training, the North Vietnamese Army* (NVA) armored units were
no match for either the U.S. or ARVN groups, but the NVA made effective use
of 57mm recoilless rifles, RPG–2 and RPG–7 rocket grenades, and the Soviet
"Sagger" wire-guided missiles. In the Final Offensive (see Ho Chi Minh Campaign) of 1975, the 700 NVA tanks overran the 350 ARVN tanks.

Sources: Simon Dunstan, *Vietnam Tracks: Armor in Battle, 1945–1975*, 1982; Donn
A. Starry, *Mounted Combat in Vietnam*, 1979; Ian Vhoog, "Land Forces in Vietnam,"
in John S. Bowman, ed., *The Vietnam War: An Almanac*, 1985.

ARMY, UNITED STATES

Throughout the Vietnam War, the main burden of battle fell on the United
States Army. More than 65 percent of the American personnel wounded or killed
in action in Vietnam were serving in the army. Between 1961 and 1975, 30,868
army personnel died from hostile action in Vietnam, and 7,193 died nonhostile
deaths. A total of 201,536 army personnel were wounded in action in Vietnam.
The commander of the Military Assistance Command, Vietnam* was an army
general. Throughout the course of the war, the army deployed to Vietnam a total
of 81 infantry battalions,* 3 tank battalions, 12 cavalry squadrons,* 70 artillery
and air defense artillery battalions, and 142 aviation companies and air cavalry*
troops.

Sources: Harry G. Summers, Jr., *Vietnam War Almanac*, 1985; Shelby L. Stanton,
Vietnam Order of Battle, 1981; Andrew F. Krepinevich, Jr., *The Army and Vietnam*,
1986.

ARMY OF THE REPUBLIC OF VIETNAM

In December 1972, the Army of the Republic of Vietnam (ARVN) had a
combat strength of nearly 500,000 troops, of which 108,000 were regular troops,
377,000 Regional* and Popular Forces,* and 14,000 Border Rangers. Those
troops were divided into eleven infantry divisions (1st, 2nd, 3rd, 5th, 7th, 9th,
18th, 21st, 22nd, 23rd, and 25th), one marine division, and one parachutist
division. Those divisions* were divided into a total of 18 armored cavalry
squadrons, 124 infantry battalions, 9 marine battalions, 55 Ranger battalions,

68 artillery battalions, 40 engineer battalions, 16 signal battalions, and 12 military police battalions. By that time, ARVN had suffered more than 190,000 troops killed in action during the war.

ARVN had its beginnings as the Vietnamese National Army,* which the French created in 1950. By the end of 1951 it totaled 38,000 troops. After the fall of Dien Bien Phu* and the rise to power of Ngo Dinh Diem* in 1954 and 1955, the Vietnamese National Army became the nucleus of the Army of the Republic of Vietnam. By the end of 1959, the ARVN had grown to 234,000 troops, and it remained that size until 1964, when a major buildup began in order to fight off the Vietcong.* At the end of 1964 ARVN totaled more than 500,000 troops, and that total increased to 720,000 at the end of 1966, 780,000 at the end of 1967, 800,000 at the end of 1968, 875,000 at the end of 1969, 940,000 at the end of 1970, and 1,000,000 at the end of 1972, of which half were considered combat strength.

Inside ARVN, there were a number of top-flight military units, the equal to any fighting in the war. Those included the ARVN Airborne Division,* the 1st Infantry Division,* and the ARVN Marines.* Time and time again they distinguished themselves during the war. Nevertheless, many of the ARVN units suffered from serious problems. All too often, military officers had been selected for their political connections, not their tactical abilities, and many ARVN units suffered from severe leadership problems. Although the United States tried to work on military training, many of the ARVN units were also characterized by poor, inconsistent training. ARVN soldiers often suffered terrible morale problems because enlistments were involuntary and tours of duty indefinite, because they hesitated to fight long distances away from their home villages, because they too often witnessed corruption on the part of their officers, and because they frequently had little sense of esprit de corps or deep convictions about the purpose of the war. But the real problem behind ARVN was the political instability of the government of the Republic of Vietnam.* Corruption, political assassination, fraudulent elections, and constant political infighting undermined the credibility of the civilian government and helped incapacitate the military. Still, it is important to remember that ARVN forces suffered 243,000 soldiers killed in action and another 507,000 seriously wounded during the war, and such figures contradict the conclusions of many that South Vietnamese soldiers were characterized by cowardice in face of the enemy.

Sources: Dong Van Khuyen, *The RVNAF*, 1980; Shelby L. Stanton, *Vietnam Order of Battle*, 1981; Ian Vhoog, "Land Forces in Vietnam and Their Weapons," in John S. Bowman, ed., *The Vietnam War: An Almanac*, 1985.

ARTILLERY

During the Vietnam War the United States Army* deployed sixty-five artillery battalions and five air defense battalions to Vietnam. In addition, there were ten artillery battalions from the United States Marines* and United States naval bombardment* from the Seventh Fleet* in the South China Sea. By the end of the war the Army of the Republic of Vietnam* had sixty-four artillery battalions. South Korea* supplied six artillery battalions, Thailand* three, and the Philippines* and Australia* one each. The primary artillery weapons employed in Vietnam included: (1) the M109, a 155mm self-propelled howitzer with a range of 14,600 meters; (2) the M107, a 175mm gun with a range of 32,600 meters; (3) the M110, an 8-inch self-propelled howitzer with a range of 16,800 meters; (4) the M114A1, a 155mm howitzer with a range of 14,600 meters; (5) the M102, a 105mm howitzer with a range of 11,500 meters; (6) the M108, a 105mm light howitzer with a range of 11,500 meters; and (7) the M101A1, an older 105mm howitzer with a range of 11,000 meters.

Sources: David Ewing Ott, *Field Artillery, 1954–1973*, 1975; Shelby L. Stanton, *Vietnam Order of Battle*, 1981; Edgar C. Doleman, Jr., *The Vietnam Experience: Tools of War*, 1984.

ARVN   *See* Army of the Republic of Vietnam

ARVN AIRBORNE DIVISION

The ARVN (*see* Army of the Republic of Vietnam) Airborne Division was first organized into the French Union Forces* as individual battalions.* Four airborne battalions were committed to Dien Bien Phu* and they distinguished themselves. After the Geneva Conference (*see* Geneva Accords) of 1954, Vietnamese units were integrated into the ARVN, with Vietnamese officers replacing the French. In the mid–1960s the airborne battalions were organized into independent brigades,* and in 1968 into the Airborne Division. They made a number of parachute assaults between 1950 and 1975. The ARVN Airborne Division was widely considered the best unit in the South Vietnamese military and the equal of any military unit in Southeast Asia. In 1966 General Nguyen Cao Ky* sent airborne units to subdue rebellious units in I Corps* during the "Buddhist* crisis." Against the North Vietnamese Army* (NVA) and Vietcong,* the airborne troops were used as a "fire brigade." The ARVN Airborne Division was one of the few units to serve in all four tactical zones.

During the Tet Offensive,* the division fought extremely well, tenaciously holding key positions. At Tan Son Nhut Air Base,* an airborne training battalion was deployed to close a breach in ARVN lines where NVA-Vietcong forces were entering the base. They closed the breach and decisively defeated the attacking forces. The battalion received numerous decorations. In 1969 the division was paired with the U.S. 1st Cavalry* in joint operations along the Cambodian border (*see* Kampuchea), spearheading the 1970 Cambodian invasion (*see* Operation Binh Tay). In 1971 the division suffered heavy casualties in the ill-conceived Laotian invasion (Lam Son 719).* During the 1972 Eastertide Offensive,* and again throughout 1974, the division saw heavy combat in I Corps. As the 1975 Final Offensive (*see* Ho Chi Minh Campaign) overran I Corps, the division was withdrawn to defend Saigon,* where they provided the last organized resistance against the NVA.

While other South Vietnamese units were ineffective, wilting under fire, the Airborne Division and a handful of other elite units fought well, even heroically. They were well-trained, well-equipped, and well-led. The French instilled the airborne esprit de corps which the division never lost. Division commanders gave troops the security of knowing that the unit took care of their families while they were away and if they were killed, and of them if they were disabled.

Sources: Bruce Palmer, Jr., *The 25-Year War*, 1984; Shelby L. Stanton, *The Rise and Fall of an American Army: U.S. Ground Troops in Vietnam, 1965–1973*, 1985; Dong Van Khuyen, *The RVNAF*, 1980; Cao Van Vien and Dong Van Khuyen, *Reflections of the Vietnam War*, 1980.

Samuel Freeman

ARVN 1ST INFANTRY DIVISION
The 1st Infantry Division was second only to the Airborne Division* as an elite ARVN (*see* Army of the Republic of Vietnam) unit. Stationed in I Corps,* the 1st Division was responsible for protecting five northern provinces against Vietcong* attack and North Vietnamese Army* (NVA) infiltration from Laos* and across the Demilitarizied Zone* (DMZ). It was a formidable task given the rugged terrain. The 1st Division was often assisted by other elite ARVN units, including the Airborne Division, Marines,* and Rangers, as well as by U.S. units, particularly marines and the 101st Airborne Division.* The 1st Division saw heavy combat during the war. I Corps was sparsely populated with only two major cities—Hue* and Da Nang.* Given a strong Vietcong presence in I Corps, and resistance by ARVN troops to serving away from home, it was always difficult to maintain sufficient manpower. Elite ARVN units were used to being shifted around the country. Hue, the imperial capital and always resistive to Saigon's* authority, was a center for Buddhist* opposition to Ngo Dinh Diem* and subsequent rulers of South Vietnam. Da Nang was an important port city often influenced by events in Hue. During the 1966 Buddhist crisis, the 1st Division sided with the Buddhists, and Nguyen Cao Ky* sent the Airborne Division in to restore government authority. American advisers reacted with horror as ARVN's two best units prepared to battle each other. The disaster was averted when Ky promised elections.

The 1st Division participated in the ill-conceived 1971 Laotian invasion. It bore the brunt of the 1972 Eastertide Offensive,* as well as the "strategic raids" of 1974 which left it in a weakened condition as the Final Offensive approached (*see* Ho Chi Minh Campaign). With I Corps collapsing, Nguyen Van Thieu's* abrupt troop movements and indecisive orders made the situation impossible. The 1st Division was completely exposed and overwhelmed.

Sources: Bruce Palmer, Jr., *The 25-Year War: America's Military Role in Vietnam*, 1984; Clark Dougan and David Fulghum, *The Vietnam Experience: The Fall of the South*,

1985; Shelby L. Stanton, *The Rise and Fall of an American Army: U.S. Ground Troops in Vietnam, 1965–1973*, 1985; Cao Van Vien, *The Final Collapse*, 1983.

Samuel Freeman

ARVN MARINES

One of ARVN's (*see* Army of the Republic of Vietnam) three best units, the marines served in all four Corps Tactical Zones, and most extensively in I Corps.* Organized into six battalions* with one battalion of artillery, the marines were given additional artillery and upgraded to a division in October 1968. Marine units fought well during the Tet Offensive* but were plagued with desertions, and 1969 was devoted to rebuilding. They did not participate in the 1970 Cambodian invasion (*see* Operation Binh Tay), but were involved in the 1971 Laotian invasion (*see* Lam Son 719), being assigned to secure the southern flank. Fighting on unfamiliar and extremely difficult terrain, against a superior enemy force, the marines took heavy casualties. Although some units did not perform up to expectation and panic gripped some during the retreat, it is a testimony to the marines (as well as the 1st Infantry Division* and the Airborne Division*) that they did not surrender and were not wiped out as the North Vietnamese Army* (NVA) made every effort to encircle and annihilate ARVN's three best divisions.

During the 1972 Eastertide Offensive,* I Corps Marines delayed NVA forces, enabling Saigon*—which responded too slowly—to counterattack. While the 3rd Infantry Division disintegrated—one regiment surrendered without a fight— no marine unit surrendered or broke. One battalion of 300 was reduced in two days to 69 men. They fought, maneuvered, regrouped, and fought again, continuing to fight as a unit despite decimation. Although badly mauled marine units participated in the counterattack, they ultimately regained Quang Tri City and most of I Corps. In face of the NVA's 1975 Final Offensive (*see* Ho Chi Minh Campaign), I and II Corps* collapsed. ARVN units evaporated. Nguyen Van Thieu's* interference and indecisive orders prevented any possibility of an effective defense. Marine units which were still operative were redeployed to III Corps* for the futile defense of Saigon.*

Sources: Shelby L. Stanton, *The Rise and Fall of an American Army: U.S. Ground Troops in Vietnam, 1965–1973*, 1985; Bruce Palmer, Jr., *The 25-Year War*, 1984; G. H. Turley, *The Easter Offensive*, 1985; Clark Dougan and David Fulghum, *The Vietnam Experience: The Fall of the South*, 1985.

Samuel Freeman

A SHAU VALLEY

The A Shau Valley is located in Thua Thien Province of I Corps* near the Laotian border. Actually several valleys and mountains, the A Shau Valley was one of the principal entry points to South Vietnam of the Ho Chi Minh Trail.* It was an area that was critical to the North Vietnamese since it was the conduit for supplies, additional troops, and communications for units of the North Vietnamese Army* (NVA) and Vietcong* (VC) operating in I Corps. Because of its importance to the NVA and VC, it was the target of repeated major operations by allied forces, especially the U.S. 101st Airborne Division.* Likewise, it was defended vigorously by the NVA and VC. Consequently, the A Shau Valley was the scene of much fighting throughout the war, and it acquired a fearsome reputation for soldiers on both sides. Being a veteran of A Shau Valley operations became a mark of distinction among combat veterans. Although each American effort to staunch the shipment of men and materiel through the A Shau Valley was successful for a brief period of time, the net effect was a series of transitory decreases in the flow followed by increases until the next American operation. Since the U.S. strategy for fighting the enemy did not include occupying remote and sparsely populated areas, the enemy often lost military battles but subsequently was able to reinfiltrate an area when the Americans left the battlefield. The most famous battle of the A Shau Valley was Operation Apache Snow,* also known as Hamburger Hill.*

Sources: Samuel Lipsman, *Fighting for Time*, 1983; Willard Pearson, *The War in the Northern Provinces, 1966–1968*, 1975; Shelby L. Stanton, *The Rise and Fall of an American Army: U.S. Ground Troops in Vietnam, 1965–1973*, 1985.

Stafford T. Thomas

ATROCITIES

Unlike earlier wars in the United States, the conflict in Vietnam brought home to most Americans the fact that their country, as well as the enemy, was capable of committing atrocities. The case of William Calley* and the massacre at My Lai* was the most intense example, but the press regularly circulated stories of civilian casualties, torture and executions of Vietcong* prisoners, throwing Vietcong prisoners of war* out of helicopters, and cutting off the ears of Vietcong* and North Vietnamese dead. As a guerrilla war without fronts, and fought in a distant land against a different ethnic group, the Vietnam War was ripe for atrocities. American soldiers, tired and frustrated about the environment and the nature of the conflict, angry about losing comrades and being unable to separate the Vietcong from civilians, came to look upon all Vietnamese as combatants. Approximately 10 percent of all American casualties were from booby traps,* and during lulls in formal military engagements that rate was even higher. American soldiers often developed feelings of deep hostility for the Vietnamese. Between 1965 and 1973, 278 army and marine soldiers were convicted of serious offenses—murder, rape, and negligent homicide—against Vietnamese civilians, but civilian casualties in the field—from accident and atrocities—were far higher. The press, which was more active in the Vietnam War than in any earlier conflict in American history, was also more able than ever to carry the story of the war back home.

But Americans were not alone in committing atrocities. Terrorism was a major weapon used by the Vietcong in promoting their cause. More than 25,000 people were part of the Vietcong Security Service, and between 1957 and 1972 they were responsible for nearly 37,000 assassinations and nearly 60,000 kidnappings—usually government officials, religious leaders, civil servants, teachers, and prospective draftees. Vietcong terrorism was also used to guarantee a lack of cooperation among peasants and villagers for the pacification programs of the United States (see Rural Reconstruction) and South Vietnam (see Accelerated Pacification Campaign).

Finally, civilian atrocities commonly resulted from indiscriminate bombing or shelling of major cities. The Vietcong and North Vietnamese killed large numbers of civilians in their artillery barrages against Saigon,* Hue,* and Da Nang,* and the United States killed large numbers of civilians in its bombing raids against Hanoi* and Haiphong. Even conservative estimates of civilian deaths in Vietnam total more than 250,000 people during the war. The magnitude of the atrocities, on both sides, during the war in Vietnam helped reinforce in the mind of the American public that the conflict in Southeast Asia was a futile, brutalizing effort from which the United States ought to withdraw.

Sources: Guenter Lewy, *America in Vietnam*, 1978; Philip Caputo, *A Rumor of War*, 1977; Peter D. Trooboff, ed., *Law and Responsibility in Warfare: The Vietnam Experience*, 1975.

ATTRITION   *See* War of Attrition

AUGUST REVOLUTION   *See* Bao Dai

AUSTRALIA

Because of its charter membership in the Southeast Asia Treaty Organization,* Australia found herself drawn into the American sphere of influence in the Pacific. And it was a role she did not resent. After the French defeat at Dien Bien Phu* in 1954, the Australians steadily warned the United States that the fall of South Vietnam would threaten democracies throughout Asia. Australian officials believed the domino theory.* As early as 1962, Australia had sent thirty military advisers to work with the ARVN (see Army of the Republic of Vietnam) on jungle and guerrilla tactics. After the Gulf of Tonkin Resolution* in 1964, Australia increased its troop contingent in South Vietnam to 1,300 people, with a large combat battalion at Bien Hoa.* Under pressure from Washington in 1965 and 1966, Australia increased that commitment, eventually to more than 8,000 troops at its peak in October 1967. Australian Prime Minister Harold Holt consistently offered his support to Lyndon Johnson,* politically as well as militarily, even to the point of using a conscription system to supply its troop commitment. Next to the South Koreans, Australia provided the most military support to the United States in the conflict.

Sources: Stanley Karnow, *Vietnam: A History*, 1983; Peter King, *Australia's Vietnam*, 1983; Stanley Robert Larsen and James Lawton Collins, Jr., *Allied Participation in Vietnam*, 1975.

· B ·

B–52 BOMBER

The B–52 is regarded by experts as the most successful military aircraft ever produced. It began entering service in the mid–1950s, and by 1959 had replaced the awesome but obsolete B–36 as the backbone of Strategic Air Command's (SAC) heavy bomber force. Its primary mission was nuclear deterrence through retaliation. The B–52 has been amazingly adaptable. It was initially designed to achieve very high-altitude penetration of enemy airspace. But when that concept was rendered obsolete by the development of accurate surface-to-air missiles (SAMs),* the B–52 was redesigned and reconstructed for low-altitude penetration. It has undergone eight major design changes since first flown in 1952, from B–52A to B–52H. Literally, although much the same in appearance, the most recent version is a radically different aircraft, superior in every way to the first models.

When the Vietnam situation began to deteriorate in 1964, key SAC commanders began pressing for SAC to get involved in any U.S. action in Vietnam. But the first problem was one of mission. How could a heavy strategic bomber designed to carry nuclear bombs be used in Vietnam? The answer was to modify the B–52 again. Two B–52 units, the 320th Bomb Wing and the 2nd Bomb Wing, had their aircraft modified to carry ''iron bombs,'' i.e., conventional high explosive bombs. After a second modification, each B–52 used in Vietnam could carry eighty-four 500-pound bombs internally and twenty-four 750-pound bombs on underwing racks, for a 3,000-mile nonstop range. The two bomb wings were deployed to operate from Guam as the 133rd Provisional Wing. Later, additional units were deployed to Thailand* and Okinawa to reduce in-flight time, and thus warning time.

The first B–52 raids against a target in South Vietnam (and the first war action for the B–52) took place on June 18, 1965. The target was a Vietcong* jungle sanctuary. The results were not encouraging. Two B–52s collided in flight to the target and were lost in the Pacific Ocean. The results of the bombing could not be evaluated because the area was controlled by the Vietcong. Although the press criticized the use of B–52s, ground commanders were much impressed with the potential of the B–52. Previous attempts to use tactical bombers and fighter-bombers (*see* fighters) to disrupt enemy troop concentrations and supply depots had not been successful. But the B–52 was a veritable flying boxcar, and the effect of a squadron-size attack was to create a virtual Armageddon on the ground.

Ironically, the most effective use of the B–52 in Vietnam was for tactical support of ground troops. B–52s were called in to disrupt enemy troop concentrations and supply areas with devastating effect. B–52 raids were also flown against targets in North Vietnam, Cambodia (*see* Kampuchea), and Laos.* General William Westmoreland* considered the B–52s essential to U.S. efforts in Vietnam. From June 1965 until August 1973, when operations ceased, B–52s flew 124,532 sorties* which successfully dropped their bomb loads on target. Thirty-one B–52s were lost, eighteen shot down by the enemy (all over North Vietnam), and thirteen lost to operational problems.

Sources: Carl Berger, [ed.], *The United States Air Force in Southeast Asia, 1961–1973*, 1984; Andrew W. Waters, *All the U.S. Air Force Airplanes, 1907–1983*, 1983; R. Bruce Harley, *A Short History of Strategic Bombardment*, 1971.

Joseph M. Rowe, Jr.

BA CUT   *See* Hoa Hao

BAEZ, JOAN

Joan Baez was born in Staten Island, New York, on January 9, 1941. She excelled in music, and after her father began teaching physics at Harvard in the late 1950s, she turned to folk music, singing in local coffeehouses. Baez received several recording contracts after the Newport Folk Festival. Her liberal politics and belief in peace and disarmament made her a natural antiwar* leader when the Vietnam conflict escalated in the 1960s. Baez refused to pay her income taxes in 1966 to protest the war and was arrested in Oakland, California, in 1967 for picketing in front of the Northern California Draft Induction Center. Baez married draft* resister David Harris, and together they led a number of protest movements in the late 1960s and early 1970s. In 1973 Baez culminated her antiwar activities with a visit to Hanoi,* and after the visit she reported that American air raids had caused widespread destruction of Hanoi as well as wiping out part of an American POW* camp.

Sources: Charles Mortiz, ed., *Current Biography*, 1964; Stanley Millet, *South Vietnam-U.S. Communist Confrontation in Southeast Asia*, 1973; Nancy Zaroulis and Gerald

Sullivan, *Who Spoke Up? American Protest Against the War in Vietnam, 1963–1975*, 1984.

Sally Smith

BA GIA, BATTLE OF (1965)

On May 29, 1965, a contingent of more than one thousand Vietcong* attacked three battalions of South Vietnamese troops at the hamlet of Ba Gia near Quang Ngai. The ARVN (*see* Army of the Republic of Vietnam) troops panicked and fled the battlefield, leaving behind their weapons and uniforms. The Vietcong were driven out of Ba Gia by concentrated rocket and napalm* fire from U.S. F–100 Super Sabres and A–1 Skyraiders.* South Vietnamese troops reoccupied Ba Gia early in June, but on July 4, after only ninety minutes of battle, the Vietcong had driven them out again. Even though his own troops were standing by at the Quang Ngai airfield, General Nguyen Chanh Thi* requested the assistance of United States Marines,* who attacked and dislodged the Vietcong. Along with several other engagements in the late spring of 1965, Ba Gia convinced U.S. policymakers that South Vietnamese forces would need massive American military assistance if they were to stave off a Vietcong takeover.

Source: Terrence Maitland and Peter McInerney, *A Contagion of War*, 1983.

BALL, GEORGE WILDMAN

George Ball was born in Des Moines, Iowa, on December 21, 1909. He took both his undergraduate and law degrees at Northwestern University in 1930 and 1933, and then joined the general counsel's office of the Department of the Treasury. Between 1935 and 1942 Ball practiced law in Chicago, and in 1942 he became associate general counsel with the Lend Lease Administration. In 1944 President Franklin D. Roosevelt* named him director of the U.S. Strategic Bombing Survey in London. After the war Ball returned to private law practice in Washington, D.C., and in 1961 he became under secretary of state for economic affairs in the Kennedy* administration. Later in the year Kennedy named him under secretary of state, and Ball became an influential figure in the American diplomatic establishment. Between 1961 and 1966, Ball was an opponent of American involvement in the Vietnam War. He opposed the troop buildup occurring during the Kennedy administration and repeatedly argued that the regime of Ngo Dinh Diem* in South Vietnam was hopelessly corrupt, that a land war in Indochina* was not in the strategic interests of the United States, and that the objective of creating a viable, democratic nation there was unreachable. After the Gulf of Tonkin incident* in the summer of 1964, Ball opposed American bombing* of North Vietnam, and he maintained that position throughout 1965 and 1966. From his experience as head of the U.S. Strategic Bombing Survey, Ball was convinced that American bombing would only make the North Vietnamese more committed to their political and military objectives. Frustrated about the drift of American policy, Ball resigned from the State Department in September 1966 and returned to his law practice. In 1968, after the Tet Offensive,* President Lyndon B. Johnson* appointed Ball a member of the Senior Advisory Group to evaluate American policy in Southeast Asia. Taking their cue from Ball's long-held position, the Senior Advisory Group urged disengagement from Vietnam. In 1969, Ball became a senior partner in the Lehman Brothers investment firm. He is the author of a number of books, including *The Discipline of Power* (1968), *Diplomacy in a Crowded World* (1976), and *The Past Has Another Pattern* (1982).

Sources: *Who's Who in America, 1984–1985*, 1985; George W. Ball, *Diplomacy in a Crowded World*, 1976; David Halberstam, *The Best and the Brightest*, 1972; Herbert Schandler, *The Unmaking of a President: Lyndon Johnson and Vietnam*, 1977.

THE BAMBOO BED

The Bamboo Bed is the title of William Eastlake's surrealistic 1969 Vietnam War novel. Beginning the novel with the suicide of Madame Dieudonne after she hears of the death of her American Ranger lover Captain Clancy, Eastlake tries to describe the absurdity of the war with implausible fantasy images: peace-loving hippie flower children wandering aimlessly through the Indochinese jungles; helicopter pilots having sex with medevac* nurses* while airborne; American Rangers topped with Roman helmets and accompanied by drummer boys airlifted into French-Vietnamese villas. Although not altogether successful, the novel was an early literary effort to expose the contradictions inherent in the Vietnam War.

Sources: William Eastlake, *The Bamboo Bed*, 1969; Philip D. Beidler, *American Literature and the Experience of Vietnam*, 1982.

BAN ME THUOT

Ban Me Thuot is the capital city of Darlac Province and the largest urban concentration in the Central Highlands. Its 1970 population was estimated at over 65,000 people. In 1975, Ban Me Thuot was the central objective in the NVA's (*see* North Vietnamese Army) attempt to seize the Central Highlands during the Final Offensive (*see* Ho Chi Minh Campaign). Known as Campaign 275, the assault on Ban Me Thuot was led by General Van Tien Dung,* commander of ten NVA divisions. On March 10, 1975, Dung had the NVA 10th, 316th, and 320th Divisions move on Ban Me Thuot and the ARVN 23rd Division (*see* Army of the Republic of Vietnam). Intense fighting lasted for two days, but on March 12, 1975, the NVA were in control of the city. The fall of Ban Me Thuot had great strategic significance because there were no ARVN troops left between the NVA soldiers in Ban Me Thuot and the South China Sea. The North Vietnamese had an unprecedented opportunity to cut South Vietnam in half. Eventually, of course, they abandoned that strategy and concentrated on the April massive assault on Saigon.*

Sources: Alan Dawson, *55 Days: The Fall of South Vietnam*, 1977; Van Tien Dung, *Our Great Spring Victory*, 1977; Clark Dougan and David Fulghum, *The Vietnam Experience: The Fall of the South*, 1985.

BAN ME THUOT, BATTLE OF (1975)   *See* Ban Me Thuot

BAO DAI

Bao Dai, the last emperor of Annam,* was born Prince Nguyen Vinh Thuy on October 22, 1913, to the Emperor Khai Dinh. He became emperor in 1925 at the age of twelve, but did not actually assume the throne until 1932, after spending ten years in France* receiving an education. The empire of Annam was essentially a powerless entity, however, because the French Treaty of Protectorate in 1884 had limited the powers of the emperor and the Convention of 1925 had stripped away all the rest. But on becoming emperor, Bao Dai hoped to create a modernized imperial government and induce France to establish a true protectorate, with limited independence, over Vietnam. He remained emperor until 1945. During the Japanese occupation of Vietnam, Bao Dai cooperated with the invaders and earned the ire of the anti-French, Communist Vietminh.*

When news of the Japanese surrender reached Vietnam in August 1945, peasants began attacking Japanese installations and food storage facilities, and Vietminh leaders began moving into positions of power. In Hanoi* Ho Chi Minh* formed the National Liberation Committee, named himself president, and hoped to greet the returning Allies from a position of power. Vietminh groups in the southern part of Vietnam battled with the Cao Dai* and Hoa Hao,* and in Annam, at the imperial palace in Hue,* demanded the abdication of Bao Dai. Known as the August Revolution, the transfer of power from the Japanese to various Vietnamese groups toppled Bao Dai from the throne, leaving Ho Chi Minh's Vietminh followers in control.

Bao Dai lived in Paris between 1945 and 1949, but returned to Vietnam in 1949 after a provisional government in 1948 had reunited Cochin China,* Annam, and Tonkin.* But he was little more than a French puppet. After the Battle of Dien Bien Phu* and expulsion of the French in 1954, Bao Dai lost his base of power, and a national referendum in 1955 stripped him of his office as chief of state and turned power over to Ngo Dinh Diem.* Bao was then exiled to France.

Sources: Ellen J. Hammer, *The Struggle for Indochina, 1940–1955*, 1966; Virginia Thompson, *French Indochina*, 1937; Joseph Buttinger, *Vietnam: A Dragon Embattled*, 2 vols., 1967.

Terry Martin

BATTALION

A battalion is an organizational institution in the army and marine corps. Commanded by a lieutenant colonel, an infantry battalion usually has around 900 people, and an artillery battalion about 500 people. During the Vietnam War, American battalions were usually much smaller than that.

Sources: Shelby Stanton, *Vietnam Order of Battle*, 1981; Harry G. Summers, Jr., *Vietnam War Almanac*, 1985.

BATTERY

A battery in the army or marine corps is an artillery unit of approximately 100 people commanded by a captain. In the Vietnam War there were howitzer batteries, search light batteries, machine gun batteries, and target acquisition batteries.

Sources: Harry G. Summers, Jr., *Vietnam War Almanac*, 1985; Shelby L. Stanton, *Vietnam Order of Battle*, 1981.

BAY VIEN   *See* Le Van Vien

BEEHIVE AMMUNITION

"Beehive ammunition" was used by U.S. forces in Vietnam as ammunition for rockets, howitzers, and recoilless rifles. The rounds were filled with thousands of small metal fléchettes which exploded in a 30-degree arc.

Source: Edgar C. Doleman, Jr., *The Vietnam Experience: Tools of War*, 1984.

BEN HAI RIVER

The Ben Hai River is the frontier boundary between North and South Vietnam, dividing the two countries between July 22, 1954, and April 29, 1975, when South Vietnam fell. Generally paralleling the seventeenth parallel (*see* Geneva Accords), the Ben Hai River comes out of the Laotian highlands and runs into the South China Sea.

Source: *Webster's Geographical Dictionary*, 1969.

BEN SUC

Ben Suc was a village of perhaps 5,500 people located along the Saigon River in Binh Duong Province. About 30 miles northwest of Saigon,* Ben Suc was in the heart of the Iron Triangle* and a center of activity for the Vietcong.* ARVN (*see* Army of the Republic of Vietnam) soldiers had kept an outpost at Ben Suc between 1955 and 1964 until Vietcong troops ousted them. After that, the Vietcong received the active cooperation of the village inhabitants. Between 1965 and 1967, ARVN troops, assisted by massive American air strikes—phosphorus bombs, napalm,* and B–52* assaults, tried unsuccessfully to retake Ben Suc. Late in 1966, American officials launched Operation Cedar Falls* to wipe out Vietcong resistance in the Iron Triangle. Although Ben Suc lay just beyond the northwestern tip of the Iron Triangle, it was an important objective for American troops in Operation Cedar Falls. In the end the village of Ben Suc became a notorious example of the futility of American military policy in South Vietnam.

On January 8, 1967, sixty troop-carrying helicopters took off from the Dau Tieng airstrip and deposited 420 soldiers right in the middle of Ben Suc. Since Ben Suc was reputedly the headquarters for Vietcong control of the Iron Triangle, the American soldiers expected intense resistance. Instead, they encountered only sporadic small arms fire. The villagers were evacuated from the village and taken to a new refugee camp at Phy Loi near Phu Cuong. The 1st Engineer Battalion of the 1st Infantry Division,* then moved into Ben Suc with Rome plows,* tankdozers, and M–48 antimine tanks and leveled the village, destroying every home and building and bulldozing all the mango, jackfruit, and grapefruit fields. Miles of tunnels used by the Vietcong were destroyed at the same time. Two days after the end of Operation Cedar Falls on January 26, Vietcong were back in the area. At home the American press reacted to the razing of Ben Suc with outrage. Less than 30 miles from Saigon, U.S. and ARVN troops, after destroying a village and turning nearly six thousand people into refugees, had not been able to prevent Vietcong control of the area. Although Operation Cedar Falls was a blow to the Vietcong in the area of the Iron Triangle, it also raised serious doubts among the American press and American policymakers about the effectiveness of both pacification (*see* Rural Reconstruction) and the "search and destroy"* strategy.

Sources: Jonathan Schell, *The Village of Ben Suc*, 1967; Bernard William Rogers, *Cedar Falls–Junction City: A Turning Point*, 1974.

BEN TRE

Ben Tre was the capital city of the Kien Hoa Province in IV Corps.* South of Saigon,* Kien Hoa Province borders the Vietnamese coast along the South China Sea. Ben Tre became temporarily famous in 1968 when Vietcong* forces captured the city during the Tet Offensive.* Overwhelming American and South Vietnamese forces, bolstered by massive air strikes, recaptured Ben Tre, but the artillery and air strikes all but destroyed the town, killing an estimated 550 people and wounding 1,200 more. The battle for Ben Tre was not much different from countless other struggles during the Vietnam War, except for the famous quote of an American major when asked by journalist Peter Arnett to justify the indiscriminate use of explosives. His remark, "It became necessary to destroy the town in order to save it," was widely quoted in the world press and became a symbol, to antiwar* activists, of the bankruptcy of U.S. policy in Southeast Asia.

Sources: Clark Dougan and Stephen Weiss, *The Vietnam Experience: Nineteen Sixty-Eight*, 1983; Max Hastings, *The Fire This Time: America's Year of Crisis*, 1969; Peter Braestrup, *Big Story: How the American Press and Television Reported and Interpreted the Crisis of Tet 1968 in Vietnam and Washington*, 1983.

BERGER, SAMUEL DAVID

Born in New York City on December 6, 1911, Samuel Berger received the Ph.D. degree from the University of Wisconsin in 1934 and joined the State Department after several years in the field of statistics and labor economics. His first assignment at State was as a labor officer in 1945 at the U.S. embassy in London. After several diplomatic assignments to Japan, New Zealand, and

Greece, Berger became ambassador to South Korea in 1961. He was named deputy ambassador to South Vietnam in 1968, and he remained in that post until 1972. Berger's role was liaison between President Ngyuen Van Thieu,* the United States, and the South Vietnamese military. Above all else, Berger wanted to maintain a stable civilian government in South Vietnam, with the military playing only a secondary political role. As such, Berger was a staunch supporter of Thieu and believed the U.S. military effort in Southeast Asia could lead to a permanent, anti-Communist government in Saigon.* Berger supported the invasion of Cambodia (*see* Kampuchea) in 1970 and helped plan the disastrous Lam Son 719* ARVN (*see* Army of the Republic of Vietnam) invasion of Laos* in 1971. Berger left Saigon in 1972 and went to work for the Foreign Service Institute.

Sources: Department of State, *Biographic Register*, 1974; Clark Dougan and Steven Weiss, *The Vietnam Experience: Nineteen Sixty-Eight*, 1983.

BERRIGAN, DANIEL

Born in Virginia, Minnesota, on May 9, 1921, Father Daniel Berrigan was a prominent figure in the New Catholic Left of the 1960s and a leading opponent of the Vietnam War and Selective Service system. He entered training for the Roman Catholic priesthood in 1939 and was ordained on June 19, 1952, as a member of the Society of Jesus. A prolific writer and poet, Berrigan won the Lamont Prize for his first poetry collection, *Time Without Number*, in 1957. As a professor of New Testament studies at Le Moyne College in Syracuse, New York, from 1957 to 1963, he encouraged students to become involved in work with the poor, civil rights, and pacifism. One of his students became the first person convicted for burning a draft* card. With James H. Forest, Thomas C. Cornell, and Philip Berrigan,* he founded the Catholic Peace Fellowship in 1964. A year later, he helped found the interdenominational Clergy and Laity Concerned About Vietnam.* In February 1967, he went to Hanoi,* North Vietnam, with Howard Zinn of Boston University to help gain the release of three captured U.S. pilots. On the afternoon of May 17, 1968, Berrigan, his brother Philip, and seven others entered Selective Service Board 33 in Knights of Columbus hall in Catonsville, Maryland. There they removed several hundred 1-A draft records from filing cabinets, threw them into trash cans, burned them with homemade napalm* in the parking lot outside, and then awaited arrest. The "Catonsville Nine" were found guilty of conspiracy and destruction of government property. Berrigan was sentenced to three years in prison. He received considerable notoriety, however, when he refused to surrender on April 9, 1970, to begin serving his sentence. He went underground and made periodic public appearances at religious services and antiwar* rallies, and was even interviewed by NBC-TV news on June 4. He was finally apprehended by the FBI on Block Island on August 11, 1970, and sent to the federal prison at Danbury, Connecticut. On January 12, 1971, he was named as an unindicted coconspirator on charges of conspiring to kidnap Henry Kissinger* and to blow up the heating systems of federal buildings in Washington, D.C. Berrigan was paroled on January 26, 1972, because of poor health. After the war, he largely receded from public view but remained supportive of causes associated with pacificism and the poor. He also distressed some followers by voicing opposition to abortion, along with war and capital punishment. On January 19, 1976, he began serving a sixty-day jail sentence rather than pay a fine for digging a hole in the White House lawn on November 26, 1975, in protest of the proliferation of nuclear weapons. In 1980, he was one of the "Plowshares Eight" who were arrested and convicted for hammering on two nuclear warhead cones and pouring blood on desks and files at the General Electric Re-entry Division plant in King of Prussia, Pennsylvania, on September 9. The convictions were upheld and prison sentences reinstated by the Supreme Court of Pennsylvania in November 1985. Further appeals were being pursued in 1986.

Sources: Daniel Berrigan, S.J., *No Bars to Manhood*, 1970; Nancy Zaroulis and Gerald Sullivan, *Who Spoke Up? American Protest Against the War in Vietnam, 1963–1975*, 1984; Charles A. Meconis, *With Clumsy Grace: The American Catholic Left, 1961–1975*, 1979.

John Kincaid

BERRIGAN, PHILIP (FRANCIS)

Born in Two Harbors, Minnesota, on October 5, 1923, Philip Berrigan was a leading member of the New Catholic Left and prominent opponent of the Vietnam War and Selective Service system. While attending St. Michael's College in Toronto, he was drafted in January 1943. He served with the U.S. Army artillery and infantry in World War II, and received a battlefield promotion to second lieutenant for service in some of the most savage battles on the European front. After earning a B.A. in English at the College of the Holy Cross, Worcester, Massachusetts, he was ordained into the Society of Jesus in 1955. Assigned to New Orleans, he earned a B.S. in secondary education at Loyola University of the South and an M.S. at Xavier University. For six years, he taught at St. Augustine High School in New Orleans's black ghetto. After he became quite controversial locally for his activity in the black civil rights movement, his superiors transferred him to a seminary in Newburgh, New York. There, in 1964, he founded the Emergency Citizens' Group Concerned About Vietnam. He also helped to found the Catholic Peace Fellowship in 1964. Again, his superiors transferred him, this time to St. Peter Claver Church in the black ghetto of Baltimore, Maryland. He then founded the Baltimore Interfaith Peace Mission. On October 27, 1967, Berrigan and three other activists entered the Selective Service office at the Baltimore Customs House and, in front of startled workers, poured jars of duck blood onto draft* files. Berrigan thus became the first Roman Catholic priest in the United States to be sentenced to prison for a political crime. While awaiting sentencing, however, he and eight others, including his brother Daniel,* entered Selective Service Board 33 at a Knights of Columbus hall in Catonsville, Maryland, on the afternoon of May 17, 1968. They removed 1-A records from filing cabinets, carried them out onto the parking lot in wire waste-baskets, and burned the records with homemade napalm.* Berrigan was convicted of conspiracy and destruction of government property and sentenced to three and a half years in prison, to be served concurrently with a six-year sentence he had already begun to serve for his first protest action against the draft. He was granted bail but refused to surrender to authorities on April 9, 1970. FBI agents apprehended him on April 21. On January 12, 1971, he and six others were indicted by a federal grand jury for conspiring to blow up the heating systems of federal buildings in Washington, D.C., and to kidnap Henry Kissinger.* The trial jury found Berrigan guilty on one charge of having a letter smuggled out of prison to codefendant Sister Elizabeth McAlister. The jury deadlocked on the other charges—ten for acquittal and two for conviction. Berrigan was sentenced to two years in prison. The conspiracy charges were dismissed upon a motion for mistrial from the U.S. Department of Justice; the smuggling conviction was later overturned by a Circuit Court of Appeals. Berrigan was paroled from the Danbury federal prison on December 20, 1972. On May 30, 1973, he announced that he and Elizabeth McAlister had privately married themselves in 1969. McAlister gave birth to a daughter on April 1, 1974. On October 4, 1975, Berrigan and twenty-one others were arrested for pouring a red liquid on military aircraft being exhibited at Rentschler Airport in East Hartford, Connecticut. Charges were dropped, however, when Pratt & Whitney Aircraft said that the liquid had been cleaned off the aircraft with soap and water. Berrigan continued to protest U.S. nuclear policies. On November 26, 1975, he and eight others dug a hole in the White House lawn in protest of nuclear weapons proliferation. He served sixty days in jail rather than pay a fine for what he called this "act of conscience." Five years later, he was one of the "Plowshares Eight" who were arrested and convicted for hammering on two nuclear warhead cones and pouring blood on desks and files at the General Electric Re-entry Division plant in King of Prussia, Pennsylvania, on September 9, 1980. The convictions were still on appeal in 1986.

Sources: William O'Rourk, *The Harrisburg 7 and the New Catholic Left*, 1972; Charles A. Meconis, *With Clumsy Grace: The American Catholic Left, 1961–1975*, 1979; Thomas E. Quigley, ed., *American Catholics and Vietnam*, 1968.

John Kincaid

BETTER TIMES THAN THESE

Better Times Than These is the title of Winston Groom's 1978 novel about Vietnam. It centers on Bravo Company, a group of soldiers sent to Vietnam in 1966. The book covers their training and long ocean voyage to Vietnam, as well as a month of brutal combat in the field. *Better Times Than These* comes out of the genre of World War II novels, even though it is an unrelenting tale of mutinous soldiers, incompetent officers, and ugly atrocities.

Sources: Winston Groom, *Better Times Than These*, 1978; Philip D. Beidler, *American Literature and the Experience of Vietnam*, 1982.

BIDAULT, GEORGES

Georges Bidault was born on October 5, 1899, in Moulins, France. During World War II he was president of the National Council of Resistance, and after the war he rose through the conservative political ranks. Between 1949 and 1952 he served as president of the Mouvement Républicain Populaire. Bidault was premier of France* between June and November 1946 and extracted from President Harry Truman* a promise that the United States supported the return of the French to Indochina.* He returned as premier between October 1949 and June 1950. During his years of power Bidault was a strong advocate of the French Empire and took a conservative approach to imperial problems in Indochina and Algeria, insisting that France maintain her commitments there. Throughout the 1950s and early 1960s he was a vigorous supporter of General Charles de Gaulle, but he lost favor after 1962 for demanding the maintenance of French Algeria. Georges Bidault died on January 27, 1983.

Sources: James J. Cooke, *France 1789–1962*, 1975; Georges Bidault, *Resistance: The Political Autobiography of Georges Bidault*, 1967; *New York Times*, January 28, 1983.

BIEN HOA, BATTLE OF (1964)

Bien Hoa, the capital city of Bien Hoa Province, is located approximately 20 miles north of Saigon* on the Dong Nai River. Early in the war, the United States constructed a large airfield and military headquarters just outside Bien Hoa, and on November 1, 1964, the Vietcong* attacked the installation. Since the Gulf of Tonkin incident* in August 1964 and the subsequent bombing* of North Vietnam, the Indochinese conflict had been consuming increasing amounts of time and resources in Washington, as well as in the public mind. Vietcong sappers attacked the base, destroying five aircraft and killing four American soldiers. Although the administration did not respond immediately to the attack, it was becoming more and more clear that if the United States was going to conduct an air war over North and South Vietnam, with aircraft and personnel stationed in the south, regular ground troops would be required to defend those installations. Escalation of the conflict became one indirect consequence of the attack on Bien Hoa in 1964.

Sources: *New York Times*, November 2–4, 1964, p. 1; George W. Ball, "Top Secret: The Prophecy the President Rejected," *The Atlantic*, 230 (July 1972), 35–49.

THE BIG V

The Big V is the title of William Pelfry's 1972 Vietnam War novel. It is the account, written in diary form, of Henry Winstead, a young draftee serving in Vietnam. Written from an antiwar* perspective, *The Big V* is conventional within that genre in its exposure of the violence and futility of the military effort in Vietnam.

Sources: William Pelfry, *The Big V*, 1972; Philip D. Beidler, *American Literature and the Experience of Vietnam*, 1982.

BINH XUYEN

With their stronghold in the Cholon* section near Saigon,* the Binh Xuyen were drug smugglers who traditionally traded support for legal protection of their rackets, whether they were dealing with the French Empire or the Vietminh* nationalists. Their trade was prostitution, gambling casinos, and opium dens. In post–World War II Vietnam, the Binh Xuyen became a powerful political faction under the leadership of Bay Vien (*see* Le Van Vien). In 1945 the Binh Xuyen provided terrorists to the Vietminh, who assassinated more than 150 French civilians, including women and children. Emperor Bao Dai,* in order to generate the funds necessary to sustain his government, readily accepted money from the Binh Xuyen, who received legal protection for their rackets in return. Bao Dai made Bay Vien a general in the Vietnamese army and gave him complete authority over the casinos, prostitution, opium traffic, gold smuggling, currency manipulation, and other rackets. The French accepted Bay Vien's authority and even used his private Binh Xuyen army to fight against the Vietminh. By the early 1950s, the Binh Xuyen army had reached more than 40,000 soldiers and it was a major political-military faction in southern Vietnam.

In the spring of 1955, after securing control of the new government of South Vietnam, Ngo Dinh Diem* decided to crush the political and religious factions in the South—like the Hoa Hao* and Cao Dai*—and one of the most powerful was the Binh Xuyen. On April 27, 1955, Diem ordered Bay Vien and the Binh Xuyen to remove its troops from Saigon, and when they refused, Diem attacked. The battle raged inside the city, killing more than 500 people and leaving 25,000 without homes. The French and Bao Dai tried to assist the Binh Xuyen, but Diem prevailed. By the end of May, Bay Vien had fled to Paris and the Binh Xuyen army had been driven into the Mekong Delta,* where many of them joined the Vietcong* guerrillas.

Sources: Stanley Karnow, *Vietnam: A History*, 1983; Denis Warner, *The Last Confucian*, 1963; Edward Doyle and Samuel Lipsman, *The Vietnam Experience: Passing the Torch*, 1981; Charles A. Joiner, *The Politics of Massacre: Political Processes in South Vietnam*, 1974.

BLACK SOLDIERS

Because the Vietnam War coincided with the militant stage of the civil rights movement, the role played by blacks in the Indochinese conflict became a major controversy. Existing draft* regulations in 1965 provided exemptions to young men attending college or working in certain critical occupations, both of which discriminated in favor of middle-class whites. Black leaders like Martin Luther King, Jr.,* argued that young blacks were more likely to be drafted than whites, and, once drafted, more likely to get dangerous infantry assignments. They were correct. Although blacks constituted about 13 percent of the American population in 1966, they had sustained more than 20 percent of the combat deaths in Vietnam up to that time. Concerned about those percentages and about the diversion of assets away from domestic problems, King condemned Vietnam as a racist war in 1967. Even before that, heavyweight champion Muhammad Ali* had startled the nation by saying "I ain't got nothing against them Vietcong"* and later refusing to be drafted.

The criticisms did not fall on deaf ears. After 1967 both the United States Army* and the Marine Corps* made conscious efforts to reduce black battlefield casualties, and by the end of the American combat effort in 1972, blacks had sustained approximately 5,700 of the 47,200 battlefield deaths of U.S. personnel—about 12 percent of the total.

Sources: Martin Binkin et al., *Blacks in the Military*, 1982; Lawrence M. Baskir and William A. Strauss, *Chance and Circumstance: The Draft, the War, and the Vietnam Generation*, 1978; Wallace Terry, *Bloods: An Oral History of the Vietnam War by Black Veterans*, 1984; Stanley Goff and Robert Sandfors, *Brothers: Black Soldiers in the Nam*, 1982.

BLUM, LÉON

Léon Blum was born April 9, 1872, and became one of the leading French socialists. He was elected a deputy in the national legislature in 1919. Blum was Jewish, and that created some political problems for him over the years, but his gentility and commitment to democracy and peaceful change enabled him to succeed politically despite the prevailing anti-Semitism. Blum became prime minister in 1936 and again in 1938, and he was responsible for a variety of left-wing, social welfare measures. Openly sympathetic with the Communists in the Spanish Civil War, Blum was arrested by the Vichy government in 1940 and deported to Germany, where he was imprisoned. After the war Blum served as president of the Council of Ministers from 1946 to 1947 and generally advocated independence for Vietnam. Léon Blum died on March 30, 1950.

Sources: James J. Cooke, *France 1789–1962*, 1975; Louise Dalby, *Leon Blum: Evolution of a Socialist*, 1963.

"BOAT PEOPLE"

The term "boat people" became a euphemism for Vietnamese refugees* fleeing Vietnam after the fall of Saigon* in 1975. Although some of the refugees made their way to freedom overland through Laos* and Cambodia (*see* Kampuchea) into Thailand,* most of them left in small boats hoping to make it to Indonesia, Malaysia, Thailand, or the Philippines.* Demographers now estimate that more than a million people fled Vietnam by boat, earning the title of "boat people." Their voyages were beset with danger. Pirates in the South China Sea regularly victimized them, and Indonesia and Malaysia frequently rejected them even when they did make landfall. Tens of thousands drowned at sea. Although exact statistics are difficult to obtain, perhaps 250,000 Vietnamese "boat people" died on the South China Sea from various causes.

Sources: "No More Room for Refugees," *Time*, May 10, 1982; Muriel Stanek, *We Came from Vietnam*, 1985; Darrel Montero, *Vietnamese Americans: Patterns of Resettlement and Socioeconomic Adjustment in the United States*, 1979; Bruce Grant, *The Boat People*, 1979.

BODY COUNT

Because the Vietnam War was a guerrilla conflict without front lines and territorial objectives, and with shifting defensive positions, it became impossible to use geography as a reliable index of progress. Instead, Secretary of Defense Robert McNamara* and General William Westmoreland* came to rely on the body count—the number of Vietcong* and North Vietnamese soldiers killed— to evaluate the progress of the war. But a number of factors made the body count figures unreliable. Combat conditions often required estimates of enemy killed, often from aerial observation or memory. It was also very difficult to distinguish between Vietcong and civilian Vietnamese casualties. Counts were often duplicated; and American officers, desperate for good efficiency reports, were known to exaggerate the body counts. Until 1968 American military officials accepted "probable kills" as the body count figure. By the time of the Tet Offensive,* however, Defense Department studies indicated that body count figures were probably 30 percent inflated. Civilian officials were also concerned because the Vietcong and North Vietnamese lost only one-sixth as many weapons as they did people, at least according to the body count figures. Such a discrepancy meant either that large numbers of civilians were killed along with the Vietcong, that the body count figures were seriously inflated, or both. At the end of the war, U.S. officials estimated that 666,000 Vietcong and North Vietnamese had died during combat in South Vietnam between 1965 and 1974, and that American air strikes had killed 65,000 people in North Vietnam. Vo Nguyen Giap* estimated that by 1969 his Communist forces had lost 500,000 men killed in action.

Sources: Phil Caputo, *A Rumor of War*, 1977; Guenter Lewy, *American in Vietnam*, 1978; John E. Mueller, "The Search for the 'Breaking Point' in Vietnam: The Statistics of a Deadly Quarrel," *International Studies Quarterly* 24 (December 1980): 497–519.

BODY COUNT

Body Count is the title of William Huggett's 1973 novel about the Vietnam War. It focuses on Lt. Chris Hawkins, who takes over a Marine platoon as an inexperienced officer. The book deals with the violence, racial tensions, and morale problems of the war, but also shows how Hawkins grows as a leader. It concludes with a bloody assault on a hilltop North Vietnamese Army* position in I Corps,* and the abandonment of the position one day after the victory.

Sources: William Turner Huggett, *Body Count*, 1973; Philip D. Beidler, *American Literature and the Experience of Vietnam*, 1982.

BOMBING OF SOUTHEAST ASIA

At the end of World War II, Vietnam was one of several nations which were artificially divided into sectors by the victorious allies. The United States was instrumental in the creation of the capitalistic Republic of South Vietnam, while the Soviet Union established the leftist nation North Vietnam. Each portion of Vietnam held differing political beliefs and sought to unify the nation under its rule. The United States developed a close relationship with South Vietnam during the 1950s, and as difficulties with leftist North Vietnam grew during the early 1960s, so did American commitments. Eventually, by the late 1960s, the United States had assumed the primary responsibilities of conducting the defense of South Vietnam.

The first clash between North Vietnamese and American forces occurred on August 2, 1964, when a North Vietnamese force attacked an American naval vessel patrolling the Gulf of Tonkin.* Two nights later, American destroyers were attacked along the Vietnamese coast. With these attacks, President Lyndon Baines Johnson* ordered a retaliatory bombing strike against a North Vietnamese supply depot on August 5. The president then requested and Congress approved the Gulf of Tonkin Resolution* on August 7, 1964, granting President Johnson the authority to use all measures necessary to assist South Vietnam in defending its territory. These actions set the stage for extended bombing operations against enemy targets in North Vietnam.

From the very beginning of bombing operations against enemy targets, the United States Air Force* (USAF) experienced difficulties. Bombardment campaigns in Vietnam were substantially different from those of World War I and II, and even materially different from those of Korea. First, the president was intensely concerned with the complexities and necessities of fighting a limited war, limited both in size and scope, and maintained firm control over all phases of planning and execution. Coordination of all bombing operations involved not only military planners but also senior State Department, Defense Department, cabinet, and numerous other government officials. Second, air force bombing doctrine underwent a striking alteration during the war as the practical differences between air interdiction and strategic bombing against North Vietnam were muted. In this conflict, all types of bombers and fighters* worked together to bomb transportation, supply, and industrial targets not just in North Vietnam but in the allied nation as well. Third, because of the limited nature of the war in Southeast Asia, any bombing activity could never be decisive.

The initial air strikes, code-named Operation Rolling Thunder,* were limited primarily to enemy radar and bridges below the twentieth parallel. As the effort expanded, however, President Johnson ordered the bombing of most metropolitan areas in North Vietnam. The first of these expanded attacks took place on May 22, 1965, when USAF F–105s* bombed the North Vietnamese barracks at Quang Soui. While the first strikes were made by tactical aircraft, the most spectacular and destructive aircraft used in the air war were B–52* strategic bombers. These aircraft operated essentially from six large airfields in Thailand.* The USAF bomber and support presence in Thailand grew from about 1,000 personnel and 83 aircraft in early 1965 to a peak of about 55,000 personnel and 600 aircraft by the time of the Tet Offensive* in January and February 1968.

From the first handful of strikes into enemy territory in 1965 until the USAF and Navy* sorties* were halted by presidential decree on October 31, 1968, the aircraft struck at bridges, vehicles, rolling stock, military posts, assembly plants, supply depots, vessels, antiaircraft and radar sites, railroads, and highways. During nearly four years of bombing, USAF, Navy, Marine,* and South Vietnamese aircraft had flown about 304,000 tactical and 2,380 B–52 sorties and dropped 643,000 tons of bombs on enemy targets.

Although the bombing halt was stopped for several months during the winter of 1968–1969, after President Richard M. Nixon* assumed office, the bombing resumed. President Nixon was responsible for the most controversial bombing operation of the war, taking place in Cambodia (*see* Kampuchea) after spring 1969 (*see* Operation Menu). American military leaders had long complained that leftist forces were using Cambodian jungles near the Vietnamese border as safe havens from which to stage hit-and-run attacks against American and South Vietnamese forces. President Nixon was convinced by military leaders that he could cripple North Vietnam by destroying its Cambodian sanctuaries.*

Accordingly, on March 18, 1969—operating under cover of special security and reporting procedures—a B–52 bombing campaign in Cambodia began. The sorties, all of which were flown at night, were directed by ground control units, ensuring that not even the aircrews were told to follow explicitly all directions for the bomb release from the ground control personnel. In all, between March 18, 1969, and May 26, 1970, the B–52s flew 4,308 sorties and dropped 120,578 tons of bombs on enemy base camps in Cambodia.

These bombings temporarily hampered North Vietnamese efforts in Cambodia, but they also expanded the war into Cambodia as the North Vietnamese retaliated. By April 26, 1970, for instance, North Vietnam had taken control of large areas of the country, and appeared on the verge of toppling the Cambodian government. This action prompted an American and South Vietnamese invasion of Cambodia to preserve the friendly government. During a three-month period, April 29 to June 30, 1970, these forces temporarily threw back the North Vietnamese, but with their withdrawal North Vietnam attacked Cambodia again. Throughout these operations, the USAF provided bombing support to the Cambodian Army in its defensive activity, but it was insufficient. Not long after the withdrawal of the United States from Southeast Asia, the Cambodian government fell and the puppet state of Kampuchea* was created by North Vietnam.

As bombing in Cambodia, Laos,* and North Vietnam continued between 1969 and 1972, so did peace negotiations in Paris.* On January 23, 1973, the Paris negotiators signed a nine-point cease-fire agreement. This agreement provided for a cease-fire of all combat operations, the return of all American and allied prisoners of war, establishment of a commission to supervise the truce, and affirmation of the national rights of South Vietnam, Laos, and Cambodia. The United States also tacitly recognized the presence of about 100,000 North Vietnamese troops in South Vietnam. During the period of the negotiation, the USAF had flown 51,000 tactical and 9,800 B–52 bombing sorties against North Vietnam, dropping 124,000 tons of bombs by tactical aircraft and 109,000 tons by B–52s. During the same period, these forces flew additional sorties against enemy positions in Laos and Cambodia. Cumulatively, between June 1965 and

August 1973, the Strategic Air Command's B–52s flew 126,615 bombing sorties and the tactical forces flew more than 400,000 bombing sorties, in the process dropping 6,162,000 tons of munitions on enemy positions. By contrast, the total tonnage of explosives dropped in World War II had been 2,150,000 tons.

Sources: David A. Anderton, *The History of the U.S. Air Force*, 1981; Carl Berger, ed., *The United States Air Force in Southeast Asia, 1961–1973: An Illustrated Account*, 1977; Walter Boyne, *Boeing B–52: A Documentary History*, 1981; idem, *The Development of the Strategic Air Command: A Chronological History*, 1982; James N. Eastman, Jr., et al., eds., *Aces and Aerial Victories: The United States Air Force in Southeast Asia, 1965–1973*, 1976; Stanley Karnow, *Vietnam: A History*, 1983; James Clay Thompson, *Rolling Thunder: Understanding Policy and Program Failure*, 1980.

Roger D. Launius

BOOBY TRAPS

Booby traps—ranging from punji stakes* to a variety of grenades, mines, and explosive devices—were a common part of the Vietnam War, primarily because of the guerrilla nature of the conflict. More than one out of ten American battlefield casualties in Vietnam was the result of a booby trap of one kind or another. The most dangerous of the makeshift Vietcong* weapons were the following: a bullet buried straight up with its firing pin on a bamboo stub, activated when someone stepped on the bullet's tip; hollowed-out coconuts filled with gunpowder and triggered by a trip wire; walk bridges with ropes almost cut away so they would collapse when someone tried to cross them; underground and hidden punji stakes; bamboo stakes connected to grenades and planted at helicopter landing sites; the "Malay whip" log, attached to two trees by a rope and triggered by a trip wire, which would sweep down on entire units; and boards studded with iron barbs and buried in streambeds and rice paddies. The common use of booby traps only further alienated American troops from civilian Vietnamese, whom they did not trust and could not distinguish from the Vietcong.

Sources: Edgar C. Doleman, Jr., *The Vietnam Experience: Tools of War*, 1984; Peter Goldman and Tony Fuller, *Charlie Company: What Vietnam Did to Us*, 1983.

BOWLES, CHESTER BLISS

Chester Bowles was born on April 5, 1901, in Springfield, Massachusetts, and graduated from Yale in 1924. He established a successful advertising firm in 1929 and worked there until 1942, when he joined the Office of Price Administration. Bowles was a member of the War Production Board from 1943 to 1946. Elected governor of Connecticut in 1949, Bowles served one term and became ambassador to India in 1951. He served one term in Congress* between 1958 and 1960, and in 1961 he became under secretary of state in the Kennedy* administration. He did not last there long. A strong advocate of a negotiated settlement, based on neutrality for Vietnam, Bowles was identified as a "dove" by the Kennedy administration and fired as under secretary of state in November 1961. He was named an ambassador-at-large and traveled widely until 1963, when he replaced John K. Galbraith* as ambassador to India. He remained there until his retirement from public life in 1969. Chester Bowles died on May 23, 1986.

Sources: Chester B. Bowles, *Promises to Keep: My Years in Public Life, 1941–1969*, 1971; Lee H. Burke, *Ambassador at Large: Diplomat Extraordinary*, 1972; *New York Times*, May 24, 1986.

THE BOYS OF COMPANY C

Released in 1978, *The Boys of Company C* was a film tracing the lives of five young men—played by actors Stan Shaw, Andrew Stevens, Craig Wasson, Michael Lembeck, and James Canning—from boot camp to combat in Vietnam. They come from all walks of American life—ghettos, farms, suburbs—and discover something about themselves in Vietnam. The film was taken directly from the antiwar genre of the 1970s, and the war in Vietnam is treated as a hopeless endeavor characterized by drug abuse, crime, atrocities, political contradictions, and diplomatic absurdities. It ends in a climactic soccer match when Vietcong* guerrillas attack and disrupt the game in the middle of Saigon.*

Source: *Magill's Survey of Cinema. English Language Films*, 1981.

BRIGADE

The term "brigade" is a basic military organizational institution. During the Vietnam War, a division was organized into three brigades, with each brigade commanded by a colonel. A division consists of approximately 20,000 people. There were also separate infantry brigades functioning in the Vietnam War. The 11th,* 196th,* and 198th Infantry Brigades fought in the war until 1967, when they were brought together to reconstitute the Americal Division, or the 23rd Infantry.* The 199th Infantry Brigade* and the 173rd Airborne Brigade* continued to fight as independent entities. A number of combat support brigades, designed to provide supplies, medical care, and maintenance, also functioned in South Vietnam during the 1960s and 1970s.

Sources: Harry G. Summers, Jr., *Vietnam War Almanac*, 1985; Shelby L. Stanton, *Vietnam Order of Battle*, 1981.

BRINKS HOTEL (SAIGON)

The Brinks Hotel housed some American military officers in Saigon.* On the afternoon of Christmas Eve, 1964, two Vietcong* agents put a bomb in the basement carpark. They had reconnoitered the target painstakingly, and they managed to park a car containing the bomb without being observed or suspected. At 5:45 P.M., while the Americans were eating dinner and planning the Christmas Eve party for later that evening, the bomb exploded while one of the agents, Nguyen Thanh Xuan, casually observed from a restaurant across the street. Two American officers were killed and fifty-eight were wounded. The Brinks Hotel episode is significant for several reasons. It demonstrated the ability of the Vietcong to operate anywhere in South Vietnam, even in the capital of its enemy.

It also demonstrated the inability of that enemy to protect its citizens and allies, a vital prerequisite to successful guerrilla or insurgency warfare. Coming soon after the American bombing* of North Vietnam following the Tonkin Gulf incident,* it demonstrated the form of escalation or response that any further bombing of North Vietnam would take. Finally, it presented policymakers in Washington with a basic question that would characterize the war throughout its history: would bombing the North reduce enemy hostilities in the South? President Johnson* overruled his advisers in this instance, arguing that bombing retaliation for the Brinks Hotel attack would be politically unwise during Christmas and militarily unsound as a disproportionate response which might unnecessarily escalate the war.

The attack on the Brinks Hotel epitomized the situation for Americans in Vietnam in the mid–1960s. No place was completely safe from Vietcong acts of terrorism, and the result was uncertainty, confusion, and trepidation for allied forces. The audacity of the Vietcong attack contributed to the escalation of the war during a critical period in Washington's policy-making.

Sources: Stanley Karnow, *Vietnam: A History*, 1983; *New York Times*, December 25–28, 1964.

Stafford T. Thomas

BROWN, GEORGE SCRATCHLEY

George S. Brown was born in Montclair, New Jersey, on August 17, 1918. He graduated from the United States Military Academy in 1941, served with the Eighth Air Force in Europe during World War II, and was director of operations for the Fifth Air Force in Korea. He became air force chief of staff in March 1973, after having served as commander of the Seventh Air Force* in 1969 and 1970. In 1974 Brown became chairman of the Joint Chiefs of Staff (*see* Chairman, JCS). He was a controversial figure for a time in 1973 when, during Senate confirmation hearings, his role in the secret bombings of Cambodia (*see* Operation Menu) and Laos (*see* Lam Son 719) was discussed. Brown died on December 5, 1978.

Sources: *New York Times*, December 6, 1978; William Shawcross, *Sideshow: Kissinger, Nixon, and the Destruction of Cambodia*, 1979; Lawrence J. Korb, *The Joint Chiefs of Staff: The First Twenty-Five Years*, 1976.

BROWN, SAMUEL WINFRED

Samuel Brown was born on July 27, 1943, in Council Bluffs, Iowa. He received a bachelor's degree from the University of Redlands in 1965, a master's degree in political science from Rutgers University in 1966, and spent some time at the Harvard Divinity School in 1967 and 1968. In 1968, Brown organized student volunteers for Senator Eugene McCarthy's* presidential bid, and in 1969 he became founder and coordinator of the Vietnam Moratorium Committee. The committee sponsored antiwar* demonstrations throughout the United States in October and November of 1969 (*see* Moratorium Day demonstrations). The committee disbanded in 1970. Brown was active in support of Senator George McGovern's* presidential campaign in 1972.

Sources: Harry G. Summers, Jr., *Vietnam War Almanac*, 1985; Eugene McCarthy, *The Year of the People*, 1969; Nancy Zaroulis and Gerald Sullivan, *Who Spoke Up? American Protest Against the War in Vietnam, 1963–1975*, 1984.

BUDDHISM

Buddhism, the dominant organized religion of Vietnam, was first introduced to Indochina* in 111 B.C., when the Chinese conquered the Red River Delta. During the next thousand years, Buddhism fitted comfortably into the animist faith of common people and became the dominant popular religion. During the imperial dynasties of the middle ages, Buddhism acquired a strong political base as well, and a Buddhist hierarchy saw to it that it became a state religion, complete with tax support and positions of influence in the imperial court. By the fifteenth century Buddhism had lost some of its imperial influence to Confucianism and Taoism, but it retained its influence among common people. Not until the twentieth century did Vietnamese Buddhism enjoy a revival among intellectual elites and the upper class.

Buddhist doctrine revolved around the idea of successive lives for individuals. After suffering the challenges of life, individuals of merit would undergo successive lives through reincarnation. A cycle of birth, death, and rebirth governed individual life until one reached the state of nirvana, a condition of eternal peace. Only as an individual transcended worldly needs could he or she approach nirvana. In Vietnam, Mahayana Buddhism became the dominant religious strain. Its comfortable approach to saints and supernatural beings made it fit nicely into Vietnamese animism, and its ritual and imagery pleased the peasants. Mahayana Buddhism also viewed Gautama Buddha, founder of the religion, not as the one, single Buddha but one of a number of great teachers and leaders.

During the reign of Ngo Dinh Diem,* Roman Catholicism* assumed special prominence in Vietnamese affairs. Catholics filled key posts in the civil service, police, and military, and Roman Catholicism increased in size because of the mass influx of Catholic refugees* from North Vietnam and increased conversion rates by South Vietnamese who saw the religion as an opportunity for economic advancement and political influence. The fact that Diem rigidly repressed all political opposition, including the disorganized Buddhist leaders, contributed to a powerful resurgence of Buddhist influence. In response to the pro-Catholic, anti-Buddhist posture of Diem, Buddhists began organizing in the 1950s. They formed the General Buddhist Association in 1955 in an attempt to provide some centralized direction to Buddhist political influence, and after the assassination of Diem in 1963 they filled a political vacuum in South Vietnam. The Buddhist Reunification Congress met at Xa Loi Pagoda in Saigon* in December 1963, and the next month they organized the United Buddhist Church of Vietnam, which soon won the support of most Buddhist sects in South Vietnam.

Buddhists in Hue* and Da Nang,* led by Thich Tri Quang,* were generally quite militant in their opposition to the Saigon government, while Buddhists in Saigon, led by Thich Thien Khiet and Thich Tam Chau, were more circumspect and conservative. In South Vietnam, the Buddhists condemned communism as atheistic, denounced military governments in all forms, and rejected any political influence Roman Catholicism seemed to have. Their opposition to General Nguyen Khanh's* military government brought his downfall in August 1964, and they were similarly responsible for the collapse of Tran Van Huong's* government in January 1965. In April 1966 General Nguyen Cao Ky* transferred power to an elected body primarily because of Buddhist influence. In May 1966, the Buddhists organized military demonstrations throughout the country, complete with marches and the widely publicized self-immolations, and General Nguyen Cao Ky sent soldiers out to crush the demonstrations. Buddhist political influence would never be the same again, primarily because American military power was firmly behind the government of Nguyen Van Thieu* and Nguyen Cao Ky. Although Buddhists represented 80 percent of the South Vietnamese population, their political influence was all but eclipsed by the crushing defeat of 1966.

Sources: Harvey H. Smith et al., *Area Handbook for South Vietnam*, 1967; Sukumar Dutt, *Buddhism in East Asia*, 1966; Frances FitzGerald, *Fire in the Lake: The Vietnamese and the Americans in Vietnam*, 1972; Edgar Wickberg, *Historical Interaction of China and Vietnam*, 1969; Pierro Gheddo, *The Cross and the Bo-Tree: Catholics and Buddhists in Vietnam*, 1970.

BUI DIEM

Bui Diem was born on October 1, 1923, in Phu Ly, North Vietnam. A cousin of South Vietnamese president Nguyen Van Thieu,* Diem fled to the south in 1954 after the Geneva Accords.* He worked as a journalist until 1964 when he became an adviser to South Vietnamese Prime Minister Phan Huy Quat.* Between 1966 and 1972 Diem was ambassador to the United States, but he returned home in 1972 to serve as an adviser to President Nguyen Van Thieu. By 1975 Diem was urging Thieu to either resign or launch a major offensive against the North Vietnamese, but Thieu was indecisive. After the fall of South Vietnam in April 1975, Bui Diem fled to the United States and opened a Jewish delicatessen in Washington, D.C.

Sources: *Who's Who in the World, 1974–1975*, 1975; Stanley Karnow, *Vietnam: A History*, 1983.

BUI PHAT

As part of the Geneva Accords* of 1954 ending the war between the French and the Vietminh* and establishing two Vietnams, a 300-day armistice period allowed Vietnamese to relocate from the north to the south or from the south to the north. During that period, with the assistance of the U.S. Seventh Fleet,* more than 900,000 people, most of them Roman Catholics* from the dioceses at Phat Diem and Bui Chu in North Vietnam, relocated to South Vietnam. The refugees* became the political base of Ngo Dinh Diem* in South Vietnam. Although most of the refugees ended up in special camps, some of them settled in Saigon* across the river from the French settlement. The name of the tin-roofed ghetto was Bui Phat, a composite title taken from the bishoprics of Phat Diem and Bui Chu. Because the economy of Bui Phat revolved around the money flowing from the American military presence in South Vietnam, the population tended to resist Vietcong* and Buddhist political overtures. Any political movement threatening the American presence also threatened the livelihoods of the people of Bui Phat.

Source: Frances FitzGerald, *Fire in the Lake: The Vietnamese and Americans in Vietnam*, 1972.

BUI TIN

Born in Hue* in 1924, Bui Tin came from an aristocratic family but joined the Vietminh* in 1945. He fought with them in the battles of the Red River Valley and at Dien Bien Phu* in 1954. After the Geneva Accords* of 1954, Bui Tin became one of the leading Communists in Hanoi,* and in 1963 he went into South Vietnam to assist the Vietcong* in their struggle against the government of Ngo Dinh Diem.* Over the next ten years Tin became a colonel in the North Vietnamese Army* (NVA) and deputy editor of *Quan Doi Nhan Dan*, the NVA newspaper. When the NVA entered Saigon* on April 30, 1975, Bui Tin was the ranking NVA officer who accepted the surrender of the South Vietnamese government.

Source: John S. Bowman, ed., *The Vietnam War: An Almanac*, 1985.

BUNDY, McGEORGE

McGeorge Bundy was born on March 30, 1919, in Boston, Massachusetts. He graduated from Yale in 1940 and joined the United States Army during World War II. His primary responsibilities were logistics and the planning for the invasions of Sicily and France. Bundy came from an old New England family, and as a result enjoyed contacts with influential people in the American business and political establishment. That he was brilliant only ensured his success. Bundy left the army in 1946 and became a research assistant to former secretary of state Henry L. Stimson, and was coauthor with him of *On Active Service in Peace and War* in 1948. In 1948 Bundy served as a consultant to the Thomas Dewey presidential campaign, to the Marshall Plan implementation group in the State Department, and to the Council on Foreign Relations in New York City. He began lecturing at Harvard in 1949, and in 1953 Bundy became dean of arts and sciences at Harvard. In January 1961 President John F. Kennedy* named Bundy special assistant to the president for national security affairs. There he became a principal architect of the Vietnam escalation.

In 1965 Bundy traveled to South Vietnam for a personal assessment of the situation there, and he returned advocating large-scale bombing of North Vietnam. His recommendation soon became Operation Rolling Thunder.* One of the "best and the brightest" of the Cold Warriors, Bundy was convinced that communism had to be stopped in Southeast Asia if the rest of Asia was going to remain free. In 1966 Bundy left the administration to become head of the Ford Foundation, but he continued to serve as a consultant to Lyndon B. Johnson* as a member of the "Wise Old Men"* group. As part of that group in 1968, Bundy helped Johnson realize that the combination of the antiwar movement* at home and the difficult political and military situation in Vietnam made a negotiated settlement of the war inevitable.

Sources: David Halberstam, *The Best and the Brightest*, 1972; Leslie Gelb and Richard Betts, *The Irony of Vietnam: The System Worked*, 1979.

BUNDY, WILLIAM

William Bundy was born on September 24, 1917, in Washington, D.C. He graduated from Yale in 1939, served with the United States Army during World War II, and took a law degree from Harvard in 1947. Between 1950 and 1960 Bundy worked for the Central Intelligence Agency* (CIA). He became a member of President Dwight D. Eisenhower's* Commission on National Goals in 1960, and in 1961 President John F. Kennedy* appointed him deputy assistant secretary of defense for international security affairs. Along with his brother McGeorge Bundy,* he played an influential role in the development of American policy toward Southeast Asia. Bundy was a strong supporter of the government of Ngo Dinh Diem* in the early 1960s and an advocate of an escalating American presence in South Vietnam. He was the chief author of what became the Gulf of Tonkin Resolution* in 1964. Early in 1964 Bundy had become assistant secretary of state for Far Eastern affairs, and later in the year President Lyndon B. Johnson* asked him to head the National Security Council Working Group and make policy recommendations for the American future in Vietnam. Their recommendations eventually became Operation Rolling Thunder,* in which Bundy and his brother often personally selected the bombing targets in North Vietnam. Bundy continued opposing negotiation and favoring increased bombing of North Vietnam until 1967, when he began to moderate his position. A leading "hawk" for both the Kennedy and Johnson administrations, Bundy left the State Department in 1969 and returned to research and writing, serving for a time as editor of *Foreign Affairs*.

Sources: *Who's Who in America, 1967–68*, 1968; David Halberstam, *The Best and the Brightest*, 1972.

BUNKER, ELLSWORTH

Ellsworth Bunker was born May 11, 1894, in Yonkers, New York. He graduated from Yale in 1916, and between his graduation and 1951, he worked for the National Sugar Refining Company, serving as president from 1940 to 1948 and chairman of the board from 1948 to 1951. Bunker's diplomatic career began in 1951 when President Harry S. Truman* appointed him ambassador to Argentina, where he worked diligently and successfully in implementing a rapprochement between the Peronistas and the United States. He was ambassador to Italy between 1952 and 1953, and in 1956 became ambassador to India and Nepal, a post he held until 1961. Bunker played a major role as a troubleshooter, negotiating settlements to the Netherlands-Indonesia controversy over West Irian in 1962 and the Panama crisis in 1964. He was the American representative to the Organization of American States from 1964 to 1966 and also helped calm the angry feelings in Latin America over the American intervention in the Dominican Republic in 1965.

Bunker was appointed ambassador to South Vietnam in 1967, and he remained in that position until his resignation in 1973. Bunker was a strong supporter of the regime of Nguyen Van Thieu,* Vietnamization,* a negotiated settlement to the conflict, and the Cambodian invasion of 1970 (*see* Operation Binh Tay). Bunker became an ambassador-at-large late in 1973 and played a major role in the Panama Canal Treaties, which were signed on September 7, 1977. Ellsworth Bunker died on September 27, 1984.

Sources: Lee H. Burke, *Ambassador at Large: Diplomat Extraordinary*, 1972; *New York Times*, September 28, 1984.

"BUST CAPS"

"Busts caps" was a slang term meaning to fire a rifle. Used predominantly by U.S. Marines,* the term refers to the unique sound of the M–16 rifle,* which was the standard weapon used by American, South Vietnamese, and South Korean troops after 1964. Unlike the AK–47,* which was commonly used by Communist forces and had a bigger bullet, the relatively narrow bullet of the M–16 makes a higher-pitched noise when it is fired and sounds like a cap pistol. Thus, to "bust caps" meant to fire the M–16 rifle, and through repeated usage the term came to mean firing any kind of rifle. The term also spawned a number of derivations, such as "capping," which simply meant shooting.

Source: Mark Baker, *Nam*, 1981.

Stafford T. Thomas

• C •

C–4

C–4 was a plastic explosive popular among soldiers in Vietnam because of its various properties. It was easy to carry because of its lightweight, stable nature. It had a potent explosive power, and malleable with a texture similar to play dough, it could be formed into a shaped charge of infinite configuration. The availability of C–4 reduced the necessity of carrying a variety of explosive charges. C–4 would not explode without use of detonation devices, even when dropped, beaten, shot, or burned. It was not destabilized by water, an important consideration given the Vietnamese climate.* Because it could be safely burned, C–4 was popular with GIs, who would break off a small piece of it for heating water or C-rations. Sometimes they used it in foxholes to warm hands and feet on chilly nights. C–4 replaced sterno as the heating fuel of choice. Soldiers in the field could obtain C–4 on a resupply mission whereas sterno required a trip to the PX which, of course, was not necessarily possible.

Sources: Edgar C. Doleman, Jr., *The Vietnam Experience: Tools of War*, 1984; Al Santoli, *Everything We Had: An Oral History of the Vietnam War by Thirty-three American Soldiers Who Fought It*, 1981.

Samuel Freeman

C–5 GALAXY

The gigantic C–5 Galaxy, with its tremendous payload capability, was developed during the 1960s in response to the unprecedented dimensions of inter-theater airlift in support of U.S. forces in Vietnam. Designed as the world's largest aircraft, the C–5 first became operational with the Military Airlift Command* on December 17, 1969, and was assigned to the Transitional Training Unit at Altus Air Force Base, Oklahoma. The first operational Galaxies were delivered to the 437th Military Airlift Wing, Charleston Air Force Base, South Carolina, in June 1970, followed by delivery to the 60th Military Airlift Wing at Travis Air Force Base, California, in October 1970. The C–5s operated by the 60th Military Airlift Wing became an important force in ensuring the efficiency of the aerial supply pipeline between the United States and Southeast Asia during the latter years of the war in Vietnam.

The C–5 was especially important for Vietnam support because it could carry virtually all equipment in the United States Army's inventory at intercontinental ranges and jet speeds. It could, for instance, handle such bulky items as the 74-ton mobile scissors bridge. Additionally, in its test program the C–5 air-dropped four 40,000-pound units—a total of 160,000-pounds—in a single pass over a drop zone. It could also be loaded and unloaded simultaneously at the front and rear cargo openings, and had the capability to "kneel down" to facilitate loading directly from truck-bed levels. All these attributes made the C–5 a transport especially useful in Southeast Asia aerial resupply operations.

The task of moving essential supplies, personnel, and units between the United States and Vietnam was a staggering one, and after 1970 one in which the C–5 force figured prominently. For instance, the C–5s were instrumental in supporting the defense of South Vietnam after invasion from the north in April 1972. Teaming with C–141* aircraft and commercial carriers, C–5s moved 3,195 personnel and 1,600 tons of cargo from the United States to Vietnam between May 6 and 15, 1972. Additionally, when the Communist offensive swept through the provincial capital of Quang Tri and moved southward, the United States Army* turned to the Air Force* to deliver more tanks and armored vehicles to the South Vietnamese. In response, and within twenty-four hours, the C–5 fleet airlifted twenty-six tanks—weighing about 1.6 million pounds—in ten flights directly to Da Nang,* including six which were delivered from a repair depot in the Pacific.

As the Vietnam War drew to a close and American participation in the war phased out, Military Airlift Command C–5s were necessary to support troop movements. Following the peace agreements in January 1973, for example, C–5 and other transport aircraft were heavily involved in the withdrawal of the remaining American military personnel and equipment from Vietnam. This task involved several thousand tons of equipment and more than 20,000 personnel.

Sources: Kenneth W. Patchin, "Strategic Airlift," in Carl Berger, ed., *The United States Air Force in Southeast Asia, 1961–1973, An Illustrated Account*, 1977.

Roger D. Launius

C–7   *See* Caribou Aircraft

C–130 HERCULES

One of the principal tactical transport aircraft used in Vietnam, the C–130 Hercules proved remarkably adaptable for in-country tasks. Beginning in 1965 United States Air Force* leaders made the decision to station C–130 units under the operational control of the Pacific Air Forces (PACAF) offshore to provide much of the airlift necessary to support operations in Southeast Asia. These aircraft played a critical role in tactical operations in the theater until 1975, when they were used to assist in the evacuation of American nationals and certain South Vietnamese from Saigon.*

A key aspect of this airlift force's role in Southeast Asia was support of ground forces. For instance, during Operation New Life, beginning November 21, 1965, the 173d Airborne Brigade* of the 101st Airborne Division* made a helicopter assault on a dirt airstrip 40 miles east of Bien Hoa* Air Base. To support this operation, within an hour of the initial attack, the first C–130s landed to deliver troops and cargo. In all, some seventy C–130 sorties* brought in critical support resources during the first thirty-six hours of the operation. A second aspect of this type of support involved the aerial resupply of Khe Sanh* during the first four months of 1968. This support was indispensable to the success of the garrison's defense from an enemy siege. Seen by North Vietnam as a second Dien Bien Phu,* the 1954 siege of a northern city where the French were soundly defeated, Communist forces pressed to crush the 6,000-man marine garrison at Khe Sanh as part of the 1968 Tet Offensive.* To hold out, C–130s flew daily airdrops and low-altitude parachute extraction (LAPE) deliveries of some 12,400 tons of supplies to the garrison. Between January 21 and April 8, 1968, C–130s flew 496 airdrop, 67 extraction, and 273 landing missions. Without this tactical airlift support provided by C–130s, the Khe Sanh garrison would have been forced to surrender.

Between 1965 and 1973 Air Force C–130s moved more than five million tons of passengers and cargo in Southeast Asia. It lost fifty-three C–130s during these operations, more than half of these losses coming in the North Vietnamese offensives of 1967 and 1968.

Source: Ray L. Bowers, *The U.S. Air Force in Southeast Asia: Tactical Airlift*, 1983.

Roger D. Launius

C–141 STARLIFTER

The C–141 Starlifter has been the "workhorse" of the Military Airlift Command's* strategic airlift fleet since the mid–1960s, and was a major contributor to the successful resupply of American military forces during the Southeast Asian conflict. It was the first jet aircraft specifically designed, engineered, and built to meet military standards as a strategic troop and cargo carrier. It succeeded admirably in fulfilling the great spectrum of intertheater airlift requirements that arose because of the Vietnam experience. Used to lift combat forces over long distances, inject those forces either by airland or airdrop activities, resupply those employed forces, and extract the sick and wounded from the hostile area to far-removed medical facilities, the C–141, along with its larger C–5 aircraft, ensured the capability of the United States to resupply forces in Vietnam on a timely basis.

Indeed, it was a milestone in the modernization of the strategic airlift fleet in April 1965 when the C–141 Starlifter became operational and began flying to Southeast Asia. By 1967, the C–141 fleet had grown to more than 100 aircraft, and in 1968 the 284th and last C–141 was produced. The Starlifter could carry 67,620 pounds of cargo 4,000 miles or 20,000 pounds nonstop from California to Japan at speeds of 440 knots. By comparison, the C–124, the principal transport aircraft of the U.S. Air Force* prior to 1965, could carry only 50,000 pounds over a range of 1,000 miles or 25,000 pounds for about 2,300 miles at speeds of only 200 knots.

In responding to the urgent Southeast Asia requirements that arose with the escalation of American commitment in South Vietnam, the air force quickly found that traffic to the Pacific grew from a monthly average of 33,779 passengers and 9,123 tons of cargo in fiscal year 1965 to 65,350 passengers and 42,296 tons of cargo in fiscal year 1967. In flying about 210,000,000 miles during 1967, the Military Airlift Command flew the equivalent of 8,750 aircraft around the world and carried sufficient troops to fill every manpower space in eighty-five army infantry divisions. The C–141 airlift fleet was the major method of supporting these increases.

On several occasions during the war, the air force was called on to undertake the deployment of major army units under special conditions. The first of these, designated Operation Blue Light, came in response to the need to rush the 3rd Brigade, 25th Infantry Division from Hawaii to Pleiku, Vietnam, to offset a buildup of Communist forces late in 1965 that threatened the area. The Military Airlift Command's C–141 fleet carried the brunt of this activity, flying with C–133 aircraft 231 sorties* over a 26-day period and moving 3,000 troops and 4,700 tons of equipment some 6,000 miles to Pleiku by January 23, 1966. At the height of the airlift, a C–141 or C–133 took off from Hickam every three hours.

In mid–1969 emphasis shifted to the return of units to the United States in accordance with the president's policy of gradual American withdrawal from Vietnam, beginning with 25,000 troops before August 31. The Military Airlift Command's C–141s carried out the first redeployments through a series of operations called Keystone. In the first of these, C–141s airlifted 15,446 of the 25,000 troops plus 47.5 tons of material from Vietnam to the United States. As the president directed other incremental withdrawals over the next several years, the C–141 force responded accordingly.

Source: Kenneth W. Patchin, "Strategic Airlift," in Carl Berger, ed., *The United States Air Force in Southeast Asia, 1961–1973, An Illustrated Account*, 1977.

Roger D. Launius

CAI TANG

A Vietnamese custom widely misunderstood by American soldiers during the war, cai tang is a religious act of exhuming and reburying the bodies of dead relatives. The practice was likely to occur if the family could not afford a proper burial or if the body was buried in a hurry, a common occurrence in South Vietnam during the late 1960s and early 1970s. Usually several years after the individual's death, the family would locate the bones, wash them, and rebury them in a place more suitable as a resting place.

Sources: Ann Crawford, *Customs and Culture of Vietnam*, 1966; Gustave Dumoutier, *Annamese Religions*, 1955; Jacques Dournes, *God Loves The Pagans*, 1966.

CALLEY, WILLIAM LAWS, JR.

Born on June 8, 1943, William Calley, Jr., spent an uneventful childhood in Miami, Florida. He graduated from high school and entered Palm Beach Junior College, but after flunking out he worked as a bellhop, dishwasher, and railroad switchman until 1966 when he enlisted in the army. He went to Officers Candidate School and after graduation was ordered to Hawaii to join Company C, First Battalion, 20th Infantry, under the command of Captain Ernest L. Medina. Calley was placed in charge of the company's First Platoon.

In December 1967, Company C arrived in Vietnam and was assigned to the 11th Infantry Brigade (*see* 23rd Infantry Division). On March 16, 1968, Calley was instructed to lead a task force to Son My in Quang Ngai Province and destroy a suspected Vietcong* stronghold in the hamlet of My Lai.* During the mission, no Vietcong were encountered, although helicopter pilots circling the area reported massive civilian casualties. This information was relayed to the commanders of the 11th Infantry, Colonel Oran K. Henderson and Major General Samuel W. Foster, and after looking into the reports, they concurred that nothing unusual had taken place during the operation at My Lai.

In April 1969, a Vietnam veteran, Ronald L. Ridenhour, in a letter to President Richard Nixon,* urged an investigation into the events of March 16, 1968, at My Lai. The following November, an army board headed by Lt. General William R. Peers made an inquiry into the alleged events of that day. In the same month, William Calley was charged with the premeditated murder of 102 civilians at My Lai. Calley's defense rested upon the fact that he had received orders from Captain Medina at a briefing to destroy and kill every living being in the hamlet of My Lai because "they were all enemy." Medina denied having given the order. On March 29, 1971, William Calley was found guilty of the premeditated murder of at least twenty-two South Vietnamese civilians by an army court-martial jury. Two days later he was sentenced to life imprisonment at hard labor and dismissal from the army.

Calley's conviction immediately provoked dissension among the American people. There were public protests demanding his release because many felt he was being made a scapegoat for the army, taking the blame while his superiors escaped responsibility. Included among the protesters were Governors Jimmy Carter and George Wallace, as well as President Nixon who ordered him released from the stockade and returned to his apartment on the base while his convictions were under review. Nixon, shrewdly aware of public opinion, decided to review the case personally before the sentence could be carried out.

In August 1971, Calley's life sentence was reduced to twenty years. In April 1974, the sentence was further reduced to ten years. The following month,

President Nixon decided that further action was neither necessary nor appropriate. Finally, in November 1975, William Calley was released on parole. Public reaction to his case reflected the contradictory nature of the Vietnam War. On the one hand, the actions at My Lai, publicized by photographs in *Life* magazine, were seen as atrocities,* unacceptable to an American public convinced that only other countries, autocratic governments, committed atrocities. Yet, on the other hand, because the incident was indicative of the true nature of the war, punishment of Calley or even his superiors would have constituted condemnation of the American government itself. Perhaps Lt. General William R. Peers summed up the affair when he said, "To think that out of all those men, only one, Lt. William Calley, was brought to justice. And now, he's practically a hero. It's a tragedy."

Sources: Joseph Goldstein, Burke Marshall, and Jack Schwartz, *The My Lai Massacre and Its Cover-Up: Beyond the Reach of Law?*, 1976; W. R. Peers, *The My Lai Inquiry*, 1979; Richard Hammer, *The Court-Martial of Lieutenant Calley*, 1971; John Sack, *Lieutenant Calley: His Own Story*, 1971.

Sally Smith

CAMBODIA   *See* Kampuchea

CAMBODIA, BOMBING OF   *See* Operation Menu

CAMBODIA, INVASION OF   *See* Operation Binh Tay

CAM RANH

Cam Ranh was an independent municipality located between Khanh Hoa and Ninh Thuan provinces in South Vietnam. At the peak of the fighting during the Vietnam war, Cam Ranh had a population of nearly 105,000.

Sources: *Webster's Geographical Dictionary*, 1984; Judith Banister, *The Population of Vietnam*, 1985.

CAM RANH BAY

Cam Ranh Bay was the major port of entry for U.S. military supplies and personnel in South Vietnam. Located about 200 miles northeast of Saigon* on the southern bulge of Vietnam, it had been an important way station for navigators since the days of Marco Polo. In June 1965, the U.S. Army Corps of Engineers began improving the port with 70 miles of roads, warehouses, fuel tanks, and larger cargo-handling facilities. A new pier was shipped from South Carolina and assembled at Cam Ranh Bay, giving the facility the ability to handle six large vessels simultaneously. The port was considered so safe that Lyndon Johnson* visited there twice, which made the shock of the Vietcong* raid in 1969 even more severe. The Vietcong attack destroyed a water tower and chapel and damaged the hospital. Most patients were evacuated safely, but the United States lost two killed and ninety-eight wounded. The Vietcong escaped without a casualty. Security was tightened, and Cam Ranh Bay continued to be the major supply port for Vietnam, even after the American withdrawal in 1975. It was abandoned without a fight in June 1975.

Sources: Harvey H. Smith et al., *Area Handbook for South Vietnam*, 1967; Carroll H. Dunn, *Base Development in South Vietnam, 1965–1970*, 1972.

Barbara Wiggins

CANADA

Canada played several important roles in the Vietnam War. Despite some disagreement over figures, it is clear that large numbers of young Americans exercised the option of becoming expatriates in Canada, either temporarily or permanently, in order to avoid the Vietnam War. Canadian immigration officials suggest that approximately 30,000 Americans settled legally there between 1965 and 1972. The American exile organization AMEX argued the number was closer to 80,000—50,000 illegally and 30,000 legally. Canada was clearly an alternative for men who chose not to aid the war effort, who could not secure deferments, or who found the possibility of jail intolerable.

Canada also served, after the 1954 Geneva Accords,* as a longtime member of the International Commission for Supervision and Control in Vietnam (the ICSC), created to monitor compliance with the agreement. Soon the Canadian role in the ICSC changed, especially after it became readily apparent that the 1954 Geneva Accords would not be upheld. With access to North Vietnam, Canadian members also became conveyors of messages from the United States to Hanoi,* especially threats of escalation unless North Vietnam compromised its position. Critics of the war charged Canada with compliance, but Prime Minister Lester Pearson defended Canadian actions as attempts to bring the war to an end and keep lines of communication open.

Pearson also pointed out that cooperation with American requests helped Canada maintain access to the corridors of power in Washington, and thus enabled Canada to influence American policy. Although Canada steadfastly would not provide material aid to the war effort, she also would not condemn American actions. Harsh criticism would have alienated the Americans, while expressions of cautious support lent credibility to urgings of moderation. That Canadian voice, along with those of other NATO allies, may have prompted more restraint in American policies and hastened the eventual disengagement.

As the United States withdrew from Vietnam, the ICSC was reconstituted in 1972 as the International Commission of Control and Supervision* (ICCS), and again Canada served as a member. It had the same weaknesses as its predecessor. Communist forces were uncooperative to the point of taking military action against ICCS helicopters and refusing to allow teams to make required inspections. When Poland and Hungary, also ICCS members, hindered objective reporting on the military situation in South Vietnam, Canada resigned from the commission in 1973.

    Sources: Douglas A. Ross, *In the Interests of Peace: Canada and Vietnam, 1954–1973*, 1984; Daniel S. Papp, *Vietnam: The View from Moscow, Peking, Washington*, 1981; Charles Taylor, *Snow Job: Canada, the United States and Vietnam (1954–1973)*, 1974.

                                                                              Gary M. Bell

CAN LAO NHAN VI CACH MANG DANG

    Translated as the Revolutionary Personalist Labor party, the Can Lao was founded in 1954 after Ngo Dinh Diem* took over the government of South Vietnam. Ngo Dinh Nhu,* the brother of Ngo Dinh Diem, was a powerful person in his own right who advised his brother on all political matters. Nhu's political philosophy was known as Personalism, or Nhan Vi, a belief in the power of the state mixed with strong emphasis on the virtues of humility, submissiveness, and sacrifice. In 1954 Nhu created the Can Lao, or Personalist Labor party, from the ranks of Catholic refugees.* Eventually the party numbered more than 20,000 people, each of them occupying a position of influence in the bureaucracy and military. Nhu left direction of the Can Lao to Dr. Tran Kim Tuyen,* and they built a number of secret intelligence organizations in the Can Lao to keep Nhu informed of traitors, spies, plots, and military news. To finance the Can Lao, Nhu resorted to graft, extortion, currency racketeering, and vice throughout South Vietnam. The Can Lao went into decline after 1963, when Ngo Dinh Diem was assassinated and his regime overthrown. Nhu was killed at the same time. In 1969, many members of the Can Lao came back to power when President Nguyen Van Thieu* dismissed his cabinet and used old Can Lao members to staff his government. The Can Lao were frequently vulnerable to Vietcong* assassination attempts, and those unable to get to the United States after 1975 were imprisoned and killed when Saigon* and South Vietnam fell to the Communists.

    Sources: Frances FitzGerald, *Fire in the Lake: The Vietnamese and Americans in Vietnam*, 1972; Denis Warner, *The Last Confucian*, 1963; Joseph Buttinger, *Vietnam: A Dragon Embattled*. Vol. 2, *Vietnam at War*, 1967.

CAN THO

    Can Tho, located on Highway 4 between Saigon* and Ca Mau, is the capital city of Phong Dinh Province and the commercial center of the Mekong Delta.* Its population at the height of the Vietnam War was nearly 154,000. Can Tho became one of South Vietnam's autonomous municipalities on September 30, 1970.

    Sources: Danny J. Whitfield, *Historical and Cultural Dictionary of Vietnam*, 1976; *Webster's Geographical Dictionary*, 1984.

CAO DAI

    Cao Dai is the popular name for the Dai Dao Tam Ky Pho Do religious sect, a group of approximately 1.5 million South Vietnamese. In 1902 a young Vietnamese civil servant, Ngo Van Chieu, became involved in spiritualism and felt the supreme power of the universe, the Cao Dai, had communicated with him. Cao Dai was organized as a formal religion in 1926. An eclectic faith drawing on Christianity, Vietnamese animism, Buddhism,* and Confucianism, Cao Dai is centered in the city of Tay Ninh, about 60 miles northwest of Saigon.* The largest collection of Cao Dai adherents live in the Mekong Delta* between the Mekong River and the Song Hau Giang River. Cao Dai believed that Buddha, Jesus, and Lao-tzu were all manifestations of one divine power and religious force in the universe, and they had a great pantheon of diverse saints, ranging from Buddha and Jesus to Charlie Chaplin and Joan of Arc.

The new religion grew rapidly in the Mekong Delta, so much so that the French prohibited its export to Annam,* Cambodia (see Kampuchea), or Tonkin.* Although the sect was more interested in religious proselytizing than political activity, it did take on a general anti-French cast and became a home for many Vietnamese nationalists. Because many Cao Dai leaders had jobs in the French bureaucracy, peasants in Cochin China* became loyal to the movement since it made it easier for them to deal with the empire. In 1938, the Cao Dai established its own private army to protect the property of members, and gradually the Cao Dai became a semiautonomous state in the Mekong Delta. Stocked with Japanese, French, and American weapons, they literally controlled a large area northwest of Saigon. Generally free of Communist influence, the Cao Dai were among the most stable elements of the South Vietnamese population. Not until 1955, under military pressure, did the Cao Dai yield their independence to President Ngo Diem* of South Vietnam. Pham Cong Tac, leader of the Cao Dai, fled to Cambodia in February 1956 and South Vietnamese forces seized control of Tay Ninh. Most Cao Dai leaders were then incorporated into the South Vietnamese bureaucracy and military.

Sources: Victor L. Oliver, *Cao Dai Spiritualism: A Study of Religion in Vietnamese Society*, 1976; Denis Warner, *The Last Confucian*, 1963; Bernard Fall, "The Political Religious Sects of Vietnam," *Pacific Affairs*, 28 (1955), 235–53.

CAO VAN VIEN

Born in Laos* in 1921, Cao Van Vien was trained in the army as a paratrooper. Vien established close relations with General Nguyen Cao Ky* and became his chief of staff in 1966. Vien fled to the United States in 1975.

Source: "Clean-Up Time," *Newsweek*, 69 (February 6, 1967), 44–45.

CAPITAL DIVISION

The Republic of Korea* (ROK) sent combat forces to South Vietnam in response to President Johnson's* desire to have "more flags" supporting the war. The ROK units in Vietnam included the Capital "Tiger" Division, the 9th "White Horse" Division,* a marine brigade, and a regimental combat team. The "Tiger" Division was deployed to Vietnam in October 1965 for combat operations in II Corps,* serving in country until March 1973. It consisted of one cavalry and two infantry regiments, three battalions of 105mm howitzers and one battalion of 155mm howitzers. The division participated in the Bong

Son campaign early in 1966. For most of the war the Tiger and White Horse divisions had responsibility for protecting the II Corps coastal area and keeping roads open, primarily from Phan Rang north over 150 miles to Qui Nhon.*

ROK forces established themselves as well-trained, well-disciplined soldiers with high morale. They brooked no opposition and were ruthless with both enemy forces and the civilian population. They generally dealt harshly with prisoners and with civilians who were suspected of sympathizing with the Vietcong* or who violated the laws or regulations established by ROK commanders. Thieves, for example, were hung from meathooks. Some Americans looked on ROK troops with admiration, but critics viewed their harsh methods not as truly pacifying an area, and surely not as "winning hearts and minds," but as creating new supporters for the Vietcong.

Sources: Shelby Stanton, *The Rise and Fall of an American Army: U.S. Ground Troops in Vietnam, 1965–1973*, 1985; Harry G. Summers, Jr., *Vietnam War Almanac*, 1985; Shelby L. Stanton, *Vietnam Order of Battle*, 1981; Stanley Robert Larsen and James Lawton Collins, Jr., *Allied Participation in Vietnam*, 1975.

Samuel Freeman

CARIBOU AIRCRAFT

Manufactured by the Haviland Aircraft Corporation in Canada, the Caribou C–7 was first deployed to South Vietnam in 1964. It was a propeller-driven craft with a thirty-two passenger capacity and the ability to rapidly load and unload cargo. The United States Army* had six companies of caribou aircraft in Vietnam before control of the C–7 was shifted to the U.S. Air Force* early in 1967.

Sources: Harry G. Summers, Jr., *Vietnam War Almanac*, 1985; Shelby L. Stanton, *Vietnam Order of Battle*, 1981; Carl Berger, ed., *The United States Air Force in Southeast Asia, 1961–1973*, 1977.

CASE, CLIFFORD

Born in 1904 in Franklin Township, New Jersey, Clifford Case was a moderate-liberal congressman who, as the ranking Republican member of the Senate Foreign Relations Committee,* became a critic of the war in Vietnam. A graduate of Rutgers University (1925) and the Columbia Law School (1928), Case practiced corporate law until his election to the New Jersey Assembly in 1942. Two years later he was elected to the House of Representatives. Case resigned his congressional seat in 1953 to become president of the Fund for the Republic, and in 1954 he won election to the U.S. Senate by a margin of only 3,507 votes. He was reelected by wide margins in 1960, 1966, and 1972.

During his Senate career Case was a champion of social and civil rights programs, and in the early 1970s he was the only Republican to be given a zero rating by the conservative Americans for Constitutional Action. His committee assignments included Appropriations, Atomic Energy, Intelligence, and Foreign Relations. Case's questioning of U.S. policy in Southeast Asia began in 1967 following Senate Foreign Relations Committee hearings. He based his criticism on three points: that the war was an unwarranted extension of executive power, that the creation of a viable South Vietnamese government was impossible as U.S. forces increasingly did what the South Vietnamese should have been doing, and that the war was not winnable without the "destruction of South Vietnam and much of American might itself." Case opposed the use of funds to subsidize foreign troops in Laos* and proposed a cap on military and economic assistance to Cambodia (*see* Kampuchea). He was especially critical of the military assistance program which had been used by Presidents Johnson* and Nixon* to extend overseas commitments without congressional concurrence.

In 1978 Case was defeated in the Republican party primary by conservative Jeffrey Bell who subsequently lost to Bill Bradley in the general election. Case remained in public life as chairman of Freedom House, a forty-year-old organization dedicated to promoting freedom in the United States and abroad. Clifford Case died on March 6, 1982.

Sources: *New York Times*, March 7 and 9, 1982; George Douth, *Leaders in Profile: The United States Senate*, 1975.

David Bernstein

CASUALTIES

Because of the nature of the war in Vietnam, accurate estimates of civilian and military casualties are extremely difficult to achieve. Senator Ted Kennedy* investigated the question of civilian casualties in South Vietnam between 1965 and 1974 and estimated that 1,005,000 people were wounded and 430,000 killed by American or Vietcong*/North Vietnamese forces. Other historians with more conservative estimates calculated 800,000 wounded and approximately, 250,000 killed. Among American soldiers during the same period, 47,244 were killed in military action, while another 10,446 died from sickness or accidents. Nearly 304,000 were wounded. North Vietnamese and Vietcong military deaths totaled more than 660,000 between 1965 and 1974, while bombing* deaths in North Vietnam were probably about 65,000. Among South Vietnamese military personnel, nearly 224,000 were killed in action and another 571,000 wounded. Among Allied troops, the South Koreans (*see* Korea) suffered 4,407 soldiers killed; the Thais, 351; and the Australians* and New Zealanders,* 469.

Sources: Edward S. Herman, *Atrocities in Vietnam: Myths and Realities*, 1970; Telford Taylor, *Nuremberg and Vietnam: An American Tragedy*, 1971; Guenter Lewy, *America in Vietnam*, 1978; Harry G. Summers, Jr., *Vietnam War Almanac*, 1985.

CENTRAL HIGHLANDS

The Central Highlands, a strategically important region of South Vietnam throughout the 1960s and 1970s, is a plateau area at the southern edge of the Truong Son Mountains. Nearly one million people, primarily Montagnard* tribesmen, lived in the 20,000 square miles of the Central Highlands in 1968. The region was economically known for its production of coffee, tea, and vegetables.

Source: Gerald Cannon Hickey, *Free in the Forest: An Ethnohistory of the Vietnamese Central Highlands, 1954–1976*, 1982.

CENTRAL INTELLIGENCE AGENCY

The Central Intelligence Agency (CIA), an outgrowth of the World War II Office of Strategic Services (OSS), was established by Congress in 1947 to serve as a clearinghouse for all foreign intelligence operations. Subsequent legislation in 1949 allowed the CIA to use secret administrative procedures and even insulated it from the congressional budget process. The CIA's involvement in Vietnam began late in World War II when a special OSS team there allied itself with Ho Chi Minh* in opposing the Japanese occupation forces. After the war, the CIA supported first the French and later, until the 1963 coup d'état, the regime of Ngo Dinh Diem* Until the Geneva Accords* of 1954, a CIA team lead by Colonel Edward Lansdale,* working out of Saigon,* had conducted psychological operations and paramilitary raids against the Vietminh* and North Vietnamese. In 1961, the CIA launched its clandestine campaign in Laos,* recruiting nearly 10,000 Hmong* tribesmen to attack the Ho Chi Minh Trail* and sever the infiltration* route. Throughout the 1960s the CIA worked to destroy the Vietcong* infrastructure, particularly through the Phoenix Program,* which included military operations against the National Liberation Front (*see* Vietcong) as well as targeted assassinations of Vietcong leaders.

Early in the 1970s, the CIA came under tremendous pressure from political critics. First, revelations of CIA assassinations of Vietcong leaders raised eyebrows, as did its intervention in the internal affairs of Cuba, Chile, Iran, Laos, and a number of other countries. More severe, however, was the public reaction to President Richard Nixon's* 1967 launching of Operation CHAOS, a program of CIA surveillance of antiwar critics in the United States, a directive which violated the CIA charter. In 1974 Congress* amended the Foreign Assistance Act of 1974 to require that the CIA be used only for intelligence operations outside the United States. Both houses of Congress also established permanent oversight committees to monitor CIA activities.

Sources: William E. Colby and Peter Forbath, *Honorable Men: My Life in the CIA*, 1978; Morton Halperin et al., *The Lawless State: The Crimes of the U.S. Intelligence Agencies*, 1976; Harry Howe Ransom, *The Intelligence Establishment*, 1970; John Prados, *Presidents' Secret Wars: CIA and Pentagon Covert Operations Since World War II*, 1986; Peer da Silva, *Sub Rosa: The CIA and the Uses of Intelligence*, 1978.

CENTRAL OFFICE FOR SOUTH VIETNAM

The Central Office for South Vietnam (COSVN) was the headquarters for North Vietnamese command of Vietcong* forces. Although COSVN was nominally located in Tay Ninh Province, it was highly mobile and quite different from what most American military officials thought of as a command headquarters. COSVN consisted of a small number of senior officers and staff assistants, but it was not a fixed installation resembling U.S. Military Assistance Command, Vietnam* (MACV) headquarters. Throughout the war American officers talked longingly of ending the war by capturing COSV—crippling the Vietcong and North Vietnamese Army* (NVA). General Creighton Abrams* in 1970 remarked that the "successful destruction of COSVN headquarters in a single blow would, I believe, have a very significant impact on enemy operations throughout South Vietnam." The desire to strike at COSVN became the rationale for the bombing of Cambodia in 1969 (see Operation Menu) and the invasion of Cambodia in 1970 (see Operation Binh Tay). Supposedly it had been located and was vulnerable to B–52* strikes. Because Cambodia was a neutral nation, elaborate steps were taken to maintain secrecy, including falsification of military records. In the invasion of Cambodia, American and South Vietnamese soldiers captured large amounts of Vietcong supplies, but they never located COSVN. The primary results of the invasion were to push the Vietcong and NVA deeper into Cambodia, increase the flood of refugees* into Phnom Penh, strengthen the Khmer Rouge,* hasten the collapse of the Cambodian military, and undermine the Cambodian government. The American pursuit of COSVN became a symbol of the difficulties of fighting a guerrilla war.

Sources: William Shawcross, *Sideshow: Kissinger, Nixon, and the Destruction of Cambodia*, 1979; Malcolm Caldwell and Tan Lek, *Cambodia in the Southeast Asian War*, 1973; Jonathan Grant et al., *The Widening War in Indochina*, 1971.

Samuel Freeman

CH–21 WORK HORSE

Early versions of the Vertol CH–21 Work Horse saw action in the Korean War. During the early years of U.S. involvement in Vietnam, the CH–21 lived up to the name "Work Horse," serving as the major component of U.S. helicopter assistance to the armed forces of the Republic of Vietnam.* By the time American combat troops began playing a major role in Vietnam in the mid–1960s, the CH–21 had largely disappeared from service with regular units of the U.S. armed forces. The aircraft continued to play a role in the war, however, with Air America,* the Central Intelligence Agency's* covert air arm. One joke going around among GIs in the late 1960s was that you could go clear across Laos* without ever touching foreign soil—you could just jump from the wreck of one CH–21 to the next.

Powered by one 1,425 horsepower Wright R–1820–103 engine, the CH–21 could accommodate twelve stretchers or fourteen fully equipped troops in a passenger-cargo compartment 20 feet long and 5 feet 8 inches wide. Capable of carrying 4,700 pounds of cargo, either internally or slung beneath the fuselage, the CH–21 did yeoman service as the "work horse" of the early years of the Vietnam war.

Sources: Stanley Karnow, *Vietnam: A History*, 1983; *Jane's All The World's Aircraft*, 1957.

Nolan J. Argyle

CH–34 CHOCTAW

The first production model of the CH–34 Choctaw flew on September 20, 1954. The Choctaw was adopted by all branches of the armed forces, including the Coast Guard.* Powered by a Wright R–1820–84 radial air-cooled engine rated at 1525 horsepower, the CH–34 could carry twelve fully equipped combat troops. Equipped with a power winch and a cargo sling, the CH–34 was a versatile aircraft capable of performing a wide variety of missions. Throughout the 1960s, the Choctaw was used in Vietnam as a medium cargo carrier, troop transport, and medical evacuation (*see* medevac) aircraft. Relatively large in relation to its payload capabilities, and slow and unmaneuverable compared to later helicopters, the CH–34 proved vulnerable to enemy ground fire and was replaced as an assault aircraft by the UH–1.

Source: *Jane's All the World's Aircraft, 1963–64*, 1964.

Nolan J. Argyle

CH–37 MOJAVE

In late 1962 the U.S. Army* introduced the CH–37 to Vietnam. One flight platoon of the 19th Transportation Company, stationed in Korea,* was brought to Vietnam to provide heavy helicopter support for forces of the Republic of Vietnam.* While very few aircraft were involved, the introduction of the CH–37 marked an escalation in American involvement in the war. The CH–37 was capable of airlifting heavy equipment, including the largest artillery, into any part of the country in support of Vietnamese ground operations.

When it was introduced into service in 1956, the CH–37 Mojave was the largest, most powerful helicopter in the non-Communist world. With a cabin 30 feet 4 inches long and 7 feet 9 inches wide, the Mojave was comparable in size to the DC–3 transport. Fitted with hydraulically operated clamshell doors, the Mojave could carry three Jeeps or three quarter-ton trucks internally. Twenty-three fully equipped combat troops could be carried in the Mojave, or it could be set up to carry twenty-four litter patients and medical attendants. Large, bulky loads could be carried under the aircraft in a sling equipped with an automatic release to release its load upon touchdown.

Powered by two Pratt & Whitney R–2800 engines with 4,200 combined horse-power, the CH–37 could carry a five-ton payload at a cruising speed of 115 mph. This helicopter was one of the first ever built with retractable landing gear and night flying equipment. With its automatic stabilizing equipment, the Mojave was capable of flying under virtually any weather conditions.

Source: *Jane's All the World's Aircraft 1959–60*, 1960.

Nolan J. Argyle

CH–47 CHINOOK

The Boeing-Vertol CH-47 Chinook entered service with the U.S. Army* in the spring of 1963 at Fort Benning, Georgia. First assigned to the 11th Air Assault Division (Airmobile), the Chinook replaced the CH–37* as the main cargo helicopter for the army. When the Chinook started service with the division, the 11th Air Assault Division was developing the strategies and techniques that were later to be tried in Vietnam. Redesignated the 1st Cavalry Division* (Airmobile), this unit was later to play a key role in the army's helicopter war in Vietnam. The CH–47 was a key component of that role.

The CH–47 was powered by two Lycoming T55-L–7 engines, each delivering 2,200 SHP, driving two three-bladed rotors. With a cabin 30 feet long, 7 feet 6 inches wide, and 6 feet 6 inches high, the CH–47 has a normal payload of three tons of freight, thirty-three troops, twenty-seven paratroopers, or twenty-four litters. The rear-loading ramp can be left open or removed to enable the Chinook to transport extra-long cargo or to be used for free-drop delivery of cargo or for paratroop drops. Capable of cruising at 150 mph, the Chinook served very successfully as the major cargo helicopter of the Vietnam War.

The CH–47 was also used as a gunship in Vietnam, with a 20mm Vulcan cannon mounted to fire from the side of the aircraft. The Chinook was less successful in this role, as the vibrations from the cannon placed too much stress on the airframe, greatly shortening the useful life of the aircraft.

Source: *Jane's All the World's Aircraft, 1963–64*, 1964.

Nolan J. Argyle

CH–53

In 1962 the U.S. Navy* selected the Sikorsky CH–53 as the new heavy assault transport helicopter for the Marine Corps.* The U.S. Air Force* also selected the Sikorsky to serve a variety of roles, including transport, medical evacuation (*see* Medevac), and rescue. Deliveries of the CH–53 started in 1965, and the aircraft entered service in Vietnam in 1966.

The CH–53 has a passenger-cargo cabin 30 feet long, 7 feet 6 inches wide, and 6 feet 6 inches high, and is capable of carrying up to 18,000 pounds of freight (overload condition). A typical cargo load would be two Jeeps, two Hawk missiles, or a 105mm howitzer. The CH–53 can carry thirty-eight combat-ready troops or twenty-four stretchers.

Powered by two General Electric T64-GE–6 2,850 horsepower shaft-turbine

engines, the CH–53 has a normal cruising speed of 172 mph and a normal radius (with a four-ton load) of 115 miles.
Source: *Jane's All the World's Aircraft*, 1964.

Nolan J. Argyle

CH–54 SKYCRANE

The CH–54 Skycrane (Tarhe) was first delivered to Vietnam in 1966 and was used to carry heavy payloads. Capable of lifting up to 20,000 pounds, the CH–54 often moved heavy artillery pieces, aircraft, trucks, and army surgical center pods. During the course of the Vietnam War, the CH–54, with its two 4,500 SHP engines, retrieved more than 380 shot-down aircraft.
Sources: Richard O'Neill, ed., *An Illustrated Guide to the Modern US Army*, 1986; Shelby L. Stanton, *Vietnam Order of Battle*, 1981.

CHAIRMAN, JOINT CHIEFS OF STAFF

The Joint Chiefs of Staff was created by the National Defense Act of July 1947. Composed of the senior officer of each of the four branches of the armed services, the Joint Chiefs of Staff operates under the secretary of defense and the president of the United States. Between 1959 and 1975, six men served as chairman of the Joint Chiefs of Staff: Air Force General Nathan F. Twining (1957–60), Army General Lyman L. Lemnitzer (1960–61), Army General Maxwell D. Taylor* (1961–64), Army General Earle G. Wheeler* (1964–70), Admiral Thomas H. Moorer* (1970–74), and Air Force General George S. Brown (1974–78).*
Sources: Edward Luttwack, *The Pentagon and the Art of War*, 1985; Lawrence J. Korb, *The Joint Chiefs of Staff: The First Twenty-five Years*, 1976.

CHAMPA

Champa was an Indianized-kingdom in Southeast Asia, located approximately in central Vietnam between the Red River Delta and Mekong Delta.* To the north were the Vietnamese people; to the south were the Khmers,* or Cambodians. During the Early Han Dynasty, Champa came to the attention of the Chinese and its recorded history begins; by the fifteenth century, the kingdom had succumbed to the relentless advance of the Vietnam kingdom down the peninsula.

Champa and Vietnam marked a dividing line of sorts between Indian and Chinese cultural and political influence in Southeast Asia. Champa was a decentralized kingdom, with each coastal fishing village having a measure of independence and power. Champa augmented income and power from fishing—there was virtually no farming land—with piracy against ships operating in the South China Sea and against Vietnamese landed communities.

For a thousand years Champa was able to withstand Vietnamese expansion. Until the collapse of the T'ang Dynasty in the early tenth century, Vietnam faced Chinese imperial power on again (during the Han Dynasty) and off again (during the interregnum) and could not devote its full strength to expansion. Champa paid tribute to Chinese dynasties and hence maintained a measure of independence and power.

The situation began to change after the fall of the T'ang. Vietnam became stronger, and soon began advancing slowly from the Red River Delta down the coastline, reaching approximately the seventeenth parallel by A.D. 1000, and the city of Hue* by approximately A.D. 1400. Along with the advance of the Vietnamese, the Mongol rise to power sapped the vitality and strength of the Champa kingdom. Vietnam and Champa united temporarily to withstand the Mongols and their Chinese and Korean levies, but the centuries of constant warfare proved too great a strain. By 1471 Vietnam had conquered Champa, and the kingdom became a part of history.

Source: Michael G. Cotter, "Towards a Social History of the Vietnamese Southward Movement," *Journal of Southeast Asian History*, 9 (March 1968), 12–24.

Charles Dobbs

CHAMS

Until the early 1400s the Chams were an Indianized people living along the coast of present-day Vietnam between the Red River Delta and Mekong Delta.* The Chams reflected the differences between Indian and Chinese cultural influences in Southeast Asia. They were a seafaring people, alternating fishing and piracy, and because of their relatively martial pursuits and despite their small numbers, they were able to withstand their neighbors, the Vietnamese and the Cambodians, and for a while even threaten the Vietnam capital in Hanoi.*

For more than a thousand years the Cham people survived along with their kingdom. The Vietnamese always faced Chinese pressure, sometimes Chinese armies, occasionally Chinese control, while the Cambodians were not particularly warlike. The Chams meanwhile benefited from fishing, piracy, and trade with the islands of present-day Indonesia.

Matters considerably worsened after the collapse of the T'ang Dynasty in China. Until A.D. 900, the Vietnamese expended a considerable amount of their energy resisting the Chinese; after the T'ang collapse, the Vietnamese would have their independence secure, and would begin a thousand-year drive to control all of Indochina.* The Chams were the first barrier, and hence the first target. Vietnamese pressure crushed the Chams; the slow, inexorable march of Vietnamese farmers down the coast overwhelmed the seafaring Chams whose hold on their land was weak. By A.D. 1000, the Vietnamese had secured perhaps a third of old Champa; by the 1400s, Champa disappeared.

In the 1950s and 1960s a vestige of the old Cham people remained in Vietnam. Around Hue,* the old Champa kingdom capital, there were up to 20,000 people who made their living from the sea and were descendants of the old Chams. Along with the expulsion of Chinese-ethnic Vietnamese (*see* Chinese) after North Vietnam's May 1975 conquest of the South, presumably the old Chams have been expelled too.

Sources: John Frank Cady, *Southeast Asia: Its Historical Development*, 1958; John F. Embree, *Ethnic Groups of Northern Southeast Asia*, 1950.

                                                                    Charles Dobbs

CHAPMAN, LEONARD FIELDING, JR.

Chapman's tour as commandant of the Marine Corps* (1968–72) coincided with the withdrawal of U.S. forces under President Nixon's* Vietnamization* policy. Born in Florida in 1913, he graduated from the University of Florida with a reserve army commission which he resigned in favor of a Marine Corps commission in 1935. Chapman served in the Pacific Fleet before the war but instructed artillery classes at Quantico until 1944 when orders sent him to the staff of the 11th Artillery and combat on Peleliu.

Chapman's postwar assignments included staff duty and regimental and barracks commands in Japan and North Carolina. In Washington in the early 1960s, his staff work earned the annual merit award of the Armed Forces Management Association (1966) and the attention of President Johnson,* who promoted Chapman to commandant over the more celebrated Victor Krulak* and Lewis Walt* in 1968.

The first artillery officer to rise to the marines' top billet and a product of McNamara's* industrialized Pentagon, Chapman became known as the "cerebral commandant" and an expert in management techniques, logistics, and communications. Candidly admitting "We've got a problem," Chapman faced morale and racial problems on Okinawa and in Vietnam rear areas during his tour and retired in January 1972. A year later President Nixon* appointed him commissioner of immigration and naturalization, and he retired from that post in May 1977.

Sources: *New York Times*, 1968–1977; J. Robert Moskin, *The U.S. Marine Corps Story*, 1982.

                                                                    Dudley Acker

CHARNER, LEONARD VICTOR JOSEPH

Leonard Charner was born in February 1797 and died in February 1869. He spent his career in the French navy, and as a result of his efforts in 1861, the French secured their control of Saigon* and controlled the flow of rice into eastern Vietnam from the western provinces. He returned to France in 1862 to become a senator and he was promoted to the rank of admiral in 1864.

Source: Joseph Buttinger, *Vietnam: A Dragon Embattled*, 2 vols., 1967.

CHIANG KAI-SHEK

Chiang Kai-shek, longtime leader of the Kuomintang and Nationalists in China, was born in 1887. Chiang was trained and served in the Japanese army between 1909 and 1911, and then joined Sun Yat-Sen in the Chinese nationalist movement. After Sun Yat-Sen's death in 1925, Chiang became leader of the Kuomintang. Although the Nationalists split with the Communists in the Kuomintang in 1927, they later joined together to resist Japanese oppression in China, especially after 1937. The civil war with the Communists resumed in 1946, and Chiang, along with the other Nationalists, was expelled from China to Taiwan after the Communist victory in 1949. From 1950 to his death in 1975, Chiang served as president of Taiwan, and although he was willing, and even anxious, to provide troops to assist the American war effort in South Vietnam, U.S. policymakers resisted the idea, worried that it might bring a large-scale intervention from the People's Republic of China.

Sources: Keiji Furaya, *Chiang Kai-shek. His Life and Times*, 1981; William Morwood, *Duel for the Middle Kingdom: The Struggle Between Chiang Kai-shek and Mao Tse-tung for Control of China*, 1980.

THE CHICAGO 8

"The Chicago 8" was the name given to eight persons tried in Chicago in 1969 on charges of criminal conspiracy with intent to start a riot in August 1968. The trial was also called the Chicago Conspiracy Trial. The trial was occasioned by the massive anti–Vietnam War demonstrations held in streets and parks around the site of the Democratic party's 1968 national nominating convention,* which had opened in Chicago on August 26. Considerable violence occurred during the demonstrations; however, in December, the National Commission on the Causes and Prevention of Violence concluded that the violence was caused by a "police riot," not by the demonstrators. Despite political pressure to prosecute the alleged leaders of the Chicago demonstrations, U.S. Attorney General Ramsey Clark concluded that there was no basis for prosecution. Nevertheless, U.S. District Court Judge William J. Campbell, a friend of Chicago's Mayor Richard Daley, convened a federal grand jury to investigate the demonstrations. Under the administration of President Richard M. Nixon,* U.S. Attorney General John Mitchell agreed to prosecute the presumed demonstration leaders. An indictment was issued on March 20, 1969. The defendants were charged with violating the so-called Anti-Riot Statute or "H. Rap Brown Law," a rider that had been attached to the Civil Rights Act of 1968 in an attempt to quell rioting and civil disturbances. David T. Dellinger,* Rennard C. Davis, Thomas E. Hayden,* Abbott H. Hoffman,* Jerry C. Rubin,* Lee Weiner, John R. Froines, and Bobby G. Seale were charged with conspiracy to cross state lines with intent to cause a riot, to interfere with the performance of duties of police officers and firemen, and to teach and demonstrate the use of incendiary devices. Weiner and Froines were also charged with teaching and demonstrating incendiary devices. The other defendants were also charged with actually crossing state lines with intent to cause a riot. The trial began on September 24, 1969, before seventy-four-year-old U.S. District Court Judge Julius Jennings Hoffman. The trial was a raucous and well-publicized event. Judge Hoffman frequently denied defense motions and mispronounced the names of defendants and their attorneys. Insults and epithets were traded between the judge and the defendants and their attorneys. The defendants sought to make the Vietnam War, racism, and domestic repression the central issues of the trial. At one point, the defendants draped Vietcong* and American flags across their defense tables. When Seale's attorney was hospitalized, Seale, the only black defendant, requested a postponement of proceedings and then the right to defend himself. Judge Hoffman denied both requests. Seale protested frequently and called Hoffman a racist, a fascist, and a pig. Hoffman ordered Seale to be gagged and chained hand and foot to a metal chair. When Seale banged his chains on the chair, Hoffman placed him in a wooden chair with a larger gag over his mouth. On November 5, Hoffman declared a mistrial for Seale, severed him from the case, and sentenced him to four years in prison on sixteen contempt charges. After the jury retired to deliberate on the case of the remaining defendants, Judge Hoffman found all seven defendants and two trial lawyers, William M. Kunstler and Leonard I. Weinglass, guilty of 175 charges of criminal contempt and sentenced them to terms of imprisonment (four years and thirteen days for Kunstler and one year and eight months for Weinglass). On February 18, 1970, after five days of deliberation, the jury found all defendants not guilty of conspiracy, but found Dellinger, Davis, Hayden, Hoffman, and Rubin guilty on substantive charges of intent to riot. Each defendant was sentenced to five years in prison and fined $5,000. These convictions were overturned on November 21, 1972, by the U.S. Court of Appeals, Seventh Circuit. Contempt and conspiracy charges against Seale were dropped after a new trial. Contempt charges against the remaining defendants and their attorneys were reduced and dismissed during ten years of appeal.

Sources: Jason Epstein, *The Great Conspiracy Trial*, 1970; Clark Dougan and Steven Weiss, *The Vietnam Experience: A Nation Divided*, 1984; Nancy Zaroulis and Gerald Sullivan, *Who Spoke Up? American Protest Against the War in Vietnam, 1963–1975*, 1984.

John Kincaid

CHIEF OF NAVAL OPERATIONS

The chief of naval operations is the senior officer of the United States Navy.* Between 1959, when Admiral Arleigh Burke held the position, and the end of the Vietnam War in 1975, six men served as chief of naval operations: Admiral Arleigh Burke (1959–61); Admiral George W. Anderson (1961–63); Admiral David L. McDonald (1963–65); Admiral Thomas H. Moorer* (1965–70); Admiral Elmo Zumwalt* (1970–74); and Admiral James L. Holloway (1974–75).

Sources: John M. Collins, *U.S. Defense Planning: A Critique*, 1982; Edward J. Marolda and G. Wesley Pryce III, *A Short History of the United States Navy and the Southeast Asian Conflict, 1950–1975*, 1984.

CHIEF OF STAFF, U.S. AIR FORCE

The senior officer in the United States Air Force* is the chief of staff. Six people occupied that position between 1959 and 1975. They were General Thomas D. White (1959–61); General Curtis LeMay* (1961–65); General John

P. McConnell (1965–68); General John D. Ryan (1968–73); General George S. Brown* (1974); and General David C. Jones (1974 until after the war).

Sources: John M. Collins, *U.S. Defense Planning: A Critique*, 1982; Carl Berger, ed., *The United States Air Force in Southeast Asia, 1961–1973*, 1977.

CHIEF OF STAFF, U.S. ARMY

The post of army chief of staff is the senior officer in the United States Army,* and seven people held the position between 1959 and 1975, starting with General Maxwell Taylor.* Taylor was replaced in 1959 by General Lyman L. Lemnitzer, who served until October 1960. General George Decker succeeded Lemnitzer and served until 1962. General Earle Wheeler* became chief of staff in October 1962 and stayed there until July 1964, when General Harold K. Johnson took over the position. General William Westmoreland* replaced Johnson in 1968 and remained in office until October 1972. General Creighton Abrams* served as chief of staff until his death from cancer in 1974. General Fred C. Weyand* took over after Abrams's death.

Sources: Harry G. Summers, Jr., *Vietnam War Almanac*, 1985; James M. Collins, *U.S. Defense Planning: A Critique*, 1982.

CHIEU HOI PROGRAM

Efforts to destroy the National Liberation Front (NLF; *see* Vietcong) included the "Chieu Hoi" (Open Arms) amnesty program initiated at the insistence of American and British advisers, including Sir Robert Thompson.* The program, like all others in Vietnam, generated impressive statistics—nearly 160,000 deserters and 11,200 weapons turned in—but only meager results. The program was conducted in typical American fashion with leaflets dropped from the air in NLF-controlled areas and Vietnamese psyops (psychological operations) personnel haranguing peasants via bullhorn from hovering helicopters. Those who rallied to the government were usually low-level personnel, many of whom may not have been enthusiastic about the NLF program to begin with. The program, in part because of its failure to develop face-to-face contacts, attracted few members of the NLF political or military cadres. In fact, critics charged the program was an "R and R" for the NLF, allowing NLF soldiers to "rally" temporarily to recuperate themselves and then return to the NLF. Evidence indicates some may have "changed sides" as many as five times. Of those who rallied, however, were some who genuinely changed sides and were recruited into the GVN military (*see* Republic of Vietnam), often as Kit Carson Scouts.* Good Kit Carson scouts were highly prized by American military units because of their familiarity with guerrilla movements, tactics, and booby traps.* Unfortunately, far more of the Chieu Hoi deserters also infiltrated American and ARVN (*see* Army of the Republic of Vietnam) military units and caused serious problems.

Sources: Frances FitzGerald, *Fire in the Lake: The Vietnamese and the Americans in Vietnam*, 1972; Tran Dinh Tho, *Pacification*, 1979; Andrew F. Krepinevich, Jr., *The Army and Vietnam*, 1986.

Samuel Freeman

CHINA   *See* People's Republic of China

CHINESE

Ethnic Chinese constituted the largest minority group in South Vietnam. At the peak of the conflict, there were approximately one million Chinese living in South Vietnam, most of them in the Cholon* suburb of Saigon.* They constituted a highly prosperous group active in banking, foreign trade, real estate, and commerce. Because of centuries of conflict between the Chinese and ethnic Vietnamese, the Chinese were often resented by the larger population, but their services and skills were important to the local economy. Large numbers of Vietnamese refugees* to the United States after 1975 consisted of the ethnic Chinese escaping the economic restrictions imposed by the Socialist Republic of Vietnam.*

Sources: F. Raymond Iredell, *Vietnam: The Country and the People*, 1966; Joan Schrock et al., *Minority Groups in the Republic of Vietnam*, 1967.

CHINH PHU CACH MANG LAM THOI CONG HOA MIEN NAM VIETNAM   *See* Provisional Revolutionary Government of South Vietnam

CHOLON

Cholon is the Chinese* part of the city of Saigon.* It was originally separate from Saigon and populated exclusively by native Chinese living in Indochina* and prospering commercially. Urban growth eventually brought Cholon into the Saigon metropolitan area, and at the height of the Vietnam War the Cholon population exceeded one million people.

Sources: *Webster's Geographical Dictionary*, 1984; Joseph Buttinger, *Vietnam: A Dragon Embattled*. Vol. 2, *Vietnam at War*, 1967.

CHOMSKY, AVRAM NOAM

Noam Chomsky, a leading intellectual critic of the war in Vietnam, was born in Philadelphia on December 7, 1928. He received a B.A. from the University of Pennsylvania in 1949, specializing in language and linguistics, and the M.A. and Ph.D. in 1951 and 1955. Chomsky joined the faculty of the Massachusetts Institute of Technology in 1955 and became a full professor in 1961. He wrote several well-received books in the late 1950s and early 1960s, including *Syntactic Structures* (1957) and *Aspects of the Theory of Syntax* (1965). Chomsky openly opposed the war in Vietnam as early as 1965, speaking widely on the northeastern campus circuit in 1966 and 1967, but he really made his mark on the antiwar movement* with the publication of his *American Power and the New Mandarins* in 1969. There he argued that the United States had become intoxicated with its own military and economic power, had assumed an ideology of superiority in world politics, and was destroying a society in the name of freedom. He also accused American intellectuals of having become stooges of the business and government establishment.

Sources: *Who's Who in America, 1984–1985*, 1985; Noam Chomsky, *American Power and the New Mandarins*, 1969; Nancy Zaroulis and Gerald Sullivan, *Who Spoke Up? American Protest Against the War in Vietnam, 1963–1975*, 1984.

CHRISTMAS BOMBING OF 1972 *See* Operation Linebacker II

CHU LAI, BATTLE OF (1965) *See* Operation Starlite

CHURCH, FRANK FORRESTER

Frank Church was born in Boise, Idaho, on July 25, 1924. During World War II Church served as a military intelligence officer in China, India, and Burma, and in 1947 he graduated from Stanford University. Church attended Harvard Law School for a year, but a bout with cancer brought him back west again, and in 1950 he graduated from the Stanford University Law School. Between 1950 and 1956 Church practiced law in Idaho and was active in Democratic politics, serving as chairman of the statewide Young Democrats organization. He won the party's nomination for the U.S. Senate in 1956 and went on to upset the Republican incumbent, Herman Welker. At thirty-two, Church was the youngest member of the Senate. He quickly earned a reputation as an outspoken liberal, and by supporting majority leader Lyndon B. Johnson* on civil rights legislation, Church gained favor and was appointed to the prestigious Senate Foreign Relations Committee* in 1959. In 1960 Church supported John F. Kennedy* for the presidential nomination, and he won reelection to the Senate in 1962.

After 1965, Senator Church became increasingly apprehensive about U.S. involvement in Southeast Asia. He warned against American support for repressive regimes such as that in Vietnam unless substantial progress was made toward reform. In 1965, he repeated this warning, contending that the rift in the Communist world between the People's Republic of China* and the Soviet Union* had diminished the threat of "monolithic communism." In 1966, Church broke with the Johnson administration over Vietnam policy by calling for an end to the bombing.* In 1970, Church cosponsored the Cooper-Church Amendment* to prohibit U.S. deployment of ground forces in Cambodia (*see* Kampuchea), setting off a six-month debate in the Senate. In 1972, in reaction to the Nixon* administration's bombing of Hanoi* and Haiphong and the mining of Haiphong Harbor,* Church joined with Senator Clifford Case* of New Jersey in sponsoring a resolution seeking an end to all U.S. military activity in Southeast

Asia. The proposal was considered the first step in the eventual adoption of the War Powers Resolution* of 1973.

On the domestic front, Church chaired the Senate Select Committee on Intelligence which investigated excesses and violations of law by the Central Intelligence Agency,* Federal Bureau of Investigation, and National Security Agency under the Nixon administration. In 1976, Church made a bid for the Democratic presidential nomination, but he lost out to Governor Jimmy Carter of Georgia. In 1980, Church was defeated for reelection to the Senate. He continued to live in Washington, D.C., practicing international law until his death from cancer on April 7, 1984.

Sources: *Current Biography*, 1978, pp. 75–79; *New York Times*, April 8, 1984.

Joseph M. Rowe, Jr.

"THE CITY"   *See* Fishhook

CIVILIAN IRREGULAR DEFENSE GROUP
The Civilian Irregular Defense Group, or CIDG, was a Central Intelligence Agency* (CIA) operation initiated in 1961 to prevent Vietcong* control of Vietnamese minorities. The purpose of the program was to train the indigenous tribes of the Vietnamese interior in self-defense so the Vietcong would not be able to get control of the Central Highlands* and to relieve regular South Vietnamese army forces of the responsibility of controlling the interior. The CIA went to work with the Montagnards* first, and then gradually extended the defensive program out to such other tribes as the Khmers,* Nungs,* Cao Dai,* Hoa Hao,* and some South Vietnamese youth groups. By mid–1963 the CIDG was functioning in more than 200 tribal villages, with 12,000 people participating in the program. The CIDG programs were more popular than later counterinsurgency efforts because they did not involve resettlement of people away from their home villages.

In October 1963 the CIDG programs were removed from CIA and placed under the control of the Special Forces.* At the same time the Special Forces assumed responsibility for about 600 people in Combat Intelligence Teams and more than 5,000 Border Surveillance personnel and Mountain Scouts. A group of Civilian Airborne Rangers were militarized and worked with the CIDG. The CIDG was under the command of the Luc Luong Dac Biet—South Vietnamese Special Forces. After the switch from the CIA to the Special Forces, the CIDG became more militarily aggressive, although their main purpose remained defensive. At times the CIDG forces were hired on a contractual basis, but usually they functioned as local security units. After 1964, some CIDG units began performing commando hit-and-run raids along the border of Vietnam, Laos,* and Cambodia (*see* Kampuchea) and the Special Forces established twenty-four CIDG camps in the border area to stop North Vietnamese infiltration.* To defend some of the more remote camps, the Special Forces gave some of the CIDG groups more extensive training and named them Mobile Strike Force Commands.* When Vietnamization* took place after Richard Nixon* became president, the CIDG units were changed either into border-patrolling battalions or special units. The Cambodians became part of the Khmer Republic Army and the Nungs*, who were ethnic Chinese,* became part of the Studies and Observation Groups* program. Vietnamese CIDG units went into the South Vietnamese army. Most of the transfers came in 1970.

Sources: Francis J. Kelly, *U.S. Army Special Forces, 1961–1971*, 1973; Shelby L. Stanton, *Green Berets at War*, 1985; Kevin Generous, "Irregular Forces in Vietnam," in John S. Bowman, ed., *The Vietnam War: An Almanac*, 1985; Ngo Quang Truong, *Territorial Forces*, 1981.

CIVIL OPERATIONS AND REVOLUTIONARY DEVELOPMENT SUPPORT

Throughout the war in Vietnam, the United States paid lip service to the idea of pacification (*see* Rural Reconstruction)—converting the loyalties of South Vietnamese peasants to the government—but the major American effort in Indochina* was always military. In February 1966 Nguyen Van Thieu* and Nguyen Cao Ky* had agreed to strengthen the pacification program, and they renamed it Revolutionary Development. Several months later Ambassador Henry Cabot Lodge* established the Office of Civil Operations to manage State Department–controlled pacification efforts. In May 1967, a new agency, named CORDS, was established, meaning Civil Operations and Revolutionary Development Support. Military Assistance Command, Vietnam* (MACV) was in complete control of CORDS, removing it from State Department direction, but CORDS drew on support from the military, the Central Intelligence Agency,* the State Department, and the United States Information Agency. Robert Komer* became director of CORDS and a deputy to MACV commander William Westmoreland.* Komer established unified civilian-military advisory teams in all forty-four provinces of South Vietnam and in 250 districts. By 1969 CORDS had more than 6,500 military personnel and 1,100 civilians pursuing pacification objectives in South Vietnam. Although CORDS claimed credit for winning higher loyalties from the peasant population, most of the gains came only from peasant migration from rural areas to the major South Vietnamese cities. Actual gains in converting the population from the Vietcong* were minimal. The Tet Offensive* of 1968 became clear proof of that reality. When President Richard Nixon* came to power in 1969, the United States quickly made its decision to withdraw from Vietnam, and after that point CORDS became an afterthought. Pacification efforts continued, but U.S. officials were more interested in getting out of Vietnam than in bringing about any real reformation of the distribution of power in Vietnam. The combination of the Tet Offensive and CORDS activities in 1968 and 1969 had severely weakened the Vietcong, but the North Vietnamese Army* only filled the vacuum.

Sources: Guenter Lewy, *America in Vietnam*, 1978; Robert Komer, "Clear, Hold, and Rebuild," *Army*, 20 (May 1970), 18–23; Tran Dinh Tho, *Pacification*, 1979; Thomas Scoville, *Reorganizing for Pacification Support*, 1982; J. K. McCallum, "CORDS Pacification Organization in Vietnam: A Civilian-Military Effort," *Armed Forces and Society*, 10 (Fall 1983), 105–122; Larry E. Cable, *Conflict of Myths: The Development of American Counterinsurgency Doctrine and the Vietnam War*, 1986.

CLAYMORE

Widely used in Vietnam, the claymore antipersonnel mine was designed to produce a directionalized, fan-shaped pattern of fragments. The claymore used a curved block of C–4* explosive, shaped to blow all its force outward in a semicircular pattern. A large number of pellets were embedded in the face of the explosive, creating a devastating blast of fragments similar to the effect of an oversized shotgun.

With their directional pattern, claymores were well-suited as a perimeter-defense weapon. With electronic firing, defenders in bunkers could set claymores in a pattern to cover all approaches and fire them at will. One problem with this was the tendency of the enemy to use infiltrators to sneak into the defense perimeter before an attack and simply turn the claymores around. Then when defenders fired the mine, its fragments peppered their own position.

The Vietcong* liked to use captured claymores as booby traps.* Set off by trip wires, a claymore mounted close to the ground was capable of cutting the legs off an unwary enemy.

A more unorthodox use was found for claymores by many American GIs. The explosive burned with intense heat, and a small amount of explosive could quickly heat a can of C-rations in the field. While never designed for it, and certainly never sanctioned, claymores became one of the most popular field stoves in the war.

Source: John Quick, *Dictionary of Weapons and Military Terms*, 1973.

Nolan J. Argyle

"CLEAR AND HOLD"

"Clear and hold" operations were part of the pacification program (*see* Rural Reconstruction) during the war in Vietnam. Most observers realized that the military sweep operations—temporary efforts to attack Vietcong* and North Vietnamese installations—would not be successful in permanently eliminating the guerrilla structure in South Vietnam. "Clear and hold" operations involved military attacks on Vietcong strongholds and then permanent stationing of military units in the area after the initial engagements. Local populations would not cooperate with American or South Vietnamese soldiers if they knew they would be departing in a few days. The problem with "clear and hold" operations, of course, was the personnel requirements. General William Westmoreland* argued that "clear and hold" strategies would have worked if he had had a larger contingent of U.S. troops at his disposal. As it was, Westmoreland generally used American troops for the military sweep operations and then relied on South Vietnamese soldiers, Popular Forces,* and Regional Forces* to hold those areas. They generally proved, however, to be quite unreliable.

Sources: William C. Westmoreland, *A Soldier Reports*, 1976; Hoang Ngoc Long, *Strategy and Tactics*, 1980; Harry G. Summers, Jr., *On Strategy: A Critical Analysis of the Vietnam War*, 1982.

CLERGY AND LAITY CONCERNED

Clergy and Laity Concerned About Vietnam (CLCV) was founded in 1965 by an interdenominational group of religious leaders including Reverend John C. Bennett and Father Daniel Berrigan.* Early cochairs included Father Berrigan, Rabbi Abraham Heschel, and Dr. Martin Luther King, Jr.* CLCV followed a moderate antiwar* course, advocating a negotiated settlement and holding teach-ins, fasts, vigils, and orderly antiwar activities. They sponsored a 2,000-member demonstration at the White House in January 1967 and a February Fast for Peace with over one million reportedly participating. Although CLCV participated in events with more radical antiwar groups, it consistently resisted radical activities such as draft* card burning and violent protest.

Late in 1966 CLCV commissioned a study entitled *In the Name of America* indicting U.S. involvement in Vietnam. It was published just before the 1968 Tet Offensive.* Drawing heavily on press reports and government documents, it argued that American involvement in Vietnam violated international law, and that the United States and its allies were committing crimes against humanity. It focused on issues including uses and effects of napalm,* gas, and defoliants;* search and destroy* operations; treatment of prisoners; forced relocation and pacification programs (*see* Rural Reconstruction); and the impact of artillery, aerial, and naval bombardment.

CLCV participated in the umbrella National Mobilization Committee protesting at the 1968 Democratic National Convention* in Chicago. Like other antiwar and peace organizations, CLCV was under surveillance and subject to infiltration by government intelligence and police agencies, including the Central Intelligence Agency's* Operation CHAOS in 1969 in violation of the CIA charter prohibiting domestic operations. Reflecting its expanding focus from Vietnam to U.S. military policies in general, CLCV changed its name in 1974 to Clergy and Laity Concerned. Recently, the organization has protested high schools allowing armed forces recruiters and ROTC programs on campus without giving equal time to peace organizations; opposed the Nestlé Corporation's marketing of infant formula in Third World countries; and called for corporate divestment in South Africa.

Sources: Nancy Zaroulis and Gerald Sullivan, *Who Spoke Up? American Protest Against the War in Vietnam, 1963–1975*, 1984; Daniel L. Migliore, "The Crisis of Faith in the Aftermath of Vietnam," *The Christian Century* 90, June 13, 1973, pp. 672–677; January 23, 1980; and March 24, 1982.

Samuel Freeman

CLIFFORD, CLARK MCADAMS

Clark Clifford was born at Fort Scott, Kansas, on December 25, 1906. He attended Washington University in St. Louis and received his law degree there in 1928. Clifford practiced law in St. Louis until World War II, when he became an assistant to Harry S. Truman's* naval aide. In 1946 Clifford was named naval aide to the president. He resigned from the navy in June 1946 and joined Truman's staff as special counsel. During the next four years he became one of Truman's most trusted aides, playing key roles in the development of the Central Intelligence Agency* (CIA), the Department of Defense, the Truman Doctrine, and U.S. policy toward Israel. Clifford resigned and returned to private law practice in 1950, although he remained in Washington, D.C., as a prominent consultant. In 1960 he helped plan John F. Kennedy's* campaign strategy, and when Kennedy was elected president, Clifford headed the transition team. After the election, Kennedy named Clifford to the Foreign Intelligence Advisory Board to oversee CIA operations, and in 1963 Clifford became chairman of the board. After the assassination of Kennedy, Clifford soon broke into Lyndon B. Johnson's* inner circle. He planned Johnson's 1964 election campaign, and after the election Clifford advised the president on Vietnam, making frequent fact-finding trips to Southeast Asia and numbering himself among the "hawks."

When Secretary of Defense Robert S. McNamara* resigned in 1968, Johnson persuaded Clifford to accept the cabinet post. He became the president's chief spokesman and defender on Vietnam policy. But after sounding out the generals on the future prospects in Vietnam, Clifford was dismayed that they had no timetable for completing the struggle. They just wanted more money, more men, and more weapons. With that sad prognosis, Clifford persuaded Johnson to put a lid on manpower allocations, limit bombing raids, and start peace negotiations.

In other foreign policy problems, such as the USS *Pueblo* incident, Clifford urged a cautious and restrained response. And he assumed (incorrectly it would seem) that China and not Russia posed the major threat to U.S. interests in the future. He believed that U.S.-Soviet relations would be normalized, given time, through détente. In January 1969, the Nixon administration took office and Clifford was replaced as secretary of defense by Melvin Laird* of Wisconsin. Back in private life, Clifford became increasingly critical of the Nixon administration's policy in Vietnam. In 1970, he branded the invasion of Cambodia (*see* Operation Binh Tay) as "reckless and foolhardy," and said that Nixon's policy of Vietnamization* was "a formula for perpetual war." He advocated an accelerated withdrawal from Vietnam in order to end the U.S. role in ground fighting no later than December 31, 1970.

Sources: *Current Biography*, 1968, pp. 90–93; Thomas G. Paterson, *American Foreign Policy*, 1983; *Facts on File*, 1970, p. 344.

Joseph M. Rowe, Jr.

CLIMATES OF VIETNAM

Three distinct climatic regions are distinguishable in Vietnam between the Sino-Vietnam border in the north and the south coast along the South China Sea. All three climatic types found in Vietnam are variations of tropical climates. The Koppen climate classification system is used here, and average monthly rainfall and temperature data for three locations—Hanoi,* Hue,* and Ho Chi Minh City*—are used to show major climatic characteristics.

Highland Tropical Savanna Climate (Koppen)

Based on the Koppen climate classification system, Hanoi falls within a climatic zone of Southeastern Asia located in latitudes 20° to 25° north of the equator. This climate is described as temperate, rainy in the spring and summer, with a dry winter and a hot, humid summer. Slightly over 60 inches of the total precipitation falls in the warmer six months (April-October) of the year. The annual temperature is 23° F with the warmest monthly average in July and the coolest in January. The Cw, or "temperate-tropical wet-dry climate," is a poleward extension of the true tropical savanna (Aw). While Hanoi is not in the highlands (elev. 53 ft.), it is in a geographical position to be influenced by the highlands west and north of the city. As a result, two months out of the year have average temperatures that cool below 64.4° F and therefore cannot be classified as tropical. As one progresses south of Hanoi towards Hue, the climate becomes both tropical and monsoon in nature.

The distinct wet-dry season results in the development of a vegetation complex identified as "tropical savanna." It is characterized by open expanses of tall grasses, with shrubs, thorn bushes, and scattered trees. True forest exists in areas where a permanent water supply is available. All of this vegetation can be classified under the heading "Raingreen Vegetation." Soils are mostly yellowish or red latisols (Ultisols). Extensive leaching is common, and often the true highland soils are infertile. Frequently, local alluvial soils are quite productive and extensively used. This climatic type (Cwa), "highland tropical savanna," was greatly favored by Europeans who settled in the tropics in the nineteenth century.

Tropical Monsoon

Monsoons are found in close association with rainy tropics, generally along coast where there is a seasonal onshore flow of moist air. In Vietnam the monsoon extends southward along the coast from Vinh, to Dong Hoi, Hue, and south to Quang Ngai. The windshift occurs in September, and from then until early February the wind blows from the northeast across the South China Sea onto the north-central coast of Vietnam.

It differs from rainy tropics in that it has a distinct dry season. However, storage of soil moisture is generally sufficient to maintain a forest in dry season. Monsoons can be regarded as transitional between rainy tropics (Aw) and the wet and dry tropics (Cwa), having total rainfall comparable to the true rain forest and a precipitation regime comparable to the Aw's (tropical savanna).

The term "monsoon tropics" does not apply to all climates affected by a monsoonal wind circulation. Its use stems from the characteristic climates of monsoon Asia, but the designation "wet-and-dry tropics" is applied to those regions with less annual precipitation and a distinct dry season.

There is little difference in the temperature characteristics of the monsoon and tropical rain forest. The most noticeable, however, is the occurrence of the maximum temperature prior to the onset of the rain period. The diurnal temperature variations are greater than in the rain forest, with greatest differences occurring in the dry months.

The average precipitation in the monsoons is around 70 inches, but where orographic conditions exist, annual precipitation can be tremendous, running over 200 inches annually. Most of precipitation comes as heavy showers, especially where the orographic effect plays a major role.

Soils in the monsoon region are usually lateritic (Ultisols) and red and yellow in color. In some localized areas, they can be utilized for tropical plantation agriculture as well as subsistence agriculture.

Tropical Savanna (Koppen)

Described as the "tropical wet-dry" by Koppen, this climatic type has a wet summer controlled by moist, warm equatorial and maritime tropical air masses and a dry season dictated by continental (dry) tropical air in the winter months. In Vietnam, this climatic type extends from approximately 8° to 15° north latitude. A very distinct characteristic of the tropical savanna (Aw) is that the warmest average monthly temperature occurs in the spring, just prior to the onset of the rain season. (See the data for Ho Chi Minh City.*) There is also a distinct dry season in the winter and a wet, humid summer. In the case of Ho Chi Minh City, the annual climatic distribution is isothermal. According to the Koppen system, any location with an annual temperature range of 9° F or less is classified as "isothermal," indicated by the lowercase letter (i). The Asiatic wet-dry climate probably has a stronger monsoon control than other regions of the tropics. The vegetation of the tropical savanna is distinct and consists of coarse-textured, tall grass mixed with scattered trees and tall brush. Permanent and true forests exist along and/or around permanent streams or water bodies. Profitable agriculture is possible in the form of tropical plantations. In the case of Vietnam, rubber plantations were particularly important in the lower Mekong Delta* of the south. In addition, subsistent, riverine agriculture is important in the tropical savanna regions of Vietnam. As with the highland tropical savanna (Cwa) in the north, the vegetation of the tropical savanna (Aw) can be classified as "Raingreen vegetation." The soils are yellow and red latisols (Ultisols) but more severely leached than those in the highland tropical savanna because of warmer temperatures and more precipitation.

Sources: F. Raymond Iredell, *Vietnam: The Country and the People*, 1966; Daniel Hall, *Atlas of Southeast Asia*, 1964.

Gerald Holder

"CLUSTER BOMBS"

A major, and controversial, weapons development of the Vietnam War was the appearance of the "cluster bomb," an explosive which had a broader impact than standard bombs and was primarily an antipersonnel weapon. The CBU–24 contained 600 golf-ball-sized bombs, each with 300 steel pellets. The CBU–46 had submunition systems with fins which allowed for wider dispersal before exploding. The most common antitank cluster bomb was the MK–20, which released 9-inch darts, each containing armor-penetrating warheads. A mine CBU was the WAAPM (wide area antipersonnel munition) which, when dropped from an aircraft, shot out dozens of fine wires upon impact. When touched, the wire triggered the explosion. Finally, the FAE, or fuel air explosive, was used in the end stages of the war. An FAE was a large canister filled with a gaseous explosive. When dropped from aircraft, the FAEs sprayed out fuel at a preset altitude, creating a huge gasoline cloud, which then ignited as it descended. The "cluster bombs" generated a good deal of controversy among antiwar groups because of their major purpose: the killing and maiming of people.

Source: Edgar C. Doleman, Jr., *The Vietnam Experience: Tools of War*, 1984.

COASTAL SURVEILLANCE FORCE

A major problem facing the United States and the South Vietnamese was infiltration* of enemy men and supplies along the 1,200-mile coastline between the seventeenth parallel (*see* Geneva Accords) and the border with Cambodia (*see* Kampuchea). It was a difficult task because on any given day literally thousands of small junks were plying the rivers of South Vietnam. A tight blockade of the coast became a major American strategic concept, and the Seventh Fleet* established a Coastal Surveillance Force to maintain the blockade. At first the navy transferred former destroyer escorts from the North Atlantic to serve as radar picket ships in the South China Sea. A number of coastal surveillance centers were set up along the South Vietnamese coast. Late in 1965 P–5 Marlin seaplanes and P–3A Orion aircraft were patrolling the coast up to 150 miles offshore, while Coast Guard Squadron One, equipped with nearly 100 50-foot "Swift" boats and 26 83-foot cutters were patrolling closer to shore. Operation Game Warden* involved use of a riverine force to monitor boat and ship movements on the interior rivers. The Coastal Surveillance Force's work off the coast of South Vietnam was code-named Operation Market Time* beginning in July 1967.

Sources: Victor Croizat, *The Brown Water Navy: The River and Coastal War in Indo-China and Vietnam, 1948–1972*, 1984; Antony Preston, "The Naval War in Vietnam," in John S. Bowman, ed., *The Vietnam War: An Almanac*, 1985.

COAST GUARD, UNITED STATES

The origins of the Coast Guard go back to the Revenue Cutter Service, a military organization founded shortly after the American Revolution and assigned to cooperation with the United States Navy in 1799. The modern Coast Guard was formed in 1915 when the Revenue Cutter Service and the Life-Saving Service were merged. The Lighthouse Service merged with the Coast Guard in 1939, and in 1942 the Bureau of Navigation and the Steamboat Inspection were added to the Coast Guard. The Coast Guard was financed out of the Treasury Department until 1967, when it became part of the Department of Transportation. At the direction of the president of the United States, the Coast Guard serves within the United States Navy.* On April 30, 1965, President Lyndon Johnson* designated Coast Guard Squadron One to be assigned to Vietnam. In 1965 and 1966, twenty-six Coast Guard patrol boats were deployed to the coast of the South China Sea, where they engaged in coastal surveillance using Da Nang,* Qui Nhon,* Nha Trang,* Vung Tau,* and An Thoi as bases. Coast Guard Squadron Three went to South Vietnam in 1967. During the war the Coast Guard vessels boarded approximately 250,000 small craft, usually sampans and junks, and participated in 6,000 support missions. Their main objective was to stop the infiltration* of supplies to the Vietcong.* In January 1969 South Vietnamese crews began operating the cutters, and in 1971 and 1972 all of the cutters were turned over to South Vietnam.

Sources: Edward J. Marolda and G. Wesley Pryce III, *A Short History of the United States Navy and the Southeast Asian Conflict, 1950–1975*, 1984; Stephen Evans, *The United States Coast Guard, 1790–1915*; Eugene Tulich, *The United States Coast Guard in Southeast Asia During the Vietnam Conflict*, 1975.

COCHIN CHINA

Geographers divided Vietnam into three general areas: Tonkin,* Annam,* and Cochin China. Cochin China comprises the six southern provinces of Vietnam. In the mid-sixteenth century, Portuguese adventurers referred to Vietnam as Cauchichina, taking "Cauchi" from "Giao Chi," the Chinese term for Vietnam, and then added the term "China" to separate it from their Cochin colony in India. By the nineteenth century, the French were using the term "Cochin China" to refer only to the southern part of Vietnam. The economy of Cochin China was dominated by the Mekong Delta.* Unlike the Red River in Tonkin, the Mekong River is more regular in its flow, not given to flooding, and far more predictable. The largest city of Cochin China was Saigon,* now known as Ho Chi Minh City.* Located approximately 40 miles inland from the coast, Saigon is connected to the South China Sea by the tidal Dong Nai River. North and east of the Mekong Delta are the forestlands of the Annamese highlands. Large regions there are still uninhabited because of extensive swamps and malaria-ridden swamps. To the west are the lowland plains of Cambodia (*see* Kampuchea), which constitute an extension of the Mekong Delta. The weather of Cochin China is usually very hot. The dry season extends from November to April, while heavy rains from May to October combine with oppressive heat. Cochin China consists of approximately 26,500 square miles.

Before the second half of the nineteenth century, Cochin China was part of China, the Khmer* Empire of Cambodia, and the Empire of Annam. The French seized Saigon in 1858, and four years later the emperor of Annam ceded the eastern portion of Cochin China to France. In 1887 the rest of Cochin China became part of the French colony. In June 1946, Cochin China became an independent republic in the new Federation of Indochina, but three years later Cochin China voted to become part of Vietnam.

Source: Milton E. Osborne, *The French Presence in Cochin China and Cambodia*, 1969.

COFFIN, WILLIAM SLOAN, JR.

William Sloan Coffin, a leading figure in the antiwar movement,* was born in New York City on June 1, 1924. He served in the army during World War II and later studied at Yale and the Union Theological Seminary. Between 1950 and 1953 he worked as a Soviet expert for the Central Intelligence Agency* (CIA), but left the CIA to complete his seminary studies at Yale. Coffin was ordained a Presbyterian minister in 1956 and in 1958 became chaplain of Yale. A political activist committed to civil rights and antipoverty causes, Coffin also became an early opponent of the Vietnam War. He traveled widely around the country calling for draft* resistance and serving as an officer of the National Emergency Committee of Clergy Concerned About Vietnam. In 1968 Coffin was indicted and convicted for conspiring to assist draft resisters, but the convictions were eventually overturned and then dropped by the Department of Justice. Coffin left Yale in 1975 to pursue new interests in lecturing and writing.

Sources: *New York Times*, October 17, 1967; Thomas Powers, *Vietnam, The War at Home*, 1984; Nancy Zaroulis and Gerald Sullivan, *Who Spoke Up? American Protest Against the War in Vietnam, 1963–1975*, 1984.

COLBY, WILLIAM EGAN

William E. Colby was born on January 4, 1920, in St. Paul, Minnesota. He graduated from Princeton in 1940, and after completing officer candidate school for the United States Army, he was assigned to the Office of Strategic Services where he worked with the French resistance. In 1947, the Office of Strategic Services became the Central Intelligence Agency.* Colby earned a law degree at Columbia University and joined the CIA in 1950. In 1959, Colby became station chief for the CIA in Saigon where he supervised recruitment of Montagnard* tribesmen and the strategic hamlet program.* Colby returned to Washington, D.C., in 1962 as head of the CIA's Far East Division. In that position he directed Air America* and the Phoenix Program.* Colby returned to South Vietnam in 1968 as a deputy to General William Westmoreland,* commander of the U.S. Military Assistance Command Vietnam.* There Colby was responsible for the Civil Operations and Rural Development Support* program and the Phoenix Program. Congressional investigations into charges of torture and assassination under the Phoenix Program brought Colby before several committees to testify where he maintained that most of the 20,000 people killed had died in combat situations. He never denied, however, that there had been assassinations under the Phoenix Program. Colby became director of the Central Intelligence Agency in 1973 and retired three years later.

Source: William Colby and Peter Forbath, *Honorable Men: My Life in the CIA*, 1978.

COLLINS, JOSEPH LAWTON

From November 3, 1954, to May 14, 1955, General J. Lawton Collins served as special U.S. representative in Vietnam, a designation that made him the de facto American ambassador in Saigon* during that period. Born on May 1, 1896, Collins graduated from West Point in 1917. After the attack on Pearl Harbor, he commanded the 25th Infantry Division in successful campaigns on Guadalcanal and New Georgia. His soldiers in the Pacific gave him the nickname "Lightning Joe." Transferred to Europe in 1944, Collins commanded the VII Corps in the Normandy invasion and the assault on Germany. From 1949 to 1953 he served with distinction as army chief of staff, and he was the U.S. representative to the Military Committee and Standing Group of the North Atlantic Treaty Organization (NATO) when President Dwight D. Eisenhower* sent him to Saigon in 1954.

Collins's mission to Vietnam came at a decisive moment in the history of U.S. involvement in Indochina.* In June 1954 Emperor Bao Dai* had selected Ngo Dinh Diem* as prime minister of the state of Vietnam. Since the partitioning of Vietnam under the Geneva Accords* of 1954 was to be only temporary, the hopes of a nationalist alternative to the Communists in the North rested on the prospects of Diem's government in the South. Collins's assignment was to assess Diem's abilities and to seek ways for the United States to assist his government. Working with General Paul Ely,* the French high commissioner in Indochina, Collins made progress in the reorganization and training of the South Vietnamese armed forces, but he soon concluded that Diem lacked the leadership qualities and experience necessary to compete with Ho Chi Minh.* In April 1955 Collins specifically recommended that the U.S. shift its support from Diem to other South Vietnamese leaders. After direct consultations in Washington between the general and Secretary of State John Foster Dulles,* a decision was reached to accept Collins's judgment. At that moment, however, Diem precipitated a hostile confrontation with his South Vietnamese opponents. The Vietnamese National Army helped Diem survive the crisis, and the prime minister's advocates in Washington sustained Dulles in reversing the decision to dump Diem.

The reaffirmation of American support for Diem wedded Washington to his regime in Saigon. In the years that followed, Collins's assessment of Diem's weaknesses proved tragically correct. Collins left Saigon in May 1955 and returned to duty with NATO. He retired from the army in 1956 and later served as an executive with Charles Pfizer & Company.

Source: J. Lawton Collins, *Lighting Joe: An Autobiography*, 1979.

David L. Anderson

COLUMBIA UNIVERSITY DEMONSTRATIONS

During the week of April 23–30, 1968, Students for a Democratic Society* (SDS) and the Students Afro-American Society (SAS) led 700 to 1,000 Columbia University students in the seizure and occupation of five campus buildings. Among the buildings occupied was Low Library, which contained the office of president Grayson Kirk. While in control of Low Library students committed several acts of vandalism including ransacking Kirk's files, ostensibly searching for secret links between the university and the military establishment. Among their demands, the demonstrators called for a halt to construction of a controversial gymnasium at Morningside Park and the severing of university ties with the Institute for Defense Analysis (IDA). The IDA was a Pentagon-sponsored group of universities that advised the government on defense strategies. Other demands dealt with the university's disciplinary policies.

The events of April 23–30 began with a rally called at the sundial, a gathering place for students, which was to start at noon, by the Columbia chapter of SDS under the leadership of Mark Rudd. The demonstrators had been called to protest disciplinary actions taken against students who had participated in a protest against the university's tie with the IDA and to demand that the university end its involvement with that organization. After an unsuccessful attempt to gain entry to Low Library, the students drifted over to Morningside Park, which had become a symbol of division between Columbia and the surrounding black community of Harlem. Following a confrontation with police, Mark Rudd, who had arrived later, led the students back to the sundial. The demonstrators then marched into Hamilton Hall to hold a sit-in. While in control of Hamilton the protesters issued their demands. They also took a hostage, Henry Coleman, the acting dean of Columbia College, who was later released unharmed. On April 24, after much discussion, the white students were asked to leave Hamilton by the SAS, who wanted to use this event to demonstrate black power and discipline. The students who left, including Rudd, occupied Low Library shortly thereafter. Eventually, various student groups occupied Fayerweather, Avery, and Mathematics halls.

Attempts to negotiate a peaceful resolution of the crisis were hampered by distrust on the part of the students and the administration. Finally, on April 30 at 1:30 A.M. one thousand New York City police cleared the buildings of demonstrators. Except for Hamilton Hall, where the black demonstrators has assured police that they would leave peacefully, the police used violence to expel the students. The Cox Commission, headed by Harvard law professor Archibald Cox and charged with investigating the events of April 23–30, concluded that violence was to be expected when students resisted arrest.

Immediately after the events of April 23–30, a university-wide strike was called by the SDS. On May 21, Mark Rudd and about 350 supporters again occupied Hamilton Hall over a dispute concerning disciplinary action against Rudd and others who had participated in the April 23–30 demonstrations. Again the police were called in to dislodge the protesters. This time the police used violence not only against the demonstrators but also against innocent bystanders. The Cox Commission characterized it as " . . . brutality for which a layman can see no justification unless it be that the way to restore order in a riot is to terrorize civilians."

Following twenty-one days of hearings beginning on May 4, 1968, and after listening to seventy-nine witnesses, the Cox Commission determined that the university's connection with the IDA had become a symbol of Columbia's participation in the Vietnam War. As such, Columbia had become a surrogate for the frustrations students felt over their inability to affect national policy on the war. The Cox Commission further concluded that while the Vietnam War was not the only grievance expressed at Columbia, it was of overriding concern for nearly all students and was a potentially explosive issue.

Source: *Crisis at Columbia: Report of the Fact-Finding Commission Appointed to Investigate the Disturbances at Columbia University in April and May 1968*, 1969.

Mike Dennis

COMBINED ACTION PLATOONS

One of the problems the United States Marines* faced in their combat activities in I Corps* was pacification (*see* Rural Reconstruction) and village security. Although designed as an assault force, the marines found themselves in static positions trying to defend territory from the Vietcong* and the North Vietnamese. In that sense they were performing a mission which had not historically been part of their function. Since security was the primary prerequisite of any pacification program, the marines developed the Combined Action Platoons (CAP) program in 1965. Under the CAP program, a marine rifle squad would operate with a South Vietnamese Regional Forces* (RF) company. Beginning in 1970, the program was changed to Combined Action Groups, in which an entire marine company was assigned to work with an RF battalion. The theory was that if the Combined Action Platoons or Groups were able to provide security, pacification efforts would succeed in winning the fidelity of the South Vietnamese peasants.

Sources: Larry E. Cable, *Conflict of Myths: The Development of American Counterinsurgency Doctrine and the Vietnam War*, 1986; Jack Shulimson, *U.S. Marines in Vietnam: An Expanding War 1966*, 1982.

COMING HOME

Coming Home was a bittersweet movie made in 1977 about the plight of American veterans of the Vietnam War and those they left behind. The film centers on Sally Hyde (Jane Fonda), the wife of a volatile marine captain (Bruce Dern) who went to Vietnam determined to uphold the honor of the nation. Sally had been a typically docile service housewife before his departure, but her husband's absence forces her to change her ways. She takes up volunteer work at the post hospital, makes new friends, and asserts her independence. More daring still, she falls in love with Luke Martin (Jon Voight), a bitter paraplegic Vietnam veteran who turns her against the war her husband is fighting.

Sally and Luke's romance is the heart of *Coming Home*. Their affair, at times perhaps a bit contrived, ultimately is both believable and poignant. It points up both the inconsistencies of personality in all the main characters and the inconsistencies of the Vietnam involvement in the 1960s. The anguish that each character expresses summarizes well that of the nation at large. Directed by Hal Ashby, *Coming Home* is an important statement of personal belief by the director and a valid description of the perspective from which many Americans viewed the conflict in the 1970s.

Source: *Magill's Survey of Cinema. English Language Films*, 1981.

Roger D. Launius

COMMANDANT, U.S. MARINE CORPS

The Marine Corps commandant is the senior officer in the United States Marine Corps.* Between the time of the first American casualty in Vietnam in 1959 and the end of the war in 1975, five men occupied the office of commandant of the Marine Corps. General Randolph Pate was replaced in 1960 by General David Shoup,* who served until January 1964. Shoup was replaced by General Wallace M. Greene,* who served until January 1968, when General Leonard Chapman* became commandant. Chapman was commandant until January 1972. General Robert Cushman* replaced Chapman and served as commandant until after the Vietnam War.

Sources: Harry G. Summers, Jr., *Vietnam War Almanac*, 1985; Shelby L. Stanton, *Vietnam Order of Battle*, 1981; Allan R. Millett, *Semper Fidelis: The History of the United States Marine Corps*, 1980.

COMMANDER, MILITARY ASSISTANCE COMMAND, VIETNAM

The Military Assistance Command, Vietnam* was established on February 8, 1962, with its headquarters in Saigon.* During the course of the war in Vietnam, four men served as commander of the Military Assistance Command, Vietnam: General Paul D. Harkins* (February 1962 to June 1964); General William C. Westmoreland* (June 1964 to July 1968); General Creighton W. Abrams* (July 1968 to June 1972); and General Frederick C. Weyand* (June 1972 to the end of the conflict).

Sources: George S. Eckhardt, *Command and Control, 1950–1969*, 1974; Shelby L. Stanton, *Vietnam Order of Battle*, 1981.

COMMANDER IN CHIEF, PACIFIC COMMAND

Also known as CINCPAC, the commander in chief of the Pacific Command changed four times during the Vietnam War. Admiral Harry D. Felt served until June 1964, when he was replaced by Admiral U. S. Grant Sharp.* Sharp stayed in the post exactly four years until Admiral John S. McCain replaced him. In September 1972 Admiral Noel Gayler took over for McCain. Gayler remained as CINCPAC until the end of the war.

Sources: U. S. Grant Sharp, *Strategy for Defeat: Vietnam in Retrospect*, 1978; Harry G. Summers, Jr., *On Strategy: A Critical Analysis of the Vietnam War*, 1982.

COMMUNIST PARTY OF VIETNAM

This party was formally established in June 1929, although its true origins predated this formal establishment. Ho Chi Minh,* originally named Nguyen Sinh Cung, was really a nationalist prior to the success of the Bolshevik Revolution of 1917. While in Paris young Ho was exposed to Marx and other socialist writers and leaders through his friendship with Jules Raveau, a veteran French Marxist. By this time he had adopted a more militant name—Nguyen Ai Quoc (Nguyen the Patriot)—and joined the Communist party.

By the 1920s French officials scrutinized Ho's revolutionary activities. In 1924 Ho went to Moscow where he met Stalin and attended the University of Oriental Workers. It is from here that Asians learned the fundamentals of Marxist-Leninism. Later in 1924 Ho moved to Canton (now with the name Ly Thuy), where he mobilized and organized Vietnamese students in southern China. Chiang Kai-shek's* betrayal of his Communist associates in 1927 forced Ho to flee. He returned to Moscow, toured Europe, and slipped into Paris secretly under the name of Duong. Ho in 1928 moved to Bangkok, where he established a school and espoused the doctrines he had preached to the Thanh Nien Cach Menh Dong Chi Hoi* (Revolutionary Youth League), an organization he created while in southern China.

The revolutionary climate inside Vietnam was not very good during the 1920s. Many of Ho's students and comrades were imprisoned for revolutionary activities. Finally in the summer of 1929, Ho organized a meeting in Hong Kong of rival Communist factions from Vietnam. Out of the meeting grew a cohesive Communist party dedicated to the overthrow of colonial rule in French Indochina. The new party Ho named the Indochinese Communist party (*see* Lao Dong party), reflecting the assembled leaders' ultimate goal of extending their control over all of Indochina.* They called for Vietnamese independence and a proletarian government.

The 1930s were a period of both growth and repression for Ho and his comrades. Although Ho eluded imprisonment by the French, his comrades Pham Van Dong* and Le Duc Tho* were not so lucky. Both ended up at the infamous prison island of Poulo Condore.* During this same period, thousands of Vietnamese peasants were tortured and killed by French authorities, because of their support of Ho's war of liberation. By the late 1930s, Ho determined that his party was too limiting and began to press his associates to form a broader movement, which in 1941 resulted in the creation of the Vietminh.* Ho Chi Minh's war against the French did not gain momentum until after World War II and ended with the surrender of Dien Bien Phu* in May 1954.

Sources: Charles Fenn, *Ho Chi Minh: A Biographical Introduction*, 1973; Peter Wiles, *Ho Chi Minh: A Political Biography*, 1968; William J. Duiker, *The Rise of Nationalism in Vietnam, 1900–1941*, 1976.

John S. Leiby

COMPANY

A company is an organizational institution commanded by a captain and consisting of two or more platoons.* It varies widely in size according to its mission. An artillery company is called a battery* and a cavalry company is called a troop.*

Sources: Harry G. Summers, Jr., *Vietnam War Almanac*, 1985; Shelby L. Stanton, *Vietnam Order of Battle*, 1981.

CONEIN, LUCIEN

Lucien Conein was born in Paris but grew up in the American midwest when his mother sent him to live with her sister, who had married a World War I veteran. In 1940, Conein volunteered for the French Army, and when France* surrendered in late June 1940, he deserted and, after some difficulty, made his way to the United States. The newly formed Office of Strategic Services, forerunner of the Central Intelligence Agency* (CIA), recruited him, and he parachuted into France to work for the resistance. When the war in Europe ended, he joined a commando group harassing the Japanese in northern Vietnam. Conein entered Hanoi* when Japan surrendered and met Ho Chi Minh* and other Vietminh* leaders. Between 1954 and 1956 Conein was back in Vietnam, this time as part of Edward G. Lansdale's* intelligence mission.

In 1962 Conein was reassigned to Vietnam, this time as an army lieutenant colonel assigned to the Interior Ministry, but his real assignment was to maintain CIA contacts with Vietnamese generals. Almost all of them trusted Conein; indeed, some of them trusted only Conein, because he once had been their commanding officer in the 1940s and early 1950s. Conein's codename in 1962 and 1963 was Lulu or Black Luigi. His major role in Vietnam then was in the military coup against Ngo Dinh Diem* in 1963. Conein knew that American support for Diem had all but disappeared, and he worked with the generals in letting them know that the United States would not look unfavorably on a change in government. The coup, complete with Diem's assassination, took place on November 1, 1963. Conein left Vietnam shortly thereafter and retired from government service early in the 1970s.

Sources: Marvin E. Gettleman et al., eds., *Vietnam and America: A Documented History*, 1985; John Prados, *Presidents' Secret Wars. CIA and Pentagon Covert Operations Since World War II*, 1986.

Charles Dobbs

CONFUCIANISM

Confucianism is a religious and moral philosophy based on the teachings of the Chinese sage Confucius, who lived in the sixth century B.C. Confucianism emphasizes worship of the family and ancestors and imposes on all people the obligation of accepting their station in life. Personal honor depends on social complacency; one has to behave in accordance with the expectations of society, and the essence of personal behavior is obedience, submissiveness, and peaceful acquiescence in the social hierarchy. As a political philosophy, Confucianism views the state as an extension of the family, with a political leader acting as a father, providing his followers with a good example, protection, and love. A leader who protects and cares for his family can automatically expect complete obedience and reverence from them. When the Chinese subjugated Vietnam in the second and third centuries B.C., Confucianism, which was rapidly permeating Chinese culture, came into Vietnam and became the dominant ideological force there. The Vietnamese emperors accepted the Chinese model of bureaucratic government based on a Confucian-trained civil service. That bureaucracy dominated Vietnamese life until the arrival of the French in the nineteenth century.

Although both Confucianism and Buddhism* coexisted in the Vietnamese spiritual world, they came into serious political conflict during the thirteenth and fourteenth centuries. Buddhists resented the control Confucians had over the civil bureaucracy, while the Confucians accused the Buddhists of exploiting peasants through religious superstition. Gradually the Buddhists were forced to retire from central political influence to their villages, pagodas, and monasteries, where they still exercised considerable authority in Vietnamese cultural life. While Buddhism was the organized religion of Vietnam, Confucianism was the moral philosophy which the Vietnamese used to govern their society.

Sources: Ellen Joy Hammer, *Vietnam, Yesterday and Today*, 1966; Sukumar Dutt, *Buddhism in East Asia*, 1966; John Frank Cady, *Southeast Asia: Its Historical Development*, 1958.

CONGRESS, UNITED STATES

The Vietnam War led to major changes in the foreign policy role of the U.S. Congress. At the beginning of the war, the Congress allowed the president a relatively free hand in foreign affairs, including the use of American armed forces abroad. By the end of the war, Congress was playing a major role in the conduct of American foreign policy.

The Constitution of the United States divides power in foreign affairs between the president and Congress, but it gives the dominant role to the president. Traditionally, presidents have taken the lead in foreign affairs, with Congress only occasionally using its powers to check presidential initiatives. This pattern continued in the aftermath of World War II. As we became involved in the Cold War, American foreign policy relations between the president and Congress were characterized by bipartisanship. Congress, arguing that partisan politics were inappropriate in foreign policy, allowed the president a great deal of freedom in the conduct of foreign policy. In the 1950s presidents committed U.S. military forces in a number of the world's trouble spots, and they generally received the full support of the Congress. While American military commitments in Korea* were under the auspices of the United Nations, and were carried out with considerable congressional involvement, most American military commitments during this era were made by the president in his role of commander in chief and involved little congressional input. Early American military involvement in Vietnam occurred within this framework. Congress allowed presidents to take the lead role in determining the size and extent of American involvement. As that involvement grew, President Johnson* instructed his assistants to draft plans to punish North Vietnam. William P. Bundy,* assistant secretary of defense, pointed out that taking military action against North Vietnam would normally require a declaration of war, something no one was prepared to do. Yet to proceed without legislative endorsement would be "unsatisfactory." He advocated obtaining a congressional resolution of the sort that had given Eisenhower* a free hand in 1955 when it appeared the Chinese Communists might attempt to seize the islands of Quemoy and Matsu. Johnson's aides began drafting such a resolution. Five months later a series of circumstances allowed that resolution to form the basis of the Gulf of Tonkin Resolution*—a resolution Johnson's aides called a virtual declaration of war.

The Gulf of Tonkin Resolution resulted from a controversial series of events in July and August of 1964, culminating with the destroyer USS *Maddox** engaging three North Vietnamese PT boats in the Gulf of Tonkin on August 2, sinking one and damaging the other two. When word of the engagement reached Johnson, he purposely downplayed the incident. Dean Rusk,* however, instructed his staff to "pull together" Bundy's draft resolution. Talking to reporters, Rusk warned North Vietnam about any repeated action. Two nights later, during a thunderstorm, the *Maddox* and USS *C. Turner Joy** intercepted messages that gave the impression of an imminent attack by the North Vietnamese. Both vessels' radar and sonar were acting erratically due to weather conditions. Both vessels recorded what they believed to be torpedo attacks on their sonars, and took evasive action. They opened fire on radar blips, and officers of the *Maddox* reported sinking two or perhaps three Communist craft. By daylight, Captain Herrick, in command of the *Maddox*, was having serious doubts that any engagement had actually occurred, and informed his superiors of his doubts. He suggested that daylight reconnaissance be conducted and completely evaluated before any further action was taken.

While the commander at the scene doubted that he had been attacked, President Johnson had no such doubts, and announced to key Democratic members of Congress that an attack had taken place, that he would retaliate against North Vietnam, and that he would ask Congress for a resolution of support. Not a single congressman present raised an objection. On August 5, 1964, Johnson sent the resolution to Congress. Polls at the time indicated that 85 percent of the American public backed the president on this issue, and Congress passed the resolution, giving the president the power to "take all necessary measures." As Johnson later quipped, the resolution was "like grandma's nightshirt—it covered everything."

As American military involvement deepened in Vietnam, public support began to wane. The Tet Offensive,* showing North Vietnamese ability to strike seemingly at will at a time when American leaders were predicting victory, represented a psychological turning point in the war. Although a military disaster for North Vietnam, the Tet Offensive resulted in a public relations coup; after Tet, Americans refused to believe anyone who said the end was in sight, and began pressing for an end to American involvement. Congress, reflecting this change in the attitudes of the public, began to assert itself in policy debates over Vietnam. In 1969 Congress passed its first restriction on presidential power in Vietnam, prohibiting the use of American combat forces in Cambodia (*see* Kampuchea) or Laos.* President Nixon,* ignoring the congressional dictate, launched a secret series of air attacks in Cambodia (*see* Operation Menu) that lasted fourteen months.

In 1973 Congress passed the War Powers Resolution,* limiting the ability of a president to commit American military forces without congressional involvement. That same year Congress voted to stop all bombing throughout Indochina.* By this time, American combat forces had been withdrawn, and American prisoners of war* held in Hanoi* had come home.

Throughout the war in Vietnam, Congress reflected public opinion in its actions. When the public was willing to give the president a free hand, Congress did so; when the public began to oppose American involvement, Congress reflected that opposition.

Sources: Thomas M. Franck and Edward Weisband, *Foreign Policy by Congress*, 1980; P. Edward Haley, *Congress and the Fall of South Vietnam and Cambodia*, 1982.

Nolan J. Argyle

CON SON ISLAND   *See* Poulo Condore

CONTAINMENT POLICY

First pronounced by George Kennan* in a 1947 article in *Foreign Affairs*, "containment" was the most important postwar American foreign policy. At first it was designed to keep Soviet expansionism under control, preferably behind its 1945 military boundaries. In the beginning, containment was nonmilitary in nature, focusing on economic and technical assistance, and it was embodied in such programs as the Marshall Plan in 1947 and 1948 to rebuild the European economies and the Truman Doctrine to provide the funds Greece and Turkey needed to fight Communist guerrillas. As the Cold War escalated in the late 1940s, however, containment took on new global, military dimensions. After the fall of China in 1949, it came to imply the encirclement of the People's Republic of China* and the Soviet Union* with a network of military alliances: the North Atlantic Treaty Organization, the Baghdad Pact, the Southeast Asia Treaty Organization,* and the enormous military buildup of the 1950s and 1960s. When the North Koreans invaded South Korea in 1950, the United States intervened in the conflict in the name of containment. Containment reached its peak during the Eisenhower* years and the tenure of Secretary of State John Foster Dulles* (1953 to 1959).

When the French were expelled from Indochina* after the Battle of Dien Bien Phu* in 1954, the United States began increasing its commitment to prevent a Communist takeover. American policymakers were applying the containment doctrine to Vietnam, assuming that Soviet and Chinese aggression were behind the North Vietnamese crusade to reunite the country. The domino theory* and the containment policy fit nicely together in the 1950s and early 1960s. Not until the mid–1960s, however, when American policymakers began to see that communism was not a single, monolithic movement orchestrated from Moscow, did the application of containment to Vietnam begin to seem counterproductive. By the late 1960s and early 1970s, American policymakers accepted the importance of colonialism and nationalism in the history of the anti-French and anti-American movements in Vietnam. By that time as well, American policymakers realized that communism was a polycentric movement requiring creative, individual responses.

Sources: John L. Gaddis, "Containment: A Reassessment," *Foreign Affairs*, 55 (July 1977), 873–87; Alexander L. George and Richard Smoke, *Deterrence in American Foreign Policy*, 1974; Douglas S. Blaufarb, *The Counterinsurgency Era: U.S. Doctrine and Performance 1950 to the Present*, 1977.

CON THIEN, BATTLE OF (1967–68)

Also known as the "Hill of Angels," Con Thien is a series of three hills, approximately 475 feet high, located south of the Demilitarized Zone* (DMZ) in eastern Quang Tri Province. Elements of the Third Marine Division* had established fixed positions on Con Thien in hopes of stopping North Vietnamese Army* (NVA) infiltration* across the DMZ and establishing McNamara's Wall, or Project Practice Nine,* an electronic barrier south of the DMZ. It was a role the marines did not like. Trained as a rapidly moving assault force, they found themselves holding down a defensive position. From mountains in the DMZ, the NVA regularly shelled the marine positions with heavy Soviet artillery. In preparation for large-scale infiltration of NVA troops into South Vietnam and

an offensive against South Vietnamese cities in 1968, General Vo Nguyen Giap*
instigated a series of border battles in 1967 to distract American and ARVN (*see*
Army of the Republic of Vietnam) attention away from the most populated areas.
These border clashes occurred near the DMZ, the Central Highlands* of the
Cambodian-Laotian-South Vietnamese border, and the rubber plantations near
the Cambodian border in III Corps.* The siege of Con Thien was the first of
the border battles.

Early in September 1967, the artillery barrage against Con Thien intensified.
The American media began to portray Con Thien as another Dien Bien Phu,*
but General William Westmoreland* launched Operation Neutralize* to relieve
the marines there. Seventh Air Force* Commander William M. Momyer* developed the SLAM* campaign, which concentrated B–52* strikes, tactical air
support, and naval bombardment on NVA positions surrounding Con Thien. By
early October 1967, when the NVA 324B Division abandoned the siege, the
United States had flown more than 4,000 sorties* against Con Thien, unloading
more than 40,000 tons of bombs. The North Vietnamese could not withstand
such firepower and gave up the battle. In the short term, the battle of Con Thien
was an American victory which left more than 2,000 North Vietnamese troops
dead. But in the long run, it did serve Vo Nguyen Giap's purpose in distracting
American attention away from the South Vietnamese cities, which would soon
face the Tet Offensive.*

Sources: Shelby L. Stanton, *The Rise and Fall of an American Army: U.S. Ground
Troops in Vietnam, 1965–1973*, 1985; William W. Momyer, *Airpower in Three Wars*,
1978.

COOPER, CHESTER

Author of *The Last Crusade* (1979), Chester Cooper was born on January 13,
1917, in Boston, Massachusetts. He attended MIT, New York University, and
Columbia, and took a Ph.D. at American University in Washington, D.C. Cooper
worked for the Central Intelligence Agency* between 1945 and 1952, and then
joined the staff of the National Security Council. Between 1963 and 1964, he
served as deputy director of intelligence, and between 1964 and 1966 he was a
member of McGeorge Bundy's* staff, where he specialized in Asian affairs.
Unlike most men in either the Johnson* or Nixon* administrations, Cooper
consistently advocated a political solution over a military solution to the conflict.
However, he also defended U.S. policies in South Vietnam, arguing that the
United States did not exert itself more with Ngo Dinh Diem* because it did not
want to play the role of colonial master. With prospects for peace negotiations
in early 1968, Cooper urged establishment of communication channels with both
the North Vietnamese and the Vietcong* and insisted that South Vietnamese
resistance to negotiations must be overcome if negotiations were to succeed. He
opposed the Cambodian invasion (*see* Operation Binh Tay) because it widened
the war and made it impossible to negotiate a genuine peace settlement in Paris
without dealing with Cambodia (*see* Kampuchea) and Laos.* One of the first to

recognize the plight of Amerasian children, Cooper recommended in 1973 that the United States offer vigorous support for UNICEF's program to care for them.

Sources: *Contemporary Authors*, vols. 29–32, 1978; Chester L. Cooper, *The Lost Crusade: America in Vietnam*, 1970.

Samuel Freeman

COOPER, JOHN SHERMAN

John Sherman Cooper was born in Somerset, Kentucky, on August 23, 1901. He graduated from Yale in 1923 and attended the Harvard Law School from 1923 to 1925. He served in the Kentucky legislature from 1928 to 1930, and then served eight years as a judge in Pulaski County. Cooper was a circuit judge in the 28th Judicial District in Kentucky (1938–46), and won a seat in the U.S. Senate in 1946. He served three terms in the Senate, 1947–48, 1952–55, and 1957–73. Between 1955 and 1956 Cooper was the U.S. ambassdor to India. He specialized in foreign affairs, and during the late 1960s he became an increasingly vocal critic of American policy in Vietnam. In 1970, after the invasion of Cambodia (*see* Operation Binh Tay), Cooper openly called for American withdrawal from Cambodia (*see* Kampuchea) and condemned the widening of the war. Along with Senator Frank Church,* Cooper sponsored the Cooper-Church Amendment* demanding a withdrawal from or cutting off all funds for military operations in Cambodia. The amendment succeeded in the Senate but failed in the House. Cooper left the Senate in 1973 and became U.S. ambassador to the German Democratic Republic. He retired from public life in 1976.

Sources: *Who's Who in America, 1984–1985*, 1985; George C. Herring, *America's Longest War: The United States in Vietnam, 1950–1975*, 1986.

COOPER-CHURCH AMENDMENT

In reaction to the invasion of Cambodia (*see* Operation Binh Tay) ordered by the Nixon* administration in 1970 without consultation with Congress,* Senators John Sherman Cooper* (Republican, Kentucky) and Frank F. Church* (Democrat, Idaho) proposed an amendment that would prohibit spending funds without congressional approval after June 1, 1970, for the purposes of keeping U.S. troops in Cambodia, for sending U.S. advisers into Cambodia, for providing combat air support for Cambodian troops, or for financing the sending of troops or advisers into Cambodia (*see* Kampuchea) by other nations.

Supporters saw the proposed amendment as an overdue attempt by Congress to reassert its constitutional control over the power to make war. The administration and its supporters in Congress denounced the amendment as an unconstitutional intrusion into the president's power as commander in chief. After bitter debate, the Senate adopted the Cooper-Church Amendment on June 30 by a vote of 58 to 37.

The amendment was attached to a foreign military sales bill. That bill also carried another amendment repealing the Gulf of Tonkin Resolution.* But the repeal was not significant because the Nixon administration cited the president's constitutional powers as commander in chief and not the Gulf of Tonkin Resolution as the basis for his war-making authority.

Sources: *Facts on File*, 1970, pp. 343–44, 359, 461–62; Paul L. Kattenburg, *The Vietnam Trauma in American Foreign Policy, 1945–1975*, 1980.

Joseph M. Rowe, Jr.

CORPS

The term "corps" has a dual meaning in the armed services. It can be used to designate any group of military personnel performing a similar function, like the Signal Corps or the Medical Corps. As an organizational element in the military, a corps is a unit made up of at least two divisions.* The corps commander, usually a lieutenant general, controls combat operations by issuing directives to division commanders and coordinating the work of artillery and cavalry groups. There were four corps operating in Vietnam during the war: the XXIV Corps,* III Marine Amphibious Force,* II Field Force Vietnam,* and I Field Force Vietnam.*

Sources: Shelby Stanton, *Vietnam Order of Battle*, 1981; Harry G. Summers, Jr., *Vietnam War Almanac*, 1985.

COUNTERINSURGENCY

Counterinsurgency is the strategy and tactics for winning a revolutionary guerrilla war. Guerrilla war is ancient, though taking its name from Spanish resistance to the Napoleonic French occupation. Revolutionary guerrilla war adds a new goal: it seeks not merely to resist another force but to overthrow it and achieve the political goal of seizing control of a country. Examples include the Mexican revolution which overthrew Porfirio Díaz, Mao Zedong's* expulsion of Chiang Kai-shek* from China, and Ho Chi Minh's* and Vo Nguyen Giap's* conquest of Vietnam.

British expert Robert Thompson* suggested five basic rules for successful counterinsurgency: the goal must be clearly that of establishing a unified country which is democratically run and stable politically and economically; one must operate according to the law rather than violating it, avoiding the use of brutality; there must be a coherent plan of operations; first priority must be to defeat political subversion rather than guerrillas; and one must make base areas secure before doing anything else. Uppermost here, and in others' admonitions, is to avoid alienating the local population. As Mao put it, "The guerrilla is the fish; the people are the water." Hence, a sixth rule: do not use foreigners, especially in a former colony. Subordinate rules include making sure of reliable intelligence regarding the enemy and cutting him off from outside aid if at all possible.

Both Frenchmen and Americans violated these precepts in their wars in Vietnam, and both lost. The French, indeed, ignored the concept of counterinsurgency, and Charles de Gaulle typified this in saying, "I know of two types of warfare: mobile warfare and positional warfare. I have never heard of revolutionary warfare."

The American approach was naive, first in believing that one merely had to instruct peasants in democracy and then in oversimplifying counterinsurgency into "winning the people over," somehow or other. At best, it represented the use of unorthodox techniques rather than real political mobilization of a people. Lyndon Johnson* ignored Roger Hilsman's* suggestion to train South Vietnamese to operate as guerrillas, though this could have kept out foreigners—American troops. Some American officials were contemptuous of the Vietnamese and hence all too willing to make the war an American one.

President John F. Kennedy* sought to develop "special forces"* capable of counterinsurgency. But his position was weak because of the narrowness of his 1960 victory, most of his advisers did not understand revolutionary war, and the U.S. Army* limited counterinsurgency largely to being an "additional duty" for all regular units. Its leaders ignored the long-published works of Samuel B. Griffith and, once committed to Vietnam, fought a technological war, highly destructive to civilians and thus arousing anti-American feelings. Members of the Central Intelligence Agency* had some grasp of the situation, but Americans in Vietnam squabbled among themselves about tactics and withheld crucial intelligence from each other.

Pacification efforts (*see* Rural Reconstruction) such as a Strategic Hamlet Program* failed because of South Vietnamese inefficiency combined with Saigon's* wish to use the program as a means of control rather than to help peasants. CORDS (Civil Operations and Revolutionary Development Support)* was organized only when insurrection had progressed too far. Also, it was meant for Saigon's use, but that government was not interested in anything that helped the peasant but not its own power. Hence, the U.S. Army took it over and again ignored the rules of counterinsurgency. The army could not buy enough time for South Vietnam to become stable and democratic because of the war's destructiveness and also because of Saigon's own antidemocratic tendencies. Most important was the fact that Vietnamese nationalism was on the side of the revolutionary guerrillas.

Sources: Douglas S. Blaufarb, *The Counterinsurgency Era: U.S. Doctrine and Performance 1950 to Present*, 1977; Lawrence E. Grinter, "South Vietnam: Pacification Denied," *Southeast Asia Spectrum* 3 (July 1975), 49–78; Larry E. Cable, *Conflict of Myths: The Development of American Counterinsurgency Doctrine and the Vietnam War*, 1986.

Robert W. Sellen

COWARD

Coward is the title of Tom Tiede's 1968 novel about the Vietnam War. The novel focuses on Private Nathan Long, a conscientious objector who protests the war with a hunger strike, undergoes a court-martial, and is sentenced to a combat tour of Vietnam, where he is captured and tortured to death by the Vietcong.* The novel is full of atrocities and the futility of the American military effort there.

Sources: Tom Tiede, *Coward*, 1968; Philip D. Beidler, *American Literature and the Experience of Vietnam*, 1982.

CREDIBILITY GAP

The term "credibility gap" referred to the discrepancies between the public pronouncements and private policies of American political leaders in the 1960s and 1970s. The idea of the credibility gap first emerged during the Lyndon Johnson* presidency in general but with the Vietnam War in particular. In February 1968 White House staffer Fred Panzer wrote a position paper explaining the psychology of the credibility gap. He blamed the phrase on "antiwar and anti-Johnson forces" who focused on the charge that Johnson lied to the American people in the election of 1964 by promising to stay out of Asian wars. The term was first used by reporter David Wise in a May 23, 1965, article for the *New York Herald Tribune*, and was popularized by a December 5, 1965, article by Murray Marder for the *Washington Post*. Talk about the credibility gap had escalated as doubts appeared about what had actually happened in the Gulf of Tonkin in August 1964 (*see* Gulf of Tonkin incident); intensified even more after the Tet Offensive* in February 1968; reached a fever pitch with the publication of the Pentagon Papers* in July 1971; and climaxed with the entire series of Watergate* revelations between 1972 and 1974.

Sources: David Culbert, "Johnson and the Media," in Robert Divine, ed., *Exploring the Johnson Years*, 1981; Peter Braestrup, *Big Story: How the American Press and Television Reported and Interpreted the Crisis of Tet 1968 in Vietnam and Washington*, 1983.

Frances Frenzel

CRONKITE, WALTER LELAND

Rising through the journalistic ranks, Walter Cronkite became the preeminent media figure of the 1960s and 1970s as correspondent and anchorman for CBS Television. Born in St. Joseph, Missouri, in 1916, Cronkite was a correspondent for United Press in World War II and joined CBS in 1950, serving as anchor and managing editor of the "CBS Evening News," 1962–81. Cronkite was widely watched and respected, and his coverage and reporting of Vietnam was seen as both reflecting and influencing American public opinion.

On September 2, 1963, in a prime-time interview with Cronkite, President John Kennedy* was critical of the South Vietnamese government then headed by Ngo Dinh Diem* and said that changes needed to be made in South Vietnam. However, Kennedy said, "I don't agree with those who say we should withdraw. That would be a great mistake. We must be patient. We must persist." In the following years, Cronkite did not publicly question this position, and his coverage was generally uncritical of Johnson* administration policies. During the Tet Offensive* of 1968, however, Cronkite made his first visit to Vietnam since 1965. Upon his return, Cronkite delivered a somber assessment on February 27, saying that it seemed certain "that the bloody experience of Vietnam is to end in stalemate.'' Rejection of the administration's optimistic forecasts by Cronkite, who had been called the ''most trusted man in America,'' sent shock waves through the government, according to George Christian, President Johnson's press secretary. Cronkite's comments especially upset Johnson, who viewed it as a turning point in American attitudes toward the administration's Vietnam policies. David Halberstam* later wrote that Johnson said that ''if he had lost Walter Cronkite he had lost Mr. Average Citizen,'' and this development helped to solidify Johnson's decision not to run for reelection.

Sources: Kathleen J. Turner, *Lyndon Johnson's Dual War: Vietnam and the Press*, 1985; David Halberstam, *The Powers That Be*, 1979.

Hoyt Purvis

C. TURNER JOY   *See* USS *C. Turner Joy*

CU CHI   *See* Tunnel Rats

CUONG DE

Cuong De, a direct descendant of Emperor Gia Long,* was born in 1882 in Vietnam but lived most of his life in Japan. The nationalist rebel Phan Boi Chau* came to know Cuong De in the early 1900s, and began to campaign for a royal, nationalist religious movement against the French. Phan Boi Chau had Prince Cuong De study in Japan instead of Europe as part of an Asian pride movement, but he eventually abandoned his support of Cuong De when he became convinced of the need for a democratic revolution. Cuong De remained for years in Japan and collaborated with the Japanese during their occupation of Indochina* between 1940 and 1945, hoping they would give him accession to the Vietnamese throne. But when World War II ended and the French returned, Cuong De's hopes were destroyed when Bao Dai* was installed as emperor. Cuong De had strong support among the Hoa Hao* and the Cao Dai* religious sects, but he never gained the power necessary to take control of the Vietnamese throne. Cuong De died in 1951.

Sources: *Webster's New Biographical Dictionary*, 1893, p. 250; Joseph Buttinger, *The Smaller Dragon: A Political History of Vietnam*, 1958.

CUSHMAN, ROBERT EVERTON, JR.

When Vice President Richard Nixon* chose Cushman as his national security adviser in 1957, he put the combat- and CIA-trained colonel on an inside track for selection as commandant of the Marine Corps* in January 1972. Born in Minnesota in 1914, Cushman graduated tenth in his 1935 Naval Academy class, served in China, and commanded the marine detachment aboard the battleship USS *Pennsylvania* when the Japanese attacked Pearl Harbor. Decorated for bravery on Bougainville and Iwo Jima, he also received a Navy Cross for valor on Guam and after the war assumed ascending staff positions at Quantico, the Pentagon, and the Central Intelligence Agency* (CIA), which he joined in 1949.

Cushman would always speak openly about his friendship with Nixon, but after leaving the White House in 1961 he built an enviable record on his own—taking command of the Third Marine Division* on Okinawa in 1961, becoming assistant chief of staff of the Marine Corps the following year, and then serving as Camp Pendleton's commander for three years before his selection to command the III Marine Amphibious Force* in April 1967. In Vietnam from 1967 to 1969, Cushman led 163,000 soldiers and marines, the largest combat force under a marine general in history, and often at the controls of a helicopter conducted the defense of Khe Sanh* and Battle for Hue* as well as the overall I Corps's* counteroffensive in the wake of the 1968 Tet Offensive.*

Nixon appointed Cushman deputy director of the CIA in 1969, and during Watergate* then-Commandant Cushman became briefly entangled in accusations concerning the alleged CIA authorization of a burglary at the offices of Daniel Ellsberg's* psychiatrist; no formal charges were brought and the matter quickly faded in the press. General Cushman served as commandant until his retirement in 1975, stressing mobility as the key to combat success and decrying the "static defense concepts" he believed had undermined the U.S. military in Vietnam. He died on January 2, 1985.

Sources: *New York Times*, January 3, 1985; Edwin H. Simmons, *The Marines in Vietnam*, 1974.

Dudley Acker

• D •

DAI VIET QUOC DAN DANG

The Dai Viet Quoc Dan Dang, or Nationalist Party of Greater Vietnam, was known as the Dai Viet and was founded in Hanoi* in 1939 by the followers of Phan Boi Chau,* the pro-Japanese, anti-French, and anti-Communist nationalist. Ho Chi Minh* outlawed the Dai Viet in 1946 and forced them into exile in South Vietnam. The Dai Viet declined in the south and fractured into several groups, but still attracted the loyalties of large numbers of civil servants. After the collapse of the Diem* regime in November 1963, the Dai Viet was revived by Phan Thong Thao and Nguyen Ton Hoan. It had a membership of approximately 20,000 people, and its strength was concentrated in Hue* and Quang Tri Province in central Vietnam. By 1965 there were three major Dai Viet factions, and their prominent leaders were Ha Thuc Ky, Nguyen Ngoc Huy, Tran Van Xuan, Dang Van Sung, and Phan Huy Quat.* Because of its internal factionalism, the Dai Viet was not able to assume political power in post-Diem South Vietnam, although Dai Viet leaders continued to occupy seats in the national legislature.

Source: Harvey H. Smith et al., *Area Handbook for South Vietnam*, 1967.

DAK TO, BATTLE OF (1967)

Located in Kontum Province in northwestern II Corps,* isolated Dak To sat astride an infiltration route into the Central Highlands* for Vietcong* and North Vietnamese Army* (NVA) forces operating out of Cambodia (*see* Kampuchea). In August 1962, Special Forces* established a border monitoring unit at Dak To to be manned by Montagnard* forces organized to watch the border. The Montagnards could not hold the outpost as the sparsely populated area fell under Vietcong control. As the United States substantially increased its military presence with the introduction of combat units, the Special Forces reestablished a camp there in August 1965.

By May 1967 the 24th NVA regiment had established a way station and supply area nearby, leading to a series of skirmishes between elements of the regiment and Special Forces–led Civilian Irregular Defense Groups.* In response to the NVA presence, elements of the 173rd Airborne Brigade* deployed in late summer to be joined by portions of the 4th Infantry Division.* A series of sharp clashes ensued, culminating in November. The explosion of the 4th Division's ammunition dump virtually leveled the camp, which was reconstructed in December. Throughout early November the American troops attacked highly fortified NVA positions—complete with elaborate tunnels and bunkers—along the elevated ridgelines. By the third week of November the battle for Dak To was centering on Hill 875, located 12 miles west of the camp. General William Westmoreland* called in more than 300 B–52* missions and 2,000 fighter-bomber sorties* to destroy the defensive positions of the 174th NVA Regiment before American troops began their ascent up the hill. Between November 19 and 23, 1967, the battle for Hill 875 raged, complete with air strikes, napalm* bursts, and hand-to-hand combat. Late in the evening of November 22, the North Vietnamese evacuated the area, and the next morning the American soldiers reached the summit. For 1967 at least, the battle for Dak To was over.

From early May to late June 1969, Dak To and nearby Ben Het were besieged by the 28th and 66th NVA regiments. Although Dak To's perimeter wire was penetrated in May, Ben Het, located to the northwest and closer to the Cambodian border, bore the brunt of the NVA attacks. Manned by irregular forces, the camps were little more than thorns in the side of the NVA, which attacked the camps with token forces while infiltrating the main body of their forces around them. The camps were kept open by the United States primarily for their symbolic political value.

Sources: Shelby L. Stanton, *Green Berets at War*, 1985; Stanley Karnow, *Vietnam: A History*, 1983; Frances FitzGerald, *Fire in the Lake: The Vietnamese and the Americans in Vietnam*, 1972.

Samuel Freeman

DA LAT

Located in Tuyen Duc Province of II Corps* in the Central Highlands,* Da Lat was one of South Vietnam's six autonomous municipalities with administrative powers similar to those of the provinces. The other cities with such status were Saigon,* Hue,* Da Nang,* Vung Tau,* and Cam Ranh.* Blessed with a cool climate on the plateau of the Central Highlands, Da Lat was a resort town for Vietnamese generals. Its population in the late 1960s was nearly 60,000 people. The Da Lat Military Academy was the Vietnamese "West Point" for officers in the Army of the Republic of Vietnam.*

Sources: Harvey Smith et al., *Area Handbook for South Vietnam*, 1967; Paul Isoart, *Le Phénomene National Vietnamien: De L'Indépendance Unitaire a L'Indépendance Fractionée*, 1961.

DA NANG

Da Nang, a port city in Quang Nam Province, was the second largest city in South Vietnam. At Western insistence, the 1954 Geneva Conference partitioned Vietnam along the seventeenth parallel (see Geneva Accords) so South Vietnam would include Da Nang and the imperial city of Hue,* a major concession since the Vietminh* controlled most of the territory between the thirteenth and seventeenth parallels. On March 8, 1965, the first U.S. combat units in Vietnam landed at Da Nang. The city became I Corps* headquarters, and a major military base, port, and resupply area for South Vietnamese and American forces.

As the war ground on, Da Nang became choked with refugees* forced to flee their ancestral homes. With no jobs and limited opportunities, many catered to the desires of military personnel—alcohol, drugs, and prostitution. A generation of South Vietnamese were turned into pushers, pimps, and prostitutes as the war tore apart the Vietnamese social fabric.

During the 1966 "Buddhist Crisis" Da Nang was the site of massive anti-government demonstrations as rebellious ARVN (see Army of the Republic of Vietnam) troops sided with the Buddhists.* Premier Nguyen Cao Ky* sent loyal troops to "liberate" Da Nang although it was secured by United States Marines* who averted a confrontation by interpositioning themselves between contentious troops.

In 1967 the Vietcong* mortared and rocketed Da Nang's air base, destroying $75 million worth of aircraft. Da Nang was attacked by Vietcong and North Vietnamese Army* (NVA) forces in the 1968 Tet Offensive.* Unlike Hue, which was attacked by much larger forces, Da Nang's defenses held. The 1975 final offensive (see Ho Chi Minh campaign) produced total chaos in Da Nang. A million refugees struggled to enter a town besieged by the NVA. Military units evaporated as soldiers sought to assist their families or attempted their own escape. With the city cut off, families loaded on to anything that would float or waded out to sea, many only to drown, as men fought desperately to get on the few aircraft that dared brave NVA antiaircraft fire. Known as Tourane by the French, Da Nang had a population of nearly 450,000 people in 1970.

Sources: George McTurnan Kahin and John W. Lewis, *The United States in Vietnam*, 1967; Harvey H. Smith et al., *Area Handbook for South Vietnam*, 1967; *Webster's Geographical Dictionary*, 1984; Carroll H. Dunn, *Base Development in South Vietnam, 1965–1970*, 1972; *Building the Bases: The History of Construction in Southeast Asia*, 1975.

Samuel Freeman

DA NANG, BATTLE OF (1975)   *See* Da Nang

DANG CONG SAN DONG DUONG   *See* Lao Dong Party

DANIEL BOONE OPERATIONS

"Daniel Boone" was the codename for U.S. Special Forces* operations into Cambodia (see Kampuchea). Teams typically included two or three Americans and about ten indigenous personnel. Operations were authorized in June 1966, but operational permission was delayed until May 1967. Their mission was to penetrate Cambodia on foot or by heliborne insertion, conduct reconnaissance, plant "sanitized self-destruct antipersonnel" mines, sabotage, and gather intelligence. Over four years there were 1,835 Daniel Boone missions with twenty-four prisoners captured. Initially the operations were limited to a small section of the Cambodian border but were expanded, encompassing the entire South Vietnam–Cambodian border to a depth of 30 kilometers (about 20 miles). Many missions were detected within hours of insertion, prompting a race to effect extraction before being cornered.

Daniel Boone teams collected information on Vietcong* and North Vietnamese border base camps, providing much of the basis for Military Assistance Command, Vietnam* requests to strike the sanctuaries,* planning the secret bombing of Cambodia (Operation Menu)* beginning in 1969, and planning the 1970 Cambodian invasion (*see* Operation Binh Tay). After the first B–52* raids, Daniel Boone teams were sent to survey the damage. They were slaughtered. Some teams then refused to go, with Americans being arrested and threatened with court-martial. Some still refused, knowing they could not be court-martialed for violating Cambodian neutrality.

Daniel Boone operations were authorized and conducted in a manner specifically intended to prevent congressional awareness. Their legality was debatable. International law recognizes "hot pursuit"* and the right of one nation, under attack by irregular forces, to attack those forces in a second nation if the second nation does not prevent cross-border attacks. U.S. law, however, prevents U.S. military and private citizens from attacking nations with which the United States is at peace and has diplomatic relations. "Daniel Boone" was renamed "Salem House" in December 1968 and "Thot Not" (pronounced "Tot Note") in 1971.

Sources: William Shawcross, *Sideshow: Kissinger, Nixon, and the Destruction of Cambodia*, 1979; Shelby L. Stanton, *Green Berets at War*, 1985.

Samuel Freeman

DAN VE

The Dan Ve were village militia units organized by the Diem* government in the late 1950s and early 1960s to provide self-defense against Vietcong* attacks. Local supporters of the Diem regime would receive weapons and ammunition, though often antiquated, and a small monthly stipend. Like so many of the programs of the Diem regime, the Dan Ve were riddled with corruption, many of the militiamen using their authority to fleece the peasants while others actually converted to the Vietcong.

Sources: Denis Warner, *The Last Confucian*, 1963; Ngo Quang Truong, *Territorial Forces*, 1981; Tran Dinh Tho, *Pacification*, 1980.

D'ARGENLIEU, GEORGES THIERRY

Born in France in 1889, Georges d'Argenlieu graduated from the French Naval

Academy and served on active duty until 1920, when he entered the Carmelite Order. He eventually became provincial of that order in 1932 but returned to active duty in the navy in 1940. Early in 1941 d'Argenlieu joined de Gaulle in London and became commander in chief of the Free French Naval Forces. He was promoted to admiral in 1943. Between August 1945 and March 1947 d'Argenlieu was the first high commissioner to Indochina.* He was highly committed to the French Empire and adamantly opposed to any negotiated settlement with the Vietminh.* After he returned from Indochina, d'Argenlieu returned to the Carmelite Order and died in 1964.

Source: Joseph Buttinger, *Vietnam: A Dragon Embattled*. Vol. 1, *From Colonialism to the Vietminh*, 1967.

THE DEER HUNTER

Michael Cimino's 1978 film *The Deer Hunter* starred Robert DeNiro, Christopher Walken, and John Savage as three friends from an eastern factory town caught up in the Vietnam War. Meryl Streep also starred as Savage's wife. The film follows the three young men from an opening wedding scene in their hometown into combat in Vietnam, their capture by the Vietcong,* their escape, and their return home. Critics viewed the film in mixed terms, some saying it was a powerful, symbolic portrait of the war, and others claiming it unfairly stereotyped the Vietnamese, particularly because of a Russian-roulette type of game that was the central symbol of the movie. *The Deer Hunter* was part of the antiwar* genre of films popular in the 1970s.

Source: *Magill's Survey of Cinema. English Language Films*, 1981.

DEFENSE ATTACHÉ OFFICE

After the U.S. Military Assistance Command, Vietnam* closed early in 1973, President Richard M. Nixon* established a Defense Attaché Office (DAO) in Saigon* to provide assistance to the South Vietnamese military. Major General John Murray of the United States Army* headed the DAO between January 1973 and June 1974, and Major General Homer Smith directed it from mid–1974 until the final withdrawal of American personnel late in April 1975.

Sources: Harry G. Summers, Jr., *Vietnam War Almanac*, 1985; William E. LeGro, *Vietnam: From Ceasefire to Capitulation*, 1981.

DEFOLIATION

"Defoliation" is the term used to describe American use of herbicides in Southeast Asia. According to the Department of Defense, three basic herbicides were commonly used. The chemical normally used for jungle defoliation was Agent Orange,* a fifty-fifty mixture of n-butyl esters of 2,4-D and 2,4,5-T. It was dissolved in an organic solvent such as diesel oil or kerosene before spray application. Agent Orange produced leaf fall in three to six weeks and lasted from seven to twelve months. During the Vietnam War, 40 million pounds of Agent Orange were sprayed over 5 million acres of forest and vegetation at a cost of $100 million. Another defoliant was Agent White, which combined picolinic acid with 2,4-D in a low-volatility amine salt formation. It produced longer control of a wide spectrum of woody plants plus the advantages of more accurate spray placements. Agent Blue, cacodylic acid, was a contact herbicide employed for rapid defoliation. It was used to keep down vegetation along roadsides and around military encampments. It was also widely sprayed on rice fields in "enemy-controlled" areas where it destroyed existing crops without affecting subsequent growth. Agent Blue withered vegetation within a few days.

Herbicides were first tested and used in Vietnam in 1961, and military defoliation became the largest known use of herbicides. The United States Air Force,* primarily the Twelfth Air Commando Squadron, carried out the defoliation. C–123 cargo planes, specially equipped for spray application, began operations in November 1961. They were the forerunners of Operation Ranch Hand,* which destroyed forest and vegetation in Vietcong* areas. Despite Defense Department claims that defoliation actually benefited small Vietnamese farmers and the forest industry, use of chemical defoliants was widely condemned as inhumane, thoughtless, environmentally dangerous, and of little strategic value.

Sources: John Lewallen, *Ecology of Devastation: Indochina*, 1971; J. B. Neilands et al., *Harvest of Death—Chemical Warfare in Vietnam and Cambodia*, 1972; William A. Buckingham, *Operation Ranch Hand: The United States Air Force and Herbicides in Southeast Asia, 1961–1971*, 1982.

Linda Casci

DELLINGER, DAVID

David Dellinger was born August 22, 1915, in Boston, Massachusetts, where his father was a conservative Republican lawyer. David graduated from Yale in 1936 with a degree in economics, studied at Oxford University and two divinity schools, and served as an associate pastor in 1939 and 1940. A pacifist, Dellinger refused to register for the draft* in 1942 and had to serve a year in prison. When he refused to report for duty in 1943, he was sentenced to two more years in prison. Between 1946 and 1967, Dellinger lived in New Jersey and owned the Libertarian Press. In 1956 he was a founder and editor of the magazine *Liberation*, which became a leading organ for radical pacifism.

In October 1965, Dellinger coordinated the Committee for a Fifth Avenue Peace Parade, the first major antiwar demonstration in New York City. In 1967 he was a judge in Bertrand Russell's unofficial "International War Crimes Tribunal" at Stockholm, which found the United States guilty of war crimes in Vietnam. In 1967 he also became chairman of the National Mobilization Committee to End the War in Vietnam,* which sponsored an antiwar march of about 150,000 people on the Pentagon in October. His passport had been revoked in 1966 when he traveled to Hanoi* to meet with Ho Chi Minh,* but he met with North Vietnamese officials again in 1968 and 1969. He then became a key link between the American peace movement and North Vietnam. As head of the

Committee of Liaison with the Families of Servicemen Detained in North Vietnam, Dellinger arranged for the release of six prisoners of war.

In August 1968, Dellinger was a leading figure in the antiwar demonstrations at the Democratic National Convention in Chicago. At the famous trial of the "Chicago Eight"* in February 1970, Dellinger was convicted of inciting to riot and contempt of court, fined $5,000, and sentenced to five years in prison. In 1972 a federal appeals court overturned the convictions.

By that time the antiwar movement* had become national in scope. In 1971, when the "New Mobe"—New Mobilization Committee to End the War in Vietnam—changed its name to the People's Coalition for Peace and Justice, Dellinger became a leader and continued his open opposition to the war. In 1975, he founded the *Seven Days* magazine to promote active resistance to war. In Stewart Alsop's words, "For Dellinger, somehow, the truth shines, still, and his ideals . . . are amazingly unfaded."

Sources: David Dellinger, *More Power Than We Know: The People's Movement Toward Democracy*, 1975; J. Anthony Likas, *The Barnyard Epithet and Other Obscenities: Notes on the Chicago Conspiracy Trial*, 1970; Jason Epstein, *The Great Conspiracy Trial: An Essay on Law, Liberty, and the Constitution*, 1970; Nancy Zaroulis and Gerald Sullivan, *Who Spoke Up? American Protest Against the War in Vietnam, 1963–1975*, 1984.

John Ricks

THE DELTA   *See* Mekong Delta

DEMILITARIZED ZONE
At the Geneva Conference (*see* Geneva Accords) in 1954, negotiators "temporarily" divided Vietnam into North Vietnam and South Vietnam. From the South China Sea to the village of Bo Ho Su, the demarcation line followed the Ben Hai River,* and from there it headed due west to the border of Laos.* It roughly followed the seventeenth parallel. A buffer zone five miles wide surrounded the line, and the entire area was designated the Demilitarized Zone, or DMZ.

Source: Robert F. Randle, *Geneva, 1954*, 1969.

DEMOCRATIC NATIONAL CONVENTION OF 1968
More than anything else, the Democratic National Convention of 1968 exposed the political divisions created by the Vietnam War. After the Tet Offensive* in February 1968 had undermined the credibility of the American war effort, Senator Eugene McCarthy* of Minnesota had almost defeated President Lyndon B. Johnson* in the New Hampshire presidential primary in March. Senator Robert Kennedy* then announced his candidacy, and at the end of March Johnson announced his decision not to seek reelection. Vice President Hubert Humphrey* and Robert Kennedy then became the front-runners for the Democratic presidential nomination. Kennedy's assassination on the night of his June primary

victory in California left the campaign in Humphrey's hands. Senator George McGovern* of South Dakota entered the race, and some liberals began touting Senator Edward Kennedy* of Massachusetts, but Humphrey was clearly the leader when the Democratic delegates met in Chicago in August 1968.

Inside the convention hall, the delegates bitterly debated the war, with pro–Johnson-Humphrey forces running the convention with an iron hand. Outside the convention hall, antiwar* protesters led by people like Tom Hayden* and David Dellinger* demonstrated against the war and against "establishment" control of the Democratic party. Chicago police, on the orders of Mayor Richard Daley, brutally attacked the crowds. Later dubbed a "police riot," the brutality on the streets of Chicago stunned a nation watching the battle on television. Hubert Humphrey secured the nomination, and he selected Senator Edmund Muskie as his running mate.

Sources: Norman Mailer, *Miami and the Siege of Chicago*, 1969; Theodore White, *The Making of the President, 1968*, 1969.

DEMOCRATIC REPUBLIC OF VIETNAM

The name "Democratic Republic of Vietnam" was the national description of the North Vietnamese government. In mid-August 1945, with the Japanese government reeling under the impact of the atomic bombs and the imminent American invasion of the mainland, Ho Chi Minh* and the Vietminh* invaded Hanoi,* and after encountering no resistance they proclaimed the establishment of the Democratic Republic of Vietnam. At the same time the French moved into Cochin China,* with the assistance of British troops, and announced their intention to return to Tonkin* in the north as well. They returned in force in February 1947, invading Hanoi and pushing more than 100,000 Vietminh into the countryside where the guerrilla war culminating in the Battle of Dien Bien Phu* in 1954 began. After the French surrender there and the division of the country at the seventeenth parallel in the Geneva Accords* of 1954, Ho Chi Minh again proclaimed the Democratic Republic of Vietnam as an independent nation-state. This time he was right. The term "Democratic Republic of Vietnam" was used until 1975, when North Vietnamese troops conquered the Republic of Vietnam* (South Vietnam). The reunited country was then given the new name "Socialist Republic of Vietnam."*

Sources: Frances FitzGerald, *Fire in the Lake: The Vietnamese and Americans in Vietnam*, 1972; Joseph Buttinger, *Vietnam: A Dragon Embattled*. Vol. 1, *From Colonialism to the Vietminh*, 1967.

DENTON, JEREMIAH

Born in 1924, Jeremiah Denton had become an outstanding naval pilot by the 1950s. In June 1965 he went to Vietnam, and one month later he was shot down about 75 miles south of Hanoi.* He spent the next seven years in North Vietnamese prisons, remaining steadfastly uncooperative with his captors. Denton came to national attention during a televised interview. While the North Vietnamese were pleased with his verbal answers, Denton was eye-blinking, in Morse code, the word "torture" to the cameras. In 1973 Commander Denton was one of the first American prisoners of war* released after the Paris Peace Accords,* and his smart salute and "reporting for duty" comment after deplaning at Clark Field in the Philippines* endeared him to the American public. In 1980 Denton became the first Republican to win a seat in the United States Senate from Alabama since Reconstruction. He was unsuccessful in his bid for reelection in 1986.

Sources: Jeremiah A. Denton, *When Hell Was In Session*, 1976; John S. Bowman, ed., *The Vietnam War: An Almanac*, 1985.

DEROS

DEROS is an acronym for Date Eligible to Return from Overseas. Every military individual assigned to duty in Southeast Asia knew in advance how long he or she would be there. For most United States Army* personnel, the normal tour of duty was 365 days, while Marines* usually served 13 months. After that date, the individual would be reassigned, usually to the United States and often to immediate separation from military service (discharge). Since leaving Vietnam safely became the fundamental objective for most troops, each individual's DEROS became a vital statistic for him or her. As an individual's DEROS approached, he/she became a "short-timer," and both anxiety and anticipation increased.

Source: Al Santoli, *Everything We Had*, 1981.

Stafford T. Thomas

DESERTION

During the Vietnam War, the highest desertion rates occurred among soldiers of the Army of the Republic of Vietnam* (ARVN). Between 1967 and 1971, more than 57,000 ARVN troops deserted. During the same period, the number of North Vietnamese and Vietcong* deserters totaled only 87,000 soldiers. Between 1965 and 1973, nearly 7,600,000 Americans served in the military in Vietnam, and the total number of desertions exceeded 550,000. All but 100,000 of those men and women returned to active duty after absences of less than one month. The others were discharged from the armed forces for desertion. Most of those cases involved non–combat-related problems. There were 32,000 cases involving failure to report to duty in Vietnam, refusal to return from rest and relaxation breaks, and unauthorized absences after completing a tour of duty in South Vietnam. There were only 5,000 cases of desertion "in country," and only 24 of those were to avoid hazardous duty. When the war ended in 1973, more than 10,000 servicemen and women were still listed as deserters, and more than 7,000 of them received amnesty from Presidents Gerald Ford* and Jimmy Carter.

Sources: Lawrence M. Baskir and William A. Strauss, *Chance and Circumstance: The Draft, the War, and the Vietnam Generation*, 1978; Guenter Lewy, *America in Vietnam*, 1978; Harry G. Summers, Jr., *Vietnam War Almanac*, 1985.

DESOTO MISSIONS

DeSoto Missions were the codename for covert U.S. naval operations. Ever since the 1950s, DeSoto Missions had been carried out against the People's Republic of China,* the Soviet Union,* and North Korea. Intelligence agents or commando units would harass coastal radar transmitters so that American electronic intelligence vessels could monitor the transmissions, measure frequencies, and pinpoint locations. In the spring of 1964 the United States Navy* began DeSoto operations off the coast of North Vietnam using South Vietnamese commando units to harass radio transmission units. The destroyer USS *Maddox** was assigned to begin the program, and it was these DeSoto Missions which led to the Gulf of Tonkin Incident* in July and August 1964.

Sources: Anthony Preston, "The Naval War in Vietnam," in John S. Bowman, ed., *The Vietnam War: An Almanac*, 1985; Edward J. Marolda and G. Wesley Pryce III, *A Short History of the United States Navy and the Southeast Asian Conflict, 1950–1975*, 1984.

DEWEY, A. PETER

Peter Dewey was the first American serviceman to be killed in Vietnam. Dewey was a member of the U.S. Office of Strategic Services (OSS), a World War II unit. One of the activities of the OSS was to work "behind the lines" with partisan groups fighting against U.S. enemies. In early 1945, one OSS detachment, the "Deer Team," parachuted into Tonkin,* made contact with Ho Chi Minh,* and assisted the Vietminh* in its guerrilla war against the Japanese. A close personal relationship developed between Ho and the Deer Team officers, and the impression resulted that the OSS was an advocate of early independence for Vietnam, under a Vietminh government. In August 1945, Dewey led another OSS detachment into Saigon,* which was then under the control of the British, who had accepted the Japanese surrender in Vietnam south of the sixteenth parallel. The British commander, Douglas D. Gracey, was faced with a near-impossible task of governing in the midst of turmoil, chaos, and confusion. Rival political and military units were operating throughout the south, and Saigon was the focal point of activity. The major parties in this setting were the British, the French, the Japanese, and various factions of Vietnamese nationalists, religious sects, and warlords. Dewey and his OSS unit were a minor group, but Dewey was sufficiently outspoken and abrasive to anger Gracey repeatedly, especially by giving the appearance of siding with the Vietminh, which the OSS in fact did. One incident in particular summarized the antagonistic relationship between Gracey and Dewey: Dewey wanted to fly an American flag on the fender of his car, but Gracey prohibited it on technical grounds. As a result, Dewey decided to leave Saigon and Vietnam. On his way to Saigon's Tan Son Nhut* Airport,

Dewey's Jeep, without the flag, was fired upon, probably by mistake, by Vietminh soldiers. Dewey was killed instantly, on September 26, 1945.

Ho Chi Minh apologized to the United States. It would be fourteen years before another U.S. soldier would be killed in Vietnam.

Source: Edward Doyle and Samuel Lipsman, *The Vietnam Experience: Passing the Torch*, 1981.

Stafford T. Thomas

DIEN BIEN PHU, BATTLE OF (1954)

General Henri Navarre (*see* Navarre Plan), the French commander in chief for Indochina,* was responsible for the decision to build an outpost in the Red River Delta and its ultimate loss. Dien Bien Phu had been a peaceful crossroads village in northwest Indochina before the French entered it to defeat Vietminh* soldiers. The French dropped paratroopers in to build the post since the only roads in were little more than trails, and all of them were controlled by the Vietminh. Navarre concentrated seventeen battalions in the main outpost, which was located in a ten mile–long river valley surrounded by hills. Navarre hoped to draw the Vietminh out into a battle where superior French firepower would overcome them. He was not really worried about the hills, even though Dien Bien Phu's two airstrips were within artillery range of them. All supplies coming into the French garrison had to come by plane. Unknown to the French, the Chinese had supplied the Vietminh with artillery and it had been carried into position on the backs of guerrillas who then reassembled it.

Between November 1953 and March 1954, General Vo Nguyen Giap,* leader of the Vietminh, tightened his noose around the French. The first artillery bombardment was a real shock to the French, and within four days three French commands had surrendered. The monsoons then arrived and turned the valley into a mudhole, rendering French tanks useless. With the airfield constantly under artillery bombardment, the French had to depend on air drops for supplies, and the Vietminh captured most of them. In March 1954, Vietminh also destroyed thirty-eight French aircraft at the airfield in Haiphong. Those planes were used to resupply Dien Bien Phu. Between late March and early May 1954 Giap attacked Dien Bien Phu repeatedly in daily assaults. Inside the French outpost, latrines overflowed, water spoiled, and food supplies ran out. Too weary to bury their dead, the French soldiers resorted to wearing masks to endure the stench. The last French command surrendered on May 7, 1954. Of the original 12,000 defenders at Dien Bien Phu, 2,293 were killed and 5,134 wounded. Survivors were herded on a long death march to Vietminh prison camps. The defeat was a bitter psychological blow to the French and inspired their permanent withdrawal from Indochina and the Geneva Accords* of 1954.

Sources: Bernard Fall, *Vietnam Witness, 1953–56*, 1966, and *Hell in a Very Small Place: The Siege of Dien Bien Phu*, 1966; Jules Roy, *The Battle of Dien Bien Phu*, 1965; Vo Nguyen Giap, *Dien Bien Phu*, 1962.

DIKES

For more than two thousand years a system of dikes has regulated water flow in the Red River Delta of northern Vietnam, and systematic construction of dikes began intensely in the thirteenth century. By the 1970s there were more than three thousand miles of dikes to protect against the monsoon floods of the Red River. During the Vietnam War, there were proposals for large-scale American bombing of the dikes during the monsoon season. Such an attack would have destroyed the system, caused widespread flooding of the Red River Delta, ruined rice crops, and drowned thousands of civilians. Because international law prohibited deliberate attacks on civilian populations, Presidents Lyndon B. Johnson* and Richard Nixon* never adopted the proposal.

Sources: Gerard Chaliand, *The Peasant of North Vietnam*, 1969; Bernard Fall, *The Two Vietnams*, 1967.

"DINK"

"Dink" was a racist reference to enemy forces or to civilians in Vietnam. The difference in usage by Americans in Vietnam of such epithets from similar epithets in previous wars was the generalized application of such words to the civilian population rather than just to enemy forces. It is generally recognized that soldiers usually dehumanize the enemy in order to help accept the reality of killing them. To some extent military training, in preparing soldiers for combat, encourages development of such an attitude. A problem occurs when dehumanization proceeds to the point where the conscience is totally numbed, enabling a soldier to become a wanton killer. Another problem occurs when the soldier begins to generalize such attitudes to the civilian population. This was very easy to do in Vietnam where it was so difficult to distinguish the enemy from the civilian population. Such generalization facilitated intentional, indiscriminate killing of civilian noncombatants and lent credit to charges by the war's critics that it was an immoral, racist conflict directed against the Vietnamese people.

Sources: Loren Baritz, *Backfire*, 1985; Peter Trooboff, *Law and Responsibility in Warfare*, 1975; Guenter Lewy, *America in Vietnam*, 1978.

Samuel Freeman

DIVISION

A division is a nearly universal military organization consisting of approximately 20,000 troops commanded by a major general. During the Vietnam War, the following U.S. divisions or elements thereof participated in the conflict: the 1st Cavalry;* the 1st,* 4th,* Fifth,* Ninth,* 23rd,* and 25th Infantry;* the 82nd* and 101st Airborne;* the 1st,* Third,* and 5th Marines;* and the Second, Seventh,* and 834th Air.*

Source: Shelby L. Stanton, *Vietnam Order of Battle*, 1981.

DIXIE STATION

"Dixie Station" was the place name for the United States Seventh Fleet's*
staging area in the South China Sea. During 1965 and 1966, Task Force 77, the
carrier strike group in the Seventh Fleet, used Dixie Station as the reference
point for its operations. Dixie Station was located at 11° N 110° E off the coast
of Cam Ranh Bay.*
Source: Harry G. Summers, Jr., *Vietnam War Almanac*, 1985.

DMZ   *See* Demilitarized Zone

DOMINO THEORY

The domino theory was first proposed by President Harry S Truman* and the
Truman Doctrine in 1946, when he argued that unless the United States provided
military aid assistance to Greece and Turkey, both countries and much of the Middle East would fall, like a row of dominoes lined up against each other, to Communist aggression. In April 1954, during the siege at Dien Bien Phu,* President
Dwight D. Eisenhower* announced the same idea about Southeast Asia, arguing
that if Vietnam fell to Communist guerrillas, the rest of the region, including
Cambodia (*see* Kampuchea), Laos,* Thailand,* and Burma, would fall as well,
and perhaps much of East Asia. Malaysia, Indonesia, New Zealand,* Australia,*
and the Philippines* would also be threatened. Presidents John F. Kennedy* and
Lyndon B. Johnson* both used the domino theory to justify the commitment of
American resources to Vietnam in the 1960s. America's strategic interests, the
theory demanded, required a strong military presence in South Vietnam.

Since the fall of South Vietnam in 1975, the domino theory has really not
been fulfilled. Armies from the Socialist Republic of Vietnam* have invaded
Cambodia and Laos, both of whom have experienced Communist takeovers, but
Thailand, Indonesia, and Malaysia have retained their pro-Western positions;
Burma is still neutral; and the integrity of Australia, New Zealand, and the
Philippines is still intact.
Sources: Russell H. Fifield, *Americans in Southeast Asia*, 1973; Richard J. Barnet,
Roots of War: The Men and Institutions Behind U.S. Foreign Policy, 1972; Gabriel
Kolko, *The Roots of American Foreign Policy*, 1969.

DONG HA

Located at the junction of Routes 1 and 9 and less than 15 kilometers from
the southern boundary of the Demilitarized Zone,* Dong Ha was a combat base
and supply center for III Marine Amphibious Force* units operating in Quang
Tri Province. An ideal site for the Third Marine Division's* headquarters, established in June 1968, the base also proved crucial to the defense of the Cua
Viet River system, through which supplies unloaded at the river's mouth on the
South China Sea were taken upstream to Dong Ha's force logistics unit and then
distributed to U.S. Marine* and Republic of Vietnam* forces.

Together with Gio Linh north on Route 1, Con Thien to the northwest, and Cam Lo west on Route 9, Dong Ha became the southeast anchor of "Leatherneck Square." In April 1968 enemy forces attacked the base, and intermittent but heavy fighting continued in the area until late summer. Meanwhile, after the marines abandoned Khe Sanh* and other northern fire bases in the same year, Dong Ha retained its role as a command and logistics center, and marines fanned out from the base conducting operations as far west as the Laotian border. The marines turned Dong Ha over to the South Vietnamese army when the Third Marine division left northern I Corps* for Okinawa in November 1969.

Sources: *The Marines in Vietnam, 1954–1973*, 1974; Willard Pearson, *The War in the Northern Provinces, 1966–1968*, 1975.

Dudley Acker

DONG HA, BATTLE OF (1968)

In the spring of 1968, after the Tet Offensive* and before the opening of the Paris peace talks,* the North Vietnamese Army* (NVA) and Vietcong* made a concerted attempt to improve their bargaining position. They conducted 119 attacks on provincial and district capitals, military installations, and major cities in South Vietnam. At Dong Ha in I Corps,* the United States Marines* maintained a supply base. It was in the northeastern area of Quang Tri Province. Late in April and early in May, the NVA 320th Division, complete with 8,000 troops, attacked Dong Ha and fought a concerted battle against an allied force of 5,000 marines and South Vietnamese troops. The North Vietnamese failed to destroy the supply base and had to retreat back across the Demilitarized Zone,* leaving behind 856 dead. Sixty-eight Americans died in the fighting.

Sources: Clark Dougan and Steven Weiss, *The Vietnam Experience: Nineteen Sixty-Eight*, 1983; Willard Pearson, *The War in the Northern Provinces, 1966–1968*, 1975; *The Marines in Vietnam, 1954–1973*, 1974.

DONG XOAI, BATTLE OF (1965)

Dong Xoai was a district capital in Phuc Long Province of III Corps.* An American Special Forces* Camp at Dong Xoai was manned by 400 Montagnard* Civilian Irregular Defense Group* troops and 24 U.S. Seebees* and soldiers. Early in the morning of June 10, 1965, approximately 1,500 Vietcong* guerrillas, armed with AK–47* rifles, grenades, and flamethrowers, attacked the camp. The defenders quickly retreated to one area of the installation, and American and South Vietnamese aircraft attacked the Vietcong with napalm* and phosphorus bombs. Soldiers from the ARVN's (*see* Army of the Republic of Vietnam) 42nd Ranger Battalion were helicoptered in, and the Vietcong retreated. At the end of the first day's fighting, 20 Americans were killed or wounded, along with 200 Vietnamese civilians and soldiers. Military Assistance Command, Vietnam* reported 700 dead Vietcong. On June 11 and 12, ARVN Rangers searched for the Vietcong, but late on June 12 the Vietcong attacked the Rangers. ARVN soldiers quickly deserted their positions and ran into the surrounding jungles, and the American advisers were airlifted out. The Battle of Dong Xoai affected American policy by undermining faith in the stability of ARVN troops and making the commitment of large numbers of American ground forces inevitable.

Source: Terence Maitland and Peter McInerney, *The Vietnam Experience: A Contagion of War*, 1983.

DRAFT

Over two million men were inducted into military service during the Vietnam War period in accordance with the Selective Service Act of 1948 and its ensuing extensions. The draft law provided for the registration of all males upon their eighteenth birthday. The president delegated authority in draft matters to the director of the Selective Service System. The director, his staff, and about 4,000 local draft boards throughout the country administered the system. Local draft boards were under the supervision of state directors, but quotas for inductees were set at the national level which made its decision relative to the number of men from each state already in the military. The Department of Defense initiated draft calls for a given number of men, based on projected enlistments and needs. Draft deferments in terms of essential activities and critical occupations were defined by the Departments of Commerce and Labor. The secretary of defense defined the standards for physical, mental, and moral acceptability for military service. Although the system operated under the regulations and standards drawn up at a national level, where the president could adjust induction numbers to meet changing political and military needs, local draft boards had considerable latitude in selecting men for service. Major inequities in the Selective Service System and its deferment procedures were recognized by both supporters and critics of the draft, but the majority of recommendations made by President Lyndon Johnson's* National Advisory Commission on Selective Service in 1967 to eliminate most deferments were not incorporated in the 1967 draft extension act. Both the inequities, where poor, rural, and minority young men were disproportionately drafted and sent to combat, and the increasing number of young men called to the draft, made the Selective Service a natural target of the antiwar movement.* Antidraft activity ranged from Stop-the-Draft week in October 1967 to break-ins of draft boards with the symbolic pouring of blood over the draft files. President Richard Nixon* ended all draft calls in December 1972, and President Gerald Ford* issued a proclamation terminating the remaining draft registration requirements in 1975. President Jimmy Carter, on January 21, 1977, pardoned all who had been convicted of violating the Selective Service Act during the Vietnam period. In 1979, President Carter reintroduced draft registration.

Sources: Lawrence M. Baskir and William A. Strauss, *Chance and Circumstance: The Draft, the War, and the Vietnam Generation*, 1978; Stephen M. Kohn, *Jailed for Peace: The History of American Draft Law Violators*, 1986.

Linda Kelly Alkana

DRV   *See* Democratic Republic of Vietnam

DULLES, JOHN FOSTER

John Foster Dulles was born February 25, 1888, in Washington, D.C. He graduated from Princeton in 1908 and took a law degree from George Washington University in 1911. His grandfather, John Foster, had been secretary of state to President Benjamin Harrison, so Dulles was raised in a diplomatically conscious family. He specialized in international law and attended the Paris Peace Conference (1919), Washington Conference (1921–22), Reparations Commission (1920s), Berlin Debt Conference (1933), and the San Francisco Conference (1945) to establish the United Nations. President Harry S. Truman* had Dulles negotiate the Japanese peace treaty in 1950–51, and in 1953 President Dwight D. Eisenhower* made Dulles secretary of state. Dulles was convinced that the United States had a mission to counteract global communism, to stop the Soviet Union* from its imperial designs. For Dulles, the world was engaged in a moral struggle between good and evil, and his penchant for such phrases as "massive retaliation," "agonizing reappraisal," and "brinkmanship" alarmed critics.

As far as Dulles was concerned, the struggle in Indochina* was only another example of Soviet evil. There was no doubt in his mind that the Soviets were manipulating Ho Chi Minh* and the Vietminh* and that French control over Vietnam had to be maintained. Dulles also expected, however, that the French would have to invest more resources in the struggle, eventually agree to grant independence to Vietnam, Laos,* and Cambodia (*see* Kampuchea) in order to eliminate any taint of colonialism, and secure allied support from the English, Australians, and New Zealanders. Early in 1954, when the Vietminh were preparing the assault on French forces at Dien Bien Phu,* Dulles joined Admiral Arthur Radford* in advocating Operation Vulture*—the American air assault on the Vietminh. Dulles was disappointed when President Eisenhower refused to approve the mission, but when Dien Bien Phu fell in 1954, Dulles argued that it would "harden, not weaken our purpose to stay united" in checking further Communist aggression. Dulles did not live to see the direct American intervention in Vietnam. After a two-year struggle with cancer, he died on May 24, 1959.

Sources: Michael Guhin, *John Foster Dulles: A Statesman and His Times*, 1972; Townsend Hoopes, *The Devil and John Foster Dulles*, 1973.

DUONG VAN DUC

Duong Van Duc was born in Sa Dec City in the Mekong Delta* in 1926. He graduated in 1946 from the Vietnam Military Academy at Da Lat* and the

French Staff School in 1953. Duong Van Duc commanded paratroopers for the Republic of Vietnam* and was promoted to brigadier general in 1956. Between 1956 and 1957 he served as minister to the Republic of Korea.* Duc was an influential force in the South Vietnamese military and participated in the abortive coup of September 1964, when his troops invaded Saigon.*

Sources: *Asia Who's Who*, 1960; Stanley Karnow, *Vietnam: A History*, 1983.

DUONG VAN MINH

Duong Van Minh, the last president of the Republic of Vietnam,* was born in 1916 in the Mekong Delta,* in what was then the French colony of Cochin China.* Trained by the French, Minh became in 1955 the ranking army officer in Ngo Dinh Diem's* newly proclaimed Republic of Vietnam. He rose to prominence a year later as a result of defeating the Mekong Delta–based Hoa Hao* sect, the leader of which was publicly guillotined. Minh's rising popularity combined with his outspokenness forced Diem to remove him from military command by "promoting" him to a largely honorific advisory position.

General Minh emerged from obscurity seven years later as the leader of a group of Vietnamese generals which staged the November 1963 military uprising that ended the regime of President Ngo Dinh Diem. During the uprising Diem and his brother Ngo Dinh Nhu* were assassinated, reportedly on Minh's orders. The generals replaced the Diem government with a Military Revolutionary Council, with Minh serving as nominal chairman. This remarkably ineffective group governed for only three months. The council, and General Minh, were ousted by a military coup led by General Nguyen Khanh* in January 1964.

After living in exile for several years, Minh returned to South Vietnam in 1968. Once there he came to be regarded as a potential leader of a non-Communist coalition of opponents of President Nguyen Van Thieu.* Minh did in fact enter the 1971 presidential election, but he withdrew from the race when events eliminated any possibility of his defeating Thieu. Minh's last appearance on the Vietnamese political stage occurred in April 1975, during the last days of the crumbling Republic of Vietnam. On April 21, Thieu resigned the presidency. His elderly vice president, Tran Van Huong,* shortly thereafter appointed Minh to the presidency as North Vietnamese units converged on Saigon.* The Minh administration lasted only two days. On April 29, 1975, Minh was taken into custody, after surrendering unconditionally to the North Vietnamese Army* unit that had occupied the presidential palace. Duong Van Minh, the last president of the Republic of Vietnam, was allowed to immigrate to France in 1983.

Sources: Frances FitzGerald, *Fire in the Lake: The Vietnamese and the Americans in Vietnam*, 1972; Stanley Karnow, *Vietnam: A History*, 1983; George C. Herring, *America's Longest War: The United States in Vietnam, 1950–1975*, 1986; Joseph Buttinger, *Vietnam: A Dragon Embattled*. Vol. 2, *Vietnam at War*, 1967.

Sean A. Kelleher

DURBOW, ELBRIDGE

Elbridge Durbow was born on September 21, 1903, in San Francisco and eventually went to Yale University where he obtained a Ph.D. in 1926. He subsequently joined the foreign service where he served in a number of minor posts around the world until after World War II. Between 1948 and 1950, however, he was an instructor at the National War College. After his stint at the War College, he was promoted and named the chief of the Division of Foreign Service Personnel.

Durbow was a career foreign service officer, and in 1957 Dwight D. Eisenhower* decided to send this seasoned diplomat to the tiny country of South Vietnam. Almost from the outset, Ambassador Durbow found much to criticize in Ngo Dinh Diem.* Of note, he would later acknowledge that the repression and corruption of the South Vietnamese regime was a catalyst to insurgency. He was also a shrewd diplomat who warned Diem that his brother, Ngo Dinh Nhu,* and his sister-in-law were damaging the government. Nhu's control of the secret police made him a most powerful man, and he used power indiscriminately.

Diem apparently did not heed Ambassador Durbow's warnings, and on December 4, 1960, he sent a message to Washington indicating that in the not too distant future the United States might be forced to support an alternative regime. Meanwhile, Diem continued to resist American pressures for reform. Most of the aid sent from the United States was used by Diem to enrich his own family and to prop up his regime. Only a very small fraction of the funds were utilized for South Vietnamese economic development.

Durbow's warnings about the unpopularity of the Diem regime finally bore fruit in November 1960. Lieutenant Colonel Vuong Van Dong staged an abortive military coup against Diem. Dong had revolted in response to Diem's arbitrary rule, his promotion of favorites, and his meddling in military operations against the insurgency. Although he succeeded in surrounding the presidential palace, Dong allowed the telephone lines to remain intact. Diem decided to wait out the dissident soldiers until loyal contingents arrived in Saigon.* Dong even went to Durbow to gain his assistance in overthrowing Diem. The ambassador, however, refused to assist Dong, knowing that Washington would never accept nor approve of Diem's overthrow with support from a U.S. ambassador. The rebellion was crushed, and Dong and other dissident soldiers fled South Vietnam.

Diem, however, was annoyed with Durbow's relationship with Dong and did not hesitate to express his displeasure with the ambassador to officials in the new Kennedy administration. John F. Kennedy* was convinced that he could gain Diem's confidence and succeed in ending the Communist threat in South Vietnam. In April 1961, Kennedy replaced Durbow with the untested Frederick Nolting* as the U.S. ambassador to South Vietnam. Durbow nonetheless was apparently correct about the intractability of the Diem regime, because in late 1963 the United States assisted in the overthrow of Diem. Durbow returned to the State Department in 1961 and remained there until his retirement in 1968.

Sources: John E. Findling, ed., *Historical Dictionary of American Diplomatic History*, 1980; Gabriel Kolko, *Anatomy of a War: Vietnam, the United States, and the Modern Historical Experience*, 1986.

John S. Leiby

DUSTOFF

"I need a dustoff" became an all-too-familiar call on the airwaves of Vietnam. Dustoff missions were medical evacuation missions (*see* medevac) using helicopters. While the term has been used to apply to all medical evacuation missions, GIs reserved the term for missions flown to pick up wounded soldiers in the field, often under fire. When a soldier was hit, the call went out for a dustoff, and any helicopter in the area without a higher priority mission could respond.

Many of the early helicopters used in Vietnam did not fare well in dustoff missions. The CH–21* and CH–34* were used in this role, but their lack of maneuverability and relatively slow speed, combined with a small door in the case of the CH–21, made them vulnerable to ground fire. During the Tet Offensive,* CH–34s flown by the U.S. Marines* in a dustoff role took heavy casualties. The UH-1* "Huey" excelled in this role, with its wide doors and ability to get in and out quickly. Still, flying dustoffs took courage on the part of the crew, as ground fire was the rule rather than the exception. The rewards, however, were great. Dustoffs allowed wounded soldiers to be brought to medical facilities much more quickly than in any other war, usually in a matter of minutes, and saved many lives.

Source: Jim Mesko, *Airmobile: The Helicopter War in Vietnam*, 1985.

Nolan J. Argyle

DYLAN, BOB

Born Robert Zimmerman in Duluth, Minnesota, on May 24, 1941, Bob Dylan (he took his name from the poet Dylan Thomas) soon became one of the most influential folk-rock artists in the world, especially after moving to New York City in the mid–1960s. As a performer Dylan refused to be categorized, be it his playing style, lifestyle, music, or political opinions. He wrote about injustice, women, drugs, and for a period about topics so obscure that no one knows exactly what he was seeking. Although he never wrote a specific song about Vietnam, he nevertheless became associated with the antiwar movement* because his songs of social consciousness, particularly "The Times They Are A-Changin' " and "Blowin' in the Wind," became anthems of a kind to a generation seeking to change America. In the 1970s Dylan continued to produce albums, but critics charged that he was not as innovative as before. Nevertheless, Dylan had a strong influence on youth and antiwar movements in the 1960s and early 1970s.

Sources: Theodore Roszak, *The Making of a Counter Culture*, 1969; Richard Flacks, *Youth and Social Change*, 1971.

Charles Dobbs

∙ E ∙

EAGLE FLIGHT

"Eagle Flight" was a term used to describe airmobile strike forces used to ambush, raid, harass, and observe enemy positions. Eagle Flights were first used in 1963 in South Vietnam, but the Fifth Special Forces Group* began using them continuously in October 1964. An Eagle Flight group consisted of five American soldiers, thirty-six Montagnard* irregular troops, a helicopter airlift, and several UH–1* gunships. Eagle Flights supported Civilian Irregular Defense Group* operations as well as regular operations of the Fifth Special Forces Group.

Sources: John S. Bowman, ed., *The Vietnam War Almanac*, 1985; Shelby L. Stanton, *The Green Berets at War*, 1985.

EASTERTIDE OFFENSIVE

Late in 1970, with Vietnamization* in full gear, the North Vietnamese began planning an all-out assault on South Vietnam. Le Duan* visited Moscow in the spring of 1971 to secure heavy weapons supplies. North Vietnam wanted to break the military stalemate in South Vietnam and, with a major victory, perhaps help defeat Richard Nixon's* reelection bid in 1972, leaving the White House open to a more moderate, even anti-Vietnam Democratic president. Throughout 1971 the Soviet Union* provided heavy supplies—trucks, surface-to-air (SAM)* missiles, tanks, and artillery—to prepare the North Vietnamese Army* (NVA) and Vietcong* for the attack.

The offensive began on March 30, 1972. Three North Vietnamese divisions, strengthened by T–54 Soviet tanks, attacked across the Demilitarized Zone* and along Highway 9 out of Laos,* with Hue* as their objective. Three more North Vietnamese divisions attacked Binh Long Province, captured Loc Ninh, and surrounded An Loc.* Other North Vietnamese troops attacked Kontum* in the Central Highlands.* Finally, two North Vietnamese divisions took control of several districts in Binh Dinh along the coast of the South China Sea. Quang

Tri Province was lost by the end of April 1972. But at that point the tide turned. ARVN (*see* Army of the Republic of Vietnam) troops held their positions 25 miles north of Hue, and the NVA was unable to take Kontum and An Loc. President Nixon had already begun bombing North Vietnam again, but on May 8, 1972, he mined Haiphong Harbor* and several other North Vietnamese ports. Fighting continued throughout the summer, with the ARVN launching a counteroffensive which recaptured Quang Tri Province. The Eastertide Offensive had failed. North Vietnam suffered more than 100,000 killed. But they still controlled more territory in South Vietnam than before and felt they were in a stronger bargaining position at the Paris negotiations.

Sources: Ngo Quang Truong, *The Easter Offensive of 1972*, 1980; G. H. Turley, *The Easter Offensive: Vietnam 1972*, 1985.

18th ENGINEER BRIGADE

The 18th Engineer Brigade was deployed to the Republic of Vietnam* in September 1965 and remained there until September 1971. It consisted of the 35th, 45th, and 937th Engineer Groups and confined its construction activities to I* and II Corps.*

Source: Shelby L. Stanton, *Vietnam Order of Battle*, 1981.

18TH MILITARY POLICE BRIGADE

The 18th Military Police Brigade went to Vietnam in September 1966 and was charged with supervision of military police throughout South Vietnam. In addition to traffic control and policing activities, the 18th Military Police Brigade provided security for convoys, highways, and bridges and supervised the evacuation of refugees.*

Source: Shelby L. Stanton, *Vietnam Order of Battle*, 1981.

834th AIR DIVISION

The 834th Air Division, stationed at Tan Son Nhut Air Base* outside Saigon,* provided tactical airlift for Seventh Air Force* operations in South Vietnam. The 834th functioned between its organization in October 1966 to its dissolution in November 1970, by which time most of its aircraft had been handed over to the South Vietnamese Air Force.*

Source: Ray L. Bowers, *The U.S. Air Force in Southeast Asia: Tactical Airlift*, 1983.

82nd AIRBORNE DIVISION

Although the Joint Chiefs of Staff (*see* Chairman, JCS) considered deploying the entire 82nd Airborne Division to Vietnam, only the 3rd Brigade ever received such orders, serving in Vietnam between February 18, 1968, and December 11, 1969. Attached to the 101st Airborne Division,* the 3rd Brigade fought in I Corps,* primarily in Hue.* Late in 1968, the 3rd Brigade was moved down to Saigon* to defend Tan Son Nhut Air Base.*

Source: Shelby L. Stanton, *Vietnam Order of Battle*, 1981.

EISENHOWER, DWIGHT DAVID

Dwight D. Eisenhower was born on October 14, 1890, in Denison, Texas. He was a West Point graduate who commanded Allied invasions of Europe during World War II, and was later army chief of staff, president of Columbia University, and commander of the North Atlantic Treaty Organization's (NATO) forces. Easily defeating Democrat Adlai Stevenson for president in 1952, Eisenhower saw his presidential role as one of creating equilibrium at home while keeping the United States involved in world affairs and avoiding nuclear war.

Eisenhower found the stalemate in French Indochina* unacceptable; it would further drain French resources and morale, and undermine the French role in NATO. A French defeat seemed even worse despite Eisenhower's view that France had caused the war by refusing to grant full independence to the Indochinese states; the domino theory* was already current, holding that defeat in Indochina would lead to Communist gains throughout Southeast Asia and the Pacific. Elected on a platform of "liberation" of Communist satellites, Eisenhower had accepted a Korean armistice that left North Korea in Communist hands. He told his cabinet that he could not give Democrats the chance to imitate Republican taunts of "who lost China?" by demanding "who lost Vietnam?" There was no way to obtain a French victory without American forces being sent to Vietnam, which Eisenhower opposed. He also vetoed as inflammatory the use of Chinese Nationalist forces from Taiwan (*see* Chiang Kai-shek). What Eisenhower really wanted was a joint U.S.-British intervention with air support and materiel but no ground troops. The British wanted nothing to do with it, so Eisenhower increased aid to France to about 75 percent of the war's cost.

Despite fervent French requests, Eisenhower limited American aid to a few aircraft and technicians. He also prepared for a deluge of demands for intervention, which he expected when Dien Bien Phu* fell, by specifying conditions for American involvement: a clear grant of independence to the Indochinese states, British and Southeast Asian participation, congressional approval, and continued French participation under American command. Historians now generally believe that Eisenhower deliberately set conditions that were impossible, believing that the United States must not destroy its anticolonial image. He was thus prepared for pressure from Vice President Richard Nixon,* Secretary of State John Foster Dulles,* and Chairman of the Joint Chiefs of Staff* Admiral Arthur Radford,* even confronting them with the risk of global and nuclear war if the United States were actually to fight in Southeast Asia.

Though Eisenhower avoided direct intervention in 1954, he did not intend to abandon the region, using the domino theory in press conferences to explain Southeast Asia's importance. Trying behind the scenes, but failing, to keep France involved after the fall of Dien Bien Phu, he continued his idea of a multilateral effort to save South Vietnam. By September 1954 the United States had created the Southeast Asia Treaty Organization* (SEATO), which Eisenhower hoped would protect the region from further Communist aggression. He also resigned himself to accepting the Geneva Accords* of 1954 partitioning

Vietnam, supposedly temporarily. Eventually that "temporary" clause was discarded when the United States refused to participate in the elections promised in the Geneva Accords. U.S. recognition of the government of Ngo Dinh Diem* led to economic and military assistance. Prophetically, while Eisenhower was still in office, a few U.S. advisers went out into the field with the South Vietnamese, exposing themselves to combat and casualties.

Eisenhower's last involvement with Vietnam came as a former president giving advice and support to Lyndon Johnson* during the escalation stage of the conflict. Eisenhower's advice followed his own earlier views: there must be multilateral aid and forces, and the Vietnamese must not depend on American troops but shoulder the bulk of the fighting themselves. While he was consistently a hawk in his approach, urging Johnson to find a way to win, Eisenhower never told Johnson that victory would be easy. He was furious when, in March 1968, Johnson withdrew from the presidential race, ended most bombing, and in effect signaled that he had given up. Dwight D. Eisenhower died on March 28, 1969.

Sources: Stephen E. Ambrose, *Eisenhower*. Vol 2, *President and Elder Statesman*, 1984; Elmo Richardson, *The Presidency of Dwight D. Eisenhower*, 1979; Robert A. Divine, *Eisenhower and the Cold War*, 1981.

Robert W. Sellen

ELECTION OF 1955 (SOUTH VIETNAM)

The 1954 Geneva Conference (*see* Geneva Accords) produced six unilateral declarations, three cease-fire agreements which were signed by the principals, and an unsigned Final Declaration which called for reunification elections to be held between July 1955 and July 1956. Whether any nations present "agreed to" the Declaration or took the election provisions seriously has been hotly debated. What is clear is that Walter Bedell Smith* issued a statement "taking note" of the Declaration and pledging the United States to support it. The Republic of Vietnam* refused to sign, making it clear they did not consider themselves bound by the Declaration.

Neither Ngo Dinh Diem,* the United States, nor France* was enthusiastic about reunification elections, first because northern Vietnam had several million more people than in the south, and second because Ho Chi Minh* had substantial popularity in the south. It was conceivable he would win a majority vote even in the south. Consequently, Diem, with the strong support of the United States, announced there would be no reunification elections because free elections were impossible. Instead there would be two plebiscites in the south to decide first whether to abolish the monarchy, and second whether to authorize drafting a new constitution. General Edward Lansdale* advised Diem how to manipulate election machinery to his own benefit, including the color of the ballots—red (signifying good luck) for Diem and green (signifying misfortune) for Emperor Bao Dai.* Lansdale also admonished Diem not to rig the election, stating that receiving 60 percent of the vote would convince Americans that Diem had a legitimate mandate. However, such a small winning margin fit neither with

Diem's absolutist nature nor with Vietnamese culture. In an election marked by massive fraud, Diem collected 605,000 votes from the 405,000 registered voters in Saigon and "won" the election with 98.2 percent of the total vote.

Sources: George McTurnen Kahin and John W. Lewis, *The United States in Vietnam*, 1967; Stanley Karnow, *Vietnam: A History*, 1983; George C. Herring, *America's Longest War: The United States and Vietnam, 1950–1975*, 1986; John C. Donnell and Charles A. Joiner, eds., *Electoral Politics in South Vietnam*, 1974.

Samuel Freeman

ELECTION OF 1967 (SOUTH VIETNAM)

Justification of U.S. policy in Vietnam often hinged on South Vietnam's being (or becoming) a democracy, necessitating elections for at least a facade of democratic structure. Ironically, Vietnam historically had elected village chiefs, but Ngo Dinh Diem* tampered with this. Nguyen Van Thieu* abolished it—all with American acquiesence. Local elections, however, don't get U.S. headlines like national elections. Although local elections might be more indicative of meaningful democracy, the United States put its money on national elections. Some argue this "top down" approach made defeat inevitable.

As a result of the Honolulu Conference of 1966,* Nguyen Cao Ky* tried to consolidate power, precipitating the 1966 "Buddhist Crisis." Denouncing American imperialism and military rule, Buddhists* brought Ky's government to the verge of collapse, ending the crisis only when they were promised elections for a National Assembly and the presidency. But seeing an electoral structure which would ensure junta control of the National Assembly, the Buddhists boycotted the elections they had demanded. Ky and Thieu opposed elections because of the remote prospect that the military's candidates would lose and because both felt the elections were an attempt by the United States to humiliate and depose them. National Assembly candidates and the electorate, despite a large turnout, were singularly apathetic—possibly because they were the eleventh and twelfth national elections since 1955 and were likely to be no more meaningful than previous ones.

The 1967 presidential election was marked by less voter fraud than the 1955* embarrassment. More accurately, it was "managed" sufficiently to ensure a Thieu-Ky victory (with 35 percent). Buddhist leaders were arrested. Press censorship was tightened. Serious opposition candidates such as General Duong Van Minh* and "neutralists" or "leftists" were banned. All candidates other than Thieu or Ky had to travel together and were at the mercy of the military for transportation. Politically unknown Truong Dinh Dzu,* a semi–peace candidate who got on the ballot by concealing his program until after the screening process, came in second with 17 percent. He was jailed shortly thereafter. There was evidence of coercing voters, multiple voting by military personnel, stuffing ballot boxes, and fraudulent vote counts—a typical "demonstration" election ultimately conducted more for its propaganda value in the United States than anything else.

Sources: Frances FitzGerald, *Fire in the Lake*, 1972; Stanley Karnow, *Vietnam; A History*, 1983; Edward Herman and Frank Borhead, *Demonstration Elections*, 1984; John C. Donnell and Charles A. Joiner, eds., *Electoral Politics in South Vietnam*, 1974.
                                                                    Samuel Freeman

ELECTION OF 1968 (U.S.)

The presidential election of 1968 was one of the stormiest in American history. Although there had been considerable opposition to a third term for President Lyndon B. Johnson,* few people in the Democratic party had any hope of wresting the presidential nomination from him until after the political disaster of the Tet Offensive* in South Vietnam, when Vietcong* and North Vietnamese troops administered a stunning setback to American forces by proving they still had the will and ability to resist. Senator Eugene McCarthy,* an antiwar Democrat from Minnesota, announced his candidacy for the presidency and to everyone's surprise, won 42 percent of the vote in the New Hampshire primary, an almost unheard-of total against an incumbent president. Four days after the March 12, 1968, New Hampshire primary, Senator Robert F. Kennedy* of New York, another antiwar Democrat, announced his candidacy, and on March 31 Lyndon B. Johnson informed the country in a television speech that he would not run for reelection.

With Johnson's decision, Vice President Hubert Humphrey* decided to seek the presidency, and the race quickly became a struggle between him and Robert Kennedy. Kennedy's assassination after the California primary on June 6 then left the nomination in Humphrey's hands. He received the nomination after a tempestuous convention in Chicago where Mayor Richard Daley's police brutally attacked antiwar* demonstrators on the streets. Richard M. Nixon* won the Republican nomination after promising a diplomatic solution to the war, and he named Spiro Agnew,* governor of Maryland, as his running mate. Alabama governor George Wallace staged a vigorous third-party campaign based on a military victory in South Vietnam and an end to federal government liberalism. He selected former Strategic Air Command chief Curtis LeMay* as his running mate.

It was a dramatically close election and Richard Nixon became the next president of the United States. The Democrats had self-destructed because of opposition to the war and the spectacle in Chicago, and George Wallace cut into their strength in the blue-collar districts of the Midwest and Northeast. Nixon received 302 electoral votes and 31,785,480 popular votes, 43.4 percent of the total, to Hubert Humphrey's 191 electoral votes and 31,275,166 popular votes, 42.7 percent of the total. George Wallace took 45 electoral votes, all in the South, and 9,906,473 popular votes, 13.5 percent of the total. Democrats kept control of the House of Representatives by 243 to 192, and the Senate by 58 to 42.

Sources: Richard B. Morris, *Encyclopedia of American History*, 1976; Clark Dougan and Stephen Weiss, *The Vietnam Experience: Nineteen Sixty-Eight*, 1983; Theodore H. White, *The Making of the President, 1968*, 1969.

ELECTION OF 1971 (SOUTH VIETNAM)

The South Vietnamese election of 1971 took place in the midst of the Paris peace talks* to end the war. Le Duc Tho,* the representative of the Democratic Republic of Vietnam,* informed Henry Kissinger* that a settlement would be easier to reach if the United States withdrew its support from Nguyen Van Thieu,* president of the Republic of Vietnam.* Vice President Nguyen Cao Ky* and army General Duong Van Minh* were challenging Nguyen Van Thieu for the presidency. The election was scheduled for October 3, 1971. North Vietnam supposed it would be easier to work out a political accommodation with someone other than Thieu. President Richard Nixon,* however, decided to stay with Thieu on the grounds of the need for stability. In the election, Thieu forced the withdrawal of Ky and Minh then decided not to run, making a sham out of the election. Running unopposed, Thieu won another term. Ellsworth Bunker,* the U.S. ambassador, was outraged at Thieu's high-handedness, but there was little he could do about it. The peace negotiations continued to stall over the status of the South Vietnamese government.

Sources: Stanley Karnow, *Vietnam: A History*, 1983; George C. Herring, *America's Longest War: The United States in Vietnam, 1950–1975*, 1986; John C. Donnell and Charles A. Joiner, eds. *Electoral Politics in South Vietnam*, 1974.

Samuel Freeman

11th ARMORED CAVALRY

The 11th Armored Cavalry deployed to Vietnam on September 8, 1966. It was also known as the "Blackhorse Regiment." At peak strength, the 11th Armored Cavalry consisted of a tank troop of 51 tanks, a howitzer battery of 18 155mm howitzers, 296 armored personnel carriers,* and 48 helicopters. By 1970 it had 3,891 personnel attached to it. Most of its effort took place in III Corps,* especially in War Zone C* of Tay Ninh Province. In January 1969, the 11th Armored Cavalry received its first detachment of M551 Sheridan tanks. Between April 1969 and June 1970 the 11th Armored Cavalry was under the control of the 1st Cavalry Division,* and in 1970 they participated in the Cambodian incursion (*see* Operation Binh Tay). The 11th Armored Cavalry left Vietnam on March 5, 1971.

Sources: Shelby L. Stanton, *Vietnam Order of Battle*, 1981; Michael D. Mahler, *Ringed in Steel: Armored Cavalry, Vietnam, 1967–68*, 1986.

11th INFANTRY BRIGADE   *See* 23rd Infantry Division

ELLSBERG, DANIEL

Daniel Ellsberg was born in Chicago on April 7, 1931. His father was a structural engineer and his mother a musician. In 1952 he graduated summa cum laude from Harvard with a degree in economics. Two years later he was commissioned a first lieutenant in the Marine Corps* where, according to Sanford J. Ungar, author of *The Papers and the Papers* (1972), he "developed an authentically military approach to America's international responsibilities.'' In 1959 Ellsberg joined the Rand Corporation* and became a specialist on game theory and risk in nuclear war. Eager to get in on decisions relating to Vietnam, he moved to Washington in August 1964 and became one of Defense Secretary Robert McNamara's* whiz kids, writing speeches and lobbying in support of the hawkish viewpoint on Vietnam. He later confessed that at times he furnished McNamara ''ten alternative lies'' to use in tight situations with the press.

In July 1965 Ellsberg volunteered to help Major General Edward Lansdale* evaluate the success of the pacification programs (*see* Rural Reconstruction) in South Vietnam. In 1967 McNamara commissioned him as one of a research task force to write a history of American-Vietnamese relations from 1945 through 1967.

Ellsberg's hypothesis was that President John Kennedy* had been led by bad advice to deepen American commitments in Vietnam. However, Ellsberg found that Kennedy acted against the counsel of many of his top aids. After looking at the whole picture of presidential actions and the advice presidents had received, he concluded that ''to a large extent it was an American President's war. No American President, Republican or Democrat, wanted to be the President who lost the war. . . . '' In 1968 he gave advice in Defense Department meetings that resulted in the bombing halt in November. Ellsberg began going to antiwar meetings and writing Senator Robert F. Kennedy's* policy statements on Vietnam during the 1968 presidential primaries. He also gave advice to president-elect Richard Nixon's* National Security adviser Henry Kissinger.*

Beset with guilt feelings because of his involvement in policy decisions and the pacification program, Ellsberg in the fall of 1969 began using a copying machine to reproduce the Pentagon study. By making it public he hoped that ''truths that changed me could help Americans free themselves and other victims from our longest war.'' Ellsberg gave a copy to Senator William Fulbright,* chairman of the Senate Foreign Relations Committee.* His increasingly public role caused Rand to pressure him to resign, which he did in late 1969 and then became a senior research associate at MIT's Center for International Studies.

After engaging in a whirlwind of antiwar activity, he became frustrated at how little influence he was able to exert. President Nixon's invasions of Cambodia (*see* Operation Binh Tay) and Laos (*see* Lam Son 719) angered him and in March 1971 triggered his leaking of the Pentagon Papers* to the *New York Times*. The *Times* began publishing excerpts and articles based on the Papers on June 13, 1971. Although the Nixon administration secured an injunction against further *Times* publication, the *Washington Post* and the *Boston Globe* continued to make the documents public. On June 30 the Supreme Court decided in favor of the *Times* and the *Post*, saying that the First Amendment presumed that there would be no prior restraint on the press.

On June 29, 1971, Ellsberg was indicted for converting government property to his personal use and illegally possessing government documents. Later the grand jury charged him with conspiracy, theft, and violation of the Espionage

Act. In the midst of the proceedings on May 11, 1973, Judge Matthew Byrne, Jr., dismissed all charges because of government misconduct, especially illegal wiretapping, breaking into the office of Ellsberg's former psychiatrist, and Nixon's attempt to influence Byrne by offering him the directorship of the Federal Bureau of Investigation. Ellsberg remained active in the antiwar movement,* and during the 1980s he became a vocal proponent of strategic arms limitations.

Sources: Daniel Ellsberg, *Papers on the War*, 1972; Peter Schrag, *Test of Loyalty*, 1974.

John Ricks

ELY, PAUL HENRY ROMAULD

Born in France* in 1897, Paul Ely was a highly respected military officer who commanded French forces in Indochina* in 1954 and 1955. Educated at the Lycée de Brest, École Spéciale Militaire de Saint Cyr, and the École Supérieure de Guerre, he worked his way through the military command system. In 1941–42, Ely was a commanding officer with the Tenth Chasseurs, and served the rest of the war as representative of the Allied High Command with the resistance movement. In 1945, Ely became commander of the infantry. He became military director to the minister of national defense in 1946, commander of the Seventh Region in 1947, and inspector general of the armed forces in 1948. Between 1950 and 1953, Ely served as the French representative to NATO, and late in 1953 was named commander in chief of the French Armed Forces in Indochina.

It was a lost cause. In 1954, as the final stage of the struggle began, Ely wanted American air support, and on March 20 he flew to Washington, D.C., to request assistance. There he warned Admiral Arthur B. Radford* and other American leaders that the "destruction of Dien Bien Phu* was likely." Direct American assistance was not forthcoming, and French forces at Dien Bien Phu surrendered on May 7, 1954. At the Geneva Accords* in 1954, Vietnam was divided into two countries, and American support replaced the French presence in the south. Ely departed South Vietnam in the spring of 1955. He served as chief general staff marshal until January 1959 and then as chief staff officer for defense until his retirement in 1961. Paul Ely died on January 19, 1975.

Sources: *International Who's Who, 1964–1965*, 1965; Joseph Buttinger, *Vietnam: A Dragon Embattled*, 2 vols., 1967.

ÉLYSÉE AGREEMENT OF 1949

The Élysée Agreement was signed on March 8, 1949, by the puppet emperor Bao Dai* and French president Vincent Auriol in Paris. The agreement declared that Vietnam was an independent nation but that France* still had authority over defensive, financial, and diplomatic matters there. The agreement also promised to incorporate Cochin China* into a unified Vietnamese nation. Bao Dai realized that the Élysée Agreement really did nothing to promote real independence, and the Vietnamese Communists under Ho Chi Minh* viewed it as a sellout and realized that any real hope of securing independence peaceably from the French was a pipe dream.

Sources: Stanley Karnow, *Vietnam: A History*, 1983; Donald Lancaster, *The Emancipation of French Indochina*, 1961; Joseph Buttinger, *The Smaller Dragon: A Political History of Vietnam*, 1958.

ENCLAVE STRATEGY

The American buildup in Vietnam precipitated a major debate within the Lyndon B. Johnson* administration about strategic commitments in Indochina.* People like Admiral Ulysses Sharp* and General William Westmoreland* wanted a rapid buildup and independent combat operations by U.S. personnel to "search and destroy"* the enemy in a war of attrition.* Under Secretary of State George Ball,* on the other hand, was suspicious about the entire American commitment in the region. Edward Lansdale* wanted the major American commitment to be directed at counterinsurgency* and pacification (*see* Rural Reconstruction). Initially, American forces secured cities and strategic military positions in a static defensive posture, but Westmoreland quickly abandoned it for the enclave strategy which was something of a compromise. Under the enclave strategy, American forces would conduct aggressive patrolling near their defensive enclaves. After gaining experience, U.S. troops would be permitted to conduct offensive operations in support of ARVN (*see* Army of the Republic of Vietnam) forces within a 50-mile radius of their enclaves. Officially that strategy lasted only a year, but it was eroded almost immediately as Westmoreland succeeded in deploying the 173rd Airborne* to the Central Highlands* and in initiating limited search and destroy operations. In 1967, sensing a stalemate, Paul Warnke,* head of International Security Affairs at the Pentagon, unsuccessfully recommended readoption of the enclave strategy to reduce casualties and costs, and to return the combat burden to the South Vietnamese.

Sources: Peter Poole, *Eight Presidents and Indochina*, 1978; William R. Corson, *The Betrayal*, 1968; Bruce Palmer, Jr., *The 25-Year War*, 1984; Andrew F. Krepinevich, Jr., *The Army and Vietnam*, 1986; Harold K. Johnson, "The Enclave Concept: A 'License to Hunt,' " *Army*, (April 1968).

Samuel Freeman

ENTHOVEN, ALAIN

Alain Enthoven was born in Seattle, Washington, on September 10, 1930. He received a degree in economics from Stanford University in 1952, studied under a Rhodes scholarship at Oxford in 1954, and received the Ph.D. in economics from MIT in 1956. Enthoven was an economist and systems analyst for the Rand Corporation* between 1956 and 1960, and after the election of John F. Kennedy* he went to the Department of Defense as a deputy assistant secretary. At the height of the Vietnam War, Enthoven was a senior assistant to Secretary of Defense Robert McNamara,* and he continually offered his opinion that the real issue in Vietnam was nationalism, not communism, and American bombing, money, and personnel would not stem the tide. Enthoven saw the war as a struggle between American public opinion, which was gradually souring on the war, the corruption of the South Vietnamese regime, and the growing strength of the Vietcong* and North Vietnamese. Consequently, Enthoven opposed the American troop buildup as futile. When the Democrats were ousted from the White House in the election of 1968,* Enthoven left Washington and joined Litton Industries as a vice president and later as president of Litton Medical Services. In 1973 he became the Marriner S. Eccles Professor of Management at Stanford University, where he still teaches.

Sources: *Who's Who in America, 1984–1985*, 1985; Stanley Karnow, *Vietnam: A History*, 1983; Alain C. Enthoven and K. Wayne Smith, *How Much Is Enough? Shaping the Defense Program, 1961–1969*, 1971.

• F •

F–4 PHANTOM II

The F–4 Phantom II, a twin-engine, all-weather, tactical fighter-bomber (*see* fighters), was one of the principal aircraft deployed to Southeast Asia. Capable of operating at speeds of more than 1,600 miles per hour and at altitudes approaching 60,000 feet, the first F–4s were deployed to participate in the air war over Vietnam in August 1964 by the United States Navy.* On August 6, 1964, in response to the Gulf of Tonkin incident,* five F–4Bs from the USS *Constellation* attacked North Vietnamese patrol boat bases. Operating from the USS *Ranger*, the USS *Coral Sea*, and the USS *Hancock*, the F–4 aircraft expanded their operations beginning on April 3, 1965, when fifty F–4Bs attacked a road bridge 65 miles south of Hanoi.

The first United States Air Force* (USAF) F–4s were deployed to Southeast Asia in early 1965. They became involved in significant air operations during the summer. For instance, on July 10, 1965, two F–4Cs shot down two MiG–17 fighters over North Vietnam with Sidewinder missiles. Additionally, in October 1965 the first RF–4s, aircraft equipped with reconnaissance equipment, were deployed to the theater. Operations expanded thereafter; by March 1966, seven USAF F–4 squadrons were in South Vietnam and three were in Thailand.* The buildup of F–4 aircraft and operations continued thereafter.

The air fighting over North Vietnam lasted from spring 1965 to January 1973, but included a long period between April 1968 and March 1972 when strikes in the north were halted or severely restricted by presidential decree. Consequently, regular air fighting by F–4s took place for approximately forty-three months during the seven-and-a-half year conflict. During their operations, USAF F–4s were credited with 107.5 air victories, Navy F–4s with 38, and Marine Corps* F–4s with one. A total of 511 F–4s from all services were lost in Southeast Asia from June 6, 1965, through June 29, 1973. Of these, 430 were combat losses, while 81 resulted from aerial or ground accidents.

Sources: Francis K. Mason, *Phantom: A Legend in Its Own Time*, 1984; *Modern Fighting Aircraft: F–4 Phantom III*, 1984.

Roger D. Launius

F–5

The F–5 was designed for smaller allied nations. Designed late in the 1950s by Northrup, the first production F–5 flew in 1963. Twelve F–5s arrived in Vietnam on October 23, 1965, for combat testing. Most of the F–5 aircraft were used by the Vietnamese Air Force.* The United States supplied them with fifty-four F–5s, and they leased another eighty from Taiwan, South Korea, and Iran in 1973. The F–5 was armed with two 20mm guns, two AIM–9B Sidewinder missiles at the wing tips, three 1,000-pound and two 750-pound bombs.

Source: Ray Wagner, *American Combat Planes*, 1982.

F–104 STARFIGHTER

The F–104 Starfighter was produced in 1956, after several years of development, by the Lockheed Aircraft Corporation as a lightweight air-superiority jet fighter to replace the aging F–100 force of Korean War–era aircraft. The F–104 entered the operational aircraft inventory of the United States Air Force* on January 26, 1958, and saw service in Southeast Asia throughout the 1960s. The first twenty-four F–104s deployed to Southeast Asia on a temporary basis beginning April 7, 1965, with one squadron standing alert at Kung Kuan, Taiwan (*see* Chiang Kai-shek), and another at Da Nang,* South Vietnam. From Da Nang, these aircraft could strike targets in both South and North Vietnam. The F–104s sustained heavy losses from enemy ground fire. They were relieved of the air defense commitment on November 21, 1965, and redeployed in December 1965. A permanent contingent of F–104s was deployed to Southeast Asia on July 5, 1966, in response to the escalation of the American commitment there. Accordingly, F–104Cs from the 479th Tactical Fighter Wing were assigned to the 435th Tactical Fighter Squadron at Udorn Royal Thai Air Base, Thailand.* These aircraft were heavily involved in combat operations throughout the theater until they were replaced in July 1967 by more efficient F–4D aircraft. During their operations in Southeast Asia, F–104s numbered a maximum of twenty-four aircraft. They flew a total of 7,083 sorties;* eight aircraft were lost, and there were no confirmed MiG victories.

Source: Marcelle S. Knaack, *Encyclopedia of U.S. Air Force Aircraft and Missile Systems*. Vol. 1, *Post-World War II Fighters*, 1978.

Roger D. Launius

F–105 THUNDERCHIEF

The F–105 Thunderchief, a supersonic, tactical fighter-bomber (*see* fighters) capable of delivering conventional and nuclear weapons, was one of the workhorses of the United States Air Force* (USAF) in Southeast Asia. The first F–105 production aircraft was delivered to the Air Force in May 1958; it incorporated the distinctive swept-forward air-intake ducts in the wing root leading edges that reduced turbulence in front of the tail section. The aircraft also had an internal bombay and positions for ordnance on wing pylons, as well as a six-barrel 20mm cannon that fired 6,000 rounds per minute. The F–105 was ultimately modified for several special missions: all-weather and night bombing, air interdiction, aerial reconnaissance, air superiority operations, and air-to-air and air-to-ground missile operations.

The F–105D, a model of the aircraft that began entering the air force inventory in the early 1960s, was the principal aircraft used for strikes on heavily defended ground targets in North Vietnam during the Southeast Asian conflict. These aircraft began to see action in the theater in early 1965, as F–105Ds, flying from Korat Air Base, Thailand,* and striking targets north of the seventeenth parallel (*see* Geneva Accords). While participating in tactical air strikes over South Vietnam in 1966 and subsequent years, they carried out more strikes against the North than any other USAF aircraft. Operating against ever-stiffening defenses, the F–105Ds also led in battle losses for USAF combat aircraft. These fighter aircraft, as well as the F–105F and F–105G configurations which began arriving in Vietnam in 1966, operated in the theater until 1973. During the eight years of operations, the maximum number of F–105 aircraft in Southeast Asia flew 137,391 sorties* and scored 27.5 confirmed victories over enemy aircraft, while sustaining 334 combat losses.

Source: J. C. Scutts, *F–105 Thunderchief*, 1981.

Roger D. Launius

F–111

Manufactured by General Dynamics, the F–111 was the most controversial aircraft in the American arsenal during the Vietnam War. Capable of delivering either nuclear weapons or conventional payloads of four 2,000-pound bombs or twelve to twenty-four 750-pound bombs, the F–111 was highly accurate because of its computerized APQ–113 attack radar and AJQ–20 inertial bombing-navigational system. The F–111 had terrain avoidance capabilities and could fly long distances at low altitudes, avoiding enemy radar contact. General Dynamics produced the F–111 and subcontracted the navy's F–111B to Grumman. Its top speed was 1,453 mph with a combat ceiling of 56,000 feet and a combat radius of 1,330 miles. On March 17, 1968, six F–111As arrived in Thailand* to attack targets in North Vietnam. After only fifty-five missions and three aircraft losses, operations were halted and the remaining F–111As returned to the United States. Serious doubts existed about the aircraft's structural stability, and all of them were retested. Between September 1972 and February 1973, two squadrons of fifty-two F–111As were redeployed and flew over 3,000 missions. Only seven were lost.

Source: Ray Wagner, *American Combat Aircraft*, 1982.

FAC   *See* Forward Air Controller

FALL, BERNARD

Author of *The Viet Minh Regime* (1956), *Le Viet Minh, 1945–1960* (1960), *Street Without Joy* (1961), *The Two Viet Nams* (1963), *Viet Nam Witness* (1966), *Hell in a Very Small Place* (1966), and *Last Reflections on a War* (1967), and editor with Marcus Raskin of *The Viet Nam Reader* (1967), Bernard Fall was a recognized authority on Vietnam and the wars fought there. Born in 1926, Fall served in World War II with the French underground until the liberation, and then with the French army until 1946. He was a research analyst at the Nuremberg War Crimes Tribunal and worked for the United Nations in the International Tracing Service. He came to the United States in 1951 on a Fulbright Scholarship, earning an M.A. and Ph.D. in political science at Syracuse University. He first went to Vietnam in 1953 to do research for his doctorate and returned for the sixth time in 1966 on a Guggenheim Fellowship. When not in Vietnam, he was a professor of international relations at Howard University.

Fall was a complex man with a passion for Vietnam. He saw both wars there as tragedies. Although deep concern about communism in Indochina* softened his criticism of both France* and the United States, Fall held to the justice of an Indochina free of foreign domination, whether it be French, American, Chinese, or Russian. A critic of both French colonialism and American intervention, Fall distinguished clearly between the policies of governments and the human beings caught in between. Fall combined meticulous scholarship with a humane writing style. He wanted to see the war as it was experienced by those condemned to fighting it, and he wrote sensitively about their travails. He loved the Vietnamese people and had great respect and admiration for the forces of the Vietminh* and National Liberation Front (NLF; *see* Vietcong). On February 21, 1967, Bernard Fall was killed in the field with a United States Marine Corps* unit when an NLF booby trap* exploded.

Sources: *New York Times*, February 22, 1967; Bernard Fall, *Hell in a Very Small Place*, 1966; *Last Reflections on a War*, 1967.

Samuel Freeman

FANK

The acronym FANK stood for Forces Armées Nationales Khmeres, or the Khmer* National Armed Forces. FANK was the military arm of the pro-American Lon Nol* government which took over Cambodia (*see* Kampuchea) after the collapse of Norodom Sihanouk's* neutral government in March 1970. FANK was defeated in 1975 when Pol Pot's* Vietnamese-trained Khmer Rouge* troops seized the Cambodian capital in Phnom Penh.

Sources: Clark Dougan and David Fulghum, *The Vietnam Experience: The Fall of the South*, 1985; William Shawcross, *Sideshow: Kissinger, Nixon, and the Destruction of Cambodia*, 1979.

FELLOWSHIP OF RECONCILIATION

The Fellowship of Reconciliation (FOR) was an important, though not very publicly visible, influence on the civil rights and antiwar movements of the late 1950s and the 1960s. Formally founded in Great Britain in 1914 and then on November 11, 1915, in the United States, the current worldwide FOR has organizations in twenty-seven countries, with an international secretariat in Brussels. The American FOR, headquartered in Nyack, New York, is a religious, predominantly Christian, pacifist association of persons who "recognize the essential unity of all humanity and have joined together to explore the power of love and truth for resolving human conflict." FOR publishes a magazine called *Fellowship* eight times a year as well as other literature. During World War I, World War II, the Korean War, the Vietnam War, and the years between those wars, FOR opposed conscription and provided support and encouragement for conscientious objectors and others wishing to protest war or refuse participation in the military. For many years, perhaps the leading spokesperson for FOR, and FOR's most well-known pacifist, was A. J. Muste* (1885–1967). Muste was among the early organizers of FOR, along with such notable reformers as Jane Addams, Scott Nearing, and Norman Thomas. In the fall of 1964, Muste and other pacifists issued the first public statement endorsing draft* resistance during the Vietnam War: the Declaration of Conscience Against the War in Vietnam. Muste died in February 1967 while helping to organize large antiwar* demonstrations that were held on April 15. Throughout its existence, FOR's greatest influence appears to have come from its enduring ability to facilitate, and provide leadership for, the formation of other reform organizations including, for example, the War Resisters League, American Civil Liberties Union, National Conference of Christians and Jews, Congress of Racial Equality, and American Committee on Africa. During the late 1950s, FOR supported the black civil rights movement in the South by participating in demonstrations and conducting workshops on nonviolence and civil disobedience. Prominent black civil rights leaders, such as James Farmer, Martin Luther King, Jr.,* and Bayard Rustin, were members of FOR. Similarly, FOR supported, provided leadership for, or helped to educate new organizations, such as Clergy and Laity Concerned* and Another Mother for Peace, that were formed to protest the war in Vietnam. After the Gulf of Tonkin incident* in 1964, FOR rallied more than 3,000 clergy to endorse a statement saying "In the Name of God Stop It." FOR members conducted long-term vigils and mounted hunger strikes against the draft and the war, and in 1970 held a month-long series of Daily Death Toll "die-ins" in front of the White House. During the war, FOR especially sought to establish ties with Buddhist* pacifists and "third force" activists in South Vietnam. Thich Nhat Hanh, a Vietnamese Buddhist monk, first came to the United States in 1965 under FOR sponsorship. FOR supported and housed the U.S. Liaison Office for the Vietnamese Buddhist Peace Delegation. After the war, FOR continued to protest the mistreatment of Buddhist pacifists and other antiwar and antimilitary activists in Vietnam. While most of the youth-based organizations as well as many others of the Vietnam era had disappeared by 1975, FOR remained active, in part because it did not deviate from its nonviolent beliefs, it had always had a reform agenda larger than the Vietnam War, and its members have been, as a group, older and more committed to pacifism as a religious philosophy. As of 1986, FOR reported a membership of 33,000 in the United States (up from some 23,000 in 1973).

Sources: Vera Brittain, *The Rebel Passion*, 1964; Nancy Zaroulis and Gerald Sullivan, *Who Spoke Up? American Protest and the War in Vietnam, 1963–1975*, 1984.

John Kincaid

FIELDS OF FIRE

Fields of Fire is the title of James Webb's 1978 novel about Vietnam. The plot follows a platoon of Marines slogging through the rice paddies and jungles outside of An Hoa, suffering violent death, horrible injuries, wretched living conditions, and poor morale because they see no rationale for the sacrifice, no reason to die. The central character is Will Goodrich, a Harvard student who enlists in the Marine Corps* Band only to be assigned by mistake to Vietnam.

Sources: James Webb, *Fields of Fire*, 1978; Philip D. Beidler, *American Literature and the Experience of Vietnam*, 1982.

FIFTH INFANTRY DIVISION

The First Brigade of the Fifth Infantry Division arrived in Vietnam on July 25, 1968, from Fort Carson, Colorado. The brigade had been involved in riot control activities in the United States early in 1968, and then had undergone reorganization as a mechanized unit. When the brigade arrived in Quang Tri of I Corps* in July, it had more than 1,300 vehicles. The brigade came under the direction of Lt. General Richard G. Stillwell and the XXIV Corps,* and worked closely with the Third Marine Division* and the 101st Airborne Division* (Airmobile) in the northern provinces of South Vietnam. The First Brigade of the Fifth Infantry Division left Vietnam on August 27, 1971.

Sources: Shelby L. Stanton, *Vietnam Order of Battle*, 1981, and *The Rise and Fall of an American Army: U.S. Ground Troops in Vietnam, 1965–1973*, 1985.

5TH MARINE DIVISION

In March 1966 the Defense Department reactivated the 5th Marine Division and thus revived a unit that had fought on Iwo Jima, participated briefly in the occupation of Japan, and ceased to exist in early 1946. When the Johnson* administration decided not to call up the Fourth Marine Division from the Organized Reserve, Major General Robert E. Cushman, Jr.,* moved over from his skeletal reserve headquarters and began drawing on the additional 55,000 volunteers and draftees authorized for the Marine Corps* by Congress* in late 1965.

The first battalion of two regimental landing teams (RLT) eventually committed to Vietnam landed north of Dong Ha* in September 1966, and by April the other two battalions of the 26th Marines were ashore and under the operational

control of the Third Marine Division.* The 26th Marines (RLT–26) won a
Presidential Unit Citation for their role in the defense of Khe Sanh* in 1968 and
later that year attached to the 1st Marine Division* for operations with the 27th
Marines (RLT–27), also of the 5th Marine Division, south of Da Nang.* The
27th Marines left I Corps* for Camp Pendleton in September 1968, but RLT–
26 remained and conducted ten special landing force operations along the coast
of southern I Corps until its return to California in the early fall of 1969. The
5th Marine Division disbanded in November of that year.

Sources: Donald L. Evans, "USMC Civil Affairs in Vietnam: A Philosophical History," in *The Marines in Vietnam, 1954–1973*, 1983; Shelby L. Stanton, *Vietnam Order
of Battle*, 1981.

Dudley Acker

FIFTH SPECIAL FORCES GROUP
Various Special Forces* groups had served tours of duty in South Vietnam
during the early 1960s; it was not until October 1964 that the Fifth Special Forces
Group was formally deployed there. The Fifth established its headquarters at
Nha Trang.* It consisted of groups of A, B, and C teams. Each twenty-man C
team was in charge of three B teams, which controlled four twelve-man A teams.
The A teams were the operational units used to head Special Forces camps,
attack and infiltrate enemy units, reconnoiter enemy positions, and call in air
strikes. There were four Fifth Special Forces Companies, one assigned to each
of the four corps tactical zones. The Fifth Special Forces Group was also responsible for directing the work of Montagnard* tribal units of the Civilian
Irregular Defense Group* (CIDG) camps. Between October 1964 and October
1969, the Fifth Special Forces Group grew from 950 U.S. personnel and 19,000
irregular troops to 3,740 U.S. troops and more than 40,000 irregulars. The Fifth
Special Forces Group also directed the Eagle Flight* program, developed the
Long Range Reconnaissance Patrol* program, supervised Projects Delta,*
Sigma,* and Omega,* and helped transform many CIDG units into Regional
Forces,* Popular Forces,* and South Vietnamese Ranger units. The Fifth Special
Forces Group was withdrawn from South Vietnam in March 1971. At the time
of its withdrawal, the Fifth Special Forces Group had also been responsible for
a wide variety of civic action and pacification projects (*see* Rural Reconstruction).
They claimed to have established 49,902 economic aid projects in Vietnam,
34,334 educational projects, 35,468 welfare projects, and 10,959 medical projects.

Sources: Shelby L. Stanton, *Vietnam Order of Battle*, 1981, and *Green Berets at War*,
1985; Francis J. Kelly, *U.S. Army Special Forces, 1961–1971*, 1973; Andrew F. Krepinevich, Jr., *The Army and Vietnam*, 1986.

FIGHTER-BOMBERS   *See* Fighters

FIGHTERS
A variety of fighters and fighter-bombers were used by the American military
forces during the Vietnam War. The mainstay of the U.S. Air Force* attack was

the Republic F–105 Thunderchief,* or "the Thud." F–105s flew more combat missions over North Vietnam than any other air force craft, but by the end of the 1960s they were being replaced by the F–4 Phantom II.* The F–4 was also used extensively by the U.S. Marines* and the Navy.* The navy and marines also made wide use of the A–4 Skyhawk* as well as the A–6 Intruder.* The air force also used the F–100 Super Sabre and the A–7 Corsair II,* for close air support. In 1967 the air force introduced six General Dynamics F–111s* to Southeast Asia, but three of them were lost almost immediately because of severe technical difficulties. They were not ready for widespread use in Vietnam until September 1972. Until the cease-fire in January 1973, the F–111s flew more than 3,000 combat missions over North Vietnam.

Sources: Carl Berger, ed., *The United States Air Force in Southeast Asia, 1961–1973*, 1977; William W. Momyer, *Airpower in Three Wars*, 1978.

FINAL OFFENSIVE   *See* Ho Chi Minh Campaign

FIRST AVIATION BRIGADE

Headquartered at Tan Son Nhut Air Base* (May 1966 to December 1967 and December 1972 to March 1973) and Long Binh* (December 1967 to December 1972), the First Aviation Brigade carried out aerial reconnaissance, medical evacuations (*see* medevac), tactical assaults, fire support, and cargo handling. At its peak strength, the First Aviation Brigade consisted of 7 aviation groups, 20 aviation battalions, 4 air cavalry squadrons, 641 fixed-wing aircraft, 441 Cobra AH–1G* attack helicopters, 311 CH–47* cargo helicopters, 635 OH–6A observation helicopters, and 2,202 UH–1* utility helicopters. The First Aviation Brigade also worked actively with the Rural Development Program in relocating Vietnamese civilians during pacification (*see* Rural Reconstruction). During its deployment to Vietnam, the First Aviation Brigade had eight commanders: Brigadier General George P. Seneff (May 1966 to November 1967); Major General Robert R. Williams (November 1967 to April 1969); Brigadier General Allen M. Burdett, Jr. (April 1969 to January 1970); Brigadier General George W. Putnam, Jr. (January 1970 to August 1970); Colonel Samuel G. Cockerham (acting) (August 1970); Brigadier General Jack W. Hemingway (August 1970 to September 1971); Brigadier General Robert N. Mackinnon (September 1971 to September 1972); and Brigadier General Jack V. Mackmull (September 1972 to March 1973).

Source: Shelby L. Stanton, *Vietnam Order of Battle*, 1981.

1ST CAVALRY DIVISION (AIRMOBILE)

Originally activated in 1921, the 1st Cavalry Division fought (dismounted) in the Pacific during World War II and later in Korea. In 1965 the division's flag was taken from Korea and presented to the experimental 11th Air Assault Division, which became the 1st Cavalry Division (Airmobile). (The former 1st Cavalry Division, still in Korea, became the new 2nd Infantry Division.) The division was deployed to South Vietnam in September 1965 and was the first full division to arrive in the country. It was almost immediately in battle in the Ia Drang Valley.* The division won a Presidential Unit Citation for its fierce fighting. During 1966 and 1967 elements of the division were engaged in numerous actions throughout the II Corps* Tactical Zone. Initially committed to operations in Binh Dinh Province in early 1968, the bulk of the division was hurriedly recommitted to the Battle for Hue* and then to the relief of the marine position at Khe Sanh.* Later in the year the division served in the A Shau Valley* before being shifted to protect the northern and western approaches to Saigon.* The division was in constant action throughout 1969, and in 1970 was a part of the American–South Vietnamese force which invaded Cambodia (see Operation Binh Tay). Most of the division left South Vietnam in April 1973. The remaining 3rd Brigade returned to Fort Hood, Texas, in June.

As the army's first airmobile division, the 1st Cavalry Division pioneered air assault tactics. It was considered one of the army's elite units in Vietnam, highly valuable because of its extreme mobility. The 1st Cavalry participated in the following operations and battles: Ia Drang Valley* (1965), Masher/White Wing/ Thang Phong II,* Paul Revere II,* Davy Crockett, Crazy Horse, Thayer, Irving,* Pershing,* Tam Quan (1967), Hue* (1968), Pegasus/Lam Son #207 (Khe Sanh),* Delaware/Lam Son #216,* Montana Raider, Toan Thang* #43, Toan Thang #44. The division suffered over 30,000 casualties during the war.

Sources: Shelby L. Stanton, *Vietnam Order of Battle*, 1981, and *The Rise and Fall of an American Army: U.S. Ground Forces in Vietnam 1965–1973*, 1985; Edward Hymoff, *The First Air Cavalry Division*, 1985; Kenneth D. Mertel, *Year of the Horse—Vietnam: First Air Cavalry in the Highlands*, 1968.

Robert S. Browning III

I CORPS

Also known as "Eye" Corps, I Corps was one of the four major military and administrative units of the South Vietnamese government in the 1960s and early 1970s. In particular, I Corps was the Central Vietnam Lowlands administrative unit and consisted of the five northernmost provinces: Quang Tri, Thua Thien, Quang Nam, Quang Tin, and Quang Ngai. The headquarters of I Corps was located in Da Nang.* The major cities in I Corps were Hue,* Quang Tri City, Da Nang,* and Chu Lai. During the Vietnam War, the major military units of the ARVN (see Army of the Republic of Vietnam) were the 1st Airborne Division,* 1st Division, 2nd Division, 3rd Division, and the 20th Tank Regiment. I Corps was also known as Military Region 1. During the course of the Vietnam War, the following U.S. military units fought in I Corps: 9th Marine Amphibious Brigade,* Third Marine Division,* III Marine Amphibious Force,* 1st Marine Division,* Americal Division,* XXIV Corps,* 1st Cavalry Division (Airmobile),* 101st Airborne Division,* First Brigade, Fifth Infantry Division,* and the 82nd Airborne Division.*

Sources: Harvey H. Smith, et al., *Area Handbook for South Vietnam*, 1967; Shelby L. Stanton, *Vietnam Order of Battle*, 1981.

I FIELD FORCE VIETNAM

Because of the increasing commitment of U.S. combat units in 1965, Military Assistance Command, Vietnam* created a provisional field force in II Corps* on August 1, 1965. It was known as Task Force ALPHA. Field Force, Vietnam grew out of Task Force ALPHA, and it was renamed I Field Force Vietnam on March 15, 1966. It was a corps*-level military organization, with operational control over U.S. and Allied forces in II Corps, but it did not carry the corps name because it was functioning inside an existing South Vietnamese corps zone. I Field Force Vietnam was headquartered at Nha Trang.* It left Vietnam on April 30, 1971, and was replaced by the Second Regional Assistance Command. The following individuals commanded I Field Force Vietnam: Lt. General Stanley R. Larsen (March 1966 to March 1968); Lt. General William R. Peers (March 1968 to March 1969); Lt. General Charles Corcoran (March 1969 to March 1970); Lt. General Arthur Collins, Jr. (March 1970 to January 1971); and Major General Charles P. Brown (January 1971 to April 1971).

Source: Shelby L. Stanton, *Vietnam Order of Battle*, 1981.

1ST INFANTRY DIVISION

The 1st Infantry Division, known as the "Big Red One," was first organized during World War I and saw extensive action during World War II in Africa, Sicily, Italy, France, Germany, and Czechoslovakia. The division arrived in Vietnam on October 2, 1965, and served in III Corps.* They fought Vietcong* forces in Binh Dinh and Tay Ninh provinces in 1966, fought in War Zone C* during 1966 and 1967 in Operation Attleboro* and Operation Junction City,* and during the Tet Offensive* defended Saigon* against Vietcong attack. The 1st Infantry Division participated in Operations Birmingham, Hollingsworth, Lexington III,* El Paso I and II,* and Toan Thang II.* Throughout much of 1969 the division worked in pacification programs (*see* Rural Reconstruction) and late in 1969 initiated Operation Keystone Bluejay—equipment transfers in preparation for departure from Vietnam. The 1st Infantry Division worked closely with the ARVN (*see* Army of the Republic of Vietnam) 5th Division to train them for combat operations. The division left Vietnam on April 15, 1970.

Sources: Shelby L. Stanton, *Vietnam Order of Battle*, 1981, and *The Rise and Fall of an American Army: U.S. Ground Troops in Vietnam, 1965–1973*, 1985.

FIRST LOGISTICAL COMMAND

The First Logistical Command arrived in Vietnam from Fort Hood on March 30, 1965, and established its headquarters in Saigon.* At first it was responsible for logistical support of all U.S. military units in II,* III,* and IV Corps,* with the United States Navy* in charge of logistics in I Corps.* In 1968, when United States Army* units became active in I Corps, the First Logistical Command assumed jurisdiction there as well. Eventually the First Logistical Command moved its headquarters to Long Binh,* and it controlled the major subordinate commands of United States Army Support Commands at Saigon,* Cam Ranh Bay,* Qui Nhon,* and Da Nang.* The First Logistical Command supervised the maintenance of the transportation system in South Vietnam; supervised ammunition, petroleum, and food supply depots; and delivered supplies to American troops on military bases and in the field. The First Logistical Command was consolidated with the United States Army Vietnam* on June 26, 1970. The First Logistical Command left Vietnam on December 7, 1970, and returned to Fort Bragg. The United States Army Vietnam assumed control of logistical support.

Sources: Joseph M. Heiser, Jr., *Logistic Support*, 1974; Shelby L. Stanton, *Vietnam Order of Battle*, 1981.

FIRST MARINE AIRCRAFT WING

The First Marine Aircraft Wing, which contained nearly 500 aircraft and helicopters, was established at Da Nang* in May 1965 and remained in Vietnam until April 1971. The First Marine Aircraft Wing was in charge of all marine aircraft operations in Vietnam.

Sources: Jack Shulimson, *U.S. Marines in Vietnam: An Expanding War 1966*, 1982; Jack Shulimson and Charles M. Johnson, *U.S. Marines in Vietnam: The Landing and the Buildup 1965*, 1978.

1ST MARINE DIVISION

Known as "The Old Breed" in the Marine Corps,* the 1st Marine Division was widely recognized as one of the best military units in the United States. It was formally organized on February 1, 1941, as the first division in the history of the Marine Corps. During World War II the 1st Marines saw action on Guadalcanal, New Guinea, New Britain, Peleliu, and Okinawa, and fought in Korea as well in 1950 and 1951. In August 1965 the headquarters of the 1st Marines was moved from Camp Pendleton, California, to Okinawa. Its 7th Marine Regiment deployed to Chu Lai* in I Corps* in August 1965, and the 1st and 2nd battalions of its 1st Marine Regiment deployed there in August and November 1965. The 1st Marine Division arrived formally in Vietnam on February 23, 1966, and it was stationed at Chu Lai. In November 1966 division headquarters were transferred to Da Nang.* By midsummer 1966, 1st Marine Division strength exceeded 17,000 men.

During 1966 the 1st Marines fought small engagements and patrolled widely in I Corps, and at the beginning of 1967 the division was evenly divided between Chu Lai and Da Nang. Fighting was especially intense in the Phuoc Ha Valley between Chu Lai and Da Nang. In March and April 1967 the 1st Marines participated in Operations Union I and II* in Quang Nam and Quang Tin provinces, and in September they fought against North Vietnamese Army* (NVA) and Vietcong* forces in Operation Swift in the same region. In 1968, the division fought in the Tet Offensive* and the Battle of Hue,* patrolled and fought widely along the border of Thua Thien and Quang Nam provinces in Operation Houston, and kept Highway 1 (see "Street Without Joy") open, especially along the Hai Van Pass.* They also engaged in Operation Mameluke Thrust in central Quang Nam Province. Early 1969 found the 1st Marine Division fighting the Vietcong and NVA in Operation Taylor Common in Quang Nam Province. They also patrolled widely throughout An Hoa Valley and Que Son Valley, protecting access routs to Da Nang. They had settled into a string of fire bases and strong points stretching from Da Nang's Monkey and Marble mountains, west to Hill 55, and then on to the An Hoa basin's "Arizona Territory."

The 1st Marine Division received two Presidential Unit Citations, the Vietnamese Cross of Gallantry with Palm, and a Republic of Vietnam* Civil Actions Award. Twenty of the division's marines, two of its corpsmen, and one navy chaplain won the Medal of Honor, and President Nixon* appeared at the 1st Marine Division's nationally televised return to Camp Pendleton, California, in April 1971.

Sources: *The Marines in Vietnam, 1954–1973*, 1974; R. Robert Moskin, *The U.S. Marine Corps Story*, 1982; Edwin H. Simmons, *The Marines in Vietnam*, 1974; Shelby L. Stanton, *Vietnam Order of Battle*, 1981, and *The Rise and Fall of an American Army: U.S. Ground Troops in Vietnam, 1965–1973*, 1985.

Dudley Acker

FIRST SIGNAL BRIGADE

Because of the increasing size and complexity of the U.S. military forces in Vietnam, the Department of the Army created the Strategic Communications Command Signal Brigade, Southeast Asia, on April 1, 1966. This unit, which was under the operational control of the United States Army Vietnam,* was redesignated the First Signal Brigade on May 26, 1966.

In the fall of 1965, General William Westmoreland* had formally protested the "fragmentation of command and control of Army Signal Units" above the field-force level. The creation of the First Signal Brigade solved this problem by bringing all long-lines communications under its contol and the control of the theater commander in Vietnam. By the end of 1968 the First Signal Brigade was larger than divisional size. It was composed of six Signal groups, twenty-two Signal battalions, and over 23,000 men. It was the largest Signal organization that the United States had ever deployed to a combat theater.

The First Signal Brigade provided a secure voice and message transmission system throughout all of South Vietnam and linked that system to Thailand* and to the Department of Defense's worldwide communications network. This network provided cable, line-of-sight, tropospheric scatter, and satellite communications support to all U.S. military units—Army,* Navy,* Marine,* Air Force,* and Coast Guard.* By 1970 the communications system was so highly refined that direct-distance dialing was possible even into the most remote areas.

Source: Thomas M. Rienzi, *Vietnam Studies: Communications-Electronics, 1962–1970*, 1972.

David L. Anderson

FISHHOOK

The term "Fishhook" referred to a geographical region in Cambodia (*see* Kampuchea) approximately 50 miles northwest of Saigon.* American military and political officials had long suspected that Central Office for South Vietnam* (COSVN), the central headquarters of the Vietcong,* was located in the Fishhook, although Central Intelligence Agency* and other intelligence officers doubted. Nevertheless, the Fishhook was a sanctuary for Vietcong and North Vietnamese Army* (NVA) forces attacking South Vietnam, and in 1970 President Richard Nixon* made the region the central thrust of the Cambodian "incursion" (*see* Operation Binh Tay). A major objective of the invasion of Cambodia was to destroy Vietcong and NVA supplies. On May 1, 1970, the invasion of Fishhook was underway, with tanks and armored personnel carriers* of the 11th Armored Cavalry* crossing the border and helicopters dropping the 1st Air Cavalry* into the area. They established fire support bases throughout the Fishhook and then used those bases for search and destroy* operations, although their major objective was to locate COSVN and major supply caches. During the second week of May the 25th Infantry Division* invaded the "Dog's Head," a region approximately 30 miles southeast of the Fishhook. The 9th Infantry* also joined the invasion. President Nixon ordered American troops to confine themselves to military activity within 35 miles of the border. In the invasion, the U.S. troops captured 15 million rounds of ammunition, 143,000 rockets, 14 million pounds of rice, 23,000 weapons, 62,000 grenades, 5,500 mines, and 200,000 antiaircraft rounds. They also destroyed "The City"—11,700 Vietcong bunkers. Still, they did not locate COSVN, and the invasion triggered a storm of protest in the United States and the Kent State University* disaster.

Sources: Samuel Lipsman et al., *The Vietnam Experience: Fighting for Time*, 1983; William Shawcross, *Sideshow: Kissinger, Nixon, and the Destruction of Cambodia*, 1979.

John E. Wilson

"FIVE O'CLOCK FOLLIES"

At 5:00 P.M. daily in downtown Saigon* the Joint United States Public Affairs Office (JUSPAO) briefed reporters on the previous day's events. They were dubbed the "Five O'Clock Follies" because of the general atmosphere of confusion, difficulties in presenting detailed information providing an overview of the war, and growing suspicion that the briefings overestimated National Liberation Front (*see* Vietcong) losses and understated their successes while doing just the opposite with U.S. gains and losses. Briefing data was compiled at Tan Son Nhut* airfield's "Pentagon East" by the Military Assistance Command, Vietnam* Office of Information (MACOI). Although briefings were intended to be comprehensive, several problems made communication of information difficult. First, both MACOI and the press focused almost exclusively on U.S. operations. MACOI usually treated ARVN (*see* Army of the Republic of Vietnam) operations as adjunct to American operations, and the press, if it reported on ARVN at all, usually did so in negative terms. Western reporters seldom attended ARVN briefings held across the street from JUSPAO offices. Second, it was impossible to discuss unconventional war in the typical terms of "lines," "fronts," and "advances"; yet this was what the military, press, government officials, and public were conditioned to expect. Third, the war was being fought episodically throughout the country, making development of a comprehensive picture impossible. The media's "spot news" demands produced a war *du jour*— Khe Sanh* one day, Tay Ninh, My Lai,* or An Loc* the next. Fourth, MACOI was dependent on information from the field which might be incomplete, inaccurate, or unavailable. Fifth, most MACOI personnel had no field experience in Vietnam and seldom, if ever, ventured outside Saigon. Sixth, the war was such that reporters generally didn't know the right questions to ask. Those who knew did not attend the "Follies." They were in the field getting answers for themselves. Seventh, military personnel, straining already difficult relationships, generally regarded the press as a necessary evil. This became most evident during the Tet Offensive.* Reporters were incredulous at General William Westmoreland's standing on the grounds of the American embassy, surrounded by Vietcong* bodies, claiming victory. Since most reporters lived in Saigon's comfortable and previously safe confines feeding off MACOI handouts, they had little experience with actual combat. What they saw was disconcerting, contradicting what they were told in the "Follies."

Sources: Frances FitzGerald, *Fire in the Lake: The Vietnamese and the Americans in Vietnam*, 1972; Peter Braestrup, *Big Story*, 1983; Daniel C. Hallin, *The Uncensored War: The Media and Vietnam*, 1986.

Samuel Freeman

FLACK JACKET

A heavy, fiberglass-filled vest worn by American soldiers in the field during the Vietnam War as a protection against shrapnel, the flack jacket became the public image of the American soldier. Because of the heat of the Southeast Asian climate,* soldiers frequently wore the flack jacket while going sleeveless. The picture of the sleeveless, helmeted soldier, chest covered by the bulky flack jacket, was published or broadcast thousands of times during the Vietnam War.

Source: Al Santoli, *Everything We Had: An Oral History of the Vietnam War by Thirty-Three American Soldiers Who Fought It*, 1981.

FLEET MARINE FORCE, PACIFIC COMMAND

Based in Hawaii, Fleet Marine Force, Pacific Command (FMFPAC) was responsible for all United States Marine* forces in the Pacific theater and immediately subordinate to the United States Navy's* commander in chief of the

Pacific Command (CINCPAC), who in turn was responsible to Washington. Lacking authority to direct particular operations in Vietnam, FMFPAC nevertheless influenced the direction of the war and contributed to its planning, while its chief concerns included overseeing the provision of personnel and materiel to the theater's marines and thus providing the III Marine Amphibious Force* with an administrative and logistical link to CINCPAC. During the time of the Vietnam War, there were three FMFPAC commanders: Lt. General Victor H. Krulak* (1964–68); Lt. General Henry W. Buse, Jr. (1968–70); and William K. Jones (1970–73).

Sources: Allan R. Millett, *Semper Fidelis: The History of the United States Marine Corps*, 1980; Victor H. Krulak, *First to Fight: An Inside View of the U.S. Marine Corps*, 1984.

Dudley Acker

FLIGHT

A basic organizational element in the United States Air Force* is called a flight. A major usually commanded a flight during the Vietnam War, and it was composed of five aircraft and their crews. An air force squadron* consisted of four flights.

Source: Harry G. Summers, Jr., *Vietnam War Almanac*, 1985.

FONDA, JANE

Jane Fonda was born on December 21, 1937, in New York City. Her father, Henry, was a well-known actor and her mother, Frances Seymour, was a socialite who in a fit of depression committed suicide in 1950. Jane attended Vassar College for two years. She appeared in her first stage role opposite her father in a 1954 production of *The Country Girl* in Omaha, Nebraska. In 1958 she studied method acting under Lee Strasberg in the Actors' Studio. In 1964 Fonda went to France,* where she met and married director Roger Vadim, who tried to mold her into a sex symbol like his previous wife, Brigitte Bardot. He starred her in *The Circle of Love* (1964) and *Barbarella* (1968). The publicity posters for these films were popular pinups for American soldiers in Vietnam. Later she regretted her nude scenes, explaining that she was ''reacting against the attitude of puritanism I was brought up with.''

During 1966 and 1967 Fonda became disturbed at reports on French television that American planes were bombing Vietnamese villages and hospitals. Unhappy with her marriage and genuinely concerned about the war, she returned to the United States and worked with the Free Theater Association, which sponsored satirical antimilitary plays and skits in coffeehouses near bases all over America. She participated in demonstrations against the war throughout 1969 and 1970, and in February 1971 helped financially support the Winter Soldier Investigation* in Detroit, where more than 100 veterans testified about atrocities and war crimes they had either committed or witnessed in Vietnam. Fonda won an Academy Award for Best Actress in 1971 for her role in *Klute*.

In the summer of 1972 she went to Hanoi* and spoke with selected American prisoners and to all American soldiers in Vietnam in a radio broadcast. She posed next to an antiaircraft gun used to shoot down American pilots, and journalists, comparing her to Tokyo Rose, dubbed her "Hanoi Jane." Her visit to North Vietnam earned her the wrath of American conservatives. In 1978 Fonda won another Academy Award for Best Actress, this time for *Coming Home*. Since then Fonda has been active in a number of social and economic causes with her husband Tom Hayden,* as well as starring in "socially aware" films and producing her best-selling video *Jane Fonda's Workout Book*.

Sources: Fred Lawrence Guiles, *Jane Fonda*, 1981; Nancy Zaroulis and Gerald Sullivan, *Who Spoke Up? American Protest Against the War in Vietnam, 1963–1975*, 1984.

John Ricks

FONTAINEBLEAU CONFERENCE OF 1946

When World War II ended and the Japanese withdrew from Indochina,* the Vietnamese, under Ho Chi Minh,* declared their independence while the French expressed the intention of returning and reestablishing their imperial apparatus and government. Ho Chi Minh wanted an independent Vietnam with Cochin China,* Annam,* and Tonkin* united under one flag, and although the French at first seemed sympathetic to such an arrangement, with a united and independent Vietnam closely tied economically and politically with France,* they renounced the idea in the spring of 1946 when they established the Republic of Cochin China. Ho went to Paris in June 1946 to negotiate the future of Vietnam, and met with French officials in the Fontainebleau forest outside of Paris. At the conference, the new conservative French government under Georges Bidault* favored a French Union of former colonies tightly connected politically to France, while Ho Chi Minh preferred a much more open arrangement similar to the British Commonwealth of Nations. At the conference they also debated the problem of Cochin China, whose independence Ho viewed as a setback. The conference lasted for more than eight weeks, but Ho had no satisfaction on unification or independence. He initialed an agreement accepting a temporary modus vivendi, but resented the agreement for the rest of his life. His lifelong passion for unification of the country reached back to the Fontainebleau Conference of 1946.

Source: Joseph Buttinger, *Vietnam: A Dragon Embattled*. Vol. 2, *Vietnam at War*, 1967.

FORCED DRAFT URBANIZATION

To deprive the Vietcong* "fishes" of their civilian "sea," the United States developed a policy of depopulating rural areas and creating "free fire zones."* The displaced population was relocated to "Strategic Hamlets,"* "New Life Hamlets,"* "Really New Life Hamlets," or became refugees* in Saigon,* other cities, or the countryside. Other tactics contributing to rural depopulation included chemical warfare, destruction of Vietcong villages, and general fighting.

Before the war approximately 15 percent of the South Vietnamese population lived in cities. By 1970, 40 to 50 percent lived in cities, especially Saigon, with 30 to 35 percent of them temporary or permanent refugees. Such massive uprooting of the population bode ill for "winning the hearts and minds* of the people," especially among peasants committed to ancestor worship and family villages who saw leaving their land as a form of death. Samuel Huntington, in a 1968 issue of *Foreign Affairs*, used the term "forced draft urbanization"* to describe the counterinsurgency* tactic of rural population movement. One way to counter the rural revolutionary strategy of the Vietcong was to bring about an accelerated modernization of the Vietnamese economy. Supposedly the modernization of the Vietnamese economy—industrialization and urbanization— would destroy the rationale of Mao Zedong's* "people's wars" (*see* Wars of national liberation). According to Huntington, "In an absent-minded way, the United States . . . may well have stumbled upon the answer to 'wars of national liberation.' The effective response lies neither in the quest for a conventional military victory, nor in esoteric doctrines and gimmicks of counterinsurgency warfare. It is instead forced-draft urbanization and modernization which rapidly brings the country in question out of the phase in which a rural revolutionary movement can . . . succeed."

Source: Samuel Huntington, "The Bases of Accommodation," *Foreign Affairs*, 46 (July 1968), 642–56.

Samuel Freeman

FORD, GERALD RUDOLPH

Gerald R. Ford was born on July 14, 1913, in Omaha, Nebraska, and was raised in Grand Rapids, Michigan. He attended the University of Michigan on a football scholarship. After graduating he turned down several offers to play professional football and attended the Yale Law School. After graduating from Yale in 1940, Ford practiced law briefly until joining the navy after the Japanese attack on Pearl Harbor. Ford served on the aircraft carrier USS *Monterey* in the Pacific. He returned to Grand Rapids after the war to practice law, became active in Republican politics, and in 1948 won a congressional seat from the Fifth District in Michigan. Ford was a loyal member of the "Republican team" until 1973, when he was named vice president of the United States, filling a vacancy created by the resignation of Spiro Agnew. House minority leader since 1965, Ford had a reputation as a party regular and a reliable "hawk" concerning the Vietnam War. After Richard Nixon's* resignation in August 1974, Gerald R. Ford became the thirty-eighth president of the United States.

Since 1974 the Paris Peace Accords* had long been violated by both sides, and by autumn North Vietnam was stronger than the South. Still, Gerald Ford received overly optimistic reports from Ambassador Graham Martin* and the Defense Attaché Office.* A Congress that was antiwar and controlled by Democrats limited aid to South Vietnam, preventing its forces from using U.S. equipment and bringing on political and economic woes. North Vietnam launched attacks late in 1974 and a major offensive in March 1975. ARVN (*see* Army of the Republic of Vietnam) forces promptly collapsed. Ford requested $300 million in emergency aid in late January and another $722 million on April 10, alienating many congressmen with the "hawkish" rhetoric accompanying the request. Ford received only $300 million for evacuating Americans and for use on "humanitarian purposes." As South Vietnam collapsed, President Ford declared that the war was "finished as far as America is concerned." North Vietnamese forces entered Saigon* on May 1, 1975. Shortly thereafter, when the new Khmer Rouge* government of Cambodia (*see* Kampuchea) captured the *Mayaguez* (*see* Mayaguez incident), an American merchant vessel, Ford sent in a contingent of United States Marines* to rescue the crew, even though Cambodia had already agreed to release them. Both Ford and Secretary of State Henry Kissinger* wanted to prove that although the United States had suffered a debacle in the Vietnam War, its resolve to maintain a position of strength in Asia was still strong. In the presidential election of 1976, Gerald Ford lost narrowly to Democrat Jimmy Carter.

Sources: Arnold R. Isaacs, *Without Honor: Defeat in Vietnam and Cambodia*, 1983; Robert T. Hartman, *Palace Politics: An Inside Account of the Ford Years*, 1980; Gerald R. Ford, *A Time to Heal: The Autobiography of Gerald R. Ford*, 1979.

Robert W. Sellen

FORRESTAL, MICHAEL VINCENT

Michael V. Forrestal was born on November 26, 1927, in New York City. The son of James Forrestal, the first U.S. secretary of defense, he became an aide to W. Averell Harriman,* working on Marshall Plan affairs, and in 1953 he received a law degree from Harvard. Forrestal practiced law in New York until 1962, when he joined the White House National Security staff. In late 1962 President John F. Kennedy* sent Roger Hilsman* and Forrestal on a fact-finding mission to South Vietnam. Their "balanced" report, delivered early in 1963, struck a middle ground between the embassy's optimism and journalists' pessimism. Forrestal and Hilsman had serious reservations about ARVN's (*see* Army of the Republic of Vietnam) effectiveness, saw flaws in the Strategic Hamlet Program,* felt Ngo Dinh Diem* was increasingly isolated, and concluded that the United States and South Vietnam were "probably winning" but that the war would "probably last longer than we would like" and "cost more in terms of lives and money than we had anticipated." Their report reinforced doubt about the accuracy of official estimates of progress.

In August 1963, the first Buddhist* crisis paralyzed Diem's government as ARVN generals plotted coups. Ambassador Henry Cabot Lodge* requested instructions from Washington, but it was a weekend and most of Kennedy's key advisers were out of town. Forrestal drafted a response with Harriman and Hilsman stating the United States would no longer tolerate Ngo Dinh Nhu's* influence over Diem and called for the removal of Nhu from power. Otherwise U.S. support for Diem would end. Kennedy approved the cable but was later enraged when he found out that Secretary of Defense Robert McNamara* and Central Intelligence Agency* director John McCone had not seen it before it was sent. During the Johnson* administration, Forrestal was a member of the White House national security staff. Believing that the military's war reporting was grossly optimistic and supporting a negotiated settlement, Forrestal fell into disfavor with Johnson, was excluded from policy discussions, and resigned in 1965. He then returned to private law practice.

Sources: Nelson Lichtenstein, ed., *Political Profiles. The Kennedy Years*, 1976; Loren Baritz, *Backfire*, 1985; Michael Maclear, *The Ten Thousand Day War*, 1981.

Samuel Freeman

44TH MEDICAL BRIGADE

The 44th Medical Brigade deployed to Vietnam in April 1966 and remained there until 1970, when it was dissolved into subordinate units. The 44th Medical Brigade consisted of the 32nd Medical Depot at Long Binh;* the 43rd and 55th Medical Groups in II Corps;* the 67th Medical Group in III Corps;* and the 68th Medical Group in III and IV Corps.* The 44th Medical Brigade was responsible for medical evacuation (*see* medevac), evacuation hospitals, field hospitals, Mobile Army Surgical Hospitals, convalescent centers, and ambulance detachments.

Source: Shelby L. Stanton, *Vietnam Order of Battle*, 1981.

FORWARD AIR CONTROLLER

The forward air controller, or FAC, had the responsibility for calling in air strikes on enemy positions during the Vietnam War. Usually flying a low-level, low-speed aircraft, such as a single-engine Cessna 0–1 Bird Dog spotter plane, the FAC identified Vietcong* or North Vietnamese positions and relayed the information to attack aircraft, helicopter gunships,* or high-altitude bombers. On the ground, a forward air controller would call in similar information.

Source: Terrence Maitland and Peter McInerney, *The Vietnam Experience: A Contagion of War*, 1983.

FOUR-PARTY JOINT MILITARY COMMISSION

One of the provisions of the Paris Peace Accords* was establishment of a Four-Party Joint Military Commission (FPJMC) to supervise the withdrawal of American and allied troops from South Vietnam, implement a prisoner-of-war (POW) exchange, and maintain the existing cease-fire. At the time there were still more than 50,000 American, South Korean, Australian,* and New Zealand* troops in South Vietnam and 587 American POWs* in North Vietnamese prisons. The FPJMC formally came into existence at the end of January 1973 and consisted or representatives from South Vietnam, North Vietnam, and the United States, and the National Liberation Front (*see* Vietcong), or Provisional Revolutionary Government of South Vietnam.* The FPJMC dissolved on March 29, 1973. By that time the American and allied forces had been removed from South Vietnam and 587 American POWs had been released. The cease-fire, of course, had not been maintained because the South Vietnamese, Vietcong, and North Vietnamese were still struggling for power.

The problem of American military personnel missing-in-action had not been resolved, and on March 29, 1973, a Four-Party Joint Military Team (FPJMT) replaced the dissolved commission, with the same representation. The FPJMT was far less successful than the FPJMC had been. The Vietcong and North Vietnamese, no longer bothered by any American military presence, refused to cooperate. Not until 1974 did the United States receive any real information, and that came only with the release of two dozen bodies. The U.S. delegation to the FPJMT withdrew from Saigon* on April 10, 1975, just before the occupation of the city by North Vietnamese and Vietcong forces.

Sources: Stuart A. Harrington, *Peace With Honor*, 1984; Walter Scott Dillard, *Sixty Days to Peace*, 1982; Alan Dawson, *55 Days: The Fall of South Vietnam*, 1977.

FOUR-PARTY JOINT MILITARY TEAM   *See* Four-Party Joint Military Commission

IV CORPS

IV Corps was the southernmost of the four major military and administrative units of South Vietnam in the 1960s and early 1970s. Its headquarters were located at Can Tho in the Mekong Delta.* Also known as Military Region 4 (MR 4), IV Corps was the fourth allied tactical combat zone. It consisted of the following provinces: Chau Doc, Kien Phong, Kien Tuong, Hau Nghia, Kien Giang, An Giang, Vinh Long, Dinh Tuong, Long An, Chuong Thien, Phong Dinh, Vinh Binh, Kien Hoa, Go Cong, An Xuyen, Bac Lieu, and Ba Xuyen. The 7th and 9th ARVN Divisions (*see* Army of the Republic of Vietnam) played prominent roles in IV Corps military activities. The United States Ninth Infantry Division* operated widely throughout IV Corps, attacking Vietcong* units in their strongholds in the Plain of Reeds,* the U Minh Forest, and the Seven Mountains areas.

Sources: Shelby L. Stanton, *Vietnam Order of Battle*, 1981, and *The Rise and Fall of an American Army: U.S. Ground Troops in Vietnam, 1965–1973*, 1985.

4TH INFANTRY DIVISION

Originally formed in 1917, the 4th Infantry Division (nicknamed the "Ivy Division") served in both World Wars. The division arrived in Vietnam in September 1966 and was immediately committed to action in Operation Attleboro.* During the last months of 1966 and the first half of 1967, most of the division attempted to secure Pleiku and Kontum provinces, while the division's 3rd Brigade participated in Operation Junction City.* Later in 1967 the division's 1st and 2nd brigades participated in Operation MacArthur* in Kontum Province. In this operation elements of the 4th Division became involved in the bitter Battle of Dak To* in November. The division continued to patrol the Pleiku and Kontum provinces of the western highlands throughout 1968 and 1969. In May 1970, the division entered Cambodia (*see* Kampuchea) as part of Operation Binh Tay.* The division left Vietnam in December 1970 as part of the phased American withdrawal. During the course of the Vietnam War, the 4th Infantry Division suffered 16,844 casualties.

Source: Shelby L. Stanton, *The Rise and Fall of an American Army: U.S. Ground Forces in Vietnam, 1965–1973*, 1985.

Robert S. Browning III

FOURTH MARINE DIVISION

The Fourth Marines fought at Kwajalein, Saipan, and Tinian, and landed the first waves at Iwo Jima's southern beachhead in 1945. Disbanded in early 1946 but later reactivated as part of the Marine Corps* Organized Reserve, the Fourth Marine Division was almost completely manned and trained in 1965, and in early February 1966 Major General Robert E. Cushman, Jr.,* took command of a staff of twenty-nine officers and sixty-nine enlisted men at Camp Pendleton, California, and began planning for mobilization should the Pentagon call the division to active duty. The Johnson* administration, however, gave scant consideration to mobilizing reserve units to fight in Vietnam and in March reactivated the 5th Marine Division,* with its ranks to be filled from the expanding pool of 80,000 volunteers and 19,000 draftees allotted to the marines that year.

Sources: *The Marines in Vietnam, 1954–1973*, 1974; J. Robert Moskin, *The U.S. Marine Corps Story*, 1982.

Dudley Acker

FRAGGING

During the Vietnam War "fragging," the murder of overzealous officers and noncommissioned officers (NCOS), was estimated to have taken the lives of 1,016 officers and NCOs. The term arose because the most popular method of eliminating the victim was to roll a fragmentation grenade into his hooch or tent. A fragmentation grenade was preferred because it left no evidence; the murder weapon was destroyed along with the victim. Fragging was not new to the Vietnam War; the mutiny of Roman legions at Pannonia in A.D. 14 was marked by the murder of unpopular officers, for example. There have been recorded incidences of troops murdering unpopular officers throughout the history of warfare. In his book *A Soldier Reports*, General William Westmoreland* concluded that fragging " . . . increases when a sense of unit purpose breaks down and esprit de corps fails and when explosives and weapons are loosely controlled."

Except for a brief period in 1967–68 where soldiers in the Mekong Delta* pooled their money to pay the person who killed a marked officer or NCO, there were few fragging cases until 1969. In 1969 there were 96 documented assault cases; that number increased to 209 in 1970 and peaked in 1971 with 333 confirmed fragging incidences and 158 possible fraggings. For the most part, fragging was almost entirely confined to the army.

By 1969 the war was winding down for American soldiers, who were being pulled out and replaced by South Vietnamese troops in President Richard Nixon's* attempt to Vietnamize the war. Many American soldiers failed to see the purpose of dying in a war that their government was presumably abandoning. Many units at the platoon and squad level were refusing to obey orders that they perceived to place their lives in peril. It was this attitude of fear and frustration combined with drug use, racial tension, and the inherent inequality of the military (which afforded some special privileges because of rank) that led to fragging. In some cases, especially in rear areas, there were cases of fragging without apparent provocation. The reason could be as trivial as forcing a soldier to wear his flack jacket,* which could be perceived as harassment. Often the fragging victim would be warned first by placing a grenade pin by the entrance of his tent or attacking him with a smoke grenade. If the warning was not heeded, a fragmentation grenade would be used. Fragging was a method soldiers could use to control their officers, who would have to consider the possibility when giving orders. One second lieutenant refused an order to advance on a hill; when his men heard this, they removed a bounty they had earlier placed on his head. In the end fragging had become one symptom of a demoralized army.

Sources: Eugene Linden, "Fragging and Other Withdrawal Symptons," *Saturday Review* (January 1972), 12–17; Richard Holmes, *Acts of War: The Behavior of Men in Battle*, 1985.

Mike Dennis

FRANCE

France became involved in Vietnam because of the European missionary movement in Asia, which coincided with rising interest in trade. In the seventeenth century, Frenchmen founded both a Society of Foreign Missions and an East India Company, two vehicles of *la mission civilisatrice*, the "civilizing mission" to non-Westerners. In the 1780s a bishop's private expedition restored to power the Nguyen* family, traditional Vietnamese rulers, in the person of Gia Long,* who tolerated Christianity but whose xenophobic heir spurned Western overtures and repudiated toleration. Incidents in the 1840s and 1850s, combined with religious and business pressure, led to expeditions and the conquest of the Mekong Delta.* After the Franco-Prussian War Frenchmen were divided, some arguing that imperialist adventures merely distracted France from recovering Alsace and Lorraine, while others held that colonies could compensate for such losses while providing raw materials and markets necessary to industry. The latter won, and an 1883 expedition took all of Vietnam amid the disorder following Emperor Tu Duc's death. France even abolished the name of Vietnam, dividing it into Cochin China,* Annam,* and Tonkin.* Resistance continued into the twentieth century, but Frenchmen refused to recognize the depth of Vietnamese nationalism.

Their colonial administration was "direct," using Frenchmen instead of ruling through indigenous institutions. This meant a large French presence, ways of governing which did not fit Vietnam, and Vietnamese mostly in low-level positions. A few converts collaborated in return for nominal high status. French law destroyed traditions and was itself discredited by the jailing of political prisoners without trials. France also shifted the fiscal burden to the Vietnamese, imposing taxes and lucrative monopolies on alcohol, rice, and opium. Frenchmen and their allies took land, creating a growing and discontented peasantry, and ruthlessly exploited labor on rubber plantations and in mines. The global depression in the 1930s made the situation worse yet, but on the eve of World War II some 40,000 *colons* ignored signs of unrest. Their rules for governing were "a lot of subjugation, very little autonomy, a dash of assimilation."

French surrender in 1940 produced a "cataclysm" in Indochina,* undermining the myth of invincibility. Vichy officials, unable to act, were reduced to orating about France as a colonial power. The Free French saw the empire as an integral part of France, but could not defend it. French forces in Asia were totally inadequate to resist Japanese advances, which began in June 1940 with the demand that France stop the flow of war supplies through Haiphong to China. Governors had to accept such demands while trying to delay the erosion of French control, in July 1941 having to grant bases in south Vietnam for 50,000 Japanese troops. During the war Japan* encouraged Vietnamese nationalism and, in March 1945, took control of the colony in a coup. Emperor Bao Dai* was persuaded to declare independence and French rule had ended. Frenchmen, however, refused to recognize the fact.

When Japan surrendered in August 1945, the Vietminh* made its play for power, taking Hanoi* and organizing a national congress. Having effective independence, it proclaimed the Democratic Republic of Vietnam* on August 29. Seeking to restore French greatness, de Gaulle in Paris was committed to recovering Indochina and refused to guarantee its independence. He and his officials were ignorant of Vietnam and did not listen to those who understood it. At Japan's surrender he sent what forces he could, shaping future events by his choice of leaders. Jean Sainteny, son-in-law of former governor Albert Sarraut, was a *colon*; High Commissioner Admiral Georges Thierry d'Argenlieu* was rigid; General Jacques Leclerc was ready to fight. The arrival of British troops in the south and the rearming of liberated French soldiers in the north gave Hanoi's *colons* overconfidence; they attacked Vietnamese and violence grew. By the end of 1945 Leclerc had regained some control in the south, but the Vietminh ruled the north. It was able to hold elections, even clandestinely in Leclerc's area. D'Argenlieu's new government in Saigon* included Vietnamese, but the latter had accepted French culture and were unable to rally their countrymen. Yet Ho Chi Minh,* the Vietminh leader, found no support among French Communists, the United States supported France, and the USSR appeared to be indifferent. On March 6, 1946, he consented to French troops in the North in exchange for independence within the new French Union. But a trip to Paris for confirmation was humiliating; the independence was not real, and he returned to Hanoi to meet militants' anger. That anger and French intransigence made peace impossible. Premier Georges Bidault* allowed d'Argenlieu to use a skirmish at Haiphong late in 1946 as an excuse for a full-scale attack on the Vietminh. Violence escalated, leading to Vo Nguyen Giap's* December 19 call for resistance. The First Indochina War had begun.

Amid changing French cabinets and offers to Ho which would mean his surrender, officials in Paris paid no heed to Leclerc's warning to deal with Vietnamese nationalism. Instead, they bullied Bao Dai into accepting obviously phony independence while ignoring Ho's offer of a neutralist Vietnam. Both sides turned to the battlefield. Vietminh forces operated as guerrillas, and with Mao Zedong's* conquest of China, aid became readily available. As French casualties and costs mounted with no victory in sight, so did discontent at home. Replacement of commanders, even the appointment of renowned General Jean de Lattre de Tassigny,* was of no avail. A deadlock broke when Giap trapped French forces at Dien Bien Phu,* near Laos,* where their supply lines were long and his short. A siege ended in French surrender on May 7, 1954, and ironically, the next day delegates from nine countries met at Geneva* to begin talks to end the war.

Having suffered over 90,000 casualties on top of the disasters of World War II, the French were sick of fighting. Diplomatic deadlock ended when Pierre Mendès-France,* dedicated to ending the war, became premier and accepted the Geneva Accords.* These meant a cease-fire, a temporary division of Vietnam at the seventeenth parallel, and nationwide elections to be held in 1956. The French era in Vietnam had officially ended.

Sources: Joseph Buttinger, *Vietnam: A Dragon Embattled*, 2 vols., 1967; John Cady, *The Roots of French Imperialism in Indochina*, 1954.

Robert W. Sellen

FRANCO-VIETNAMESE ACCORDS OF 1946

After World War II, with pressure building in Indochina* for independence as well as anti-imperialist sentiment in France,* representatives of France, Tonkin,* and Annam* signed an agreement on March 6, 1946. The agreement recognized the independence of Tonkin and Annam and admitted them to the French Union, but French troops were not withdrawn. France scheduled elections in Cochin China* to measure public opinion there about unification with Tonkin and Annam. The Franco-Vietnamese Accords of 1946 were followed by the Fontainebleau Conference.*

Sources: James J. Cooke, *France 1789–1962*, 1975; Joseph Buttinger, *Vietnam: A Dragon Embattled*. Vol. 2, *Vietnam at War*, 1967.

FREEDOM BIRDS

"Freedom Birds" ("big iron birds") took GIs home to the United States. These were passenger aircraft, most under contract from private charter air services such as World Airways, which ferried troops to and from Vietnam. To Vietnam vets, these "freedom birds" represented everything desirable in life— home, family, friends, safety, and peace. Soldiers with time left in Vietnam looked upon them longingly and painfully. To those going home, they were the most beautiful sight on earth. Passengers bound for Vietnam were usually neatly dressed, quiet, and somber. A sense of dread and impending doom permeated the plane. Soldiers going home usually had a disheveled look and many were still dressed in combat fatigues. But the mood was one of relief and celebration.

The rapid passage home has been seen as a contributing force to post-traumatic stress syndrome. In previous wars soldiers had time during the long ocean voyage home to debrief themselves in conversations with other GIs. This enabled them to deal with their war experiences, and allowed them time to prepare for returning home and resuming civilian life. For some Vietnam veterans the return trip was so quick they literally were in the jungle one day and sitting at home the next, producing profound cultural shock.

Sources: Gloria Emerson, *Winners and Losers*, 1976; Rick Eilert, *For Self and Country*, 1983; John Wheeler, *Touched with Fire*, 1984.

Samuel Freeman

FREE FIRE ZONES

Free fire zones, officially designated "specified strike zones" after 1965, were described by the Defense Department as "specifically designated areas" which had been cleared "by responsible local Vietnamese authority for firing on specific military targets." They were "known enemy strongholds" and "virtually un- inhabited by noncombatants." The use of free fire zones was an attempt to structure the war along conventional military lines, with enemy forces and friendly forces occupying distinct, separate areas. When forces of the enemy had been thus isolated, they would become the targets of massive American air strikes or artillery fire.

The flaw in the logic of the free fire zone concept was that the isolation of enemy forces was accomplished by definition rather than actual physical sepa- ration from friendly inhabitants. Longtime strongholds of the Vietcong* were simply defined as being free of noncombatants. Thus anyone residing in these areas was assumed to be the enemy, regardless of sympathies or noncombatant status. In localities not identifiable as Vietcong strongholds, free fire zones were created by removing noncombatants from the area. Loudspeaker announcements, aerial leaflet drops, and sweeps by infantry units through affected hamlets were techniques used, sometimes in combination, to warn inhabitants to evacuate. Forced relocations to create free fire zones impacted such large numbers of civilians that a senior Agency for International Development official characterized them as "mass movements." Such relocation efforts were rarely effective. Some Vietnamese villagers simply could not read the warning leaflets and others were reluctant to abandon ancestral homes. Nevertheless, once inhabitants had been warned and evacuation efforts made, the affected locality was assumed to be cleared of friendly inhabitants and was designated as a free fire zone. As a military tactic, the use of free fire zones proved only marginally effective. Much more significant was the impact on American public opinion, where it became synonymous with the indiscriminate use of American artillery and air power, and thus helped fuel popular doubts concerning America's role in Vietnam.

Sources: Frances FitzGerald, *Fire in the Lake: The Vietnamese and the Americans in Vietnam*, 1972; Raphael Littauer and Norman Uphoff, eds., *The Air War in Indochina*, 1972.

Sean A. Kelleher

FREE KHMER (KHMER ISSARAK, KHMER SEREI)

The Khmer Issarak (Free Khmer) were anti-French Cambodian guerrillas formed in the western provinces of Battambang and Siem Reap (Angkor) with Thai encouragement. Although loosely affiliated with the Vietminh,* the Khmer Issarak were non-Communist. The significance of the Issarak in opposing French colonialism is debated, but they were considerably weaker than the Laotian Pathet Lao.* In 1954 at Geneva,* the Vietminh tried vainly to have Pathet Lao and Khmer Issarak delegations seated, but both were excluded because of Soviet and Chinese pressure.

Toward the end of World War II, at the request of occupying Japanese forces, Prince Sihanouk* named Son Ngoc Thanh as foreign minister and then premier. With Japan's defeat he attempted to seize power, only to be arrested and exiled by the French, who restored Sihanouk as the nominal head of state. Son Thanh joined the Khmer Issarak in Thailand,* but the Issarak dissolved with Cambodia's independence (*see* Kampuchea). Son Thanh then formed the Khmer Serei (also meaning "Free Khmer"), an anti-Sihanouk, anti-Communist guerrilla group with operations based in South Vietnam. Throughout the 1960s the Khmer Serei recruited from non-Communist Phnom Penh elites frustrated by Sihanouk's autocratic rule. Sihanouk's popularity in the countryside, however, made the Khmer Serei, like the Khmer Rouge,* little more than a nuisance for his regime.

Late in 1969 Serei units in South Vietnam "defected" to Sihanouk's army—part of a Central Intelligence Agency* (CIA) plan to undermine his government, according to Sihanouk. There were contacts between the CIA and the Khmer Serei and American military assistance and training for Khmer Serei troops, but it has not been established that the CIA was behind the defection or Sihanouk's overthrow in 1970. After the coup, Lon Nol* embraced the Khmer Serei, but Son Ngoc Thanh chose initially to remain in the field, receiving Lon Nol's permission to attack Vietcong*/ National Liberation Front sanctuaries* in eastern Cambodia. Son Ngoc then recruited forces among South Vietnam's Cambodian population. They were trained by Special Forces* in South Vietnam and flown into Cambodia. Better trained than the Cambodian army and a potential threat to Lon Nol, they were committed to major battles until decimated and eventually wiped out.

Sources: William Shawcross, *Sideshow: Kissinger, Nixon, and the Destruction of Cambodia*, 1979; Philippe Devillers and Jean Lacouture, *End of a War*, 1969; Wilfred Burchett, *The Second Indochina War*, 1970; Ben Kiernan, "How Pol Pot Came to Power: A History of Communism in Kampuchea, 1930–1975," Ph.D. diss., Monash University, 1983.

Samuel Freeman

FREE WORLD MILITARY FORCES

The term "Free World Military Forces" was used to describe those allied nations providing assistance to the Republic of Vietnam* between 1959 and 1975. Including the United States, forty nations provided military and/or economic assistance to South Vietnam. The peak troop commitments from those nations were as follows: 10 from Spain, 30 from Taiwan (*see* Chiang Kai-shek), 550 from New Zealand,* 1,576 from the Philippines,* 7,672 from Australia,* 11,568 from Thailand,* 48,869 from South Korea,* and 540,000 from the United States.

Source: Stanley Robert Larsen and James Lawton Collins, Jr., *Allied Participation in Vietnam*, 1975.

FRENCH EXPEDITIONARY CORPS

The French Expeditionary Corps was first sent to Vietnam in the 1880s, ostensibly to protect French Catholic missionaries. Although there were isolated uprisings periodically, France* colonized and controlled Indochina* for over sixty years with a few thousand soldiers—70,000 in all of Indochina when World War II began. In 1940 the French Expeditionary Corps fought a brief, bloody war with Japan, but then sat out the war after France surrendered to Germany. At the war's end, Great Britain* quickly rearmed French forces. Although this upset Vietnamese hoping for independence, they were more concerned about their ancient enemy's presence (the Chinese) in northern Vietnam. Consequently, Ho Chi Minh* permitted 15,000 French troops to enter northern Vietnam to hasten the Chinese withdrawal. France meanwhile moved to reestablish its Indochina colonies.

Relations between Ho Chi Minh and France deteriorated steadily. On December 6, 1946, the French navy bombarded Haiphong harbor and the First Indochina War began. Initially, less than 20,000 French troops confronted fewer than 50,000 Vietminh* guerrillas, but the numbers changed rapidly. French forces increased to 115,000 men in 1947 and 178,000 in 1954 (including about 30,000 Vietnamese who had been integrated into the French Expeditionary Corps). These forces were augmented by 339,000 indigenous forces. Vietminh strength also grew tremendously, to approximately 375,000 by 1954.

In December 1948, General Jean de Lattre de Tassigny* was appointed commander in chief of the French Expeditionary Corps and high commissioner in Indochina. He established the Vietnamese National Army* which became the largest part of the French Union Forces.* He predicted victory in fifteen months, and in 1950 enjoyed a victory over General Vo Nguyen Giap.* Upon de Lattre's death in January 1952, General Raoul Salan became commander in chief. His command was short-lived but significant, for he reoriented French strategy from maintaining static defensive positions to conducting mobile warfare. He was replaced in 1953 by General Henri Navarre (*see* Navarre Plan), who was perceived as better able to implement this strategy. Navarre had few hopes of winning and simply hoped to keep Laos* and arrange a negotiated settlement. But when Giap invaded Laos, Navarre overextended himself by committing troops to Dien Bien Phu.* Sensing a chance to lure Giap into a pitched battle, Navarre countermanded his mobile warfare strategy and committed the heart of French forces to a remote, poorly defensible valley surrounded by mountains. Contrary to expectations, the Vietminh hauled in heavy artillery and in 1954 defeated Navarre's French Expeditionary Corps at Dien Bien Phu, destroying the French Empire in Indochina.

Sources: Bernard Fall, *Viet Nam Witness*, 1966, and *Hell in a Very Small Place*, 1966; Ellen J. Hammer, *The Struggle for Indochina, 1940–1955*, 1966.

Samuel Freeman

FRENCH UNION FORCES

As World War II began, France* held all of Indochina* with about 70,000 poorly equipped troops. Neither the numbers nor the equipment had changed much by the beginning of the First Indochina War. Trying first to hold its colonies and then to establish (at least in name) autonomous nations within the French Union, France increased the size of the French Expeditionary Corps* (FEC) and, in 1948, established native armies, the largest of which was the Vietnamese National Army* (VNA). FEC and native forces comprised the French Union Forces.

By the spring of 1954, when General Navarre (*see* Navarre Plan) ordered the French stand at Dien Bien Phu,* French Union Forces totaled over 517,000 men, with 178,000 being members of the FEC, and the remaining 339,000 being native Indochinese. Building an army of over 300,000 from scratch in a wartime situation was no small task. Since effective combat leadership cannot be quickly produced, most VNA forces were led by French officers. While this greatly improved their fighting qualities, it hindered French efforts to convince the Vietnamese that France had abandoned its colonialist intentions. It also dramatized the problem of building independent governments (assuming France was truly willing to do so, which is debatable at best).

The French developed a plan later echoed by American military strategists. French units tied down in pacification, communication, transportation, and static defense postures would be replaced with newly trained VNA units, producing a twofold benefit. Battle-seasoned French soldiers could then carry the fight to the Vietminh* on a larger and more intense scale, and increasing the presence of the Vietnamese officials among the people would improve the Vietnamese sense of independence and will to resist "Communist aggression."

Lack of time and resources doomed the plan to failure. Furthermore, the better units of the VNA were integrated into the FEC to compensate for its shortage in manpower, again undercutting the illusion of Vietnamese independence. Despite limited time and resources, however, the Vietnamese National Army and Vietnamese units in the FEC accorded themselves well in battle, often demonstrating fighting skills and heroism equal to those of their French comrades.

Sources: Bernard Fall, *Viet-Nam Witness, 1953–66*; *Hell in a Very Small Place*, 1966; *Street Without Joy*, 1961; Ellen J. Hammer, *The Struggle for Indochina, 1940–1955*, 1966.

Samuel Freeman

"FRIENDLY FIRE"

"Friendly Fire" was a euphemism used during the war in Vietnam to describe air, artillery, or small-arms fire from American forces mistakenly directed at American positions. The term gained national prominence as the title of C.D.B. Bryan's 1976 book *Friendly Fire*, describing the death of Michael E. Mullen in Vietnam on February 18, 1970. Mullen was killed by an accidental American artillery strike, and the telegram to his parents said he had been "at a night defensive position when artillery fire from friendly forces landed on the area." In 1983 a television movie starring Carol Burnett further emphasized the term in the public consciousness.

Source: C.D.B. Bryan, *Friendly Fire*, 1976.

FULBRIGHT, JAMES WILLIAM

J. William Fulbright was born on April 9, 1905, in Sumner, Missouri. He graduated from the University of Arkansas in 1925 and then attended Oxford University as a Rhodes scholar. Fulbright took a law degree from the George Washington University Law School in 1934, and then taught law at George Washington and the University of Arkansas between 1934 and 1939. Fulbright became president of the University of Arkansas in 1939, and in 1942 was elected to Congress.* In 1945 he began a stay in the U.S. Senate which lasted for the next thirty years. In 1959 Fulbright became chairman of the Senate Foreign Relations Committee.* Although he helped Lyndon B. Johnson* shepherd the Gulf of Tonkin Resolution* through Congress in 1964, Fulbright soon became an outspoken critic of U.S. policy in Vietnam. Convinced that there was no such thing as "monolithic communism," Fulbright accused Johnson of confusing Communist aggression with nationalism in Vietnam and urged an American withdrawal. Throughout 1967 and 1968 Fulbright held public hearings of the Senate Foreign Relations Committee, giving critics of American policy in Southeast Asia a high-level forum for expressing their views. Fulbright was defeated in the Arkansas Democrat primary for the Senate in 1974 and returned to the private practice of law.

Sources: Tristram Coffin, *Senator Fulbright: Portrait of a Public Philosopher*, 1966; J. William Fulbright, *The Arrogance of Power*, 1966; *Who's Who in America, 1984–1985*, 1985.

• G •

GALBRAITH, JOHN KENNETH

John Kenneth Galbraith was born on October 15, 1908, on a farm near Iona Station, Ontario, Canada. He graduated from the University of Toronto in 1931 and received a Ph.D. in agricultural economics from the University of California at Berkeley in 1934. Galbraith began teaching at Harvard in 1934, and has remained there except for a stint at Princeton (1939–40), government work during World War II, and the editorial board of *Fortune* magazine (1943–48). He was also U.S. ambassador to India from 1961 to 1963. A prolific writer, Galbraith is the author of *The Affluent Society* (1958), *The New Industrial State* (1967), and *Money* (1977), among other books. A vigorous opponent of the war in Vietnam, Galbraith wrote *A Moderate's View of Vietnam* in 1966, arguing an enclave* policy of withdrawal to the coastal and urban areas which the United States could hold with ease. Once those regions were secure, the United States should open negotiations with Ho Chi Minh.* In 1967 Galbraith repeated those ideas in his book *How to Get Out of Vietnam*. Also in 1967, Galbraith became the chairman of Americans for Democratic Action, and lobbied against the war from that forum. He endorsed the presidential candidacy of Senator Eugene McCarthy* in 1968.

Sources: John Kenneth Galbraith, *A Life in Our Times: Memoirs*, 1981; John S. Gambs, *John Kenneth Galbraith*, 1975.

Kim Younghaus

GAVIN, JAMES

James Gavin was born on March 22, 1907, in New York City. He enlisted in the United States Army in 1924 but the next year was allowed to enroll at West Point, where he graduated in 1929. Gavin rose through the ranks and during World War II won a Silver Star, became an expert in airborne warfare, and earned the rank of lieutenant general. In 1961 President John F. Kennedy* named Gavin ambassador to France,* a post he held until 1963. During the

Vietnam War, Gavin became one of the few American military figures who voiced real misgivings about U.S. policy there. In 1966 Gavin testified before the Senate Foreign Relations Committee* and urged the Johnson* administration to adopt the "enclave strategy"*—stop escalating the war and confine American troops to easily defensible positions in the major cities and coastal locations. In 1968 Gavin published a book, *Crisis Now*, and maintained illusions he could seek the presidency, but those hopes remained impossible. He continued to urge a de-escalation of the conflict.

Sources: *Who's Who in America, 1982–1983*, 1:1174, 1982; James Gavin, *Crisis Now*, 1968; Thomas Powers, *Vietnam, The War at Home*, 1984.

GENEVA ACCORDS OF 1954

After the defeat of French forces at the Battle of Dien Bien Phu* in 1954, an international convention met in Geneva, Switzerland, between May 8 and July 21, 1954, to determine the political future of Indochina.* Delegates from the United States, the Soviet Union,* the People's Republic of China,* Great Britain,* France,* India, the State of Vietnam, the Democratic Republic of Vietnam,* Laos,* and Cambodia (*see* Kampuchea) attended the meetings. For a time the conference tried to work out some method of reuniting North and South Korea,* but all efforts failed. What the conference did manage to do was draft a number of complicated political arrangements for Vietnam. The American delegation was headed by W. Bedell Smith.*

The accords divided Vietnam at the seventeenth parallel into two countries: South Vietnam (Republic of Vietnam)* and North Vietnam (Democratic Republic of Vietnam). With the division in place, the Geneva Accords imposed a cease-fire throughout Vietnam as well as cease-fire provisions for the peaceful withdrawal of French forces from North Vietnam and Vietminh* forces from South Vietnam. New foreign troop placements were prohibited throughout Vietnam, and all troops were to be withdrawn from Laos and Cambodia. Finally, provisions were made for free elections in both North and South Vietnam in 1956, with the goal of reunification and elimination of the artificial barrier at the seventeenth parallel. An International Supervisory Commission composed of representatives from India, Canada, and Poland was established to monitor compliance with the accords. Although the United States did not sign the accords, it did agree with them and promised to avoid the use of military force in the area and to support the principle of self-determination throughout Indochina. South Vietnamese representatives also neglected to sign the accords but nevertheless expressed public support for its major provisions. By not signing the agreement, the United States had the advantage of appearing supportive without being bound by its provisions. Two years after the Geneva Conference, when it appeared that the followers of Ho Chi Minh* had majority support in North as well as South Vietnam, the United States scuttled the free elections and threw all of its economic and military support behind the South Vietnamese regime.

Sources: Robert F. Randle, *Geneva 1954*, 1969; Arnold R. Isaacs, *Without Honor: Defeat in Vietnam and Cambodia*, 1983.

GENEVA CONFERENCE OF 1954   *See* Geneva Accords of 1954

GENOVESE, EUGENE DOMINICK

Eugene Genovese was born on May 19, 1930, in Brooklyn, New York. He received a B.A. from Brooklyn College in 1955 and the M.A. and Ph.D. from Columbia University in 1956 and 1959. Genovese taught history at the Brooklyn Polytechnic Institute from 1958 to 1963. He joined the faculty of Rutgers University in 1963 and published his first book—*The Political Economy of Slavery*—in 1965. Known as a "neo-Marxist," Genovese came to national political attention in 1967 and 1968 when he protested American involvement in the Vietnam War and described the Vietcong* as a nationalistically inspired people trying to liberate their homeland from foreign domination. The ensuing controversy caused Genovese political problems at Rutgers, and he accepted a position at Sir George Williams University in Montreal in 1967. In 1969 he joined the faculty of the University of Rochester. He subsequently became one of the most well-known American historians, not just because of his politics but because of the quality of his research and writing. Genovese's books *The World the Slaveholders Made* (1969) and *Roll, Jordan, Roll* (1974) helped reshape the way American historians viewed slavery and the South.

Source: *Who's Who in America, 1984–1985*, 1985.

GIA LONG

Born in 1762 as Nguyen Phuc Anh, he became emperor of Vietnam in 1802 and adopted the name of Gia Long. With the help of French missionary Pigneau de Behaine, Nguyen Anh escaped Vietnam during the Tay Son Rebellion* and was the only surviving heir to the Nguyen* throne. In 1787, Nguyen Anh secured French assistance in crushing the Tay Son Rebellion. In return he promised unrestricted trade for the French in Cochin China.* After years of struggle, Nguyen Anh's forces defeated the Tay Son and seized control of Vietnam in 1802. Nguyen Anh then adopted the name Gia Long and established the Nguyen dynasty, which lasted until the abdication of Bao Dai* in 1955. Gia Long moved the capital of Vietnam from Hanoi* to Hue,* constructed public granaries and a working postal system, repaired the Old Mandarin Road, and brought Cambodia (*see* Kampuchea) under control as a vassal state. Gia Long died in 1820.

Sources: *Webster's New Biographical Dictionary*, 1983; Joseph Buttinger, *The Smaller Dragon: A Political History of Vietnam*, 1958.

GOING AFTER CACCIATO

Going After Cacciato is the title of Tim O'Brien's 1978 Vietnam War novel. The central character is Specialist Fourth Class Paul Berlin, who leads a cast of soldiers and Vietnamese civilians (Doc Peret, Sarkin Aung Wan, Corson, Oscar

Johnson, Eddie Lazutti, and Stink Harris) on a surrealistic pursuit of Private Cacciato, who leaves their base camp in Quang Ngai Province and goes AWOL. Cacciato then leads his pursuers on a trancelike trek across the Laotian border, through Burma, India, Afghanistan, Iran, Turkey, Greece, Yugoslavia, Austria, East and West Germany,* and France* into Paris. On the way they expose the absurdity of the war.

Sources: Tim O'Brien, *Going after Cacciato*, 1978; Philip D. Beidler, *American Literature and the Experience of Vietnam*, 1982.

GOLDBERG, ARTHUR JOSEPH

As U.S. ambassador to the United Nations (UN) from July 1965 to April 1968, Goldberg believed the Vietnam War could end only through negotiations, not continued application of force. Born in 1908 in Chicago, he worked his way through Northwestern's undergraduate and law schools and began practicing corporate and labor law in 1929. After service in the OSS during World War II, Goldberg became general counsel of the United Steelworkers and the CIO (the AFL-CIO after the 1955 merger) until tapped by President Kennedy* to serve as secretary of labor in 1961.

Kennedy appointed him to the Supreme Court the following year, and Goldberg voted with the Warren Court's "liberal" bloc until his lifelong interest in foreign affairs and concern with the direction of the war persuaded him to accept President Johnson's* offer of the UN post in July 1965. Uninformed by the White House on many critical decisions and thus often operating at odds with Johnson's Vietnam policy, Ambassador Goldberg focused his attention on finding a way to begin peace talks between Washington and Hanoi.* Although he failed to win administration accommodation to his views in that effort, Goldberg did participate in the March 1968 sessions of the "Wise Old Men,"* who reassessed Vietnam policy, recommended a bombing halt, and persuaded Johnson to announce a de-escalation at the end of the month.

Goldberg left the administration in April 1968, and Johnson responded with a cold letter that failed to praise the ambassador for his UN efforts. Goldberg then publicly broke with U.S. policy and later spoke out vigorously at the October 1969 Moratorium Day demonstrations* in Washington and other rallies.

Sources: David Halberstam, *The Best and the Brightest*, 1972; Stanley Karnow, *Vietnam: A History*, 1983; *New York Times*, 1964–1975; *Guide to the U.S. Supreme Court*, 1979.

                                                                                    Dudley Acker

GOLDWATER, BARRY MORRIS

Barry M. Goldwater was born in Phoenix, Arizona, on January 1, 1909. He attended the University of Arizona for a year after leaving high school but then worked in the family department store business. Goldwater saw active duty with the Army Air Corps as a pilot during World War II in the Asian theater. A conservative Republican, Goldwater was elected to the U.S. Senate in 1952, and in 1964 he won the Republican nomination for president. It was an inauspicious time for conservative Republicans, and Lyndon B. Johnson* defeated Goldwater in a landslide. During the election, Goldwater had adopted a very "hawkish" position on the U.S. role in Vietnam, and throughout the course of the war he argued that the United States should be willing to make a major military commitment—whatever it took, short of nuclear weapons—to support American soldiers in the field or should withdraw from the conflict. Because of the presidential nomination, Goldwater did not run for reelection to the Senate in 1964, but he was reelected in 1968, 1974, and 1980. During his Senate career, Goldwater was a vigorous supporter of a strong military effort in Vietnam and the government of South Vietnam. In the closing stages of the conflict, Goldwater called for large-scale bombing* of North Vietnam and increased financial assistance to South Vietnam. In 1986, Barry Goldwater decided not to seek reelection, and he retired from public life in 1987.

Source: Barry M. Goldwater, *With No Apologies: The Personal and Political Memoirs of United States Senator Barry Morris Goldwater*, 1979.

GO TELL THE SPARTANS

Based on Daniel Ford's novel, *Incident at Muc Wa,* Go Tell the Spartans* is perhaps the best film yet on the Vietnam War. Set in 1964 when the U.S. effort was still "advisory," it captures significant issues of the war honestly and accurately. Unlike *The Deer Hunter* and *Apocalypse Now*, *Go Tell the Spartans* presents the racism of American involvement without being racist. Rather than some film producer's imaginings of what the war was like, it presents a view Vietnam veterans, especially advisers, can relate to as truthful. The film opens with a Vietcong* suspect enduring water torture at a Regional Forces*–Popular Forces* (RF/PF) base camp. Against his better judgment, the senior American adviser is ordered to occupy a former French position at Muc Wa where over 300 French soldiers had been killed by the Vietminh* in 1953. The film then centers on the RF-PF forces and their American advisers who quickly are besieged and overrun. The significant issues captured include American contempt for the French; the role of civilians as Vietcong sympathizers; the patriotic naïveté of American forces; the arrogance of senior U.S. officers; the way in which ground was taken one day and given up the next; the emphasis on psychological operations, intelligence reports, and high-tech warfare; the sober realization of some experienced American officers and NCOs who were totally frustrated by the war; the corruption and incompetence of South Vietnamese officials; the mixed quality of South Vietnamese forces; the brutality and heroism of both South Vietnamese and American forces; and the sheer terror of night combat. Released in 1978, *Go Tell the Spartans* starred Burt Lancaster as Major Asa

Barker, the commander of a Military Advisory and Assistance Group* in Penang, South Vietnam.

Source: *Magill's Survey of Cinema. English Language Films*, 1981.

Samuel Freeman

GRAVEL, MIKE

Mike Gravel was born in Springfield, Massachusetts, on May 13, 1930. He spent one year at American International College before entering the United States Army in 1951, where he served in Germany and France. Gravel graduated from Columbia University in 1956 with a degree in economics and moved to Alaska. He won a seat in the Alaska House of Representatives in 1962, and he defeated Senator Ernest Gruening,* one of the earliest critics of the Vietnam War, in the Democratic primary. Ironically, *Time* called Gravel "hawkish" in the campaign. Gravel won the general election and eventually became an increasingly outspoken critic of the Vietnam War with the reputation as a Senate maverick. In 1971 Gravel tried unsuccessfully to read the Pentagon Papers* in the Senate chamber. Then, on June 29, 1971, Gravel convened a late session of the Building and Grounds subcommittee which he chaired. For the next three hours he read from the Pentagon Papers, sometimes crying and sobbing. Many senators opposed his actions. Subsequently, he arranged with Beacon Press to publish *The Senator Gravel Edition of the Pentagon Papers* in four volumes. Gravel also made public a copy of National Security Study Memorandum No. 1, which Daniel Ellsberg* had provided him.

Gravel's opposition to the war continued. He opposed extension of the draft* and advocated equal air time from the media to counter the Nixon* administration's position on the war. He worked to organize a War No More group. Gravel criticized Vietnamization* as "a plan to keep on our involvement for decades until we win." In 1972 Gravel tried unsuccessfully to have the Senate vote on a declaration of war against North Vietnam and to persuade the Senate to publish, in the *Congressional Record*, a secret Nixon administration study of U.S. bombing* effectiveness in Vietnam. Gravel won reelection in 1974, but he lost the senatorial primary in 1980 to Clark Gruening, Ernest's grandson.

Sources: *Biographical Directory of the American Congress, 1789–1971*, 1972; *New York Times*, November 7, 1980.

James Hindman

GREAT BRITAIN

Ever since 1945 the British have adopted a policy of relative noninvolvement with Indochina.* They were preoccupied with a contraction of their own responsibilities east of the Suez Canal; were bogged down in a counterinsurgency effort in Malaysia; were undergoing substantial reductions in defense expenditures because of economic problems; were entertaining hopes of expanding trade with Communist-bloc nations; and were dealing with a powerful left-wing movement at home which resented military adventures abroad. All these problems precluded active British intervention in the problems of Vietnam.

In 1945, in order to free American troops for the anticipated invasion of Japan, the British took the Japanese surrender in Indochina, disarmed the enemy, and reestablished the prewar supremacy of the French. The British commander, Major General Douglas Gracey, actually used, however, a combined force of British and Japanese troops to fight the Vietminh,* who were preparing to resist any reimposition of Western control over Vietnam. Still, on March 5, 1946, the British disengaged from the area. Eight years later, when President Dwight Eisenhower* sought British support for an American air strike at Dien Bien Phu,* Prime Minister Winston Churchill refused, pragmatically arguing that air strikes would accomplish little since most of Indochina was already under Vietminh control. He preferred a diplomatic solution.

In 1954, Great Britain cochaired the Geneva Conference (*see* Geneva Accords) on Vietnam, where they supported the American proposal for a division of Vietnam at the seventeenth parallel, with reunification elections to be held in two years. Privately, the British hoped, like the Americans, that the seventeenth parallel would become a recognized and permanent international boundary, with the South remaining non-Communist, out of the control of the Vietminh. When it appeared obvious that such elections would endorse the demands of Ho Chi Minh* and the Vietminh, Britain supported the U.S. decision to stall and delay those elections.

As the American involvement escalated during the Lyndon B. Johnson* administration, Prime Minister Harold Wilson refused all American requests for military support. The British sense that the United States would not prevail against the Vietcong* persisted. Sensitive to the "special relationship" that Britain had with the United States in the postwar era, but also harassed by strongly leftist elements in his own Labor party who vocally condemned the war, Wilson maintained a delicate balance between 1964 and 1970. His government gave verbal support to American policy in Southeast Asia generally, while privately calling for an end to the bombing of North Vietnam and a negotiated settlement. Wilson's conservative successor, Edward Heath, continued the policy of limited support but no formal participation.

Britain did serve, however, as an important conduit for contact between the United States and the Soviet Union.* Harold Wilson consulted frequently with Soviet leaders. The United States frequently used the British government as a sounding board, and to either convey negotiating positions to or to try to bring pressure on North Vietnam through the Soviet Union. Such contacts availed little because the United States greatly exaggerated the amount of influence the Soviet Union had with the North Vietnamese.

Sources: Harold Wilson, *A Personal Record: The Labour Government, 1964–1970*, 1971; Max Beloff, *The Future of British Foreign Policy*, 1969; J. H. Weiner and J. H. Plumb, *Great Britain: Foreign Policy and the Span of Empire, 1689–1971*. A Docu-

mentary History, 1972; George Rosie, *The British in Vietnam: How the Twenty-five Years War Began*, 1970.

Gary M. Bell

GREAT SOCIETY

The term "Great Society" became the historical description of the domestic reforms of the Lyndon B. Johnson* administration. In his 1964 State of the Union address, Johnson declared a "war on poverty," and in an address at the University of Michigan in May 1964, Johnson spoke of "the opportunity to move not only toward the rich society and the powerful society but upward to the Great Society." The Great Society, he argued, "rests on abundance and liberty for all. It demands an end to poverty and racial injustice—to which we are totally committed." The Civil Rights Act of 1964, the Voting Rights Act of 1965, the antipoverty campaign of the mid–1960s, and the Civil Rights Act of 1968 were all part of the Great Society. Eventually, the Great Society reforms, which were Johnson's favorites, ran up against the demands of the Vietnam War, which Johnson hated. His decision to continue funding domestic reforms along with increased military funding without a tax increase fueled inflation and made him even more politically vulnerable. Lyndon Johnson's Great Society died in the jungles of Vietnam.

Sources: Lawrence S. Wittner, *Cold War America. From Hiroshima to Watergate*, 1974; Doris Kearns, *Lyndon Johnson and the American Dream*, 1976.

GREEN BERETS   *See* Special Forces

THE GREEN BERETS

Robin Moore's 1965 novel *The Green Berets* was a naive but temporarily popular novel about the American war effort in Vietnam. In the book, U.S. Special Forces* troops appear as the "good guys" out to rescue South Vietnam from its own incompetence and the immoral aggression of the Vietcong* and the North Vietnamese. South Vietnamese army officers appear cowardly and venal and ARVN (*see* Army of the Republic of Vietnam) troops unreliable and quick to desert when facing combat. The Vietcong and North Vietnamese are depicted as uniformly venal and evil, bent on torture, murder, and atrocity. The book also celebrates the genius of American technology and the virtues of American democracy and capitalism. In short, *The Green Berets* is a "World War II" novel about the Vietnam war. By 1966, as the antiwar movement* gained momentum in the United States, Robin Moore's novel quickly lost credibility, becoming almost a ludicrous caricature of U.S. policy in Vietnam.

Sources: Robin Moore, *The Green Berets*, 1965; Philip D. Beidler, *American Literature and the Experience of Vietnam*, 1982.

THE GREEN BERETS

Written in 1965 when the Vietnam War was just underway at its escalated level, but released in 1968 when the antiwar movement* was at its peak, *The*

Green Berets starred John Wayne as the Green Beret (*see* Special Forces) colonel, David Janssen as a jaded journalist, and Jim Hutton as the naive, big-hearted American GI out to save the world. The film was loaded with World War II clichés, with the Vietcong* portrayed as universal savages and the Americans and South Vietnamese characterized as the epitome of goodness and mercy. Of all the films of the Vietnam era, none was a better reflection of U.S. policies in 1965, at the beginning of the conflict.

Source: *Magill's Survey of Cinema. English Language Films*, 1981.

GREENE, WALLACE MARTIN, JR.

During his tour as commandant of the Marine Corps* (1964–68), Greene became a strong public advocate of U.S. policy in Vietnam. Born in Vermont in 1907, he attended the University of Vermont for a year before entering Annapolis and taking a Marine Corps commission in 1930. In the thirties he served aboard ship, on Guam, and in China, then advanced rapidly as a staff officer in the Pacific, receiving the Legion of Merit for planning the Marshall Islands invasions in 1944. After the war he served as assistant chief of staff, Fleet Marine Force, Pacific Command* (1948–50), then on the staff of the Marine Corps Schools for two years before graduating from the National War College in 1953. Greene next served on the Joint Chiefs of Staff (*see* Chairman, JCS) for two years, becoming assistant commander of the Second Marine Division in 1955 and commander of Parris Island and Camp Lejeune in 1957. When President Kennedy* selected him to succeed David M. Shoup* in 1963, Greene had just completed four years as chief of staff of the Marine Corps.

With his troops committed to defensive tactics around Da Nang,* Phu Bai, and Chu Lai* in the late spring of 1965, Greene publicly pushed for an expanded combat role, one in which marines would not be ''sitting around on their diddybox.'' Thereafter Greene spoke optimistically of U.S. prospects in Vietnam, promoting the Combined Action Platoons,* yet acknowledging that pacification (*see* Rural Reconstruction) would take about a decade to accomplish. He retired in January 1968, on the eve of the Tet Offensive.

Sources: Robert Moskin, *The United States Marine Corps Story*, 1982; Allen R. Millett, *Semper Fidelis: The History of the United States Marine Corps*, 1980.

Dudley Acker

GROUP

A group in the United States Army* is a system of command controlling several battalions.* Subordinate to a brigade,* a group is usually part of support commands. Most commonly they are commanded by a colonel.

Source: Harry G. Summers, Jr., *Vietnam War Almanac*, 1985.

GRUENING, ERNEST HENRY

Elected to the U.S. Senate in 1959 when Alaska became a state, Gruening entered the Senate with a diverse background. Born in New York in 1887, he studied medicine but spent much of his career as a journalist, working as an editor and writer for a number of publications, including the *Nation* magazine. A major interest was Latin America, and he crusaded against U.S. military intervention and what he saw as financial exploitation in Central and South America. In the mid–1930s, he turned to government service, eventually being appointed governor of Alaska by President Franklin Roosevelt.* He became a leader of the Alaskan statehood movement.

In the Senate, Gruening, a liberal Democrat, was one of the first to question U.S. involvement in Vietnam. In a speech on March 10, 1964, Gruening deplored the waste of American lives and resources "in seeking vainly in this remote jungle to shore up self-serving corrupt dynasties or their self-imposed successors, and a people that has demonstrated that it has no will to save itself." He said that "all Vietnam is not worth the life of a single American boy" and that the loss of any American lives in Vietnam would some day "be denounced as a crime." Later that year he joined Senator Wayne Morse* in casting the only votes against the Gulf of Tonkin Resolution,* which Gruening said subverted the Constitution by giving the president "warmaking powers in the absence of a declaration of war." He remained in the Senate through 1968 and consistently opposed appropriations to support the war. He blamed his defeat by Mike Gravel* in the 1968 Democratic primary on his opposition to the war. Ironically, as a Senator, Gravel eventually became an outspoken opponent of the war. After leaving the Senate, Gruening coauthored a book, *Vietnam Folly*, calling for an "end of the folly of America's intervention and the return by the United States to principles which it has long cherished." Gruening died on June 26, 1974.

Sources: Joseph C. Goulden, *Truth Is the First Casualty*, 1969; Ernest Gruening and Herbert B. Beaser, *Vietnam Folly*, 1968; *New York Times*, June 27, 1974.

Hoyt Purvis

GUAM CONFERENCE OF 1967

In 1967 President Lyndon B. Johnson* decided to hold a high-level conference on Guam. Guam was secure yet near Saigon,* symbolized American Pacific interests, and had represented American power because of the B–52s* stationed there. Johnson, Secretary of State Dean Rusk,* Secretary of Defense Robert McNamara,* and a number of military advisers and reporters made the 16,000-mile trip to the March 20–21, 1967, conference. Ambassador Henry Cabot Lodge,* Premier Nguyen Cao Ky,* and President Nguyen Van Thieu* came from Saigon. They met at the Officers' Club on Nimitz Hill.

The president called the meeting for several reasons. He wanted to demonstrate American resolve in continuing the war effort and to introduce new personnel to the South Vietnamese leaders. In particular, Ellsworth Bunker* would replace Lodge as ambassador; Eugene Locke, a presidential friend and ambassador to Pakistan, would become Bunker's assistant; Robert Komer* would become the new deputy for Civil Operations and Revolutionary Development Support* to direct the pacification effort (*see* Rural Reconstruction); and General Creighton

W. Abrams* would become William Westmoreland's* deputy and eventual successor. At the conference, Westmoreland presented his request for 200,000 more troops, but the president, pressured by McNamara to be cautious, agreed to only 55,000 new troops. Ky and Thieu brought the new South Vietnamese constitution, just completed by the Constituent Assembly, to satisfy Johnson that they were making progress toward democracy. Ky also called for increased bombing sorties* against sanctuaries* and supply routes in Laos* and Cambodia (see Kampuchea). The president refused, and the Guam Conference became little more than a public relations event.

Source: *New York Times*, March 21–23, 1967.

James Hindman

GUERRILLAS   *See* Vietcong

GULF OF TONKIN INCIDENT (1964)
By August 1964, the United States Navy* was supporting South Vietnam's fight against North Vietnam in two programs. Operations Plan (OPLAN) 34 involved South Vietnamese naval and marine forces raiding North Vietnamese coastal installations with American advice and logistical support. Operation DeSoto involved American naval vessels patrolling international waters off the coast of North Vietnam to observe the North Vietnamese Navy and probe the North Vietnamese radar capabilities by electronic surveillance. The destroyer USS *Maddox*,* patrolling 28 miles off the North Vietnamese coast as part of DeSoto, came under attack by three North Vietnamese torpedo boats on August 2. An OPLAN 34 raid against the torpedo boat base at Loc Chao had taken place on the night of July 31, and this probably precipitated the attack on the American destroyer. The *Maddox* fired warning shots, but the torpedo boats continued attacking by launching two torpedoes. These were avoided and fire from the destroyer damaged one of the torpedo boats. Four Vought F–8E Crusaders, on patrol from the carrier USS *Ticonderoga*,* came to assist the *Maddox*. The destroyer division commander on board the *Maddox* orderd the aircraft to attack the now-retiring torpedo boats. Several strafing runs with 20mm cannons and rocket attacks with 5-inch Zuni rockets resulted in the sinking of the already-damaged torpedo boat. The destroyer USS *C. Turner Joy*,* joined the *Maddox* and the carrier USS *Constellation* proceeded to the area from Hong Kong. The two destroyers retired to an area 100 miles off the coast, and combat air patrols began.

On the evening of August 4, in very poor weather conditions, the *Maddox* identified five high-speed radar contacts as North Vietnamese torpedo boats. The details of the engagement are somewhat confused, but American naval personnel were convinced they were being attacked, reporting several torpedo wakes while maneuvering in the darkness. The *Ticonderoga* sent two Douglas A–1 Skyraiders* to assist, and between the aircraft and destroyers two torpedo boats were reported destroyed and two damaged. President Johnson* ordered retaliatory air strikes against four North Vietnamese torpedo boat bases on August 5. Aircraft from the *Ticonderoga* and *Constellation* destroyed twenty-five boats and severely damaged the support facilities. The boats destroyed amounted to one-half of the total North Vietnamese torpedo boat strength. Two American aircraft were shot down by antiaircraft fire and two were damaged. An A–4* pilot became the first American prisoner of war* in North Vietnam. On August 7, 1964, both houses of Congress* passed the Gulf of Tonkin Resolution.*

Sources: Tom Carhart, *Battles and Campaigns in Vietnam*, 1984; *Jane's Fighting Ships 1976–77*, 1978; Joseph C. Goulden, *Truth Is the First Casualty: The Gulf of Tonkin Affair—Illusion and Reality*, 1969.

Charles Angel

GULF OF TONKIN RESOLUTION

On August 4, 1964, the USS *Maddox** and its companion destroyer, the USS *C. Turner Joy*,* were ordered to the Gulf of Tonkin for electronic surveillance of North Vietnam. At 9:12 P.M. the Combat Information Center (CIC) reported the detection of fast-closing targets, apparently the repeat of an attack two days before by three North Vietnamese torpedo boats. The sonar man reported that torpedoes were in the water. At that time the *C. Turner Joy* opened fire, but the *Maddox* found no target, not even the *C. Turner Joy*. Before midnight the *Maddox* was ordered to open fire, but Patrick N. Parks, standing in the main gun director, refused to do so until he heard from the *C. Turner Joy*. The *C. Turner Joy* turned out to be the proposed target of the *Maddox*.

The attack by the North Vietnamese boats on the *Maddox* on August 2, 1964, and the supposed engagement between the *Maddox*, *C. Turner Joy*, and North Vietnamese vessels on August 4, 1964, marked the turning point in the Vietnam War. In retaliation U.S. bombers swept over North Vietnam for the first time, attacking patrol-boat bases and large oil-storage depots.

President Lyndon B. Johnson* found the Gulf of Tonkin incident* politically useful because it justified a large-scale American attack on North Vietnam, boosted South Vietnamese morale, and rallied support back at home. On August 7, 1964, Congress* passed a resolution stating that "the Congress approves and supports the determination of the President as Commander in Chief, to take all necessary measures to repel any armed attack against the forces of the United States and to prevent further aggression. . . . '' The resolution also gave the president authority to provide military assistance to any member or protocol nation of the Southeast Asia Collective Defense Treaty. The power of the resolution would expire when the president had decided that the security of the area was reasonably assured. It passed by a 416–0 vote in the House and 88–2 in the Senate. President Johnson then used the Gulf of Tonkin Resolution as his congressional authority to conduct the war in Vietnam. Six years later President Richard Nixon* used the Gulf of Tonkin Resolution to justify the invasion of Laos (*see* Lam Son 719) and Cambodia (*see* Operation Binh Tay). In the ensuing political uproar during 1970, Congress repealed the Resolution.

Sources: Joseph C. Goulden, *Truth Is the First Casualty: The Gulf of Tonkin Affair—Illusion and Reality*, 1969; Eugene Windchy, *A Documentary of the Tonkin Gulf on August 2 and August 4, 1964 and Their Consequences*, 1971.

Terry Martin

"GUNS AND BUTTER"

The term "guns and butter" was used frequently during the Vietnam War to refer to the problem of financing domestic reform programs while conducting an expensive war. President Lyndon B. Johnson's* major preoccupation was his Great Society plan to extend the net of social welfare assistance to every needy group in American society while eliminating racial, ethnic, and religious discrimination. But the attempt to maintain government spending on behalf of Great Society reforms, when combined with the enormous cost of the Vietnam War, contributed to the severe inflationary cycle of the 1970s and early 1980s. Between 1965 and 1968, when the Vietnam War assumed larger and larger dimensions, defense spending, measured in constant dollars, increased by 43 percent while government transfer payments to individuals grew by 39 percent. That was "guns and butter" policy. The unemployment rate fell to 3.8 percent in 1966, while the rate of inflation went from 1.7 to 2.9 percent. By 1969 the unemployment rate had dropped again, this time to 3.6 percent, but the inflation rate had gone to 5.4 percent. To deal with rising prices, Congress* enacted a 10 percent income tax surcharge in 1968, but the $6 billion in savings was offset by lenient monetary policies. The money supply grew by 2.8 percent in 1966 but by 6.4 percent in 1967 and 7.3 percent in 1968. By then the inflation problem was set in place.

President Richard Nixon* came into the White House in 1969 committed to reducing inflation, but he too was baffled by the problem. Defense spending as a percentage of the gross national product began to subside, from 9.5 in 1968 to 5.0 percent in 1978, but the reduction was replaced by concomitant increases in spending for Medicare, Social Security, retirement, and unemployment programs. In August 1971, President Nixon took desperate measures to control inflation by imposing wage and price restrictions and devaluing the dollar. But over the next two years, the value of the dollar dropped by more than 25 percent, increasing the prices of American imports as well as the inflation rate. The wage and price controls were ineffective. The Arab oil embargo of 1973 and subsequent dramatic increases in the price of OPEC oil only exacerbated the problem, creating the spiraling prices of the 1970s.

Source: Kenneth Bacon, "Vietnam's Legacy," *Wall Street Journal*, April 30, 1985.

GUNSHIPS

During the Vietnam War, the United States Air Force* used gunships to attack North Vietnamese and Vietcong* supply lines as well as to provide close air support for American and ARVN forces (*see* Army of the Republic of Vietnam). The air force converted three aircraft into fixed-wing gunships: C–47 Gooneybird aircraft were equipped with 7.62mm Gatling machine guns and redesignated AC–47,* also known as "Puff the Magic Dragon"; AC–119 Flying Boxcars were also equipped with 7.62mm Gatling guns; and C–130 Hercules* planes were converted to AC–130* gunships by the addition of 7.62mm Gatling guns, Vulcan Gatling guns, and 40mm Bofors cannons.

Sources: William W. Momyer, *Airpower in Three Wars*, 1978; Jack S. Ballard, *The United States Air Force in Southeast Asia: Fixed Wing Gunships, 1962–1972*, 1982.

GVN   *See* Republic of Vietnam

· H ·

HAIG, ALEXANDER MEIGS, JR.

Alexander Meigs Haig, Jr., was born on December 2, 1924. He graduated from West Point in 1947, and for a time in 1948 he worked on General Douglas MacArthur's* staff in Tokyo. There he learned a lifelong disdain for journalists and for civilian authority. After Korea, Haig spent a decade in obscure army posts, and in 1961 he earned a master's degree in international relations at Georgetown University. The theme of his master's thesis was "the role of the military man in the making of national security policy." It advocated a military czar permanently at the president's side advising on military challenges.

In 1963 Haig was chosen by Joseph Califano to work as military assistant to Secretary of the Army Cyrus R. Vance.* When Vance was appointed deputy secretary of defense under Robert S. McNamara* in 1964, Haig remained with him, becoming deputy special assistant to both the secretary and deputy secretary of defense. He became McNamara's right hand, responsible for liaison between his office and the president's office. In 1964 McNamara and his aides were steadily involved in plans for covert raids against North Vietnam and in readying U.S. escalation. He was an advocate of strong military presence in South Vietnam.

Haig arrived in Vietnam in July 1966 as G–3, an operations planning officer for the 1st Infantry Division* at Lai Khe just north of Saigon.* While there he was awarded three Distinguished Flying Crosses. As commander of the First Battalion of the 26th Infantry Regiment, he led a surprise assault on Ben Suc,* a Vietcong* refuge in the Iron Triangle.* In June 1967 Haig came home, was promoted to colonel, and received command of a cadet regiment at West Point. Late in 1968 he got a call from Henry Kissinger* to join the White House staff as his military adviser on the National Security Council. Among other duties, he screened all intelligence information to the president. Although few people knew his name, insiders began to recognize Haig as one of the most important people in Washington, D.C. By 1970 he had acquired direct access to President Richard M. Nixon* as well as the authority to conduct presidential briefings in Kissinger's absence. On September 7, 1972, Nixon promoted Haig over the heads of 240 senior officers to four-star general rank. At the same time he was designated vice-chief of staff of the United States Army.*

Haig played a central part in the final settlement with Hanoi* by convincing Nixon that his survival in office was more important than how Vietnam came out. In the peace negotiations of October 1972, Kissinger and Haig fought a war of telegrams over the settlement. Haig thought Kissinger was going too far and giving up too much. Haig advocated the 1972 Christmas bombings (*see* Operation Linebacker II) of Hanoi and Haiphong and personally delivered the ultimatum to Nguyen Van Thieu* to accept the peace agreement. In May 1973 Haig became permanent assistant to President Nixon. His power was so extensive during the Watergate* crisis that Special Prosecutor Leon Jaworski called him the country's 37½th president.

Remarkably, Haig emerged from Watergate unscathed. Journalist Jules Witcover described his actions in getting Nixon to resign as a bloodless presidential coup. Haig continued as a national security adviser to President Gerald Ford* and then returned to power in Washington as secretary of state in the first Reagan administration. In 1986 Haig was giving serious consideration to making a run for the Republican presidential nomination in the election of 1988.

Source: Roger Morris, *Haig: The General's Progress*, 1982.

Frances Frenzel

HAIPHONG HARBOR, MINING OF

Haiphong is the major port and third largest city in North Vietnam. The bulk of North Vietnam's imports arrive through the port of Haiphong, which is connected by railroad with Hanoi.* During the Vietnam War, Haiphong was a major supply depot and was heavily bombed from 1965 until 1968, when bombing* was curtailed by President Johnson.* During the attacks, much of the population was evacuated and the industry dispersed.

In 1972, the Nixon* administration sparked a major controversy when the president ordered the renewal of bombing of Hanoi and Haiphong (April 16) and the mining of Haiphong Harbor as well as other harbors and inland waterways in North Vietnam (May 9). Also, U.S. naval forces intensified raids against coastal installations and put into effect a naval blockade of the North Vietnamese coastline. In a televised speech to the nation on May 8, 1972, Nixon justified his escalation of the air and sea war as necessary to cut off the flow of supplies to North Vietnamese troops fighting in the South and to protect the lives of American forces still in Vietnam. In addition, Nixon contended that the raids and the minings were intended to pressure the North Vietnamese government into resuming serious negotiations to achieve peace in Vietnam.

In Congress,* most Republican conservatives defended the president's actions, but moderate Republicans joined with the Democratic majority's criticism of the escalation. Resolutions were introduced to end all U.S. involvement in Southeast Asia (*see* War Powers Resolution, 1973). Across the country, Nixon's actions revived the dormant antiwar movement,* and protest demonstrations were renewed.

Source: *Facts on File*, April-May 1972.

Joseph M. Rowe, Jr.

HAI VAN PASS

Highway 1 (*see* "Street Without Joy"), the main supply route along the north-south axis in South Vietnam, connected the port cities of Chu Lai and Da Nang* with Hue,* Quang Tri, and the areas south of the Demilitarized Zone.* Highway 1 ran through the Hai Van Pass at the boundary between Quang Nam and Thua Tien provinces. The supply line was critical to the American war effort, and over the years the army invested considerable effort in keeping it open, particularly when bad weather made aerial resupply of American troops impossible.

Source: Harry G. Summers, Jr., *Vietnam War Almanac*, 1985.

HALBERSTAM, DAVID

As a reporter for the *New York Times*, Halberstam won a Pulitzer Prize for his coverage of Vietnam, where he was a correspondent, 1962–64. He was a penetrating critic of the war, but in the early stages of American military involvement he said that Vietnam was a legitimate part of America's global commitment and as "a strategic country in a key area, it is perhaps one of only five or six nations in the world that are truly vital to U.S. interests." He said, "We want stability for these people, whereas the Communists actively promote inconstancy. So, we cannot abandon our efforts to help these people." However, he insisted that Americans should understand the difficult and complex nature of the struggle in Vietnam, and he told the truth by American officials. These were the themes of his book, *The Making of a Quagmire*, published in 1965. Halberstam and some of his colleagues reported on the deteriorating military situation and the problems facing the South Vietnamese government. Halberstam was criticized for his reporting of these developments in Vietnam and along with other journalists was subjected to pressure from both Washington and the Vietnamese government. President Kennedy* suggested to *Times* publisher Arthur O. Sulzberger in October 1963 that Halberstam should be removed from the Vietnam assignment because he was "too close to the story." Sulzberger refused, although Halberstam did leave Vietnam in 1964.

Born in New York in 1934, Halberstam was a Harvard graduate who joined the *Times* in 1960. In 1967 he left the *Times*. He wrote for *Harper's* magazine, and later wrote several acclaimed books including *The Best and the Brightest*, a critique of American policy in Vietnam and of American policymakers.

Sources: David Halberstam, *The Making of a Quagmire*, 1965, and *The Best and the Brightest*, 1972.

Hoyt Purvis

HALPERIN, MORTON

Morton Halperin was born in Brooklyn in 1938. He graduated from Columbia University in 1958 and earned a Ph.D. in political science from Yale in 1961. After working for the Center for International Affairs at Harvard between 1960 and 1966, Halperin went to work for the secretary of defense. The next year he became deputy assistant secretary of defense. Halperin was widely recognized as an expert in arms control, having written a number of books on the subject, including *Nuclear Weapons and Limited War*, 1960; *Strategy and Arms Control*, 1961; *A Proposal for a Ban on the Use of Nuclear Weapons*, 1961; *Arms Control and Inadvertent General War*, 1962; and *Limited War in the Nuclear Age*, 1963. Halperin quickly emerged as a critic of American policy in Vietnam, especially such domestic political imperatives as fear of appearing soft on communism, which brought about the escalation of the war. He also observed that secrecy hampered full discussion of controversial policies and possible consequences, which led Richard Nixon* into the 1970 invasion of Cambodia (*see* Operation Binh Tay) and the fire storm of protest following it. Halperin attributed the unrestrained use of herbicides and other chemical substances in Vietnam to the failure of policymakers to be precise in describing the limitations to be imposed on the use of such chemicals, as well as the tendency of those responding to the pressures of war to make maximum use of any weapon available.

In 1969 Halperin became a senior staff member in the National Security Council and a senior fellow of the Brookings Institute. Since 1974, Halperin has continued in his role as a critic of policy-making in Washington. He has concentrated on the growing discrepancy between the administration's desire that controversial policies and decisions be kept from the public in the name of national security and the public's right to know about such policies.

Sources: *Contemporary Authors*, vols. 9–12, 1974; *American Men of Science: The Social and Behavioral Sciences*, vol. 7, 1968; Morton H. Halperin, *Bureaucratic Politics and Foreign Policy*, 1974.

Joanna D. Cowden

HAMBURGER HILL

Hamburger Hill was the nickname for Dong Ap Bia, a mountain in the A Shau Valley* area of South Vietnam, southwest of Hue* near the Laotian* border. In May of 1969, units of the Army of the Republic of Vietnam* (ARVN) and the U.S. 101st Airborne Division* fought against soldiers of the North Vietnamese Army* (NVA) in Operation Apache Snow.* The battle of Dong Ap Bia lasted from May 10 to May 20. It was atypical of the combat in the Vietnam War since it involved large troop units on both sides and because the enemy did not use the tactic of maneuver but instead chose to defend his positions on Dong

Ap Bia. The result was a very bloody battle with high casualties* sustained by all units, thus prompting American troops to call the objective "Hamburger Hill."

While the enemy's tactics were atypical, the United States characteristically emphasized firepower, including heavy artillery,* napalm,* and B–52* "Arc Light"* air strikes. However, the enemy's defensive skills against this tactic, together with his tenacity, meant that eventually his positions had to be assaulted by infantry, and the result was fierce combat, often hand to hand. After eleven days, the enemy retreated to sanctuaries* in Laos. One week later, Hamburger Hill was abandoned by the victorious American troops. This was a normal consequence of battles in Vietnam, especially in areas like the A Shau Valley which were remote and sparsely populated. The basic strategy of both sides was attrition (*see* War of attrition), not occupation of captured territory.

The battle of Hamburger Hill was similar to other engagements during the war. Enemy losses were much higher than American casualties, the enemy resolved the battle by retreating without pursuit by American or ARVN forces, and the battlefield was abandoned shortly after the cessation of hostilities. However, its timing made it newsworthy, and it attracted considerable media attention. In 1969, the new president, Richard Nixon,* was implementing Vietnamization,* a policy to reduce American ground combat involvement (and casualties) and shift that responsibility to the ARVN. Hamburger Hill, reported extensively by the print and broadcast media, seemed to contradict the intent of Vietnamization. It also came to symbolize the frustration of achieving an overwhelming battlefield success without any indication that the war was being won. To many, this frustration suggested that such battles were discrete, mutually exclusive, isolated events which were unrelated to any ultimate policy goal. Hamburger Hill became the subject of intense public debate, focusing on the decision to capture Ap Bia regardless of the casualties and irrespective of its marginal significance in terms of the reasons why the United States was in Vietnam.

Sources: Samuel Lipsman et al., *The Vietnam Experience: Fighting for Time*, 1983; Shelby L. Stanton, *The Rise and Fall of an American Army: U.S. Ground Troops in Vietnam, 1965–1973*, 1985.

Stafford T. Thomas

HAMLET EVALUATION SURVEY

Developed by Robert Komer* in 1967, the Hamlet Evaluation Survey was an elaborate, computerized system for measuring the number of South Vietnamese citizens living in areas "controlled" by the Republic of Vietnam.* Using eighteen political, economic, and military variables, the Hamlet Evaluation Survey classified villages into one of five categories, depending on the depth of their loyalty to Saigon.* At the end of 1967, according to the Hamlet Evaluation Survey, more than two-thirds of the people of South Vietnam lived in villages loyal to the Republic of Vietnam. Just one more episode in the futile American pacification efforts (*see* Rural Reconstruction), the Hamlet Evaluation Survey was hopelessly optimistic and naive, and the Tet Offensive* in February 1968 exposed its gross inaccuracies.

Sources: Frances FitzGerald, *Fire in the Lake: The Vietnamese and the Americans in Vietnam*, 1972; Larry E. Cable, *Conflict of Myths: The Development of American Counterinsurgency Doctrine and the Vietnam War*, 1986.

HANOI

Located in the Red River Delta about 75 miles inland from the South China Sea, Hanoi is the capital of the Socialist Republic of Vietnam.* It was also the capital of French Indochina.* An industrial and transportation center, Hanoi was a graceful city, influenced by French architecture with spacious tree-lined boulevards. Its population in 1970 had reached 1,100,000 people.

Hanoi was the center of the post–World War II Vietnamese independence movement. Ho Chi Minh* proclaimed the Provisional Government of the Democratic Republic of Vietnam there on August 29, 1945, and three days later he proclaimed Vietnamese independence. Ironically, 500,000 people watched Ho quote the U.S. Declaration of Independence with American military personnel on the reviewing stand, American military aircraft flying overhead, and a band playing "The Star-Spangled Banner." In December 1946, after the French had returned in force, Ho Chi Minh and the Vietminh* blew up Hanoi's power station and attacked French outposts throughout the city. France* controlled Hanoi throughout the war, but as it progressed, French influence was increasingly confined to a small area around the city and in Haiphong. After the Battle of Dien Bien Phu* and the Geneva Accords* in 1954, the Vietminh regained control of Hanoi, making it the capital of the Democratic Republic of Vietnam.

Beginning in 1965 the United States launched massive bombing* campaigns against Hanoi, attacking fuel storage facilities and transportation centers, especially the Paul Doumer Bridge and the rail yards across the Red River. In 1967 the United States began air strikes against steel factories, power plants, and other industrial targets. Most industries as well as 800,000 of the city's population were relocated to rural areas. Hanoi was heavily bombed in 1972 in punishment for the Eastertide Offensive.* During the Christmas bombing of 1972 (*see* Operation Linebacker II), in which Richard Nixon* and Henry Kissinger* forced North Vietnamese leaders to fulfill the October Paris Peace Accords,* 36,000 tons of bombs were dropped on the city, killing 2,000 civilians and destroying the Bach Mai Hospital.

Sources: Paul Burbage et al., *The Battle for the Skies over North Vietnam, 1964–1972*, 1976; Lou Drendel, *Air War over Southeast Asia*, 1984; Danny J. Whitfield, *Historical and Cultural Dictionary of Vietnam*, 1976.

Samuel Freeman

HANOI HANNAH

In the tradition of Tokyo Rose, Hanoi Hannah was a North Vietnamese radio announcer broadcasting pro-Communist propaganda into South Vietnam and hoping to destroy the morale of American troops there. Most U.S. soldiers reacted with contempt or amusement to her broadcasts, and even prided themselves on having had their units mentioned in her programs. Later in the war, by emphasizing and exaggerating American casualties* and reporting the antiwar* demonstrations back in the United States, Hannah probably helped some soldiers begin to question why they were risking their lives. She particularly singled out black soldiers,* attempting to exacerbate racial animosities and convince them that they were being killed for the advantage of white men.

Source: Terrence Maitland and Peter McInerney, *The Vietnam Experience. A Contagion of War*, 1983.

Samuel Freeman

HANOI HILTON

One of numerous prisons which ultimately housed over 700 American prisoners of war* (POWs) between August 1964 and February 1973, the Hanoi Hilton (Hoa Lo Prison) was built by the French near the center of Hanoi.* Sections of the Hilton were dubbed "New Guy Village," "Heartbreak Hotel," "Little Vegas," and "Camp Unity." These sections were further subdivided and named. It is an imposing facility, occupying a city block. Walls are 4 feet thick, 20 feet high, and extended another 5 feet by electrified strands of barbed wire. Shards of glass are embedded on the wall's top. Other prisons located in or near Hanoi included the Zoo, Alcatraz, the Plantation, and the Powerplant. The Briarpatch, Camp Faith, and Camp Hope (Son Tay) were located within about 35 miles of Hanoi.

Jeremiah Denton's* cell in New Guy Village consisted of "two solid concrete beds . . . with metal-and-wood stocks at the foot of each. The one amenity was a small honey bucket (a pail that served as a toilet). . . . The concrete bunks were about 3½ feet high and 2½ feet apart. The cell was 9 feet by 8 feet. The door had a small peephole and was flanked by windows which had been covered over by a thin layer of concrete." Sanitation was poor. Cells were infested with insects and rodents. The food, by normal standards, was not fit to eat. Medical treatment was poor to nonexistent and was provided only when a captive's condition became serious or the captive became cooperative.

The North Vietnamese constantly utilized various methods to break captives psychologically, primarily to elicit confessions or information of propaganda value. Captives were not permitted to organize with a recognized chain of command as POWs generally do. Efforts were made to isolate prisoners and prohibit communications. Consequently, captives developed unobtrusive communication networks employing Morse and "tap" codes. Transmission methods included whistling softly, scratching sounds, even the cadence of sweeping with a broom. As communications networks and chains of command were established and ultimately discovered, prisoners were moved to different units and even to different prisons to break them up or punish the uncooperative. Prisoners were subjected to torture, but not for military information until later in the war.

Sometimes this occurred in their cells, but the Hilton and other prisons also had rooms especially for interrogation and torture. Torture took many forms, from various deprivations such as not being permitted to bathe, to beatings, extended darkness, isolation, shackling (often in contorted positions), and psychological torture.

While U.S. commanders were concerned that prisons inadvertently might be hit during the 1972 Christmas bombing (*see* Operation Linebacker II), prisoners welcomed the bombing and its attendant risks. As a settlement neared, conditions at the Hilton and other prisons improved markedly. Captives were given new clothes, were permitted to organize and to bathe and exercise regularly, and were given much-improved medical attention and food.

Sources: Jeremiah Denton, *When Hell Was in Session*, 1982; Benjamin F. Schemmer, *The Raid*, 1976.

Samuel Freeman

HARKINS, PAUL DONAL

Paul D. Harkins was born in Boston, Massachusetts, on May 15, 1904. After graduating from West Point in 1929, Harkins took a cavalry assignment, served as deputy chief of staff of George Patton's Third Army in World War II, and then was chief of staff of the Eighth Army in Korea. General Paul Harkins served as the first commander of Military Assistance Command, Vietnam* (MACV). He occupied that post between February 1962 and June 1964. Harkins was a strong supporter of Ngo Dinh Diem,* although the South Vietnamese president usually ignored his advice. Harkin's opposition to the coup that eventually toppled the Diem regime put him at odds with U.S. State Department officials in Saigon,* most notably Ambassador Henry Cabot Lodge.*

In the two decades after his departure from Vietnam, Harkins was criticized for his overly optimistic reports to Washington regarding the military and political situation there. This occasionally brought him into conflict with American military officers in the field, who often held much more pessimistic views of the South Vietnamese situation. Harkins retired from active duty in 1964 when General William Westmoreland* replaced him at MACV. Harkins died on August 21, 1984.

Sources: *New York Times*, August 22, 1984; David Halberstam, *The Best and the Brightest*, 1972; George S. Eckhardt, *Command and Control, 1950–1969*, 1974.

Sean A. Kelleher

HARRIMAN, WILLIAM AVERELL

William Averell Harriman was born in New York City on November 15, 1891, to one of America's most well-known families. After graduating from Yale in 1913, Harriman went to work for the Union Pacific Railroad. In 1917 he organized the Merchant Shipbuilding Company, made a fortune during World War I, and by the mid–1920s owned the largest merchant fleet in the country. He became chairman of the board of the Illinois Central Railroad in 1931 and the Union Pacific Railroad in 1932. During World War II Harriman represented the Lend Lease program to the British and the Soviets, and he became ambassador to the Soviet Union* in 1943. He served briefly as ambassador to Great Britain* in 1946 before being named secretary of commerce in President Harry S. Truman's* cabinet. In 1948 Harriman was named as the official U.S. representative in Europe for the Marshall Plan. He was the U.S. representative to NATO in 1951, elected governor of New York in 1954, and during the Kennedy* administration served as an ambassador-at-large and assistant secretary of state for Far Eastern affairs. Between 1963 and 1965, Harriman was under secretary of state for political affairs.

In 1962 Harriman had played a key role in negotiating the settlement in Laos,* and he had serious doubts about the efficacy of any military solution in Vietnam. Harriman had been a supporter of the containment policy* in Europe, but he saw Asia in different terms. By 1963 Harriman was privately condemning the corruption of the Diem* regime and urging Kennedy to disassociate the United States from him. President Lyndon B. Johnson* appointed Harriman an ambassador-at-large in 1965 with responsibility for Southeast Asia. Harriman traveled throughout the world in 1965 and 1966 trying to gather support for the American war effort in Vietnam and trying to work out the details for peace talks. By that time his own faith in the war was dead. Early in 1968 Harriman took an active part in the "Wise Old Men"* group which advised President Johnson to negotiate a settlement to the war and withdraw American troops. In May 1968, when the Paris peace talks* began, Harriman went there as the chief American negotiator. He remained in Paris until Henry Cabot Lodge* replaced him in January 1969. Throughout the Nixon* administration, Harriman urged American fidelity to a strict withdrawal timetable. W. Averell Harriman died on July 26, 1986.

Sources: Lee H. Burke, *Ambassador at Large: Diplomat Extraordinary*, 1972; *New York Times*, July 27, 1986; Walter Isaacson and Evan Thomas, *The Wise Men: Six Friends and the World They Made*, 1986.

HARTKE, VANCE

Vance Hartke was born in Stendal, Indiana, on May 31, 1919. He took his undergraduate degree from Evansville College and a law degree from Indiana University, and between 1948 and 1958 he practiced law in Evansville. Hartke served as mayor of Evansville between 1956 and 1958, and he entered the U.S. Senate as a Democrat in 1958, where he served until 1976. Hartke was an avid supporter of Lyndon B. Johnson's* Great Society* programs, and the president counted him as one of his most loyal followers in Congress* until early 1966, when Hartke began questioning American involvement in Vietnam. In January 1966, when Hartke signed a letter to the president with a number of his colleagues, asking Johnson to not resume the bombing* of North Vietnam and to work toward a diplomatic settlement, the president was enraged. He publicly criticized Hartke and actively worked to limit his patronage opportunities. Johnson also saw to it that several of Hartke's followers were fired from government jobs. It mattered little, and Hartke continued to question the depth of the American involvement in Southeast Asia. Hartke left the Senate in 1976 and moved to Virginia.

Sources: *Who's Who in American Politics, 1985–1986*, 1986; Stanley Karnow, *Vietnam: A History*, 1983.

HATFIELD, MARK ODUM

Mark Hatfield was born in Dalles, Oregon, on July 12, 1922. He graduated from Willamette University in 1943 and took a master's degree from Stanford in 1948. Hatfield then taught political science at Willamette between 1950 and 1956. He was a state legislator in Oregon from 1951 to 1957, secretary of state from 1957 to 1959, and governor of Oregon from 1959 to 1967. Hatfield won election to the U.S. Senate as a Republican in 1966. Hatfield's career in the Senate was marked by a vigorous opposition to the Vietnam War. By 1967 he was criticizing the scale of the American military effort in Indochina,* and he also became a frequent critic of the Nixon* administration's handling of the war. In Hatfield's opinion, Nixon and Kissinger* were unnecessarily lengthening the American stay there. When Nixon authorized the invasion of Cambodia (*see* Operation Binh Tay), Hatfield spoke militantly against it and sponsored, along with Senator George McGovern,* a Senate amendment cutting off funds for the Vietnam War after December 31, 1971. The amendment never passed. Hatfield also opposed the military draft* and called for the establishment of a voluntary army.

Sources: *Who's Who in America, 1984–1985*, 1985; Mark Hatfield, *Conflict and Conscience*, 1971; Mark Hatfield, *Amnesty: The Unsettled Question of Vietnam*, 1973.

HATFIELD-McGOVERN AMENDMENT

Late in April 1970, President Richard Nixon* had approved a combined American–South Vietnamese invasion of Cambodia (*see* Operation Binh Tay) to attack Vietcong* and North Vietnamese sanctuaries* there. To many Americans the invasion—Nixon called it an "incursion"—seemed a dangerous escalation of the war, and widespread protest demonstrations erupted across the country. Especially violent confrontations between students and National Guard troops occurred at Kent State University* in Ohio and Jackson State University in Mississippi. During the first week of May more than 100,000 protesters gathered in Washington, D.C., to denounce the invasion. Outraged at not being consulted about the invasion, the Senate symbolically protested by terminating the Gulf of Tonkin Resolution* in June 1970. Senator George McGovern* of South Dakota and Senator Mark Hatfield* of Oregon jointly sponsored an amendment requiring a total American withdrawal from South Vietnam by the end of 1971. Although the Hatfield-McGovern Amendment failed to pass in the Senate, it was an indication of the frustration large numbers of Americans felt about the war.

Sources: George Herring, *America's Longest War: The United States and Vietnam, 1950–1975*, 1986; William Shawcross, *Sideshow: Kissinger, Nixon, and the Destruction of Cambodia*, 1979.

HAYDEN, THOMAS EMMETT

Thomas Hayden was born on December 12, 1940, in Royal Oak, Michigan, the only child of Catholic parents in a conservative working-class neighborhood. In December 1961, as a University of Michigan student, Hayden had helped found the Students for a Democratic Society* (SDS) and drafted the Port Huron Statement: "We are the people of this generation, bred in at least modest comfort, housed now in universities, looking uncomfortably to a world we inherit." At first SDS was not much more to the left than the liberal wing of the Democratic party. But under the pressure of the civil rights movement and opposition to the Vietnam War, Hayden's politics gradually became more and more radical. By the fall of 1965 SDS was organizing against the draft* and was accused of sabotaging the war effort. In 1966 and 1967 SDS escalated its campus demonstrations and protest marches. Hayden met with North Vietnamese representatives in Czechoslovakia in 1967, where the release of American prisoners of war* (POWs) was discussed. He later flew to Cambodia (*see* Kampuchea) and escorted three released prisoners home.

In 1968, Hayden joined Rennie Davis* in planning the National Mobilization Committee's anti-Vietnam demonstrations at the Democratic National Convention in 1968. The protesters were assaulted by the Chicago police, but Hayden was later arrested and became one of the "Chicago 7"* defendants charged with conspiracy. Although he was convicted, the decision was later overturned on appeal. After the trial, Hayden joined actress Jane Fonda* on the antiwar circuit, and they were married in January 1973. After that Hayden began to change his radical image and entered California politics. He ran a surprisingly close race against Senator John Tunney in the senatorial primary in 1976, and in 1979 he and Fonda established the Campaign for Economic Democracy, a movement designed to secure popular control over major corporations. Dubbed the "Mork and Mindy" of the left in a column by George Will, they made appearances dressed conservatively and toned down their rhetoric from the militancy of the 1960s. Hayden won a seat in the California state legislature in 1980, and explained his political evolution by saying: "The radical or reformer sets a climate. The politician inherits the constituency that the reformer created. My problem is to be both."

Sources: Charles Moritz, "Tom Hayden," *Current Biography*, 1976; Tom Hayden, *The American Future: New Visions Beyond Old Frontiers*, 1980; Nancy Zaroulis and Gerald Sullivan, *Who Spoke Up? American Protest Against the Vietnam War, 1963–1975*, 1984.

Frances Frenzel

HEARTS AND MINDS

An Academy Award winner for Best Documentary in 1974, *Hearts and Minds* was a controversial film examining U.S. involvement in Vietnam. By interviewing

American policymakers, Vietnamese leaders, veterans, and Vietnamese peasants, the film looks at the war in terms of American culture, the World War II
experience, and global politics. In one sense the film is balanced, devoting equal
time to the war's supporters and critics. Harry S. Truman,* Dwight D. Eisenhower,* John F. Kennedy,* Lyndon B. Johnson,* Richard M. Nixon,* and
William Westmoreland* present rationales supporting the war, while Clark Clifford,* Daniel Ellsberg,* and J. William Fulbright* oppose it. Navy lieutenant
and POW (1966–73) George Coker (fifty-five bombing missions) explains the
war in terms of Communist aggression, and former fighter-bomber pilot Captain
Randy Floyd (ninety-eight bombing missions) explains it in terms of human
beings. Other veterans, including paraplegic Robert Mueller and double amputee
William Marshall, explain their views before, during, and after Vietnam.

In another sense, the film was not balanced. Graphic war footage includes the
most famous and damning of the war. Colonel Nguyen Ngoc Loan,* Saigon*
chief of police, is shown summarily executing a Vietcong* suspect during the
1968 Tet Offensive.* A young girl, Kim Phuc, her burns clearly visible, is
shown running down a road nude, having torn off her burning clothes after the
pagoda in which she had taken refuge was napalmed. While there are scenes of
hamlets being bombed and put to flame by GIs as villagers beg for mercy, of
Vietnamese being tortured, of disabled and mutilated Vietnamese and Americans,
of Vietnamese recounting the destruction of their homes and loss of loved ones
due to American bombardment, there are few scenes of Vietcong/North Vietnamese Army* violence, and virtually none of the injuries they inflicted on the
civilian population. Critics of the film were outraged by what they saw as blatant
bias. After footage in which a Vietnamese family demonstrably mourns the death
of an ARVN soldier (see Army of the Republic of Vietnam), with his son crying
and hugging his picture and his mother attempting to crawl into the grave with
him, General William Westmoreland is shown saying "The Oriental doesn't put
the same high price on life as does the Westerner. Life is plentiful; life is cheap
in the Orient. And as the philosophy of the Orient expresses itself, life is not
important." Those who praised the film, however, felt its spirit matched the
nature of the American war effort in Vietnam. There is thought-provoking irony
footage in celebrations of our own war for independence, or a minister before
the "big game" praying for victory with a high school football team, or Colonel
George S. Patton III's account of a memorial service for fallen comrades in
which he concludes that his men are "a bloody good bunch of killers."

Source: "Hearts and Minds," *Variety*, May 15, 1974.

Samuel Freeman

"HEARTS AND MINDS" (Phrase)

In 1965 President Lyndon B. Johnson* paraphrased John Adams's description
of the American Revolution: "The Revolution was effected before the war
commenced. The Revolution was in the minds and hearts of the people." About
Vietnam, Johnson said: "So we must be ready to fight in Vietnam, but the
ultimate victory will depend on the hearts and minds of the people who actually

live out there." Eventually, however, the United States did not win the hearts and minds of the Vietnamese people, and the war became a conflict over the hearts and minds of the American people.

Military apologists argued that the war was lost because Washington misperceived it as a guerrilla/civil war rather than conventional war instigated, directed, and ultimately fought by North Vietnam. To them the emphasis on pacification (*see* Rural Reconstruction) was misplaced, resulting in misallocation of resources away from fighting the war, inappropriate strategy aimed at ferreting out guerrilla bands when main-force, hard-core North Vietnamese Army* units were the real problem, allowing invading forces sanctuaries* which guaranteed they could never be defeated, and a media focus which caused Americans to misunderstand and lose patience with the war. According to Harry G. Summers, the war was not in "the hearts and minds of the . . . people but the guns and bullets of the North Vietnamese Army."

Most observers, however, accepted the counterarguments of military and pacification professionals like William Corson (*The Betrayal*, 1968) and Cincinnatus (*Self-Destruction*, 1981), who argued that "every strike that levels a village or cuts a road or kills innocent civilians contributes to the ultimate victory even if . . . the guerrillas lose both ground and men. For all such military operations, by their very nature and destructiveness, alienate the people among whom they occur." That sentiment was shared by people like CIA director William Colby and pacification expert Robert Komer.* Robert Taber (*The War of the Flea*, 1965) said there "is only one way of defeating an insurgent people who will not surrender, and that is extermination. There is only one way to control a territory that harbours resistance, and that is to turn it into a desert. Where these means cannot, for whatever reason, be used, the war is lost."

But unwillingness to understand, much less respect, either pacification or the Vietnamese people, permeated the American command structure. American military personnel were either paternalistic or racist in their attitudes toward the Vietnamese; if U.S.-ARVN military violence did not turn the Vietnamese peasants against the United States, those attitudes surely did. Ultimately the war became a battle for the American people's "hearts and minds." The Vietnamese could refuse defeat. They understood that Americans would tire of a war they did not and could not understand, that eventually enough body bags would return, that there were limits to the resources the United States could squander in Vietnam. When that day came, the Americans would leave, just as had the Chinese and French before them.

Sources: Larry E. Cable, *Conflict of Myths: The Development of American Counterinsurgency Doctrine and the Vietnam War*, 1986; Andrew F. Krepinevich, Jr., *The Army and Vietnam*, 1986; Frances FitzGerald, *Fire in the Lake: The Vietnamese and the Americans in Vietnam*, 1972.

Samuel Freeman

HELICOPTER GUNSHIPS

Early U.S. helicopter operation in Vietnam met limited resistance from enemy small arms fire, causing the U.S. Army* to begin arming helicopters in an attempt to suppress ground fire. A .30 caliber machine gun was mounted in the forward door of CH–21s* to give them the ability to suppress ground fire during landing operations. As the weapon had a limited arc of fire and the CH–21 suffered from poor maneuverability, this attempt was not very successful. The army then decided to arm the new UH–1As* and organized a test unit, the Utility Tactical Transport Helicopter Company. Fifteen UH–1As were equipped with two .30 caliber machine guns and sixteen 2.75-inch rockets and sent to Thailand* for training. In November 1962, this unit was assigned to Tan Son Nhut Air Base* in Vietnam, where it began flying in support of U.S. Army CH–21 units.

Originally designated as "escorts," these helicopters were to pioneer the helicopter gunship role in Vietnam. As this role expanded, the term "escort" was dropped in favor of "gunship" or the nickname given to them by GIs, "hog." The UH–1s continued to provide most of the gunships used in Vietnam, although other helicopters also were used in this role. In a typical airmobile assault, gunships would make passes over landing zones to soften them up and draw enemy fire before the slicks* carrying troops came in.

As enemy ground weapons improved, the need for increased firepower from helicopter gunships became apparent. More sophisticated rocket packs, .50 caliber machine guns, and the M–75 grenade launcher became standard equipment for the UH–1s; and the CH–47,* capable of carrying more weight, was turned into a gunship, using G.E. miniguns capable of firing 2,000 rounds per minute of 7.62mm shells either through the side windows or through the rear doors. As the need for increased firepower was recognized, the 1st Cavalry Division* received three heavily modified CH–47s. These "Go-Go Birds" were fitted with a grenade launcher capable of firing 200 rounds per minute of 40mm high explosive in the nose, rocket pods and cannon mounted on side sponsons, and .50 caliber machine guns firing through windows and the rear cargo hatch. In response to Vietcong* use of .50 caliber machine guns as antiaircraft weapons, a number of UH–1s were fitted with M24A 20mm cannons. These cannons enabled the UH–1s to stay out of range of enemy ground fire, while delivering 2,000 rounds per minute of fire.

The UH–1 provided the basic frame for the first helicopter designed as a gunship, the AH–1G* Cobra. Using the basic components of the UH–1 allowed the army to develop this gunship in only six months. Cobras began serving in Vietnam in 1967. Heavily armed with a variety of weapons and equipped with sophisticated, new "sight-guided" aiming systems, the Cobra proved a highly effective gunship. Cannons, grenade launchers, or machine guns could be mounted in turrets, giving them the capability of swinging through a 230-degree arc. The weapons were aimed by the gunner "looking-in" the target, with the turret swinging to follow his head.

Overall, helicopter gunships proved their worth in Vietnam, providing ground forces with close support cover in a way fixed-wing aircraft could not.

Sources: *Jane's All the World's Aircraft: 1970–71*, 1971; Jim Mesko, *Airmobile: The Helicopter War in Vietnam*, 1985.

Nolan J. Argyle

"HELICOPTER VALLEY"

"Helicopter Valley" was a nickname given to the Song Ngan Valley in 1966. Located in Quang Tri Province just south of the Demilitarized Zone,* Song Ngan Valley became famous on July 15, 1966, when a squadron of CH–46* helicopters carried the 3rd Battalion, 4th Marines of the Third Marine Division* as part of Operation Hastings* to stop North Vietnamese infiltration* of South Vietnam. The third wave of CH–46s fell into a disaster when two of them collided and crashed. Another CH–46, desperately trying to avoid the collision, crashed into the jungle. North Vietnamese snipers then destroyed a fourth CH–46. Panic-stricken marines trying to escape the crashed helicopters were slashed to death by the whirling blades. Among marines, the Song Ngan Valley carried the name "Helicopter Valley" after those incidents on July 15, 1966.

Sources: Edward Doyle and Samuel Lipsman, *The Vietnam Experience: America Takes Over, 1965–1967*, 1985; Willard Pearson, *The War in the Northern Provinces, 1966–1968*, 1975.

HELICOPTER WAR

The helicopter became the primary symbol of the U.S. military presence in Vietnam. No other weapon system attained the high degree of visibility or identification with the war that the helicopter did. The ubiquitous "Huey" (UH–1)* emerged as the unofficial symbol of U.S. involvement.

Helicopters were first used in Vietnam by the French, mainly for medical evacuation. The French had determined to begin using large numbers of helicopters for troop movements to offset the superior mobility of the Vietminh,* but the French defeat at Dien Bien Phu* ended those plans.

American combat involvement in Vietnam started and ended with helicopters. In December of 1961 the 8th and 57th Transportation Companies arrived in Vietnam. Flying the Piasecki H–21 (later the Vertol and then Boeing-Vertol CH–21*), these units flew combat missions supporting the Army of the Republic of Vietnam* (ARVN), thus becoming the first U.S. troops to officially serve in a direct combat role. These units were followed by a U.S. Marine* helicopter squadron flying CH–34s* and by a U.S. Army* medical detachment using UH–1s for medical evacuation (*see* medevac). In the fall of 1962, fifteen armed UH–1s arrived in Vietnam to serve as the first of the helicopter gunships of the war.

The first major offensive operation using American helicopters occurred on January 2, 1963, when ten CH–21s, escorted by five Huey gunships, were used to place ARVN forces in a ring around Ap Bac in an attempt to trap and eliminate a major enemy unit. Lacking fixed-wing* air cover, the units took heavy losses, including the loss of five helicopters. The enemy forces were able to withdraw from Ap Bac successfully. Thus the first airmobile assault of the Vietnam War was a failure. Lessons were drawn from this failure, including the need to coordinate airmobile assaults with bombing and strafing runs by fixed-wing aircraft. As helicopter gunships improved, the need for fixed-wing support declined.

Faced with early failure in the attempt to use a new concept of airmobile fighting, the U.S. Army established a test division to work out effective techniques. The division was established at Ft. Benning, Georgia, as the 11th Air Assault Division. This division constantly exchanged personnel with units in Vietnam in an attempt to analyze and perfect airmobile techniques. In 1965 one of these units in Vietnam, the 173rd Airborne Brigade,* teamed with a number of helicopter units in launching a series of airmobile assaults which were seen as highly successful. By October of 1965, the 11th Air Assault Division, now combined with major elements of the 2nd Infantry Division and redesignated the 1st Cavalry Division (Airmobile)* was in place at An Khe in South Vietnam's Central Highlands. They constructed the world's largest helipad (known as the "golf course" as it always had at least eighteen holes in it from rocket and mortar attacks), and the U.S. Army was ready to launch the helicopter war in earnest.

In November 1965 the 1st Cavalry fought its first major battles with the North Vietnamese Army* (NVA). The NVA launched an attack designed to draw out ARVN forces and ambush them in the Central Highlands.* The NVA then planned to drive across the center of South Vietnam, cutting the country in half. First Cavalry forces, supporting the ARVN units, engaged the enemy in a series of battles known as the Battle of Ia Drang* Valley. NVA attempts to isolate American and ARVN units and hit them with superior forces were constantly thwarted by the 1st Cavalry's ability to move units rapidly with helicopters. At the end of the campaign, the NVA had lost 1,800 troops while the 1st Cavalry lost 240 men and four helicopters. The pattern of conflict in the helicopter war had been established.

By the late 1960s the U.S. Army had 4,000 aircraft serving in Vietnam, including 3,600 helicopters. These were organized into four types of units. Airmobile divisions, starting with the 1st Cavalry Division and joined in 1968 by the converted 101st Airborne,* were fully equipped with their own helicopters under their direct control. Regular infantry divisions had organic aviation units attached to them, normally of battalion* strength. A number of helicopter companies were assigned directly to Military Assistance Command, Vietnam* and a number of other helicopter units were assigned directly to special units such as engineer, signal, or support groups.

Operation Delaware,* conducted in the A Shau Valley* in 1966, represented a turning point in the helicopter war. This was the biggest airmobile operation to date, and was seen by U.S. forces as a major success. However, they lost more aircraft than expected, and it appeared that the NVA had, in a little more than a year, begun to adapt their tactics to fit within the helicopter war. In 1971 the United States was involved in the last major airmobile offensive operation of the war in Lam Son 719,* an attempt to clear the NVA from an area extending from Khe Sanh* into Laos.* Ground forces were provided by the ARVN, with U.S. support limited primarily to helicopters. Lam Son 719 failed to meet any of its objectives, with ARVN troops bogging down in heavy fighting.

The last major involvement of U.S. forces in Vietnam was defensive, and involved helicopter gunships. In the spring of 1972, the NVA launched major assaults supported by heavy armor, including T–54 tanks. A major factor in a successful ARVN defense was the presence of U.S. helicopter gunships armed with antitank weapons (see M–72), including TOW missiles.

In 1975, South Vietnam collapsed. Americans witnessed the panic, as they had witnessed much of the helicopter war, on their television screens. Graphic images of hovering U.S. helicopters evacuating personnel from the American embassy, and of other helicopters, both U.S. and ARVN, crashing into the sea after dropping their passengers on ships, represented the end of American involvement in South Vietnam. A CH–53* involved in the evacuation crashed into the sea, killing two U.S. marines—the last U.S. casualties of the Vietnam War.

American combat involvement in Vietnam began and ended with helicopters. Early attempts using U.S. helicopters and ARVN troops proved unsatisfactory; the same combination at the end of the war, as represented in Lam Son 719, proved equally ineffective. Yet the helicopter war concept of airmobile units did prove its value, and remains a key component of American military strategy.

Sources: *The Encyclopedia of Air Warfare*, 1974; Jim Mesko, *Airmobile: The Helicopter War in Vietnam*, 1985.

Nolan J. Argyle

HELMS, RICHARD McGARRAH

Richard Helms was born in St. Davids, Pennsylvania, on March 30, 1913. After graduating from Williams College in 1935, he became a staff correspondent for UPI and joined the *Indianapolis Times* in 1937. Helms stayed with the *Times* until 1942, when he was assigned by the United States Navy* to work with the Office of Strategic Services (OSS). After the war Helms stayed on with the OSS when it became the Central Intelligence Agency* (CIA). During the years of the Vietnam War between 1965 and 1973, Helms was deputy director and then director of the CIA. When the war reached its late stages in the early 1970s, Helms came under siege from critics protesting clandestine CIA activities in Indochina*—secret armies, assassination squads, sponsored coup d'états, and domestic surveillance. As a result of congressional hearings, new legislation required the CIA to secure presidential approval of all covert operations, surrender documents to public scrutiny as long as it did not compromise agents in the field, stop surveillance of Americans abroad unless national security required it, and cease all domestic surveillance. Helms was forced to appear before a number of House and Senate committees in the mid–1970s as the legislation was evolving. Between 1973 and 1976, he also served as ambassador to Iran.

Sources: *Who's Who in America, 1984–1985*, 1985; Thomas W. Powers, *The Man Who Kept the Secrets*, 1979; Morton H. Halperin et al., *The Lawless State: The Crimes of the U.S. Intelligence Agencies*, 1976; John Prados, *Presidents' Secret Wars: CIA and Pentagon Covert Operations Since World War II*, 1986.

HERBICIDES   *See* Agent Orange; Defoliation; Operation Ranch Hand

HIGH NATIONAL COUNCIL

Between November 1963, with the assassination of Ngo Dinh Diem,* and Nguyen Van Thieu's* rise to power in June 1965, a succession of civilian and military governments assumed power in Saigon.* In September 1964, a military regime headed by General Nguyen Khanh* appointed a seventeen-member High National Council, representing a variety of political groups, to draft a new constitution. The constitution was ready on October 20, 1964, and the High National Council appointed Phan Khac Suu* as chief of state and Tran Van Huong* as prime minister. Buddhist* groups immediately began demonstrating against the High National Council; and on December 18, thirty young generals, led by Nguyen Khanh, formed an Armed Forces Council, dissolved the High National Council, and in January 1965 dismissed Prime Minister Huong.

Source: Harvey H. Smith et al., *Area Handbook for South Vietnam*, 1967.

HIGHWAY 1   *See* "Street Without Joy"

"HILL OF ANGELS"   *See* Con Thien, Battle of

HILSMAN, ROGER

Roger Hilsman was born in Waco, Texas, on November 23, 1919. He graduated from West Point in 1943 and joined the Office of Strategic Services working behind Japanese lines in Asia. After the war Hilsman stayed with the Central Intelligence Agency,* and in 1951 received a Ph.D. in international relations from Yale. Between 1950 and 1953 Hilsman worked on NATO development in Europe, spent the years between 1953 and 1956 with the Center for International Studies at Princeton, and then joined the Library of Congress. He wrote widely on foreign affairs, and his books *Strategic Intelligence and National Decisions* (1956) and *Alliance Policy in the Cold War* (1959) made him an influential figure in Washington. In 1961 Hilsman became director of the bureau of intelligence and research for the Department of State. As early as 1961 Hilsman was warning policymakers that military action alone would not solve guerrilla wars in underdeveloped countries; that popular support gained through economic development and political reform was indispensable. In 1963 Hilsman was promoted to assistant secretary of state for Far Eastern affairs. Along with Michael Forrestal,* Hilsman went to Vietnam on a fact-finding mission in 1963, and their Hilsman-Forrestal Report* concluded that the American commitment in Vietnam would be a difficult and long-term problem. Hilsman also urged John Kennedy* to exploit the growing rift between the Soviet Union* and China by seeking a normalization of relations with the People's Republic of China.*

After the assassination of President Kennedy, Hilsman resigned from the government to resume his academic career, teaching at Columbia University. In 1967, he published a well-received account of foreign policy during the Kennedy administration, *To Move a Nation*. A major contention was that Kennedy intended, after the election of 1964, to work for the neutralization of Vietnam, as had already been done in Laos,* and thus extricate the United States from that quagmire.

Sources: *Current Biography*, 1964, pp. 194–196; *Current Authors*, 1969; Roger Hilsman, *To Move a Nation*, 1967.

Joseph M. Rowe, Jr.

HILSMAN-FORRESTAL REPORT

Early in 1963, concerned about contradictory reports about Vietnam coming from military officials and journalists, President John F. Kennedy* dispatched State Department Far East expert Roger Hilsman* and White House staffer Michael Forrestal* to Vietnam on a fact-finding mission. In their report, they argued that American policies in Southeast Asia should be continued, but they argued that the ARVN (*see* Army of the Republic of Vietnam) was weakened by severe corruption and morale problems, that Ngo Dinh Diem* was becoming increasingly isolated from the Vietnamese masses, and that the American commitment there would be longer than originally anticipated. The overall tone of the report, however, was optimistic and contributed to the escalation of the American effort in Vietnam.

Source: George C. Herring, *America's Longest War: The United States in Vietnam, 1950–1975*, 1986.

HMONG

The Hmong, also known as Meo or Miao, were Laotian tribal people living in the mountains of North Vietnam and Laos.* They constituted about 15 percent of the Laotian population in the early 1970s, totaling more than 300,000 people. Speaking a Sino-Tibetan dialect, the Hmong were relatively late arrivals to Laos and Vietnam, migrating from China in the nineteenth century. Over the years the Vietnamese and the French were in frequent conflict with them, and the Hmong were often recruited by all sides in the Vietnamese conflict. During the 1960s and 1970s, the Central Intelligence Agency* raised a Hmong army, led by General Vang Pao, to attack the Ho Chi Minh Trail* as it passed through Laos, and over the years they sustained heavy casualties. After the end of the Vietnam War, large numbers of Hmong immigrated to the United States, settling in the western states.

Sources: George Kahin, "Minorities in the Democratic Republic of Vietnam," *Asian Survey* 12 (July 1972); Donald P. Whitaker, *Area Handbook for Laos*, 1972; John Prados, *Presidents' Secret Wars: CIA and Pentagon Covert Operations Since World War II*, 1986.

HOA HAO

The Hoa Hao movement, a major but independent Buddhist sect prominent in the Mekong Delta,* was founded in 1919 by Huynh Phu So.* After a sickly youth, he entered a monastery in 1939; when he received what he termed a miraculous cure, he founded the sect. The movement had strong anti-French overtones, which the Japanese exploited between 1940 and 1945. A variant of Theravada Buddhism,* the Hoa Hao emphasized the importance of faith as opposed to experience, prayer four times daily, and veneration of Buddha, ancestors, and national heroes. By the late 1940s and 1950s, the Hoa Hao had more than one million followers and were a force to be reckoned with in South Vietnam, the only political movement with roots in the Vietnamese peasantry sufficient to rival Communist influence. In April 1947, Communist guerrillas (*see* Vietcong) among the Vietminh* assassinated Huynh Phu So, and leadership of the movement shifted to Ba Cut, a powerful man who directed the Hoa Hao army in South Vietnam.

But it was just that Hoa Hao independence, particularly its military strength and independent army, which bothered other political elements in South Vietnam. The anti-Communist government of South Vietnam, like the Communist Vietminh, resented the independence of the Hoa Hao, and in 1955 they launched a military campaign against them. After extensive resistance, the Hoa Hao were subdued and conquered, and Ba Cut was arrested in April 1956 and executed in July. The Hoa Hao remained a strong religious presence in South Vietnam, but their status as an independent military power was over.

Source: Bernard B. Fall, "The Political Religious Sects of Vietnam," *Pacific Affairs* 28 (1958), 235–53.

HOANG VAN HOAN

Hoang Van Hoan was born in Nghe An Province in central Vietnam in 1905, and joined the Vietnam Youth Revolutionary League in 1926. Under pressure from the French, he fled to China and became a founding member of the Lao Dong party* in 1930. Hoan was active in the Vietminh* after World War II and served as ambassador to the People's Republic of China* for several years in the 1950s. In 1958 Hoang Van Hoan became vice president of the National Assembly Standing Committee of the Democratic Republic of Vietnam.* Between 1951 and 1982 Van Hoan was also a member of the Central Committee and Politburo of the Democratic Republic of Vietnam.

Sources: Central Intelligence Agency, *Who's Who in North Vietnam*, 1969; Joseph Buttinger, *Vietnam: A Dragon Embattled*. Vol. 2, *Vietnam at War*, 1967.

HO CHI MINH

Ho Chi Minh was born as Nguyen Sinh Cung on May 19, 1890, in Nghe An Province of central Vietnam. His father, Nguyen Sinh Sac, had achieved mandarin status through diligent study but abandoned his family to become an itinerant teacher. Ho attended school in Hue,* where his lifelong quest for

Vietnamese independence was first launched. Moving south in 1909, Ho Chi Minh, now calling himself Van Ba, taught school in a number of villages, worked in Saigon,* and in 1911 signed on aboard a French freighter. In 1912 Ho left Vietnam and did not return for thirty years. He sailed around the world for three years, and lived one year in the United States—Brooklyn. Known as Nguyen Tat Thanh, Ho then moved to London and from there to Paris, where he became a founding member of the French Communist party in 1920. By then Ho Chi Minh was speaking and writing avidly on his major ideological theory—that anticolonial* nationalism and socioeconomic revolution were inseparable.

Suspicious of the Vietnamese nationalist among them, French security forces began tracking Ho Chi Minh's movements, and in 1924 he moved to Moscow, met the leaders of the Soviet Union,* studied for several months at the University of Oriental Workers, and then moved on to Canton. In southern China Ho Chi Minh organized the Thanh Nien Cach Menh Dong Chi Hoi* (Revolutionary Youth League) to campaign for Vietnamese independence, and in 1930 the Indochinese Communist party (*see* Lao Dong party). Throughout the 1930s Ho Chi Minh wandered widely throughout the world, spending time in China, the Soviet Union, Thailand,* and Asia. When the Japanese invaded Indochina* in 1940, Ho Chi Minh began allying himself with the Allied powers; Japanese domination of Vietnam, in his mind, was no better than the French Empire. Assuming the name Ho Chi Minh, he returned to Vietnam in May 1941 and established the Viet Nam Doc Lap Dong Minh Hoi* (League for Vietnamese Independence), or the Vietminh.* During World War II Ho cultivated his relationship with the United States, especially with OSS agents fighting against the Japanese in Indochina; and when the war ended in 1945, Ho was widely recognized as the most prominent native leader in Vietnam. He declared Vietnamese independence on September 2, 1945, using language from the U.S. Declaration of Independence to punctuate his proclamation. When the French returned to Vietnam in 1946, Ho was prepared to work out an arrangement for Vietnamese independence within a French union—somewhat like the British Commonwealth—but his plans never materialized and broke down at the Fontainebleau Conference* in May 1946, when Ho traveled to Paris. By late 1946 the Vietminh were at war with French forces. Ho Chi Minh formed the Democratic Republic of Vietnam* in 1950, quickly won recognition from most Soviet-bloc countries, and finally won true independence in May 1954 when Vo Nguyen Giap* and the Vietminh defeated the French at Dien Bien Phu.*

Between 1954 and 1960, Ho Chi Minh consolidated his power in the north and waited to see if the government of Ngo Dinh Diem* in South Vietnam would collapse. When American military and economic assistance sustained the Diem regime, Ho organized the National Liberation Front, or Vietcong,* in 1960, began construction of the Ho Chi Minh Trail* through Laos* and Cambodia (*see* Kampuchea) into South Vietnam, and began providing money and supplies to the Pathet Lao* in Laos and the Khmer Rouge* in Cambodia. Absolutely indefatigable in his drive for Vietnamese unification and independence, and often brutal in his implementation of revolution, Ho Chi Minh was the "father of his country." He died on September 2, 1969, and Vietcong and North Vietnamese Army* troops memorialized him in May 1975 when they invaded Saigon and renamed it Ho Chi Minh City.*

Sources: David Halberstam, *Ho*, 1971; Charles Fenn, *Ho Chi Minh: A Biographical Introduction*, 1973; Stanley Karnow, *Vietnam: A History*, 1983.

HO CHI MINH CAMPAIGN (1975)

Under the direction of General Van Tien Dung,* the Ho Chi Minh Campaign was the final assault on Saigon* between April 26 and April 30, 1975. During late March and early April, Dung moved eighteen North Vietnamese Army* (NVA) divisions into place within a 40-mile radius of Saigon. Poised due east of Saigon were the 3rd, 304th, 325th, and 324B divisions, with the objective of taking out the ARVN (*see* Army of the Republic of Vietnam) 1st Airborne Brigade at Ba Ria and the 951st ARVN Ranger Group and 4th Airborne Brigade near Long Thanh. Northeast of Saigon, Dung placed the 6th, 7th, and 314th divisions and assigned them the assault on Bien Hoa.* To the north, the 320B, 312th, and 338th divisions were assigned the conquest of the ARVN 5th Division at Ben Cat and the ARVN 9th Ranger Brigade at Lai Thieu. Northwest of Saigon, Dung had the 70th, 316th, 320th, and 968th divisions ready to pounce on ARVN 25th Division at Trang Bang and Cu Chi. In the west, the 3rd, 5th, 9th, and 16th North Vietnamese divisions were charged with an assault on the ARVN 22nd Division at Tan An and Ben Luc and with a direct attack on the ARVN 7th and 8th Ranger brigades outside of Saigon. In the southwest, the NVA 8th Division prepared to attack the ARVN 7th Division at My Tho.* Dung's attack plan worked flawlessly. The fighting was intense, but ARVN units kept falling back into an increasingly tight circle around Saigon. On April 29 the city was coming under intense artillery barrages, and NVA units had entered the outskirts of the city. The last Americans were evacuated on April 30, and the North Vietnamese took control of Saigon. The Ho Chi Minh Campaign, and the war, was over.

Sources: Alan Dawson, *55 Days: The Fall of South Vietnam*, 1977; David Butler, *The Fall of Saigon: Scenes from the Sudden End of a Long War*, 1985.

HO CHI MINH CITY

When they finally overran South Vietnam in 1975, North Vietnamese took control of Saigon* and quickly renamed it Ho Chi Minh City, in honor of Ho Chi Minh,* the father of Vietnamese nationalism, who had died in 1969.

Source: Stanley Karnow, *Vietnam: A History*, 1983.

HO CHI MINH TRAIL

In May 1959 the Communist leadership in Hanoi* decided the time had come to step up guerrilla efforts (*see* Vietcong) in South Vietnam, and they formed Group 559 to investigate enlarging the traditional series of trails through the mountains and jungles from the panhandle of North Vietnam into Laos,* southward into Cambodia (*see* Kampuchea), and then emptying into South Vietnam. In time Hanoi intended to use the so-called Ho Chi Minh Trail to take control of the war in the south and to conquer South Vietnam. By 1964 the Ho Chi Minh Trail remained primitive, requiring a physically arduous, exhausting trip, and it was incapable of handling large numbers of troops. It took more than a month of hard marching to cover its several hundred miles.

When the United States commenced its vast logistical buildup in 1964, North Vietnam began expanding the trail and increasing its capacity, and that effort continued until the final North Vietnamese victory in 1975. Within a year, the Ho Chi Minh Trail became a well-marked series of jungle roads, capable of handling heavy trucks and other vehicles, replete with necessary support facilities, mostly built underground to escape American detection and air strikes. There were hospitals with sanitary operating rooms, fuel storage tanks, and vast supply caches. While the north's logistical capability remained limited, North Vietnamese Army* (NVA) divisions required less than fifteen tons of supplies each day.

By 1967 the entire trail system became a key to the war's progress. North Vietnam was moving more than 20,000 troops a month. United States Army Special Forces* operated advance camps near the trail outlets in the south; CIA-recruited Hmong* tribesmen sought to cut the trail in the north; and thousands of sorties* by a variety of aircraft sought to interdict the flow of men and materiel, though all without much success. A 1971 South Vietnamese Army invasion up Route 9 into Laos to cut the trail was a failure, resulting in rout of the troops. By 1975 the trail contained major fuel pipelines, and it was able to support more than a dozen full NVA divisions, an amazing feat.

Sources: James Clay Thompson, *Rolling Thunder*, 1980; Ralph Littauer and Norman Uphoff, eds., *The Air War in Indochina*, 1972; Jon M. Van Dyke, *North Vietnam's Strategy for Survival*, 1972.

Charles Dobbs

HOFFMAN, ABBIE

Abbie Hoffman was born on November 30, 1936, at Worcester, Massachusetts. He graduated from Brandeis University in 1959 with a degree in psychology, studied for a time at the University of California at Berkeley, and began his political activism in 1960 protesting capital punishment. Between 1963 and 1965, Hoffman was active in the civil rights movement, and in 1964 he joined the Student Non-Violent Coordinating Committee and worked actively in Mississippi and Georgia. By late 1965, when he became active in the antiwar movement,* Hoffman's personality was characterized by a need to be noticed, frenetic activity, a missionary-martyr complex, a large ego, frequent use of LSD and marijuana, and a commitment to the counterculture. He rejected mainstream values, preached revolution, and hoped to discredit American values through ridicule, outrageous behavior, and black humor.

By 1967 Hoffman was living on the Lower East Side of New York City working against the Vietnam War. He claimed to have serious goals but hoped to have fun achieving them. For example, he created pandemonium on the floor of the New York Stock Exchange by throwing dollar bills from the balcony and seeing brokers scramble after them. He combined farce with seriousness in his antiwar activities, on one occasion publicly trying to "exorcise" the Pentagon of its evil spirits. Early in 1968 Hoffman participated in the occupation of Columbia University* and, in August, played an important role in organizing the demonstrations at the Democratic National Convention* in Chicago. While in Chicago, Hoffman joined with Ed Sanders, Jerry Rubin,* and Paul Krassner in founding the Youth International party—"Yippies"—in an attempt to fuse the hippie and antiwar movements. The Yippies sponsored songs, speeches, a "nude-in" in Chicago, and nominated a pig named Pigasus as their presidential candidate. Hoffman was arrested at the Chicago airport for carrying a pocket knife. In 1969, Hoffman became one of the famous "Chicago 7"* because of his arrest on charges of conspiring to disrupt the Democratic convention. Although he was acquitted on those charges, he was convicted of contempt for his disruptive courtroom behavior. Eventually even those charges were dropped.

Hoffman joined the campus lecture circuit, speaking against the war, but in 1973 police arrested him for selling cocaine to undercover agents. Hoffman jumped bail, went underground, dyed his hair, and underwent plastic surgery. His antiwar protests ended. Hoffman turned himself in to the authorities in 1980, entering a work release program in 1981. After his release from the program, Hoffman went on the campus lecture circuit, averaging seventy speeches a year. In 1986, he was working for Radio Free USA and writing a book, *Steal This Urine Test*, a manual on how to tamper with drug test equipment. Late in November 1986, he was arrested for protesting Central Intelligence Agency* employment recruitment on the campus of the University of Massachusetts at Amherst.

Sources: Harry G. Summers, Jr., *Vietnam War Almanac*, 1985; "Hoffman Survives," *USA Today*, November 28, 1986; Mitchell Cohen and Dennis Hale, eds., *The New Student Left: An Anthology*, 1966.

James Hindman

HONOLULU CONFERENCE OF 1965

Late in April 1965, with the military and political situation in South Vietnam deteriorating, the Joint Chiefs of Staff (*see* Chairman, JCS), Secretary of Defense Robert McNamara,* Ambassador to South Vietnam Maxwell Taylor,* and Assistant Secretary for Far Eastern Affairs William Bundy* met in Honolulu to develop a strategy for escalation of the American involvement in Indochina.* As a result of the conference, President Lyndon Johnson* agreed to use American combat forces to supplement the South Vietnamese army. He decided to send approximately 40,000 additional American soldiers. They would be used in the "enclave strategy,"* which restricted their operations to within 50 miles of their base area. No troops would be sent to the Central Highlands.* Along with these nine United States Marine* and Army* battalions, Australia* agreed to send one battalion and South Korea* three. The possibility of future troop commitments was left open, as was the option of invading the Central Highlands. The commitment of large contingents of ground troops was a turning point in the war, a shift away from counterinsurgency* and an air war over the North to a large-scale ground war in the South.

Source: Edward W. Knappman, ed., *U.S.-Communist Confrontation in Southeast Asia*, 1974.

Gloria F. Collins

HONOLULU CONFERENCE OF 1966

President Lyndon B. Johnson* announced on February 4, 1966, that he would consult with representatives of South Vietnam in Honolulu, Hawaii. The president was accompanied to the conference (February 6–8) by Secretary of Defense Robert McNamara,* Ambassador to South Vietnam Henry Cabot Lodge, Jr.,* General William Westmoreland,* and Special Adviser General Maxwell Taylor.* At the conference, Johnson and his associates met with Nguyen Cao Ky* and Nguyen Van Thieu,* South Vietnam's top leaders. The American press argued that Johnson's decision to hold the conference was designed to counter Senator J. William Fulbright's* announcement on February 3, 1966, that the Senate Foreign Relations Committee* would open hearings on U.S. policies in Southeast Asia. At the conference, Johnson assured Ky and Thieu that American resolve was firm, but that the U.S. commitment would be politically easier to sustain if the South Vietnamese could reform their own government. During the conference they also discussed economic questions, the resumption of bombing* of North Vietnam, and the possibility of the People's Republic of China* entering the war. At the end of the meeting the participants released the Declaration of Honolulu, a joint communiqué in which both governments promised to work for peace, political reform, refugee* resettlement, economic growth, and control of inflation. It also called for defeat of the Vietcong* and self-determination for the people of South Vietnam.

Source: Joseph Buttinger, *Vietnam: A Dragon Embattled*. Vol. 2, *Vietnam at War*, 1967.

Gloria Collins

HOOPES, TOWNSEND

Townsend Hoopes was born on April 28, 1922, in Duluth, Minnesota. He graduated from Yale in 1944. During the 1950s Hoopes was a consultant with the State Department, and in January 1965 President Lyndon Johnson* appointed Hoopes assistant secretary of defense. In October 1967 Hoopes became under secretary of the U.S. Air Force.* When Secretary of Defense Robert S. Mc-Namara* resigned in February 1968 and was replaced by Clark Clifford,* Hoopes gained influence and eventually helped convince Clifford that the Vietnam War was unwinnable and that the United States should disengage as quickly as possible. Hoopes helped supply information for the well-known *New York Times* story of March 12, 1968, that the Joint Chiefs of Staff (*see* Chairman, JCS) were asking for another 206,000 troops and that administration officials were dismayed. In 1969 Hoopes recounted the period in *The Limits of Intervention.*

Source: Townsend Hoopes, *The Limits of Intervention*, 1969.

Charles Dobbs

HOP TAC

Hop Tac was the nickname for the short-lived pacification program (*see* Rural Reconstruction) General William Westmoreland* tried to implement around Saigon* in 1964. Shortly after arriving in South Vietnam and during his first year there, Westmoreland tried to pacify the guerrilla-held provinces around Saigon. The idea was to use South Vietnamese troops to move out from Saigon, eliminating all Vietcong* and distributing American supplies to win the loyalties of the peasants. The French had earlier tried a similar policy—called *quadrillage*—which involved pacifying small quadrants of rural areas at a time and hoping to maintain their loyalties. Westmoreland's program was the first in a long string of American failures at guerrilla pacification. ARVN (*see* Army of the Republic of Vietnam) soldiers frequently deserted to escape confrontation with the Vietcong, especially after they had left the II Corps* area where their families lived. The South Vietnamese also failed to deliver the supplies which might have convinced the peasantry to remain loyal. Westmoreland abandoned Hop Tac in mid–1965 after losing all his faith in the abilities of South Vietnamese troops.

Sources: Frances FitzGerald, *Fire in the Lake: The Vietnamese and the Americans in Vietnam*, 1972; Larry E. Cable, *Conflict of Myths: The Development of American Counterinsurgency Doctrine and the Vietnam War*, 1986.

HO THI THIEN

Born in 1908 in Nha Trang, Ho Thi Thien gained international attention on May 30, 1966, when she committed suicide in front of the United Buddhist Church in Saigon.* Ho Thi Thien was a Buddhist nun protesting the political corruption and anti-Buddhist posture (*see* Buddhism) of the regime of Nguyen Cao Ky.*

Source: *New York Times*, May 30, 1966.

"HOT PURSUIT" POLICY

In 1965, when the war in Vietnam escalated, the North Vietnamese increased the infiltration of men and supplies along the Sihanouk Trail out of Cambodia (*see* Kampuchea) and the Ho Chi Minh Trail* out of Laos.* American military officers in Vietnam proposed a blockade of Sihanoukville (Phnom Penh) and military assaults on North Vietnamese and Vietcong* sanctuaries* inside Cambodia. They also wanted approval to impose the "hot pursuit" policy, allowing American and South Vietnamese military units to follow retreating enemy forces across the border into Cambodia. At the time the Cambodian government, under the direction of Norodom Sihanouk,* was officially neutral, and the U.S. State Department was reluctant to widen the conflict. Consequently, President Lyndon B. Johnson* did not approve the Sihanoukville blockade, the attack on the sanctuaries, or the "hot pursuit" policy. The debate became a moot question, however, in 1970 when President Richard M. Nixon* approved the massive bombing (see Operation Menu) and military "incursion" into Cambodia (see Operation Binh Tay) to attack Vietcong and North Vietnamese sanctuaries.

Sources: Terrence Maitland and Peter McInerney, *The Vietnam Experience: A Contagion of War*, 1983; William Shawcross, *Sideshow: Kissinger, Nixon, and the Destruction of Cambodia*, 1979.

HUE

First built by Emperor Gia Long* early in the nineteenth century, Hue was the imperial capital of Vietnam between 1802 and 1945. It is located on Highway 1 (see "Street Without Joy"), about 420 miles south of Hanoi* and 670 miles north of Saigon.* Hue was an independent municipality under the Republic of Vietnam* and had a population of more than 205,000 when the war ended in 1975. The city suffered extensive damage during the Tet Offensive* of 1968 but remains today a cultural center for all of Vietnam.

Sources: Joseph Buttinger, *The Smaller Dragon*, 1958, and *Vietnam: A Dragon Embattled*. Vol. 2, *Vietnam at War*, 1967.

HUE, BATTLE OF (1968)

For the Vietcong* and North Vietnamese, Hue* was a city with tremendous historical significance. Formerly the imperial capital of a united Vietnam, the center of Vietnamese cultural and religious life, and capital of Thua Thien Province, Hue became an important symbol in the struggle for dominance of Indochina.* It was also a difficult city to defend. Isolated by the Annamese mountain chain and bordered by Laos* to the west and the Demilitarized Zone* to the north, Hue was without access to a major port for resupply. Still, before the Tet Offensive,* Hue was considered secure for South Vietnam. That all ended on January 31, 1968.

At 3:40 A.M. that morning North Vietnamese Army* (NVA) artillery began pounding the city. Elements of the NVA 6th Regiment simultaneously attacked Military Assistance Command, Vietnam* (MACV) headquarters in Hue and ARVN 1st Division headquarters. Other NVA troops blockaded Highway 1 (see "Street Without Joy") north and south of the city and attacked several hundred other sites in the city. By daylight, the Vietcong flag was flying atop the Imperial Citadel of the Nguyen* emperors. Hue had fallen to the Communists.

The American and Army of the Republic of Vietnam* (ARVN) counterattack on Hue began almost immediately, with huge volumes of artillery, naval bombardment, and air strikes reducing much of Hue to rubble while elements of the 1st Air Cavalry Division,* the 101st Airborne Division,* the ARVN 1st Division, the U.S. 1st Marines,* and ARVN Rangers and Marines engaged in house-to-house, hand-to-hand combat with NVA troops and Vietcong. The Imperial Citadel was not recaptured from the Communists until February 24, 1968. Hue had been devastated. More than 50 percent of the city had been totally destroyed, and 116,000 people of a total population of 140,000 had been rendered homeless. Nearly 6,000 civilians were dead or missing, and several thousand more were assassinated outright during the Vietcong occupation. The NVA and Vietcong suffered 5,000 dead; the United States, 216 dead and 1,364 seriously wounded; and ARVN, 384 dead and 1,830 seriously wounded. Like the Tet Offensive in general, the battle for Hue was a tactical defeat for the Communists as well as a strategic victory. In taking control of the city, if only for several weeks, they had proven that MACV predictions of an imminent Communist collapse were totally groundless, undermining American faith in the credibility of political and military leaders. Hue in particular, and Tet in general, was indeed the turning point in the war.

Sources: Clark Dougan and Steven Weiss, *The Vietnam Experience: Nineteen Sixty-Eight*, 1983; Don Oberdorfer, *Tet!*, 1971; James R. Bullington, "And Here See Hue!," *Foreign Service Journal* (November 1968), pp. 18–21, 48–49; Keith W. Nolan, *The Battle for Hue: Tet, 1968*, 1973.

HUE, BATTLE OF (1975)

In March 1975, on the eve of the North Vietnamese assault on South Vietnam, Hue* was defended by the 369th Marine Brigade to the west, the ARVN (*see* Army of the Republic of Vietnam) 1st Division and 15th Ranger Group to the South, and the 14th Ranger Group to the north. The ARVN commander of I Corps* was Lt. General Ngo Quang Truong. North Vietnamese Army* (NVA) troops in the B–4 Front Group and elements of the 341st Division were poised by March 19 at the My Chanh River north of Hue, while the NVA 325C and 324B divisions were preparing to descend out of the Central Highlands* to attack the ARVN 1st Division and 15th Ranger Group. NVA artillery attacks were increasing in intensity throughout March, and large numbers of refugees* were fleeing the city, heading south along Highway 1 (*see* "Street Without Joy") toward Da Nang.*

On March 20, 1975, confusing orders reached General Truong from South Vietnam President Nguyen Van Thieu,* which Truong interpreted as a demand for sacrificing the defense of Hue in order to hold the line at Da Nang. At the same time, the NVA General Staff ordered a drive to cut Highway 1 and isolate Hue. The 324B and 325C divisions drove through the ARVN 1st Division and 15th Ranger Group by March 23, cutting Hue off from Da Nang. On March 24, General Truong began evacuating ARVN forces from Hue. NVA troops entered the city the same day.

Sources: Clark Dougan and David Fulghum, *The Vietnam Experience: The Fall of the South*, 1985; Van Tien Dung, *Our Great Spring Victory*, 1977; Alan Dawson, *55 Days: The Fall of South Vietnam*, 1977.

HUMPHREY, HUBERT HORATIO

Born in 1911 in Wallace, South Dakota, Hubert Humphrey worked as a pharmacist before graduating magna cum laude in 1939 from the University of Minnesota. In 1941 Humphrey received a master's degree from Louisiana State University, and then he returned and taught for a year at the University of Minnesota. He began his public career as head of the Minnesota Branch of the Federal War Production Administration (1941–43), assistant regional director of the War Manpower Progress Commission (1943), and teacher in the Army Air Force training program at Macalester College in Minneapolis (1943–44). As a Democrat rooted in agrarian populism and small-town bourgeoisie, Humphrey was an unsuccessful candidate for mayor of Minneapolis in 1943, but in 1944 he worked to merge the state's Democratic and Farm Labor parties. Political success followed. After a stint as Franklin D. Roosevelt's* Minnesota campaign manager in 1944, Humphrey was elected mayor of Minneapolis on the Democratic–Farm Labor ticket. He was reelected in 1947 by the largest plurality in city history.

Humphrey entered the national scene at the Democratic presidential nominating convention of 1948 in Philadelphia by leading the successful effort for a strong civil rights plank in the party platform. That fall Humphrey was elected to the U.S. Senate, defeating incumbent Republican Joseph H. Ball. Although somewhat brash and indefatigable in his advocacy of civil rights, Humphrey entered the Senate's inner circle, especially after his reelection in 1954 and 1960. His Senate career was devoted to the causes of civil rights, medicare, and pro-labor legislation. Humphrey had been a founding member of the Americans for Democratic Action and served as its president in 1949 and 1950, so his liberal credentials were impeccable.

As an advocate of containment,* Humphrey was an early and ardent supporter of American intervention in Vietnam. He accepted the domino theory* and believed the United States must take a stand in Southeast Asia if communism was not to spread across the globe. Humphrey accepted a spot on Lyndon B. Johnson's* 1964 presidential ticket, and as vice president one of his prime duties was to marshal support for the increased direct involvement of U.S. armed forces in Vietnam. As the escalation continued between 1965 and 1968, Humphrey was continuously heckled as he became one of the few administration spokesmen willing to publicly defend the war effort.

Increasing domestic discontent over the war led to rival presidential bids by Democratic Senators Robert F. Kennedy* and Eugene McCarthy* in 1968, both of whom challenged Johnson for the nomination. Johnson's withdrawal from the contest in March 1968 surprised the nation, including Vice President Humphrey, who fell heir to Johnson's formidable political support within the party. Shunning the open primaries, Humphrey built up support among the urban party machines and state party organizations, and after the assassination of Robert F. Kennedy and the disruptive nominating convention in Chicago, Humphrey was the Democratic candidate. Burdened by his association with a failing war policy, subject to intensive harassment on the campaign trail yet loyal to the president who was ultimately responsible for his candidacy, Humphrey finally made a last-minute effort in the campaign to distance himself from Johnson's war policy by calling for a negotiated settlement. Humphrey's moderate change of heart was one of many factors which narrowed the race with Republican candidate Richard M. Nixon* and third-party candidate George Wallace. Although a decided winner in the electoral vote, Nixon's victory margin in 1968 was only 43.4 percent of the popular vote to 42.7 percent for Humphrey and 13.5 percent for Wallace.

In 1970 Humphrey was reelected to the U.S. Senate. A short-lived effort to promote a 1972 presidential candidacy received no significant support within the party. Reelected to the Senate in 1976, Humphrey's main goal was full-employment legislation which designated the government as the employer of last resort. In a 1974 interview Humphrey commented on U.S. policy in Vietnam. He noted that very often big powers "miscalculate . . . overestimating our power to control events. . . . Power tends to be a substitute for judgment and wisdom." Humphrey died of cancer on January 13, 1978.

Sources: *New York Times*, January 14, 1978; George Donth, *Leaders in Profile: The United States Senate*, 1975; Carl Solberg, *Hubert Humphrey: A Political Biography*, 1984.

David Bernstein

HUYNH PHU SO

Born in the Mekong Delta* village of Hoa Hao in 1919, Huynh Phu So had a youth besieged by illness until he entered a monastery in 1939 where he experienced what he termed a miraculous cure. Using his considerable oratorical skills as well as expertise in herbal medicine and acupuncture, Huynh Phu So founded a new Buddhist sect, the Hoa Hao.* He quickly converted thousands of peasants south of Saigon,* stressing the importance of inner experience and the irrelevancy of external evidence. Each member of the Hoa Hao was expected to pray four times daily to Buddha, ancestors, and national heroes. Worried about his growing influence, the French arrested and imprisoned him in a mental hospital in 1940, where he converted his physician and a number of staff people. The French intended to exile him to Laos,* but by then the Japanese had taken over Indochina,* and Huynh Phu So was placed under house arrest in Saigon. The Japanese allowed him to see disciples and continue to direct his religious work. By then Huynh Phu So had an army of nearly 50,000. After World War II, Huynh Phu So established the Dan Xa, or Social Democratic party, and the Hoa Hao had become a powerful political-religious sect in southern Vietnam. The movement continued to grow, and by the mid–1950s the Hoa Hao and Cao Dai* were very influential in the Mekong Delta, with strong sympathies among perhaps half the area's six million people. In April 1947, Vietminh* guerrillas killed Huynh Phu So. No comparable leader appeared among the Hoa Hao to replace him.

Sources: Bernard Fall, "The Political Religious Sects of Vietnam," *Pacific Affairs* 28 (1955), 235–53; Joseph Buttinger, *Vietnam: A Dragon Embattled*. Vol. 2, *Vietnam at War*, 1967.

HUYNH TAN PHAT

Huynh Tan Phat was born in 1913 just outside of My Tho* in Dinh Tuong Province. He went to school at Hanoi University and became actively involved in anti-French nationalism. During the years of Ngo Dinh Diem's* reign over the Republic of Vietnam,* Huynh Tan Phat became active in the National Liberation Front (*see* Vietcong), becoming its secretary-general in 1964. In 1969 he became president of the Provisional Revolutionary Government of South Vietnam.*

Source: Danny J. Whitfield, *Historical and Cultural Dictionary of Vietnam*, 1976.

• I •

IA DRANG VALLEY   *See* Ia Drang Valley, Battle of (1965)

IA DRANG VALLEY, BATTLE OF (1965)

The battle of the Ia Drang Valley began with a North Vietnamese attack on the Special Forces* camp at Plei Me in the Central Highlands* on October 19, 1965. The brand-new 1st Cavalry Division,* responsible for the security of the Central Highlands and the critical Highway 19 which ran through them toward the coast, was ordered to the relief of Plei Me, even though the division had not yet finished developing its airmobile tactics. The operation was code-named Silver Bayonet. Using airmobility, the division's 1st Brigade was able to fly over a North Vietnamese ambush and relieve the Special Forces camp. The North Vietnamese Army* troops deployed in the ambush now had to flee back toward their base camps near the Cambodian border in the Chu Phong mountains. In their retreat they were harried constantly from the air by the 1st Cavalry Division.

In early November the division's 3rd Brigade began a ''search and destroy''* operation intended to break up the North Vietnamese concentration and destroy the NVA forces in the Ia Drang Valley and the nearby mountains. On November 14 the 1st Battalion of the 7th Cavalry unwittingly landed in the midst of a large body of North Vietnamese troops, bringing on an intense and bloody two-day battle. Fighting was so fierce that relief forces had to land a considerable distance from the action, and for the first time American ground forces were directly supported by B–52* strikes. The 2nd Battalion of the 7th Cavalry was ambushed while moving toward the scene of the original fighting, bringing on another daylong battle in which some American units, cut off and surrounded, were almost wiped out. The rest of the American forces managed to hang on to their positions with the assistance of air strikes and artillery fire. On November 18, the North Vietnamese broke off the action and withdrew. The 1st Cavalry Division returned to its base at An Khe on November 26. In the fighting, the division lost some 300 men killed. North Vietnamese dead totaled some 1,770 in the entire campaign.

Sources: Shelby L. Stanton, *The Rise and Fall of an American Army: U.S. Ground Forces in Vietnam, 1965–1973*, 1985; Thomas D. Boettcher, *Vietnam: The Valor and the Sorrow*, 1985; John Albright et al., *Seven Firefights in Vietnam*, 1970.

Robert S. Browning III

INCIDENT AT MUC WA

Incident at Muc Wa was the title of Daniel Ford's 1967 novel on the Vietnam War. The book centers on Corporal Stephen Courcey, a demolitions expert who has just arrived in Vietnam. Along with several other American soldiers, he establishes an outpost at Muc Wa. The novel proceeds to expose the absurdities of the war through tragicomedy. Courcey's girlfriend from the states shows up at Muc Wa as a war correspondent, but she is unable to meet him because he is off in the jungles with a visiting general and army captain who are trying to earn their Combat Infantry Badges. The novel provides a caricature of stupid officers fighting a war for the wrong reasons. In the end, the troops at Muc Wa fight off a Vietcong* attack, and the Vietcong, in Ford's words, finally "exfiltrate" the area. In the end, Courcey is killed in action.

Sources: Daniel Ford, *Incident at Muc Wa*, 1967; Philip D. Beidler, *American Literature and the Vietnam Experience*, 1982.

INDOCHINA

"Indochina" is the name Westerners have traditionally applied to parts of Southeast Asia, including Vietnam, Cambodia (*see* Kampuchea), and Laos.* Under French rule its area was about 288,000 square miles, 10 percent larger than Texas. A spine of mountains runs from northwest to southeast from the Chinese border to the sea near Nha Trang,* with peaks rising from 8,524 feet north of Pleiku to 10,308 feet near China. Interspersed with plateaus, mountains also run from the coast at Nha Trang southwesterly to within 100 miles of Saigon.* Cambodia is largely a basin, surrounded on the north by the Dangrek Range, on the southwest by the Cardamom and Elephant ranges, and on the east by Vietnam's highlands and the Mekong Delta.* The north's significant river valley is that of the Song Koi, or Red. The Mekong River, which rises in China, flows southward through Laos, then forms the Laotian-Thai border, and finally flows through Cambodia and southern Vietnam to the South China Sea south of Ho Chi Minh City* (Saigon). Light soil in the hills is easily eroded, but the river valleys are highly fertile. Traditional culture came to terms with the environment of heat, monsoon, and disease, depending upon pigs, forest trees, rice, and water buffalo to help in cultivation.

Paleolithic man was present in northern Vietnam over 10,000 years ago, neolithic man overspread the entire region from about 8000 to 5000 B.C., and a bronze age culture ranged from coastal Indochina to Indonesia from about 500 to 300 B.C. The people who were Proto-Vietnamese formed a kingdom known variously as Vat Lang and Au Loc, perhaps as early as 500 B.C., and this was conquered by Han Dynasty Chinese by 111 B.C. With brief moments of independence, it remained Chinese until A.D. 940, having come to be known as Nam-Viet. Despite a brief Ming Dynasty reconquest from 1407 to 1427, Vietnam emerged as a permanently independent entity. Buddhism* had become an increasing influence, though Confucianism* from China remained significant, especially for the mandarin rulers.

Indian influence had entered the southern part of Indochina by A.D. 100, being fairly strong in the kingdom of Champa,* established about that time. With internal troubles in India by the end of the sixth century A.D., the Khmers* emerged as the strongest people in southern Indochina, with monumental architecture on the Indian model in the reign of Isarnavarman I (616–635). During the ninth century the Khmers established themselves near Tonle Sap (the "great lake"), founding Angkor and the empire that bore its name. Angkor endured repeated attacks by Champa and Thailand,* gradually decaying. The city itself was taken and looted by a Thai army in 1431, effectively ending the Khmer Empire. By this time Hinayana Buddhism was replacing the original god-king cult with its imported elements of the Hindu cult of Shiva. The Khmer collapse liberated the region now known as Laos, most of which Angkor had controlled. The new kingdom of Lan Xang appeared, which had to fight off Burmese attacks and where Thai influence became dominant by the end of the eighteenth century.

By this time Vietnam, with increasing population based on successful rice culture, had completed its own conquest of the coastal region, which was won, slice by slice, from Champa and then Cambodia, the less imposing successor to Angkor. Vietnam reduced Cambodia to a vassal state, exacting tribute, and dividing it into three residencies, each under a Vietnamese proconsul. There was attempted Vietnamization of Cambodian culture, the monarchy was in effect abolished, and total conquest was prevented only by the imposition of French control of the region. (For that era, see France.) Vietnamese influence did not control more mountainous and Thai-influenced Laos, and especially in the mountains, there remained tribes of other ethnic groups, ranging from the Sino-Tibetan Meo to the Malay Chams.

The population of Indochina at the end of the French era in 1954 was about 26,800,000, of whom some 21,000,000 were Vietnamese, 3,000,000 Cambodians, 1,000,000 Moi and Kha, 600,000 Laotians, 600,000 Chinese,* 300,000 Man and Meo, 200,000 Muong, 100,000 Cham,* and 40,000 Europeans.

Sources: Bernard Philippe Groslier, *Indochina*, 1966; John F. Cody, "The French Colonial Regime in Vietnam," *Current History* 50 (1966), 72–78, 115; Ellen J. Hammer, *The Struggle for Indochina, 1940–1955*, 1966.

Robert W. Sellen

INDOCHINESE COMMUNIST PARTY *See* Lao Dong Party

INFILTRATION

Throughout the years of the Vietnam War, one of the major U.S. challenges was stopping the infiltration of men and supplies into South Vietnam by the

North Vietnamese. Between 1959 and 1975, North Vietnam sent supplies and reinforcements to the Vietcong* and North Vietnamese soldiers by three means: along the Ho Chi Minh Trail* down through the Laotian panhandle to the eastern border of Cambodia (*see* Kampuchea) and then along smaller branches into the A Shau Valley,* Ia Drang Valley,* and War Zone C;* from Sihanoukville in neutral Cambodia by truck to bases along the Cambodian and Laotian border; and by small ships and junks down the coast of the South China Sea and then upriver in various regions of the Republic of Vietnam.* After 1970, when Lon Nol* deposed Prince Sihanouk* and realigned Cambodia with the United States, that infiltration route through Sihanoukville was shut off. Nevertheless, despite the elimination of that route and the application of enormous American firepower along the Ho Chi Minh Trail and the South China Sea, North Vietnam still managed to ship supplies. Between 1959 and 1964, North Vietnam infiltrated more than 30,000 personnel into South Vietnam, and that number increased to 36,000 in 1965, 92,000 in 1966, and 101,000 in 1967. By 1968 North Vietnam was able to send more than 10,000 troops a month into South Vietnam, and enough food to feed them and ammunition to equip them, along the Ho Chi Minh Trail and through the American blockade of the South China Sea.

Source: William E. LeGro, *Vietnam from Ceasefire to Capitulation*, 1981.

INFLATION   *See* "Guns and Butter"

INTERNATIONAL COMMISSION OF CONTROL AND SUPERVISION

One of the provisions of the Paris Accords* of 1973 was establishment of a four-nation International Commission of Control and Supervision (ICCS). It replaced the International Control Commission (ICC), a three-country body established by the Geneva Conference* of 1954. The ICC was composed of Canada,* India, and Poland. The Paris Accords provided for those three nations to continue on the new ICCS, but India declined and was replaced by Indonesia. Hungary became the fourth member. Canada withdrew in August 1973 when she realized the North Vietnamese were still intent on taking over South Vietnam. Iran then became the fourth member. The ICCS headquarters were located near Saigon* at Tan Son Nhut Air Base.* It had no power and became the butt of jokes among the Americans, South Vietnamese, and North Vietnamese vying for control in Southeast Asia.

Sources: Walter Scott Dillard, *Sixty Days to Peace*, 1982; Ramesh Thakur, *Peacekeeping in Vietnam: Canada, India, Poland, and the International Commission*, 1984.

INVASION OF CAMBODIA   *See* Operation Binh Tay

INVASION OF LAOS   *See* Lam Son 719

IRON TRIANGLE (WAR ZONE D)

The Iron Triangle was a National Liberation Front (NLF; *see* Vietcong) stronghold 20 miles northwest of Saigon* which had been built by the Vietminh* twenty years before in the war aginst French colonialism. Serving as a supply depot and staging area with a vast underground complex including command headquarters, dining halls, hospital rooms, munitions factories, and living quarters, it was never cleared by the French, nor was it successfully neutralized by the United States or ARVN (*see* Army of the Republic of Vietnam). Located between Saigon, Tay Ninh, and Song Be cities, the Triangle comprised about 125 square miles and included portions of Bien Hoa, Binh Duong, Phuoc Long, Long Khanh, and Hau Nghia provinces. It was generally bounded by the Saigon River, the Song (river) Thi Thinh north of Bien Hoa, and the Than Dien Forest in Binh Duong Province. The area was heavily forested, consisting of jungle and rubber plantations and containing a few small villages and hamlets, the most strategic being Ben Suc,* which had been under NLF control since 1964.

In January 1967 the United States and ARVN mounted the war's first major combined operation and the first U.S. corps-size operation. Operation Cedar Falls* deployed 32,000 troops against the Triangle. Its "search and destroy"* objective was to engage and eliminate enemy forces, destroy base camps and supplies, remove all noncombatants along with possessions and livestock to strategic hamlets,* and completely destroy four principal villages. Extensive underground complexes were found, and large quantities of supplies and papers were captured. The complete U.S. arsenal was employed—intensive bombing, flamethrowers, chemical warfare (defoliants and the first authorized major use of CS, or tear, gas), and land-clearing Rome plows. Units participating in Cedar Falls included the 173rd Airborne Brigade,* the 196th* and 199th* Infantry brigades, elements of the 1st* and 25th* Infantry divisions, the 11th Armored Cavalry Regiment,* and the ARVN 5th Ranger Group.

There was little fighting as the NLF fled to sanctuaries* in Cambodia (*see* Kampuchea) until the operation was finished. However, the destruction, chronicled in Jonathan Schell's *The Village of Ben Suc*, was considerable. About 7,000 refugees* were created and the region was made uninhabitable to anyone other than NLF-NVA forces. The operation's magnitude increased NLF utilization of Cambodian sanctuaries; however, they did return to rebuild camps which became springboards for the assault on Saigon during the Tet Offensive,* 1968. Subsequent operations against the Iron Triangle included Uniontown,* Atlas Wedge,* and Toan Thang.*

Sources: Stanley Karnow, *Vietnam: A History*, 1983; Shelby Stanton, *The Rise and Fall of an American Army: U.S. Ground Troops in Vietnam, 1965–1973*, 1985; Andrew F. Krepinevich, Jr., *The Army and Vietnam*, 1986.

Samuel Freeman

• J •

JAPAN

Japan played several important roles in the Vietnam conflict. Historically, the original drive for Vietnamese independence received substantial impetus from Japanese occupation during World War II. When Japan conquered Indochina* in 1941, it chose to leave French bureaucrats in nominal control, belying Japanese wartime propaganda of "Asia for the Asians" and greatly reinforcing Vietnamese anticolonialism.* Supported with U.S. supplies and advice, the Vietminh* had fought against Japanese occupation forces, becoming popular heroes in the process and the de facto government in the countryside. When the French returned to power in 1946, the Vietminh simply turned their nationalist energies against them. Japan's rhetoric and occupation policies had accelerated the movement for Vietnamese independence.

Japan also served as a primary rationale for U.S. intervention in Vietnam after the French debacle at Dien Bien Phu* in 1954. China had become a Communist state in 1949; the Korean War had seemingly demonstrated the expansionist nature of communism between 1950 and 1953; and a containment*-oriented American foreign policy worried about Communist aggression in Southeast Asia. If Vietnam fell to communism, the United States argued, a sequence of disastrous events would follow: both Japan and the United States would lose access to Indochina's natural resources; Japanese economic expansion would be curtailed since Indochinese markets would be closed; and Japan would be forced into an accommodation with both the Soviet Union* and the People's Republic of China.* Japan was the United States's closest ally in Asia and had to be protected through American intervention in Vietnam. Finally, the United States had to prove to the Soviet Union, the Chinese, and the other nations of the world its commitment to stopping communism.

During the war itself, Japan played only a peripheral role. Despite the U.S.-Japanese security treaty of 1960, Japan resisted American blandishments to become more involved in the conflict. They viewed the American commitment in Vietnam as excessive and ultimately as a dangerous mistake. Japan's role in the conflict was confined to playing host to the Seventh Fleet* and various U.S. air wings, and permitting U.S. personnel to find necessary hospitalization and rest and recreation. Potent leftist elements periodically provoked domestic turmoil over such issues as hospitalized American soldiers in Japan conveying virulent tropical diseases to Japanese civilians or the dangers of expanding airports, especially at Narita, which could then be used for American air operations against Vietnam. The leftists were never successful, however, in convincing the Japanese public that the United States was engaged in a racist war in Vietnam. Japan also adopted a conservative posture for fear of inciting her Communist neighbors in North Korea and China. Finally, Japan wanted to maintain commerce with North Vietnam. It was the presence of Japanese ships in Haiphong which restrained initial American plans to bomb and mine the harbor.

The irony, of course, is that the Vietnam War may actually have hastened the Japanese accommodation with the Soviet Union and the People's Republic of China. With Vietnam monopolizing U.S. diplomatic interests, with the articulation of the Nixon Doctrine* in 1969, and with the shock of not being consulted about Henry Kissinger's* secret initiatives to the People's Republic of China, Japan felt free, even compelled, to adopt a more independent diplomatic course in Asia. Although Japan remains solidly pro-Western, she is more wary about her relations with the United States and more independent in her dealings with the major powers.

Sources: Stanley Robert Larsen and James Lawton Collins, Jr., *Vietnam Studies: Allied Participation in Vietnam*, 1975; Frank Gibney, *Japan: The Fragile Superpower*, 1975; Edwin O. Reischauer, *Japan: Story of a Nation*, 1974; John K. Emmerson, *Arms, Yen and Power*, 1971.

                                                                Gary M. Bell

JASON STUDY

By the spring of 1966, Secretary of Defense Robert McNamara* was beginning to have serious misgivings about the nature of the war in Vietnam. Two of his closest civilian aides—John McNaughton and Adam Yarmolinksy—began searching for alternatives to the war, and in the summer of 1966, with the assistance of the Institute of Defense Analysis, a think tank, they organized a conference of perhaps fifty leading scholars at Wellesley, Massachusetts. They met there throughout the summer of 1966, and their collective report came to be known as the Jason Study. The major conclusion of the report was that American air strikes on Vietnam were having little effect and might even be counterproductive. Because much of North Vietnam was a subsistence, agricultural economy, air strikes did not sufficiently disrupt economic affairs. The flow of supplies into South Vietnam was not materially affected by air strikes, and the People's Republic of China* and the Soviet Union* quickly replaced any supplies lost. Worse still, the volume of supplies making their way into the south had actually increased since the bombing* began, and the morale of the North Vietnamese had measurably stiffened. The Jason Study confirmed many of McNamara's growing suspicions about the war and converted him into an advocate of negotiation and an end to the bombing of North Vietnam.

Source: Stanley Karnow, *Vietnam: A History*, 1983.

JAVITS, JACOB KOPPEL

Jacob Javits was born in New York City on May 18, 1904. He took a law degree from New York University in 1927, practiced law privately, and served in the United States Army during World War II. In 1946 Javits was elected to Congress,* and he won a seat in the U.S. Senate in 1956. A liberal Republican, Javits became a leading Republican critic of the Vietnam War. He supported both the Cooper-Church Amendment* and the Hatfield-McGovern Amendment,* and in 1970 he sponsored legislation to restrict the ability of the president to conduct war without congressional authorization. It was passed over Richard Nixon's* veto in 1973 and was known as the War Powers Resolution.* In 1980 Javits lost the Republican primary in New York. Since then he has suffered from amyotrophic lateralsclerosis, or Lou Gehrig's disease.

Sources: Jacob Javits, *Who Makes War: The President versus Congress*, 1973; *Biographical Directory of American Congresses*, 1971.

JOHNS HOPKINS SPEECH

On April 7, 1966, amidst widespread opposition to the Vietnam War, President Lyndon B. Johnson* delivered a speech at Johns Hopkins University and offered to hold "unconditional discussions" with the North Vietnamese about ending the conflict. Johnson also held out the proverbial diplomatic "carrot," offering a billion-dollar economic development program for the Mekong Delta.* The only hitch in the offer, of course, was Johnson's insistence that the United States would not negotiate with the National Liberation Front (*see* Vietcong) and was committed to the existence of a non-Communist, independent South Vietnam.

Sources: George C. Herring, *America's Longest War: The United States and Vietnam, 1950–1975*, 1986; *New York Times*, April 8, 1966.

Dudley Acker

JOHNSON, HAROLD KEITH

Harold Keith Johnson was born on February 22, 1912, in Bowesmont, North Dakota. He graduated from the United States Military Academy at West Point in 1933, and spent all of World War II in a Japanese prisoner-of-war camp after participating in the Bataan death march. Johnson saw active duty in the Korean War. He rose up through army ranks until July 6, 1964, when he was appointed army chief of staff. Johnson retired from the army in 1968 and died on September 24, 1983.

Source: *New York Times*, September 25, 1983.

JOHNSON, LYNDON BAINES

Lyndon Baines Johnson was born on August 27, 1908, in the Hill Country of central Texas and was raised in Johnson City. He attended Southwest State Teachers College, took a year off to teach school in Cotulla, Texas, and then graduated in 1930. Johnson taught school briefly in Houston before becoming assistant to the newly elected congressman from the Fourteenth District in Texas, Richard M. Kleberg. As a congressional aide, Johnson excelled at meeting and cultivating people, especially Congressman Sam T. Rayburn, the dean of the Texas delegation. After serving two years as the state director of the National Youth Administration, Johnson won his own seat in Congress,* and served there until 1949. He was elected to the U.S. Senate in 1948 in an election marked for its bitterness and fraud. Johnson became majority leader of the Senate in 1955 and earned a formidable reputation as a legislative strategist. After failing to win the Democratic presidential nomination in 1960, Johnson accepted a position as running mate with John F. Kennedy,* and he became vice president of the United States in 1961. When Kennedy was assassinated on November 22, 1963, Johnson became the thirty-sixth president of the United States.

As president, Johnson earned impeccable liberal credentials for his support of civil rights and antipoverty programs, but his Great Society administration was politically destroyed in the jungles of Southeast Asia. Accepting the official U.S. view of the Vietnam War as one of pure Communist aggression, Johnson ignored anti-Western feelings and the serious flaws of the Saigon* governments, and allowed himself to be trapped into escalation. He limited genuine consultation to "hawks," most of whom also failed to grasp Vietnamese realities, and unlike Kennedy, Johnson did not know how to question their advice. His queries to them were confined to techniques and amounts; he assumed the correctness of American military involvement. Johnson also allowed his goals to escalate from stopping aggression to "winning," presumably by destroying both the enemy's forces and will to continue.

Consequently, he obtained from Congress the Gulf of Tonkin Resolution* in August 1964, which authorized him "to take all necessary measures to repel any armed attack against the forces of the United States and to prevent further aggression," a virtual blank check. Johnson consistently reacted vigorously to attacks on American personnel or installations, beginning and increasing the bombing* of North Vietnam, sending ever more troops into South Vietnam, and allowing them to fight on the ground independently of ARVN forces (see Army of the Republic of Vietnam). Johnson paid lip service to the idea of a negotiated settlement, but he ignored warnings by such advisers as George Ball,* who understood the power of Vietnamese nationalism. By 1968 Johnson had more than 540,000 troops in Vietnam, plus powerful naval forces off the coast and B–52s* bombing from bases in Guam, Okinawa, and Thailand.*

The enemy fought on, but Johnson refused to admit that his strategy of attrition (see war of attrition) was not working. He replaced Robert McNamara* as secretary of defense when the latter began to turn "dovish." Late in January and early February 1968, the Vietcong* and North Vietnamese Army* launched the Tet Offensive,* hitting Saigon* and thirty provincial capitals, and despite heavy casualties, they earned a strategic victory by demoralizing American public opinion. When, after Tet, General William Westmoreland* requested 206,000 more American troops, Johnson asked Clark Clifford,* his new secretary of defense, to evaluate the request. Clifford asked Pentagon officials if more troops would guarantee a victory in South Vietnam, and when they hedged their answers, he advised Johnson to seek peace. Johnson was enraged and almost fired Clifford. Stunned by his near defeat at the hands of Senator Eugene McCarthy* in the New Hampshire presidential primary, and depressed about the prospects of Senator Robert Kennedy* of New York seeking the Democratic presidential nomination, Johnson withdrew from the campaign at the end of March and announced a bombing halt and a willingness to seek a negotiated settlement. He then quibbled over such details as a meeting place for peace talks which, when they began in Paris in May, dragged on inconclusively until the end of his term. Johnson left the White House in January 1969 and retired to his Texas ranch, where he died on January 22, 1973.

Sources: Robert W. Sellen, "Old Assumptions versus New Realities: Lyndon Johnson and Foreign Policy," *International Journal* 28 (Spring 1973), 205–229; Robert A. Caro, *The Years of Lyndon Johnson: The Path to Power*, 1982; and Doris Kearns, *Lyndon Johnson and the American Dream*, 1976.

Robert W. Sellen

JOINT CHIEFS OF STAFF   *See* Chairman, Joint Chiefs of Staff

JOINT GENERAL STAFF

The Joint General Staff (JGS) was the South Vietnamese equivalent of the U.S. Joint Chiefs of Staff (JCS; *see* Chairman, JCS). JGS headquarters were in Saigon.* The major difference between the JGS and the JCS was that the JGS had direct operational control over the South Vietnamese forces. United States commanders of the Military Assistance Command, Vietnam,* especially Generals William Westmoreland* and Creighton Abrams,* cooperated closely with, but did not control, the JGS.

Source: William C. Westmoreland, *A Soldier Reports*, 1976.

. K .

KAMPUCHEA

Covering nearly 70,000 square miles in Southeast Asia, Kampuchea (formerly Cambodia) had a 1985 population of 6,180,000. The country is a great basin composed of one gigantic alluvial floodplain formed by numerous streams. Near the center of the basin is a huge, shallow lake called Tonle Sap. It has hundreds of tributaries flowing in, and the lake drains southeast into the Mekong River via a complex system of distributaries. However, when the Mekong floods, the drainage is reversed and the river backs into Tonle Sap. Three-quarters of Kampuchea is heavily forested, and rice is cultivated on 80 percent of the arable land.

Approximately 85 percent of the people are ethnic Khmer.* The vast majority of them are small farmers raising rice. About 9 percent of the population are ethnic Vietnamese and 5 percent ethnic Chinese,* and both of these groups dominate commerce and industry. Ethnic conflicts between the Khmer and the Vietnamese are fundamental to an understanding of Kampuchean history. Anciently, the Khmer occupied much of the Mekong Delta* in southern Vietnam, but as the ethnic Vietnamese expanded out of northern Vietnam in the sixteenth century, they pushed the Khmer west back into Kampuchea. Both countries were under French rule until 1954, but even after independence the expansionary pressures of the ethnic Vietnamese on the Khmer continued. That pressure precipitated the 1970 coup d'état, the 1975 triumph of the Khmer Rouge,* and the genocidal rage of Pol Pot* in the late 1970s.

Prince Norodom Sihanouk* became head of state in Cambodia in 1954, and he walked a neutralist tightrope between the Vietnamese-backed Khmer Rouge Communists and the American-backed South Vietnamese. His prime minister Lon Nol,* however, was bitterly anti-Communist and resented the willingness of Sihanouk to allow Vietcong* and North Vietnamese Army* (NVA) troops to occupy sanctuaries* in eastern Cambodia and infiltrate supplies and personnel into South Vietnam via the Ho Chi Minh Trail.* Sihanouk tolerated their presence there only because he feared a North Vietnamese invasion and the triumph of the Khmer Rouge if he tried to drive Vietcong and NVA soldiers out. Beginning in 1969 he secretly allowed the United States to begin bombing enemy targets inside Cambodia (*see* Operation Menu). In March 1970 Sihanouk traveled to France, and while he was gone Lon Nol engineered a coup d'état. The National Assembly displaced Sihanouk, and Lon Nol became the new head of state. Lon Nol then tacitly agreed to the U.S. invasion of Cambodia in April 1970. Prince Sihanouk fled to the People's Republic of China* and announced his support for the Khmer Rouge.

In October 1970 Lon Nol abolished the monarchy and proclaimed a republic, but in effect he had become the dictator of Cambodia. His administration was marked by extraordinary corruption and ineptitude, and his 1971 stroke left him unable to maintain control of the government. Pol Pot and the Khmer Rouge made steady gains in the countryside. In the spring of 1975 the Khmer Rouge surrounded the Cambodian capital of Phnom Penh. Lon Nol fled to Hawaii early in April 1975, and the Khmer Rouge overran the capital later in the month. They then renamed the country Kampuchea, its ancient name.

Pol Pot, the leader of the Khmer Rouge, then declared "Year Zero" and began forcibly depopulating all Kampuchean cities, forcing everyone into rural labor camps and murdering anyone and everyone with ties to the French, Norodom Sihanouk, and Lon Nol. The killings assumed genocidal dimensions, with up to two million people dying between 1975 and 1979. Astonished by the brutality of Pol Pot, worried about the political stability of the regime, and still interested in their ancient quest for dominance of the Khmer people, the Vietnamese went on the march again when soldiers of the Socialist Republic of Vietnam* invaded Kampuchea in 1979. They drove to the capital and Pol Pot fled back into the jungles, organizing remnants of the Khmer Rouge into a new guerrilla force fighting against the Vietnamese occupation force.

Sources: William Shawcross, *Sideshow: Kissinger, Nixon, and the Destruction of Cambodia*, 1979; Michael Vickery, *Cambodia, 1975–1982*, 1984; William Shawcross, *The Quality of Mercy. Cambodia, Holocaust, and the Modern Conscience*, 1984; Ben Kiernan, "How Pol Pot Came to Power," Ph.D. diss., 1986.

Gerald L. Holder

KATTENBURG, PAUL

Born in Austria in 1922, Paul Kattenburg immigrated to the United States in 1940 and earned degrees at the University of North Carolina (B.S.), Georgetown University (M.A.), and Yale (Ph.D.). Between 1952 and 1956 he served in the State Department as an Indochina* research analyst and between 1963 and 1964 as Vietnam desk officer. At a meeting of the National Security Council* on August 31, 1963, Paul Kattenburg became the first known American official to recommend withdrawal from Vietnam. He had traveled to South Vietnam many times on State Department business in the 1950s and early 1960s, and he became convinced that the regime of Ngo Dinh Diem* would never survive and that the Vietcong* would eventually prevail. His recommendation was summarily rejected by Dean Rusk* and Robert McNamara,* and Kattenburg was quickly cut off from the advisory–decision-making process on Vietnam. After he left public service, Kattenburg became the Charles L. Jacobsen Professor of Public Affairs at the University of South Carolina.

Sources: Stanley Karnow, *Vietnam: A History*, 1983; *New York Times*, June 25, 1971.

Samuel Freeman

KATZENBACH, NICHOLAS

Nicholas Katzenbach was born in Philadelphia in 1922. He attended Princeton until joining the army in 1942 and spent most of the war in Italian and German POW camps. When the war was over, he returned to Princeton and was allowed to graduate in 1945 by taking special examinations. Katzenbach then received a law degree from Yale in 1947. A Rhodes scholarship took him to Oxford between 1947 and 1949, and he then returned to the United States to practice law. In 1952 Katzenbach joined the law faculty at Yale, and between 1956 and 1960 he was professor of law at the University of Chicago Law School. With the election of John F. Kennedy* in 1960, Katzenbach came to Washington as an assistant attorney general where he specialized in civil rights issues. He helped draft the Civil Rights Acts of 1964 and 1965. Katzenbach's reputation for composure under pressure was enhanced in December 1962 when he negotiated the release of prisoners captured by Cuba during the Bay of Pigs invasion in 1961.

When he became under secretary of state in 1966, Katzenbach, who had no direct experience with foreign policy, spent his early months reading files and briefs and in discussion with his colleagues. Yet his experience in the Department of State was less successful than in the office of the attorney general. In an early session with the Senate Foreign Relations Committee,* Katzenbach provoked dismay among those who believed that he would continue in the tradition of his predecessor, George Ball,* who did not favor the escalation of the war. Katzenbach, when asked by the committee to interpret the 1964 Gulf of Tonkin Resolution,* argued that in its wording, it supported President Johnson's* right to escalate the war as he saw fit. In this and other situations, Katzenbach's analytical approach and propensity to reconcile opposing viewpoints led his former admirer to see him as a mere functionary, unwilling to argue against a doubtful policy. Katzenbach has been a senior vice president and general counsel for IBM since 1969.

Sources: U. S. Navasky, "No. 2 Man at State is a Cooler-Downer," *New York Times Magazine*, December 24, 1967; *Who's Who in Finance and Industry, 1985–86*, 1985.

Joanna D. Cowden

KENNAN, GEORGE FROST

Born in Milwaukee, Wisconsin, on February 16, 1904, George Kennan attended Princeton University and joined the Foreign Service of the State Department in 1926. He served as U.S. ambassador to the Soviet Union* in the early 1950s and became an expert on Russian affairs. In a 1947 article in the journal *Foreign Affairs*, Kennan became the father of the containment policy,* a foreign policy strategy to keep the Soviet Union behind her 1945 military boundaries. The Truman Doctrine, Marshall Plan, NATO, Berlin Airlift, and the other regional treaty organizations were all examples of containment. Since 1956 Kennan has worked as a professor of historical studies at the Institute for Advanced Studies at Princeton. Among his many books are *Russia Leaves the War*, *American Diplomacy 1900–1950*, and *Realities of American Foreign Policy*.

By the 1960s, however, Kennan was becoming a minority voice in foreign policy circles because of his conviction that the containment policy was being indiscriminately applied to too many unique situations. In Vietnam, he was convinced that nationalism, not communism, was the moving force behind the rebellion, and from the beginning he opposed U.S. involvement in the war. He argued that it was a mistake for the United States to ally itself with a corrupt regime incapable of winning the confidence of most South Vietnamese. Kennan also harbored serious doubts about whether the United States could administer a military defeat to the Vietcong* and North Vietnamese using only conventional weapons. On February 10, 1966, Kennan testified before the Senate Foreign Relations Committee,* arguing that since the region was not of military or industrial importance, and that since the area would remain philosophically independent of Russian or Chinese influence, the United States should withdraw as soon as possible.

Sources: George Kennan, *Memoirs, 1950–1963*, 1972; David Halberstam, *The Best and the Brightest*, 1972.

Kim Younghaus

KENNEDY, EDWARD MOORE

Edward Moore Kennedy was born in Boston, Massachusetts, on February 22, 1932. He graduated from Harvard University in 1956 and then took a law degree at the University of Virginia in 1959. In 1962, with his brother John* serving as president of the United States and his other brother Robert serving as attorney general in the Kennedy cabinet, Edward Kennedy won election as a U.S. senator. In the Senate he staked out his own political ground with expertise in labor, judicial, and medical issues, but after the assassination of Robert Kennedy* in 1968, Edward inherited the mantle of his anti-Vietnam commitment. He flirted with a run for the presidency in 1968, and his campaign book *Decisions for a Decade* outspokenly opposed the American commitment in Vietnam, condemned the "search and destroy"* strategy, and called for military defense of limited sanctuaries.* By 1969 Kennedy was openly critical of the Nixon* administration's continuing commitment to the struggle in Vietnam, and he also condemned the "gross corruption" of the government of the Republic of Vietnam.* But that year the incident at Chappaquidick Island and the death of Mary Jo Kopekne all but destroyed Kennedy's presidential chances. He criticized the Nixon administration for the Cambodian invasion (*see* Operation Binh Tay) in 1970 and began calling for an immediate withdrawal of American forces from Southeast Asia. Kennedy tried to make presidential runs in the primaries of 1972, 1976, and 1980 but failed in each of them. He was reelected to the Senate in 1968, 1974, 1980, and 1986.

Sources: John Galloway, *The Kennedys and Vietnam*, 1971; Edward M. Kennedy, *Decisions for a Decade*, 1968.

KENNEDY, JOHN FITZGERALD

John F. Kennedy was born in Brookline, Massachusetts, on May 29, 1917. He graduated from Harvard in 1940 and served in the Pacific with the United States Navy during World War II. He inherited the political mantle of the Kennedy family in Massachusetts, especially after his older brother Joseph was killed in Europe during the war, and in 1946 he was elected to Congress. He won a seat as a Democrat in the U.S. Senate in 1952, came close to winning a spot as Adlai Stevenson's vice presidential running mate in the election of 1956, and in 1960 defeated Richard Nixon* for the presidency.

Kennedy's involvement with Vietnam, in one way or another, had existed well back into the 1950s. He was a relatively typical Cold Warrior, urging Eisenhower* to resist Communist expansion in Indochina.* When it was clear the French would withdraw, Kennedy urged Eisenhower to back the government of Roman Catholic Ngo Dinh Diem* in South Vietnam. When Kennedy became president in 1961, he asked the United States Army* to develop counterinsurgency* forces and General Maxwell D. Taylor* to oversee the program. In 1963 Kennedy announced that "now is the time" and "Vietnam is the place" for a firm stand against Communist aggression. Kennedy also replaced Army Chief of Staff General George Decker with General Earl Wheeler,* who was more of a supporter of counterinsurgency tactics.

Believing in the domino theory* and committed to containment policies,* Kennedy was gradually drawn deeply into the Vietnamese quagmire. He ended up following a middle road, primarily because the advice he received from civilian and military advisers was so contradictory. By 1963 there were more than 16,000 U.S. economic and military advisers in South Vietnam and the political and military situation was already deteriorating. Some U.S. officials in Washington and Saigon* urged support for an army coup in Vietnam; some urged stronger backing for Ngo Dinh Diem; a few people like Chester Cooper* urged withdrawal. Kennedy, tired of the manifest corruption of the Diem regime, opted for the coup but was surprised when news came in of Diem's assassination. Years later, Kennedy supporters claimed that he was seriously considering a military withdrawal from Vietnam, but that he was waiting for the end of the 1964 election so Republicans would not be able to accuse him of being soft on communism. Kennedy's critics, as well as Lyndon B. Johnson* loyalists, disagree, arguing that Kennedy was too much of a Cold Warrior to have considered such an option, and that he had steadily escalated the conflict in Indochina throughout his administration. John F. Kennedy was assassinated on November 22, 1963.

Sources: Arthur M. Schlesinger, Jr., *A Thousand Days: John F. Kennedy in the White House*, 1965; David Halberstam, *The Best and the Brightest*, 1972; William J. Rust, *Kennedy in Vietnam*, 1985; Bruce Miroff, *Pragmatic Illusions: The Presidential Politics of John F. Kennedy*, 1976.

Charles Dobbs

KENNEDY, ROBERT FRANCIS

At age forty-two, while campaigning for the 1968 Democratic presidential nomination, Kennedy was assassinated by Sirhan Sirhan in Los Angeles, dying on June 6, 1968. Born in Boston in 1925, he graduated from Harvard and the University of Virginia Law School. He managed the successful presidential campaign of his brother John* in 1960, and served as attorney general during his brother's presidency and then under President Lyndon Johnson.* In 1964 he resigned and was elected to the U.S. Senate from New York. He remained a senator until his death.

In 1962, when his brother was president, Robert Kennedy said, "we are going to win in Vietnam. We will remain here until we do win," although he played a very limited role in Vietnam policy while he was attorney general. He initially supported Johnson administration Vietnam policies; however, as a senator he had increasingly dissented from Johnson's policies, particularly after the resumption of bombing* of North Vietnam in 1966. Nonetheless, Robert Kennedy had refrained from making an open break with Johnson until he announced his candidacy for the presidency on March 16, 1968. He said that he wanted to end the bloodshed in Vietnam. "In private talks and in public I have tried in vain to alter our course in Vietnam before it further saps our spirit and our manpower, further raises the risks of wider war, and further destroys the country and the people it was meant to save." In his campaign he opposed further military escalation in Vietnam and U.S. bombing of the North. However, he did not enter the race until after Eugene McCarthy* had made a strong showing against Lyndon Johnson in the New Hampshire primary. Two weeks later, Johnson said he would not seek reelection. Just before he was murdered, Kennedy had won the California Democratic primary, and was making a strong bid for his party's presidential nomination.

Sources: Arthur M. Schlesinger, Jr., *Robert Kennedy and His Times*, 1978; David Halberstam, *The Unfinished Odyssey of Robert Kennedy*, 1968.

Hoyt Purvis

KENT STATE UNIVERSITY

After President Richard M. Nixon* announced that American and South Vietnamese soldiers had invaded Cambodia (*see* Kampuchea) on April 30, 1970, to eliminate Vietcong* base camps and stop the infiltration* of materiel and personnel from North Vietnam, students across the country demonstrated against the escalation of the war. On May 1, 1970, students at Kent State University in Ohio marched against the war and rioted, shattering windows, lighting fires, and damaging cars. The next night some of them arsoned the ROTC building on campus. When firemen arrived to put out the blaze, some students seized the firehoses and turned them on the firemen. Governor James Rhodes ordered in the National Guard, declared martial law, and announced that campus violence must come to an end. Rhodes felt the rioters were part of a revolutionary group and he ordered that students not be allowed to assemble in groups on the campus until the disturbances were over.

Around noon on May 4, 1970, antiwar* protesters staged another rally. Campus police asked them a number of times to disperse, and when they refused, armed guardsmen advanced on them. A group of students began hurling chunks of concrete and rock at the guardsmen, and the guardsmen reacted with tear gas grenades. Apparently one of the guardsmen thought he heard a sniper shot and he opened fire. Others joined him, some of them firing directly into the crowd of students. They fired a total of thirty-five rounds at students approximately sixty feet away. Four students died and fourteen were wounded. The incident triggered hundreds of college protest movements and a march on Washington, D.C., on May 9, 1970. The guardsmen were brought to trial but found not guilty.

Sources: Weldon Brown, *The Last Chopper*, 1976; Clark Dougan and Steven Weiss, *The Vietnam Experience: A Nation Divided*, 1984; James Michener, *Kent State: What Happened and Why*, 1971; Richard E. Peterson and John Bilorsky, *May 1970: The Campus Aftermath of Cambodia and Kent State*, 1971.

Gloria Collins

KHAM DUC AIRLIFT EVACUATION

As early as April 1968 intelligence analysts began to observe signs that the Kham Duc Special Forces Camp near the Laotian border 50 miles southeast of Da Nang* was being threatened in a way similar to that of the Khe Sanh* base. By early May it appeared that large contingents of Vietcong* and North Vietnamese units were preparing to attack, and beginning May 10, American commanders reinforced the installation. On May 10–11, 1968, American and Allied forces at Kham Duc found themselves under intense artillery, mortar, and recoilless rifle attacks. Losses on May 10 alone were heavy: fifteen killed, fifty-two wounded, and sixty-four missing in action. As a result of these losses, the prospect of increased activity by the enemy, and the relatively poor defensive potential of the base, General William Westmoreland* ordered the evacuation of Kham Duc.

The evacuation of the garrison at Kham Duc on May 12, 1968, was one of the most spectacular operations of the war. Intermittently through much of the day, United States Army* and Marine* helicopters lifted out survivors, while allied air strikes held off the enemy on all sides. While under constant attack early in the morning, a C–130* landed to pick up evacuees. It received heavy damage while on the landing strip and was able to carry out only three passengers because fuel was streaming from the fuselage through shrapnel holes. A C–123 transport, however, was able to make a successful morning pickup of several evacuees. In the early afternoon, three C–130s attempted pickups. Enemy fire detroyed one after it took off with more than 100 civilian passengers; another, crippled in landing, was abandoned. Only the third made a successful landing and evacuation. Then, late in the afternoon, three additional C–130s succeeded in bringing out the last of the garrison. Of the 1,500 survivors of Kham Duc, the United States Air Force* flew out more than 500, nearly all in the final crucial minutes before the outpost fell.

One final evacuation mission took place, when a C–130 landed at the now enemy-controlled Kham Duc landing strip to bring in a three-man air force control team. By the time the team realized that all Allied forces had been withdrawn, the C–130 carrying them had already departed. To rescue this team a C–123 landed under heavy fire and successfully removed them.

Source: Alan L. Gropman, *Airpower and the Airlift Evacuation of Kham Duc*, 1979.

Roger D. Launius

KHE SANH

Khe Sanh is a town in Quang Tri Province located on Highway 9 between Laos* and Dong Ha.* It is just below the Demilitarized Zone* along the Laotian border. For seventy-five days late in 1967 and early in 1968, Khe Sanh was the site of one of the most publicized battles of the Vietnam War, where American and South Vietnamese forces inflicted a major military defeat on Vietcong* and North Vietnamese forces.

Sources: Moyers S. Shore II, *The Battle for Khe Sanh*, 1969; Bernard C. Nalty, *Air Power and the Fight for Khe Sanh*, 1973.

KHE SANH, BATTLE OF (1967–68)

Khe Sanh, located 18 miles south of the Demilitarized Zone* and 8 miles east of the Laotian border in Quang Tri Province, had been a small Special Forces* base since 1962, but General William Westmoreland* in 1965 took note of its strategic significance as well. For him Khe Sanh could be used for clandestine operations into Laos* or a major invasion of Laos, reconnaissance flights over the Ho Chi Minh Trail,* and as a base for cutting off North Vietnamese Army* (NVA) infiltration* into South Vietnam along Route 9. When NVA infiltration increased in 1966, Westmoreland had a Seabee* unit extend the airstrip and had the United States Marines* send a battalion* (lst Battalion, 3rd Marines) to Khe Sanh. In the spring of 1967 Khe Sanh was garrisoned by the 1st Battalion of the 26th Marines. Intelligence estimates also began pointing a massive increase in traffic along the Ho Chi Minh Trail, and American military officials assumed the North Vietnamese were planning a large-scale invasion, with Khe Sanh a key point in the attack.

That was just what the North Vietnamese wanted them to assume. They were actually planning the Tet Offensive* for 1968, and as a preliminary to that offensive they wanted to draw American troops away from the major population centers of South Vietnam to diversionary battles in remote areas. In October and November NVA soldiers attacked the marines at Con Thien* as well as Loc Ninh and Song Be near Saigon,* and Dak To* in the Central Highlands.* Late in 1967, military intelligence indicated that the NVA 325C Division was northwest of Khe Sanh; the 304th Division was southwest; and elements of the 324th and 320th divisions were close enough to provide reinforcements. In all it appeared that 25,000 to 40,000 NVA regulars were prepared to engage American forces in a head-on military confrontation. In response, General Westmoreland prepared Operation Niagara,* an armada of more than 5,000 aircraft and helicopters to pulverize NVA troops in an unprecedented artillery bombardment. He also had 6,000 U.S. Marines sent in to defend Khe Sanh. The NVA seige of Khe Sanh began on January 21, 1968.

For the next ten days President Lyndon B. Johnson* debated the question of whether to hold Khe Sanh. General Maxwell Taylor* argued that it ought to be abandoned because of its isolated position and because the North Vietnamese would be able to overrun it if they really decided to accept the casualties necessary to do so. Westmoreland wanted it held at all costs, so the siege of Khe Sanh began to build up as another similitude of Dien Bien Phu.* Johnson sided with Westmoreland, and the Military Assistance Command, Vietnam* commander then initiated Operation Niagara. In the next two months the United States unloaded more than 100,000 tons of explosives on the five-square miles surrounding Khe Sanh.

But on January 31, 1968, the battle for Khe Sanh was absorbed by the much larger scale confrontation between U.S., ARVN, Vietcong, and NVA troops in the Tet Offensive. The marines at Khe Sanh were expecting a full-scale NVA attack, but the only constant was artillery bombardment. Cargo planes and helicopters kept the base minimally supplied. The attack never came. Early in March the NVA abandoned the siege. Westmoreland then launched Operation Pegasus* to relieve Khe Sanh. The 1st Cavalry Division (Airmobile)* moved in and reopened Route 9. In mid-June 1968, the marines left Khe Sanh. The North Vietnamese had failed to overrun the site, but the larger Tet Offensive had succeeded in politically demoralizing the American public and undermining the American military effort.

Source: Robert Pisor, *The End of the Line: The Siege of Khe Sanh*, 1982.

KHMER KAMPUCHEA KRON

With 700,000 people, the Khmer* were one of the largest minority groups in the Republic of Vietnam.* Most of them were concentrated in the Mekong Delta* region of southwestern South Vietnam. In the seventeenth century ethnic Vietnamese had expanded out of Annam* into Khmer land and wrested it from them. Ever since, the ethnic and territorial rivalry between the Vietnamese and Khmer of Cambodia (see Kampuchea) has been intense. Kampuchea Kron was the name given to the Khmer areas of southern Vietnam. During the 1950s an armed band of ethnic Cambodian soldiers, known as the Khmer Kampuchea Kron, began fighting against the regime of Ngo Dinh Diem,* demanding the return of Khmer land to Cambodia. By the early 1960s, U.S. Special Forces* had convinced the Khmer Kampuchea Kron to fight against the Vietcong* and North Vietnamese, and large numbers of the Khmer Kampuchea Kron were incorporated into Civilian Irregular Defense Group* military units. After the fall of South Vietnam in 1975, the Khmer Kampuchea Kron often fought as guerrillas against the troops of the Socialist Republic of Vietnam,* whom they viewed as aggressors out to destroy all of Cambodia (Kampuchea).

Sources: Michael Vickery, *Cambodia, 1975–1982*, 1984; Joan L. Schrock et al., *Minority Groups in the Republic of Vietnam*, 1967.

KHMER ROUGE

Khmer Rouge means "Red Cambodians," and is the term describing the Communist party in Kampuchea* (Cambodia). The Khmer Rouge was first organized by Vietnamese Communists from both North and South Vietnam, and they waged guerrilla war against the neutral government of Prince Norodom Sihanouk.* Until 1969, the North Vietnamese gave only tacit support to the Khmer Rouge because Sihanouk allowed them to ship military equipment and supplies through the Cambodian port at Kompong Som and across the country by truck to Communist bases along the Laotian and Cambodian borders with South Vietnam. But the North Vietnamese were angered when Prince Sihanouk agreed to Operation Menu,* the secret U.S. bombing of those bases in 1969. They increased their support of the Khmer Rouge, and substantially increased it in 1970 when General Lon Nol,* an American supporter, deposed Sihanouk. Between 1970 and 1975 the Khmer Rouge strengthened its position in Cambodia, isolating Lon Nol's Cambodian army to city fortresses and forcing their surrender in 1975.

Led by Pol Pot,* formerly Saloth Sar, the Khmer Rouge then imposed a genocidal reign of terror throughout Cambodia, depopulating the cities in the hope of creating an agrarian utopia, and murdering more than two million people in the process. By that time the Khmer Rouge had become a threat and an embarrassment to the North Vietnamese, and in December 1978, they conquered most of Cambodia, forcing the Khmer Rouge to withdraw to remote jungles to resume their guerrilla activities, this time against their Vietnamese enemies.

Sources: William Shawcross, *Sideshow: Kissinger, Nixon, and the Destruction of Cambodia*, 1979; François Ponchaud, *Cambodia: Year Zero*, 1978; Ben Kiernan, "How Pol Pot Came to Power," Ph.D., diss., 1986; William Shawcross, *The Quality of Mercy: Cambodia, Holocaust, and the Modern Conscience*, 1984.

KHMERS

The Khmers, an ethnic minority group numbering approximately 700,000 people, are similar in history and culture to the people of Cambodia (see Kampuchea). It was not until the eighteenth century, when Vietnamese control reached the Mekong Delta,* that the Khmers became part of Vietnam. They were concentrated northwest of Saigon* around Tay Ninh, southwest of Saigon around Phu Vinh, and throughout An Xuyen Province. While most Vietnamese are faithful to Mahayana Buddhism,* the Khmers are Hinayana Buddhists. Taller, darker, and less Mongoloid than the Vietnamese, the Khmers were distinguished in dress by tight, buttoned-down jackets and skirts with a lower end brought forward between the legs and tucked in at the waist. During the 1960s and 1970s, tens of thousands of Khmers escaped the fighting in Vietnam by fleeing across the border into Cambodia. The Vietnamese tended to look down upon the Khmers as a primitive, less civilized people than themselves.

Source: Harvey Smith et al., *Area Handbook for South Vietnam*, 1967.

KHRUSHCHEV, NIKITA

Premier of the Soviet Union* between 1958 and 1964, Nikita Khrushchev was born in 1894 and gradually rose to power in the Communist party after joining it in 1918. Khrushchev was a loyal follower of Josef Stalin, became a member of the Central Committee in 1934, and joined the Politburo in 1939. After Stalin's death in 1953, Khrushchev won a power struggle with Georgy Malenkov and became first secretary of the Communist party. He was ultimately removed as premier in 1964, primarily because of continuing Soviet problems with the People's Republic of China,* terrible agricultural harvests, and the apparent diplomatic defeat of the Soviet Union in the Cuban missile crisis of 1962. Khrushchev was troubled by the increasing American commitment in Vietnam during the early 1960s, but he genuinely did not want to see a major military conflict in Southeast Asia, primarily because he had no idea of what role China would play in it. In 1964, when the North Vietnamese came to Moscow with requests for huge increases in military support, Khrushchev agreed, but only if the North Vietnamese would consider a negotiated settlement with the United States. But when Khrushchev was removed from office in October 1964, all hopes for negotiations died. Khrushchev then lived in obscurity until his death in 1971.

Source: Carl A. Linden, *Khrushchev & the Soviet Leaders, 1957–1964*, 1966.

KIA

"KIA" was the acronym for "Killed in Action." Technically, any serviceman or servicewoman who died as a result of wounds sustained in action with enemy forces was classified KIA. This included wounds inflicted in a variety of ways, both conventional (e.g., bullets, artillery shells, grenades, and mortar rounds) and unconventional (e.g., booby traps* and mines). This classification did not include deaths due to circumstances unrelated to combat, such as traffic accidents, homicides, snake bites, and aircraft crashes due to faulty maintenance. Consequently, while the Vietnam Memorial "wall" lists the names of over 58,000

American servicemen and servicewomen who died in Southeast Asia between 1959 and 1975, nearly 11,000 were not technically killed in action.

Sources: Ronald J. Glasser, *365 Days*, 1971; Harry G. Summers, Jr., *Vietnam War Almanac*, 1985.

Stafford T. Thomas

THE KILLING AT NGO THO

The Killing at Ngo Tho is the title of Gene D. Moore's 1967 novel about the Vietnam War. The book centers on a Colonel Scott Leonard, who is a military adviser to General Huang Huu-Lac of ARVN (*see* Army of the Republic of Vietnam). Their headquarters is at Ngo Tho, near the Cambodian border (*see* Kampuchea). Leonard and Huang have a good working relationship, but when Vietcong* infiltrate the base, Leonard suspects treachery from Huang's staff. Leonard convinces the general to cooperate, and together they locate the traitor and destroy the Vietcong in the base.

Sources: Gene D. Moore, *The Killing at Ngo Tho*, 1967; Philip D. Beidler, *American Literature and the Experience of Vietnam*, 1982.

THE KILLING FIELDS

Released in 1984, *The Killing Fields* was directed by David Puttnam and starred Sam Waterson as *New York Times* journalist Sydney Schanberg, John Malkovich as a photojournalist, and Haing Ngor as Dith Pran, Schanberg's Cambodian associate. The film is set in Cambodia (*see* Kampuchea) in 1975 when the Khmer Rouge* overran Phnom Penh. Pran chooses to remain behind with Schanberg and then is unable to be evacuated with the foreign journalists. The rest of the film portrays Pran's struggle for survival and eventual escape from Pol Pot's* genocidal "Year Zero" campaign, in which the Khmer Rouge annihilated up to two million Cambodians. Pran eventually escapes out of Cambodia via Thailand* and the film ends with Pran and Schanberg meeting again in a Thai refugee camp.

Source: Samuel G. Freedman, "*The Killing Fields*," *New York Times*, October 28, 1984.

THE KILLING ZONE

Written by William Crawford Woods, *The Killing Zone* was published in 1970. As David Halberstam* wrote in *The Best and the Brightest*, the Vietnam War was a consequence of liberal extremism, the belief that power and technology could achieve military as well as political ends. Vietnam was high-tech warfare, and in the end the United States discovered it had not been enough. In *The Killing Zone*, Woods writes of a training camp where an outdated professional soldier must train new recruits in the new age of warfare. But in the end there is a grisly training camp accident where several young soldiers are accidentally killed when a computer at the base incorrectly orders the use of live rounds in a training exercise. The novel exposes the intellectual arrogance of the programmers, systems analysts, accountants, statisticians, and experts who organized and conducted the Vietnam War.

Sources: William Crawford Woods, *The Killing Zone*, 1970; Philip D. Beidler, *American Literature and the Experience of Vietnam*, 1982.

KING, MARTIN LUTHER, JR.

Martin Luther King, Jr., was born on January 15, 1929, in Atlanta, Georgia. He graduated from Morehouse College in 1948 and the Crozer Theological Seminary in 1951, and then took a Ph.D. in theology from Boston University in 1955. King rocketed into the national consciousness as leader of the Montgomery bus boycott in 1955 and 1956, and in 1957 he established the Southern Christian Leadership Conference to fight segregation. In 1960 King was one of the founding members of the Student Nonviolent Coordinating Committee. Inspired by the passive disobedience of Mahatma Gandhi in India, King applied those same tactics to the American South, leading demonstrations, sit-ins, boycotts, and protest marches. By 1965, when the Vietnam War escalation began, King was the premier civil rights leader in the United States.

From the very beginning of the conflict in Vietnam, King had serious misgivings about it, seeing it as a misguided effort on the part of the United States which the Third World would interpret as simply another attempt by the white, industrialized West to colonize the rest of the world. King was also disturbed by the effect of the draft* on the black community and the inordinately large numbers of casualties black soldiers* were sustaining in 1965 and 1966. In 1967, King openly protested the Vietnam War and linked the civil rights and antiwar movements* together, a step which earned him the ire of President Lyndon Johnson* and most civil rights leaders. Other civil rights leaders, both black and white, worried that linking the two movements would only dissipate the force of the campaign for equality. But King was convinced that the Vietnam War was diverting financial and emotional resources away from domestic programs and into a futile effort abroad. By 1968 the rest of the country was slowly coming around to King's point of view, but his voice was stilled by an assassin on April 4, 1968.

Sources: Lenwood G. Davis, *I Have a Dream: The Life and Times of Martin Luther King, Jr.*, 1973; Stephen B. Oates, *Let the Trumpet Sound: The Life of Martin Luther King, Jr.*, 1982.

KISSINGER, HENRY ALFRED

Henry A. Kissinger was born in Fürth, Germany, on May 27, 1923, and his family emigrated to the United States in 1938, fleeing Nazi persecution of German Jews. He joined the army during World War II and spent time in occupied Germany after the conflict working in the military bureaucracy. Kissinger returned to the United States and pursued his education, eventually receiving a Ph.D. from Harvard in 1954. Specializing in diplomacy, Kissinger wrote his doctoral dissertation on the Congress of Vienna (1815), displaying his appreciation for power politics and his disdain for the moralistic assumptions which, in his opinion, so frequently prevent long-term solutions to nationalistic rivalries. Kissinger taught at Harvard during the 1950s and early 1960s, and during those years he was a leading figure in the rise of "nuclear strategy" among intellectuals who considered thermonuclear weapons a reality which must be coordinated in any realistic defense policy. Kissinger's 1957 book *Nuclear War and Foreign Policy* argued that tactical nuclear weapons could be considered a highly useful tool in defense strategy. Filmmaker Stanley Kubrick used Kissinger as the model for the deranged Dr. Strangelove in his 1964 movie of the same name. Kissinger served as a consultant to both the Kennedy* and Johnson* administrations in the 1960s, and acquired a larger political profile between 1964 and 1968 as a foreign policy aide to Governor Nelson Rockefeller of New York, who was unsuccessfully pursuing the presidency. Before his inauguration in January 1969, President Richard M. Nixon* appointed Kissinger special assistant for national security affairs.

From the very beginning, both Kissinger and Nixon took the middle road about Vietnam, realizing that military victory was impossible but refusing to implement a unilateral withdrawal. They wanted to turn the war over to the South Vietnamese while maintaining the international credibility of the United States. Vietnamization,* the policy they proposed in June 1969, became the institutional reflection of their middle-of-the-road approach. Simultaneously with a gradual, phased withdrawal of American troops, the United States would hand over war materiel to the South Vietnamese and continue to provide them naval and air support. Kissinger realized that the government of South Vietnam was notoriously corrupt and probably incapable of defeating the Vietcong* and North Vietnamese, so he intended, through the threat of military escalation and the carrot stick of U.S. economic assistance, to convince North Vietnam to settle the conflict.

Between 1969 and 1973, Henry Kissinger was the central figure in the diplomatic effort to restore peace in Southeast Asia. He held secret talks with officials from North Vietnam, the National Liberation Front (*see* Vietcong), the Soviet Union,* and the People's Republic of China* between 1969 and 1973 while the official peace talks were going on in Paris. The negotiations were complicated by the rigidity of both sides: the North Vietnamese insisted on a complete halt of American bombing* of North Vietnam, total withdrawal of U.S. troops from South Vietnam, removal of Nguyen Van Thieu* as president of South Vietnam, and participation of the National Liberation Front (NLF) in any new government in South Vietnam. The United States demanded a mutual withdrawal of American and North Vietnamese troops from South Vietnam, refused to abandon Nguyen Van Thieu, and insisted that the NLF be excluded from the political process in South Vietnam.

Progress in the peace talks did not really come until 1972. Adept at power politics, Kissinger was intent on exploiting the rivalry between the Soviet Union and the People's Republic of China, and he secretly visited Beijing in July 1971 to prepare for Nixon's famous February 1972 trip there. Similarly, Kissinger pursued a policy of détente with the Soviet Union, which Nixon followed up on with his summit meeting in Moscow in May 1972. By that time pressure to end the war in Vietnam was becoming overwhelming. Both Kissinger and Nixon realized the conflict in Southeast Asia was retarding their efforts to reach an accommodation with China and the Soviet Union; and the antiwar movement* at home, particularly after the invasion of Cambodia (*see* Kampuchea) in 1970, was demanding an end to the conflict.

In the summer of 1972 the peace talks finally began to yield results, but only because of major modifications in the U.S. negotiating position. Kissinger was dealing head-to-head with Le Duc Tho,* North Vietnam's negotiator, and in October 1972 they reached an agreement. The United States agreed to halt the bombing of North Vietnam, allow the NLF to participate in the political process in South Vietnam, let North Vietnamese Army* (NVA) troops remain in place in South Vietnam, and withdraw all American troops. The North Vietnamese agreed to a prisoner-of-war* exchange and dropped their demand that Nguyen Van Thieu be removed from office in South Vietnam. When the North Vietnamese appeared in November 1972 to be stepping back from their October agreement, Nixon ordered massive bombing of Hanoi* and Haiphong, as well as mining of Haiphong Harbor.* In January 1973, Le Duc Tho agreed to uphold the October 1972 settlement. The two nations signed a formal agreement on January 27, 1973.

In September 1973, Nixon named Kissinger the new secretary of state, but by that time the Watergate* scandal had compromised the administration's ability to pursue either its domestic or foreign policy agenda. After Nixon's resignation in August 1974, Kissinger remained in office, serving as secretary of state under President Gerald Ford* and engineering the ill-advised attack on Cambodia in 1975 after the *Mayaguez** incident. Kissinger left the State Department in January 1977 when President Jimmy Carter and the Democrats assumed the reins of power. Since then Kissinger has lectured and written widely about American foreign policy.

Sources: William Shawcross, *Sideshow: Kissinger, Nixon, and the Destruction of Cambodia*, 1979; Seymour Hersh, *The Price of Power: Kissinger in the Nixon White House*, 1983; Henry A. Kissinger, *White House Years*, 1979, and *Years of Upheaval*, 1982.

KIT CARSON SCOUTS

Kit Carson Scouts were former Vietcong* guerrillas who had "rallied" to the government, often under the Chieu Hoi Program,* and who were willing to act as scouts for U.S. units. New scouts would be closely watched and regarded with suspicion, for they could not always be trusted. Some "rallied" only to work for the Vietcong as spies or to lead U.S. units into traps. However, most were very reliable, risking and often losing their lives for the units they served. Consequently, good Kit Carson Scouts were highly prized and treated accordingly by their units. They had familiarity with the terrain and culture, understood Vietcong tactics in establishing ambushes, and could identify booby traps.* They also recognized Vietcong base and assembly areas from indicators Americans did not notice. Finally, Kit Carson Scouts were able to identify Vietcong collaborators in villages as well as Vietcong masquerading as civilians.

Source: Peter Goldman and Tony Fuller, *Charlie Company*, 1983.

Samuel Freeman

KOMER, ROBERT WILLIAM

Robert William Komer was born on February 23, 1922, in Chicago, Illinois. He graduated from Harvard in 1942 and then received an M.B.A. there in 1947 after serving in the army during World War II. Komer joined the Central Intelligence Agency* (CIA) in 1947 and remained there until 1960. At the CIA, Komer was a Middle East expert. He was appointed to the National Security Council* in 1960, serving there as a Middle East expert, and in 1965 Komer became a deputy special assistant to President Lyndon B. Johnson.* One year later he was promoted to special assistant. Considered by journalist David Halberstam* to be one of "the best and the brightest," Komer invested all his energies in the Vietnam conflict, and became one of the most optimistic advisers on Johnson's staff, always insisting the United States could win the war if only it could secure the support of the Vietnamese people. Komer believed military counterinsurgency* had to be combined with social and economic development, and in May 1967 the president sent him to Vietnam where he was appointed civilian deputy to the commander of the Military Assistance Command, Vietnam.* Working directly with General William Westmoreland,* Komer established the Civil Operations and Revolutionary Development Support* (CORDS) program to increase local support for the American war effort. Although Komer believed the ultimate answer in Vietnam was not a military one, his development program failed. After the Tet Offensive,* administration officials put more pressure on Komer for results, so he established the Accelerated Pacification Program* and the Phoenix Program,* which was a CIA-sponsored program to assassinate Vietcong* and their sympathizers. Komer was appointed ambassador to Turkey in 1968, and he joined the Rand Corporation* as an analyst in 1969. Komer stayed with Rand until 1977, when the Democrats returned to the White House under Jimmy Carter. He was appointed as NATO adviser in 1977 and as under secretary for policy in the Defense Department in 1979. When Ronald Reagan came to the White House in 1981, Komer left government service to become a lecturer at George Washington University.

Sources: David Halberstam, *The Best and the Brightest*, 1972; *Who's Who in America, 1984–1985*, 1985; Guenter Lewy, *America in Vietnam*, 1978; Andrew F. Krepinevich, Jr., *The Army and Vietnam*, 1986; John Prados, *Presidents' Secret Wars: CIA and Pentagon Covert Operations Since World War II*, 1986; Robert W. Komer, *Bureaucracy Does Its Thing: Institutional Constraints on US-GVN Performance*, 1972.

KOREA

During the Vietnam War, the Republic of Korea sent more combat troops to South Vietnam than any other American ally. A South Korean liaison unit came to Vietnam in the summer of 1964, and between 1965 and late 1966 their Capital Division,* Ninth Infantry Division, and Second Marine Brigade arrived. South Koreans concentrated their combat efforts in II Corps.* By 1969 there were nearly 49,000 South Koreans fighting in South Vietnam. During the entire war, the South Koreans suffered 4,407 combat deaths. The Capital and Ninth divisions were withdrawn from South Vietnam in March 1973. South Korea's loyalty to the American war effort in South Vietnam, even though most Korean officials did not think the war was politically winnable, was a direct function of the close relationship existing between the two countries since the Korean War (1950–53).

Source: Stanley Robert Larsen and James Lawton Collins, Jr., *Allied Participation in Vietnam*, 1981.

KOSYGIN, ALEKSEI NIKOLAYEVICH

A Soviet politician who assisted the North Vietnamese with weaponry during the 1960s, Kosygin was born in St. Petersburg (now Leningrad) on February 20, 1904. After completing his schooling, he volunteered for the Red Army in 1919. In 1921 Kosygin was released from military service and thereupon entered the Leningrad Co-Operative Technicum, where he gained firsthand knowledge of the politics of Soviet Russia. Between 1929 and 1935, young Kosygin was a student at the Leningrad-Kirov Textile Institute. During the 1940s he became a protégé of Josef Stalin and eventually became a deputy premier. In 1953, however, he was removed from his deputy premiership after Stalin's death. But Khrushchev* brought him back, and in 1964 Kosygin was elected chairman of the USSR Council of Ministers.

In 1965 Kosygin became directly involved in North Vietnam's struggle against the U.S. The Soviet premier departed from Moscow in February 1965 destined for Hanoi.* Before his departure from Moscow he had been reluctant to expand Soviet military aid to the North Vietnamese Communists. He tried to pressure the Hanoi leadership into accepting the possibility of negotiations to end the conflict. While Kosygin was in Hanoi, however, the United States launched air attacks upon Dong Hoi (near Hanoi), which prompted the Soviet premier to reconsider his stance on the Vietnamese conflict.

Upon his return to Moscow, Kosygin told reporters that the United States were the aggressors in Vietnam—calling the American bombing* of North Vietnam "Hitlerite." The Soviet premier felt compelled to defend the USSR's "anti-imperialist" image and thus acquiesced to the Hanoi leadership's request for sophisticated military hardware. Within ten days after his return to Moscow, Soviet surface-to-air missiles (SAM)* arrived in Hanoi. Kosygin also warned in press releases that the Soviet Union* could not have normal relations with the United States as long as they were involved in aggression in Vietnam. The Soviet

Union continued to send more and more weapons to the North Vietnamese as the U.S. commitment to South Vietnam widened.

By 1967 the Johnson* administration was wearying of the Vietnam War, although not to the extent of abandoning their South Vietnamese allies. A series of letters were exchanged between Johnson and Ho Chi Minh.* These proposals were not firmly thought out, except for the idea of negotiations taking place. Lyndon Johnson insisted that only if North Vietnam ended its hostilities in the South would the United States be willing to end the bombing and enter negotiations to bring the war to a close. The Hanoi regime, on the other hand, refused to even consider talks until a bombing halt was in effect. In early February 1967 Kosygin visited London where Prime Minister Harold Wilson tried to get the Soviet premier to bring pressure on Hanoi to negotiate. Before the meeting Johnson had indicated a willingness to compromise; however, now he insisted on a tougher line toward Hanoi. Only if the North ceased its operations in the South would the United States negotiate. Although Kosygin did pass along these proposals, the North Vietnamese remained silent and thus ended what Wilson called a "historic opportunity." Kosygin would not again act as a broker in the conflict and continued to work at his desk in Moscow until his death in late 1980.

Sources: *Current Biography*, November 1965; Stanley Karnow, *Vietnam: A History*, 1983; *New York Times*, December 21, 1980; Robin Edmonds, *Soviet Foreign Policy, 1962–1973: The Paradox of a Superpower*, 1975; Leif Rosenberger, *The Soviet Union and Vietnam: An Uneasy Alliance*, 1986.

John S. Leiby

KRULAK, VICTOR

In command of the Fleet Marine Force, Pacific* (FMFPAC) from 1964 to 1968, "Brute" Krulak was responsible for all marine units in the Pacific area. Born in 1913, Krulak graduated from Annapolis in 1934, observed Japanese operations in China in the late 1930s, and commanded a parachute battalion in a diversionary attack on Choiseul Island during the Bougainville Campaign in 1943. Wounded and awarded a Navy Cross for valor, Krulak then served as a division operations officer on Okinawa and returned to China at the war's end to assist in the Japanese surrender. In Washington in the late 1940s he worked with staffs seeking to preserve Marine Corps autonomy during the unification battles, and during the Korean War he helped plan the Inchon landing (1950) and later served as chief of staff of the 1st Marine Division* until 1951.

From 1962 to 1964, as the special assistant for counterinsurgency* to the Joint Chiefs of Staff (*see* Chairman, JCS), Krulak gained a reputation as the "military's most skilled bureaucratic player in Washington at the time, a figure of immense import in the constant struggle over Vietnam." Diminutive in size (5'4", 134 lbs) but not in military stature, he had no real operational authority as commander of FMFPAC, but his fifty-four visits in country and lengthy staff experience made him a force to reckon with among top commanders and their civilian counterparts in Washington. Krulak's memoir details the conflict of strategies characteristic of the command and political systems that oversaw the war effort.

In 1968 a faction of officers at Marine Headquarters pushed a Krulak nomination for commandant, but the general—along with fellow competitor Lewis Walt*—lost this battle to Leonard F. Chapman.* Krulak then retired, joined the Copely Newspaper Service, earned a Ph.D. from the University of San Diego (1970), and wrote a weekly syndicated column in addition to numerous articles and two books on international and military affairs.

Sources: David Halberstam, *The Best and the Brightest*, 1972; Victor H. Krulak, *First to Fight: An Inside View of the U.S. Marine Corps*, 1984.

Dudley Acker

• **L** •

LAIRD, MELVIN R.

Born on September 1, 1922, Melvin R. Laird was a Republican congressman from Wisconsin, 1953–69 and secretary of defense (1969–72) in the Nixon* administration. Melvin Laird was chosen by Nixon as secretary of defense because, as a veteran congressman, he had much influence in the U.S. Congress* which Nixon believed could be used to diminish criticism from that quarter. Laird believed that he should have direct access to the president. Nixon's national security adviser, Henry Kissinger,* feared Laird's influence on Nixon and hence did not want the kind of access the secretary desired. Kissinger established an indirect channel between the White House and Joint Chiefs of Staff (*see* Chairman, JCS) to offset some of Laird's power and influence.

Almost from the outset of his tenure as secretary of defense Laird began to lobby for troop reductions from Vietnam. He believed that Nixon's goodwill on Capitol Hill would run thin unless the president demonstrated his commitment in curtailing U.S. involvement in South Vietnam. And signs of congressional impatience were apparent in the spring of 1969. There was the normal partisan criticism, however; even the Senate Republican whip, Hugh Scott, called for the withdrawal of large numbers of troops from Vietnam. Nixon, on the other hand, had promised the American public "peace with honor" but could not accept huge troop reductions unless military conditions changed in South Vietnam.

By late 1969, Laird was pressing for a precise timetable of troop reductions so that by the end of 1971 the United States would have only 206,000 men in South Vietnam. Laird's insistence on troop reductions annoyed Kissinger, who worried that his bargaining position was being damaged by Laird. Kissinger went as far as warning Nixon that the South Vietnamese could not yet carry on the war themselves. Kissinger moreover had his assistants concoct or draft a contingency plan to knock the North Vietnamese out of the war. The proposal included massive bombing* attacks on North Vietnam. Laird intervened and warned Nixon that if the plan was implemented, domestic opposition to the war would mount, particularly from congressional sources. Nixon shelved the idea although it would be resurrected in the winter of 1972.

Laird meanwhile continued to press for disengagement and coined the term "Vietnamization."* The defense secretary even visited South Vietnam and came away with the conviction that the South Vietnamese could defend themselves. Laird's appraisal was supported by Sir Robert Thompson,* the British guerrilla warfare specialist. As protests mounted against Nixon's Vietnam policy, Laird responded to critics that Vietnamization was the top priority of the administration. Laird avoided conflict and was convinced that the American public was tired of the war. When military officials pressed for massive incursions into Cambodia (*see* Kampuchea) in 1970, he urged restraint. He was vetoed, however, by Nixon and Kissinger. Laird would and did advise restraint in the winter of 1972, when Nixon decided on mining Haiphong Harbor* and using B–52* attacks to bring the North Vietnamese to the conference table. Laird decided to leave the Nixon administration at the end of the president's first term.

Sources: *Who's Who in America*, 1984–1985; Allen E. Goodman, *The Lost Peace*, 1978; Stanley Karnow, *Vietnam: A History*, 1983; Melvin R. Laird, *The Nixon Doctrine*, 1972.

John S. Leiby

LAM SON

Lam Son is a small village in Thanh Hoa Province and the birthplace of Le Loi,* the famous Vietnamese nationalist who defeated a contingent of invading Chinese forces in 1428. Le Loi is one of the most famous names in Vietnamese history. During the Vietnam War, ARVN (*see* Army of the Republic of Vietnam) forces frequently used Lam Son as a codename to describe their military operations or their phase of joint military operations with U.S. forces. Operation Lam Son 719,* for example, was the codename for the 1971 ARVN invasion of Laos.* Lam Son 246 was the ARVN phase of Operation Somerset Plain,* the 101st Airborne Division's* assault on the A Shau Valley* in 1968. Lam Son 216 was the ARVN portion of Operation Delaware,* the 7th Cavalry's attack on the A Shau Valley that same year. Use of the codename Lam Son in ARVN operations was a symbolic act designating South Vietnam as the "true" descendant of Vietnamese nationalism.

Sources: David G. Marr, *Vietnamese Anticolonialism, 1885–1925*, 1981; Joseph Buttinger, *The Smaller Dragon: A Political History of Vietnam*, 1958; Shelby L. Stanton, *The Rise and Fall of an American Army: U.S. Ground Forces in Vietnam, 1965–1973*, 1985.

LAM SON 719

Lam Son 719 was the operational name for the disastrous Laotian invasion of February 1971. Nixon* and Kissinger* anticipated heavy infiltration* of men and materiel during the 1971 dry season in preparation for a major North Vietnamese Army* (NVA) offensive during the 1972 elections.* Also hoping to test Vietnamization,* they proposed a major ARVN (see Army of the Republic of Vietnam) initiative for 1971. They initially proposed invading Cambodia (see Kampuchea) or North Vietnam, but General Creighton Abrams* and President Nguyen Van Thieu* favored cutting the Ho Chi Minh Trail* in Laos* along Route 9.

The invasion proved to be an unmitigated disaster. Planning was confined to a few people in Washington and Saigon,* and the invasion units were given minimal notice and planning time. Congressional restrictions prohibited American ground troops in Cambodia and Laos, preventing American advisers from accompanying their units and coordinating artillery, helicopter, and tactical air support. Despite American predictions that four divisions would be necessary to secure the road from the border to Tchepone (the objective), ARVN committed only two divisions. The NVA had four seasoned divisions in opposition. The terrain was rugged, restricting ground movement and limiting flight patterns— all to the NVA's advantage. NVA artillery had greater range, and their familiarity with the terrain gave them a fire direction advantage. Finally, the weather was unusually rainy, impeding air support and resupply.

ARVN's best units were committed—1st Infantry,* Airborne,* Marines,* and Rangers. But the NVA was not surprised, and they drew ARVN away from U.S. artillery, lengthening ARVN supply lines and marshaling resources for a counterattack. Seizing the opportunity to annihilate ARVN's best units, the NVA would have succeeded except for massive U.S. air strikes and American helicopter pilots' ability to extract beleaguered units. Lam Son 719 proved the failure of Vietnamization. ARVN's best units suffered 50 percent casualties. Morale plummeted. It became obvious ARVN was hard-pressed to stand alone. The NVA buildup was not stemmed; their 1972 offensive was furious, initially successful and foreshadowed 1975's Final Offensive (see Ho Chi Minh Campaign).

Sources: Bruce Palmer, Jr., *The 25-Year War: America's Military Role in Vietnam*, 1984; Nguyen Duy Hinh, *Lam Son 719*, 1981; David Fulghum and Terrence Maitland, *The Vietnam Experience: South Vietnam on Trial*, 1984; Keith William Nolan, *Into Laos. The Story of Dewey Canyon II/Lam Son 719*, 1986.

Samuel Freeman

LAND REFORM

At the time of the Geneva Accords* of 1954, approximately 60 percent of Vietnamese peasants were landless and another 20 percent owned less than two acres of land. The desire to own land or acquire more land was almost universal in South Vietnam. Tenant farmers paid an average of 34 percent of their annual crop to landlords for use of the land. The Vietcong* had made a strong appeal to South Vietnamese peasants by distributing the land of absentee landlords in the early 1950s, but after Ngo Dinh Diem* took over in 1954, landlords regained control of their property. In areas they controlled, the Vietcong redistributed land and gained a stronger following from peasant farmers. Between January 1968 and December 1969, under the direction of President Nguyen Van Thieu,* the government of the Republic of Vietnam* began a modest land reform program in which 50,000 families received government land. Thieu also prohibited local officials from restoring land to former landlords. On March 26, 1970, the Republic of Vietnam, at Thieu's urging, passed the Land-to-the-Tiller Act which provided for an end to rent payments and the issuing of ownership titles to the peasants currently working the land. The maximum amount of land anyone could own was 37 acres. By 1972, the Land-to-the-Tiller Act had provided land titles to 400,000 formerly landless peasants, and the land they received totaled more than 1,500,000 acres. The number of farm tenants in South Vietnam was reduced from 60 to 34 percent of the population. By 1973 all but 7 percent of the farmers in South Vietnam owned their own land. The Vietcong had for all intents and purposes lost a major issue alienating the peasants from the government of the Republic of Vietnam.

Source: Guenter Lewy, *America in Vietnam*, 1978.

LANIEL, JOSEPH

Born in France in 1889, Joseph Laniel was educated at the École Gerson, Lyćee Janson de Sailly, and the University of Paris. Active in the resistance movement during World War II, Laniel founded the Parti Républicain de la Liberté in 1946. Between 1940 and 1948, he served as secretary of state. Elected minister of state in 1952, Laniel rose to become prime minister of France* in June 1953, where he presided over the collapse of the French Indochinese empire. A right-wing politician, Laniel tried to implement the Navarre Plan* and accepted $400 million in American aid toward that end, but the defeat at Dien Bien Phu* ended his dreams. Laniel was firmly committed to Bao Dai* and did not want Vietnam divided, but he had no power to implement his wishes. His government collapsed before the Geneva Accords* were completed, and Laniel was replaced as prime minister by Pierre Mendès-France.* Laniel died in April 1975.

Sources: *International Who's Who, 1964–1965*, 1965; *Who Was Who in America*, vol. 6, 1976; Joseph Buttinger, *Vietnam: A Dragon Embattled*. Vol. 2, *Vietnam at War*, 1967.

LANSDALE, EDWARD GEARY

Born in 1908 and a graduate of UCLA, Lansdale was an air force officer and agent for the Central Intelligence Agency.* Lansdale had been an architect of the successful counterguerrilla and counterinsurgency* effort in the Philippines* in the early 1950s. Consequently, he was assigned to Vietnam in 1954, following the Geneva Accords* that ended the First Indochinese War between the Vietminh* and France.* His initial assignment was to plan, coordinate, and implement a psychological warfare ("psywar") campaign in North Vietnam in the 1954–56 period. His campaign was a mixture of successes and failures, but it did contribute to the large exodus of people from North to South Vietnam. Following 1956, Lansdale became a close personal friend of Ngo Dinh Diem,* the president of the Republic of Vietnam.* He also became one of the very few Americans to whom Diem listened. This rapport between Diem and Lansdale was unofficial and bypassed normal channels of diplomatic relations, which resulted in great distrust of Lansdale by various diplomatic, military, and civilian representatives of the U.S. government. However, Lansdale's record in the Philippines, his successes in covert action operations in Vietnam, and his relationship with a recalcitrant and often unresponsive Diem made him a valuable policy conduit for both the Eisenhower* and Kennedy* administrations. Lansdale's views on the evolving situation in Vietnam in the 1950s and early 1960s were influential in Washington, even though they often conflicted with other perceptions from Americans in Vietnam who resented Lansdale's presence. Thus, Lansdale is significant because he manifested not only the clandestine, informal relations between the United States and South Vietnam that existed simultaneously and often in contradiction to the overt, official relations, but also the intense contest for influence over policy between the numerous American government agencies functioning in South Vietnam. Lansdale was basically the father of American counterinsurgency programs in Vietnam. Although he was considered a candidate for ambassador to South Vietnam by President John F. Kennedy, the appointment was vetoed by Secretary of Defense Robert McNamara.* Between 1965 and 1968 Lansdale served as a special assistant at the U.S. Embassy in Saigon.*

Sources: John Prados, *Presidents' Secret Wars: CIA and Pentagon Covert Operations Since World War II*, 1986; Edward Geary Lansdale, *In the Midst of Wars: An American's Mission to Southeast Asia*, 1972.

Stafford T. Thomas

LAO DONG PARTY

Ho Chi Minh,* although he was a Communist, understood the fragmented nature of Vietnamese society. He had, with his comrades Le Duc Tho,* Pham Van Dong,* Le Duan,* and Vo Nguyen Giap,* created the Indochinese Communist party in 1929. The creation of this party, however, did not result in total cohesion among Vietnam's many political leaders. During the 1940s and after World War II, Ho Chi Minh determined that nationalism would be the catalyst to bring about the demise of French rule. He worked tirelessly to mobilize Vietnamese resistance against the French, and after 1941 it was his own Vietminh* which he believed would be the vehicle for ending French dominion in Vietnam.

But as a leader Ho understood by 1952 that neither the exclusive Communist party nor the Vietminh were entirely capable of bringing all of Vietnamese society into union to end French rule. In 1952 he changed the name of the Communist party to the Lao Dong, or Workers' party. At the same time he merged it with the Lien Viet, or the National United Front. Ho believed that by these moves nationalist sentiment would rise throughout Vietnam. Through the apparatus of the Lao Dong party, during the 1950s Ho introduced land reform, education, health care, and other reforms in the provinces held by the Vietminh. Even though he gained additional support among the Vietnamese populace, the demise of the French presence in Vietnam was decided on the battlefield at Dien Bien Phu.*

Probably the severest test of the Lao Dong party came during the 1950s in North Vietnam over the program collectivization. Peasants revolted against this program in several provinces. The Communists, however, crushed each revolt, believing that they were contrived from abroad. Ho Chi Minh urged moderation and even had the leader of the Lao Dong party, Truong Chinh,* removed from his post. Le Duan* became the new leader or head of the Lao Dong party, which he continued to head until his death in July 1986. Under the tutelage of Le Duan, however, the programs created by the Lao Dong party were cautiously introduced to prevent future rebellions. In reality, the Lao Dong party is the Communist party, which wields great power in contemporary Vietnam.

Sources: George C. Herring, *America's Longest War*, 1986; Donald Lancaster, *The Emancipation of French Indochina*, 1961; John T. McAlister, Jr., *Vietnam: The Origins of Revolution*, 1969.

John S. Leiby

LAOS

Covering 92,429 square miles in mountainous Southeast Asia, Laos is one of the most underdeveloped nations in the Third World. Its population of 3,775,000 people in 1985 were primarily engaged in rice cultivation, and more than 80 percent of them are illiterate. The largest Laotian city is Vientiane, with 138,000 people, but the capital city is Luang Prabang, with a population of 45,000. Approximately 75 percent of the population is ethnic Lao or Kha, and 25 percent consists of tribes of Thais who have spilled over from the Khorant Plateau of eastern Thailand.* During the Vietnam War, the country was engaged in a civil war between the Communist-backed Pathet Lao* and the forces of Souvana Phouma,* but along with Cambodia (*see* Kampuchea) and South Vietnam, Laos fell to the Communists in 1975.

Sources: *Webster's Geographical Dictionary*, 1984; Charles A. Stevenson, *The End of Nowhere: American Policy Toward Laos Since 1954*, 1973.

Gerald L. Holder

LAOS, INVASION OF   *See* Lam Son 719

LATTRE DE TASSIGNY, JEAN JOSEPH DE

Jean Joseph de Lattre de Tassigny was born in 1889 in the Vendée at Mouilleron-en-Pareds, France.* He saw active duty in World War I as well as in Morocco between 1921 and 1926. He was promoted to general in 1939 but was imprisoned by the Germans in 1940. He escaped in 1943 and joined the Fighting French. After the war Tassigny became chief of staff and was the prime mover behind building the Vietnamese National Army.* He returned to France in 1951 because of illness and died on January 11, 1952.

Sources: James J. Cooke, *France, 1789–1962*, 1975; Joseph Buttinger, *Vietnam: A Dragon Embattled*. Vol. 2, *Vietnam at War*, 1967.

LA VANG BASILICA

The La Vang Basilica was completed in 1900 as a monument to the alleged appearance of the Virgin Mary to a group of persecuted Roman Catholics* in 1798. It was located about four miles outside of Quang Tri City in Quang Tri Province. The basilica was a favorite pilgrimage site for Vietnamese Catholics until its destruction during the Eastertide Offensive in 1972.*

Source: Danny J. Whitfield, *Historical and Cultural Dictionary of Vietnam*, 1976.

LAVELLE, JOHN DANIEL

John D. Lavelle was born on September 9, 1916, in Cleveland, Ohio. He graduated from John Carroll University in 1938 and spent World War II as a pilot in the Army Air Corps. After the war Lavelle rose up through air force ranks and in July 1971 took command of the Seventh Air Force* in Saigon.* Late in 1972 Lavelle was forced to testify before both the House and Senate Armed Services committees concerning his activities in 1971 and 1972. Although U.S. pilots were allowed to conduct "protective reaction strikes"* against North Vietnamese installations after October 31, 1968, Lavelle was charged with ordering dozens of unauthorized missions against North Vietnam. Lavelle argued before the committees that he was encouraged to carry out secret attacks against North Vietnam by his superiors, but no formal proof of his charges could be found. Because of the secret raids, Lavelle was relieved of his command of the Seventh Air Force in April 1972. He retired from active duty and died on July 10, 1979.

Sources: Guenter Lewy, *America in Vietnam*, 1978; *New York Times*, July 11, 1979.

LE DUAN

Secretary-general of the Communist party of Vietnam* and noted revolutionary leader in twentieth-century Vietnam, Le Duan was born in Quang Tri Province in central Vietnam on April 4, 1907, and eventually found his way to Hanoi.* Le Duan, as a young man, was a political activist who advocated the end of French colonial rule in Indochina.* Because of his anti-French activities, he was imprisoned between 1931 and 1936 and then between 1940 and 1945. He also began to follow the leadership of Ho Chi Minh* and later became one of Ho's most trusted aides.

Because of his faithful service to the Vietminh* movement, Le Duan rose rapidly within the Communist party hierarchy. In 1952 he headed the Vietminh military command in southern Vietnam and ultimately conducted a war of attrition against the French. With the defeat of the French in 1954, Le Duan was catapulted into prominence and in 1959 was made secretary-general of the Lao Dong party*

(Workers' party). And then in 1960 he was named first secretary of the Lao Dong party.

Meanwhile, as a consequence of the Geneva Conference* of 1954, Vietnam was divided temporarily into two political entities. Elections were promised but never held. A puppet regime under Ngo Dinh Diem* governed South Vietnam while Ho Chi Minh, with Le Duan at his side, secured North Vietnam under the dominance of the Communist party. By 1959 Vietnam once again was involved in conflict but this time between revolutionaries in the south who received aid from the north and the Diem regime which received assistance from the United States.

Le Duan advocated a total war against the Diem regime by the Vietcong.* He made a secret trip to the south in 1959 and found that the insurgents faced annihilation unless they resorted to urban and rural terrorism. His report resulted in a redirection of the war in the south. Between 1959 and 1961, the Vietcong, as a consequence of directives from Hanoi, embarked on a massive campaign of terrorism and assassination in the south.

Le Duan continued to exert increasing influence upon the conduct of the war. After a few years of limited guerrilla warfare in the south, Le Duan, along with other members of the Hanoi politburo, decided that in order to achieve victory they would have to adopt a conventional war akin to that which they had waged against the French. He noted in 1965 that whenever they had been offensive in warfare they had succeeded in driving out foreign aggressors, and Le Duan believed this would hold true with the Americans.

As the war progressed and American public opinion faltered, Le Duan became increasingly convinced that he and the Hanoi leadership would prevail in the south. With the end of the Johnson* administration, negotiations were held in Paris to end the conflict. For years both sides bantered around the conference table about the terms of a cease-fire. Meanwhile, Ho Chi Minh's health faltered and on September 2, 1969, he died. Thus the mantle of power passed on to veteran nationalist fighters such as Le Duan, Pham Van Dong,* and Vo Nguyen Giap.* All of these men believed that the defeat of the United States and South Vietnam was their sacred mission. Le Duan finally realized his dream in 1975 with the fall of Saigon.* He died on July 10, 1986.

Sources: *Who's Who in the World*, 1985; Jon M. Van Dyke, *North Vietnam's Strategy for Survival*, 1972; Vo Nguyen Giap, *Big Victory, Big Task*, 1967; *New York Times*, July 11, 1986.

John S. Leiby

LE DUC THO

Born in 1910 in Nam Ha Province in Tonkin,* Le Duc Tho was North Vietnam's principal negotiator at the Paris peace talks.* The son of a French functionary in the Vietnamese colonial government, Le was educated in French schools before joining the revolution. He spent years in jail and hiding because of his revolutionary activities and helped found both the Indochinese Communist party (*see* Lao Dong party) and the Vietminh.* During the French Indochina War he was chief commissar for southern Vietnam and maintained primary responsibility for the region after U.S. intervention ended.

The Paris peace talks formally began on May 13, 1968, and deadlocked immediately. Le insisted that U.S. bombing of North Vietnam must stop before anything else could be negotiated. While his position was firm, Le apparently had considerable discretion in how to pursue negotiations until Ho Chi Minh's* death in September 1969. After that, North Vietnamese decision making became collegial and Le reported to the collective leadership. Beginning February 21, 1970, Le met secretly with Henry Kissinger* for two years. Seeing the military and political struggles as part of the same overall conflict, Le maintained a negotiating position throughout that any agreement must simultaneously resolve both issues. Furthermore, any armistice must include replacement of Nguyen Van Thieu's* government with a coalition which included the National Liberation Front (*see* Vietcong).

In order to effect American withdrawal from Vietnam, Le ultimately made concessions on these points. The principal provision of the October 1972 agreement allowed Thieu to remain in power with 150,000 North Vietnamese Army* troops remaining in South Vietnam. Thieu angrily rejected the agreement, and all sides sought "modifications." Renewed negotiations stalled in December. They were soon back on track, however, and an agreement almost identical to the October agreement was signed in Paris on January 27, 1973. Although the cease-fire never took place, Nixon* proclaimed "peace with honor." The settlement really provided only a face-saving "decent interval" before the Vietnamese finally settled the issue among themselves. With the agreements being roundly violated by all parties, Le Duc Tho and Henry Kissinger attempted in June 1973 to effect better observance of them, but there were no substantive results. Both men were awarded the Nobel Peace Prize, but Tho refused to accept, contending it would be inappropriate until there was genuine peace in Vietnam. In 1975 Le Duc Tho returned to South Vietnam to oversee the final assault on Saigon.* Between 1975 and 1986, he served on the politburo in Hanoi* and as the Lao Dong party's* chief theoretician, but he resigned his post in December 1986 because of continuing economic troubles in the Socialist Republic of Vietnam.*

Sources: Stanley Karnow, *Vietnam: A History*, 1983; Joseph Buttinger, *Vietnam: A Dragon Embattled*, 2 vols., 1967; Henry Kissinger, *Years of Upheaval*, 1982; *Washington Post*, December 18, 1986.

Samuel Freeman

LE LOI

Le Loi was emperor of Vietnam from 1428 until his death in 1443. Le Loi led the independence movement which successfully expelled the Chinese in 1428. Le founded the dynasty which ruled Vietnam for more than three centuries until the Tay Son Rebellion* displaced them in the 1770s and 1780s.

Source: Joseph Buttinger, *The Smaller Dragon: A Political History of Vietnam*, 1958.

LEMAY, CURTIS EMERSON

Curtis E. LeMay was born on November 15, 1906, in Columbus, Ohio. He joined the Army Air Corps in 1928 and was commissioned as a second lieutenant in 1930. He rose to the rank of major general in 1943 when he commanded the 305th Bomber Group and 20th Bomber Command in the European theater during World War II, and received command of the 21st Bomber Command in the Marianas in 1945 and advanced to commanding general of the 20th Air Force at Guam. LeMay became a legend because of his unorthodox methods. In Europe he had his bombers abandon the usual zigzag pattern of flight to avoid flack so they could have more accurate runs, and in the Pacific he removed the guns from the bombers in order to carry heavier payloads. In Japan LeMay opposed dropping the atomic bombs because he believed more firebomb raids would secure a surrender. After World War II LeMay rose through the ranks of the air force, becoming head of the Strategic Air Command in 1957 and air force chief of staff in 1961, a position he held until his retirement in 1965. LeMay came out of retirement to serve as George Wallace's vice presidential running mate in the election of 1968,* and his position on Vietnam was hardline. LeMay urged the United States to bring all of its firepower to bear, even nuclear weapons if necessary, on the North Vietnamese to end the war quickly. He said that the United States was capable of "bombing Vietnam back into the stone age" and that the North Vietnamese should be aware of such power. LeMay felt any settlement in the Far East should protect free governments from Communist takeovers.

Sources: McKinley Kantor, *Mission With LeMay*, 1965; *Who's Who in America, 1974– 1975*, 1975.

LE THANH NGHI

Born in 1915, Le Thanh Nghi turned to anti-French nationalism as a student and was an early member of the Lao Dong party* and the Vietminh.* In 1974 he became the deputy premier of the Democratic Republic of Vietnam,* and in 1976 assumed that same position in the new Socialist Republic of Vietnam.*

Sources: *International Who's Who, 1981–1982*, 1982; *Who's Who in Socialist Countries*, 1978.

LE VAN VIEN

Before World War II, Le Van Vien, also known as Bay Vien, was an illiterate chauffeur in the employ of the French colonialists. In the chaotic days at the end of the war, he organized a gang of Saigon* river pirates that eventually became known as the Binh Xuyen,* which was the name of the neighborhood in Cholon* where Le Van Vien had his headquarters. For two years he collaborated with the Vietminh* against the French. He was, in fact, deputy Vietminh commander for Cochin China* and was responsible for some notorious anti-French atrocities. In a characteristically expedient move, he switched sides in 1947 when the French agreed to recognize his gang as a "sect" similar to the

Cao Dai* and Hoa Hao* religions. They also commissioned him as a colonel and later a general in the Vietnamese National Army.* In 1954 Emperor Bao Dai* gave Vien control of the national police.

The source of Le Van Vien's wealth and power was his control of the vice establishment in Saigon and Cholon. His huge gambling complex, the Grande Monde in Cholon, brought in millions of piasters that he shared with Bao Dai. He owned the largest brothel in Asia, the so-called Hall of Mirrors, and had his own opium factory to supply his numerous opium dens. His empire also included Saigon's best department stores, a fleet of riverboats, and many houses and other real estate holdings.

After becoming prime minister in 1954, Ngo Dinh Diem* recognized Le Van Vien as the most immediate threat to his authority, and consequently the prime minister instigated a showdown with the vice lord in April 1955. The national army forced the Binh Xuyen out of Saigon. Le Van Vien escaped to France and never returned to Vietnam.

Source: Bernard Fall, "The Political-Religious Sects of Viet-Nam," *Pacific Affairs* 28 (September 1955), 235–53.

David L. Anderson

LIGHT ANTITANK WEAPON *See* M–72

"LIGHT AT THE END OF THE TUNNEL"
First used by General William Westmoreland* at a televised press conference on November 17, 1967, to describe the imminent demise of Vietcong* resistance and an end to the war in Southeast Asia, the term "light at the end of the tunnel" eventually was converted by journalists into a sarcastic reference to American leadership, both political and military. Between 1967 and 1975 the term was used hundreds of times in magazine and newspaper articles to describe how misguided U.S. policies were and how American officials basically misunderstood the nature of the war. The term had a fitting climax in 1975 when a GI leaving Vietnam at the end of the conflict showed a poster to a United Press cameraman. The poster had a light bulb shining from a tunnel.

Source: David Culbert, "Johnson and the Media," in Robert A. Divine, ed., *Exploring the Johnson Years*, 1981.

THE LIONHEADS
The Lionheads is the title of Josiah Bunting's 1972 novel about the Vietnam War. Written as a military history, the novel focuses on George Lemming, commanding general of the 12th Infantry Division (nicknamed "The Lionheads"). The time frame is March and April 1968, when U.S. forces were still reacting from the Tet Offensive.* It is a fairly standard account of military operations, with most critics commenting that the book was strong on explaining combat operations but weak on characterizations.

Sources: Josiah Bunting, *The Lionheads*, 1972; Philip D. Beidler, *American Literature and the Experience of Vietnam*, 1982.

LIPPMANN, WALTER

Walter Lippmann was born on September 21, 1889, in New York City. He graduated from Harvard in 1910 and in 1914 helped found the *New Republic*. Lippmann joined the editorial staff of the *New York Herald Tribune* in 1931, and over the years he became one of the country's most influential syndicated columnists. During the 1950s Lippmann worried about the moralisms which infected the Cold War debate, preferring a foreign policy based on concrete political, economic, and strategic needs. He initially praised Lyndon Johnson's* handling of the war in Vietnam, especially after the Gulf of Tonkin incident* in 1964, but Lippmann was too much an advocate of a negotiated settlement to be content with the 1965 escalation of the American commitment. He also doubted whether Vietnam was really enough of a strategic interest to the United States to justify the resources the war was consuming. Between 1965 and 1973 Lippmann continued to call for de-escalation. Walter Lippmann died on December 14, 1974.

Sources: *New York Times*, December 15, 1974; Ronald Steele, *Walter Lippmann and the American Century*, 1980.

LOC NINH, BATTLE OF (1967)

As part of his strategic preparation for the Tet Offensive* in 1968, General Vo Nguyen Giap* began attacking isolated American outposts in the fall of 1967. Located in Binh Long Province, nine miles east of the Cambodian border, was Loc Ninh, a military outpost defended by three Civilian Irregular Defense Group* companies, a company of Regional Forces,* and a Popular Forces* platoon. On October 29, 1967, two regiments of the 9th Vietcong Division came out of their base in Cambodia (*see* Kampuchea) and attacked the base at Loc Ninh. They encountered strong resistance from the local forces, and on November 1, ARVN (*see* Army of the Republic of Vietnam) forces and troops from the American 1st Brigade of the 1st Infantry Division* came in to reinforce them. On November 7 the Vietcong abandoned the struggle, leaving 850 dead. Along with generally unsuccessful attacks at places like Dak To* and Song Be, the Vietcong* defeat at Loc Binh encouraged American military officials to believe that at long last the enemy was trying to use conventional tactics. Actually, the attacks brought on a dispersal of allied forces out of the cities and into the countryside, just what Giap had hoped would occur so that the upcoming Tet Offensive would have more impact.

Source: Edward Doyle and Samuel Lipsman, *The Vietnam Experience. America Takes Over, 1965–1967*, 1985.

LODGE, HENRY CABOT, JR.

Henry Cabot Lodge, Jr., was born on July 5, 1902, in Nahant, Massachusetts. He graduated from Harvard in 1924 and went to work as a journalist for the

Boston *Evening Transcript* and then the *New York Herald Tribune*. Lodge traveled widely and spent time in Vietnam analyzing and writing about the nature of the French Empire there. In 1932, Lodge won a seat in the Massachusetts legislature, and in 1936 he was elected as a Republican to the U.S. Senate, and he served there, except for a two-year military stint during World War II, until 1953. He lost his Senate seat in the election of 1952 to John F. Kennedy,* and in 1953 President Dwight Eisenhower* named Lodge ambassador to the United Nations. Lodge held that post until 1960. He was Richard Nixon's* running mate in their unsuccessful presidential bid in 1960, and on June 27, 1963, John F. Kennedy named Lodge ambassador to the Republic of Vietnam.*

In many ways Lodge was a perfect choice. He had spent time visiting and writing about Indochina,* spoke fluent French, and as a Republican, he might deflect GOP criticism of John F. Kennedy's foreign policies in Vietnam. Lodge was not long in Vietnam before he decided that Ngo Dinh Diem* had to go— his pride, arrogance, and unbridled ambition and greed would never allow him to effect the reforms necessary to prevent a Vietcong takeover. Lodge was enraged at Diem's attacks on the Buddhists* in August 1963, and he began advocating strongly the overthrow of the Diem government. Kennedy turned the matter over to Lodge after giving his approval, and after a good deal of intrigue the coup took place, with the Central Intelligence Agency* working with the military officers in ARVN (*see* Army of the Republic of Vietnam) responsible for it. Lodge was horrified at the assassination of Diem.

During the next six months, when political instability plagued the South Vietnamese regime, Lodge tired of the struggle, and he resigned as ambassador in the spring of 1964. He was also planning a bid for the GOP presidential nomination in 1964. In 1965 President Lyndon B. Johnson* got Lodge to accept the ambassadorship to South Vietnam again, and he remained in Saigon* until 1967. Between 1967 and 1969 Lodge was ambassador-at-large for the United States and ambassador to West Germany.* He tried in vain to negotiate with the Vietcong* and North Vietnamese as head of the U.S. delegation to the Paris peace talks* in 1969 and 1970, but he resigned that post in 1970 to become special envoy to the Vatican. Lodge returned from the Vatican in 1975. He died on February 27, 1985.

Sources: William C. Widenor, *Henry Cabot Lodge and the Search for an American Foreign Policy*, 1980; *New York Times*, February 28, 1985.

LOH–6

In 1965 the U.S. Army* selected the Hughes Model 369 helicopter as the next generation of light observation helicopters. The LOH–6 began service in Vietnam in 1967.

The LOH–6 had an enclosed aluminum semi-monocoque fuselage with side-by-side crew seats for two in front and fold-down seats for two in the rear. With the rear seats folded, four combat troops could ride in the rear cargo compartment. Powered by an Allison T63 shaft-turbine engine delivering 317 SHP, the LOH–

6 could cruise at 143 mph. The aircraft could be armed with a variety of weapons, including twin machine guns, the M–75 grenade launcher capable of firing 220 rounds per minute of 40mm shells, and the 7.62mm six-barrel machine gun capable of firing 2,000 rounds per minute.

With its relatively high speed and maneuverability, the LOH–6 made an excellent flying command center, and was widely used for convoy control and as an airborne artillery spotter. The LOH–6 was also widely used as a gunship* in support of ground operations. Overall, the LOH–6 proved a versatile addition to the helicopter war in Vietnam.

Source: *Jane's All the World's Aircraft: 1966–1967*, 1967.

Nolan J. Argyle

LONG BINH

Long Binh was a major United States Army* supply facility constructed just outside the city of Bien Hoa,* about 20 miles north of Saigon.* The headquarters of II Field Force Vietnam* and the III ARVN Corps were located at Long Binh, as was the Long Binh Jail—the "LBJ." Vietcong* attacked the Long Binh complex during the Tet Offensive* in 1968, the Post-Tet Offensive in 1969, and again, successfully, during the Final Offensive (*see* Ho Chi Minh Campaign) of 1975.

Sources: Al Santoli, *Everything We Had: An Oral History of the Vietnam War by Thirty-Three American Soldiers Who Fought It*, 1981; Shelby L. Stanton, *The Rise and Fall of an American Army: U.S. Ground Troops in Vietnam, 1965–1973*, 1985.

LONG RANGE RECONNAISSANCE PATROLS

Long Range Reconnaissance Patrols (LRRPs, pronounced "Lurps") were developed in response to specific combat conditions in Vietnam—a war without "lines" or "fronts" against a guerrilla army in rugged jungle terrain. The Vietcong* were found only when they wanted to be—when they initiated combat; therefore, finding Vietcong or North Vietnamese Army* (NVA) forces tended to be more difficult than defeating them. LRRPs were developed to overcome these problems. LRRPs were small units—ten to twelve men, although sometimes as large as a platoon* (about forty men)—patrolling a few days to a couple of weeks at a time. They neither occupied nor established fixed positions and usually were not resupplied. They traveled light, carried a minimum of food, and foraged off the land. To facilitate extended days in the field, lightweight freeze-dried LRRP rations were developed. They were preferred over traditional C-rations because they were lighter, less bulky, and tasted better.

Generally, LRRPs avoided enemy contact. Small in number and operating independent of larger units, LRRPs were not equipped to engage the enemy. Their missions included collecting intelligence on Vietcong-NVA base camps, supply areas, trail networks and troop movements, bomb damage assessments, fire direction, capturing soldiers for interrogation, rescuing downed flight crews, laying booby traps,* and sabotage.

Initially, divisions developed their own LRRP units, usually one LRRP platoon with squads operating independently or in combination depending on the mission. Some divisions developed LRRP companies comprised of two platoons. The Special Forces,* under Project Delta,* made extensive use of LRRPs and established a training center at Nha Trang* for Special Forces and regular Army LRRPs. Special Forces LRRP teams typically consisted of two or three Americans plus indigenous personnel. The Australian Task Force included a squadron of Special Air Service commandos who served as LRRPs, and some ARVN divisions (*see* Army of the Republic of Vietnam) also developed LRRP units.

Two criticisms of the military's performance in Vietnam were that greater use was not made of LRRPs and that greater use was not made of rifle companies similarly operating in the field independently over extended periods of time with minimal or no resupply. For the most part, such units were highly successful.

Sources: Harry G. Summers, Jr., *Vietnam War Almanac*, 1985; Shelby L. Stanton, *Green Berets at War*, 1985; Cincinnatus, *Self-Destruction*, 1981; Andrew F. Krepinevich, Jr., *The Army and Vietnam*, 1986.

Samuel Freeman

LON NOL

Born in French-controlled Cambodia (*see* Kampuchea) in 1913, Lon Nol was educated at a series of French colonial schools. Between 1935 and 1954 Lon Nol held a number of political and military positions in the French colonial administration and became close to Prince Norodom Sihanouk.* After independence the United States provided small amounts of assistance to Cambodia through a small military mission, resulting in close ties between Minister of National Defense Lon Nol and the United States. In 1966 Lon Nol became premier of Cambodia. Although a trusted member of Sihanouk's government, Lon Nol nevertheless criticized Sihanouk for allowing Vietcong* and North Vietnamese Army* troops to have sanctuaries* in eastern Cambodia. When Prince Sihanouk went to France* in January 1970, he entrusted the country to Prime Minister Lon Nol and Deputy Prime Minister Prince Sisowath Sirik Matak. Both were long on ambition, short on ability, and vehemently anti-Communist. Lon Nol, tired of Sihanouk's neutrality in the Indochinese conflict, engineered a coup in which the National Assembly ousted Sihanouk and placed Lon Nol in complete power.

Sihanouk charged that the March 1970 coup was instigated by the Central Intelligence Agency.* The accusation has not been proven, but Lon Nol was in contact with members of the Nixon* administration. Lon Nol proved incapable of organizing the government. In inciting the coup, he unleashed historical conflicts between Cambodians and resident Vietnamese. Quickly losing control, the anti-Vietnamese rage became rampages resulting in the deaths of several hundred Vietnamese. The American invasion of Cambodia in 1970 (*see* Operation Binh Tay) had further alienated the population, and they rallied to the Khmer Rouge.* By 1971 the Khmer Rouge controlled most of the country. In

LOWENSTEIN, ALLARD KENNETH

1975 they triumphed and the government of Lon Nol collapsed on April 17. Lon Nol fled to Hawaii.

Sources: Wilfred Burchett, *The Second Indochina War*, 1970; *Who's Who in the Far East and Australasia, 1970–1971*, 1971; William Shawcross, *Sideshow: Kissinger, Nixon, and the Destruction of Cambodia*, 1979; John Prados, *Presidents' Secret Wars: CIA and Pentagon Covert Operations Since World War II*, 1986.

Samuel Freeman

LOWENSTEIN, ALLARD KENNETH

Born in Newark, New Jersey, January 16, 1929, Allard K. Lowenstein was the principal figure in the "Dump Johnson" campaign in 1967–68. Lowenstein received a B.A. from the University of North Carolina in 1949 and an LL.B. from Yale Law School in 1954. Lowenstein had become president of the National Student Association in 1951, and remained prominent in that organization through the 1960s. In the early 1960s, he gave legal aid to jailed civil rights workers in the South; recruited student volunteers for voter registration campaigns in Mississippi; advised the Reverend Martin Luther King, Jr.,* and the Southern Christian Leadership Conference; and actively supported the Student Nonviolent Coordinating Committee. He was a civilian observer of the 1966 elections in the Dominican Republic and the 1967 elections* in South Vietnam. When he returned from Vietnam, Lowenstein formed the Conference of Concerned Democrats and the Coalition for a Democratic Alternative to oppose President Lyndon B. Johnson's* Vietnam War policies and promote a "Dump Johnson" movement among Democrats. In November 1967, Lowenstein announced support for Senator Eugene McCarthy* for president and pledged to mobilize an army of youth volunteers. Lowenstein's "Dump Johnson" campaign was apparently a factor in the president's decision not to seek reelection in 1968. At the Democratic National Convention* in Chicago in 1968, he led a Coalition for an Open Convention opposing the nomination of Hubert H. Humphrey.* In the same year, Lowenstein was elected to the U.S. House of Representatives from Long Beach, Long Island. In Congress,* he supported liberal legislation and opposed the Vietnam War. As a result, Lowenstein was included on President Richard M. Nixon's* "enemies" list. He was defeated for reelection in 1970 after the New York legislature gerrymandered his district. He then served as chairman of Americans for Democratic Action in 1971–73 and continued to be an active supporter of liberal causes during the 1970s. Lowenstein was shot to death on March 14, 1980.

Sources: Roland Turner, ed., *The Annual Obituary 1980*, 1981; *New York Times*, March 15, 1980; Nancy Zaroulis and Gerald Sullivan, *Who Spoke Up? American Protest Against the Vietnam War, 1963–1975*, 1984.

LUCE, HENRY ROBINSON

Henry Robinson Luce was born in Tengchow, China, to missionary parents on April 3, 1898. He graduated from Yale in 1920 and helped establish *Time* magazine in 1927. A strong supporter of Chiang Kai-shek* and the conservative movement in Asia, Luce in particular and *Time* in general, along with the associated magazines *Fortune* and *Life*, supported the American war effort in Vietnam, reporting news favorable to the cause and editorializing frequently in favor of the Johnson* administration. Henry Luce died on February 28, 1967, and under the new direction of Hedley Donovan, *Time* magazine shifted its position and began criticizing the conduct of the war.

Sources: *New York Times*, March 1, 1967; John Kobler, *Luce*, 1968; W. A. Swanberg, *Luce and His Empire*, 1972.

LUONG NGOC QUYEN

Luong Ngoc Quyen was born in Hanoi* in 1885. He was a student in Japan and became a disciple of the ardent Vietnamese nationalist Phan Boi Chau.* He traveled widely throughout China, and in 1916 the British arrested him in Hong Kong and turned him over to the French. While in prison, Luong Ngoc Quyen engineered the unsuccessful Thai Nguyen rebellion north of Hanoi in 1917. The rebellion was crushed by the French and Luong died in the fighting, but in the process he became a martyr to Vietnamese nationalism.

Source: William J. Duiker, *The Rise of Nationalism in Vietnam, 1900–1941*, 1976.

LYND, STAUGHTON

Born in 1929 to the famous sociologists Robert and Helen Lynd, Staughton Lynd graduated from Harvard in 1951 and in 1953, when faced with the draft,* declared himself a conscientious objector. He was designated a noncombatant. In 1961 Lynd began teaching at Spelman College in Atlanta and also earned a Ph.D. in history from Columbia in 1965. While in Atlanta, Lynd worked with Howard Zinn in 1962 to organize the Student Nonviolent Coordinating Committee and protested the actions of the Kennedy* administration during the Cuban missile crisis. Lynd was a civil rights activist throughout the early 1960s. In 1965 he was appointed an assistant professor of history at Yale.

His protest against the Vietnam War took two forms. The first was his refusal in 1965 to pay $300 in income tax, which he described as an act of civil disobedience. The second, and more dramatic, was a trip to North Vietnam in 1965 with Tom Hayden.* While in North Vietnam, Lynd described the war as immoral, illegal, and antidemocratic. The visit brought on a public, rhetorical battle with Yale president Kingman Brewster, who accused Lynd of "aiding the enemy." Lynd took a leave of absence from Yale, realizing he probably would not receive tenure, but then was unable to locate another position in higher education. He then went to law school at the University of Chicago and earned a degree in 1976. His law practice specializes in cases involving working-class people.

Sources: John Corry, " 'We Must Say Yes to Our Souls': Staughton Lynd: Spokesman for the New Left," *New York Times Magazine*, January 23, 1966; Joseph Lelyveld, "A Touch of Class," *New York Times Magazine*, August 14, 1977.

Joanna D. Cowden

LZ

"LZ" is slang for "landing zone" or, in the military alphabet, "lima zula." While technically "LZ" referred to a landing area for any type of aircraft, it was almost always used to designate a place where helicopters could land, dispatch troops and/or cargo, receive troops and/or cargo, and depart. Because the terrain was often covered by jungle or rain forest, LZs often had to be created by removing threatening obstacles to the thin-skinned helicopters. This was done in a variety of ways, depending on the circumstances. For instance, chain saws were often used, but if the forestation was too dense, a 15,000-pound bomb (known as the "Daisy Cutter") could be dropped to create an instant LZ.

In Vietnam, the helicopter became the primary means of getting troops into battle, supplying them during their stay in the field, evacuating the wounded and dead, and finally removing the survivors after battle. Consequently, LZs became a focal point of combat activity. Upon initiation of contact with the enemy, the first objective was to make the LZ as secure and safe as possible. Likewise, the enemy could be expected to make the LZ so hazardous that helicopters could not accomplish their basic mission of combat troop support. For helicopter crews flying into an LZ, the critical question was whether it was "hot" (actively contested by the enemy, in which case the helicopter was bound to be the principal target) or "cold" (safe and secure from enemy hostilities).

Source: Robert Mason, *Chickenhawk*, 1983.

Stafford T. Thomas

• M •

M

In 1967 John Sack published his novel *M,* the first in a series of anti-Vietnam War novels. The novel focuses on M Company, a training unit of American soldiers, and follows them from basic training at Fort Dix, New Jersey, through several months of combat in Vietnam. Sack juxtaposes Specialist 4 Demirgian, a gung ho American soldier committed to the philosophical rationale of the war, with the corruption of ARVN troops (*see* Army of the Republic of Vietnam), the inability to distinguish between Vietcong* and civilians, and the unbelievably poor morale among U.S. soldiers. The novel climaxes in the tragic killing of a Vietnamese girl by an American grenade lobbed into a shelter to kill Vietcong.*

Sources: John Sack, *M,* 1967; Philip D. Beidler, *American Literature and the Experience of Vietnam,* 1982; Review of *M* by Neil Sheehan, *New York Times Book Review,* May 14, 1967.

M–14 RIFLE

The M–14 rifle was adopted by the U.S. Army* in 1957, with delivery beginning in 1959. The M–14 was the result of a decade-long search for a placement rifle for the M–1 used in World War II. As such, the M–14 was the army's standard weapon at the start of the Vietnam era. However, it was rapidly replaced by the M–16 as the basic infantry rifle and weapon of choice in Vietnam.

Development of the M–14 reflected a century-old tradition of emphasizing marksmanship in the U.S. Army. The army sought a heavy caliber weapon, accurate at ranges up to 1,000 yards. Yet tactics evolved in World War II and in the Korean War emphasized firepower over marksmanship, and the M–14 was an uneasy compromise between the two.

A major factor in the development of the M–14 was the decision to standardize weapons used by NATO forces. All infantry weapons developed were expected to share ammunition. The British military, finding that few British troops in

World War II had attempted to fire on targets over 300 yards away, and that, indeed, fewer still had bothered trying to aim their rifles, pushed for a small, lightweight assault rifle firing a small-caliber round but with a high rate of fire. They developed a fine weapon meeting these characteristics, the EM–2, and tried to push it as the standard infantry weapon for NATO. The U.S. Army, with a tradition of marksmanship, balked at the weapon, and forced NATO to adopt the 7.62mm (.30 caliber) round as a standard. The M–14 was the American version of this rifle.

M–16s* had also been adopted by the army in limited numbers, and their early success in Vietnam led the army to reverse their position, dropping the M–14 in favor of the M–16—a lightweight assault rifle firing a light-caliber 5.56mm shell with a high rate of fire, much to the confusion and consternation of our NATO allies.

Source: Thomas L. McNaugher, "Marksmanship, McNamara, and the M–16 Rifle: Innovation in Military Organizations," *Public Policy* 28 (Winter 1980), 1–38.

Nolan J. Argyle

M–16 RIFLE

The adoption of the M–16 as the basic infantry weapon of the U.S. armed forces represented a break with over a hundred years of military tradition, and was, in large part, a direct result of the war in Vietnam.

The M–16 has been called one of the success stories of the twentieth century. Now one of the best known infantry weapons in the Western world, it was developed as a private venture by an unknown company employing only one designer. Developed for Armalite by Eugene Stoner in the mid–1950s as the AR–15, the weapon was designed to take advantage of modern manufacturing techniques and materials. The metal components of the weapon were stamped, pressed, or forged rather than using the traditional methods of machining and casting. Plastics were used in place of traditional wood. Mechanically, the M–16 varied from other automatic or semiautomatic weapons. It is gas-operated, but rather than using the conventional piston, the gas is led through a tube directly into the bolt carrier. The drawback to this design is that it can lead to the action fouling up—something that happened frequently in the early days of its use in Vietnam. Furthermore, troops using the weapon had a tendency to tape two clips together, so that when they emptied one they could simply pull out the clip, turn it over, and start firing again. This caused the clips to hang and jam the action. Kept clean and fed with single clips, the M–16 proved to be a highly reliable weapon.

While it did prove to be a highly respected, reliable weapon, the M–16 was not at first considered suitable for the American infantryman. The U.S. Army* adopted its first rifle as standard equipment in 1855 (earlier weapons had been smooth-bore weapons, lacking the accuracy given by rifled barrels). From this time on the army stressed accuracy over long distance—marksmanship—over rate of fire in selecting weapons. The American infantryman was expected to be a sharpshooter, and therefore needed a weapon with hitting power at long range. In light of the Civil War experience with rifled weapons, the army published a training manual stressing that what counted was the number of hits, not the number of shots fired, and that such hits should be made out to a range of 1,000 yards or more. This led to an emphasis on heavy-caliber weapons. Then in the 1950s, American military forces started to standardize their weapons and equipment with other NATO armed forces, so that ammunition could be interchangeable. It was decided to adopt the British-developed 7.62mm cartridge as the basic cartridge for infantry weapons. Reflecting these two concerns, the U.S. Army developed the M–14* as its next-generation infantry weapon, and started to supply field units with that weapon. It was in this context that the Armalite weapon was introduced.

In 1962, Defense Secretary Robert McNamara* sought to interest the army in the M–16. Having just developed the M–14, the army showed little interest in adopting the weapon. The M–16 fired a 5.56mm slug that gained its hitting power from its muzzle velocity of 3,250 feet per/second. As the slug lost speed, its hitting power dropped, giving it an effective range of only about 400 yards. Further, the light slug was easily diverted from its path by any object it encountered, including twigs, therefore affecting its accuracy over long distances. Its strong point was not marksmanship but a high rate of fire. With its straight-line design (a line drawn through the barrel would hit the rifleman at the shoulder, instead of above as in traditional designs) the M–16 could be held on target even in automatic fire, allowing the soldier to spray a target. In short, the M–16 did not fit within the army's traditions.

While the army failed to adopt the M–16, the U.S. Air Forces* did adopt the weapon for its security forces. More important, the army did purchase the weapon for special units, including some of the Special Forces.* These units saw the first direct combat action by U.S. troops in Vietnam, and they found the M–16 far superior to the M–14 for the type of fighting they were doing. In jungle fighting, firepower was far more important than marksmanship. Just 39 inches in length and weighing only 6 pounds 5 ounces, the M–16 was an easy weapon to carry and bring into action quickly. In 1967, the army reversed its long tradition and adopted the M–16, much to the consternation of NATO. By this time, the weapon was being manufactured by Colt Arms. Several million M–16s have been manufactured over the past two decades, and the weapon is now the most widely used infantry weapon in the world.

Sources: Thomas L. McNaugher, "Marksmanship, McNamara and the M–16 Rifle: Innovation in Military Organization," *Public Policy* 28 (Winter 1980), 1–38; *The Illustrated Encyclopedia of 20th Century Weapons and Warfare,* 1969.

Nolan J. Argyle

M–60 MACHINE GUN

The M–60 machine gun was designed to replace both the .30 caliber Browning light machine gun and the .50 caliber heavy machine gun for the U.S. armed forces. Mounted on a tripod, the M–60 served as a heavy machine gun, used primarily to defend fixed positions. As a light machine gun, the M–60 used a folding bipod attached to the barrel. Although Vietnam saw its first major use, the weapon's design dates back to World War II, incorporating the belt-feed mechanism of the German MG 42 machine gun and the operating mechanism of the German MG 42 automatic rifle. Although it does not have selective-fire capabilities, it does have a low cyclic rate of 600 rounds per minute, which permits firing single rounds. The weapon is gas-operated, with a muzzle velocity of 2,800 feet per second and a maximum effective range of 3,500 yards. Far smaller and lighter than its predecessors at 43.73 inches in length and 23.05 pounds, the M–60 is the first truly portable machine gun in the U.S. arsenal. Capable of being fired from the hip while moving, the M–60 proved well-suited to the type of fighting found in Vietnam.

Source: John Quick, *Dictionary of Weapons and Military Terms,* 1973.

Nolan J. Argyle

M–72

The M–72, or Light Antitank Weapon (LAW), was a high-explosive rocket used by U.S. and South Vietnamese forces to destroy Vietcong* and North Vietnamese bunkers. Lightweight and approximately three feet long, the M–72 was perfectly suited for infantry assaults.

Source: Harry G. Summers, Jr., *Vietnam War Almanac,* 1985.

M–79

The M–79 grenade launcher was introduced in the early 1960s, just as the war in Vietnam was heating up and starting to take more U.S. military attention. The M–79 represented a vast improvement over earlier rifle-fired grenades. Looking like a single-barrel, break-open shotgun, the M–79 was only 28.6 inches long and weighed just 6 pounds, 2 ounces, making it a highly portable weapon capable of being carried and fired by light infantry on the move. The M–79 fired a 9-ounce, 40mm shell with various warheads, including antipersonnel, armor-piercing, and white phosphorus. With an effective range of 400 meters and far greater accuracy than the older rifle-fired grenades, the M–79 gave the field soldier a potent weapon against enemy bunkers and troop concentrations. An automatic version, the M–75, was capable of firing 220 rounds per minute with a range of 2,000 meters. The M–75 was often mounted in a remote-control turret for helicopter use.

Source: John Quick, *Dictionary of Weapons and Military Terms,* 1973.

Nolan J. Argyle

MAAG   *See* Military Assistance and Advisory Group

MacARTHUR, DOUGLAS

The child of a military family, Douglas MacArthur was born on January 26, 1880, on an army base near Little Rock, Arkansas. He graduated from West

Point in 1903, and then served with distinction in the Philippines, Mexico, and with the Rainbow Division in World War I. After the war, MacArthur became commandant of West Point. He was promoted to general in 1930, and in 1935 went to the Philippines as a military adviser. During World War II he was commander in chief of army forces in the Pacific, and after the war virtually ruled Japan as head of the occupation forces. MacArthur drafted the new Japanese constitution and then established a democratic government and economic revival in Japan. MacArthur took command of UN forces in South Korea* in 1950 after the North Korean invasion, reversed the invasion with the amphibious assault at Inchon, and then lost his command because of insubordination in 1951, after the Chinese had entered the conflict and he had refused to accept President Harry S. Truman's* vision of a limited conflict. MacArthur then retired from the army. Before his death on April 5, 1964, MacArthur frequently expressed to his associates, as well as to President John F. Kennedy*, his misgivings about the United States becoming involved in a protracted guerrilla war in Southeast Asia.

Source: William Manchester, *American Caesar: Douglas MacArthur, 1880–1964,* 1978.

McCAIN, JOHN SIDNEY, JR.

Commander in chief of Pacific naval forces (1968–72), John McCain was the youngest son of another full admiral. He was born on January 17, 1911, in Council Bluffs, Iowa. He grew up in Washington, D.C., where he attended Central High School. After completing high school he entered the United States Naval Academy at Annapolis at the tender age of sixteen. In 1931 he graduated from Annapolis nearly at the bottom of his class.

McCain's first tour of duty was on the battleship *Oklahoma,* and he subsequently served on submarines between 1933 and 1938. After his stint on submarines he became an instructor of electrical engineering at the Naval Academy. With the outbreak of World War II, McCain entered combat aboard the USS *Skipjack,* a submarine, and subsequently commanded submarines in both the Atlantic and Pacific. After the war he became records director of the Bureau of Naval Personnel until 1949.

During the 1950s McCain successfully served aboard the USS *St. Paul* as its executive officer. His next assignments followed in succession: director of navy undersea warfare research and development; commander of Submarine Squadron 6; commander of the attack transport USS *Monrovia*; director of progress analysis in the Office of the Chief of Naval Operations; commanding officer of the USS *Albany*; and chief of legislative liaison for the secretary of the navy. McCain was promoted to rear admiral in 1959 and to vice admiral four years later.

During the early 1960s McCain was part of the Atlantic Fleet's amphibious command, eventually rising to its entire command in 1965. Admiral McCain took part in the U.S. intervention in the Dominican Republic in 1965. He finally succeeded retiring Admiral Ulysses S. Grant Sharp* as commander in chief, Pacific Command* on July 31, 1968. McCain was a hard-liner on the Vietnam

War and believed that the Communists were using the Vietnamese conflict to further their expansionist aims. In the fall of 1972 it was McCain who urged that President Nixon* take drastic measures against North Vietnam. He supported the resumption of bombing* as well as the mining of Haiphong Harbor* to bring the North Vietnamese to the conference table. McCain, before 1972, was a strong and vocal proponent of the Nixon administration's Vietnamization* program. Yet by the fall of 1972, McCain was weary of his longtime service to the country and consequently decided to return to the Naval Academy as an instructor of electrical engineering. He retired in 1972 and died on March 22, 1981.

Sources: *Current Biography,* November 1970; *Washington Post,* March 24, 1981; *Congressional Record,* October 3, 1972; *New York Times,* March 23, 1981.

John S. Leiby

McCARTHY, EUGENE JOSEPH

Elected to the U.S. House of Representatives in 1948 and to the Senate in 1958 from his native state of Minnesota, McCarthy became an outspoken opponent of the Vietnam War. Born in Watkins, Minnesota, on March 29, 1916, he was a schoolteacher and college professor before being elected to Congress. He served on the Senate Foreign Relations Committee,* and after supporting the Gulf of Tonkin Resolution* and generally refraining from criticism of Johnson* administration policies in Vietnam, by 1967 he had become a leading critic of the war.

On November 30, 1967, McCarthy announced as a candidate for the 1968 Democratic presidential nomination against President Johnson, emphasizing his support for a negotiated settlement of the war. He said the war was draining "the material and moral resources of the country from our really pressing problems." Viewed as more of a scholar than a politician, McCarthy surprised the experts. He demonstrated the political potential of the antiwar movement* and was a rallying point for youthful opponents of the war. His strong showing against Johnson in the New Hampshire primary on March 12, 1968, was a major factor in Robert Kennedy's* decision to become a candidate for the presidential nomination and in Johnson's decision not to seek reelection. McCarthy remained in the race for the nomination through the Democratic National Convention in Chicago, where he was defeated by Vice President Hubert Humphrey.* McCarthy left the Senate after completing his second term in 1970.

Sources: Eugene McCarthy, *The Year of the People,* 1969; Theodore H. White, *The Making of the President 1968,* 1969.

Hoyt Purvis

McGEE, GALE WILLIAM

Gale McGee was born in Lincoln, Nebraska, in 1915. He graduated from the Nebraska State Teachers College in 1936 and eventually earned a Ph.D. in history from the University of Chicago. Between 1938 and 1948 he taught at a number of colleges, until his appointment as professor of history at the University of

Wyoming. McGee served as a legislative assistant to Democratic Senator Joseph O'Mahoney in 1955 and 1956, and in 1958 he won election to the U.S. Senate. During the years of the Vietnam War, McGee was one of the Senate's most articulate "hawks," generally supporting the American military presence in Southeast Asia. McGee served in the Senate until 1977. He had been defeated in the election of 1976 by Malcolm Wallop. After his 1976 defeat, McGee served from 1977 to 1981 as a permanent representative to the Organization of American States. He is the author of *The Responsibility of World Power* (1968).

Sources: *Current Biography*, 1961; "Democrats," *Time*, January 17, 1969, p. 19; *The Almanac of American Politics, 1982*, 1982.

Joanna D. Cowden

McGOVERN, GEORGE STANLEY

George Stanley McGovern was born in Avon, South Dakota, on July 19, 1922. He served as a pilot with the Army Air Force during World War II and received his B.A. from Dakota Wesleyan University in 1945. McGovern went on to earn the M.A. and Ph.D. in history from Northwestern University in 1949 and 1953. He taught at Dakota Wesleyan between 1949 and 1953, and then served for two years as executive secretary of the South Dakota Democratic party. McGovern was elected to Congress* in 1956, and in 1961 accepted President John F. Kennedy's* offer to direct the Food for Peace program. McGovern was elected to the U.S. Senate in 1963 and served there until 1981. In 1968, after the assassination of Robert F. Kennedy,* McGovern staged a belated run for the Democratic presidential nomination, emphasizing opposition to the war in Vietnam and the need to reinforce Great Society* programs. He lost the nomination to Hubert Humphrey,* but between 1968 and 1972 McGovern was a leading figure in the restructuring of the Democratic party, de-emphasizing the power of the urban machines and the South in favor of women and minorities. McGovern won the Democratic presidential nomination in 1972, campaigning on the theme of an immediate, unilateral withdrawal from Vietnam, but he suffered a landslide defeat at the hands of President Richard M. Nixon* in the general election.

Sources: George S. McGovern, *A Time of War, A Time of Peace*, 1968; *Who's Who in America, 1984–1985*, 1985; Theodore White, *The Making of the President, 1972*, 1973; Robert Sam Anson, *McGovern: A Biography*, 1972.

McNAMARA, ROBERT STRANGE

Robert S. McNamara was born on June 9, 1916, in San Francisco, California. He graduated from the University of California at Berkeley in 1937 and then received his M.B.A. from Harvard in 1939. An expert in systems management and statistics, McNamara served in administrative positions with the Army Air Corps during World War II, and after the war he joined the Ford Motor Company, where he rose rapidly through management ranks as one of the new generation of whiz kids. In 1960, at the age of forty-four, McNamara was named president of Ford Motor Company. President-elect John F. Kennedy* had his eye on McNamara, however, and offered him the cabinet post of secretary of defense. McNamara came to Washington, D.C., in 1961 and remained there until his resignation from the Pentagon in 1968.

Robert McNamara proved to be one of the most influential figures in the history of the Vietnam War. Blessed with a keen, analytical mind and a supreme confidence in the efficacy of modern technology, McNamara became a primary architect of American policy in Vietnam, exercising both logistical and operational control over the war, presiding over the initial buildup, and eventually losing all faith in the American effort there. McNamara was a leading exponent of counterinsurgency,* the Gulf of Tonkin Resolution,* and bombing* of North Vietnam in 1964 and 1965, as well as the large-scale commitment of ground troops to South Vietnam. To stop infiltration* from North Vietnam along the Ho Chi Minh Trail* and across the Demilitarized Zone,* McNamara called for the construction of an electronic barrier across Southeast Asia—a system of devices to alert the United States of any breach of security at any time. Dubbed "McNamara's Wall" (see Project Practice Nine) by skeptical journalists, the proposal was never implemented, but it did show the naïveté of McNamara's faith in modern technology.

By 1966, however, McNamara had become somewhat skeptical of the American war effort in Vietnam. He was astonished at the resilience of the North Vietnamese and the relative lack of effect American bombing had, especially on their extraordinary ability to move men and material down the Ho Chi Minh Trail into South Vietnam. McNamara was also surprised at the level of casualties the Vietcong* and North Vietnamese Army* were willing to accept, and he knew, statistician that he was, how their commitment upset the basic philosophy behind the American war of attrition* there. Finally, McNamara grew positively disgusted with the corruption of South Vietnamese officials, the instability of their government, and their lack of sensitivity to democratic principles. Between 1961 and 1966 McNamara visited South Vietnam eight times, and by the end of 1966 he realized that American casualties were too high for the results achieved. No end of the war was in sight.

By 1967 McNamara was advocating a negotiated settlement to the conflict, pushing on President Lyndon Johnson* a diplomatic solution to the problem. Understandably, the president was upset. For years he had accepted the counsel and advice of these "experts," the "best and the brightest" in David Halberstam's* words, and now they were essentially admitting they had been wrong, after the troop totals had reached more than 500,000 soldiers and more than 30,000 Americans were dead. As McNamara's skepticism grew throughout 1967, so did Johnson's frustration, and in November 1967 he asked McNamara to resign his defense post. By that time McNamara was advocating an end to bombing the north, a cap on American troop strength in Vietnam, and gradually turning the war over to the South Vietnamese. After leaving the Department of

Defense, McNamara became president of the World Bank, a position he held until his retirement in 1983.

Sources: David Halberstam, *The Best and the Brightest*, 1972; Gregory Palmer, *The McNamara Strategy and the Vietnam War: Program Budgeting in the Pentagon, 1960–1968*, 1978.

McNAMARA'S WALL   *See* Project Practice Nine

McNAUGHTON, JOHN THEODORE

Born on November 21, 1921, John McNaughton was one of Robert McNamara's* whiz kids brought into the Department of Defense to make it more efficient. McNaughton was a former Harvard Law School professor and one of McNamara's closest civilian advisers when the United States embarked on its Vietnamese venture. After President Johnson* received the Gulf of Tonkin Resolution in August 1964, he was among the hard-liners who urged serious action against North Vietnam. Of course, the Johnson administration decided that any military operations against North Vietnam would be taken after the November 1964 elections.

McNaughton agreed with Maxwell Taylor's* assertions that only direct intervention by the United States would save South Vietnam from almost certain takeover by the Communists. He recommended that combat units be introduced and that air bases be constructed in South Vietnam. McNaughton also suggested that naval forces be stationed in the Gulf of Tonkin to provoke the North Vietnamese and hence give the United States justification to punish the Hanoi* regime. Although McNaughton was a hard-liner, he did urge some restraint so as not to damage Johnson's image with the American public. In March 1965, after U.S. combat forces had been deployed in South Vietnam, McNaughton asserted that only these forces, with accompanying reinforcements, could avert defeat of the South Vietnamese. He supported continuing escalation at least until American public opinion soured on the Vietnam War.

By late 1967, however, McNaughton began to question America's role in Vietnam. Throughout the summer of 1966, he had been part of a think tank institute which drafted the Jason Study.* This study found that U.S. actions in Vietnam had failed. Because of their primitive economy, North Vietnam had not been materially damaged by U.S. air raids. Instead of destroying their morale, the air raids had strengthened patriotism and nationalism among the Hanoi leadership. The study found in addition that the North Vietnamese had increased their infiltration* into the south. Such conclusions alarmed McNamara and made him more pessimistic about the U.S. involvement. McNaughton, in private conversations with McNamara, warned in the summer of 1967 that the Vietnam War was fast becoming so serious that its consequences "could cause the worst split in our people in more than a century." McNaughton, however, did not live to see his prophecy fulfilled. In July 1967, he and his family were killed in an air crash, only a short time before he was to become the secretary of the navy.

Sources: "Career's End," *Newsweek,* July 31, 1967; *New York Times,* July 18, 1967; Stanley Karnow, *Vietnam: A History,* 1983.

John S. Leiby

MACV   *See* Military Assistance Command, Vietnam

MADDOX   *See* USS *Maddox*

MANSFIELD, MICHAEL JOSEPH

Successor to Lyndon Johnson* as majority leader of the U.S. Senate, Mike Mansfield served in that position from 1961 until 1977, the longest-serving majority leader in Senate history. Born in New York City on March 16, 1903, he grew up in Montana, enlisted in the navy at age fifteen and later served with the marines. His military service took him to Asia, and he developed a deep interest in the Far East. He taught Far Eastern history at the University of Montana before being elected to the U.S. House of Representatives as a Democrat in 1942. He served on the House Foreign Affairs Committee, and when elected to the Senate in 1952, he became a member of the Foreign Relations Committee.*

Mansfield was an early supporter of Ngo Dinh Diem* in Vietnam. However, when the majority leader visited Vietnam in 1962 at President Kennedy's* request, he returned with a pessimistic assessment of developments there. Under the Johnson* administration, he also made several visits to Southeast Asia and expressed increasing concern about the escalation of the war. He cautioned that the United States should learn from the French experience in Vietnam, and in 1965 he advised President Johnson against a major commitment of American troops. As his efforts to convince Johnson that a negotiated settlement rather than further military action was the proper course proved futile, Mansfield became a public opponent of the war. He was even more critical as the war continued under the Nixon* administration and became a champion of the reassertion of congressional foreign policy powers. He backed the 1970 Cooper-Church* and Hatfield-McGovern* amendments, and in 1971 his amendment calling for withdrawal of U.S. military forces within nine months (subject to the release of American prisoners of war)* passed the Senate but was defeated in the House. He did not seek reelection in 1976, and in 1977 was named by President Carter as U.S. ambassador to Japan, a position he retained under the Reagan administration.

Sources: David Halberstam, *The Best and the Brightest,* 1972; Stanley Karnow, *Vietnam,* 1983.

Hoyt Purvis

MAO ZEDONG

Born in Hunan in 1893, Mao Zedong came from peasant roots. As a young man he journeyed to Beijing and found employment as a library assistant at Beijing National University. There he was caught up in revolutionary fervor and joined the Chinese Communist party. In the 1920s Mao began to articulate his view that the future of revolution in China rested with the peasantry and not with the working poor in major cities, for there were too few of them. After the famous Long March of 1934–35, Mao established himself in Yenan in northwest China and became a folk hero during World War II because of his aggressive tactics against the Japanese. He led the Communists to victory in the Chinese Civil War and in 1949 became chairman of the Communist party and of the People's Republic of China.*

Afraid that revolutionary principles and zeal were waning in China by the 1960s, Mao launched the Cultural Revolution in 1966 and fueled its fanatical attacks on Chinese intellectuals until 1969. China was thrown into such turmoil that it had little opportunity to assist the North Vietnamese and Vietcong,* beyond some weapons shipments, in their struggle against the United States. The long ethnic rivalry between Chinese* and Vietnamese in Southeast Asia would probably have precluded any unified front anyway. After 1969 more practical Chinese leaders brought the Cultural Revolution to an end, and Mao Zedong spent his last years in retirement. He died in 1976.

Sources: *Webster's New Biographical Dictionary*, 1983; Daniel S. Papp, *Vietnam: The View from Moscow, Peking, Washington*, 1981.

Charles Dobbs

MARINE COMBINED ACTION PLATOONS

First formed in the fall of 1965 to support the South Vietnamese government's Revolutionary Development Program and III Marine Amphibious Force's* (MAF) budding civic action policy, Marine Combined Action Platoons (CAP) became an integral, well-publicized part of the "other war"—the effort to gain the confidence of villagers and thus deny the Vietcong* (VC) a critical base of support. Limited to defending airfields during the first several months of deployment, marine patrols found booby traps,* mines, and snipers to be constant and costly reminders of an unseen VC presence. Responding with modest medical and construction projects based on marine experiences in the Caribbean islands and Central America, marine civic action eventually won enthusiastic support in Saigon* and Washington and tapped resources from all major I Corps* commands to build schools, roads, and hospitals.

Marine CAP supplemented civic action by integrating U.S. Marine Corps* units with Republic of Vietnam* Popular Forces* (PF), with whom the Americans would train, share rations and quarters, and fight side by side. Typically, a squad of marines plus a navy corpsman would be integrated into a PF platoon and assigned to a particular hamlet to "win hearts and minds"* and cultivate intelligence sources.

III MAF organized these units under a G–5 or civil affairs section in Da Nang,* and the program grew rapidly with four Combined Action Battalions deployed in Vietnam between October 1967 and July 1970. The last Marine

CAP withdrew when marine ground and air operations ceased in the spring of 1971.

Sources: *The Marines in Vietnam, 1954–1973*, 1983; Shelby L. Stanton, *Vietnam Order of Battle*, 1981; Larry E. Cable, *Conflict of Myths: The Development of American Counterinsurgency Doctrine and the Vietnam War*, 1986; Russell H. Stolfi, *U.S. Marine Corps Civil Action Efforts in Vietnam, March 1965-March 1966*, 1968.

Dudley Acker

MARINE CORPS, UNITED STATES

In the decade between the Geneva Accords* of 1954 and the first overt commitment of U.S. combat troops (two marine battalions at Da Nang*) in March 1965, marines helped establish the Vietnamese Marine Corps and also served with the U.S. Military Assistance and Advisory Group* in Saigon,* two helicopter squadrons and a radio company sent to the theater in 1962, as advisers to Republic of Vietnam* infantry units, and in small security forces at air bases and the U.S. embassy. Before South Vietnam collapsed in 1975, marines who had spent at least part of the normal thirteen-month tour in country numbered over 450,000.

While mines, booby traps,* and sniper rounds accounted for a high percentage of early marine casualties,* after the rapid buildup in I Corps* in 1966–67 small arms fire and fragments accounted for almost 90 percent of the deaths and wounds suffered by marine personnel. Peaking at 85,520 marines in country in 1968 (almost one-third of the Marine Corps's total strength at the time), in six years marine units lost almost 15,000 killed and 89,000 wounded in action compared to the 20,000 killed and 70,000 wounded fighting the Japanese in World War II. Marines accounted for 28.4 percent of the casualties, 33.5 percent of those wounded and hospitalized, 4.7 percent of the POWs,* and 8 percent of the MIAs among American forces in the theater.

Fifty-seven Medals of Honor were awarded to twelve marine officers and forty-five enlisted men, thirteen of whom survived to attend their ceremonies; and marines captured 4,098 prisoners (not including Vietcong* suspects and civilian detainees) and 22,879 weapons, and reported killing approximately 86,000 enemy soldiers and guerrillas.

Marines units deployed to Vietnam included two divisions reinforced by two regimental landing teams, a reinforced air wing, several battalion landing teams afloat and on call with the Seventh Fleet,* plus small units detached to the U.S. Army* or guarding the U.S. embassy and naval installations in the Saigon area. This force broke down into 24 infantry regiments, 2 reconnaissance battalions, 2 force reconnaissance companies, 4 armored battalions, more than 10 battalions of artillery, 4 combined action battalions, 2 antitank battalions, 26 aircraft squadrons (approximately 500 helicopters, fighters,* and fighter-bombers), and 5 battalions each of engineers and motor transport personnel. Two medical battalions and a hospital company supplemented the hundreds of U.S. Navy* doctors, corpsmen, and nurses attached to marine units.

While the Marine Corps's worldwide strength peaked at 317,400 in 1968 and thus fell short of the 485,113 figure set in World War II, over 730,000 marines served during the Vietnam era compared to about 600,000 in the war against Japan.* Peacetime personnel policies remained in effect from 1965 to 1973 and accounted for the disparities in numbers between the two wars. In Vietnam, marines served twelve- and thirteen-month tours, then rotated back to "the world." Except those who extended for six-month increments or chose to reenlist, Marines were not required to serve for the duration of the conflict as in earlier years. Fleet Marine Force, Pacific Command* thus required some 9 to 10 thousand troops to keep the marine war going, and between 85,000 and 120,000* men and women enlisted, were drafted into, or left the Marine Corps in each of the six years before its units withdrew in the spring of 1971.

Sources: *The Marines in Vietnam, 1954–1973*, 1983; Shelby L. Stanton, *Vietnam Order of Battle*, 1981; J. Robert Moskin, *The U.S. Marine Corps Story*, 1982.

Dudley Acker

MARINE CORPS RECRUIT DEPOTS

When asked what made their service special, marines usually repy, "boot camp"—during the Vietnam era eight to twelve weeks of intense indoctrination designed to supplant civilian values and introduce recruits to the rudiments of the Marine Corps's* mission and tradition. Training began abruptly in a receiving barracks where shorn "boots" met their drill instructors (DIs), noncommissioned officers who then double-timed them through several days of showers, dental work, inoculations, and the issue of uniforms, rifles, 782-gear, and *The Guidebook for Marines,* parts of which had to be memorized and recited loudly and in unison.

The regimen changed occasionally during the war but at any time included Marine Corps's history, physical fitness, marksmanship, and daily doses of close-order drill on "the grinder"—a few acres of sun-baked tarmac on which DIs called cadence and resorted to other techniques to instill discipline. A meticulous final inspection followed by a family-oriented graduation ceremony capped Marine Corps Recruit Depot (MCRD) training, and no longer called "boots," the marines then received orders to an Infantry Training Regiment (ITR) at Camp Lejeune, North Carolina, or Camp Pendleton, California.

MCRD, Parris Island, South Carolina: First established in 1911 at the Marine Barracks, Port Royal Naval Station, recruit training moved after two months to the Norfolk (Virginia) Naval Yard and then back to the barracks in 1915; the name of the base became Parris Island in 1919. Located amid salt marshes between Charleston and Savannah, the base is hot, humid, and under attack by sand fleas in summer, but rarely cold enough to suspend training during its damp winters.

MCRD, San Diego, California: Dubbed "Hollywood Marines" by those trained at Parris Island, San Diego recruits at least enjoyed a dry, moderate climate year round. The Marine Corps first established Camp Howard on a nearby island in 1914 and moved to the mainland later that year, selecting a permanent site for the future recruit depot in 1919. In 1923 boot training shifted from Mare Island in San Francisco Bay to San Diego, where the supervision of recruits from western states continued through World War II, Korea, and Vietnam.

Source: V. Keith Fleming, ''Welcome to the Marines: Boot Camp Training,'' in Ashley Brown, ed., *The U.S. Marines in Action,* 1986.

Dudley Acker

MARTIN, GRAHAM ANDERSON

Born in Mars Hill, North Carolina, on September 12, 1912, Graham Martin graduated from Wake Forest University in 1932 and joined the National Recovery Administration in 1933 as an aide to W. Averell Harriman.* After working in various New Deal agencies during the 1930s and serving in the Army Air Corps during World War II, Martin went to the State Department in 1947 as a foreign service officer. He was assigned to Paris for eight years, worked as a special assistant to Douglas Dillon, under secretary of state, between 1957 and 1959, and became ambassador to Thailand* in 1963. He was successful there in building a strong military relationship between the United States and the Thais, and in 1969 Martin became ambassador to Italy. An avowed anti-Communist, Martin was named to replace Ellsworth Bunker* as ambassador to Vietnam in 1973.

Martin's stay in Vietnam was a disaster. He carried a powerful emotional burden as ambassador because his wife's son had been killed in the war, and Martin was much too abrupt for Nguyen Van Thieu,* who needed constant reassuring and praise. Martin also disregarded the problem of official corruption in the South Vietnamese government, which bled local villages and generated more support for the Vietcong.* Finally, Martin tended to exaggerate the strength of the American position in South Vietnam. Right up to the end, Martin believed that the South Vietnamese government in general and the city of Saigon* in particular could survive the North Vietnamese and Vietcong assault in the spring of 1975. Holding on to the embassy flag, Martin and his wife climbed to the roof of the embassy on April 29, 1975, and fled the country. Before his retirement from the State Department, Martin served as a special assistant to Secretary of State Henry Kissinger* and an ambassador-at-large for the Pacific.

Sources: Tad Szulc, *An Illusion of Peace,* 1978; *New York Times,* April 2, 1973; May 2, 1976; and August 26, 1976.

MAT TRAN DAN TOC GIAI PHONG MIEN NAM   *See* Vietcong

MAYAGUEZ INCIDENT

On May 12, 1975, a Cambodian gunboat seized the SS *Mayaguez,* an American merchant ship, in transit from Hong Kong to Thailand.* The ship and its thirty-nine-member crew were taken seven miles to the Cambodian island of Poulo Wai. The Khmer* government of Cambodia (*see* Kampuchea) claimed the *Mayaguez* was captured inside Cambodian territorial waters while engaged on a spy mission for the United States. President Gerald Ford* responded that the Cambodian action was an "act of piracy" and demanded the release of the ship and its crew. When appeals to the People's Republic of China* and the United Nations to use their influence to persuade Cambodia to release the crew appeared to fail, Ford prepared for a military response.

On May 14, 200 U.S. Marines* were landed on Koh Tang Island by helicopter assault to rescue the *Mayaguez* crew, who were presumed to be there. The assault force encountered heavy Cambodian resistance and were able to advance no further than the beach. In a simultaneous operation a marine boarding party from the USS *Holt* seized the empty *Mayaguez* (on May 13 the crew had been moved to the Cambodian mainland). While military operations were underway, the Cambodian government released the crew of the *Mayaguez* along with five Thai fishermen who had been captured earlier and charged with spying for the United States. The announcement of the release was made at 7:07 P.M. EDT on Cambodian radio and by 11:00 P.M. the *Mayaguez* crew had been taken aboard the USS *Wilson* from a Thai fishing boat. Subsequently, at 11:16 P.M. President Ford ordered a halt to offensive operations and a withdrawal of all forces. However, planned air strikes of the Cambodian mainland were still carried out. Rescue of the marines on Tang Island was delayed because heavy Cambodian gunfire drove off the evacuation helicopters. It was not until naval gunfire support could be used that the marines were finally evacuated on the morning of May 15. The operation resulted in fifteen dead and fifty wounded.

Foreign and domestic reactions to the United States were generally favorable or neutral, although actual casualty figures were not immediately released. It later came to light that Secretary of State Henry Kissinger* kept a possible diplomatic option a secret from the National Security Council.* The Chinese apparently were using their influence to gain release of the crew and were expecting success. General Brent Scowcroft, deputy of national security affairs, later admitted that the United States had responded harshly in an attempt to show that although the United States had recently withdrawn from Southeast Asia, it was prepared to protect its interest abroad.

Sources: Chris Lamb, "Belief Systems and Decision Making in the *Mayaguez* Incident," *Political Science Quarterly* 99 (Winter 1984–85), 681–702; Roy Rowan, *The Four Days of Mayaguez*, 1975.

Mike Dennis

MEDEVAC

"Medevac" was an acronym for medical evacuation, almost always associated with evacuation of casualties by helicopter during or after a battle. Consequently, the helicopters used for these missions also were called "medevac helicopters," or simply "medevacs." The use of the helicopter in a variety of missions was a distinguishing feature of the Vietnam War. For American and Allied troops, the sound of the helicopter was perhaps the most nearly ubiquitous sound of the war. Usually, it evoked positive feelings for troops in the field, since the helicopter almost always meant relief in some form, be it additional troop reinforcements; supplies such as ammunition, food, and medicine; or evacuation of the wounded and/or dead. The medevac helicopter was an especially important factor in enhancing and sustaining troop morale in the field. Soldiers knew that if they were wounded, the probability was high that they would be transported quickly to a field hospital. Statistics suggest the validity of this assumption: nearly 98 percent of those wounded in action were evacuated from the battlefield alive, and no battlefield was more than one hour's flying time from a hospital. Medevac helicopter crews often had to fly into "hot" landing zones to evacuate the wounded, and all of those involved in evacuating wounded under such conditions were at great risk to becoming casualties. The use of the helicopter for medical evacuation contributed substantially to the military performance of American and Allied troops during the Vietnam War, and medevacs resulted in many wounded being saved who might otherwise have died from wounds. A synonym for medevac was "dustoff," used after the death of Lieutenant Paul B. Kelley in 1964. Kelley's radio call sign was "dustoff," and he was killed on a medevac mission. The term was used to refer to medevac missions and medevac helicopters after that.

Source: Robert Mason, *Chickenhawk*, 1983.

Stafford T. Thomas

MEDICAL SUPPORT

Because of major improvements in medical support facilities and evacuation of the wounded, less than 19 percent of soldiers died from combat wounds in the Vietnam War, compared to 26 percent in the Korean War and 29 percent in World War II. Helicopters quickly evacuated wounded troops to base camp hospitals, MASH units, field hospitals, and hospital ships off the coast of the South China Sea. Also, because of major improvements in pharmaceutical care against infectious diseases, death or disability from malaria, hepatitis, and intestinal disorders was well below the rates of Korea and World War II.

Source: Spurgeon Neel, *Vietnam Studies: Medical Support of the U.S. Army in Vietnam, 1965–1970*, 1973.

MEDINA, ERNEST L.

Ernest L. Medina was born in Springer, New Mexico, in 1936. His mother died when he was only a few months old and shortly thereafter his father sent him to Montrose, Colorado, where he was reared by his grandparents. To supplement his grandparents' meager income he worked as a soda jerk, a paperboy, and in a local supermarket.

When Medina was sixteen years old, he lied about his age to enlist in the National Guard, where he served until 1956, when at the age of twenty he entered the army as a private. In March 1964, after serving eight years, Medina was commissioned a second lieutenant, graduating fourth out of a class of more than two hundred from Officer Candidate School at Fort Benning, Georgia. After his second tour of duty in Germany, where he met his wife Barbara, an East German refugee, he was ordered to Hawaii in December of 1966. Medina was promoted to captain and given command of Charlie Company, which was a part of the 11th Infantry Brigade (*see* 23rd Infantry Division). In December of 1967 the 11th Brigade was flown to Vietnam.

While in Vietnam Medina won the Bronze and Silver stars for valor. On March 10, 1970, Medina was charged with murder, manslaughter, and assault as a result of the March 16, 1968, massacre at My Lai* 4 hamlet. On September 22, 1970, a jury of five officers cleared him of all charges. Subsequently, Medina resigned his commission from the army on October 15, 1971, explaining, "I cannot wear the uniform with the same pride I had before."

Source: Seymour M. Hersh, *My Lai 4: Report on the Massacre and its Aftermath*, 1970.

Mike Dennis

MEKONG DELTA

The Mekong Delta area of Vietnam technically extends from Go Cong Province all the way down to the Ca Mau Peninsula, the area drained by the Mekong River as it reaches the South China Sea. Sometimes the Vam Co, Saigon,* and Dong Nai rivers are also included in the region known as the Mekong Delta, giving it a total of more than 26,000 square miles. The Mekong Delta area is known for its elaborate system of rivers and canals as well as its rice cultivation. Formed by silt deposits, the soil is extremely fertile, and at the mouth of the Mekong River the sediment extends the shoreline by an average of 250 feet a year. The Mekong Delta area is inhabited primarily by ethnic Vietnamese, with large concentrations of Khmers* in the southwestern areas. The Mekong Delta was included in the IV Corps* Tactical Zone during the Vietnam War.

Source: Danny J. Whitfield, *Historical and Cultural Dictionary of Vietnam*, 1976.

MEKONG RIVER PROJECT

Known officially as the Mekong River Basin Development Project, the Mekong River Project was launched in 1957 by the United Nations Economic Commission for Asia and the Far East. Designed after the successful Tennessee Valley Authority of the 1930s, the Mekong River Project involved Laos,* Cambodia (*see* Kampuchea), Thailand,* and the Republic of Vietnam,* but Burma and the Democratic Republic of Vietnam* refused to participate. Surveys began in 1958 under the direction of the four-nation committee, headquartered in Bangkok. By the early 1970s, the Mekong River Project had completed three dams providing for flood control and hydroelectric power.

Sources: Harvey H. Smith, et al. *Area Handbook for South Vietnam*, 1967; "The Mekong Project," *Impact* 8 (1963), 168–180; Danny J. Whitfield, *Historical and Cultural Dictionary of Vietnam*, 1976.

MENDENHALL, JOSEPH

Born in 1920 and a graduate of the Harvard Law School, Joseph Mendenhall was a career diplomat in the State Department, where he worked with the Marshall Plan and Vietnamese affairs. He served in the American embassy at Saigon* between 1959 and 1962; was director of Far Eastern affairs in Washington, D.C., between 1964 and 1965; was director of the U.S. Agency for International Development* (USAID) mission in Vientiane, Laos,* between 1965 and 1968; and served first as deputy then as acting assistant administrator of USAID Vietnam in Washington between 1968 and 1969. In 1963 President John F. Kennedy* sent Mendenhall and General Victor Krulak* to Saigon to assess the situation in Vietnam; Krulak decided the war was being aggressively pursued and could be won, while Mendenhall decided that the regime of Ngo Dinh Diem* was near collapse. Mendenhall reported that educated, urban Vietnamese were more interested in eliminating Diem than in fighting the Vietcong* and that there was a ''virtual breakdown of the civil government in Saigon.'' He warned of a religious war between Catholics* and Buddhists* and saw no chance of defeating the Vietcong unless ''as a minimum, Nhu [Diem's brother] withdrew or was removed from the government.'' When Mendenhall and Krulak returned, John Kennedy remarked, ''You two did visit the same country, didn't you?''

Source: Stanley Karnow, *Vietnam: A History,* 1983.

Samuel Freeman

MENDÈS-FRANCE, PIERRE

An unconventional political figure who became prime minister of France* at age forty-seven during the 1954 Geneva Conference,* Mendès-France believed France's position in world affairs depended upon withdrawal from the war in Indochina.* He had been urging direct negotiations with Ho Chi Minh* and was opposed to the United States becoming militarily involved in Vietnam. In the National Assembly on June 10, 1954, he called for a complete change in French policy ''to make it sure that France's aim is not the intervention of the United States, but an honorable end of the terrible conflict. . . . France should play for a straightforward peace with the Vietminh.'' A week later the longtime critic of the Indochina war was chosen to head the government. He immediately pledged to obtain a cease-fire and imposed a deadline of four weeks, saying that he would resign otherwise. He told the French people, ''If you want war we shall have to send draftees, your own sons, to the battlefields of Indochina. If you want peace, I shall bring you a cease-fire agreement by July 20 or resign.'' He met his deadline, the negotiations including some secret meetings with Zhou Enlai,* China's representative at the talks. The armistice agreement included the provisional partitioning of Vietnam at the seventeenth parallel (*see* Geneva Accords). Mendès-France remained in office only a short time thereafter. His government fell in February 1955 during controversy over French policy in North Africa.

Born in Paris in 1907, he was first elected to the Chamber of Deputies in 1932 and held key positions in a number of French governments. He died in 1982.

Sources: Jean Lacouture, *Pierre Mendès-France*, 1985; Alexander Werth, *Lost Statesman*, 1958.

Hoyt Purvis

MIA   *See* Prisoners of War

MICHIGAN STATE UNIVERSITY ADVISORY GROUP

Headed by Wesley Fishel, the Michigan State University Advisory Group (MSUAG) contracted with the South Vietnamese government to train civil servants, civil guards, and police, reforming the National Administration Institute along American lines, reorganizing Ngo Dinh Diem's* administration, studying social problems, and issuing reports and recommendations to South Vietnamese and American policymakers. The MSUAG functioned between 1954 and 1961. Fishel was a strong supporter of Ngo Dinh Diem. Given to social science jargon, Fishel extracted democratic principles from virtually all of Diem's oppressive and authoritarian actions and claimed that the internal Communist threat left Diem no choice. Shortcomings in South Vietnam's exercise of democracy were explained away with such statements as the "people of Southeast Asia are not, generally speaking, sufficiently sophisticated to understand what we mean by democracy." According to Fishel, South Vietnam needed strong leadership, not democracy. He defended corruption on the grounds that all Asian governments were corrupt. Early in the 1960s, the program was dissolved when Michigan State University refused to restrain returning scholars who openly criticized the South Vietnamese government.

Sources: Bernard Fall, *The Two Viet-Nams: A Social and Political Analysis*, 1963; Frances Fitzgerald, *Fire in the Lake: The Vietnamese and the Americans in Vietnam*, 1972.

Samuel Freeman

"MIKE" FORCES   *See* MOBILE STRIKE FORCE COMMAND

MILITARY AIRLIFT COMMAND

From headquarters at Scott Air Force Base, Illinois, the Military Airlift Command (MAC) directed during the Vietnam era some 90,000 active-duty military and civilians as well as more than 1,000 aircraft at more than 340 locations in 26 countries. Created as the Air Transport Command just before World War II, MAC was redesignated the Military Air Transport Service in 1947 and received its present designation in 1966. It held responsibilities throughout the era for airlift support of American forces throughout the world, and in supporting these requirements managed air bases not just within the United States but also at such far-flung places as Clark Air Base, the Philippines;* Ramstein Air Base, Federal Republic of Germany; and Hickam Air Force Base, Hawaii.

MAC's assigned airlift capability—all configured to handle passengers, supplies, and equipment—rested during the early Vietnam era essentially on an aging fleet of C–124 transports, slow C–133 aircraft, and C–130* and C–135 cargo aircraft which were more suited to tactical airlift roles. Some of the great difficulties MAC personnel faced in supporting Southeast Asia requirements with these aircraft were their relatively small cargo capacities and, especially, the lengthy flying times necessary to travel across the Pacific. For example, a round-trip between Travis Air Force Base, California, a major departure port, and Saigon* in the prop-driven C–24 normally required about ninety-five flying hours.

As a result of the difficulties inherent in resupplying a large overseas force by air, MAC officials during the 1950s moved toward the replacement of these prop-driven transports with jet cargo aircraft. Accordingly, a milestone in Southeast Asia strategic airlift support was realized in April 1965 when the C–141 Starlifter* became operational. This jet cargo transport could carry 67,620 pounds of cargo across the Pacific at speeds in excess of 440 knots per hour. A second improvement came with the deployment of the C–5 Galaxy,* an enlarged version of thge C–141, beginning in December 1969. These two aircraft greatly enhanced MAC's ability to supply American forces in Southeast Asia over a massive logistics pipeline halfway around the globe.

Charged with strategic airlift in support of military operations in Southeast Asia between American escalation in 1965 and withdrawal of forces in 1973, MAC used all types of aircraft at its disposal to develop and operate a complex airlift system that spanned more than 15,000 miles between the United States and American bases in the Pacific and on the Asian mainland. This reliance on strategic airlift stemmed from the disabilities of ship movements to support an ever-larger and more sophisticated military mission to South Vietnam. Moreover, the lack of suitable ports, roads, and railways hampered the ready distribution of personnel and war material in Southeast Asia. It was not uncommon, for instance, during the 1965–66 force buildup for ships to wait in harbors for days or weeks to be unloaded.

In responding to the urgent Southeast Asian theater requirements during the American escalation of operations, the U.S. Air Force* quickly found that traffic to the Pacific grew from a monthly average of 33,779 passengers and 9,123 tons of cargo in fiscal year 1965 to 65,350 passengers and 42,296 tons of cargo in fiscal year 1967. Similar rises were experienced until 1969, when reductions in military support began to take place. Throughout the conflict in Southeast Asia, MAC personnel offered unique airlift support to American military forces in the theater. Only with the collapse of South Vietnam in 1975 did MAC airlift into that nation finally end.

Source: Kenneth W. Patchin, "Strategic Airlift," in Carl Berger, ed., *The United States Air Force in Southeast Asia, 1961–1973, An Illustrated Account*, 1977.

Roger D. Launius

MILITARY ASSISTANCE AND ADVISORY GROUP

The U.S. government created the Military Assistance and Advisory Group (MAAG), Indochina,* in 1950 to process, monitor, and evaluate American military aid to the French forces fighting in Southeast Asia. As originally conceived, it numbered about sixty men and was headed by a general officer. The French commanders resented MAAG's presence and hindered its operations. At first, the American group's mission was not to train or advise the Vietnamese National Army* (VNA), but by the time of the Battle of Dien Bien Phu,* those activities were under consideration by American and French officials. After the Geneva Conference (*see* Geneva Accords), specific Franco-American discussions began on the future relationship between MAAG and VNA. In 1955, MAAG, Indochina, became MAAG, Vietnam, and a separate MAAG was established in Cambodia (*see* Kampuchea). In 1955 and 1956, MAAG, Vietnam, took over from the French the training and organizing of VNA. Using various legal pretexts to avoid overt violation of limits set at Geneva on foreign troops, the number of American advisers grew to almost 700 in the late 1950s.

The task facing MAAG was enormous. The South Vietnamese Army that it inherited from the French was poorly trained, equipped, and led. Furthermore, the Vietnamese often viewed the American advisers as interlopers just as they had the French colonialists. Despite these difficulties, by 1960 MAAG had shaped the South Vietnamese Army into what appeared on paper to be an efficient force. The reality, however, was that the army still lacked good leadership, and President Ngo Dinh Diem* constantly frustrated MAAG by selecting his commanders on the basis of loyalty rather than merit.

By the time John F. Kennedy* became president of the United States in 1961, the role and effectiveness of MAAG was under review. Following military doctrine developed during World War II and the Korean War, MAAG had prepared the South Vietnamese Army to fight a conventional war with little attention to guerrilla tactics. The growing strength of the Communist insurgency in South Vietnam in the early 1960s necessitated a change in doctrine. As part of Kennedy's move to a counterinsurgency* effort, the administration replaced MAAG with the Military Assistance Command, Vietnam* (MACV), in 1962.

Source: Ronald H. Spector, *United States Army in Vietnam: Advice and Support: The Early Years, 1941–1960*, 1983.

David L. Anderson

MILITARY ASSISTANCE COMMAND, VIETNAM

Located at Tan Son Nhut Air Base* outside Saigon,* the U.S. Military Assistance Command, Vietnam (MACV), was a unified command subject to the direction of the Commander in Chief, Pacific.* The MACV commander was responsible for all American military activities in Vietnam. MACV was first established at Saigon on February 8, 1962, after President John F. Kennedy* had ordered an increase in U.S. military personnel. The Military Advisory and Assistance Group* (MAAG), which had been in Vietnam since November 1955, remained in charge of advising ARVN (*see* Army of the Republic of Vietnam), but on May 15, 1964, MACV succeeded MAAG in that responsibility as well. Between that reorganization on May 15, 1964, and its departure from Vietnam on March 29,1973, MACV directed the United States Army, Vietnam;* Naval Forces Vietnam;* the Seventh Air Force;* III Marine Amphibious Force;* the Fifth Special Forces Group*; I Field Force Vietnam;* II Field Force Vietnam;* the XXIV Corps;* and a variety of pacification programs (*see* Rural Reconstruction). Four people commanded MACV: General Paul Harkins* (February 1962 to June 1964); General William Westmoreland* (June 1964 to July 1968); General Creighton Abrams* (July 1968 to June 1972); and General Frederick Weyand* (June 1972 to March 1973).

Sources: Shelby L. Stanton, *Vietnam Order of Battle*, 1981; Bruce Palmer, Jr., *The 25-Year War: America's Military Role in Vietnam*, 1984; George S. Eckhardt, *Command and Control, 1950–1969*, 1981.

MILITARY REGIONS

Until July 1970, U.S. military officials divided South Vietnam into four major geographical zones, known as corps tactical areas. They were designated I Corps,* II Corps,* III Corps,* and IV Corps.* After July 1970 a new designation was used. Military Region I, or MR I, was the new designation for I Corps. MR II referred to II Corps, MR III to III Corps, and MR IV to IV Corps.

Source: Harry G. Summers, Jr., *Vietnam War Almanac*, 1985.

MILITARY SEALIFT COMMAND

The Military Sealift Command was a United States Navy* operation responsible for shipping fuel, food, clothing, and weapons to Vietnam in support of the American war effort. At its peak the Military Sealift Command operated more than 500 ships, including fuel tankers, LSTs, aircraft ferries, tugboats, and troop carriers. At the end of the war in 1975, the Military Sealift Command helped evacuate more than 40,000 refugees* from South Vietnam.

Source: Edward J. Marolda and G. Wesley Pryce III, *A Short History of the United States Navy and the Southeast Asian Conflict, 1950–1975*, 1984.

MISSING IN ACTION   *See* Prisoners of War

MISSING IN ACTION

Distributed by MGM/United Artists in 1983 and 1984, *Missing in Action* starred Chuck Norris as Special Forces* leader James Braddock, who had escaped from a Vietnamese prisoner of war* (POW) camp after ten years imprisonment.

After the war is over in 1975, Braddock returns to Vietnam as part of an American fact-finding mission, but is frustrated with the lying and posturing of the sadistic General Tran (played by James Hong), who denies knowledge of any remaining American prisoners in Vietnam. Braddock leaves the mission, heads into Thailand* where he purchases enough weapons to become a one-man army, and then returns to Vietnam and rescues a group of American POWs. *Missing in Action*, a precursor to *Rambo*, was one of the genre of action films in the 1980s celebrating the sacrifices American soldiers made during the Vietnam War.

MISSING IN ACTION 2: THE BEGINNING

Released by MGM/United Artists in 1985, *Missing in Action 2: The Beginning* starred Chuck Norris as American Special Forces* soldier James Braddock, who is captured and spends ten years in a Vietnamese prisoner of war camp before escaping. Dubbed a "prequel" to *Missing in Action, Missing in Action 2* told the story of Braddock in the period before the scenes depicted in *Missing in Action*. Like *Rambo, Missing in Action*, and *Uncommon Valor, Missing in Action 2* portrayed the American effort in Vietnam as a noble one spoiled only by politicians back home who refused to give American soldiers the total support they needed to win.

MOBILE GUERRILLA FORCES

Designed to fight Vietcong* insurgency, the Mobile Guerrilla Forces (MGF) evolved out of the special reconnaissance projects—Projects Delta,* Omega,* and Sigma*—established in 1965 and 1966. Each MGF consisted of a 12-man A-Team of Special Forces,* a 150-man mobile guerrilla company, and a 34-man combat reconnaissance platoon. The MGF operated for extended periods of time in Communist-controlled regions of South Vietnam and Cambodia (*see* Kampuchea). Basically they were hit-and-run units giving the North Vietnamese and Vietcong* a taste of their own tactical medicine. The MGF operations were known as "Blackjack Missions" and existed between October 1966 and July 1967, when they became part of the Mobile Strike Forces.

Source: Francis J. Kelly, *U.S. Special Forces, 1961–1971*, 1973.

MOBILE RIVERINE FORCE

Because of the extent of the Mekong Delta,* nearly 90 percent of the lines of communication in South Vietnam was by river and canals. More than 50,000 junks operated in the Mekong Delta, providing Vietcong* guerrillas with the ability to ship supplies and move about undetected. To interdict that guerrilla effort, the United States Navy* implemented Operation Game Warden* in 1965 and established Task Force 116 under the command of Captain Burton B. Witham, Jr., to carry it out. In 1967 Task Force 117 was established to attack the Vietcong in the Mekong Delta and the Rung Sat Swamp* area. Eventually, several hundred armed small craft—31-foot fiberglass PBRs, air-cushion vehicles,* reconditioned World War II landing craft, motorized junks, LCM6 mechanized landing craft, and amphibious troop carriers—operated with Task Forces 116 and 117. In June 1967 the Mobile Riverine Force was established by joining the existing naval riverine forces with the United States Army* Ninth Infantry's Riverine Forces. Blessed with 5,000 highly mobile troops, the Mobile Riverine Force was capable of moving the soldiers up river more than 150 miles within a day's time. The Mobile Riverine Force was headquartered first at Vung Tau* in III Corps* but moved to a Seabee*-constructed base at Dong Tam about five miles from My Tho* in the Mekong Delta. Between 1969 and 1971 the Mobile Riverine Force was turned over to ARVN (*see* Army of the Republic of Vietnam) as part of Vietnamization.*

Sources: William B. Fulton, *Riverine Operations, 1966–1969*, 1973; Victor Croizat, *The Brown Water Navy: The River and Coastal War in Indo-China and Vietnam, 1948–1972*, 1984.

MOBILE STRIKE FORCE COMMAND

In June 1965, the Military Assistance Command, Vietnam,* established Mobile Strike Force Commands in each of the four Corps Tactical Zones and at the Fifth Special Forces Group* headquarters at Nha Trang.* Each of these "Mike" forces consisted of a Special Forces* twelve-man A-Team, several Civilian Irregular Defense Group* battalions, a reconaissance company, and a Nung* or Cambodian airborne company. They were all under the direction of Special Forces commanders. The Mobile Strike Force Commands operated until the withdrawal of the Fifth Special Forces Group from South Vietnam in 1971.

Sources: John S. Bowman, ed., *The Vietnam War Almanac*, 1985; Shelby L. Stanton, *Green Berets at War*, 1985; Andrew F. Krepinevich, Jr., *The Army and Vietnam*, 1986.

MOMYER, WILLIAM WALLACE

William W. Momyer was born on September 23, 1916, in Muskogee, Oklahoma. He graduated from the University of Washington in 1937, joined the Army Air Corps in 1938, and saw action in North Africa and Italy during World War II. Momyer climbed through the ranks of the United States Air Force* officer corps after World War II, and in 1966 was given command of the Seventh Air Force* in Vietnam, where he supervised the air war over Southeast Asia. Momyer left South Vietnam in the summer of 1968 and retired from the air force in 1973.

Sources: *Who's Who in America, 1968–1969*, 1969; William W. Momyer, *Airpower in Three Wars*, 1978; John Morrocco, *The Vietnam Experience. Thunder From Above: Air War, 1941–1968*, 1985.

MONTAGNARDS

The Montagnards, or "mountain people," were primitive tribes occupying the Central Highlands* of Vietnam. Before World War II, the Montagnards were isolated from the conflict in Indochina,* except for periodic tribute payments they made to a series of emperors. During the nineteenth and early twentieth centuries, French imperial officials continued the policy of general neglect. But when the Vietminh* began their assault on the French Empire again in 1946, General Vo Nguyen Giap* declared the Central Highlands* crucial to the expulsion of the French and conquest of the South. Through the 1940s, 1950s, and 1960s, competing armies tried to woo the Montagnards, and the North Vietnamese proved more successful than the South Vietnamese or the Americans. After 1954 Ho Chi Minh* brought more than 10,000 Montagnards to Hanoi* for training as teachers, medical assistants, soldiers, and political agents; established open, self-governing zones in the North for the mountain people; and gave the tribes representation in the National Assembly. The South Vietnamese took another approach, trying to assimilate the Montagnards through relocation, reservations, and cultural pressure. The fact that South Vietnam also put Catholic refugees* on Montagnard land only further alienated the mountain people. Some Montagnard tribes, like the Hre and the Rhade, were loyal to the United States and South Vietnam, but they were exceptions rather than the rule. By 1975, the Montagnards had suffered the loss of their land and cultural isolation, facing the disintegration of their village lifestyle. More than 200,000 of them had died in the conflict, and 85 percent of all Montagnards had been displaced from their tribal lands.

Sources: Gerald C. Hickey, *Free in the Forest: An Ethnohistory of the Vietnamese Central Highlands, 1954–1976*, 1982; Robert L. Mole, *The Montagnards of South Vietnam: A Study of Nine Tribes*, 1970.

MOORE, ROBERT

Robert Moore was born October 21, 1909, in Charlotte, North Carolina, and graduated from the United States Naval Academy in 1932. He fought in both the Atlantic and Pacific during World War II, and in 1961 he had achieved the rank of rear admiral. In 1964, Moore was transferred to the attack aircraft carriers with the Seventh Fleet* in the South China Sea. He was on board the USS *Ticonderoga** during the Gulf of Tonkin incident* in July and August 1964, and he assumed command of the task force President Lyndon Johnson* ordered to bomb North Vietnam. Robert Moore retired from the navy in 1967.

Sources: *Who's Who in America, 1966*, 1966; Eugene C. Windchy, *Tonkin Gulf*, 1971.

MOORER, THOMAS HINMAN

Thomas Moorer was born in 1912 in Mount Willing, Alabama. He graduated from the United States Naval Academy and served on warships between 1933 and 1935 and in aviation squadrons between 1936 and 1943. Moorer commanded a bombing squadron in 1943, and between 1943 and 1945 he served as a gunnery and tactical officer on the staff of the commander of the Naval Air Force. Moorer had a variety of assignments in the late 1940s and early 1950s, serving as executive officer on the aircraft carrier *Midway* and receiving the rank of captain in 1952. Between 1953 and 1962 Moorer was successively on the staff of the commander of the Naval Air Force, Atlantic Fleet; aide to the assistant secretary of the navy; commander of the USS *Salisbury Sound*; and a strategic planner for the chief of naval operations. He was promoted to rear admiral in 1958 and in 1962 became commander of the Seventh Fleet.* Moorer became commander in chief of the Atlantic Fleet and head of NATO in 1965. In 1967 he was named chief of naval operations and, in 1970, chairman of the Joint Chiefs of Staff (*see* Chairman, JCS). He was a soft-spoken, competent leader who relied on his diplomatic and problem-solving skills. Moorer retired in 1974.

Sources: *International Who's Who, 1984–1985*, 1984; "Armed Forces," *Time* 96, February 26, 1965, p. 16, and 85, July 6, 1970, p. 21; Henry Kissinger, *White House Years*, 1979; Richard K. Betts, *Soldiers, Sailors and Cold War Crises*, 1977; Lawrence J. Korb, *The Joint Chiefs of Staff: The First Twenty-Five Years*, 1976.

Joanna D. Cowden

MORATORIUM DAY DEMONSTRATIONS (1969)

The Moratorium Day demonstrations on October 15, 1969, constituted the largest public protest at that time in American history. The demonstrations were organized by the Vietnam Moratorium Committee, which was founded on June 30, 1969, in order to galvanize a majority position against the war through a nationwide demonstration in October with plans for one additional day of demonstrations on each successive month until there were satisfactory peace negotiations and a firm American commitment to withdraw from Vietnam. This timetable of demonstrations was conceived by peace campaign veterans Sam Brown,* Marge Sklencar, David Hawk, and David Mixner in an effort to counter the anarchic and violent protest seen in the Chicago demonstrations in 1968 (*see* Democratic National Convention), and to take the antiwar movement* into the communities where people who had never protested before could respectably offer their opposition to the war in Vietnam. At the same time, the reconstituted New Mobilization Committee to End the War in Vietnam was preparing for renewed antiwar demonstrations. Working in an uneasy collaboration, the two groups developed a moderate and mainstream approach, whereby organizers generated a grass-roots structure in dozens of cities across the nation, garnered bipartisan endorsements from a multitude of senators and congressional representatives, and got their message to the people through ads in the *New York Times* and press conferences. Millions of people participated in the October 15 Moratorium. The activities, in an effort to suspend "business as usual," varied: many people, including some GIs in Vietnam, wore black armbands to show their opposition to the war; others shone their car headlights; some passed out leaflets door to door; over 100,000 people massed on the Boston Commons; New York City Mayor Lindsay decreed the day a day of mourning and ordered the city's flags to be at half-staff; the two largest unions, the Teamsters and the Auto Workers, teamed up with the Chemical Workers to support the Moratorium; a quarter of a million people marched in Washington, D.C.; and Coretta Scott King led a candlelight vigil through the capital. Countless speakers from Benjamin Spock,* to former Supreme Court Justice Arthur Goldberg,* to activist David Dellinger* and diplomat Averell Harriman,* all voiced their opposition to the war. The White House attempted to dampen the sense of goodwill and unity the Moratorium demonstrated by releasing a message of support for it by North Vietnam Premier Pham Van Dong,* but the enormous numbers and the moderate nature of the protest demonstrated overwhelming nationwide opposition to the war. President Nixon's* "silent majority" speech* two weeks later attempted to downplay mainstream opposition to the war, but the Moratorium demonstrations in November surpassed the October 15 demonstrations in number. The Vietnam Moratorium Committee was disbanded in April 1970.

Sources: Nancy Zaroulis and Gerald Sullivan, *Who Spoke Up? American Protest Against the War in Vietnam 1963–1975,* 1984; Charles DeBenedetti, *The Peace Reform in American History,* 1980.

Linda Kelly Alkana

MORSE, WAYNE LYMAN

Known as a maverick who frequently stood alone and refused to compromise, Wayne Morse was elected to the U.S. Senate in 1942 and served through 1968. Born in Madison, Wisconsin on October 20, 1900, he received a law degree from the University of Oregon. Elected to the Senate from Oregon as a Republican, he became an independent in 1952 and in 1955 joined the Democrats.

He was an early and outspoken critic of U.S. military involvement in Vietnam, but his irascible style and reputation as a gadfly left him without much influence. He argued vigorously against the 1964 Gulf of Tonkin Resolution.* Morse was the first to suggest that the Johnson* administration was not revealing the full story of the Gulf of Tonkin incident.* He charged that the United States was acting as a "provocateur" in Vietnam. Morse criticized the administration for not referring the matter to the United Nations. He asserted that the place to settle the controversy "is not by way of the proposed predated declaration of war, giving to the President the power to make war without a declaration of war. The place to settle it is around the conference tables."

Morse argued that the resolution represented an illegal abridgment of the Constitution, and warned at the time of its passage that President Johnson would interpret it broadly. He said those senators who voted for it "will live to regret it." But he was joined only by Senator Ernest Gruening* in voting against the resolution. He later predicted that the Tonkin controversy would continue for decades.

During the remainder of his last term in the Senate, Morse repeatedly opposed Johnson administration policies in Vietnam and in 1967 failed in an effort to repeal the Gulf of Tonkin Resolution. Morse lost a reelection bid in 1968. He died in 1974.

Sources: Anthony Austin, *The President's War*, 1971; *Congressional Record*, August 6–7, 1974; *New York Times*, July 21, 1974.

Hoyt Purvis

MORTARS

Mortars are muzzle-loaded, either smooth- or rifle-bored, high-angle fire weapons. Small, light, and easier to move than artillery, the mortars used in Vietnam varied in range up to a maximum of 5,650 meters for the 4.2 inch ("four-deuce") usually mounted on vehicles or emplaced at fire bases, with U.S. forces also deploying the smaller, troop-carried 81mm and 60mm at the battalion and company levels, respectively. Commonly used mortar ammunition included high explosive (either impact or proximity fused) for use against troops and light material; white phosphorus ("willy-pete") for screening, signaling, and incendiary action; illumination; and tactical gas rounds.

The Vietcong* and North Vietnamese Army* often captured allied ordnance, and their 82mm mortar, rather than the more cumbersome 120mm model, became a choice weapon because it also fired U.S.-made 81mm rounds. With sympathetic villagers to pace off the dimensions of U.S. positions, Communist gunners proved accurate and elusive. Relying on the weapon's high-angle trajectory, mortarmen would "hang" several rounds in the air toward a target then quickly disassemble and move or bury their mortar before radar or visual sighting could direct and adjust effective counterbattery fire.

Source: Edgar C. Doleman, Jr., *The Vietnam Experience: Tools of War*, 1984.

Dudley Acker

MU GIA PASS

Located in Quang Binh Province, the Mu Gia Pass was part of the Truong Son Mountain Range and a strategic route for North Vietnamese supplies making their way into South Vietnam during the years of the war. Throughout the 1960s the pass was subjected to massive American bombing in an attempt to cut off the flow of supplies.

Source: Danny J. Whitfield, *Historical and Cultural Dictionary of Vietnam*, 1976.

MUSTE, ABRAHAM JOHANNES

A. J. Muste was born in the Netherlands on January 8, 1885, and immigrated to the United States in 1891. He attended Hope College in Michigan and in 1909 became a minister in the Dutch Reformed Church. Inspired by Quaker writings and the suffering of the industrial poor, Muste was an avowed pacifist by 1915. He joined the Fellowship of Reconciliation,* a nondenominational pacifist group, in 1915. From 1926 to 1929 Muste served as national chairman of the Fellowship of Reconciliation, and from 1940 to 1953 as its executive secretary. He openly opposed both World War I and II. In 1957 Muste helped found the Committee for Nonviolent Action, which protested nuclear proliferation through mass demonstrations, and was elected its first national chairman.

When the United States increased its involvement in Vietnam, Muste was one of the earliest critics. He was the keynote speaker at one of the first antiwar* rallies, held on December 20, 1964, in New York City. Throughout 1965 and 1966 Muste appeared at dozens of antiwar rallies, vigils, and demonstrations, and in 1966 he was expelled from South Vietnam after leading a demonstration in Saigon.* In November 1966, at the age of eighty-two, Muste became chairman of the Spring Mobilization to End the War in Vietnam.* He visited North Vietnam and spoke with Ho Chi Minh* in January 1967, and died on February 11, 1967.

Sources: Jo Ann Robinson, *Abraham Went Out,* 1981; *New York Times,* February 12, 1967; Nancy Zaroulis and Gerald Sullivan, *Who Spoke Up? American Protest Against the War in Vietnam, 1963–1975,* 1984.

John Ricks

MY LAI

Because the American public prided itself on its humanity during war, the My Lai incident was a particularly painful part of the conflict in Vietnam. My Lai was a small rural hamlet of about 700 people located in the Son My district of Quang Ngai Province, situated on the northeast coast of South Vietnam. It was believed to be one of the toughest Vietcong* strongholds in the area. In the spring of 1967, search and destroy* operations, led by Task Force Oregon (*see* 23rd Infantry Division), began in Quang Ngai Province. In September 1967, the newly created Americal Division (*see* 23rd Infantry Division) went to relieve Task Force Oregon, continuing the mission to ''sanitize'' the region. In December, Charlie Company led by Captain Ernest L. Medina* went in to assist the operation. Because of continual attacks by unseen enemies, the duty inspired questionable judgement and intensified emotions on the part of American troops. They had seen comrades killed and maimed by mines, bombs, and booby traps* with the perpetrators melting into Vietnamese village life. The virtual impossibility of differentiating between Vietnamese peasants and Vietcong* guerrillas led, at the bare minimum, to a contempt for all Vietnamese people. It also provided the backdrop for the My Lai massacre.

On the morning of March 16, 1968, a short artillery barrage fell on the village of My Lai to ''soften'' it up for the clean sweep to be made by Charlie Company. Lt. William Calley* and his 1st Platoon boarded helicopters and landed on an airstrip 150 meters west of My Lai. Following this, the 2nd and 3rd platoons arrived, led by Lt. Stephen Brooks and Lt. Jeffrey La Crosse. A plan was formulated calling for Calley's 1st Platoon to approach the hamlet from the north. La Crosse's 3rd Platoon, accompanied by commander Captain Medina, would stay behind at the airstrip to establish communication with headquarters and direct operations. Additional protection was afforded by helicopter gunships circling My Lai at 1,000 feet.

Upon entering the village neither platoon met with enemy fire; there was no resistance. Calley ordered his men to round up all of the civilians at the center of the village. At this point accounts of the incident begin to differ. It seems that Calley opened fire on the civilians and ordered his men to do the same. Then his platoon moved through the village, systematically shooting anything that moved. No Vietcong ever appeared. The body count was estimated at 400 to 500, but Calley was eventually charged with the deaths of 122. One man who shot himself in the foot was the only American casualty. Radio messages were sent back and forth among combat pilots and crewmen flying over My Lai. These were monitored by high-ranking officers such as Major General Samuel Koster and Colonel Oran K. Henderson during the course of the morning, and yet no senior officers made an attempt to investigate or stop the massacre. A report filed two weeks later referred to the attack as "well planned, well executed, and successful."

The incident was successfully concealed until Ronald Ridenhour wrote a letter in 1969 to President Nixon* and a number of congressmen and Defense Department officials. The letter prompted an investigation and the indictment of twelve officers and enlisted men on charges either of murder or of assault with intent to commit murder. Lt. William Calley was found guilty of murder while all the others were either acquitted or had charges dismissed.

While the actual events of March 16, 1968, may never be completely clear, My Lai represents a landmark in American history for two reasons. First, such atrocities have traditionally been committed by countries considered uncivilized and barbaric—categories Americans did not see themselves fitting. Second, in broader and more encompassing terms, My Lai reveals the nature of the war as it was fought by the U.S. military and supported by the U.S. government—conduct which violated America's basic moral principles. With her reputation tainted, America could no longer rightfully claim her virtuous position at the head of other world powers.

Sources: Gerald Kurland, *The My Lai Massacre*, 1973; Richard Hammer, *The Court Martial of Lieutenant Calley*, 1971; Seymour Hersh, *My Lai 4: A Report on the Massacre and Its Aftermath*, 1970.

Sally Smith

MY THO

My Tho is the capital city of Dinh-Tuong Province. Located along Highway 4 between Saigon* and Ca Mau, My Tho was first founded by Chinese refugees* fleeing from Taiwan. With a population of nearly 100,000, My Tho became one of South Vietnam's autonomous principalities in September 1970. During the Tet Offensive* in 1968, Vietcong* forces occupied My Tho, and in response U.S. bombers and artillery reduced a full third of the city to rubble.

Sources: *Webster's Geographical Dictionary*, 1984.

· N ·

NAPALM

Napalm is jellied gasoline. Its name is an acronym of naphthenic and palmitic acids, which are used in its manufacture. Although used in World War II and the Korean War, napalm became (in)famous in Vietnam where it was used in three capacities. Perhaps its most visual use was being dropped from aircraft in large canisters which tumbled lazily to earth. Exploding on impact, it engulfed large areas in flame, sucking up all the oxygen and emitting intense heat, thick black smoke, and a smell which no one exposed to it will ever forget. Dropping napalm from high-speed jet aircraft was not very accurate, resulting in numerous instances of "friendly" (Allied) and/or civilian casualties. A second use of napalm was in flamethrowers—by both U.S.-ARVN (*see* Army of the Republic of Vietnam) and Vietcong*-North Vietnamese Army* forces—which were very effective in clearing bunkers. If the flames could not be directed to penetrate the bunker, they could bathe the bunker in fire, consuming all the oxygen and suffocating those inside. Flamethrowers also were used in destroying "enemy" villages. Napalm was used in base camp and fire base perimeter defense. Barrels of napalm would be buried under concertina wire (coils of barbed wire standing two-three feet high and stretched around the perimeter). As troops massed to breach the wire, the barrels would be detonated, incinerating anyone in the immediate area—and dampening the attackers' enthusiasm. A terrifying, effective weapon, napalm's properties are such that it clings to whatever it touches. Smothering it is the only effective way to put it out. Trying to wipe it off only spreads it around, expanding the burn area. The rapid consumption of oxygen can cause suffocation, and the intense heat can produce severe burns without actual contact. The noise, smoke, and smell are terrifying in themselves.

Source: Edgar C. Doleman, Jr., *The Vietnam Experience: Tools of War*, 1984.

Samuel Freeman

NATIONAL COORDINATING COMMITTEE TO END THE WAR IN VIETNAM

The Madison, Wisconsin-based National Coordinating Committee to End the War in Vietnam (NCC) was a short-lived umbrella organization formed in August 1965 in order to mobilize nationwide activity against the war in Vietnam and to coordinate the over thirty disparate local antiwar groups which had sprung up in protest of President Johnson's* escalation of the war in February 1965. Its roots lay in the Assembly of Unrepresented People, an organization which linked social injustice to the war in Vietnam. The NCC sponsored the International Days of Protest in October 1965, which involved about 100,000 people nationwide and included a massive rally at Berkeley with a teach-in at the Oakland Army Base, a parade of twenty to twenty-five thousand people down 5th Avenue in New York, and the first draft card burning since Johnson had signed the order making such burnings a felony. The NCC, which included an uneasy coalition of the Old and New Left, antiwar liberals and different pacifist groups, disbanded in January 1966 because of splits within the organization about whether to remain an umbrella group or to reorganize as a national organization making immediate withdrawal from Vietnam the group's basic priority. The NCC's last action was to call for another International Day of Protest in March 1966. The large size and international scope of the second International Day of Protest showed the increasing power of the antiwar movement* and the growing unpopularity of the war.

Sources: Nancy Zaroulis and Gerald Sullivan, *Who Spoke Up? American Protest Against the War in Vietnam 1963–1975*, 1984; Charles DeBenedetti, *The Peace Reform in American History*, 1980.

Linda Kelly Alkana

NATIONAL COUNCIL OF RECONCILIATION AND CONCORD

One provision of the Paris Peace Accords* was creation of a tripartite National Council of Reconciliation and Concord. The accords called for a withdrawal of all American troops within sixty days of the cease-fire, return of all prisoners of war,* and establishment of the National Council of Reconciliation and Concord. The National Council, composed of representatives of the United States, the Democratic Republic of Vietnam,* the Republic of Vietnam,* and the Provisional Revolutionary Government of South Vietnam,* would then negotiate a political settlement throughout Vietnam. That, of course, was the stickiest negotiating point and one that was never concluded. The National Council never got off the ground in 1973, and any hope for a final political settlement died with the North Vietnamese offensive in 1975.

Sources: Guenter Lewy, *America in Vietnam*, 1978; George C. Herring, *America's Longest War: The United States in Vietnam, 1950–1975*, 1985; Walter Scott Dillard, *Sixty Days to Peace*, 1982.

NATIONAL LEADERSHIP COUNCIL

Between the assassination of Ngo Dinh Diem* in November 1963 and the rise of the ruling junta of Nguyen Cao Ky* in June 1965, South Vietnam had experienced wave after wave of political instability. On June 12, 1965, Generals Nguyen Van Thieu,* Nguyen Cao Ky, and Nguyen Huu Co* declared the establishment of a National Leadership Council to rule the Republic of Vietnam.* The three military leaders subsequently expanded the National Leadership Council to ten members and elected Nguyen Cao Ky as chief executive of the council. Ky eventually used his position as head of the council to become the new premier of the Republic of Vietnam. The National Leadership Council functioned until the regular elections in 1967,* when Nguyen Van Thieu became the new president of the Republic of Vietnam.

Source: Frances FitzGerald, *Fire in the Lake: The Vietnamese and the Americans in Vietnam*, 1972.

NATIONAL LIBERATION FRONT   *See* Vietcong

NATIONAL SECURITY ADVISER

In 1947, as the Cold War and fear of communism gained momentum in the United States, Congress* passed the National Security Act, which consolidated the armed services into a new Department of Defense, established the Central Intelligence Agency,* and formed the National Security Council (NSC).* The national security adviser is the head of the NSC administrative staff and is known as the assistant to the president for national security affairs. During the years of the Vietnam War, four men served as the national security adviser. Gordon Gray served under President Dwight Eisenhower* and left the position in January 1961. McGeorge Bundy* took over under President John Kennedy* and served until April 1966, when Walt W. Rostow* assumed the post. With the election and then the inauguration of Richard Nixon* in January 1969, Rostow left the National Security Council and was replaced by Henry Kissinger.* Kissinger served there until November 1975.

Sources: George C. Herring, *America's Longest War: The United States and Vietnam, 1950–1975*, 1985; Paul L. Kattenburg, *The Vietnam Trauma in American Foreign Policy, 1945–1975*, 1980.

NATIONAL SECURITY COUNCIL

Created by the National Security Act of 1947, the National Security Council (NSC) consisted of the president, the vice president, the secretaries of defense and state, and the director of the Office of Emergency Planning. Under Presidents John F. Kennedy* and Lyndon B. Johnson,* the NSC had little power because these two presidents essentially bypassed it in policy-making, but between 1969 and 1977 the NSC became the major foreign policy body in the United States. President Richard M. Nixon* named Henry Kissinger* as national security adviser, and Kissinger added the head of the Central Intelligence Agency* and the Joint Chiefs of Staff (*see* Chairman of JCS) to the NSC on an informal basis. Nixon allowed the NSC to supplant completely the Department of State in Vietnam War decisions, and it remained that way until mid–1973, when Kissinger replaced William P. Rogers* as secretary of state.

Sources: Richard A. Johnson, *The Administration of United States Foreign Policy,* 1971; Tad Szulc, *The Illusion of Peace,* 1978.

NATIONALIST PARTY OF GREATER VIETNAM   *See* Dai Viet Quoc Dan Dang

NAVAL FORCES VIETNAM

The office of the commander of Naval Forces Vietnam existed between April 1, 1966, and March 29, 1973, to direct the U.S. naval effort along the coast of the South China Sea. Naval Forces Vietnam supervised Task Forces 115, 116, and 117 (*see* Mobile Riverine Force), involving coastal surveillance and river operations, as well as the Coast Guard* patrols and the Seabees.* Seventh Fleet* operations farther off the coast, however, were under the direct command of the commander in chief, Pacific Command,* in Hawaii.

Sources: Edward J. Marolda and G. Wesley Pryce III, *A Short History of the United States Navy and the Southeast Asian Conflict, 1950–1975,* 1984.

NAVAL BOMBARDMENT

Between the summer of 1965 and early fall of 1972, the Seventh Fleet* occupied positions off the coast of North and South Vietnam. Task Force 70.8, part of the Seventh Fleet, was charged with shore bombardment operations. Except for a six-month stay of the battleship USS *New Jersey* in 1968–69, Task Force 70.8 was composed primarily of cruisers and destroyers. The ships provided artillery support for U.S. and South Vietnamese troops, and attacked important targets within range in North Vietnam. Most of Task Force 70.8 shore bombardment took place in I Corps.*

Sources: Edward J. Marolda and G. Wesley Pryce III, *A Short History of the United States Navy and the Southeast Asian Conflict, 1950–1975,* 1984.

NAVARRE, HENRI   *See* Navarre Plan

NAVARRE PLAN

A career army officer, Henry Navarre was appointed commander of French forces in Indochina* in May 1953. Major General René Cogny became his deputy. Together they developed the so-called Navarre Plan to end the crisis in Vietnam. The plan proposed a major strengthening of the Vietnamese National

Army,* the addition of nine new French battalions to the Indochinese theater, withdrawal of scattered French forces, and the launching of a major offensive in the Red River Delta against the Vietminh.* The United States agreed to support the Navarre Plan in 1953 with nearly $400 million in assistance. Eventually, Navarre committed his augmented forces to the village of Dien Bien Phu* in northwestern Vietnam, hoping the Vietminh would stage a frontal attack on the French valley outpost. The rest was history. General Vo Nguyen Giap* inflicted a complete defeat on the French army and destroyed the French Empire in Indochina.

Sources: Joseph Buttinger, *Vietnam: A Dragon Embattled.* Vol. 2, *Vietnam at War,* 1967; Jules Roy, *The Battle of Dien Bien Phu,* 1965.

NAVY, UNITED STATES

The United States Navy played a direct role in the conflict in Vietnam from 1964 to 1975. The Seventh Fleet* was responsible for naval operations in the South China Sea and over Indochina.* During the war the navy performed three major functions. First, aircraft attack carriers flew tens of thousands of sorties* over North Vietnam, South Vietnam, Laos,* and Cambodia (*see* Kampuchea). The F–4 Phantom,* A–4 Skyhawk,* A–1 Skyraider,* and A–6 Intruder* were the primary naval aircraft involved in the attack on the Vietcong* and North Vietnam. Second, cruisers and destroyers, and for a while the battleship *New Jersey,* were responsible for naval artillery bombardment in support of U.S., South Korean,* and ARVN troops (*see* Army of the Republic of Vietnam). Finally, a host of smaller craft were responsible for patrolling the coast of the South China Sea and the major river systems in South Vietnam to interdict enemy supplies. During the course of the war, naval personnel suffered 1,574 killed in action and 4,180 wounded.

Sources: Edward J. Marolda and G. Wesley Pryce III, *A Short History of the United States Navy and the Southeast Asia Conflict, 1950–1975,* 1984.

NEUTRALITY

The question of neutrality was a difficult one during the Vietnam War, especially as it related to Laos* and Cambodia (*see* Kampuchea). Both Laos and Cambodia claimed neutrality in the conflict between the United States and Vietnam, but at the same time the North Vietnamese consistently used both countries to provide troops and supplies in South Vietnam. North Vietnam began constructing the Ho Chi Minh Trail* in 1959, and eventually it reached all through the panhandle of southern Laos and the eastern parts of Cambodia into South Vietnam. The United States ostensibly honored the neutrality of Laos and Cambodia, but throughout the conflict worked to stop the flow of supplies. International law requires neutral nations to prevent their own exploitation by a belligerent, which both Laos and Cambodia failed to do, and the United States eventually justified all of its interventions there—the White Star Mobile Training Teams* between 1959 and 1962, Operation Barrel Roll* in 1964, Operation

Steel Tiger* and Operation Tiger Hound in 1965, Operation Rolling Thunder* in the 1960s, and the 1970 and 1971 "incursion" into Cambodia and Laos— on the grounds that if a neutral nation did not stop a belligerent from using its territory for hostile purposes, the other belligerent was not obligated to respect political neutrality. Neutrality proved to be an empty phrase during the Vietnam War.

Sources: Arnold R. Isaacs, *Without Honor: Defeat in Vietnam and Cambodia*, 1983.

NEUTRALIZE

"Neutralize" was one of the first and most commonly used euphemisms used to describe assassination. However, the term originated considerably before Vietnam and was frequently used in a context both broader than and different from assassination—physical targets or enemy positions to be destroyed by aerial bombardment or artillery. In Vietnam the term was also used to designate "unfriendly" hamlets hiding Vietcong,* and those hamlets were subject to destruction. If pacification efforts (*see* Rural Reconstruction) continuously failed, a decision might be made to "neutralize" the hamlet by relocating the inhabitants to a government-controlled area, perhaps a New Life Hamlet,* and destroying the hamlet, often by burning it down, giving rise to the phrase "zippo war."* Often the results of such neutralizations were negative in that innocent civilians were killed either because of mistaken identity or false or erroneous information providing the basis for targeting.

Sources: Jonathan Schell, *The Village of Ben Suc,* 1967; Richard Hammer, *One Morning in the War,* 1970.

Samuel Freeman

NEW LIFE HAMLETS

Part of the Civil Operations and Revolutionary Development Support* pacification program (*see* Rural Reconstruction), New Life Hamlets were one of a succession of hamlet development programs beginning with Strategic Hamlets* and continuing through "Ap Doi Moi" (Really New Life Hamlets), which followed the New Life Hamlet program. Each was intended to deprive the Vietcong* "fish" of the civilian "sea" by relocating civilians from the countryside to secured, fortified hamlets. Revolutionary Development (RD) cadres lived and worked among hamlet residents and tried to teach them about the Republic of Vietnam,* hoping to earn their respect and build their loyalty. In practice, the New Life Hamlet program was riddled with corruption. It ignored the sacred nature of the land and the people's worship of their ancestors. To leave ancestral land was to die. Resources were inadequate or unavailable. Pacification priorities were always subordinate to military needs, and security was uniformly inadequate. The RD cadres, even when present and not corrupt, were undertrained. Paid and supplied by Saigon,* they were dependent on and had to please Saigon officials, not the villagers. Hastily constructed in Vietcong areas, the hamlets were usually infiltrated. In sum, the program was poorly conceived and even more poorly executed.

Source: Larry E. Cable, *Conflict of Myths: The Development of American Counterinsurgency Doctrine and the Vietnam War*, 1986.

Samuel Freeman

NEWPORT

The major American troop buildup between 1965 and 1968 required enormous logistical resources. By 1968 nearly 45 percent of all American military personnel in South Vietnam were support troops, and more than five million tons of goods were shipped into the country. Because of inadequate port facilities, American merchant ships in 1965 usually had a twenty-day waiting period to be unloaded. To eliminate that backlog, the United States constructed major deep-water ports at Cam Ranh Bay,* Da Nang,* Qui Nhon,* and Newport, near Saigon.* The port at Newport just outside Saigon relieved the congestion there after its construction was completed in 1967. Newport handled more than 150,000 tons of supplies each month. It was under the direction of the army transportation corps.

Sources: Carroll H. Dunn, *Base Development in South Vietnam, 1965–1970*, 1972; Edwin B. Hooper, *Mobility, Support, Endurance: A Story of Naval Operational Logistics in the Vietnam War, 1965–1968*, 1972.

NEW YORK TIMES CO. v *UNITED STATES*, 403 U.S. 713 (1971)

In this decision, the U.S. Supreme Court upheld the First Amendment right of the *New York Times* and the *Washington Post* to publish excerpts from a U.S. Defense Department study marked Top Secret and entitled *History of U.S. Decision-Making Process on Vietnam Policy*, popularly known as the Pentagon Papers.* The *New York Times* began to publish excerpts from the Pentagon Papers on Sunday, June 13. On the evening of June 14, after White House consultation, U.S. Attorney General John Mitchell asked the *New York Times* to stop publishing excerpts from the Pentagon Papers on the ground that publication violated the Espionage Act. The *Times* refused to comply, saying "that it is in the interest of the people of this country to be informed of the material contained in this series of articles." The Department of Justice obtained a temporary restraining order against the *Times*. The newspaper appealed to the U.S. Supreme Court on June 24. While the *Times* was restrained from publishing excerpts from the Pentagon Papers, the *Washington Post* began to publish portions of the study. The *Post* distributed extracts to some 345 client publications through the *Washington Post-Los Angeles Times* News Service. The Department of Justice obtained a temporary restraining order against the *Post*, and then appealed to the U.S. Supreme Court when the U.S. Court of Appeals for the District of Columbia ruled that the *Post* had a constitutional right to publish the material. Extracts from the Pentagon Papers were also published by the *Boston Globe*, the *Los Angeles Times*, the *St. Louis Post-Dispatch*, the *Christian Science Monitor*, and a number of other newspapers during June 22–29. The Department of Justice obtained a restraining order against the *St. Louis Post-Dispatch* on June 26. On that day, the U.S. Supreme Court heard public oral arguments from Solicitor General Erwin Griswold for the United States, Alexander Bickel for the *Times,* and William Glendon for the *Post.* In an extraordinary flourish of activity, the Court rendered a 6–3 decision on June 30 and issued a short per curiam opinion for the Court, with Justices Burger, Harlan, and Blackmun dissenting. The decision was accompanied by nine opinions. The per curiam opinion held that the United States had not overcome the heavy presumption against the constitutional validity of any prior restraint on the press. Justices Black and Douglas took a nearly absolute view of a First Amendment prohibition of prior restraint on newspapers. Justices Brennan, Marshall, Stewart, and White acknowledged that there could be conditions that would justify a prior restraint on press publication of national security information. Such conditions were not, in their view, present in this case. Chief Justice Burger objected to the "unseemly haste" with which the Court handled the cases of the *Times* and the *Post.* Justices Harlan and Blackmun also objected to the "frenzied train of events [that] took place in the name of the presumption against prior restraints created by the First Amendment." The dissenting justices believed that publication of the Pentagon Papers should have been delayed until an assessment could be made of their potential effect on national defense and security. The *New York Times* and the *Washington Post* hailed the decision as a victory for freedom of the press and resumed publication of excerpts of the Pentagon Papers on July 1.

Source: Sanford J. Ungar, *The Papers and The Papers,* 1972.

John Kincaid

NEW ZEALAND

A charter member of the Southeast Asia Treaty Organization,* New Zealand was reluctant to become too deeply involved in the Vietnam War, simply on the grounds of limited resources and limited political support at home, and because the war was more than two thousand miles away. Nevertheless, New Zealand did make a troop commitment to the conflict. Eventually, New Zealand sent about a thousand soldiers and artillery support troops to South Vietnam because they wanted to prove their allegiance to American collective security arrangements in the Pacific and because they genuinely did not want to see a Communist takeover of Vietnam, Cambodia (*see* Kampuchea), and Laos.*

Sources: Stanley Robert Larsen and James Lawton Collins, Jr., *Allied Participation in Vietnam,* 1975; Shelby L. Stanton, *Vietnam Order of Battle,* 1981.

NGHE TINH UPRISING

Communism appeared for the first time in Vietnam in Nghe An and Ha Tinh provinces in 1930 and 1931. The worldwide depression had driven down the price of rice by more than 50 percent, and tax revolts were spreading throughout the countryside. Peasants in Nghe An Province joined with discontented factory workers, protesting capitalism and French imperialism. They formed a "Red

Soviet'' in Nghe An Province on September 12, 1930. Public demonstrations were widespread until French aircraft attacked a crowd of 6,000 protesters, killing more than 200 of them. The protests then went underground, but the movement weakened because of the famine which hit Vietnam in 1930 and 1931. The French went after leaders of the Indochinese Communist party (see Lao Dong party) with a vengeance, arresting 1,000 of them and executing 80. The uprising is known as the Nghe Tinh Uprising because of its strength throughout Nghe An and Ha Tinh provinces.

Source: William J. Duiker, *The Rise of Nationalism in Vietnam, 1900–1941,* 1976.

NGO DINH CAN

Ngo Dinh Can was the younger brother of Ngo Dinh Diem* and Ngo Dinh Nhu,* and from the Ngo family compound in Hue,* he ruled central Vietnam as a virtual warlord or feudal baron. Although Can held no official position, he was the de facto governor of the Hue region, and his actual power under the Diem administration was as extensive in his area as was that of Nhu in the Saigon* region. The dividing line between the two brothers' domains was Phan Thiet Province. The youngest brother, Ngo Dinh Luyen, resided abroad as South Vietnam's ambassador to Great Britain.*

Unlike his brothers, Can did not have a Western education, never traveled abroad, and seldom left his native Hue, where he lived with the clan's widowed matriarch. He lived in a simple, reclusive style, despite many reports that he had used his position for personal enrichment. Employing his own secret police network, Can exercised a severe, even brutal, domination over central Vietnam. His local authority was largely independent of Saigon, and at times he was at odds with his brothers. Overall, however, the brothers worked together to maintain their power. Following the assassination of Diem and Nhu in 1963, the new regime arrested, tried, and executed Can.

Sources: Robert G. Scigliano, *South Viet-Nam: Nation Under Stress,* 1963; Terrence Maitland and Stephen Weiss, *The Vietnam Experience: Raising the Stakes,* 1982.

David L. Anderson

NGO DINH DIEM

Son of a counselor to Emperor Thanh Thai, Ngo Dihn Diem* was born in 1901 and claimed to descend from mandarins—a claim disputed by some. The third of six sons, Diem graduated first in his class from a Catholic school in Hue* and studied for the civil service at a French college in Hanoi.* Rising rapidly through administrative ranks, he became minister of the interior in 1933 but resigned two months later because of French unwillingness to grant Vietnam greater autonomy. An ardent nationalist and early opponent of communism, Diem retired from public life for twenty years, having nothing further to do with the French and refusing offers from the Japanese during World War II. His anticommunism strengthened when Vietminh* forces killed one of his brothers and a nephew. Diem refused Ho Chi Minh's* offer to join his government,

denouncing him as a "criminal." In 1950 Diem went to the United States where
he met Cardinal Spellman and Senators John Kennedy* and Mike Mansfield.*
These contacts served Diem well when he accepted Emperor Bao Dai's* 1954
offer to become prime minister of what would become the Republic of Vietnam.*
One of Diem's first acts was to request American assistance.

Diem might be described as a brilliant incompetent who beat the odds longer
than anyone thought possible. Given his twenty-year retirement, he was not well-
known in Vietnam and had no following outside the Catholic* community in an
overwhelmingly Buddhist* nation. Reclusive and paranoid, he depended almost
exclusively on his family, refused to delegate authority, and did little to build
a broadly based, popular government. Diem was surprisingly adept in meeting
challenges to his government. In 1955 he rejected the reunification elections
specified in the Geneva Accords,* disposed of Emperor Bao Dai in a fraudulent
election (winning 98.2 percent of the vote), neutralized the Cao Dai* and Hoa
Hao* religious sects, and defeated the Binh Xuyen* in open combat. He survived
a 1960 coup attempt which rendered him even more dependent on his immediate
family, especially his brother Ngo Dinh Nhu.*

Administratively, Diem could not set priorities, choosing to spend a long
afternoon with a journalist while members of his government and the military
waited for audiences. Governing through repression and intrigue, he quickly
killed or imprisoned the remaining Vietminh* infrastructure along with most
other potential opponents. His oppressiveness and refusal to implement reforms
tried the patience of the United States, which flirted with dumping him as early
as 1955. By 1963, however, he was finished. The final blow was Ngo Dinh
Nhu's vicious attacks on Buddhist dissidents and the ensuing national paralysis.
Although not involved in the coup, the United States signaled that it would
accept a change in government. On November 1, the generals moved; Diem and
his brother were murdered the next day.

After the coup, Diem was vilified, but Vietnamese attitudes toward Diem
changed in the 1970s as the United States withdrew and South Vietnam's fate
became obvious. In South Vietnam's final weeks Diem was rehabilitated as a
courageous nationalist tragically victimized by the United States.

Sources: Denis Warner, *The Last Confucian*, 1963; *Who's Who in the Far East and
Australasia, 1961–1962*, 1962; Marvin Kalb and Elie Abel, *Roots of Involvement: The
U.S. in Asia, 1784–1971*, 1971.

                                                                      Samuel Freeman

NGO DINH NHU

Born in 1910, Ngo Dinh Nhu was educated at the École des Chartes in Paris
and then worked in the French colonial bureaucracy until penalized for nationalist
activities. A master at organization, Nhu orchestrated Saigon* demonstrations
in September 1954 advocating a "third force" alternative to French colonialism
or Ho Chi Minh.* The Can Lao Nhan Vi Cach Mang Dang* was his primary
effort at mass organization. Unfortunately, Nhu's "personalism" was based on

a misinterpretation of French thinking and was so alien to Vietnamese thought and culture that no one understood it. The party was organized along the lines of Communist cells complete with fascist-styled storm troopers and an elaborate intelligence network. Nhu used the party to maintain the authority of the Ngo family rather than building democratic institutions or national unity.

Nhu recommended and administered the Strategic Hamlet Program.* Like everything else in the Diem regime, it was poorly administered and riddled with corruption. Obsessed with numbers, Nhu pushed the construction of strategic hamlets more rapidly than they could be assimilated, often in unsecured areas. Government promises for equipment, material, and money were not kept. Villagers often had to pay bribes to receive promised supplies. The Vietcong* quickly subverted many hamlets; others simply disintegrated.

As head of the secret police, Nhu created thirteen internal intelligence units which spied on one another as well as on potential dissidents. He also commanded Vietnamese Special Forces,* effectively his personal army. With these resources Nhu frustrated numerous efforts to depose his brother, Ngo Dinh Diem,* who always viewed internal dissent as more threatening than the Vietcong. The corruption, brutality, and intrigue caught up with the Diem regime in 1963 when Nhu took on the Buddhists.* After Nhu's Special Forces attacked Buddhist pagodas, the United States notified plotting generals that it would accept a coup. On November 1 the generals moved. Diem and Nhu were murdered that next day.

Source: Stanley Karnow, *Vietnam: A History,* 1983; Thomas D. Boettcher, *Vietnam: The Valor and the Sorrow,* 1985; Denis Warner, *The Last Confucian,* 1963.

Samuel Freeman

MADAME NGO DINH NHU

Born as Tran Le Xuan (Beautiful Spring) in 1924 to a completely Gallicized Vietnamese family which had enriched itself in service to the French colonialists, Le Xuan dropped out of Hanoi's* Lycée Albert Sarraut. She was fluent in French but never learned to write in Vietnamese. In 1944 Tran Le Xuan married Ngo Dinh Nhu,* and because Ngo Dinh Diem* never married, she was essentially the first lady of the Republic of Vietnam.* Powerful in her own right, Madame Nhu issued decrees having the force of law banning divorce, adultery, prostitution, dancing, boxing, beauty contests, and fortune-telling, among other things. Considering herself a feminist, she lectured on women's issues and commanded her own paramilitary organization, the Women's Solidarity Movement.

Madame Nhu saw herself as the reincarnation of the Trung sisters, ancient leaders in the struggle for independence from China,* but she was more a reincarnation of Marie Antoinette. She was incredibly insensitive to and uncaring about anyone outside the ruling clique or the sufferings that Diem's inept, corrupt, and increasingly brutal government imposed on the people. When Buddhist monks, including Thich Quang Duc,* and a nun immolated themselves protesting Diem's government, she airily referred to them as Buddhist "barbeques." Nhu encouraged her outrageousness by adding that "if the Buddhists want to have another barbecue, I will be glad to supply the gasoline." Such statements helped consolidate U.S. opposition to Diem, paving the way for the November 1963 coup. Madame Nhu was traveling in the United States, campaigning for support for the Diem regime, in November 1963 when Diem and her husband were assassinated. She then returned to a widowhood in Rome.

Sources: Frances FitzGerald, *Fire in the Lake: The Vietnamese and the Americans in Vietnam,* 1972; Stanley Karnow, *Vietnam: A History,* 1983; Thomas D. Boettcher, *Vietnam, The Valor and the Sorrow,* 1985; *New York Times,* October 28–31, November 1–2, 1963.

Samuel Freeman

NGO DINH THUC

Ngo Dinh Thuc was the older brother of Ngo Dinh Diem,* and the second oldest of the six Ngo brothers. The Vietminh* killed Ngo Dinh Khoi in 1945, and Thuc then became the senior male in the Ngo clan. Although the family was devoutly Catholic, Vietnam's Confucian* traditions meant that Thuc, the family elder, had considerable authority within the family and took proprietary interest in the welfare of all its members.

Under the influence of his father, Ngo Dinh Kha, who had once studied for the priesthood, Ngo Dinh Thuc entered the seminary in his youth. He rose steadily in the Roman Catholic* hierarchy in Vietnam and eventually became the bishop of Vinh Long. He shared his brother Diem's distaste for Emperor Bao Dai's* seeming collaboration with the French colonialists, and in 1950 the two brothers traveled to America and Europe to meet influential Catholics and to promote themselves as anticolonial and anti-Communist Vietnamese. When Diem became prime minister in 1954, these contacts and this Ngo family image in the West proved very valuable to the new regime.

By the end of the 1950s, Thuc was Archbishop of Hue* and dean of the Catholic episcopacy in Vietnam. He held no official post in his brother's government, but as leader of the Catholic clergy, he was in an excellent position to promote the interests both of the Church and the Ngo family. The Vatican declined to make him Arch-bishop of Saigon* in order to keep some discreet distance between Thuc and Diem, but the prelate still spent considerable time in the capital city advising his brothers and managing the Church's real estate. In the fall of 1963, the Vatican ordered Thuc to Rome to answer for his conduct during the government's violent suppression of the Buddhists.* Consequently, he was out of Vietnam at the time of the coup against Diem. He never returned to Vietnam, and the Church eventually excommunicated him for religious extremism.

Sources: Joseph Buttinger, *Vietnam: A Dragon Embattled.* Vol. 2, *Vietnam at War,* 1967; Anthony T. Bouscaren, *The Last of the Mandarins: Diem of Vietnam,* 1965; David Halberstam, *The Making of a Quagmire,* 1965.

David L. Anderson

NGUYEN

The Nguyen were the dynastic family in control of Annam* and Cochin China* during the seventeenth and eighteenth centuries. In the sixteenth century, the

Trinh family, another warlord group, took control of Vietnam from the Le clan, and by 1620 the Nguyen clan had separated from the Trinh* family and dominated Annam. Throughout the 1600s the Trinh tried unsuccessfully to bring the Nguyen back under control, but they were never able to penetrate the large walls the Nguyen had constructed near the seventeenth parallel (*see* Geneva Accords). Gradually the Nguyen moved south, colonizing the Mekong Delta* and bringing the Cham* and Khmer* people under Annamite culture. By the 1700s the Nguyen had taken over parts of Thailand,* Laos,* and Cambodia (*see* Kampuchea), and were anxious to dominate all of Indochina.* The Tay Son Rebellion* temporarily displaced them in the late eighteenth century, but under Nguyen Gia Long* they reestablished their control. Indeed, because the Tay Son Rebellion had crushed the Trinh family in the north, Gia Long was able to unite all of Vietnam under a Nguyen dynasty which remained in power until the abdication of Bao Dai* in 1955. Only the arrival of the French Empire and later the Japanese and Americans stopped Nguyen expansion. Although the Nguyen had nationalist sympathies and resented foreign control over Vietnam, they tended to cooperate with foreign rulers—French, Japanese, or American—in order to maintain their own positions of wealth and influence. Blessed with a Confucian,* elitist mentality, they continued to occupy important political positions in South Vietnam during the 1950s, 1960s, and 1970s. The most prominent family representative then was Nguyen Cao Ky,* head of the South Vietnamese Air Force.*

Source: Joseph Buttinger, *The Smaller Dragon: A Political History of Vietnam,* 1958.

NGUYEN CAO KY

Nguyen Cao Ky was born on September 8, 1930, in Son Tay, Tonkin,* near Hanoi.* Ky was drafted into the Vietnamese National Army in 1950, served with distinction, and rose to the rank of lieutenant. He was trained as a pilot in France* and Algeria in 1953 and 1954, and during the regime of Ngo Dinh Diem* he became an officer, eventually a lieutenant general, in the South Vietnamese Air Force.* Flamboyant and with an iron will, Ky first came to prominence in 1964 when he threatened to conduct an air strike against the headquarters of Nguyen Khanh* because of all the squabbling during the military regime. Ky finally agreed to cooperate after a dressing-down by U.S. ambassador Maxwell Taylor,* and in 1965 he became prime minister, sharing power with General Nguyen Van Thieu.* A dedicated elitist with decidedly Western tastes, Ky imposed brutal restrictions on the Buddhists*—far more than even Ngo Dinh Diem had imposed—and invited their wrath. Throughout 1966 the Buddhists demanded Ky's ouster, but Ky continued in power. In 1967, he agreed, with considerable support from the United States, to let Thieu become the sole head of state, with Ky serving as vice president. Although Ky had promised Lyndon Johnson* he would strive to bring about a "social revolution" in Vietnam, he had no intention of upsetting the status quo of corruption and power which was enriching him and his family. Between 1967 and 1971, Ky's influence was gradually eclipsed as Thieu consolidated his own power, and in 1971, Thieu disqualified Ky from challenging him for the presidency of South Vietnam.

Nguyen Cao Ky fled South Vietnam before the Final Offensive (*see* Ho Chi Minh Campaign) and opened a liquor store in southern California.

Sources: David Halberstam, *The Best and the Brightest,* 1972; Nguyen Cao Ky, *Twenty Years and Twenty Days,* 1976; George C. Herring, *America's Longest War: The United States in Vietnam, 1950–1975,* 1986.

Samuel Freeman

NGUYEN CHANH THI

Nguyen Chanh Thi was born in central Vietnam in 1923 and became a career military officer in the Army of the Republic of Vietnam.* In 1960, as a colonel, Thi worked surreptitiously in an unsuccessful coup attempt against Ngo Dinh Diem.* Although loyal to the concept of an independent South Vietnam, Nguyen Chanh Thi was also a Buddhist* who resented Diem's attacks on the church. By 1965 Thi had risen to command I Corps,* and there he formed a close relationship with Buddhist leader Thich Tri Quang.* As Buddhist opposition to the government of Nguyen Cao Ky* mounted, Thi became more and more vulnerable. In 1966, Ky dismissed Thi as I Corps* commander, put him under house arrest in Saigon,* and triggered countrywide Buddhist protest demonstrations. Nguyen Chanh Thi was exiled to the United States.

Source: "Central Figures in the Struggle for Leadership of Vietnam," *U.S. News & World Report* (March 28, 1966), 14.

NGUYEN CHI THANH

Nguyen Chi Thanh, the North Vietnamese commander in charge of operations in South Vietnam, was born in 1914 in central Vietnam. He attended school in Hanoi* and became a schoolteacher before World War II, but he joined the Vietminh* after the war and began fighting first the French and then the Americans in South Vietnam. In 1965, Thanh was infiltrated into South Vietnam to take control of North Vietnamese and Vietcong* troop movements. He operated out of Tay Ninh Province, where he headed the Central Office for South Vietnam.* Thanh was committed to defeating South Vietnamese and American troops through conventional means on an early timetable, but as they accumulated heavy losses in 1965 and 1966, General Vo Nguyen Giap* switched to more emphasis on guerrilla operations and a political victory over the Americans. Nguyen Chi Thanh died on July 8, 1967, in a Hanoi hospital.

Source: *New York Times,* July 9, 1967.

NGUYEN CO THACH

Nguyen Co Thach, a veteran North Vietnamese politician, was active in anti-French activities as a student in the 1930s, and with the Vietminh* in the 1940s and 1950s. He began a diplomatic career in 1954 with the creation of the Democratic Republic of Vietnam.* Between 1956 and 1960, Thach served as ambassador to India and headed the Vietnamese delegation to the Geneva convention in 1962. After the fall of South Vietnam in 1975, Thach became assistant and then minister of foreign affairs for the Socialist Republic of Vietnam.*

Source: *International Who's Who, 1982–1983,* 1983.

NGUYEN DUY TRINH

Nguyen Duy Trinh was born in the village of Nghi Loc, in Nghe An Province, in 1910. He joined the New Vietnam Revolutionary party as an eighteen-year-old student in 1918, and was a member of the Communist party as early as 1930. Trinh was imprisoned for anti-French activities in 1928 in Saigon,* was released in 1930, and was imprisoned in Kontum again between 1932 and 1945. Upon his release at the end of World War II, Trinh immediately organized anti-French uprisings in Vinh and Hue,* and in 1951 was selected as a member of the Central Committee of the Vietnam Workers' party. After the expulsion of the French from Indochina* in 1954, Trinh became secretary of the Central Committee of the Vietnam Workers' party, and deputy prime minister of North Vietnam in 1960, where he served until 1975. Trinh served concurrently as minister of foreign affairs between 1965 and 1975. After the fall of South Vietnam in 1975, Trinh became a member of the politburo of the Socialist Republic of Vietnam.*

Source: *Who's Who in the Socialist Countries,* 1978.

NGUYEN HUU CO

Nguyen Huu Co was a native of South Vietnam born in 1925. He rose quickly through the ranks of the Army of the Republic of Vietnam,* and was one of thirteen generals who replaced Ngo Dinh Diem* in 1963. After two years of political instability for South Vietnam, Co was one of the ten generals who helped put Nguyen Cao Ky* in power in 1965. Co was widely known as an excellent field commander who was also hopelessly corrupt, accumulating a fortune by accepting payments from draft dodgers and selling military appointments. When he was ousted from power and exiled to Taiwan in 1967, Nguyen Huu Co was serving as defense secretary and deputy premier.

Source: "Clean-Up Time," *Newsweek* (February 6, 1967), 44–45.

NGUYEN HUU THO

Nguyen Huu Tho was born on July 10, 1910, in the Cholon* suburb of Saigon.* A French-educated Saigon attorney, Tho was a revolutionary with middle-class credentials. Between 1945 and 1954 he fought against French forces in Vietnam, protested American involvement in the conflict as early as 1950, and spent two years in a prison for anti-French activity from 1950 to 1952. He was arrested in 1961 for establishing the Saigon-Cholon Peace Movement, escaped from the control of the Diem* government, and became chairman of the central committee of the National Liberation Front (*see* Vietcong) in 1962. By June 1970 Tho was chairman of the consultative council of the Provisional

Revolutionary Government of South Vietnam,* and entered Saigon with North Vietnamese forces in 1975.

Source: *The International Who's Who, 1976–77,* 1976.

NGUYEN KHANH

Born in 1927, Nguyen Khanh grew up to be an incorrigible, untrustworthy schemer. He had quit school in 1943 and joined the Vietminh* in their campaign against the Japanese and the French, but the Vietminh soon expelled him. Khanh then went over to the French, who trained him for an officer's position in the Vietnamese National Army.* In 1954 Khanh came to the support of Ngo Dinh Diem,* but in 1963 he also participated in the coup against him. Khanh then participated in a bloodless coup in January 1964 which put him in control of the government of South Vietnam. For the next year South Vietnam deteriorated under his convoluted leadership, with the Vietcong* gaining strength and his own government torn apart by corruption and internecine political warfare. In February 1965, Generals Nguyen Cao Ky* and Nguyen Van Thieu* ousted Khanh for good. He was exiled to the United States and took up residence in Palm Beach, Florida.

Sources: *Who's Who in the Far East and Australasia, 1964–1965,* 1965; Stanley Karnow, *Vietnam: A History,* 1983; Frances FitzGerald, *Fire in the Lake: The Vietnamese and the Americans in Vietnam,* 1972.

Samuel Freeman

NGUYEN LUONG BANG

Nguyen Luong Bang was born in Hai Hung Province in North Vietnam in 1904. He worked as a sailor before joining Ho Chi Minh's* Revolutionary Youth League (*see* Thanh Nien Cach Menh Dong Chi Hoi) in 1925. Bang was a founding member of the Indochinese Communist party (*see* Lao Dong party) in 1930. Between 1931 and 1943 he spent most of his time in French prisons, escaping in 1932 but being recaptured in 1933. Bang escaped again in 1943 and fled to China.* Between 1952 and 1956 he was the ambassador to the Soviet Union* for the Democratic Republic of Vietnam.* Bang became vice president of the Democratic Republic of Vietnam in 1969.

Source: U.S. State Department, *Who's Who in North Vietnam,* 1972.

NGUYEN NGOC LOAN

General Nguyen Ngoc Loan achieved infamy with the filmed summary execution of a Vietcong* suspect in Saigon* during the Tet Offensive* in 1968. Widely reported in the United States, it contributed to the American people's increasing revulsion with the war. Loan attempted to justify the execution, explaining that the man had murdered a friend and his family. Nevertheless, the execution was in keeping with his reputation for ruthlessness, corruption, and brutality.

A northern-born Catholic, Loan first came into prominence in 1966 as a colonel while serving as Saigon's chief of police—a lucrative position which enabled him to control Saigon's extortion racket. Faced with the "Buddhist Crisis," Nguyen Cao Ky* placed him in charge of subduing rebellious I Corps.* With loyal troops reenforced by tanks and airborne units, Loan attacked Da Nang* pagodas which lodged resisting Buddhists* and military units. In a series of firefights ending May 22, Loan regained control of the city, killing hundreds of rebel troops and about 100 civilians in the process. He then proceeded to lay siege to Hue,* prompting self-immolations by nine Buddhist priests and nuns in protest. After Loan pacified Hue, Ky instigated a public relations campaign to soften resentments. Prominent members of the uprising were treated leniently. Colonel Loan was ordered to clean up Hue, and he jailed hundreds who remained behind bars for years without trial. Loan's efforts were rewarded with promotion to general and chief of the national police shortly thereafter. After the fall of South Vietnam in 1975, Loan fled to the United States.

Sources: Frances FitzGerald, *Fire in the Lake: The Vietnamese and the Americans in Vietnam,* 1972; *New York Times,* February 1–2, 1968.

Samuel Freeman

NGUYEN PHU DUC

Nguyen Phu Duc was born on November 13, 1924, in Son Tay, and he was educated at the University of Hanoi* and the Harvard Law School. During the 1960s, Nguyen Phu Duc was a diplomat in active support of the South Vietnamese government. He served as special assistant for foreign affairs to President Nguyen Van Thieu* in 1968; acted as envoy to Thailand,* Laos,* Indonesia, and the United States between 1969 and 1972; and participated in the Paris peace talks* of 1968 and 1973. Duc was named minister of foreign affairs in 1973, and between 1974 and 1975 he was ambassador to Belgium.

Source: *International Who's Who, 1982–1983,* 1983.

NGUYEN THI BINH

Nguyen Thi Binh was born in 1927 to a middle-class Saigon* family. As a student she became a strident nationalist, opposing first French rule, Japanese occupation, and finally the American presence. Between 1951 and 1954 Nguyen Thi Binh spent three years in a French prison for anti-French and anti-American activities, and after 1954 was a bitter opponent of the regime of Ngo Dinh Diem.* Nguyen Thi Binh joined the National Liberation Front (NLF; *see* Vietcong) soon after its creation in December 1960, and in 1962 she had risen to membership in its central committee. Binh traveled around the world explaining the NLF position and opposing U.S. involvement in the war. At the same time she worked as a representative, and between 1963 and 1966, as head of the Women's Liberation Association, a group promoting the rights of Vietnamese women in the struggle for revolution. In 1968, Binh appeared in Paris as head of the NLF delegation at the peace talks.* For the next four years Binh served as the public NLF spokesman, and after the collapse of the South Vietnamese government in 1975, she was named minister of education for the Socialist Republic of Vietnam.*

Sources: John S. Bowman, ed., *The Vietnam War Almanac*, 1985; *Encyclopedia of the Third World*, 3:1929–31, 1982.

NGUYEN VAN BINH

Nguyen Van Binh was born on September 1, 1910, in Saigon* and was educated at the Roman Catholic Seminary of Saigon and in Rome. He was ordained a Roman Catholic priest in 1937 and served in parishes in Duc Hoa and Can Dat. He was ordained a bishop in 1955 and served for six years as the Apostolic Vicar of Can Tho* until being named Archbishop of Saigon in 1961, a position he still held in the 1980s.

Source: *Who's Who in the Far East and Australasia, 1981–1982*, 1982.

NGUYEN VAN HINH

In an effort to counter the military strength of the Vietminh,* the French began in 1951 the creation of the Vietnamese National Army* (VNA). General Nguyen Van Hinh, as chief of staff, was the commander of this force from its inception until November 1954. Hinh was the son of Nguyen Van Tam, a prominent Vietnamese collaborator with the French and one of Emperor Bao Dai's* prime ministers. Like his father, Hinh was a French citizen. He was also an officer in the French armed forces, had a French wife, and preferred the French way of life. In the eyes of the Vietnamese he was French, and his command of the VNA made a mockery of the notion of an independent Vietnamese army. Because of its colonialist stigma, the VNA under Hinh never became the efficient and inspired anti-Vietminh force that the French and many Vietnamese desired.

In 1954 Hinh openly challenged Ngo Dinh Diem's* authority as prime minister. Defying demands by Diem that he leave the country, the general plotted with gangsters and religious sects around Saigon to oust the prime minister. Diem responded with his own enticements to the sects. Hoping to maintain a stable government in Saigon* to combat the Communists in the North, the Americans warned that a coup by Hinh would mean the end of U.S. assistance to South Vietnam. Faced with that prospect, Bao Dai ordered Hinh to come to France,* and the general reluctantly complied. Hinh returned once to Vietnam in 1955 when Diem's authority seemed threatened but soon fled the country when Diem's forces prevailed. Hinh was then given a high position in the French army.

Source: Joseph Buttinger, *Vietnam: A Dragon Embattled*. Vol. 2, *Vietnam at War*, 1967.

David L. Anderson

NGUYEN VAN LINH

Nguyen Van Linh was born in 1913 in North Vietnam. A longtime member of the central committee of the Lao Dong party,* Nguyen Van Linh was a bitter opponent of the French Empire as well as the subsequent Japanese and American occupations of Vietnam. Between 1976 and 1981 Linh served as secretary of the Communist party of Vietnam.

Source: *International Who's Who, 1982–1983*, 1983.

NGUYEN VAN THIEU

Nguyen Van Thieu was born in 1923 in Tri Thuy village in Ninh Thuan Province. Nguyen Van Thieu distinguished himself against the Vietminh* after graduating from the Vietnamese Military Academy as an infantry lieutenant in 1949. Thieu also graduated from the United States Command and General Staff College in 1957. His major commands in the Army of the Republic of Vietnam* (ARVN), beginning in 1959, included the 21st Infantry Division, commandant of the National Military Academy, the ARVN 1st Infantry Division,* and the 5th Infantry Division. He led a brigade of the 5th Division against Diem's presidential guard during the 1963 coup. Thieu continued to rise in power after the overthrow of Ngo Dinh Diem* and was instrumental, along with General Nguyen Cao Ky,* in bringing General Nguyen Khanh* to power in January 1964. By February 1965 Ky and Thieu had positioned themselves to take over the government. Surprisingly, the Ky-Thieu government was South Vietnam's longest. Although Ky originally was premier and Thieu was chief of state and commander in chief of the armed forces, Thieu outmaneuvered Ky to become the presidential candidate (with Ky as his vice president) in the 1967 elections.

While Thieu would have been more acceptable to the United States than Ky in 1965, they were about equally acceptable by 1967. The primary American concern was that they not run against each other, splitting the military and raising prospects for a civilian government or more coups. A Thieu-Ky ticket ensured military unity and their victory. However, Thieu managed only 35 percent of the vote with a surprise peace candidate running an unexpectedly strong second in elections marred by double voting by military personnel and stuffed ballot boxes. When Ky attempted to run against him for president in 1971, Thieu outmaneuvered him again, disqualifying his candidacy on a technicality. Eliminating Ky prompted General Duong Van ''Big'' Minh* to withdraw, leaving Thieu to run unopposed and to head the government until just before its collapse in April 1975.

Thieu bitterly opposed the proposed 1972 peace agreement. Calling it a sellout, he delayed its signing until January 1973. To gain Thieu's assent, some minor modifications were effected. More important, Nixon* made secret promises regarding future American military support. In August 1974 Nixon resigned rather than face impeachment and Gerald Ford* became president. Congress* passed the War Powers Resolution* and other legislation restricting American involvement in Southeast Asia. When Thieu asked the United States to honor Nixon's promises, President Ford had neither the authority nor the sense of obligation to provide assistance. For the first time Thieu and South Vietnam stood alone.

The stability of Thieu's regime did not result from his establishing a popular government. Like its predecessors, it was noted for corruption, incompetence, and oppression. Stability resulted from Thieu's keeping the Vietnamese military command either unable or unwilling to mount a successful coup. This depended largely on his maintaining the confidence of the United States. At bottom it was the American military and American money which kept South Vietnam afloat, as demonstrated by its rapid disintegration once the support was terminated. Some criticize the United States for not coming to Thieu's assistance in 1975; however, a strong case can be made that since South Vietnam had failed to build a viable government after a massive twenty-five-year effort, there were no meaningful prospects for ever building one. President Thieu now lives in Great Britain.

Sources: *Who's Who in the Far East and Australasia, 1974–1975*, 1975; Stanley Karnow, *Vietnam: A History*, 1983; Edward Doyle and Terrence Maitland, *The Vietnam Experience: The Aftermath, 1975–1985*, 1985.

Samuel Freeman

NHA TRANG

Nha Trang, 15 miles north of Cam Ranh Bay* in Khanh Hoa Province, was a major logistic base for the supply of American military forces and headquarters for the Fifth Special Forces Group* and the I Field Force Vietnam.* Nha Trang had a population of 194,969 in 1971. It was made an autonomous municipality in October 1970.

Sources: Harvey H. Smith, et al, *Area Handbook for South Vietnam*, 1967; Danny J. Whitfield, *Historical and Cultural Dictionary of Vietnam*, 1976.

NINTH INFANTRY DIVISION

The Ninth Infantry Division was created in 1940 and during World War II saw combat in North Africa, Italy, France, and Germany. Known as "Old Reliables," the Ninth was deactivated in 1946, reactivated in 1947, deactivated in 1962, and reactivated again in 1966 and deployed to Vietnam on December 16 that year. In 1967 the Ninth Division fought in Dinh Tuong and Long An provinces, the Saigon* area during the Tet Offensive* and post-Tet campaigns of 1968, and widely throughout IV Corps* in 1969. One brigade of the Ninth Infantry Division participated in the Mobile Riverine Force,* which searched and fought against Vietcong* units in the Mekong Delta.* During its stay in Vietnam, the Ninth Infantry Division was commanded by four men: Major General George S. Eckhardt (December 1966-June 1967); Major General George G. O'Connor (June 1967-February 1968); Major General Julian J. Ewell (February 1968-April 1969); and Major General Harris W. Hollis (April 1969-August 1969). The 1st and 2nd brigades of the Ninth Infantry left Vietnam on August 27, 1969, and the 3rd Brigade remained behind, assigned to the 25th Infantry Division.* The 3rd Brigade left Vietnam on October 11, 1970.

Sources: Shelby L. Stanton, *Vietnam Order of Battle*, 1981, and *The Rise and Fall of an American Army: U.S. Ground Troops in Vietnam, 1965–1973*, 1985.

9TH MARINE AMPHIBIOUS BRIGADE

When the North Vietnamese Army* (NVA) attacked in force across the Demilitarized Zone* in late March 1972, the 9th Marine Amphibious Brigade (MAB) provided troops and aircraft off the coast ready to attack NVA-controlled areas south or north of the seventeenth parallel (*see* Geneva Accords), support ARVN forces (*see* Army of the Republic of Vietnam), and if necessary evacuate U.S. military personnel and material in South Vietnam's northern provinces. The deployment of 9th MAB revived the Marine Corps's* traditional amphibious role, and with marine aircraft sent ashore to provide support for ARVN infantry, 9th MAB also dispatched a battalion landing team (BLT) to provide security for the air bases at Bien Hoa and Nam Phong.

In 1975 the Seventh Fleet* and 9th MAB conducted Operation Frequent Wind* (April 29–30) to evacuate U.S. personnel and friendly South Vietnamese from Saigon.* Ninth MAB provided several ground security units and sixty-eight transport helicopters to lift thousands off the roof of the U.S. embassy and out of Tan Son Nhut Air Base,* and two of the brigade's officers died when their CH–46* helicopter crashed into the South China Sea on the last day of the Vietnam War. But 9th MAB took more casualties two weeks later when—two hours after the unannounced release of the crew of the SS *Mayaguez* (*see Mayaguez* incident)—elements of one of its BLTs unwittingly landed on Koh Tang island and met fierce resistance from Cambodian forces. The Marine Corps role in Indochina* thus ended in a bloody but futile daylong battle.

Sources: Edwin H. Simmons, "Marine Corps Operations in Vietnam, 1969–1972," and Richard E. Carey and David A. Quinlan, "Frequent Wind," in *The Marines in Vietnam, 1954–1973*, 1983; J. Robert Moskin, *The U.S. Marine Corps Story*, 1982.

Dudley Acker

9TH MARINE EXPEDITIONARY BRIGADE

The August 1964 Gulf of Tonkin incident* led to the transformation of the 9th Marine Expeditionary Brigade (MEB) from a paper organization into the deployable 6,000-man air and ground force from which two infantry battalions made the initial sea and air landings to secure Da Nang's* air base in March 1965. Despite this commitment of combat troops, the Washington-Military Assistance Command, Vietnam* landing directive stated that marines "will not, repeat, will not, engage in day-to-day actions against the Vietcong," and overall responsibility for both offensive and defensive operations in the vicinity temporarily remained with ARVN commanders (*see* Army of the Republic of Vietnam).

In early May, however, 9th MEB established two more bases on the coast at Chu Lai and Phu Bai, 57 miles south and 30 miles north of Da Nang, respectively. Sensitive to reviving memories of the French debacle through use of the term "expeditionary," 9th MEB became the III Marine Amphibious Force* on the seventh of that month.

316   NITZE, PAUL HENRY

Sources: Jack Shulimson and Edward F. Wells, "The Marine Experience in Vietnam, 1965–71: First In, First Out," in *The Marines in Vietnam, 1954–1973*, 1983; Philip Caputo, *A Rumor of War*, 1977.

Dudley Acker

NITZE, PAUL HENRY

Paul H. Nitze was born in Amherst, Massachusetts, on January 16, 1907. He graduated cum laude from Harvard in 1928 and shortly thereafter became a vice president for the investment banking firm of Dillon, Reed, and Company. In 1940 Nitze became assistant to James V. Forrestal, under secretary of the navy. In 1941 he was named financial director of the Office of the Coordinator of Inter-American Affairs, then under Nelson Rockefeller's direction. During World War II, Nitze served on the Board of Economic Warfare and the Foreign Economic Administration, and after the war he was vice chairman of the U.S. Strategic Bombing Survey. Nitze moved to the State Department in 1946, helped develop the Marshall Plan, and in 1949 succeeded George Kennan* as head of the State Department's policy planning staff. In 1956, Nitze wrote *U.S. Foreign Policy, 1945–1955*.

In 1960 President John F. Kennedy* appointed Nitze assistant secretary of defense for international security affairs, where he specialized in disarmament and military assistance plans. Nitze was secretary of the navy between 1963 and 1967, and deputy secretary of defense between 1967 and 1969. In that position he helped draft the San Antonio Formula* and served on the Ad Hoc Task Force on Vietnam,* where he advised against further escalation of the war for fear of intervention from the People's Republic of China.* Nitze resigned from the Defense Department when Richard Nixon* entered the White House in January 1969, although he served until 1974 as a member of the U.S. delegation to the Strategic Arms Limitation Talks. In 1981 Nitze was named head of the U.S. delegation to the Intermediate Range Nuclear Forces Negotiations with the Soviet Union, and in 1984 as arms control adviser to Secretary of State George Schultz.

Sources: *Current Biography*, 1962; *International Who's Who 1984–85*, 1984; "Brinksmanship on a Hot Border," *Time* 113, February 26, 1979, pp. 39–40.

Joanna D. Cowden

NIXON, RICHARD MILHOUS

Richard M. Nixon was born on January 9, 1913, in Yorba Linda, California. He graduated from Whittier College in 1934 and then took a law degree at Duke in 1937. Nixon practiced law in Whittier, California, between 1937 and 1942, and was active in the naval reserve during World War II. He won a seat in Congress, as a Republican, in 1946, and then rose to prominence in 1949 pushing the treason case against Alger Hiss for the House Un-American Activities Committee. A conservative, anti-Communist Republican, Nixon won a seat in the U.S. Senate in 1950. In 1952 Dwight D. Eisenhower* selected Nixon as his vice presidential running mate, and Nixon survived a controversy over personal use of campaign funds to become vice president of the United States. In 1960, he lost a narrow election for president to Democrat John F. Kennedy,* and in 1962 he lost a bid for the governorship of California to incumbent Democrat Pat Brown. Most observers assumed Nixon's political career was over, but while practicing law he spoke widely on behalf of Republican candidates and causes, and in 1968 he won the GOP presidential nomination. By then the Democratic party was self-destructing over Vietnam, and in the general election, promising a new plan to end the war, Nixon narrowly defeated Hubert Humphrey.*

Although Nixon's political career had taken a hard-line, ideological tone over the years, especially in foreign policy, he proved to be a pragmatic president willing to explore a variety of initiatives. Until 1967, he had supported the American commitment in Vietnam, but he became more critical as the election politics of 1968 heated up. By the time he took office in 1969, Nixon, along with his national security adviser, Henry Kissinger,* was convinced the war must come to an end. But they wanted no ignominious withdrawal either. Anything less than an "honorable" peace would compromise their grand design to reach an accommodation with the People's Republic of China* and the Soviet Union* without abandoning traditional allies.

The Nixon-Kissinger approach to peace came to be known as Vietnamization* and rested on several major assumptions: (1) the government of Nguyen Van Thieu* was stable and was prepared to assume more responsibility for conduct of the war; (2) South Vietnamese troops would gradually replace American troops in combat operations and American troops would simultaneously be withdrawn; (3) the American withdrawal must not bear the slightest taint of defeat; (4) there must be no coalition government with the Vietcong* in the South; (5) all prisoners of war* (POWs) would have to be returned; and (6) the withdrawal of all North Vietnamese troops from South Vietnam would have to be carried out before the United States would terminate its support of the Republic of Vietnam.*

In the ongoing peace talks in Paris* as well as the secret diplomacy of Henry Kissinger, the North Vietnamese refused to cooperate, insisting on an unconditional withdrawal of all American troops and creation of a coalition government, without Nguyen Van Thieu, in South Vietnam. Nixon initiated large-scale bombing of infiltration* routes in Cambodia (see Operation Menu) and strategic targets in North Vietnam, but it had little impact on the negotiations. The pace of Vietnamization quickened. Most American combat troops were removed between 1969 and 1972, and massive amounts of military equipment were handed over to South Vietnam. In 1970 Nixon launched an "incursion" into Cambodia (see Operation Binh Tay) by American and ARVN troops (see Army of the Republic of Vietnam) to attack Vietcong and North Vietnamese sanctuaries* there, but the invasion triggered a storm of protest, as well as the tragedy at Kent State University.* In 1971 he ordered an invasion of Laos (see Lam Son 719) to sever North Vietnamese supply lines, but it too did little to stop the flow of supplies.

In March 1972, conscious of the upcoming presidential election and anxious to fulfill his promise of ending the war, Nixon was ready to make some concessions, and the North Vietnamese were equally ready to intensify their commitment to the fall of the South. They launched a massive invasion of South Vietnam, and in response Nixon unleashed massive bombing of the Democratic Republic of Vietnam.* Late in 1972 negotiations finally became serious, but only because the United States surrendered on most major points. Nixon was anxious to get an agreement before the election. He agreed to a coalition government in South Vietnam, complete withdrawal of American troops, leaving North Vietnamese troops in place, and exchanges of all prisoners of war. The treaty was concluded late in October, and Nixon won reelection in November, defeating George McGovern.* In December 1972, when North Vietnam appeared to be dragging its feet on the POW issue, Nixon ordered a new round of massive Christmas bombings (*see* Operation Linebacker II), and North Vietnam acquiesced. In March 1973, in what will surely be remembered as the high point of the Nixon administration, the American POWs came home. After that, the Watergate* quagmire gradually destroyed the Nixon presidency, forcing his resignation in August 1974.

Sources: Fawn Brodie, *Richard Nixon: The Shaping of His Character,* 1983; Henry Kissinger, *Years of Upheaval,* 1982; Theodore S. White, *Breach of Faith. The Fall of Richard Nixon,* 1976; Richard Nixon, *RN: The Memoirs of Richard Nixon,* 1978, and *No More Vietnams,* 1985.

NIXON DOCTRINE

Facing enormous political pressure because of economic problems, squeezes on the federal budget, antiwar opposition, and a new spirit of neo-isolationism, President Richard Nixon* announced the Nixon Doctrine in a talk with journalists on Guam on July 25, 1969. While maintaining the protection of Southeast Asia and Japan by the "nuclear umbrella," the United States insisted that Asian soldiers, rather than American troops, would have to carry the burden of land warfare in the future. The Nixon Doctrine would not go into effect until after American disengagement from Vietnam, and would not modify any existing U.S. commitments to the Southeast Asia Treaty Organization* or any bilateral commitments to Japan,* South Korea,* Taiwan (*see* Chiang Kai-Shek), or the Philippines.* Critics charged that the Nixon Doctrine was based on a continuation of the containment policy* and actually made the United States more dependent on its Asian allies and more vulnerable to political instability in the area. President Nixon invoked the doctrine in 1971 to justify increased American economic and military assistance to Iran.

Source: Earl C. Ravenal, "The Nixon Doctrine and Our Asian Commitments," *Foreign Affairs* 49 (1971), 201–17.

NOLTING, FREDERICK ERNEST

Born on August 24, 1911, in Richmond, Virginia, Frederick Nolting received the B.A. from the University of Virginia in 1933, an M.A. from Harvard in

1941, and a Ph.D. from the University of Virginia in 1942. After service in the navy during World War II, Nolting joined the State Department, serving in a series of minor positions until his appointment to the NATO delegation in 1955. Dwight D. Eisenhower* named him the alternate permanent representative to NATO in 1957, and then appointed him ambassador to South Vietnam in 1961. Nolting developed a close and supportive relationship with President Ngo Dinh Diem* and worked diligently to get him as much American military and economic assistance as possible. But during the Kennedy* administration, American officials gradually lost faith in Diem, doubting whether he had the inclination or the temperament to win broad support among Vietnamese peasants. Kennedy replaced Nolting with Henry Cabot Lodge, Jr.,* in 1963 after growing dissatisfied with Nolting's unwavering support of Diem and his unwillingness to clearly describe the deterioration of Diem's political position. Nolting resigned from the State Department and joined the investment firm of Morgan Guaranty Trust Company. He stayed there until 1970, when he joined the faculty of the University of Virginia to direct the White Burkett Miller Center for Public Affairs.

Sources: David Halberstam, *The Best and the Brightest*, 1972; *Who's Who in America, 1978–1979*, 1979.

NORTH VIETNAM   *See* Democratic Republic of Vietnam

NORTH VIETNAMESE ARMY

At the outset of the war in Vietnam, most American soldiers anticipated a fairly quick end to the conflict because they expected the North Vietnamese Army (NVA) to be little match for U.S. firepower. By 1975, the American military respected the NVA as one of the finest armies, man for man, in the world. In 1950, the NVA, though not yet officially named, consisted of three infantry divisions of perhaps 35,000 troops. They were commanded by Vo Nguyen Giap.* That army engaged the French and finally defeated them in 1954 at the battle of Dien Bien Phu.*

The NVA was formally organized in 1954 after the Geneva Accords.* By 1964 the NVA totaled fifteen infantry divisions armed with World War II-vintage weapons. During the next decade, supplied by the Soviet Union* and the People's Republic of China,* the NVA grew to nearly 600,000 men organized into eighteen infantry divisions. In 1968, they had used PT–76 Soviet tanks, and by 1975 they had a total of four armored regiments equipped with nearly one thousand Soviet-made T–34, T–54, T–59, and PT–76 tanks. The NVA also consisted of ten artillery regiments, twenty independent infantry regiments, twenty-four antiaircraft regiments, and fifteen SAM regiments. Despite early denials, more than half of the NVA was deployed in South Vietnam, Laos,* and Cambodia (*see* Kampuchea) in the late 1960s and early 1970s, and the other half invaded South Vietnam in 1975 for the final conquest (*see* Ho Chi Minh Campaign).

Sources: Anthony Robinson, ed., *The Weapons of the Vietnam War*, 1983; International Institute for Strategic Studies, *The Military Balance 1963–64*, 1963 and *The Military Balance 1974–75*, 1975.

NUNG

The Nung were a Sino-Tibetan minority group of more than 300,000 people living in North Vietnam. A small number, perhaps 15,000, resided in the Central Highlands* of South Vietnam. Originating in the Western Canton River area of China, the Nung migrated to Tonkin* in the nineteenth century and intermarried with Muong and Thai people. In 1955 Ngo Dinh Diem* raised three battalions of Nung soldiers to fight the Binh Xuyen* and Hoa Hao* sect. During the 1960s, the Fifth Special Forces Group* continued to train and equip the Nung tribesmen, and eventually came to consider them a superb fighting force against the Vietcong* and North Vietnamese Army.*

Sources: Alan Houghton Brokrick, *Little China: The Annamese Lands*, 1942; Shelby L. Stanton, *Vietnam Order of Battle*, 1981; Joseph Buttinger, *Vietnam: A Dragon Embattled*. Vol. 2, *Vietnam at War*, 1967.

NURSES (WOMEN) IN VIETNAM

The majority of the approximately 10,000 U.S. women* who served in Vietnam were army nurses. (These numbers are subject to debate. The Department of Defense claims there were around 7,000 women in Vietnam. Other estimates range as high as 55,000.) All army nurses were volunteers; many specified Vietnam service. They received six weeks basic training at Fort Sam Houston, Texas, and were assigned one-year stints in Vietnam hospitals and Mobile Army Surgical Hospital (MASH) units. Many of the nurses were fresh graduates from three-year nursing hospitals. Some were sent to train South Vietnamese nurses, but the majority worked with the casualties* of the war who had been helicoptered to hospitals where the emergency skills of the nurses were most needed. Many army nurses shared experiences with other veterans: the shock of the consequences of conflict in Vietnam, their problematic return to a country that did not understand their participation or experiences, high incidences of Post-Traumatic Stress Syndrome,* and denial of their work in Vietnam. Oral histories and autobiographies reveal that American nurses in Vietnam also experienced a sense of isolation from their male counterparts in Vietnam and their female counterparts back home, as well as an anger at the absence of Veterans Administration and veterans' service group support upon their return. Nurse veterans are responsible for forming a Women's Veterans project within the Vietnam Veterans of America* (VVA) to press for financial, educational, and health benefits for women veterans. Others are organizing a Vietnam Women's Memorial Project to acknowledge and honor the work of nurses in Vietnam.

Sources: Lynda Van Devanter and Christopher Morgan, *Home Before Morning*, 1983; Shelley Saywell, *Women in War*; Carol Lynn Mithers, "Missing in Action: Women Warriors in Vietnam," *Cultural Critique* (Spring 1986).

Linda Kelly Alkana

NVA *See* North Vietnamese Army

• O •

O'DANIEL, JOHN W.

Lieutenant General John W. O'Daniel was chief of the United States Army Military Assistance and Advisory Group* (MAAG), Indochina, from March 1954 to October 1955. "Iron Mike" O'Daniel was a hard-charging combat veteran of both world wars and the Korean War.

In 1953 he was commander of the U.S. Army, Pacific, when the Joint Chiefs of Staff (*see* Chairman, JCS) selected him to head a special mission to Vietnam to assess French needs for military aid. He made a second inspection trip later in 1953 before becoming chief of MAAG in 1954. His initial reports on the French effort in Indochina* were positive. After the French defeat at Dien Bien Phu,* however, he became one of the key American officials in implementing the transfer of South Vietnamese military training and support from France* to the United States. While in Vietnam, he developed a high regard for Ngo Dinh Diem* and for the potential of the South Vietnamese military. After his retirement from the U.S. Army in 1955, he became one of the founders of the American Friends of Vietnam,* a highly effective lobby for American support of the Diem government.

Source: Ronald H. Spector, *Advice and Support: The Early Years, 1941–1960*, 1983.

David L. Anderson

OFFICE OF CIVIL OPERATIONS

A forerunner of CORDS (Civil Operations and Revolutionary Development Support),* the Office of Civil Operations was established in November 1966 by Ambassador Henry Cabot Lodge, Jr.,* to pursue the goal of pacification (*see* Rural Reconstruction) in South Vietnam. At that time pacification fell under the general direction of the embassy in the Republic of Vietnam,* but when CORDS was established in May 1967, that effort passed to the control of the Military Assistance Command, Vietnam.*

Sources: Larry E. Cable, *Conflict of Myths: The Development of American Counter-insurgency Doctrine and the Vietnam War*, 1986; Andrew F. Krepinevich, Jr., *The Army and Vietnam*, 1986.

101ST AIRBORNE DIVISION (AIRMOBILE)

From the very beginning of the conflict to the end of American combat operations in Vietnam, the 101st Airborne Division (Airmobile) was one of the elite U.S. military units. The 1st Brigade of the 101st arrived in Vietnam on July 29, 1965, and fought in the II Corps* Tactical Zone. In 1966 the brigade fought in Phu Yen and Kontum provinces. The 1st Brigade became part of Task Force Oregon (*see* 23rd Infantry Division), along with the 3rd Brigade of the 25th Infantry Division* and the 196th Light Infantry Brigade,* to fight in Quang Ngai and Quang Tin provinces and allow the United States Marines* to move north closer to the Demilitarized Zone.* On November 18, 1967, the 1st Brigade rejoined the 101st Airborne Division.

The 101st Airborne Division deployed to Vietnam on November 19, 1967. Known as the "Screaming Eagles," the 101st had an illustrious history, especially at the Battle of the Bulge in World War II. By 1967 the division was completing its transition from parachutist to airmobile tactics. At first committed to III Corps,* the 101st was moved to Hue* during the Tet Offensive,* and in April and May 1968 the unit ranged widely throughout Thua Thien and Quang Tri provinces. In mid–1968, the 3rd Brigade fought around Dak To* and then joined the 25th Infantry Division in defense of Saigon.* It was redeployed to I Corps* in September 1968. The 101st participated in Operation Texas Star* throughout 1970, and in 1971 joined ARVN (*see* Army of the Republic of Vietnam) in Operation Jefferson Glenn,* the last American offensive action of the war. Later in 1971 the 101st supported ARVN in Lam Son 719*—the ill-fated invasion of Laos.* The 101st Airborne Division left Vietnam on March 10, 1972.

Sources: Shelby L. Stanton, *Vietnam Order of Battle*, 1981, and *The Rise and Fall of an American Army: U.S. Ground Troops in Vietnam, 1965–1973*, 1985; Willard Pearson, *The War in the Northern Provinces, 1966–1968*, 1975; John J. Tolson, *Airmobility, 1961–1971*, 1973.

199TH LIGHT INFANTRY BRIGADE

The 199th Light Infantry Brigade was formed at Fort Benning, Georgia, in 1966, and arrived in South Vietnam that December. The brigade assumed responsibility for Operation Fairfax,* defending the approaches to Saigon,* until late 1967. In December 1967, the brigade undertook Operation Uniontown,* a sweep into War Zone D (*see* Iron Triangle) near Bien Hoa.* During the Tet Offensive* the brigade defended Bien Hoa airfield together with the Long Binh* post complex and the headquarters of II Field Force Vietnam.* However, elements of the brigade were used to recapture the Pho Tho racetrack in Saigon and, together with other American and South Vietnamese troops, held the area during two days of house-to-house fighting. During most of 1968, the 199th

Light Infantry Brigade continued to patrol the area around Bien Hoa in support of a series of joint American-Vietnamese operations known as Operation Toan Thang* (or "Total Victory"). The brigade also supported the invasion of Cambodia (*see* Operation Binh Tay) in May 1970. The 199th Light Infantry Brigade was withdrawn from South Vietnam in the fall of 1970 and was deactivated at Fort Benning in October. The 199th sustained more than 3,200 casualties during its stay in South Vietnam.

Sources: Shelby L. Stanton, *Vietnam Order of Battle*, 1981, and *The Rise and Fall of an American Army: U.S. Ground Forces in Vietnam, 1965–1973*, 1985.

Robert S. Browning III

196TH LIGHT INFANTRY BRIGADE

Raised at Fort Devens, Massachusetts, in 1965, the 196th Light Infantry Brigade arrived in South Vietnam in August 1966. The brigade's first major combat came during Operation Attleboro* in October and November 1966. In the spring of 1967 the brigade was assigned to a divisional task force in the I Corps* Tactical Zone named Task Force Oregon (*see* 23rd Infantry Division). Task Force Oregon became the Americal Division (*see* 23rd Infantry Division) in September 1967. When the Americal Division was withdrawn from South Vietnam in 1971, the 196th Light Infantry Brigade was reconstituted as a separate provisional brigade. This provisional brigade was withdrawn from South Vietnam in June 1972. It was the last American combat brigade to leave the country. The 196th Light Infantry Brigade participated in the following operations and battles: Attleboro, Cedar Falls,* Junction City,* Malheur,* Hill 63 (1967), Nhi Ha (1968), Tien Phuoc (1969), and Frederick Hill. During its tour in South Vietnam, the 196th Light Infantry sustained nearly 7,000 casualties.

Sources: Shelby L. Stanton, *Vietnam Order of Battle*, 1981, and *The Rise and Fall of an American Army: U.S. Ground Forces in Vietnam, 1965–1973*, 1985.

Robert S. Browning III

173RD AIRBORNE BRIGADE

The 173rd Airborne, formed in 1963 and stationed in Okinawa as the Pacific's ready-action strike force, was the first major United States Army* combat unit in Vietnam. The brigade arrived in country on May 7, 1965. It was supposed to serve in South Vietnam only temporarily until a brigade of the 101st Airborne* could be deployed from the United States, but that was changed by the brigade's completion of early combat operations. Aside from periodic duty in III Corps,* the 173rd operated primarily in northern II Corps.* The 2nd Battalion of the 173rd conducted the only major U.S. airborne assault of the war in III Corps in 1967 during Operation Junction City.* Unlike most infantry brigades, which have three battalions, the 173rd had only two. Occasionally it was augmented with a "round out" battalion such as the 1st Battalion of the Royal Australian Regiment. In 1969 the brigade's battalions were mated with the 22nd and 24th

ARVN (*see* Army of the Republic of Vietnam) Infantry divisions for joint operations.

The 173rd was affectionately known as "Sky Soldiers" and as "The Herd" or "Two Shades of Soul" because of its comaraderie and excellent relations between black and white troops. It won a Presidential Unit Citation in 1967 for taking infamous Hill 875 from the North Vietnamese Army* on Thanksgiving Day in 1967 just outside of Dak To.* Establishing itself quickly as a battle-seasoned unit with aggressive leadership, the 173rd took great pride in its abilities. It participated in many operations, including Marauder, Crimp, Attleboro,* Hawthorne,* Cedar Falls,* Junction City, Greeley, and MacArthur.* It also paid for its aggressiveness. The 173rd Airborne Brigade sustained more casualties in its seven years in Vietnam than did the entire divisions of either the 82nd* or 101st Airborne during World War II. The 173rd Airborne Brigade left Vietnam on August 25, 1971.

Sources: Shelby L. Stanton, *Vietnam Order of Battle*, 1981, and *The Rise and Fall of an American Army: U.S. Ground Troops in Vietnam, 1965–1973*, 1985; Harry G. Summers, Jr., *Vietnam War Almanac*, 1985.

Samuel Freeman

ONE TO COUNT CADENCE

One to Count Cadence is the title of James Crumley's 1969 Vietnam War novel. The story centers on a ten-man communications detachment stationed first at Clark Air Base in the Philippines* and then in Vietnam during the early stages of the war. A Sergeant "Slag" Krummel is the narrator, and his foil is Joe Morning, a classic, self-destructive loser. The novel exposes the gratuitous violence of military life—bars, brothels, fights, and profanity—as well as the futility of the war in Vietnam. The novel concludes with the communications team, decimated by combat in Vietnam, returning to the Philippines, where Morning joins the Huk rebellion.

Sources: James Crumley, *One to Count Cadence*, 1969; Philip D. Beidler, *American Literature and the Experience of Vietnam*, 1982.

ONE VERY HOT DAY

One Very Hot Day is the title of David Halberstam's* 1967 Vietnam War novel. Written at an early stage of American involvement in the escalated war, *One Very Hot Day* traces three characters—the American captain Beaupre, the Vietnamese lieutenant Thuong, and the black American Ranger captain Redfern—on one day in the hot, wet, sticky, despair-ridden atmosphere of the Vietnam War. When one of Beaupre's men, a Lieutenant Anderson, dies in an ambush, Beaupre is unable to find any reason for the death, any meaning to a dead American in some nowhere-place called Ap Than Thoi. A likable young American soldier had died for nothing on a hot day in nowhere. Such is the theme of *One Very Hot Day*.

Sources: Philip D. Beidler, *American Literature and the Experience of Vietnam*, 1982; David Halberstam, *One Very Hot Day*, 1967.

OPERATION ABILENE

Operation Abilene was a sweep of Phuoc Tuy Province mounted by elements of the 1st Infantry Division* in April 1966. Such sweeps were intended to put pressure on the Vietcong* and demonstrate the United States army's* willingness to take the offensive into the jungle.

Source: Shelby L. Stanton, *Rise and Fall of an American Army: U.S. Ground Forces in Vietnam, 1965–1973*, 1985.

Robert S. Browning III

OPERATION ALA MOANA

Operation Ala Moana was the codename for the combat operations of the 25th Infantry Division* in December 1966. General William Westmoreland* wanted to keep the Vietcong* away from major rice-producing areas near Saigon* and in the Ho Bo Woods in III Corps.* Operation Ala Moana was launched on December 1, 1966, and continued into 1967, although most of the combat action shifted then to Hau Nghia Province. Operation Ala Moana was a preliminary to Operation Cedar Falls.*

Source: Shelby L. Stanton, *The Rise and Fall of an American Army: U.S. Ground Troops in Vietnam, 1965–1973*, 1985.

OPERATION APACHE SNOW

Operation Apache Snow was the codename for the combat activities of the 9th Marine Regiment and elements of the 101st Airborne (Airmobile) Division* in Thua Thien Province of I Corps* between May 10 and June 7, 1969. The most important and controversial phase of Operation Apache Snow was the Battle of Ap Bia, or Hamburger Hill.

Source: Shelby L. Stanton, *The Rise and Fall of an American Army: U.S. Ground Troops in Vietnam, 1965–1973*, 1985.

OPERATION ATLAS WEDGE

Operation Atlas Wedge was the codename for the engagement between Colonel George S. Patton's 11th Armored Cavalry* and elements of the North Vietnamese Army* (NVA) 7th Division in the abandoned Michelin rubber plantation near Saigon* between March 17 and 26, 1969. The 11th Armored Cavalry destroyed huge bunkers in the area and fought intense battles with the North Vietnamese before the NVA withdrawal.

Source: Shelby L. Stanton, *The Rise and Fall of an American Army: U.S. Ground Troops in Vietnam, 1965–1973*, 1985.

OPERATION ATTLEBORO

Operation Attleboro, conducted in War Zone C* between September 14 and November 24, 1966, was the first field test of the army's doctrine of "search and destroy."* Initiated by the 196th Light Infantry Brigade,* Operation Attleboro had the objective of discovering the location(s) of the Vietcong,* or North Vietnamese base areas, and forcing the enemy to fight. There was no important contact in this operation until October 19, when the brigade discovered a major base area and severe fighting erupted. By November 6, the American units involved included (in addition to the 196th Light Infantry Brigade) the 1st and 2nd battalions of the 27th Infantry Regiment (25th Infantry Division),* the 173rd Airborne Brigade,* and two brigades of the 1st Infantry Division.* By November 15, the 9th Vietcong Division was able to successfully disengage. The United States Army* reported 1,106 enemy casualties.

Sources: Shelby L. Stanton, *The Rise and Fall of an American Army: U.S. Ground Forces in Vietnam, 1965–1973*, 1985; S. L. A. Marshall, *Ambush: The Battle of Dau Tieng, Also Called The Battle of Dong Ming Chau, War Zone C, Operation Attleboro, and Other Deadfalls in South Vietnam*, 1969.

Robert S. Browning III

OPERATION BABYLIFT

With the imminent takeover of South Vietnam by Communist forces in 1975, President Gerald R. Ford,* announced that the United States would evacuate some 2,000 Vietnamese orphans to the United States. At a press conference in San Diego, California, on April 3, 1975, he commented: "I have directed . . . that C–5A aircraft and other aircraft especially equipped to care for these orphans during the flight be sent to Saigon. I expect these flights to begin within the next 36 to 48 hours. These orphans will be flown to Travis Air Force Base in California, and other bases on the West Coast, and cared for in those locations."

Hours after the presidential statement, the dramatic humanitarian airlift, named Operation Babylift, began. On April 4, 1975, the first Babylift aircraft, a Military Airlift Command* C–5 en route from Clark Air Base, the Philippines,* landed at Tan Son Nhut Air Base* in Saigon*; unloaded its military cargo; and was on its way back to the Philippines with 314 persons onboard. Unfortunately, what started out as a routine flight ended in tragedy when the aircraft crashed approximately fourteen minutes after takeoff. Of the 314 aboard, 138 were killed. It was a tragic beginning that fortunately was not repeated in other flights.

Although Babylift got off to a bad start, the operation gathered momentum thereafter and was conducted without further mishap. By noon the next day, five C–141s* and other aircraft had moved 141 orphans and 137 evacuees and escorts from Saigon to Clark Air Base. During subsequent days the flow of aircraft to and from Saigon continued at a steady pace as Vietnamese refugees* were transported to homes in the United States. Between April 5 and May 9, 1975, Operation Babylift aircraft evacuated 2,678 Vietnamese and Cambodian orphans to the homes of sponsors in the United States.

Sources: "Global Humanitarian Airlift," Military Airlift Command Fact Sheet, February 1983; Dick J. Burkard, *Military Airlift Command: Historical Handbook, 1941–1984*, 1984.

Roger D. Launius

OPERATION BARREL ROLL

Operation Barrel Roll was the codename given to American air operations over northern Laos* from December 1964 to February 1973. The aircraft involved included both U.S. Navy* and Air Force* fighters,* as well as air force bombers (including B–52s*) and fixed-wing gunships.* For political reasons, the American government did not inform the public of these operations until American aircraft were lost, at which time it was announced that the Americans were flying escort missions at the request of the Royal Laotian government.

Sources: John S. Bowman, ed., *The Vietnam War: An Almanac*, 1985; P. Frank Futrell, *Aces and Aerial Victories: The United States Air Force in Southeast Asia*, 1976.

Robert S. Browning III

OPERATION BEAU CHARGER   *See* Project Nine

OPERATION BINH TAY

Operation Binh Tay was the codename for combined U.S.-ARVN (*see* Army of the Republic of Vietnam) combat activities in Cambodia (*see* Kampuchea) in 1970. On May 6, 1970, as part of the Cambodian "incursion," the 4th Infantry Division* combined with the 49th ARVN Regiment in attacking Vietcong* and North Vietnamese Army* positions in Cambodia. On May 16, 1970, the 4th Infantry Division turned Operation Binh Tay completely over to ARVN troops, who continued it until mid-June without making significant enemy contact.

Sources: Shelby L. Stanton, *The Rise and Fall of an American Army: U.S. Ground Troops in Vietnam, 1965–1973*, 1985; William Shawcross, *Sideshow: Kissinger, Nixon, and the Destruction of Cambodia*, 1979; Tom Carhart, *Battles and Campaigns in Vietnam*, 1984.

OPERATION BLUE LIGHT   *See* C–141 Starlifter

OPERATION BOLO

Operation Bolo was the codename given to the U.S. Air Force* effort to eliminate North Vietnamese MiG–21 strength. Since American aircraft were prohibited from attacking the airfields from which the MiGs operated (until April 1967), it was necessary to lure the MiGs into the air. F–4C aircraft were equipped with F–105* electronic pods in an effort to confuse North Vietnamese radar. The operation was mounted on January 2, 1967, from Ubon Air Base in Thailand.* Seven MiG–21s were shot down and the remainder temporarily withdrawn from action. No American aircraft were lost.

Source: P. Frank Futrell, *Aces and Aerial Victories: The U.S. Air Force in Southeast Asia*, 1976.

Robert S. Browning III

OPERATION BRAVO

Late in October 1963, as the political support for his regime was rapidly crumbling, Ngo Dinh Diem* hatched an elaborate plot to shore up his crumbling position. Known as Operation Bravo I and Bravo II, the plan involved staging a fake revolt in Saigon,* with Diem and his brother Ngo Dinh Nhu* fleeing to the countryside. The rebels would conduct demonstrations, orchestrate "revolutionary" broadcasts from the Saigon radio station, and even assassinate several local officials. All this, known as Bravo I, would continue for several days. Bravo II would then go into effect, with Diem and Nhu marching back into Saigon and crushing the "rebellion," proving that only they were capable of keeping the Republic of Vietnam* out of Communist hands. Although both Diem and Nhu thought the operation was underway early in November, military officials responsible for conducting Operations Bravo I and II were actually plotting, with tacit American support, a coup d'état against the regime. The coup was successful and Ngo Dinh Diem and Ngo Dinh Nhu were assassinated. Operations Bravo I and II had failed.

Sources: Stanley Karnow, *Vietnam: A History*, 1983; Denis Warner, *The Last Confucian*, 1963; Tran Van Don, *Our Endless War*, 1972.

OPERATION BUFFALO

Operation Buffalo was the codename for a brief combat action by elements of the Third Marine Division* near the Demilitarized Zone* in I Corps.* The operation lasted between July 2 and July 14, 1967, and resulted in just over 700 enemy casualties.

Sources: Shelby L. Stanton, *Vietnam Order of Battle*, 1981; Willard Pearson, *The War in the Northern Provinces, 1966–1968*, 1975.

OPERATION CEDAR FALLS

A major "search and destroy"* effort by U.S. troops in January 1967, Operation Cedar Falls, named after the hometown of an early Vietnam War recipient of the Medal of Honor (posthumously), was aimed at the Iron Triangle,* located only 20 miles northwest of the outskirts of Saigon.* A 60-square-mile area of rice paddies, dense jungle, rubber plantations, and an extremely sophisticated complex of underground tunnels, the Iron Triangle had been controlled by the Vietcong* (VC) since the late 1950s and was characterized as a "dagger pointed at the heart of Saigon." Destruction of the VC infrastructure in the Iron Triangle was the basic military objective of Cedar Falls. The fundamental plan of Cedar Falls was the "hammer-and-anvil" tactic, in which a blocking force of American troops would be landed by helicopter at one edge of the area and then a second force (the "hammer") would drive the enemy against this "anvil." In order for this tactic to work, the entire area had to first be cleared of innocent civilians so that a free fire zone could be created. In this way, *any* Vietnamese in the area would be assumed to be a Vietcong.

Operation Cedar Falls began on January 8, 1967, with the forced evacuation and total destruction of Ben Suc,* an Iron Triangle village that was a haven for VC. The next phase was saturation bombing and artillery fire, after which the infantry swept the Iron Triangle using the hammer-and-anvil tactic. The tunnel complex was a particular target, and approximately 500 tunnels, running for some 12 miles underground, were discovered and destroyed. Operation Cedar Falls lasted eighteen days and was declared a success. The VC lost 775 veteran soldiers while American losses were approximately 250. The enemy bastion was seized, and the Vietcong were eliminated from the Iron Triangle. The major allied units involved in the operation were the 1st* and 25th* Infantry divisions,* the 173rd Airborne Brigade,* the 11th Armored Cavalry,* and several ARVN units (*see* Army of the Republic of Vietnam). However, since basic strategy did not include occupation of captured territory, Allied troops did not stay in the Iron Triangle after Cedar Falls. Given the enemy's tenacity and resiliency, within six months the Vietcong had returned in strength, and the local inhabitants were more hostile and resentful of the allies; they had also become more supportive of the enemy than before the occupation. The Iron Triangle became a major staging area for the Tet Offensive* attacks on Saigon on January 31, 1968, illustrating the frustration that characterized American military successes throughout the war: to defeat the enemy thoroughly only to find him reappearing sometime after the engagement.

Sources: Jonathan Schell, *The Village of Ben Suc*, 1967; Bernard William Rogers, *Cedar Falls–Junction City: A Turning Point*, 1974.

Stafford T. Thomas

OPERATION CHAOS   *See* Central Intelligence Agency

OPERATION COMMANDO HUNT

Commando Hunt was the codename for combined U.S. Navy,* Marine,* and Air Force* air assaults on infiltration* routes along the Ho Chi Minh Trail* in the Laotian panhandle. The air strikes began in 1968 and continued until January 1973, but they had little or no effect on the volume of materiel and the number of troops brought into South Vietnam by the North Vietnamese.

Sources: Tom Carhart, *Battles and Campaigns in Vietnam*, 1984; John Morrocco, *The Vietnam Experience. Rain of Fire: Air War, 1969–1973*, 1985.

OPERATION DEFIANT STAND

Operation Defiant Stand was the codename for a combined United States Navy,* United States Marine Corps,* Korean Marines, and ARVN (*see* Army of the Republic of Vietnam) amphibious assault on Barrier Island south of Da

Nang.* Vietcong* responded with only light resistance when the landing force swept through the island on September 7, 1969.

Source: Shelby L. Stanton, *The Rise and Fall of an American Army: U.S. Ground Troops in Vietnam, 1965–1973*, 1985.

OPERATION DELAWARE

Operation Delaware was the codename for a combined United States Army*–ARVN (*see* Army of the Republic of Vietnam) combat operation in the A Shau Valley.* The ARVN portion of the operation was dubbed Operation Lam Son 216. Elements of the 1st Cavalry Division (Airmobile),* 101st Airborne Division (Airmobile),* the 196th Light Infantry Brigade,* the ARVN 1st Division, and the ARVN Airborne Task Force Bravo participated in the operation, which took place between April 19 and May 17, 1968. Although the operation resulted in nearly 900 enemy casualties, American forces sustained heavy helicopter losses and never really dealt a death blow to Vietcong* and North Vietnamese Army* forces in the A Shau Valley.

Sources: Shelby L. Stanton, *Vietnam Order of Battle*, 1981, and *The Rise and Fall of an American Army: U.S. Ground Troops in Vietnam, 1965–1973*, 1985; Willard Pearson, *The War in the Northern Provinces, 1966–1968*, 1975.

OPERATION DEWEY CANYON

Operation Dewey Canyon was the codename for the combat activities of the 9th Marine Regiment in I Corps* between January 22 and March 18, 1969. The marine objective was to cut a North Vietnamese Army* (NVA) supply route which came into Vietnam from Laos* and moved through the Da Krong Valley and the A Shau Valley.* During the course of Operation Dewey Canyon, marines flew more than 13,000 sorties* in air support of the campaign, and the 9th Marine Regiment discovered more than 500 tons of NVA weapons and ammunition, along with inflicting more than 1,335 casualties on the North Vietnamese.

Sources: Shelby L. Stanton, *Vietnam Order of Battle*, 1981, and *The Rise and Fall of an American Army: U.S. Ground Troops in Vietnam, 1965–1973*, 1985; Keith William Nolan, *Into Laos. The Story of Dewey Canyon II/Lam Son 719*, 1986.

OPERATION DOUBLE EAGLE

Operation Double Eagle was launched by United States Marines* in I Corps* on January 28, 1966. The 4th Marines and the 7th Marines, two regiments garrisoned at Chu Lai in Quang Tin Province, joined with the 2nd ARVN Division (*see* Army of the Republic of Vietnam) to drive south into Quang Ngai Province, where they hoped to trap a large contingent of Vietcong*–North Vietnamese Army* (NVA) troops between them and the U.S. Army 1st Cavalry Division* and 22nd ARVN Division's operations in Binh Dinh Province. The marines made an amphibious assault at Thach Tru, a coastal point approximately 20 miles south of Quang Ngai, and then drove inland. For the next five weeks, the marines searched in vain for significant Vietcong–VNA contacts, encountering little more than occasional sniper fire. Early in March, the marines called off Operation Double Eagle.

Sources: Shelby L. Stanton, *The Rise and Fall of an American Army: U.S. Ground Troops in Vietnam, 1965–1973*, 1985; Willard Pearson, *The War in the Northern Provinces, 1966–1968*, 1975; Jack Shulimson, *U.S. Marines in Vietnam: An Expanding War 1966*, 1982.

OPERATION EAGLE PULL

Eagle Pull was the codename for the U.S. effort to evacuate American diplomatic and military officials from Cambodia (*see* Kampuchea) in 1975. With the Khmer Rouge* surrounding and invading Phnom Penh, the capital city of Cambodia, naval helicopters from the Seventh Fleet,* leaving their ships in the South China Sea, landed on the embassy grounds and removed 276 people, most of them Cambodian and American embassy employees and their families.

Sources: Arnold R. Isaacs, *Without Honor: Defeat in Vietnam and Cambodia*, 1983; William Shawcross, *Sideshow: Kissinger, Nixon, and the Destruction of Cambodia*, 1979.

OPERATION EL PASO

Operation El Paso was the codename for combat activities of the U.S. 1st Infantry Division* and the ARVN (*see* Army of the Republic of Vietnam) 5th Infantry Division in Binh Long Province of III Corps.* Early in May 1966, American intelligence officers received news of an impending attack by the Vietcong* (VC) 9th Division on the Special Forces* base at Loc Ninh. Operation El Paso I was designed to locate the VC 9th Division, but it was largely a fruitless endeavor. So on June 2, 1966, the 1st Division went deep into War Zone C* in search of the Vietcong. By that time Military Assistance Command, Vietnam* (MACV) hoped the operation would prevent the Vietcong from offensive operations during the monsoon season. Operation El Paso II ended on July 13, 1966, by which time MACV claimed to have killed 855 Vietcong.

Source: Shelby L. Stanton, *The Rise and Fall of an American Army: U.S. Ground Troops in Vietnam, 1965–1973*, 1985.

OPERATION ENHANCE PLUS

Operation Enhance Plus was the codename for a crash program late in 1972 to transfer huge volumes of military equipment to the South Vietnamese. In October 1972, when it became apparent that a negotiated settlement with the Vietcong* and North Vietnamese was possible, Secretary of State Henry Kissinger* had the Pentagon launch Operation Enhance Plus, a six-week program to deliver $2 billion in military equipment, as well as control over American military bases in South Vietnam, to the government of Nguyen Van Thieu.* Kissinger also asked Thieu to take military control of as much territory in South Vietnam as possible, all of this based on the premise that U.S. military influence there would shortly be discontinued. Operation Enhance Plus supervised the equipment transfer. By the end of 1972, with goods shipped in from the United

States, Taiwan (see Chiang Kai-shek), South Korea,* and the Philippines,* South Vietnam had acquired one of the largest aircraft and naval armadas in the world.

Sources: Stanley Karnow, *Vietnam: A History*, 1983; Nguyen Duy Hinh, *Vietnamization and the Cease-Fire*, 1980; Henry Kissinger, *Years of Upheaval*, 1982.

OPERATION ENTERPRISE

Operation Enterprise was the codename for combined U.S.-ARVN (see Army of the Republic of Vietnam) military activities in Long An Province in 1967 and 1968. Launched on February 13, 1967, Operation Enterprise was designed to clear the Vietcong* (VC) out of Long An Province. The 9th Infantry Division,* several ARVN elements, and groups of Regional Forces* and Popular Forces* participated in the operation. The operation continued until March 11, 1968, and although Military Assistance Command, Vietnam* claimed more than 2,000 VC casualties, the campaign had not achieved its objective of clearing the VC out of Long An Province. They remained popular in provincial villages and retained a powerful presence throughout the area, even after the losses the Tet Offensive* had brought to them.

Sources: Shelby L. Stanton, *Vietnam Order of Battle*, 1981, and *The Rise and Fall of an American Army: U.S. Ground Troops in Vietnam, 1965–1973*, 1985.

OPERATION FAIRFAX

Operation Fairfax was the codename given to combined United States Army* and ARVN (see Army of the Republic of Vietnam) combat operations outside Saigon* in 1967. It was an early experiment in Vietnamization* in which ARVN forces were supposed to gradually assume responsibility for the campaign. The 199th Light Infantry Brigade* joined with the 5th ARVN Ranger Group, and both groups patrolled the region surrounding Saigon. The main objective of Operation Fairfax was to enable the South Vietnamese to assume responsibility for defending Saigon. The operation began in January 1967, and by November ARVN troops had assumed primary responsibility for the combat patrols. The Tet Offensive* in January 1968 demonstrated clearly that ARVN troops had not achieved the capability of defending the country's capital city against Vietcong* attack.

Source: Shelby L. Stanton, *The Rise and Fall of an American Army: U.S. Ground Troops in Vietnam, 1965–1973*, 1985.

OPERATION FARMGATE

In April 1961, the United States Air Force* created the 4400th Combat Crew Training Squadron, also called "Jungle Jim," and stationed it at Elgin Air Force Base in Florida. In October 1961, half of the 4400th Combat Squadron received a new codename—Farmgate—and were deployed to an old French air base at Bien Hoa, just 15 miles northeast of Saigon.* Farmgate trained Vietnamese pilots to fly A–1H Skyraiders,* dropped propaganda leaflets over Vietcong* territory, and supplied Vietnamese Ranger camps and Civilian Irregular Defense

Group* camps along the Laotian and Cambodian borders. At first Farmgate pilots provided only covert support to Vietnamese operations. They had to fly with Vietnamese copilots in Vietnamese aircraft.

The American pilots chafed under their restrictions, and by 1964 almost ninety of them were flying combat missions for South Vietnam. When Captain Edwin G. Shank was shot down and killed piloting a T–28 aircraft in May 1964, the press got wind of the combat operations and criticized the Department of Defense. Operation Farmgate continued after the press revelations, but Secretary of Defense Robert McNamara* strictly confined its duties to training missions.

Source: John Morrocco, *The Vietnam Experience. Thunder From Above: Air War, 1941–1968*, 1985.

OPERATION FRANCIS MARION

Operation Francis Marion was the codename for operations by the 4th Infantry Division* in the Ia Drang Valley* from April to October 1967. The 4th Infantry Division had the responsibility of patrolling the Cambodian border to prevent North Vietnamese forces from pushing into the Central Highlands.* During Operation Francis Marion, elements of the 4th Infantry Division fought in eight battles and numerous smaller skirmishes. The heaviest fighting took place in May, June, and July. On May 18, Company B of the 1st Battalion, 8th Infantry, lost twenty-nine killed and thirty-one wounded in an ambush; and over a two-day period from May 20 to 22, the 1st Battalion, 8th Infantry, and the 3rd Battalion, 12th Infantry, were subjected to a series of fierce assaults by North Vietnamese regulars. In October 1967, Operation Francis Marion was incorporated into Operation Greeley, and the two operations were renamed Operation MacArthur.*

Source: Shelby L. Stanton, *The Rise and Fall of an American Army: U.S. Ground Forces in Vietnam, 1965–1973*, 1985.

Robert S. Browning III

OPERATION FREEDOM DEAL   *See* Operation Menu

OPERATION FREQUENT WIND

Operation Frequent Wind was the codename for the United States Navy's* evacuation of American personnel and Vietnamese civilians from Saigon* in April 1975. The U.S. aircraft carriers *Enterprise* and *Coral Sea* supplied the necessary air cover, and Operation Frequent Wind commenced in the morning of April 29, 1975. The two primary evacuation locations were Tan Son Nhut Air Base* and the U.S. embassy in Saigon. More than 7,100 American and South Vietnamese military and civilian personnel were helicoptered out of Saigon to ships of Task Force 76 of the Seventh Fleet.* The Military Sealift Command* and ships of the South Vietnamese Navy,* along with hundreds of sampans and junks, also ferried thousands of Vietnamese civilians and military personnel out of South Vietnam. When Operation Frequent Wind was over, more than 80,000

people had been evacuated from South Vietnam and taken to the Philippines*
and Guam.

Sources: Thomas G. Tobin, et al, *Last Flight from Saigon*, 1978; Edward J. Marolda
and G. Wesley Pryce III, *A Short History of the United States Navy and the Southeast
Asian Conflict, 1950–1975*, 1984.

OPERATION GAME WARDEN

Launched in December 1965, Operation Game Warden was the codename of
the United States Navy* program to patrol approximately three thousand miles
of rivers and canals in South Vietnam, especially in the Mekong Delta,* in order
to prevent the Vietcong* and North Vietnamese from moving personnel and
materiel along the inland waterways. Task Force 116 of the United States Navy,
also known as the Riverine Assault Force (*see* Mobile Riverine Force), conducted
the operation. The task force used air-cushion vehicles,* helicopters, minesweepers, fiberglass boats, and LST landing ships to attack the Vietcong and
North Vietnamese on the rivers and streams of South Vietnam.

Sources: William B. Fulton, *Riverine Operations, 1966–1969*, 1973; Victor Croizat,
*The Brown Water Navy: The River and Coastal War in Indochina and Vietnam, 1948–
1972*, 1984.

OPERATION GREELEY   *See* Operation MacArthur

OPERATION HARVEST MOON

Operation Harvest Moon was the codename for a joint United States Marine*
and ARVN (*see* Army for the Republic of Vietnam) operation intended to trap
the Vietcong* in the Phuoc Ha Valley in December 1965. The operation began
on December 8 when the 11th ARVN Ranger Battalion and the 1st Battalion of
the 5th ARVN Regiment were ambushed and overrun by the Vietcong. A marine
counterattack began on December 9, encountering fierce resistance and forcing
the deployment of eventually three marine battalions. On December 12–14, B–
52* strikes were made in support of the ground effort, and follow-up ground
forces encountered little immediate resistance, although the 2nd Battalion of the
7th Marines was ambushed on December 18 and suffered heavy casualties before
a combination of artillery and close air support forced the Vietcong to disengage.

Sources: Shelby Stanton, *The Rise and Fall of an American Army: U.S. Ground Troops
in Vietnam, 1965–1973*, 1985; Jack Shulimson and Charles M. Johnson, *U.S. Marines
in Vietnam: The Landing and the Buildup 1965*, 1978.

Robert S. Browning

OPERATION HASTINGS

Operation Hastings was the codename for a gruelling battle between a joint
U.S. Marine*–South Vietnamese force and the 324B North Vietnamese regular
division in July 1966. Six marine battalions and five ARVN battalions (*see* Army
of the Republic of Vietnam) were ultimately committed to the struggle, which

began on July 7. The most intensive fighting took place on July 28 in the Song Ngan Valley, which the marines had nicknamed "Helicopter Valley"* after a number of helicopters were either shot down or crashed there. Operation Hastings was a typical marine operation of 1966, in which the marines attempted to defend the I Corps* Tactical Zone by attacking any large-scale enemy troop concentration they discovered, using helicopter mobility to bring in large numbers of troops quickly. Although some of the marine encounters are labeled as distinct operations, the fighting was more or less continuous. Operation Hastings officially ended on August 3, but was immediately succeeded by Operation Prairie.*

Sources: Shelby L. Stanton, *The Rise and Fall of an American Army: U.S. Ground Forces in Vietnam, 1965–1973*, 1985; Willard Pearson, *The War in the Northern Provinces, 1966–1968*, 1975; S. L. A. Marshall, *Battles in the Monsoon: Campaigning in the Central Highlands, South Vietnam, Summer 1966*, 1966.

Robert S. Browning III

OPERATION HAWTHORNE

Operation Hawthorne was the codename for combat activities of the 1st Brigade of the 101st Airborne Division* in Kontum Province during June 1966. Designed to rescue the Tou Morong Regional Force, which was surrounded by the 24th NVA Regiment (*see* North Vietnamese Army), Operation Hawthorne was launched on June 2, 1966, and concluded on June 20, 1966. Along with the 1st Battalion of the 42nd ARVN Regiment and the 21st ARVN Ranger Battalion (*see* Army of the Republic of Vietnam), the 1st Brigade succeeded in reaching the outpost and withdrawing the isolated troops. More than 460 air strikes, including 36 B–52* sorties,* were called in on NVA troops. On June 20, 1966, the NVA 24th Regiment withdrew from the area, having sustained approximately 530 casualties.

Sources: Shelby L. Stanton, *Vietnam Order of Battle*, 1981, and *The Rise and Fall of an American Army: U.S. Ground Troops in Vietnam, 1965–1973*, 1985; S. L. A. Marshall, *Battles in the Monsoon: Campaigning in the Central Highlands, South Vietnam, Summer 1966*, 1966.

OPERATION HICKORY   *See* Project Practice Nine

OPERATION HOMECOMING

On January 27, 1973, Henry Kissinger,* assistant to the president for national security affairs, concluded a cease-fire with representatives of North Vietnam which provided for the withdrawal of American military forces from South Vietnam. Part of the agreement also provided for the release of nearly 600 American prisoners of war* (POWs) held by North Vietnam and its allies. This gave rise to Operation Homecoming, the return of POWs from Southeast Asia to their homes in the United States. The operation was divided into three phases. First, there was to be the initial reception of prisoners at three release sites: prisoners held by the Vietcong* were to be flown by helicopter to Saigon*; those held in North Vietnam were to be released at Hanoi*; and three POWs in China were to be freed in Hong Kong. All groups were to be flown to Clark Air Base, the Philippines.* Second, at Clark Air Base these individuals were to be processed through a reception center, debriefed, and examined by physicians. Third, the former POWs were to be flown to military hospitals for recovery. Beginning on February 12, 1973, the first of these POWs were released at Hanoi and the last were turned over to American officials on March 29. In all, 591 POWs were released.

Source: Carl Berger, "American POWs and Operation Homecoming," in Carl Berger, ed., *The United States Air Force in Southeast Asia, 1961–1973: An Illustrated Account*, 1984.

Roger D. Launius

OPERATION IRVING

Operation Irving was the codename for the 1st Cavalry (Airmobile) Division's* activities in Binh Dinh Province of II Corps* between October 2 and October 24, 1966. Charged with clearing Vietcong* and North Vietnamese Army* elements out of the Phu Cat Mountain area, Operation Irving combined the 1st Cavalry with Republic of Korea* troops. When the operation was concluded on October 24, Military Assistance Command, Vietnam* claimed that Irving had inflicted 681 casualties on the enemy.

Sources: Shelby L. Stanton, *Vietnam Order of Battle*, 1981, and *The Rise and Fall of an American Army: U.S. Ground Troops in Vietnam, 1965–1973*, 1985; Kenneth D. Mertel, *Year of the Horse—Vietnam: First Air Cavalry in the Highlands*, 1968.

OPERATION JEFFERSON GLENN

Launched on September 5, 1970, and continuing until October 8, 1971, Operation Jefferson Glenn was the codename for the combined activities of the 101st Airborne Division* and the ARVN 1st Infantry Division (*see* Army of the Republic of Vietnam) in Thua Thien Province. During the 399 days of the operation, Allied forces established several fire bases in the coastal lowlands of Thua Thien Province and fought against regular North Vietnamese Army* troops. Gradually the 101st Airborne disengaged and turned the fighting over to ARVN troops. The North Vietnamese and Vietcong* sustained more than 2,000 casualties before the operation was terminated. Operation Jefferson Glenn was the last major U.S. ground combat operation in the Vietnam War.

Sources: Shelby L. Stanton, *Vietnam Order of Battle*, 1981, and *The Rise and Fall of an American Army: U.S. Ground Troops in Vietnam, 1965–1973*, 1985.

OPERATION JUNCTION CITY

Operation Junction City was the codename for the 1967 combined United States Army*–ARVN (*see* Army of the Republic of Vietnam) search and destroy* campaign in War Zone C* of Tay Ninh Province. At its time, Junction City was the largest military operation of the war, involving twenty-two American and

ARVN battalions—elements of the 1st,* 4th,* and 25th* Infantry divisions,* 196th Light Infantry Brigade,* 11th Armored Cavalry,* and the 173rd Airborne Brigade.* Military Assistance Command, Vietnam* launched Operation Junction City on February 22, 1967, one month after the conclusion of Operation Cedar Falls.* Junction City continued until May 14, 1967. It was successful in attacking Vietcong* (VC) strongholds in War Zone C. By the end of the operation, the VC had taken nearly 3,000 casualties. But instead of making the VC vulnerable by eliminating their secure areas in War Zone C, Junction City had different results. The VC 9th Division simply withdrew from War Zone C and moved across the Cambodian border (*see* Kampuchea) where they could regroup and be resupplied. That added a new strategic dimension to the war. The question of how to deal with the Cambodian sanctuary* preoccupied American policy-makers throughout the war.

Sources: Shelby L. Stanton, *Vietnam Order of Battle*, 1981, and *The Rise and Fall of an American Army: U.S. Ground Troops in Vietnam, 1965–1973*, 1985; Bernard William Rogers, *Cedar Falls–Junction City: A Turning Point*, 1974.

OPERATION KEYSTONE   *See* C–141 Starlifter

OPERATION KINGFISHER

Operation Kingfisher was the codename for a three-month operation by the Third Marine Division* in the I Corps* Tactical Zone beginning in July 1967. This operation was one of a number of marine operations that summer designed to interrupt North Vietnamese Army* infiltration* of the Demilitarized Zone* and to support efforts to build a manned and electronic barrier across South Vietnam which was expected to prevent, or reduce in effectiveness, any large-scale movement of enemy troops. This barrier project was initially codenamed Project Practice Nine,* was renamed Project Illinois City in June 1967, and was finally entitled Project Dye Marker a month later. The cost of Operation Kingfisher was 340 U.S. Marines killed and 3,086 wounded.

Sources: Allan R. Millett, *Semper Fidelis: The History of the United States Marine Corps*, 1980; Shelby L. Stanton, *The Rise and Fall of an American Army: U.S. Ground Forces in Vietnam, 1965–1973*, 1985.

Robert S. Browning III

OPERATION LEXINGTON III

Operation Lexington III was the codename for battles of the 1st Battalion of the 18th Infantry in the Rung Sat* Special Zone between April 17, 1966, and June 9, 1966. Although Operation Lexington III resulted in the destruction of large numbers of Vietcong* sampans, movement in the waist-deep mangrove swamps prevented large-scale engagement of ground troops. The onset of the summer monsoons brought Operation Lexington III to an end.

Source: Shelby L. Stanton, *The Rise and Fall of an American Army: Ground Troops in Vietnam, 1965–1973*, 1985.

OPERATION LINEBACKER I

On Good Friday, March 30, 1972, three North Vietnamese Army* (NVA) divisions crossed the Demilitarized Zone* (DMZ) and invaded the Republic of Vietnam.* Before the Easter weekend was over, 120,000 NVA regulars with 200 armored vehicles were in South Vietnam. Launched to strengthen Hanoi's negotiating position at Paris, the invasion prompted the second major bombing* campaign over North Vietnam by the United States. Named Linebacker I, the operation continued nearly nine months and involved nearly all United States Air Force* assets in the theater. B–52* Arc Light* bombing missions against infiltration* routes and staging areas increased, and B–52 forces already in the theater were strengthened by additional aircraft deployments to Guam. At the same time tactical air power forces were also reinforced. Over the next few weeks U.S. Marine* air squadrons deployed to several staging bases; Navy* carrier support doubled; and Air Force tactical air units rejoined the war from Korea* and the United States. The major priority of returning tactical air units was to support South Vietnamese forces directly so that the ground battle in South Vietnam could be stabilized.

On April 2, 1972, President Richard Nixon* authorized air strikes against military targets and logistic supply points north of the DMZ to the parallel at 17°25'; this was increased to 18°N on April 4 and to 19°N on April 6. On April 9, fifteen B–52s struck railroad and supply depots at Vinh, the first use of B–52s in North Vietnam since October 28, 1968. Three days later, eighteen B–52s struck Bai Thuong airfield. On the weekend of April 15–16, navy and air force aircraft bombed military storage areas surrounding Hanoi* and Haiphong.

As with most military operations, these attacks had several purposes. They disrupted the flow of war supplies supporting the invasion of South Vietnam; warned Hanoi that if it persisted in the invasion, it would face mounting raids in the north; and demonstrated continuing American support for the government of South Vietnam. Furthermore, these attacks were intended to persuade the North Vietnamese to seek a political rather than a purely military resolution of the conflict.

When the initial Linebacker I bombing operations brought further North Vietnamese intransigence, President Nixon announced that the North Vietnamese ports of Haiphong, Cam Pha, Hon Gai, and Thanh Hoa, as well as smaller inlets harboring North Vietnamese patrol boats, would be mined. The mines were laid on May 9 and activated two days later. Simultaneously, Nixon announced that Linebacker I air operations throughout North Vietnam would continue until a formal cessation of hostilities could be secured. Throughout the spring and summer of 1972, Linebacker I operations continued. In the fall North Vietnam indicated a willingness to negotiate, and on October 22, 1972, Nixon ended Linebacker I.

Sources: W. Hays Parks, "Linebacker and the Law of War," *Air University Review* 34 (January-February 1983), 2–30; Robert Frank Futrell et al., *Aces and Aerial Victories: The United States Air Force in Southeast Asia, 1965–1973*, 1976.

Roger D. Launius

OPERATION LINEBACKER II

On October 22, 1972, when it seemed the Paris peace talks* were leading to an agreement, the United States halted air operations above the twentieth parallel. This end of Operation Linebacker I* provided a breathing spell for the North Vietnamese, who quickly strengthened air defenses in Hanoi* and Haiphong. By mid-December, Hanoi had repaired rail lines to China* and adjusted its supply routing to compensate for the naval mine blockade. The restored rail lines were capable of handling 16,000 tons of supplies per day, or 2.5 times Hanoi's needs. Simultaneous with the cessation of bombing,* negotiations between North Vietnam and the United States stalled amid indications that Hanoi might renew its offensive in South Vietnam. By early December, an agreement that had appeared so near five weeks earlier was in a shambles. President Richard Nixon* then launched Operation Linebacker II, a final eleven-day bombing campaign which was one of the heaviest aerial assaults of the war. The United States Air Force* used F–105,* F–4,* F–111,* and for the first time B–52* aircraft to attack Hanoi and Haiphong. Tactical aircraft flew more than 1,000 sorties* and the B–52s about 740, most them against rail yards, power plants, communication facilities, air defense radar sites, docks and shipping facilities, petroleum stores, ammunition supply depots, air bases, and transportation facilities.

The North Vietnamese retaliated with most of their inventory of about 1,000 surface-to-air missiles (SAM)* and a heavy barrage of antiaircraft fire. The countermeasures were ineffective. Only twenty-seven aircraft were lost; however, eighteen B–52s were destroyed or badly damaged by missiles. In spite of this, the air attacks continued, and by December 28 North Vietnamese defenses had been all but obliterated. During the last two days of the campaign American aircraft flew over Hanoi and Haiphong without suffering any losses. The North Vietnamese lost eight aircraft in aerial fighting during the Linebacker II campaign, as well as suffering substantial collateral damage in the raids.

Partially as a result of Linebacker II's success, negotiations resumed with Henry Kissinger* and Le Duc Tho* in Paris on January 8, 1973. While the diplomats talked, American air attacks were restricted and confined south of the twentieth parallel. United States Air Force, Navy,* and Marine* fighters* flew about twenty sorties per day with B–52s, adding thirty-six to the daily total. On January 23, 1973, the Paris negotiators signed a nine-point cease-fire agreement effective January 28, 1973. The air power displayed in Linebacker II had played a significant role in extracting this agreement to end the war.

Sources: W. Hays Parks, "Linebacker and the Law of War," *Air University Review* 34 (January-February 1983), 2–30; Robert Frank Futrell et al., *Aces and Aerial Victories: The United States Air Force in Southeast Asia, 1965–1973,* 1976.

Roger D. Launius

OPERATION MacARTHUR

Operation MacArthur was the codename for combat operations of the 4th Infantry Division* in the western highlands of South Vietnam between October 12, 1967, and January 31, 1969. It began as Operation Greeley back in June 1967 when two paratrooper battalions of the 173rd Airborne Brigade* were airlifted into Dak To* to relieve a Special Forces* camp there. Elements of the 1st Cavalry Division,* the 42nd ARVN Regiment, and the 5th and 8th ARVN Airborne battalions (*see* Army of the Republic of Vietnam) were also engaged in the early campaign. Operation Greeley became part of Operation MacArthur in October 1967. Operation MacArthur then became the battle for Dak To in 1967. United States and ARVN forces ultimately prevailed at Dak To, driving the North Vietnamese Army* back into Laos,* but in 1968 they returned, and Operation MacArthur continued until early in 1969. When the operation ended, Military Assistance Command, Vietnam* claimed a total of 5,731 enemy casualties.

Sources: Shelby L. Stanton, *Vietnam Order of Battle,* 1981, and *The Rise and Fall of an American Army: U.S. Ground Troops in Vietnam, 1965–1973,* 1985.

OPERATION MALHEUR

Operation Malheur was the codename for two operations of Task Force Oregon (*see* 23rd Infantry Division) in the spring of 1967. To help fight Vietcong* and North Vietnamese Army* (NVA) elements in the southern reaches of I Corps,* General William Westmoreland* decided early in 1967 to bring together three separate army brigades. Dubbed Task Force Oregon, the division-sized unit consisted of the 1st Brigade of the 101st Airborne Division,* the 196th Light Infantry Brigade,* and the 3rd Brigade of the 25th Division.* Westmoreland hoped Task Force Oregon would increase security in the coastal areas, keep Route 1 open to commercial and military traffic, and relieve pressure in the northern reaches of Binh Dinh Province. Operation Malheur I, the first combat operation of the task force, was launched on May 11, 1967. It continued through July 1967 in the area of Duc Pho. Although they engaged in numerous firefights and called in repeated air strikes, they had little more success than uncovering large amounts of Vietcong and NVA food and ammunition. Operation Malheur II, launched late in July and concluded early in August 1967, was equally unsuccessful in engaging any large enemy forces. Task Force Oregon, however, did meet Westmoreland's objective of increasing security in southern I Corps and maintaining the integrity of Route 1.

Sources: Shelby L. Stanton, *The Rise and Fall of an American Army: U.S. Ground Troops in Vietnam, 1965–1973*, 1985, and *Vietnam Order of Battle*, 1981; Willard Pearson, *The War in the Northern Provinces, 1966–1968*, 1975.

OPERATION MARKET TIME

Operation Market Time was the codename for United States Navy* operations in the South China Sea to prevent the North Vietnamese from supplying the Vietcong* and North Vietnamese Army* by coastal infiltration.* Operation Market Time began on March 11, 1965, and placed a picket line of ships from the United States Navy, United States Coast Guard,* and South Vietnamese Navy* along the 1,000-mile coast of the South China Sea in South Vietnam. They regularly boarded and inspected the more than 50,000 junks operating off the coast and along the major rivers. General William Westmoreland* estimated that Operation Market Time was so successful that between 1965 and the end of 1966, the Vietcong lost the ability to resupply themselves by sea. In 1965 70 percent of their supplies came in through the South Vietnamese coast and 30 percent along the Ho Chi Minh Trail,* but by 1967 only 10 percent of their supplies were being infiltrated from the coast.

Source: Edward J. Marolda and G. Wesley Pryce III, *A Short History of the United States Navy and the Southeast Asian Conflict, 1956–1975*, 1984.

OPERATION MASHER/WHITE WING

In January 1966 Major General Harry W. O. Kinnard received orders to use his 1st Cavalry Division (Airmobile),* stationed near An Khe, to eliminate Vietcong* and North Vietnamese Army* forces from four valleys in northeastern Binh Dinh Province. The 1st Cavalry Division was assisted by the ARVN (*see* Army of the Republic of Vietnam) Airborne Brigade, the 22nd ARVN Division, and the 1st Regiment of the Republic of Korea's Capital Division.* Known as the Bong Son campaign, the mission was codenamed Operation Masher. That codename was changed to Operation White Wing on February 4, 1966. The operation lasted from late January to March 6, 1966, by which time the North Vietnamese had abandoned the region. They would return, and the United States would subsequently launch Operations Davy Crockett, Crazy Horse, Irving,* and Thayer to attack them again.

Sources: Shelby L. Stanton, *The Rise and Fall of an American Army: U.S. Ground Troops in Vietnam, 1965–1973*, 1985; Willard Pearson, *The War in the Northern Provinces, 1966–1968*, 1975; *The 1st Air Cavalry Division: Vietnam, August 1965 to December 1969*, 1970.

OPERATION MASSACHUSETTS STRIKER

Operation Massachusetts Striker was the codename for the 101st Airborne (Airmobile) Division's* activities in the A Shau Valley* between March 1 and May 8, 1969. In their sweep operations through the valley, the 101st discovered an enormous North Vietnamese Army* (NVA) logistical base, complete with ammunition dumps, underground oil depots, motor pool repair facilities, and a field hospital, all concealed in the jungles. The discovery of such a large NVA logistical investment convinced the Military Assistance Command, Vietnam* to launch a larger combat operation in the area, which led to Operation Apache Snow.*

Sources: Shelby L. Stanton, *Vietnam Order of Battle*, 1981, and *The Rise and Fall of an American Army: U.S. Ground Troops in Vietnam, 1965–1973*, 1985.

OPERATION MAYFLOWER

Operation Mayflower was the codename for a diplomatic initiative President Lyndon B. Johnson* launched on May 13, 1966, in an attempt to bring the North Vietnamese to the negotiating table. He stopped the bombing* of North Vietnam and instructed Foy Kohler, the U.S. ambassador to the Soviet Union,* to meet with the North Vietnamese delegation in Moscow and propose peace negotiations. The North Vietnamese summarily refused to even meet with Kohler, and on May 15, 1968, Johnson terminated Operation Mayflower and resumed the bombing.

Sources: Stanley Karnow, *Vietnam: A History*, 1983; *New York Times*, May 13–15, 17–19, 1966.

OPERATION MENU

On March 18, 1969, the U.S. Air Force* began Operation Menu, a series of secret, illegal B–52* bombings of National Liberation Front (NLF; *see* Vietcong) and North Vietnamese Army* (NVA) sanctuaries* in eastern Cambodia (*see* Kampuchea). It continued for fifteen months until the Cambodian invasion (May 1970), when it was renamed Operation Freedom Deal and expanded to include "targets" throughout Cambodia. Freedom Deal continued until Congress* prohibited funds for bombing Cambodia effective August 15, 1973. By their end 16,527 sorties* had been flown and 383,851 tons of bombs dropped.

General Creighton Abrams* had wanted to attack sanctuaries for some time; however, President Lyndon Johnson* repeatedly refused permission. When Richard Nixon* became president in January 1969, these requests were resubmitted with the justifications that striking sanctuaries would reduce NLF-NVA offensive capabilities and the Central Office for South Vietnam* (COSVN) (the NLF–NVA command structure) had been located and could be destroyed by either ground or air attack. After initial hesitation, Nixon approved, for reasons of his own. The bombing was to "signal" Hanoi* that Nixon was "tougher" than Johnson and to lend credence to the "mad man" image he wanted to create among North Vietnamese leaders.

"Menu" was a series of attacks (meals) against NLF-NVA Base Areas: "Breakfast"—Base Area 353, 25 square kilometers near the Fishhook,* inhabited by 1,640 Cambodians (U.S. military population estimates) and the supposed headquarters of COSVN; "Lunch"—Base Area 609, located on the Laotian-Cambodian-Vietnamese borders and inhabited by 198 Cambodians; "Snack"— Base Area 351, 101 square kilometers in the Fishhook including one town and

383 Cambodians; "Dinner"—Base Area 352, located in the Fishhook including one town and 770 Cambodians; and "Dessert"—Base Area 350, located north of the Fishhook with 120 Cambodians. The military did not recommend bombing Base Areas 354, 704, and 707 because they had substantial Cambodian populations. Nonetheless, Base Area 704 was authorized as "Supper" with 247 B–52* missions flown against it. In March 1970 Nixon authorized expanded bombing of Laos,* including B–52 raids against the Plain of Jars.

Officially, Military Assistance Command, Vietnam* claimed the Base Areas were not inhabited by Cambodian civilians, but private military reports indicated awareness of civilian presence and expectations of civilian casualties. These reports contended that although casualties should be light because the Base Areas were sparsely populated and Cambodians lived apart from the NLF-NVA, "some Cambodian casualties would be sustained . . . [and] the surprise effect of attacks would tend to increase casualties . . . [due to] probable lack of protective shelter around Cambodian homes." The number of Cambodians killed is unknown.

Nixon, very concerned that Operation Menu not become public knowledge, ordered elaborate security measures which included falsification of military records, an offense punishable by court-martial under Article 107 of *The Uniform Code of Military Justice*, so there was absolutely no record of the bombings having occurred. Nixon and Henry Kissinger's* justification was that secrecy was necessary to protect Cambodia's Prince Norodom Sihanouk,* who gave his "tacit consent." They do not provide evidence to support this proposition, and Prince Sihanouk vehemently denies he consented, tacitly or otherwise.

Sources: William Shawcross, *Sideshow: Kissinger, Nixon, and the Destruction of Cambodia*, 1979; John Morrocco, *The Vietnam Experience. Rain of Fire: Air War, 1969–1973*, 1984.

Samuel Freeman

OPERATION NEUTRALIZE

Operation Neutralize was the codename for the combined United States Air Force,* Army,* and Navy* operation to relieve the siege of Con Thien* in September and October of 1967. To relieve the Third Marine Division* at Con Thien from the assault by the North Vietnamese Army* (NVA) 325C and 324B divisions, General William Momyer,* commander of the Seventh Air Force,* developed the SLAM* approach (seek, locate, annihilate, and monitor). It involved a coordinated heavy fire support, using naval artillery bombardment, tactical air support, B–52* bombing, and artillery fire, leveled at NVA forces outside Con Thien. Operation Neutralize became the codename. Launched on September 11, 1967, Operation Neutralize lasted until October 31, 1967, during which 4,000 aircraft sorties* unloaded 40,000 tons of bombs on an area about the size of Manhattan. North Vietnamese forces could not stand the firepower, and they ended the siege of Con Thien at the end of October.

Sources: Terrence Maitland and Peter McInerney, *The Vietnam Experience: A Contagion of War*, 1983; John Morrocco, *The Vietnam Experience. Thunder From Above: Air War, 1941–1968*, 1985.

OPERATION NEVADA EAGLE

Operation Nevada Eagle was the codename for the activities of the 101st Airborne Division (Airmobile)* in Thua Thien Province of I Corps* between May 17, 1968, and February 28, 1969. During those eight and a half months of combat, often involving heavy booby-trap* casualties and search and destroy* sweeps, the 101st Airborne claimed to have inflicted 3,299 casualties on Vietcong* and North Vietnamese Army* forces.

Sources: Shelby L. Stanton, *Vietnam Order of Battle*, 1981, and *The Rise and Fall of an American Army: U.S. Ground Troops in Vietnam, 1965–1973*, 1985.

OPERATION NIAGARA

Operation Niagara was the codename for a joint U.S. Air Force,* Navy,* and Marine* air assault on Khe Sanh* between January 14 and March 31, 1968. North Vietnamese Army* (NVA) forces had put the marine base at Khe Sanh under siege, and President Lyndon B. Johnson* feared that a defeat there would resemble the French debacle at Dien Bien Phu* fourteen years earlier. Committed to maintaining the marine base at Khe Sanh, the United States launched Operation Niagara. Air force, navy, and marine pilots flew more than 5,000 tactical fighter-bomber (*see* fighters) and B–52* sorties* over Khe Sanh during the next ten weeks, unloading more than 100,000 tons of bombs on NVA forces and eventually forcing the North Vietnamese to end the siege.

Sources: Carl Berger, ed., *The United States Air Force in Southeast Asia, 1961–1973*, 1977; Rober Pisor, *The End of the Line: The Siege of Khe Sanh*, 1982; Moyers S. Shore II, *The Battle for Khe Sanh*, 1969.

OPERATION PAUL REVERE

Operation Paul Revere was the codename for four combat operations (I, II, III, and IV) of the 4th Infantry Division,* 25th Infantry Division,* and 1st Cavalry Division (Airmobile)* in Pleiku Province in 1966. Operation Paul Revere I commenced on May 19, 1966, and Operation Paul Revere IV concluded on December 30, 1966. Fighting with the North Vietnamese Army* 1st Division was conducted near the Cambodian border (*see* Kampuchea) throughout the campaigns, but American forces were unable to cross the border in pursuit of North Vietnamese forces. When the Paul Revere operations were concluded at the end of the year, the 4th and 25th Infantry divisions, along with the 1st Cavalry (Airmobile) were claiming more than 4,000 enemy casualties.

Sources: Shelby L. Stanton, *Vietnam Order of Battle*, 1981, and *The Rise and Fall of an American Army: U.S. Ground Troops in Vietnam, 1965–1973*, 1985; Willard Pearson, *The War in the Northern Provinces, 1966–1968*, 1975; Tom Carhart, *Battles and Campaigns in Vietnam*, 1984.

OPERATION PEGASUS

Operation Pegasus was the codename for the 1st Cavalry Division (Airmobile)* operation to relieve the siege of Khe Sanh* in April 1968. United States Marine* and ARVN (*see* Army of the Republic of Vietnam) units assisted in the operation.

The ARVN dimension was codenamed Operation Lam Son 207. Operation Pegasus was launched on April 1, 1968, and concluded on April 15, 1968, when the siege of Khe Sanh was over.

Sources: Shelby L. Stanton, *The Rise and Fall of an American Army: U.S. Ground Troops in Vietnam, 1965–1973*, 1985; *The 1st Air Cavalry Division: Vietnam, August 1965 to December 1969*, 1970.

OPERATION PENNSYLVANIA

Operation Pennsylvania was the codename for an unofficial but State Department–approved visit to Hanoi* by Herbert Marcovich, a French biologist, and Raymond Aubrac, a worker with the Food and Agriculture Organization. Aubrac knew Ho Chi Minh* personally and offered to visit with him in Hanoi. Henry Kissinger* knew of the visit and acted as a go-between for the State Department and Aubrac. Aubrac and Marcovich went to Hanoi in July 1967, visited with Ho Chi Minh and Pham Van Dong,* and returned expressing positive hopes for a negotiated settlement, although little came of the visit. The North Vietnamese were committed to reunification of the two countries, and were willing to negotiate if that goal was a real possibility. In 1967 it was not, at least given the diplomatic position of the United States.

Sources: Stanley Karnow, *Vietnam: A History*, 1983; Henry Kissinger, *White House Years*, 1979.

OPERATION PERSHING

Operation Pershing was the codename for the combat activities of the 1st Cavalry Division (Airmobile)* in Binh Dinh Province of II Corps.* Launched on February 11, 1967, Operation Pershing was designed to attack the Vietcong* (VC) and North Vietnamese Army* (NVA) 610th Division. Operation Pershing continued for nearly a year, inflicting more than 5,400 casualties on VC and NVA forces. The 1st Cavalry Division's activities had been so successful that when the Tet Offensive* erupted in February 1968, Binh Dinh Province was one of the quietest areas in South Vietnam.

Sources: Shelby L. Stanton, *The Rise and Fall of an American Army: U.S. Ground Troops in Vietnam, 1965–1973*, 1985; Willard Pearson, *The War in the Northern Provinces, 1966–1968*, 1975; *The 1st Air Cavalry Division: Vietnam, August 1965 to December 1969*, 1970.

OPERATION PIRANHA

Operation Piranha was the codename for a joint United States Marine* and ARVN (*see* Army of the Republic of Vietnam) amphibious-heliborne assault on Vietcong* positions on the Batangan Peninsula in September 1965. It was an attempt to repeat the success of Operation Starlite* and was marked by the destruction of a major Vietcong stronghold.

Source: Shelby L. Stanton, *The Rise and Fall of an American Army. U.S. Ground Troops in Vietnam, 1965–1973*, 1985.

Robert S. Browning III

OPERATION PRAIRIE

Operation Prairie was the codename for the combat activities of the Third Marine Division* in the Con Thien* and Gio Linh regions of I Corps* in 1966 and early 1967. The Marines were concerned with stopping the North Vietnamese Army* (NVA) 324B Division from crossing the Demilitarized Zone* and invading Quang Tri Province. Operation Prairie, following on the heels of Operation Hastings,* was launched on August 3, 1966, and continued until January 31, 1967. A second stage of Operation Prairie commenced on February 1, 1967, and concluded on March 18, 1967. In both stages of the operation, the Third Division killed more than 2,000 NVA soldiers. The marines succeeded in driving the North Vietnamese back across the Ben Hai River,* but the NVA units only regrouped, reequipped, and recrossed back into South Vietnam later in 1967.

Sources: Shelby L. Stanton, *Vietnam Order of Battle*, 1981, and *The Rise and Fall of an American Army: U.S. Ground Troops in Vietnam, 1965–1973*, 1985; Willard Pearson, *The War in the Northern Provinces, 1966–1968*, 1975; Jack Shulimson, *U.S. Marines in Vietnam: An Expanding War 1966*, 1982.

OPERATION RANCH HAND

Operation Ranch Hand, the codename for a U.S. Air Force* mission to spray herbicides in Southeast Asia between 1961 and 1971, arose out of the military necessity of destroying the jungle cover and food of the Vietcong.* Herbicides, or weed-killing chemicals, had long been used in American agriculture, spread both by ground and aerial methods. Many American military leaders also recognized the potentials of such chemicals for combat situations, but refrained from using them either because of legal restrictions made in treaty or because of possible in-kind retaliations. In 1961, President Ngo Dinh Diem* of South Vietnam ended this long-standing proscription, however, and asked the U.S. Air Force to conduct such defoliant operations in his nation.

Diem's request launched a debate over the morality of using herbicides that raged for years. On one side, some policymakers argued that herbicides offered an economical and efficient means of defoliating* enemy hiding areas. Others, however, doubted the chemicals' effectiveness, suggested that their use would needlessly alienate South Vietnamese villagers, and argued that the chemicals posed serious ecological problems for all living organisms coming in contact with them. Virtually all individuals noted that the use of such defoliants could lead to terrific adverse publicity; almost certainly it would foster charges of barbarism and brutality. Accepting these risks, President John F. Kennedy* approved the use of herbicides in southeast Asia in November 1961.

Operation Ranch Hand officially commenced in January 1962. The U.S. Air Force's Tactical Air Command was initially directed to deploy six C–123 transports modified with crop-dusting equipment and sufficient supplies for four-month operations to South Vietnam to conduct this mission. After movement to Bien Hoa* Air Base, outside Saigon,* the Ranch Hand pilots flew their first familiarization flights over targeted areas on January 10 and 11, 1962. The first air force operational Ranch Hand missions took place on January 13, 1962, as two C–123 aircraft sprayed land near Route 15 south and east of Saigon.

At first the use of herbicides was very carefully governed by the Military Assistance Command, Vietnam* (MACV), but gradually limitations were re-laxed and the spraying became more frequent and covered larger areas. In addition to the use of defoliants in South Vietnam, the air force conducted Ranch Hand missions in Laos* between December 1965 and September 1969. From the beginning of this operation until its official termination in February 1971 by General Creighton W. Abrams, Jr.,* MACV commander, the air force dissem-inated 19.22 million gallons of herbicides in South Vietnam, according to a 1974 National Research Council study. Approximately 5.96 million acres in the nation had been sprayed during the operation, including 36 percent of its mangrove forests. An additional 417,420 gallons were sprayed on 65,972 hectares in Laos between 1965 and 1969.

Sources: William A. Buckingham, Jr., *Operation Ranch Hand: The United States Air Force and Herbicides in Southeast Asia, 1961–1971*, 1982.

Roger D. Launius

OPERATION ROLLING THUNDER

Operation Rolling Thunder was the codename for American bombing* attacks on strategic targets within North Vietnam. The raids began in an effort to persuade the North Vietnamese to cease their support of the war in the south by forcing them to pay a direct and increasing cost. Since American political leaders hoped to persuade the North Vietnamese quickly and at little cost to either side, President Lyndon B. Johnson* rejected a plan for a concentrated sixteen-day campaign and opted instead for a program of gradually escalated raids beginning in March 1965. There were seven phases to the Rolling Thunder campaign, separated by halts to see if the North Vietnamese were willing to begin negotiations, and usually marked by changes in the type and geographic location of the targets being attacked.

Before May 1965, only targets south of the twentieth parallel could be attacked. When Phase II began in May, American pilots were still ordered to hit no targets within 30 miles of Hanoi* or the Chinese borders, or within 10 miles of Haiphong. For a brief period in early 1966 American air strikes were once again confined to the area just north of the seventeenth parallel (*see* Geneva Accords), but in April 1966 the operational area was expanded to all of North Vietnam, while the target list was expanded to include oil storage facilities near Hanoi. Phase Five, which began in February 1967, consisted of intensive bombing attacks on Hanoi area factories, railroad yards, power plants, and airfields. Following an-other Christmas halt, attacks on Hanoi resumed in January 1968, but American aircraft were hampered by bad weather and by the need to support ground operations in the south in the wake of the Tet Offensive.* On April 1, 1968, all attacks north of the nineteenth parallel ceased, and all Rolling Thunder raids stopped on November 1. Throughout the Rolling Thunder campaign, target selection was closely controlled by the White House (from a list of potential targets supplied by the Joint Chiefs of Staff; (*see* Chairman, JCS). During the entire campaign, American aircraft dropped over 640,000 tons of bombs; 922 American aircraft were lost.

Sources: R. Frank Futrell et al., *Aces and Aerial Victories: The U.S. Air Force in Southeast Asia*, 1981; John Morrocco, *The Vietnam Experience. Thunder From Above: Air War, 1941–1968*, 1985.

Robert S. Browning III

OPERATION SCOTLAND

Operation Scotland was the codename for two Third Marine Division* actions in I Corps* in 1967 and 1968. Launched on November 1, 1967, Operation Scotland centered on the Khe Sanh* region of Quang Tri Province. It continued until March 31, 1968, inflicting 1,561 casualties on Vietcong* and North Vietnamese Army* (NVA) forces. Operation Scotland came to an end when Operation Pegasus* began on April 1, 1968. Elements of the Third Marine Division and the 7th Cavalry engaged North Vietnamese regulars near Khe Sanh. South Vietnamese paratroopers joined the action. Operation Pegasus was the codename for the relief of the siege of Khe Sanh. When Operation Pegasus ended in April 1968, Operation Scotland II began, with the Third Marine Division continuing its operations around Khe Sanh. Operation Scotland II lasted until February 28, 1969. Operations Scotland and Scotland II accounted for a total of nearly 4,900 NVA casualties.

Sources: Shelby L. Stanton, *Vietnam Order of Battle*, 1981, and *The Rise and Fall of an American Army: U.S. Ground Troops in Vietnam, 1965–1973*, 1985; Willard Pearson, *The War in the Northern Provinces, 1966–1968*, 1975.

OPERATION SEA DRAGON

A U.S. Navy* counterpart to the Air Force's* Rolling Thunder* campaign, Operation Sea Dragon was the codename for an operation to cut North Vietnamese supply lines. Operation Sea Dragon began in October 1966 and ended in October 1968. Cruisers and destroyers dominated the operation, except for a brief stay by the battleship *New Jersey*. The naval vessels ranged up and down the coast of North Vietnam, shelling shore batteries, supply routes, and communication stations, and sinking small North Vietnamese ships running supplies south. Operation Sea Dragon came to an end when President Lyndon B. Johnson* was trying to secure a negotiated settlement at the Paris peace talks.*

Source: Edward J. Marolda and G. Wesley Pryce III, *A Short History of the United States Navy and the Southeast Asian Conflict, 1950–1975*, 1984.

OPERATION SHINING BRASS

Operation Shining Brass was the codename for the first U.S. Special Forces* infiltration of Laos* to locate and disrupt the Ho Chi Minh Trail.* In October 1965 a Special Forces team conducted the operation and, after locating an ammunition depot, called in a series of F–105* air strikes. They withdrew after several days, satisfied that they had located the Ho Chi Minh Trail and destroyed an ammunition cache, but disappointed that they had not encountered any Vietcong* or North Vietnamese soldiers, except for sniper fire.

Sources: Terrence Maitland and Peter McInerney, *The Vietnam Experience: A Contagion of War*, 1983; Shelby L. Stanton, *The Green Berets at War*, 1985; Charles M. Simpson, *Inside the Green Berets: The First Thirty Years*, 1983; Francis J. Kelly, *U.S. Army Special Forces, 1961–1971*, 1973.

OPERATION SILVER BAYONET   *See* Ia Drang Valley, Battle of

OPERATION SOMERSET PLAIN

Operation Somerset Plain was the codename for a combined 101st Airborne Division* and ARVN (*see* Army of the Republic of Vietnam) 1st Regiment combat operation in the A Shau Valley* in August 1968. The ARVN portion of the operation was codenamed Lam Son 246. Little contact was made with North Vietnamese Army* forces, and the allied force evacuated the area on August 18 and 19, 1968.

Source: Shelby L. Stanton, *The Rise and Fall of an American Army: U.S. Ground Troops in Vietnam, 1965–1973*, 1985.

OPERATION STARLITE (STARLIGHT)

Operation Starlite was the codename for a U.S. Marine* combined land-air-amphibious operation aimed at destroying the 1st Vietcong* Regiment on the Van Tuong Peninsula in August 1965. The operation began on August 18 when the 3rd Battalion of the Third Marine Division* came ashore while the 2nd Battalion of the Fourth Marine Division* flew into landing zones to the west. Fighting was fierce as the marines moved from one Vietcong defensive position to the next. Nevertheless, by August 19 the 1st Vietcong Regiment was pinned along the coast and destroyed through a combination of ground fire, air strikes, and naval gunfire. Operation Starlite marked the first large battle between American forces and Vietcong main force groups. Its success encouraged the marines to follow up with a similar operation (codenamed Operation Piranha*) the following month.

Sources: Shelby Stanton, *The Rise and Fall of an American Army. U.S. Ground Troops in Vietnam, 1965–1973*, 1985; Jack Shulimson and Charles M. Johnson, *U.S. Marines in Vietnam: The Landing and the Buildup 1965*, 1978.

Robert S. Browning III

OPERATION STEEL TIGER

Operation Steel Tiger was the codename for U.S. air operations over the Ho Chi Minh Trail* in the northern Laotian panhandle. Operation Steel Tiger began in April 1965 and involved both U.S. Air Force* and Navy* aircraft flying from bases in Thailand* and South Vietnam, as well as aircraft carriers in the South China Sea. Although all types of aircraft flew on these interdiction missions (including B–52* bombers), the most effective aircraft were air force fixed-wing gunships,* particularly the AC–130* Spectre.

A subsidiary operation intended to interdict the Ho Chi Minh Trail in the southern Laotian panhandle was codenamed Operation Tiger Hound. Operation Tiger Hound began in December 1965. In 1968 both Operation Steel Tiger and Operation Tiger Hound were increased to cover the entire Ho Chi Minh Trail. At that time the codename was changed to Operation Commando Hunt.* Commando Hunt campaigns were numbered in series, and American military officials estimated that some 20,000 trucks were destroyed in Commando Hunt 5. Although at times the flow of men and supplies along the Ho Chi Minh Trail was slowed to a trickle by the air campaigns, the trail was never completely closed.

Sources: William W. Momyer, *Airpower in Three Wars*, 1978; Thomas D. Boettcher, *Vietnam: The Valor and the Sorrow*, 1985; John Morrocco, *The Vietnam Experience. Thunder From Above: Air War, 1941–1968*, 1985, and *The Vietnam Experience. Rain of Fire: Air War, 1969–1973*, 1984.

Robert S. Browning III

OPERATION SUNRISE

Operation Sunrise was the codename for an early attempt at pacification (*see* Rural Reconstruction). In March 1962, South Vietnam leader Ngo Dinh Diem* launched a pilot project in Binh Duong Province north of Saigon.* ARVN troops (*see* Army of the Republic of Vietnam) attempted to establish five strategic hamlets* and move peasants off their ancestral homelands to the new communities in the Ben Cat district. The peasants were reluctant to move, however, because of religious ties to ancestral land, coercive ARVN methods, government corruption and unwillingness to deliver the promised payments and resources, and the fact that the hamlets were located far from market areas where rice could be sold. Operation Sunrise was a failure.

Sources: Stanley Karnow, *Vietnam: A History*, 1983; Frances FitzGerald, *Fire in the Lake: The Vietnamese and the Americans in Vietnam*, 1972.

OPERATION TALON VISE   *See* Operation Frequent Wind

OPERATION TEXAS

Operation Texas was the codename for a combined Army of the Republic of Vietnam* (ARVN) and United States Marine* combat operation to relieve the North Vietnamese Army* siege of a South Vietnamese Regional Forces* outpost at An Hoa, approximately fifteen miles south of Chu Lai in Quang Ngai Province. On March 19, 1966, the Vietcong 1st Regiment attacked the An Hoa base, and marine helicopters quickly brought reinforcements and evacuated the wounded. On March 20, the 3rd Battalion of the 7th Marines and the 5th ARVN Airborne

Battalion joined in the engagement. The 2nd Battalion of the Fourth Marines* came in later, trapping the enemy between the base and the new marine positions. The Vietcong* were annihilated.

Sources: Shelby L. Stanton, *The Rise and Fall of an American Army: U.S. Ground Troops in Vietnam, 1965–1973*, 1985; Willard Pearson, *The War in the Northern Provinces, 1966–1968*, 1975.

OPERATION TEXAS STAR

Operation Texas Star was the codename for combined U.S.-ARVN (*see* Army of the Republic of Vietnam) military operations in I Corps* between April 1 and September 5, 1970. In cooperation with the ARVN 1st Infantry Division, the 101st Airborne Division (Airmobile)* conducted pacification (*see* Rural Reconstruction) and development programs as well as offensive operations against North Vietnamese Army* forces in Quang Tri and Thua Thien provinces. At the conclusion of Operation Texas Star, the Military Assistance Command, Vietnam* claimed 1,782 casualties inflicted on the North Vietnamese.

Source: Shelby L. Stanton, *Vietnam Order of Battle*, 1981.

OPERATION TIGER HOUND   *See* Operation Steel Tiger

OPERATION TOAN THANG

Operation Toan Thang was the codename for a massive allied combat operation outside Saigon* in 1968. The Tet Offensive,* with its attacks on Saigon, had shown how vulnerable and tentative the American presence in South Vietnam still was, and U.S. military officials were determined to prevent any repetition of the successful Vietcong* raids on the capital. Military Assistance Command, Vietnam* (MACV) launched Operation Toan Thang on April 8, 1968, using seventy-nine U.S. and ARVN battalions (*see* Army of the Republic of Vietnam). The units formed a security ring around Saigon and set out to destroy all Vietcong and North Vietnamese Army* (NVA) troops in what was known as the Capital Military District. When the NVA and Vietcong launched the Mini-Tet Offensive in May 1968, Operation Toan Thang successfully prevented any major successful attacks on Saigon, except for the detonation of 100 pounds of explosives outside a Saigon radio and television complex. When Operation Toan Thang was concluded on May 31, 1968, when the Mini-Tet Offensive ended, MACV claimed to have inflicted 7,645 casualties on Vietcong and NVA forces.

Sources: Shelby L. Stanton, *Vietnam Order of Battle*, 1981 and *The Rise and Fall of an American Army: U.S. Ground Forces in Vietnam, 1965–1973*, 1985; Tom Carhart, *Battles and Campaigns in Vietnam*, 1984.

OPERATION TRAN HUNG DAO

Operations Tran Hung Dao I and Tran Hung Dao II were conducted by the South Vietnamese during and just after the Tet Offensive* of 1968. Both involved several Vietnamese marine, ranger, and airborne battalions fighting Vietcong* in the Saigon* area. The ARVN (*see* Army of the Republic of Vietnam) 5th Ranger Group encountered particularly bitter fighting in Cholon.* Tran Hung Dao I commenced on February 5 and concluded on February 17, 1968, and Tran Hung Dao II started on February 17 and finished on March 8, 1968, the day after the last Vietcong resistance in Cholon had been eliminated. In both operations, ARVN forces claimed credit for 1,666 enemy casualties. Although Operations Tran Hung Dao I and II had successfully repelled Vietcong forces from Saigon and Cholon, they had indicated how vulnerable South Vietnam still was to guerrilla activity.

Sources: Shelby L. Stanton, *Vietnam Order of Battle*, 1981; Don Oberdofer, *Tet!*, 1971.

OPERATION UNION

Operations Union I and II were codenames for combat activities of the 1st Marine Division* in Quang Nam and Quang Tin provinces during 1967. The Vietcong* were particularly strong between Chu Lai and Da Nang* in the Phuoc Ha Valley, as was the North Vietnamese Army* (NVA) 2nd Division. Operation Union I, involving the 1st and 3rd battalions of the 1st Marines and the 3rd Battalion of the 5th Marines,* began on April 21, 1967, and continued until May 17, 1967. Operation Union II commenced on May 25, 1967, and concluded on June 5, 1967. The marines claimed to have inflicted 1,566 casualties on the enemy in both operations before the NVA retreated.

Sources: Shelby L. Stanton, *Vietnam Order of Battle*, 1981, and *The Rise and Fall of an American Army: U.S. Ground Troops in Vietnam, 1965–1973*, 1985.

OPERATION UNIONTOWN

Operation Uniontown was the codename for the combat activities of the 199th Light Infantry Brigade* in Bien Hoa Province. Launched on December 17, 1967, Operation Uniontown had as its objective a clearing of the Vietcong* from the Bien Hoa area. Operation Uniontown became part of the larger American reaction to the Tet Offensive* in February 1968, and when the operation was concluded on March 8, 1968, the 199th Infantry Brigade claimed 922 Vietcong casualties. As for clearing the Vietcong out of Bien Hoa Province, Operation Uniontown dealt them a savage, but not a lethal, blow.

Source: Shelby L. Stanton, *Vietnam Order of Battle*, 1981.

OPERATION UTAH

Operation Utah was the codename for a combined U.S. Marine* and ARVN (*see* Army of the Republic of Vietnam) assault in Quang Ngai Province between March 4 and March 8, 1966. North Vietnamese Army* (NVA) regular troops of the 36th NVA Regiment were operating south of Chu Lai. Five marine battalions from the 1st,* 4th,* and 7th Marines air-assaulted into an area just outside Quang Ngai City, and after several days in heavy fighting, they drove the NVA out of the region, inflicting more than 600 casualties on them.

Sources: Shelby L. Stanton, *Vietnam Order of Battle*, 1981, and *The Rise and Fall of an American Army: U.S. Ground Troops in Vietnam, 1965–1973*, 1985; Jack Shulimson, *U.S. Marines in Vietnam: An Expanding War 1966*, 1982.

OPERATION VULTURE

Late in March 1954, General Paul Ely,* the French chief of staff, flew to Washington to request American air support in Indochina* if the Chinese intervened on the side of the Vietminh.* Admiral Arthur W. Radford,* chairman of the Joint Chiefs of Staff (*see* Chairman, JCS), then unveiled to Ely what he called Operation Vulture, a series of American air strikes around Dien Bien Phu* aimed at severing Vietminh communications, destroying their artillery, and ending the siege there. Radford told Ely the French would have to make a formal request for such assistance. If such a request came through, 200 American aircraft from the carriers *Essex* and *Boxer*, both stationed in the South China Sea, would conduct the air strike. But when Operation Vulture encountered congressional opposition, President Dwight Eisenhower,* over Radford's objections, argued that he would approve the air strike only with formal congressional approval as well as verbal support from NATO allies. At that point the French withdrew their request, afraid that any multinational approach would reduce their control over the military campaign in Indochina. Operation Vulture never came to pass.

Sources: Philippe Devillers and Jean Lacouture. *End of a War: Indochina, 1954*, 1969; Bernard B. Fall, *Hell in a Very Small Place: The Siege of Dien Bien Phu*, 1967; Melvin Gurtov, *The First Vietnam Crisis: Chinese Communist Strategy and United States Involvement, 1953–54*, 1967; John Prados, *The Sky Would Fall: Operation Vulture, The U.S. Bombing Mission in Indochina*, 1983.

OPERATION WHEELER/WALLOWA

Operation Wheeler/Wallowa was the codename for the yearlong operations of the Americal Division (23rd Infantry Division*) in Quang Nam and Quang Tin provinces of I Corps.* Launched on November 11, 1967, Operation Wheeler/Wallowa continued until November 11, 1968, and resulted in more than 10,000 Vietcong* and North Vietnamese Army* casualties.

Sources: Shelby L. Stanton, *Vietnam Order of Battle*, 1981; Willard Pearson, *The War in the Northern Provinces, 1966–1968*, 1975.

OPERATION WHITE STAR

Operation White Star was the codename for the 1959 Special Forces* program to organize Hmong* (Meo) tribesmen in Laos* to serve as a resistance force against Vietcong* and North Vietnamese infiltration* and supply routes in Laos and along the Laotian-Vietnam border. Operation White Star formally ended in 1962 after the Geneva agreements settling the Laotian controversy, but U.S. Special Forces continued to work closely with Hmong tribesmen throughout the 1960s.

Sources: Douglas Blaufarb, *The Counterinsurgency Era: U.S. Doctrine and Performance*, 1977; Shelby L. Stanton, *Green Berets at War*, 1985; John Prados, *Presidents' Secret Wars: CIA and Pentagon Covert Operations Since World War II*, 1986.

OPERATION YELLOWSTONE

Operation Yellowstone was the codename for combat operations of the 25th Infantry Division* in War Zone C* between December 8, 1966, and February 24, 1967. Although they encountered frequent Vietcong* mortar attacks, ground combat was relatively light, except for some intense confrontations early in January. The major consequence of Operation Yellowstone, aside from the 1,254 casualties the 25th Division claimed to have inflicted on the Vietcong, was to confirm that Tay Ninh Province (War Zone C) continued to be a major stronghold of the Vietcong.

Source: Shelby L. Stanton, *The Rise and Fall of an American Army: U.S. Ground Troops in Vietnam, 1965–1973*, 1985.

• P •

PACIFICATION   *See* Rural Reconstruction

PACIFIC COMMAND

Pacific Command, or PACOM, was located in Hawaii. It was a unified command headquarters responsible for joint military operations in Asia and the Pacific. Four individuals served as commander in chief of the Pacific Command during the Vietnam War: Admiral Harry D. Felt until June 1964; Admiral Ulysses S. Sharp* until July 1968; Admiral John S. McCain* until September 1972; and Admiral Noel Gayler until the end of the war.

Sources: George S. Eckhardt, *Command and Control, 1950–1969*, 1974; Bruce Palmer, Jr., *The 25-Year War: America's Military Role in Vietnam*, 1984.

PARIS PEACE ACCORDS (1973)

In the aftermath of the so-called Christmas bombing (*see* Operation Linebacker II) of Hanoi* and Haiphong in December 1972, American Henry Kissinger* and North Vietnamese Le Duc Tho* resumed peace talks on January 8 in Paris and after two weeks of intensive negotiations finally settled on an agreement on January 23. Two days later, on January 25, 1973, cease-fire agreements were formally signed in Paris, and another chapter in the fighting in Indochina* had closed.

The agreement of January 1973 differed little from an abortive one of October 1972 which had been unacceptable to South Vietnamese President Nguyen Van Thieu.* The agreement called for a cease-fire, American troop withdrawal, prisoner exchanges (especially of the American pilots shot down over North Vietnam), but permitted Vietnamese troops on both sides to remain in place. That tacit recognition of Communist military strength meant that the South Vietnamese government had to maintain its territorial integrity without American ground support against an enemy with more than 100,000 main force troops in the south. The agreement also called for an eventual compromise government reflecting the military balance in the south.

Years later the North Vietnamese claimed that the United States reneged on the agreement, for they claimed in secret protocols—for which there is no proof save for their claims—that Richard Nixon* agreed to supply billions of dollars in economic assistance to rebuild the North. Still it is clear that the North Vietnamese never intended to live by the agreements, merely waiting for the propitious time to invade the South. Nixon accepted the agreement and felt he could intervene with air power and military supplies. Such intervention would maintain the balance of power in Vietnam.

Sources: Allan E. Goodman, *The Lost Peace: America's Search for a Negotiated Settlement of the Vietnam War*, 1978; Walter Scott Dillard, *Sixty Days to Peace*, 1982; Seymour Hersh, *The Price of Power: Kissinger in the Nixon White House*, 1983.

Charles Dobbs

PARIS PEACE TALKS

Formal discussions between representatives of the United States and the Democratic Republic of Vietnam* began in Paris on May 13, 1968, and continued intermittently until January 25, 1973, when Henry Kissinger* and Le Duc Tho* signed the Paris Peace Accords* ending the war. The talks developed out of a painful reassessment of American policy by President Lyndon B. Johnson* in the aftermath of the Communist Tet Offensive* in 1968. After receiving Secretary of Defense Clark Clifford's* report in mid-March that the United States could not win the war, Johnson stunned a nationwide audience on March 31, 1968, announcing he would seek peace in Vietnam and not seek renomination or reelection in 1968. After several weeks of preparatory talks, the Paris peace talks commenced on May 13, 1968.

From the outset, the talks were fraught with difficulties. The chief American negotiater was W. Averell Harriman* until January 1969 and then Henry Cabot Lodge.* Le Duc Tho headed the North Vietnamese delegation throughout the negotiations. Nguyen Thi Binh* headed the National Liberation Front (NLF; *see* Vietcong) delegation. During Johnson's presidency, the United States approached the talks believing it held the advantage in Vietnam and thus continually insisted on mutual withdrawal of American and North Vietnamese forces, leaving the Saigon* government in control. The North Vietnamese and NLF, of course, refused to accept an arrangement. The impasse in the two negotiating positions was symbolized by a month-long debate over the size and shape of the table the two sides would sit at once formal negotiations began. Later, during the Nixon* administration, the United States operated from a belief that, whether it held the advantage or not, it had to remain firm to impress the Soviet Union* and the People's Republic of China* that the United States had not lost its will to resist Communist aggression. Meanwhile, the North Vietnamese remained unyielding in their negotiating position. They wanted all foreign military forces removed from Indochina,* and they would not admit to any division of Vietnam. Eventually this test of wills would prove uneven: the United States would weaken while the North Vietnamese leadership would accept tremendous losses in manpower and devastation of their homeland to stay the course.

By 1971 Henry Kissinger and Richard Nixon had decided to pursue secret negotiations to end the war. The Paris peace talks were too public, and since the United States was willing to make concessions to the North Vietnamese and NLF point of view, Kissinger and Nixon felt secret negotiations would better preserve American credibility. Those secret negotiations reached fruition in the fall of 1972 and the final arrangement was signed on January 25, 1973.

Sources: Allan E. Goodman, *The Lost Peace: America's Search for a Negotiated Settlement of the Vietnam War*, 1978; Walter Scott Dillard, *Sixty Days to Peace*, 1982.

Charles Dobbs

PARROT'S BEAK

The Parrot's Beak illustrates the complexities, both political and logistic, surrounding the war in Vietnam. The Parrot's Beak is a region of Cambodia (*see* Kampuchea) jutting into South Vietnam west of Saigon* and north of the Mekong River. Vietcong* and North Vietnamese units established a presence in the region early in the Vietnam War, giving them a safe haven close to major population centers in South Vietnam. After becoming independent from France,* Cambodia had been ruled by Prince Norodom Sihanouk.* Early in his rule, Sihanouk had sought close ties with the United States to offset Cambodia's two centuries-old enemies: Thailand* and Vietnam. As American interests became increasingly identified with South Vietnam, Sihanouk sought closer ties with the People's Republic of China* as a means of countering Vietnamese influence. At the same time, he allowed the North Vietnamese to establish a presence along the Cambodian-Vietnamese border, with a major presence in the Parrot's Beak. Sihanouk believed that the Chinese would restrain them from violating Cambodian sovereignty. This strategy came apart as China sank into increased isolation during Mao Zedong's* Cultural Revolution.

In late 1967, the North Vietnamese were building up forces inside Cambodia in preparation for 1968's Tet Offensive.* General William Westmoreland* pressed President Lyndon Johnson* to approve American ground assaults against the enemy in Cambodia. Sihanouk began once again to court American support. In an interview with the *Washington Post* in December 1967, Sihanouk stated he would grant the United States the right of "hot pursuit" against the North Vietnamese and Vietcong inside Cambodia—as long as no Cambodians were harmed. Sihanouk suggested that Johnson send Senator Mike Mansfield,* whom he labeled "a just and courageous man whom we consider a friend," to Cambodia to discuss the issue. Johnson, however, was reluctant to expand the war, and nothing came of this overture.

After Richard Nixon's* inauguration, the question of sanctuaries* in Cambodia became a major policy issue. General Creighton Abrams,* Westmoreland's successor, reported that the Communists had recently moved forty thousand fresh troops into the area, and were supplying them largely by sea through the port of Sihanoukville, on the Gulf of Siam. In February 1969, Nixon ordered the bombing of Cambodia in retaliation for increased Communist attacks from that area. The bombing, dubbed Operation Menu,* was seen as a short-term operation. In fact, it continued for fourteen months.

The operation was conducted in total secrecy, with only a few sympathetic members of Congress* informed of the actions. Then an enterprising *New York Times* correspondent broke the story. Finally acknowledged in 1973, the air strikes fueled demands for impeachment of Nixon in Congress, and helped win the support needed to pass the War Powers Resolution Act.*

As a result of American air action in the Parrot's Beak, the North Vietnamese began preparing for Sihanouk to turn against them completely by arming and training guerrillas of the Khmer Rouge,* the Cambodian Communist movement. At the same time, Sihanouk was losing the support of the Cambodian military and middle class. In 1970, while Sihanouk was in France, he was removed by Lon Nol,* setting Cambodia on a long downward road from which it has yet to recover.

Sources: Shelby L. Stanton, *The Rise and Fall of an American Army: U.S. Ground Troops in Vietnam, 1965–1973*, 1985; William Shawcross, *Sideshow: Kissinger, Nixon, and the Destruction of Cambodia*, 1979; Stanley Karnow, *Vietnam: A History*, 1983.

Nolan J. Argyle

"PASSAGE TO FREEDOM"

In 1954, when the Geneva Accords* divided Indochina* at the seventeenth parallel into North and South Vietnam, Roman Catholic leaders in the north openly urged Catholic peasants to relocate to South Vietnam, where they thought the Church would have a more hospitable reception. Approximately 900,000 Roman Catholics* relocated to South Vietnam. The South Vietnamese government, headed by northerner Ngo Dinh Diem,* received the refugees* with open arms, and the United States assisted the relocation by providing a task force of fifty ships to help move the people. Reception centers, financed by the United States and the South Vietnamese government, offered the refugees food, clothing, and medical assistance. The program to relocate the refugees was called the "Passage to Freedom" by U.S. officials.

Source: Gertrude Samuels, "Passage to Freedom," *National Geographic* 107 (June 1955), 858–74.

PATHET LAO

Nominally led by Prince Souphanouvong, the Pathet Lao (Land of the Lao) evolved from Ho Chi Minh's* Indochinese Communist party (*see* Lao Dong party). Educated in France* as an engineer, Prince Souphanouvong affiliated with the Vietminh* while working in Vietnam. The deplorable conditions resulting from French colonial rule made Souphanouvong a radical nationalist in favor of armed revolt. With Vietminh assistance, he helped build nationalist political and military organizations which briefly governed Laos* in 1945. During the First Indochina War, the Pathet Lao worked closely with the Vietminh. At Dien Bien Phu* Pathet Lao forces occupied blocking positions to prevent French reinforcements. Although the Vietminh argued determinedly for Pathet Lao and Khmer Issarak* (pro-Vietminh Cambodian nationalists) representation at the 1954 Geneva conference (*see* Geneva Accords), France and the United States absolutely refused. Pressured by China* and the Soviets, the Vietminh yielded amid charges by Laotian and Cambodian nationalists that they had been sold out to gain Western acceptance of Vietminh control of at least northern Vietnam. Pathet Lao exclusion resulted in a Laotian settlement which reflected neither its political nor military strength.

Throughout the 1950s and into the 1960s, Prince Souvanna Phouma* and his half brother Prince Souphanouvong tried to establish a unified government. Their efforts were sabotaged repeatedly by American determination to deny the Pathet Lao any participation in the national government. The unwillingness of premier Souvana Phouma to deploy the Royal Laotian Army against the Pathet Lao promoted U.S. funding of a rightist mercenary army, led by General Phoumi Nosavan, which attacked both the Pathet Lao and the Royal Laotian Army. To American dismay, the brothers joined forces, defeating Phoumi's mercenaries, and provoking the "Laotian Crisis" and the 1962 Geneva agreements on Laos.

Continued American intervention prevented Pathet Lao participation in the coalition government agreed upon at Geneva. The Pathet Lao retreated to two northern provinces and the eastern border where North Vietnamese Army* forces controlled the Ho Chi Minh Trail.* The United States initiated a "secret war" against both the Trail and the Pathet Lao through extensive bombing (over two million tons—slightly less tonnage than was dropped in all of World War II), establishing Special Forces* camps, and raising a mercenary army among Meo Hmong* tribesmen. These actions effectively partitioned Laos until a Pathet Lao–dominated coalition government was established in 1974. It was replaced by the Lao People's Democratic Republic in December 1975.

Sources: Philippe Devillers and Jean Lacouture, *End of A War*, 1969; Peter Poole, *Eight Presidents and Indochina*, 1978; Wilfred Bruchett, *The Second Indochina War*, 1970; Bernard Fall, *The Two Viet Nams*, 1967; Paul F. Langer and Joseph J. Zasloff, *North Vietnam and the Pathet Lao: Partners in the Struggle for Laos*, 1970; Charles A. Stevenson, *The End of Nowhere: American Policy Toward Laos Since 1954*, 1973.

Samuel Freeman

PATHFINDERS

Trained at the Airborne School at Ft. Benning, Georgia, Pathfinders (known as "black hats" because of their black baseball caps) were the U.S. Army's equivalent of combat air traffic controllers. Working in small teams, they were parachuted or helicopter-inserted into hostile terrain to direct air traffic. They were utilized anytime an operation employed substantial numbers of aircraft, including airborne or heliborne combat assaults, major search and destroy* operations, establishing forward artillery fire bases, or extracting large enemy caches. Since ground travel was time-consuming and forfeited the element of surprise, and since roads were subject to mining and ambush, the United States relied heavily on airmobile operations. The skies were often crowded with gunships,* helicopters, and helicopter-gunships; and without Pathfinders serious accidents were likely. Pathfinders' responsibilities included indentifying drop zones for airborne operations, landing zones—or LZs*—for heliborne operations, supervising the clearing and securing of LZs for heliborne operations, determining flight approaches to these zones, establishing and operating navigational aids, coordinating various types of aircraft and the sorties* of aircraft over their operational area, and occasionally fire direction for tactical aircraft and artillery, especially final preparation fires prior to heliborne combat assault operations. Pathfinders were used most extensively by airborne and airmobile forces including the 82nd,* 101st,* and ARVN (*see* Army of the Republic of Vietnam) Airborne Divisions,* the 173rd Airborne Brigade,* and the U.S. Marines.*

Sources: Bernard W. Rogers, *Cedar Falls–Junction City: A Turning Point*, 1974; John J. Tolson, *Airmobility, 1961–1971*, 1973; Shelby L. Stanton, *The Green Berets at War*, 1985.

Samuel Freeman

PENTAGON PAPERS

On Sunday, June 13, 1971, the *New York Times* began publishing a series of articles based upon a several-thousand-page, secret Defense Department account of American involvement in Indochina.* Within a few days the Justice Department obtained a temporary restraining order barring further publication on the grounds of national security, and the so-called Pentagon Papers became another flash point between liberals and conservatives in the great Vietnam debate. In 1967, Secretary of Defense Robert McNamara* had ordered a history of U.S. involvement, and the project was completed in 1968. In 1971, the secret history became public knowledge. The previous year, one of the coauthors of the history, a Rand Corporation* employee named Daniel Ellsberg,* had begun photocopying thousands of pages and giving them to J. William Fulbright,* chairman of the Senate Foreign Relations Committee.* The next year Ellsberg provided a complete set to the *New York Times*. Efforts by the Nixon* administration could not dissuade the paper from publishing excerpts of the history.

By a vote of 6 to 3, the U.S. Supreme Court overturned the temporary restraining order on June 30, 1971, and permitted publication, noting that the freedoms of speech and press were at stake. Publication of the Pentagon Papers became a cause célèbre primarily because they revealed duplicity in the Johnson* administration—government officials telling the public one thing and actively pursuing different military and political policies, in particular being involved in Indochina sooner and to a greater extent than the public had once assumed.

Sources: John P. Roche, "The Pentagon Papers," in *Sentenced to Life*, 1974; Peter Schrag, *Test of Loyalty*, 1974.

Charles Dobbs

PENTAGON PAPERS TRIAL

The Pentagon Papers Trial was the popular name given to the 1972–73 trial of Daniel Ellsberg* and Anthony J. Russo.* The defendants were charged with conspiracy, espionage, and conversion of government property (theft) for photocopying in 1969 substantial portions of a forty-seven-volume study commissioned by U.S. Secretary of Defense Robert S. McNamara* in 1967 and entitled *History of U.S. Decision-making Process on Vietnam Policy*, otherwise known as the Pentagon Papers.* Criminal charges against Ellsberg came after the *New York Times* and other newspapers published excerpts of the Pentagon Papers in June and July 1971. Contrary to common belief, Ellsberg and Russo were not indicted for giving the Pentagon Papers to any newspapers. They were indicted for temporarily removing the Pentagon Papers from the premises of the Rand Corporation* in Santa Barbara, California, and for photocopying the documents at an advertising agency owned by Russo's friend, Lynda Sinay. Ellsberg was first indicted on June 25, 1971. He surrendered to federal authorities in Boston on June 28.

A new indictment was returned in secret on December 29, 1971, charging Ellsberg and Russo with fifteen counts of conspiracy, espionage, and theft. Listed as unindicted coconspirators were Lynda Sinay and Vu Van Thai, a former South Vietnamese ambassador to the United States. The charges against Ellsberg carried maximum penalties of 115 years imprisonment and $120,000 in fines. Those against Russo carried maximum penalties of 35 years imprisonment and $40,000 in fines. During the trial, however, federal district court judge William Byrne directed an acquittal on one espionage count against Ellsberg and Russo. The trial began in Los Angeles on July 10, 1972, with selection of the jury. On July 24, Judge Byrne revealed that the United States had filed a wiretap transcript of a conversation by a member of the defense team, but ruled that the contents need not be disclosed because they did not bear on the case. The Supreme Court upheld the judge in November. Jury selection began in January 1973. Several key questions animated the four-month trial: (1) Can citizens be prosecuted for conspiracy to obstruct the executive branch's function of controlling the dissemination of classified documents when there is no statute authorizing the president to classify general national security information or making it a crime to duplicate or release such information to the public? (2) Can a citizen lawfully be prosecuted for duplicating or disseminating information that was improperly marked "Top Secret"? (3) Since the defendants had not given the Pentagon Papers to a foreign nation, could they be prosecuted for espionage? (4) Can citizens be prosecuted for espionage for leaking classified information if their only intent is to inform the public of what they believe is government misconduct? (5) Did photocopying the documents constitute theft? (6) What was stolen—physical documents or information? (7) Who owned the copied documents: the federal government, the Rand Corporation, or the three former Defense Department officials who possessed the documents and gave Ellsberg permission to study them? Key testimony in the trial centered on these questions as well as the judge's instruction that the government prove that the published information injured the United States or helped a foreign nation. On May 11, 1973, however, at the close of testimony, Judge Byrne dismissed all charges against Ellsberg and Russo and declared a mistrial because of "improper government conduct" which offends a "sense of justice." Among other things, a White House unit, with Central Intelligence Agency* assistance, had burglarized the office of Ellsberg's psychiatrist in 1971 in search of information damaging to Ellsberg; FBI wiretap transcripts of telephone conversations by Ellsberg in 1969 and 1970 had disappeared; and presidential assistant John Ehrlichman had offered Judge Byrne the directorship of the FBI during the trial. A poll of jurors after the mistrial indicated that most would have voted for acquittal.

Source: Peter Schrag, *Test of Loyalty*, 1974.

John Kincaid

PEOPLE'S LIBERATION ARMY   *See* People's Republic of China

PEOPLE'S REPUBLIC OF CHINA

On October 1, 1949, Mao Zedong's* victorious Communist forces proclaimed the People's Republic of China in Beijing, the traditional capital. The next twenty-five years would be as tumultuous as the preceding twenty-five years of civil war. After the Chinese intervention in the Korean War, the United States attempted to freeze the People's Republic out of the international community, erecting a series of regional security pacts and mutual defense treaties among surrounding nations. In return, the Chinese predicted the demise of capitalism and American global hegemony, declaring "wars of national liberation"* throughout the world. Their own People's Liberation Army was a model. Although the People's Liberation Army eventually became huge and questionable in quality, it was unsurpassed in its ability, through tightly controlled discipline and mass appeal, to politicize large numbers of people. Mao Zedong predicted that mass uprisings and guerrilla wars in capitalist countries would bring about the revolution Karl Marx had predicted.

Ho Chi Minh's* People's Army of Vietnam was modeled on the People's Liberation Army, but after that the resemblance stopped. Although the United States feared the intervention of the Chinese in the Vietnam conflict, just as had happened in Korea,* the People's Republic of China was not inclined to do so. For centuries an intense and often bloody rivalry had raged between the Vietnamese and the Chinese, and the North Vietnamese would have viewed any Chinese military intervention into Indochina as simply a pretext for renewing the domination of the peninsula they had once enjoyed. Also, in 1962 Mao had plunged the Chinese people into the Great Proletarian Cultural Revolution. Mao gained control of the army and let loose a rampaging horde of young Red Guards to terrorize government officials, scientists, and teachers. The Cultural Revolution so destabilized Chinese society that concerted military effort in Indochina was not really possible. Finally, by 1971 the Chinese began to fear Soviet and even Vietnamese power more than American power, which seemed to be ebbing. With increasingly powerful Vietnamese forces to her south and Soviet forces aligned all along her long northern borders, Chinese leaders decided to seek a rapprochement with the United States. Richard Nixon* and Henry Kissinger* exploited that decision and normalized diplomatic relations in 1972. Although the Chinese provided some weapons and economic assistance to the North Vietnamese during the course of the war, they never posed the threat to the United States that they had twenty years earlier in Korea.

Sources: *China, Vietnam, and the United States*, 1966; King C. Chen, *Vietnam and China, 1938–1954*, 1969; Stanley Karnow, *Vietnam: A History*, 1983.

Charles Dobbs

PEOPLE'S REVOLUTIONARY PARTY   *See* Lao Dong Party

PEOPLE'S SELF-DEFENSE FORCE

The People's Self-Defense Force (PSDF) was an unpaid, part-time militia in the Republic of Vietnam* designed to prevent Vietcong* infiltration* and village dominance. Although the Republic of Vietnam claimed there were more than four million members of the PSDF in 1972, those numbers were highly inflated because they included all men between the ages of 16 and 17 and 39 and 50. Commitment to the PSDF was often weak and the Vietcong were known for infiltrating the group.

Sources: Guenter Lewy, *America in Vietnam*, 1978; Ngo Quang Truong, *Territorial Forces*, 1981.

PEOPLE'S WARS   *See* Wars of National Liberation

PF   *See* Popular Forces

PHAM HUNG

Pham Hung was born in Hanoi in 1911. He joined the Communist party just after he turned twenty and spent the next forty years fighting against the succession of French, Japanese, and American forces occupying Vietnam. By 1963 Hung was a member of the central committee of the Lao Dong party.* When the final assault on South Vietnam began in 1975, Hung was the senior North Vietnamese politburo member in the south. General Van Tien Dung* was military commander of the final assault, and Hung was the chief political commissar. He became part of the Provisional Revolutionary Government* in 1975 and of the ruling politburo of the new Socialist Republic of Vietnam.*

Source: *Who's Who in the Socialist Countries*, 1978.

PHAM NGOC THAO

Pham Ngoc Thao was born in 1922 to Roman Catholic parents. While still a student Thao began absorbing anti-French attitudes, and after World War II he joined the Vietcong.* When the Geneva Accords* were concluded in 1954, Thao decided to stay in South Vietnam and he became a captain in the army. Loyal to General Nguyen Khanh* and opposed to Ngo Dinh Diem,* Thao enjoyed a brief popularity in 1964 when Khanh was in control of the military junta in Saigon,* but after Khanh's resignation later in the year, Thao was exiled to the United States as press attaché to ambassador Tran Thien Khiem.* When Thao tried to return to South Vietnam in 1965 to lead a coup against the government, he disappeared under mysterious circumstances and was never seen again. Most political observers in Saigon assumed that General Nguyen Van Thieu* had seen to his death.

Sources: *Newsweek*, 65 (March 1, 1965), 21–22; Frances FitzGerald, *Fire in the Lake: The Vietnamese and the Americans in Vietnam*, 1972.

PHAM VAN DONG

Pham Van Dong was born on March 1, 1906, in Quang Nam Province. At the time Quang Nam Province was part of the French protectorate of Annam.* Dong's family had an educated, mandarin background, and he was educated at the French lycée academy at Hue,* where two of his classmates were Vo Nguyen Giap* and Ngo Dinh Diem.* As a student Dong became active in nationalist groups and eventually defined himself as a revolutionary bent on the expulsion of the French. In 1930 French authorities arrested him for sedition, and he spent the next eight years in prison. He finally fled to China* where he met Ho Chi Minh* and became one of the founding fathers of the Lao Dong party.* For the next four decades, along with Ho Chi Minh and Vo Nguyen Giap, Dong was among the triumvirate which dominated North Vietnamese politics.

Pham Van Dong was active in the Vietminh* during their struggle against the Japanese during World War II and the French between 1946 and 1954, and he served as the leader of the Vietnamese delegation to the Geneva Conference (*see* Geneva Accords) in 1954. Dong was Ho Chi Minh's prime minister from 1950 to Ho's death in September 1969, and after his death Dong emerged as the most public figure in North Vietnam. Between 1969 and 1975 Dong released several diplomatic initiatives, always insisting on an American withdrawal, and frequently gave interviews to the Western press. Pham Van Dong played a key role in the Paris Peace Accords* of 1973 in which the United States agreed to withdraw from South Vietnam with a concurrent withdrawal of North Vietnamese forces. After the conquest of South Vietnam in 1975, Pham Van Dong was appointed prime minister of the Socialist Republic of Vietnam.* He remained at that post until December 1986, when a series of economic setbacks in the Socialist Republic of Vietnam forced his resignation.

Sources: *Who's Who in the Socialist Countries*, 1978; Joseph Buttinger, *Vietnam: A Dragon Embattled*. Vol. 2, *Vietnam at War*, 1967; *Washington Post*, December 18, 1986.

PHAN BOI CHAU

Originally named Phan Van San, Phan Boi Chau was born in 1867 in the central province of Nghe An, Vietnam. After passing the mandarin examinations in 1900, Phan Boi Chau began organizing resistance movements against the French. At first he wanted the restoration of a royal Vietnamese government, and he threw his support behind Prince Cuong De,* a direct descendant of Gia Long* of the Nguyen* dynasty. After the Japanese victory over Russia in 1904, Phan Boi Chau felt the support of Japan* was necessary to Vietnam, so both he and Cuong De went to live in Japan and study. Phan Boi Chau met with Japanese leaders who urged him to send young men to Japan for military and political training, and in 1907 he organized the "Exodus to the East," a program which sent more than two hundred young Vietnamese to study in Japan.

By then, however, Phan Boi Chau was growing more sympathetic with Chinese philosophers committed to democratic reform, and his royalist schemes to restore Cuong De to the Vietnamese throne waned. Instead of a return to the inflexibility of the mandarin bureaucracy, Vietnamese independence would come only through mass participation. He attempted a rebellion against the French which failed late in 1907, and led to the execution of thirteen of Phan Boi Chau's followers. He had remained in Japan during the revolt, but fled to Siam after the French began demanding his extradiction. Phan and his resistance group, Duy Tan Hoi (founded in 1904), continued to play an important role in Vietnamese nationalism. He was imprisoned between 1912 and 1917 for establishing a new nationalist group, the Viet Nam Quang Phuc Hoi, and the unsuccessful assassination attempt on Albert Sarraut. Phan Boi Chau was a major figure in Vietnamese rebellion against the French because his political organizations rallied mass insurgency and his East Asia United League at least gave the Vietnamese a visible profile among nationalists in Japan, China,* Korea,* India, and the Philippines.*

French agents constantly tracked Phan after the 1907 revolt, and he maintained his freedom, albeit a furtive one, until 1925 when they caught up with him in Shanghai. Charged with sedition, Phan Boi Chau was extradited to Hanoi,* tried and convicted of sedition, and placed under house arrest in Hue.* He died fifteen years later in 1940.

Sources: *Webster's New Biographical Dictionary*, 1983; David G. Marr, *Vietnamese Anticolonialism, 1885–1925*, 1971; Joseph Buttinger, *Vietnam: A Dragon Embattled*. Vol. 1, *From Colonialism to the Vietminh*, 1967.

PHAN CHAU TRINH

Born in central Vietnam in 1872, Phan Chau Trinh came from a wealthy, scholarly, landowning family. His father was loyal to Emperor Ham Nghi, fought in the Scholar's Revolt, but was killed in 1885 by other dissidents who considered him a traitor. Phan Chau Trinh studied the Chinese classics under the tutorship of his brother, and by 1901 he had earned the most prestigious mandarin degree. He met Phan Boi Chau* in 1903 and in 1905 resigned his position in the mandarin

366   PHAN DINH PHUNG

bureaucracy. He quickly split company with Phan Boi Chau because he had no faith in Japanese benevolence, and instead of viewing the French as the major enemy of Vietnamese independence, he blamed the mandarin bureaucracy and imperial family. Phan Chau Trinh preferred the French to the Nguyen* clan. Allying himself with French anticolonialists,* Phan Chau Trinh called for the destruction of the mandarin bureaucracy and its replacement with a modern educational and legal system. He also advocated industrialization of Vietnam. Phan Chau Trinh eschewed the radical violence of Phan Boi Chau, but his trust in the power of French liberals proved naive. France* arrested him for revolutionary activity* in 1908 and kept him in prison until 1911, when he went to live in France. For the next ten years Phan Chau Trinh met with French liberals and journalists, and became a symbol of Vietnamese nationalism, but he lacked broad peasant support. Phan Chau Trinh died in 1926.

Sources: Joseph Buttinger, *The Smaller Dragon: A Political History of Vietnam*, 1958; *Webster's New Biographical Dictionary*, 1983.

PHAN DINH PHUNG

Born in 1847, Phan Dinh Phung became one of the most prominent of the nineteenth-century Vietnamese nationalists. He rose to power at the imperial court of Tu Duc. Although he was banished from the imperial court because of his eventual opposition to the accession of Ham Nghi to the imperial throne, Phan Dinh Phung organized his own guerrilla army, retreated into the mountains of central Vietnam, and for nearly a decade regularly attacked the French throughout a region extending from Thanh Hoa Province in the north to Quang Binh in the south. Phan Dinh Phung died of dysentery in 1896, but his life and career became a rallying point and patriotic memory for three generations of Vietnamese nationalists.

Sources: *Webster's New Biographical Dictionary*, 1983; Stanley Karnow, *Vietnam: A History*, 1983; Joseph Buttinger, *Vietnam: A Dragon Embattled*. Vol. 1, *From Colonialism to the Vietminh*, 1967.

PHAN HUY QUAT

From February 16 to June 12, 1965, Phan Huy Quat was prime minister of South Vietnam. An able and reform-minded civilian politician, Quat served as a transitional leader between General Nguyen Khanh* and Air Marshal Nguyen Cao Ky.* Born in 1901 in northern Vietnam, Quat received a medical degree in Hanoi* in 1937 and operated a maternity clinic there until 1945. He became one of the founders of the Dai Viet Quoc Dan Dang,* or Nationalist party of Greater Vietnam. In the early 1950s, he held several cabinet posts including minister of defense. Ngo Dinh Diem* viewed him as a serious rival and refused to give him a cabinet post after 1954. In 1955 the United States came very close to endorsing Quat as a replacement for Diem. Quat was one of the signers of the ''Caravelle'' petition urging reform in April 1960 and was arrested but later released by Diem's government in November 1960.

After Diem's death in 1963, Quat was finally included in South Vietnam's cabinet. Early in 1965 the Armed Forces Council forced Nguyen Khanh out of power, and the military group supported the selection of Quat as prime minister. Quat attempted to structure a representative cabinet and to cultivate the goodwill of the military, but he was unable to overcome the factional intrigues among Buddhists,* Catholics,* and other groups in Saigon.* When Quat finally came to an impasse with elderly Chief of State Phan Khac Suu,* the military forced Quat to resign, and Nguyen Cao Ky* became prime minister. Quat was a well-known opponent of communism. After Hanoi's victory in 1975, attempts to get him out of Vietnam proved unsuccessful, and he was killed.

Source: Robert Shaplen, *The Lost Revolution*, 1965.

David L. Anderson

PHAN KHAC SUU

Phan Khac Suu was born in My Tho* in the Mekong Delta* in 1905. The son of a prosperous farmer, Suu studied engineering in Paris during the 1920s. He returned to Saigon* in 1930 and took an engineering job with the French government, but at night he was actively engaged in anti-French nationalist activities. The French imprisoned him at Poulo Condore* between 1940 and 1945. Suu was a devout member of the Cao Dai* religion who served briefly in 1954 as minister of agriculture under Ngo Dinh Diem.* After cooperating in the abortive coup against Diem in 1960, Suu spent three more years in prison. He was released after Diem's assassination and became chief of state of South Vietnam in 1964–65 and president of the Constituent Assembly in 1966–67. During the last years before his death in 1970, Suu was an opponent of Generals Nguyen Cao Ky* and Nguyen Van Thieu.*

Source: *New York Times*, May 25, 1970.

PHAN QUANG DAN

Phan Quang Dan was born on November 6, 1918, in Nghe An. He received an M.D. degree from the University of Hanoi in 1945 and later studied at the Sorbonne in Paris and at Harvard University. An intense anti-Communist, Phan Quang Dan was a political adviser to Bao Dai* in the late 1940s. He relocated to South Vietnam after 1954 and taught at the Medical School of Saigon.* He practiced medicine in a working-class neighborhood in Saigon and won election to the Constituent Assembly in 1955. An outspoken opponent of Ngo Dinh Diem,* he was not allowed to assume his seat in the Assembly and instead spent time undergoing torture as a political prisoner. Later in the 1960s Phan Quang Dan spoke out against the corruption of the Thieu-Ky government even while opposing the Communists.

Sources: *Asia Who's Who*, 1960; Frances FitzGerald, *Fire in the Lake: The Vietnamese and the Americans in Vietnam*, 1972; Joseph Buttinger, *Vietnam: A Dragon Embattled*. Vol. 2, *Vietnam at War*, 1967.

PHILIPPINES

The Philippines played a dual role in the Vietnam War. The location of the giant military complexes of Subic Bay Naval Base and Clark Air Base within the Philippines virtually assured that this country would serve as the primary non-U.S. staging area for the war. Virtually all naval aircraft and ordnance passed through Subic. It served as the main repair station for the Seventh Fleet,* playing host to 1,600 military personnel and 9,000 sailors at any one time. Similarly, Clark Air Base saw such an increase in traffic that a reserve air base on Mactan Island was made operational in order to handle some of the volume. Clark became the hub for all U.S. military air traffic in the western Pacific and the operational hope of the 13th Air Force.

The second role for the Philippines was support for the war effort. Manila had always been a strong champion of South Vietnam, which the Philippines considered the key to the future political direction of Southeast Asia. In June 1964 Defense Minister Tran Thien Khiem* of South Vietnam visited the Philippines in return for which Manila sent thirty-four Filipino doctors to Saigon.* Later in 1964 the Philippines reiterated its support for the defense of Southeast Asia in general and Vietnam in particular under the SEATO agreements. In September 1965, Manila served as the center for the American-sponsored Asian People's Anti-Communist League, which condemned North Vietnamese aggression in South Vietnam. In October 1966, the Philippines hosted a summit of all the nations that had troops in South Vietnam to assess the prospects for peace there. North Vietnam, of course, refused to attend.

Increasing American military involvement in South Vietnam led to the "Many Flags Program" of 1965, in which the United States asked for troop commitments from its allies. Australia,* New Zealand,* and South Korea* quickly responded. President Lyndon B. Johnson* especially wanted Filipino participation. The new president of the Philippines, Ferdinand Marcos, initially refused; but after visits from Vice President Hubert Humphrey,* Senator Mike Mansfield,* Secretary of State Dean Rusk,* and Ambassador W. Averell Harriman,* he relented. On February 19, 1966, Marcos announced that a combat engineering battalion of 2,000 men would be sent. They served until October 4, 1969, when increasing Filipino opposition to the Vietnam War forced their withdrawal. Marcos's support for the war, however, was not motivated simply by feelings of national security. He negotiated aggressively for $39 million in additional American aid as well as sizable contributions of equipment to the Philippine military. Marcos also made sure that Filipino troops had full access to U.S. military PXs, which they exploited, and that the United States employ Filipino civilians in Vietnam.

The Philippines contributed to the Vietnam War in another, less direct way. During the 1950s, the United States had supported the highly successful Filipino fight against the Communist-led Hukbalahap (Huk) insurrection. This included engineering the ascendancy of the strongly pro-U.S. Ramon Magsaysay to the Philippine presidency. As Paul Nitze* noted in 1965, the Philippine experience demonstrated conclusively that guerrillas could be suppressed. In a very real sense, the Philippines became a model for the American role in South Vietnam.

After the end of the war and the triumph of North Vietnam in 1975, the Philippines became even more important to U.S. interests. The Socialist Republic of Vietnam* permitted a large Soviet naval presence in Cam Ranh Bay* and a significant Soviet air presence at Da Nang.* Subic Bay and Clark military facilities are now considered a counterweight of inestimable importance.

Sources: William J. Pomeroy, *An American Made Tragedy: Neo-Colonialism and Dictatorship in the Philippines*, 1974; James Gregor, *Crisis in the Philippines: A Threat to U.S. Interests*, 1984; Man Mohini Kaul, *The Philippines and South East Asia*, 1978.

Gary M. Bell

PHOENIX PROGRAM

An effort by the government of (South) Vietnam (GVN; *see* Republic of Vietnam) and the Central Intelligence Agency* (CIA) to gather intelligence on the Vietcong* infrastructure (VCI) and to coordinate a counterinsurgency* effort against that VCI, Phoenix was actually an attempt to use the same techniques and tactics that had proven effective for the Vietcong. The three basic objectives of Phoenix were to identity Vietcong (VC), gain the support and cooperation of local Vietnamese in combatting the VC, and eventually reduce the military and political activities of the enemy. Phoenix was characterized primarily by its bureaucratic nature. To be successful, it had to decrease the endemic political contests that so characterized South Vietnam. A unified and coordinated effort was necessary before the GVN could gain legitimacy and loyalty, which were essential factors in diminishing the enemy's political and military effectiveness.

Phoenix was aimed at the VC "shadow government" (policymakers and policy implementers). Its first task was to identify individual members of the VCI. It then sought to "neutralize" those individuals, through arrest, conversion, or death. While basically a GVN program, Phoenix relied heavily on American support. The CIA provided essential advice and personnel for the intelligence-gathering aspects of the program. The Civil Operations and Revolutionary Development Support* (CORDS) assisted in the effort to coordinate Phoenix activities both among the numerous and varied GVN governmental units and with the village and hamlet officials.

The Phoenix Program faced major obstacles. Coordination was a continuing difficulty, corruption was prevalent, and the quota system adopted for identifying members of the VCI meant that any Vietnamese was at risk. Begun in 1968 under the direction of Robert Komer* and William Colby, Phoenix lasted until 1972 and was only marginally successful. Although these years coincided with a precipitous decline in VC activity and effectiveness, Phoenix was not a major factor in that decline. Rather, the debilitation of the VC was due to normal losses of a military nature, especially the Tet Offensive,* which was a disaster for the Vietcong, who lost approximately 80 percent of their military forces in a six-week period of massive conventional attacks.

Phoenix did result in the identification and neutralization of over 20,000 individuals in South Vietnam. However, inconsistent record keeping, abuse of the program in resolving personal disputes, the use of Phoenix to maintain a favored position by removing political adversaries, and the quota system meant that many of those neutralized were not Vietcong.

Sources: Samuel Lipsman et al., *The Vietnam Experience: Fighting for Time*, 1983; John Prados, *Presidents' Secret Wars: CIA and Pentagon Covert Operations Since World War II*, 1986.

Stafford T. Thomas

PHU BAI

Located 45 miles north of Da Nang* near Hue,* Phu Bai was an important American military installation between 1965 and 1972. An air and marine base was established at Phu Bai in the spring of 1965. In April the 9th Marine Expeditionary Brigade,* along with the 3rd Battalion of the Fourth Marines,* was stationed at Phu Bai, along with ten UH–34* helicopters. Eventually Phu Bai became home to Marine Air Group 39, with its seventy-five helicopters and fixed-wing aircraft. Phu Bai fell to the Vietcong* after the American withdrawal from Vietnam in 1972.

Sources: Edward Doyle and Samuel Lipsman, *The Vietnam Experience: America Takes Over, 1965–1967*, 1985; Carroll H. Dunn, *Base Development in South Vietnam 1965–1970*, 1972.

PHUOC BINH

Phuoc Binh (also known as "Song Be" after the Be River), capital of Phuoc Long Province, was located in the northern tip of II Corps,* at the foot of the Central Highlands* in mountainous terrain. Amost due west of Snoul, Cambodia (*see* Kampuchea), a major Vietcong* and North Vietnamese Army* (NVA) supply base, Phuoc Binh was a frequent target for enemy attack. Surrounded by mountains which were never cleared of Vietcong-NVA forces, the city and military compounds were rocketed so frequently that it was appropriately called "rocket alley."

In May 1965 Phuoc Binh was defended by an ARVN (*see* Army of the Republic of Vietnam) Ranger Battalion and an American Special Forces* detachment. A Vietcong attack put the Rangers to rout. The Special Forces held their compound only after hand-to-hand combat. In October 1967, as a prelude to the 1968 Tet Offensive,* Vietcong-NVA forces mounted a series of attacks in rural areas including Phuoc Binh to draw U.S. forces away from population centers. The Phuoc Binh attack was successfully repelled, but the city was attacked again during the Tet Offensive. The city was virtually destroyed in the fighting.

Engineers, supported by U.S. infantry, opened the road from Long Binh* to Phuoc Binh early in 1969 for the first time in three years. Phuoc Binh's remoteness, coupled with difficult terrain and proximity to the Iron Triangle,* made continuous Vietcong-NVA interdiction of the main highway easy, necessitating resupply by air. Phuoc Binh was the first provincial capital to fall during the 1975 Final Offensive (*see* Ho Chi Minh Campaign). The province was lightly defended, making it an ideal diversion for the main offensive in II Corps. Phuoc Binh's fall reportedly was facilitated by ARVN corruption so great that infantry units had to pay artillery units for fire support.

Sources: Shelby L. Stanton, *The Rise and Fall of an American Army. U.S. Ground Troops in Vietnam, 1965–1973*, 1985; Stanley Karnow, *Vietnam: A History*, 1983; Bruce Palmer, Jr., *The 25-Year War*, 1984.

Samuel Freeman

PHUOC LONG   *See* Phuoc Binh

PIASTER

Before World War II, the currency used throughout French Indochina* was the piaster, a money directly tied to the franc. Issued by the Bank of Indochina, the piaster was the first currency used nationwide in Vietnam. A severe inflation hit the piaster during the Japanese occupation of World War II because the Vichy France* government issued large volumes of unsecured piasters. The French revalued the piaster to 17 francs in 1946, an official rate of 21 piasters to the U.S. dollar, but it actually sold on the free market for 65 piasters to the dollar. A new piaster was issued in 1949 after the unification of Vietnam, Laos,* and Cambodia (*see* Kampuchea), but it was devalued in 1952. In 1954 the Republic of Vietnam* withdrew from the franc zone, and in 1955 the South Vietnamese government began issuing a new, independent piaster, whose value was supported by the United States.

Source: Harvey H. Smith et al., *Area Handbook for South Vietnam*, 1967.

PIGNON, LEON

Léon Pignon was born on April 19, 1908, and educated at the École Coloniale. During the 1930s he worked for the Ministry for the Colonies and spent time in Tonkin.* Strongly committed to the idea of the French Empire, Pignon always saw independence for Vietnam as the height of folly. Pignon spent time in a German prison during World War II, and after the war was federal commissioner for foreign affairs in 1946–47 and commissioner of the republic in Cambodia (*see* Kampuchea) in 1947–48. He succeeded Georges d'Argenlieu* and Emile Bollaert* as high commissioner for Indochina* in 1948–50. Pignon hated the Vietminh* and would not hear of negotiating with them. Between 1950 and 1954 he served as a delegate to the United Nations Trusteeship Council, and between 1954 and 1959 as director of political affairs for the Ministry of French Overseas Territories. Léon Pignon died on April 4, 1976.

Sources: *International Who's Who 1976–77*, 1977; Joseph Buttinger, *Vietnam: A Dragon Embattled*. Vol. 2, *Vietnam at War*, 1967.

PLAIN OF REEDS

The Plain of Reeds was a flat, brush-covered region covering nearly 2,500 square miles in Kien Phong and Kien Tuong provinces and parts of Dinh Tuong, Long An, and Hau Nghia provinces. The Vietcong* used the Plain of Reeds as a base area for military operations against American and South Vietnamese forces.

Source: Danny Whitfield, *Historical and Cultural Dictionary of Vietnam*, 1976.

PLATOON

Commanded by a lieutenant, a platoon is an organizational unit composed of two or more squads.* A sergeant is usually second in command.

Source: Shelby L. Stanton, *Vietnam Order of Battle*, 1981.

PLATOON

Platoon is a gritty, grunt's-eye view of the Vietnam War. Directed by Oliver Stone, a Vietnam veteran, the film focuses on the war in 1967 as two sergeants, one brutal and the other compassionate, struggle for influence and as a new recruit witnesses combat and atrocities committed by and against his platoon. Unlike the surrealistic *Apocalypse Now*,* the jingoism of *Rambo*,* and the overt antiwar attitudes of *Coming Home*,* *Platoon* was widely recognized by critics during its late 1986 release as the best and most realistic of the Vietnam War films.

Source: "Vietnam Images," *USA Today*, January 2, 1987.

PLEIKU

Located in the Central Highlands* and bordered by Cambodia (*see* Kampuchea), Pleiku City is the capital of Pleiku Province and was II Corps* Tactical Zone headquarters. Pleiku City also was regional market for mountain tribes, and its strategic location made it the center of a large U.S.-ARVN (*see* Army of the Republic of Vietnam) military complex. The province endured heavy fighting throughout the war. On February 7, 1965, National Liberation Front (NLF; *see* Vietcong) forces attacked Camp Holloway and Pleiku's airfield, killing 9 and wounding 128 Americans. Coupled with NLF attacks on American personnel at Qui Nhon,* this served as Lyndon Johnson's* justification for regularizing the air war and committing U.S. combat units to South Vietnam. Why the NLF attacked Pleiku and why the United States responded as it did are debatable. Some say the attack was the logical consequence of guerrilla war. Others see an attempt by North Vietnam to gain leverage with the Soviets, and as a "coup" for China. Some, citing Johnson's "I've had enough of this," see the American response resulting from having been pushed too far. Others, citing McGorge Bundy's* "Pleikus are like streetcars" (one comes along every few minutes), contend the Americanization of the war had already been decided—the attack was only a pretext.

The first major battle between U.S. and North Vietnamese Army* (NVA) forces occurred in Pleiku Province's Ia Drang Valley* in November 1965. Elements of the 1st Cavalry Division* and the NVA's 32nd, 33rd, and 66th regiments were locked in heavy combat for three days before NVA forces withdrew. Pleiku City was rocketed and mortared in the summer of 1967 as the NLF and NVA prepared for the 1968 Tet Offensive.* It also was the scene of heavy fighting during Tet. In the Final Offensive (*see* Ho Chi Minh Campaign), the NVA made a diversionary attack against Pleiku and Kontum while three divisions prepared for the main assault against Ban Me Thuot.* After Ban Me Thuot fell, Nguyen Van Thieu* ordered Pleiku's abandonment. The rout had begun.

Sources: Shelby L. Stanton, *The Rise and Fall of an American Army: U.S. Ground Troops in Vietnam, 1965–1973*, 1985; Jean Lacouture, *Vietnam Between Two Truces*, 1966; George C. Herring, *America's Longest War: The United States in Vietnam, 1950–1975*, 1986.

Samuel Freeman

"POINT"

"Point" was a term used during the Vietnam War to describe an individual or unit advancing in front of the main body of troops. The purpose of the "point" was to draw enemy fire and allow the main body of soldiers to then attack.

Source: Al Santoli, *Everything We Had: An Oral History of the Vietnam War By Thirty-Three Soldiers Who Fought It*, 1981.

POL POT

Born in Cambodia (*see* Kampuchea) as Saloth Sar in 1928, Pol Pot left his peasant background and as a teenager during the 1940s joined the forces of Ho Chi Minh* in fighting both the Japanese and the French. He became secretary of the Cambodian communist party in 1963, and during that same year he retreated into the Cambodian jungles and formed the Khmer Rouge* guerrillas. They opposed the government of Norodom Sihanouk,* and the American invasion of Cambodia in 1970 (*see* Operation Binh Tay) greatly swelled their numbers, giving them the strength to depose the government of Lon Nol* in 1975. At that point Pol Pot initiated a genocidal campaign matched only by Adolf Hitler's World War II assault on Jews and East Europeans. Dreaming of a preindustrial, agricultural utopia, Pol Pot decided to eliminate cities, intellectuals, professionals, and the Cambodian middle class. He completely evacuated the capital city of Phnom Penh and declared "Year Zero." During the next three years the Khmer Rouge obliterated libraries, temples, cities, schools, and colleges, and turned the entire country into a large concentration camp. An estimated two million people perished in his crusade for utopia. In 1978, the Vietnamese invaded Cambodia and deposed Pol Pot, creating the People's Republic of Kampuchea in its place. Pol Pot retreated into the jungles with what was left of the Khmer Rouge and continued guerrilla warfare against the new government.

Sources: Michael Vickery, *Cambodia, 1975–1982*, 1984; John Barron and Paul Anthony, *Murder of a Gentle Land*, 1977; Ben Kiernan, "How Pol Pot Came to Power," Ph.D. diss., 1986; William Shawcross, *Sideshow: Kissinger, Nixon, and the Destruction of Cambodia*, 1979, and *The Quality of Mercy: Cambodia, Holocaust, and the Modern Conscience*, 1984.

POPULAR FORCES

The Popular Forces were paramilitary units, along with the Regional Forces,* and helped constitute the Territorial Forces* of South Vietnam. Unlike the Regional Forces, they were nonuniformed, static units charged with village and hamlet defense. They were first activated in 1955 and were under the operational control of the province chief. In 1964 they became part of the South Vietnamese Army, commanded by the Joint General Staff.* After 1969, when U.S. military units began their gradual withdrawal, the Popular Forces were often removed from their home villages and attached to main ARVN (*see* Army of the Republic of Vietnam) units for combat with the Vietcong* and North Vietnamese. Along with the Regional Forces, the Popular Forces suffered more than eighty thousand killed between 1965 and 1973.

Source: Ngo Quang Truong, *Territorial Forces*, 1981.

PORTER, WILLIAM JAMES

Born in England in 1914, Porter obtained a clerk's position in the American diplomatic mission in Baghdad, and for the next ten years served in Beirut, Lebanon, Baghdad, Damascus, and Jerusalem. A specialist in the Middle East, Porter became ambassador to Algeria in 1962, and later was assigned in 1965 as deputy ambassador to South Vietnam. This unusual position was created so that Porter, an experienced diplomat, could work with the ambassadors assigned to that post.

Porter's assignment was to bring order to the so-called pacification program (*see* Rural Reconstruction) recently established in South Vietnam. The object was to attract the loyalty of the Vietnamese people through the efforts of trained workers in health, education, and agriculture strategically located throughout the country. The program was not working efficiently because there were different agencies involved, including the Central Intelligence Agency,* the United States Information Agency, and the Agency for International Development,* which were duplicating one another's efforts. Porter's attempt to coordinate the program was short-lived because, after eighteen months, it was transferred from the embassy to the Military Assistance Command,* and he was reassigned as ambassador to South Korea.

Porter's most significant role in the Vietnam War was as provider of information and advice to President Lyndon Johnson* and as negotiator in the Paris peace talks.* Porter, drawing upon his earlier experience with insurgency in Morocco and Algeria, pointed out that in the uprisings in those two countries, there had been considerable popular support. The Vietcong,* he noted, had not mobilized such support. His reports buttressed Johnson's belief that a policy of escalation was in order because the struggle against the Vietcong could be won.

In 1970, the aggressive diplomatic style that Porter had developed stood him in good stead, for he was called on to explain to a Senate subcommittee the expenditure, kept secret, of one billion dollars on the 50,000 troops sent to South Vietnam since 1965. Again, in the following year, he drew upon his skill at negotiation when asked to explain to the South Vietnamese the withdrawal of 20,000 of the 50,000 American troops located in Vietnam.

In 1971, he was named as a delegate to the Paris peace talks with North Vietnam then in progress. His task was to work out detailed arrangements to buttress the broad agreements between Henry Kissinger* and Le Duc Tho,* the North Vietnamese negotiator. Porter's most significant contribution to the Paris talks was his unwillingness to allow his opponents to use them as a stage for propaganda statements. His unconventional approach helped to break the deadlock that had stalled progress in these negotiations. According to a *Time* report, Porter "changed the once patient and restrained U.S. style in Paris" by taking the verbal offensive and talking tough. In 1973, President Richard Nixon* named him as under secretary of state for political affairs and in 1974, ambassador to Canada. His last post, 1975 to 1977, was as ambassador to Saudi Arabia.

Sources: *Current Biography Yearbook*, 1974; "People," *Time*, January 17, 1972, 26–27; *International Who's Who, 1983–1984*, 47th ed., 1983.

Joanna D. Cowden

POST-TRAUMATIC STRESS DISORDER

Between 1954 and 1975, more than 2,800,000 Americans served in Vietnam, and nearly one million of them saw combat. Because of its unique nature—a guerrilla conflict (*see* Vietcong), a war of attrition,* intense opposition at home, and the youthful age of the average soldier (nineteen)—the Vietnam War exacted a high toll from its participants. Most of the American combatants experienced to one degree or another a serious psychological disorder characterized by emotional numbness, severe flashbacks and recurring nightmares, periodic panic and depression, and sometimes violent behavior. In earlier wars the disorder had other names—"shell shock" in World War I, "battle fatigue" in World War II, "operational exhaustion" in the Korea War, but the Vietnam variety was more severe because the war was such a traumatic event in American society. Risking their lives, sometimes killing and maiming civilians, the Vietnam veterans then came home to a hostile country convinced their sacrifice had been a waste at best and murder at worst. In 1980, with the third edition of its *Diagnostic and Statistical Manual of Mental Disorders*, the American Psychiatric Association named the Vietnam veteran disease PTSD, or Post-Traumatic Stress Disorder. In December 1979 the Veterans Administration opened the first Vet Center staffed with social workers, psychologists, and paraprofessionals. By January 1985 there were 135 Vet Centers across the country and more than 200,000 veterans had sought treatment there.

Source: John Langone, "The War That Has No Ending," *Discover* 6 (June 1985), 44–54.

POULO CONDORE

Poulo Condore is an island approximately 75 miles off the southeast of the Ca Mau Peninsula in the South China Sea. In February 1861 a French invasion force reached Vietnam, and by July they had seized Saigon.* After one year they were firmly in control of the three surrounding provinces: Dinh Tuong, Gia Dinh, and Bien Hoa. In June 1862 Emperor Tu Duc agreed to a peace treaty. He had little choice, since a dynastic rebellion against him had erupted in Tonkin.* As part of the treaty, France* gained control of Poulo Condore, $4 million, religious freedom, free access to port facilities at Tourane (Da Nang),* and the right to veto any foreign alliances Vietnam tried to establish. The French constructed an infamous prison on Poulo Condore to incarcerate politically rebellious nationalists. Such prominent anti-imperialists as Phan Chu Trinh,* Pham Van Dong,* and Le Duc Tho* all spent years in the underground cells, suffering from heat, hunger, and disease. After the expulsion of the French, the South Vietnamese government used the prison to hold Vietcong* guerrillas, Communist sympathizers, and North Vietnamese prisoners of war. By that time Poulo Condore was known by its Vietnamese name—Con Son Island. It became famous in 1970 when revelations of the "tiger cages"* received international press coverage. The "tiger cages" were the prison cells at the Con Son Correctional Center.

Sources: Stanley Karnow, *Vietnam: A History*, 1983; *New York Times*, July 8, 1970.

THE PRISONERS OF QUAI DONG

The Prisoners of Quai Dong is the title of Victor Kolpacoff's 1967 novel describing a prison camp in North Vietnam inhabited by American prisoners of war* (POWs) and their North Vietnamese captors. Through the lens of an interrogation room, where Americans are regularly tortured to extract confessions, Kolpacoff eventually describes everyone there—American POWs, Vietnamese officials, and innocent witnesses—as equally prisoners of the Vietnam War.

Sources: Victor Kolpacoff, *The Prisoners of Quai Dong*, 1967; Philip D. Beidler, *American Literature and the Experience of Vietnam*, 1982.

PRISONERS OF WAR

The question of American prisoners of war (POWs) in Southeast Asia was one of the most difficult and controversial of the war. Return of the POWs was a central demand in the American negotiating position with the North Vietnamese and Vietcong* between 1965 and 1972, and North Vietnam exploited that bargaining chip for all it was worth. Eventually, the United States compromised on its opposition to a coalition government in South Vietnam and its insistence on a withdrawal of North Vietnamese troops, but continued to insist on the return of all American POWs. That was arranged in the 1972 Paris Peace Accords,* and between February and April 1973, North Vietnam returned 566 American military POWs and 25 civilian POWs (*see* Operation Homecoming). Although the Democratic Republic of Vietnam* said it agreed with the 1949 Geneva Convention on treatment of prisoners of war, the American POWs were subject to torture, malnutrition, inadequate medical treatment, political manipulation, and generally inhumane treatment.

Despite the return of the POWs, there were still another 2,483 Americans still unaccounted for during the Southeast Asian conflict. They were either captured or killed, or were deserters somewhere in North Vietnam, South Vietnam, Laos,* or Cambodia (*see* Kampuchea). By mid–1986, North Vietman had returned the remains of 104 Americans who allegedly died during captivity or in aircraft crashes and firefights. The problem of these Americans listed as missing in action (MIA) continues to remain a controversial issue for two reasons. (1) There are continuing rumors of Americans still held captive in Vietnam, Laos, or Cambodia, and the American public, as well as the families of those listed as missing in action, maintains pressure for a resolution of the issue. Groups such as the National League of Families of American POWs and MIAs in Southeast Asia keep political pressure on government officials to demand cooperation from the Socialist Republic of Vietnam.* (2) The large discrepancy between the number missing and the number of prisoners actually returned leaves a huge question about just how many American POWs died during confinement in North Vietnamese, Cambodian, Laotian, or Vietcong prisons—how many died of starvation, torture, murder, and neglect.

Sources: Reader's Digest, *POW: A Definitive History of the American Prisoner of War Experience in Vietnam, 1964–1973*, 1976; Guenter Lewy, *America in Vietnam*, 1978; Department of Defense, *POW-MIA Fact Book*, 1985.

PROJECT DELTA

In May 1964 the Studies and Observation Groups* launched Project Leaping Lena, a program to train Civilian Irregular Defense Group* and elite Vietnamese troops in long-range reconnaissance patrol* (LRRP) tactics. One year later the LRRP training program was reassigned to the Fifth Special Forces Group,* which redesignated it Project Delta. Composed of 450 troops divided into twelve reconnaissance teams, twelve Roadrunner teams (indigenous South Vietnamese who dressed as Vietcong* or North Vietnamese and infiltrated their units), a security company composed of ethnic Nung* troops, and the 91st ARVN Ranger Battalion (*see* Army of the Republic of Vietnam). They gathered intelligence on North Vietnamese and Vietcong units, evaluated bomb and artillery damage, and conducted raids. Project Delta was also known as Detachment B–52. After September 1966, Project Delta also included training regular U.S. infantry in LRRP tactics.

Source: Francis J. Kelly, *U.S. Army Special Forces, 1961–1971*, 1973.

PROJECT DYE MARKER   *See* Project Practice Nine

PROJECT ILLINOIS CITY   *See* Project Practice Nine

PROJECT OMEGA

Encouraged by the success of Project Delta* in 1965, General William West-moreland* had the Fifth Special Forces Group* launch Project Omega in August 1966. Known as Detachment B–50, Project Omega consisted of approximately 900 Civilian Irregular Defense Group* troops and 125 U.S. personnel. It was headquartered at Ban Me Thuot* in II Corps.* Project Omega gathered intelligence on enemy positions, called in air strikes and evaluated bombing damage, and conducted special raids against the North Vietnamese and Vietcong.* Project Omega evolved into the Mobile Guerrilla Force* concept in 1967 and was absorbed into the Studies and Observation Group's* program in November 1967.

Source: Francis J. Kelly. *U.S. Army Special Forces, 1961–1971*, 1973.

PROJECT PRACTICE NINE

Project Practice Nine was the codename for the Department of Defense's plan to install an electronic infiltration barrier across Vietnam, just south of the Demilitarized Zone* (DMZ), from the South China Sea to Laos.* Popularly known as the "Electric Fence" or "McNamara's Wall," the barrier was to consist of a strip of bulldozed jungle laced with mines, electronic sensors, booby traps,* and obstacles. The Defense Department was convinced that construction of the barrier would eliminate the need for larger troop reinforcements in I Corps,* so William Westmoreland* and the Military Assistance Command, Vietnam* (MACV) endorsed the concept. The Marine Corps* was totally opposed. They thought it would be expensive and probably unworkable—that the technology would not really stop infiltration.* Worse, they were convinced Project Practice Nine would drastically change their role in the war, taking them away from mobile assaults to requiring them to defend static positions along the barrier. But the Defense Department rejected the marine arguments, and in the spring of 1967 the Third Marine Division* began preparing for construction of the barrier.

In order to prepare for construction of the barrier, the Third Marine Division had to launch sweep and clear operations in May 1967. On May 18, a combined Marine-ARVN (*see* Army of the Republic of Vietnam) force attacked into the southern reaches of the DMZ. Five ARVN battalions invaded in the Lam Son 54 portion of the operation. The 1st Battalion of the Third Marines pushed into the DMZ in Operation Beau Charger, and in the west, Operation Hickory saw the 2nd and 3rd Battalions of the 9th Marines, the 2nd Battalion of the 26th Marines, the 3rd Battalion of the Fourth Marines,* and the 2nd Battalion of the Third Marines engaged in the sweep. They were fighting the 31st, 32nd, and 812th NVA Regiments of the North Vietnamese Army* (NVA). They evacuated large numbers of civilians from the area, engaged in hard fighting with the NVA, and destroyed massive bunker and tunnel complexes. The initial sweep operations were concluded at the end of May. In June 1967 Project Practice Nine was renamed Project Illinois City, and it was renamed again in July 1967, this time Project Dye Marker. Although some test stages of the barrier were constructed, Secretary of Defense Robert McNamara's* dream of a barrier all the way across Vietnam never came to be. It was too ambitious, too expensive, and too naive, all of which became abundantly clear in 1968 with the Tet Offensive* and the siege of Khe Sanh.*

Sources: Shelby L. Stanton, *The Rise and Fall of an American Army: U.S. Ground Troops in Vietnam, 1965–1973*, 1985; Gregory Palmer, *The McNamara Strategy and the Vietnam War: Program Budgeting in the Pentagon, 1960–1968*, 1978; Lloyd Norman, "McNamara's Fence: Our Eyes and Ears Along the DMZ," *Army* 18 (August 1968), pp. 28–33.

PROJECT SIGMA

Encouraged by the success of Project Delta* in 1965, General William Westmoreland* had the Fifth Special Forces Group* launch Project Sigma in August 1966. Known as Detachment–56, Project Sigma consisted of approximately 900 Civilian Irregular Defense Group* troops and 125 U.S. personnel. It was headquartered at Ho Ngoc Nau outside Saigon.* Project Sigma gathered intelligence on enemy positions, called in air strikes and evaluated bombing damage, and conducted special raids against the North Vietnamese and Vietcong.* Project Sigma evolved into the Mobile Guerrilla Force* concept in 1967 and was absorbed into the Studies and Observation Group's* program in November 1967.

Source: Francis J. Kelly, *U.S. Army Special Forces, 1961–1971*, 1973.

PROTECTIVE REACTION STRIKES

On October 31, 1968, as part of a general, informal agreement reached in Paris between negotiators for the United States and North Vietnam, naval and air force "offensive" strikes against the Democratic Republic of Vietnam* were stopped. The United States continued reconnaissance flights over North Vietnam, and when those flights were fired upon, the U.S. Air Force* began sending armed escorts with them. Those escorts fired on the antiaircraft installations attacking the reconnaissance planes, although the U.S. strikes had to be confined to areas south of the nineteenth parallel. In April 1970, the United States authorized air strikes on North Vietnamese SAM* and antiaircraft installations protecting the Ho Chi Minh Trail* from American bombing.* Those strikes had to occur south of the twentieth parallel. Department of Defense spokesmen referred to them as "protective reaction strikes." Other "protective reaction strikes" were used in 1970 to stop North Vietnamese infiltration* across the Demilitarized Zone.* More than 1,100 sorties* occurred in 1970 as part of the "protective reaction" program.

Sources: John Morrocco, *The Vietnam Experience. Rain of Fire: Air War, 1969–1973*, 1984; Peter Mersky and Norman Polmar, *The Naval Air War in Vietnam*, 1981.

PROVISIONAL REVOLUTIONARY GOVERNMENT OF SOUTH VIETNAM

The Provisional Revolutionary Government of South Vietnam was the name taken by the National Liberation Front (NLF; *See* Vietcong) in 1969. It was the Communist government in South Vietnam until 1975 when North Vietnamese forces reunited the country. Its primary spokesperson was Nguyen Thi Binh,* longtime foreign minister for the NLF.

Sources: Douglas Pike, *History of the Vietnamese Communist Party*, 1978, and *The Viet Cong Strategy of Terror*, 1970.

PROXMIRE, WILLIAM

When Republican Senator Joe McCarthy died in 1957, Wisconsin voters replaced him with Democrat William Proxmire, a former state assemblyman and three-time gubernatorial loser. Born in 1915 in Illinois, Proxmire attended the Hill School, majored in literature at Yale and finance at Harvard, rose to master sergeant before receiving a commission in the Army Counter Intelligence Corps in World War II, and in 1946 married Elsie Rockefeller (John D.'s granddaughter) before earning an M.A. in public administration at Harvard.

In the Senate Proxmire quickly gained a reputation as a maverick—he opposed both "excessive" military spending and liberal domestic legislation (except civil rights) and even attacked small projects dear to his party's leadership. He supported intervention in Vietnam through 1965 and, according to an authorized biography, "was flying with the fiercest of hawks." Proxmire criticized Lyndon Johnson's* handling of the war in 1966 and after the Tet Offensive* in early 1968 broke completely with administration policy. "Tet," he said later, "made me very suspicious." Unsuccessful attempts to legislate an end to the war followed, with Proxmire urging that funding cease for B–52* and defoliation* missions. Through the Nixon* years he continued to speak against the war and also led Senate opposition to the C–5A cargo plane. While Proxmire's transition from hawk to dove roughly paralleled shifting public opinion on the war, a skeptical approach to Pentagon spending has been and remains a consistent feature of his work in the Senate.

Sources: *Who's Who in American Politics, 1985–1986*, 1986; George C. Herring, *America's Longest War. The United States and Vietnam 1950–1975*, 1986; *New York Times*, 1957–1975.

Dudley Acker

PSYCHOLOGICAL OPERATIONS

During the war in Vietnam, the United States Information Agency (USIA), directing the Joint U.S. Public Affairs Office, and several military units invested an enormous amount of resources in "psyops," or psychological operations— propaganda campaigns aimed at the North Vietnamese, the Vietcong,* and the South Vietnamese. Between 1965 and 1972, the United States dropped fifty billion leaflets on North and South Vietnam, and on the Ho Chi Minh Trail* in

Laos* and Cambodia (*see* Kampuchea)—all with the goal of building an anti-Communist nationalism, supporting the Chieu Hoi program,* or breaking the will of the North Vietnamese to resist. They inundated South Vietnam with posters, banners, newspaper articles, magazines, brochures, comic books, bumper stickers, and matchbook covers, all urging the Vietcong and the North Vietnamese to end the fighting. The USIA also filled the available airwaves with anti-Communist radio broadcasts.

Military operations were also extensive. The Psychological Operations Directorate of the Military Assistance Command, Vietnam* coordinated propaganda campaigns. The U.S. Air Force* dropped leaflets and the Navy* handed out brochures during routine searches of merchant craft and used loudspeaker broadcasts from patrol craft. The U.S. Army eventually had four psyops battalions—the 6th Psychological Operations Battalion in III Corps,* the 7th Psychological Operations Battalion in I Corps,* the 8th Psychological Operations Battalion in II Corps,* and the 10th Psychological Operations Battalion in IV Corps.* Each battalion had its own printing plant, photographic and tape recording production equipment, and loudspeaker trucks.

Sources: Robert W. Chandler, *War of Ideas: The U.S. Propaganda Campaign in Vietnam*, 1981; Shelby L. Stanton, *Vietnam Order of Battle*, 1981.

PUEBLO   *See* USS *Pueblo*

"PUFF THE MAGIC DRAGON"   *See* AC–47 Gunship

PUNJI STAKES

Until 1965 the Vietcong* made or captured 90 percent of its weaponry, necessitating imaginative utilization of natural resources, including bamboo. Punji stakes were lengths of bamboo cut into strips, sharpened to a point, and hardened over flame. These hardened sticks, which could penetrate soles of combat boots and which might be coated with feces or some infection-causing substance, were used as passive and offensive weapons. They were excellent substitutes for concertina (coils of barbed wire) in defending fixed positions. Punji stakes were often driven into the bottoms of shallow holes, then carefully camouflaged so an unsuspecting soldier would step on them, impaling his foot. Holes often were dug near obstacles, channeling a person's foot to that spot. Sticks were driven into rice paddies, to be stepped on as troops moved through them, and mounted on saplings which were bent over and camouflaged. An unwary soldier would activate a trip mechanism, releasing the sapling which would fly up, piercing him with sticks. They were mounted on platforms suspended in trees. Activating the trip mechanism caused the platform to sail down, perforating another victim.

Such booby traps* were highly effective because they took both a physical and psychological toll. The Vietcong were more interested in wounding soldiers than killing them because wounded soldiers required attention. Units stopped their movement; medevacs* were called in for more seriously wounded soldiers, giving away a unit's position. Booby traps were a major advantage for the Vietcong and often helped compensate for lack of firepower.

Sources: George McTurnan Kahin and John W. Lewis, *The United States in Vietnam*, 1967; Al Santoli, *Everything We Had: An Oral History of the Vietnam War by Thirty-Three Americans Who Fought It*, 1981; Edgar C. Doleman, Jr., *The Vietnam Experience: Tools of War*, 1984.

Samuel Freeman

· Q ·

QUANG TRI, BATTLE OF (1972)

On March 30, 1972, as part of the Eastertide Offensive,* four North Vietnamese divisions attacked across the Demilitarized Zone* into Quang Tri Province. The North Vietnamese Army* (NVA) had moved long-range 130mm artillery just north of the Cam Lo–Cua Viet River bringing Quang Tri City and an area five miles south of the city under bombardment. NVA forces, backed by that artillery and amphibious PT–76 tanks, brought Quang Tri City under siege from three separate directions. Internecine rivalries between the Army of the Republic of Vietnam* (ARVN) and South Vietnamese Marine* commanders, as well as friction between U.S. advisers and ARVN officers, weakened the defensive effort. Cloud cover during the first two weeks of April inhibited American air support, and even though the weather cleared in mid-April and B–52* strikes were heavy, the North Vietnamese crossed the Cam Lo–Cua Viet River barrier and invaded on a broad front. NVA artillery were also striking hard at ARVN forces south of Quang Tri City. On April 27, 1972, the cloud cover returned and the NVA 304th Division attacked Quang Tri City. Thousands of South Vietnamese refugees* began fleeing the city along Highway 1 (*see* "Street Without Joy") toward Hue,* and the North Vietnamese targeted the 130mm guns on the road. By April 30 the North Vietnamese were indiscriminately shelling the capital city. On May 1 they took the city. The rest of the province fell under North Vietnamese control two days later.

But the Eastertide Offensive then stalled and degenerated into a stalemate. Not until the end of the summer did the South Vietnamese, buoyed by massive B–52 air support, launch the counteroffensive. In house-to-house combat, the South Vietnamese recaptured Quang Tri City on September 15, 1972, suffering more than five thousand casualties in the process. The fighting and bombing almost completely obliterated Quang Tri City.

Source: G. H. Turley, *The Easter Offensive: Vietnam, 1972*, 1985.

QUEEN'S COBRAS

"Queen's Cobras" was the name used to describe the crack infantry regiment sent to South Vietnam by Thailand* in the fall of 1967. The troops fought alongside American soldiers in III Corps* before their removal almost one year later.

Source: Harry G. Summers, Jr., *Vietnam War Almanac*, 1985.

QUI NHON

Qui Nhon was the capital city of Binh Dinh Province in South Vietnam. At the peak of the fighting in Vietnam during the late 1960s, Qui Nhon had a population of more than 188,000. Located on the coast just off Highway 1 (*see* "Street Without Joy"), Qui Nhon is 420 miles north of Saigon.* Before the arrival of large numbers of American ground troops, Qui Nhon was a small fishing and commercial port. Military engineers deepened the harbor, constructed supply and petroleum depots, and transformed Qui Nhon into a major supply base. Service support for the nearly 100,000 American, South Vietnamese, and Korean* troops operating in the northern reaches of II Corps* came from Qui Nhon. The Capitol Division* of the South Korean army had its headquarters in Qui Nhon. The port and supply depot was part of the American effort to keep land routes open between the coast and the Central Highlands.*

Sources: Harvey H. Smith, et al., *Area Handbook for South Vietnam*, 1967; Shelby L. Stanton, *Vietnam Order of Battle*, 1981; Carroll H. Dunn, *Base Development in South Vietnam, 1965–1970*, 1972.

• R •

RADFORD, ARTHUR WILLIAM

As chairman of the U.S. Joint Chiefs of Staff (JCS; *see* Chairman, JCS) in 1954, Admiral Arthur W. Radford played a central role in the determination of American options during the decisive French battle of Dien Bien Phu.* Radford was born on February 27, 1896, and was a 1916 graduate of the Naval Academy. After World War I he became an aviator, and his own career advancement and the growth of naval aviation formed a virtually parallel history. During World War II he commanded a carrier group and a carrier division. After the war he rose to the command of the Pacific Fleet and to the chairmanship of the JCS in August 1953.

Radford had great confidence in the key role of air power in modern warfare, and he was a forceful advocate of this view in the Eisenhower* administration's deliberations on Vietnam in 1954. In March 1954 the Vietminh* army began its attack on the French garrison at Dien Bien Phu. Washington already was considering the implications of a French defeat, and as the battlefield conditions worsened, a decision on how to help the French was urgent. French Chief of Staff General Paul Ely* came to Washington and conferred directly with Radford. The admiral discussed a plan, Operation Vulture,* in which American carrier-based aircraft could inflict a massive air strike on the Vietminh forces besieging Dien Bien Phu. Upon his return to Paris, Ely believed that Radford had made a commitment to the plan, but Radford insisted that he had only raised the possibility. President Eisenhower refused to authorize an American bombardment without allied support, and in early May the Vietminh overran the outpost. Radford was chairman of the JCS until his retirement in August 1957. He died in 1973.

Sources: Arthur W. Radford, *From Pearl Harbor to Vietnam: The Memoirs of Admiral Arthur W. Radford*, 1980; John Prados, *The Sky Would Fall: Operation Vulture, The U.S. Bombing Mission in Indochina, 1954*, 1983.

David L. Anderson

RADIO HANOI   *See* Hanoi Hannah

RAMBO

Written and directed by Sylvester Stallone, *Rambo* is a sequel to Stallone's 1983 hit *First Blood*. In the film *Rambo*, Stallone plays the role of a Vietnam veteran imprisoned for wrecking a small Oregon town after the local police chief and deputies harassed him. Richard Crenna, playing the role of Rambo's former Green Beret commander, springs him, literally, from a rock pile for a special mission in "Nam." Single-handedly, Rambo reenters Vietnam and rescues a group of American prisoners of war* (POWs) still languishing in bamboo cage cells. As it turns out, the rescue project had only been intended as a political gesture by politicians back home to do something about the POW-MIA issue. Rambo surprises them by winning another Congressional Medal of Honor, bringing home his comrades, and threatening the mission chief whom he considers a stooge for the politicians who lost the first war in Vietnam. Riding a crest of American patriotism and nationalism, *Rambo* was a runaway box-office smash in 1985, the most successful of the Vietnam-genre films spawned in the 1980s.

RAND CORPORATION

Rand Corporation is a nonprofit think tank designed to analyze issues of national importance to the United States. Rand emerged at the end of World War II when it was organized as an adjunct of Douglas Aircraft Company in Santa Monica, California. The name was derived from combining the words *Research and D*evelopment. Rand separated from Douglas Aircraft in 1948 and was incorporated under the laws of California as a private, nonprofit corporation. Rand concentrated on "operation research," first focusing on the operational employment of existing weapon systems and later broadening out into more general tasks concerned with the allocation of resources for national security purposes. By the 1950s Rand was developing "systems analysis" as its major focus for such clients as the U.S. Air Force, Department of Defense, and the State Department. During the 1960s, Rand's major effort was on the Vietnam War. It provided copious studies of Saigon* politics, the National Liberation Front (*see* Vietcong), the organization of combat villages, command structures in North Vietnam, weapons effectiveness, and negotiation strategies. Rand studies were heavily employed by American officials in developing military and political policy in Southeast Asia.

Sources: L. R. Smith, *The Rand Corporation*, 1966; Mike Gravel, ed., *Pentagon Papers*, 1971.

Linda Casci

REEDUCATION CAMPAIGNS

The term "Reeducation" has become a euphemism for concentration camps, imprisonment, and brainwashing by totalitarian states in the twentieth century. After the end of the Vietnam War in 1975, both the Socialist Republic of Vietnam* and the Pol Pot* government in Kampuchea* (Cambodia) implemented widespread reeducation campaigns to punish and/or reorient citizens closely associated with the U.S. war effort or the governments of the Republic of Vietnam* and Lon Nol* in Cambodia. In Vietnam, more than 400,000 Vietnamese were placed in reeducation camps, most of whom died there. The government of Pol Pot in Kampuchea was even more brutal, placing more than one million citizens into camps before executing them in a genocidal orgy.

Sources: Nguyen Long, with Harry Kendall, *After Saigon Fell*, 1981; Ginette Sagan and Stephen Denney, *Violations of Human Rights in the Socialist Republic of Vietnam*, 1983; Michael Vickery, *Cambodia, 1975–1982*, 1984.

REFUGEES

Throughout and even after the war in Vietnam, the issue of displaced refugees posed a critical economic, political, and military problem for the United States. As part of the Geneva Accords* of 1954, a one-year period was established for relocation across the seventeenth parallel dividing North and South Vietnam. Between 80,000 and 100,000 South Vietnamese, mostly Vietminh,* moved from the south to the north, while nearly one million northerners, mostly Roman Catholics,* moved into South Vietnam. Both the United States and France* provided ships to assist the mass migration. Many of them ended up for a time in refugee camps, but they eventually became an intense anti-Communist constituency in South Vietnam.

But the refugee situation became a critical problem after the American escalation of the war in 1965. Between December 1965 and June 1967, more than 1,200,000 people in South Vietnam were officially listed as refugees. Between 1964 and 1969, a total of 3,500,000 South Vietnamese had been refugees for a period of time. Several million others were temporarily displaced from their homes by the war itself. They were placed in refugee camps where living conditions were abominable. The migration began in earnest in 1964 when severe flooding drove 100,000 people from their homes in South Vietnam. In 1965, when the fighting increased, tens of thousands more were displaced. Finally, the United States and the government of South Vietnam began large-scale relocations of the population. Between 1966 and 1970 they pursued the policy of creating free fire zones,* areas where peasants had been removed and military commanders could attack with abandon, assuming any people left behind had to be North Vietnamese or Vietcong.* The relocations supposedly denied the

388

Vietcong sources of income, food, and labor and military recruits; cleared the battlefield of innocent civilians; and allowed military commanders a free hand in the use of firepower. The relocated people, however, often ended up in dismal refugee camps where resentment and alienation accumulated against the United States and the Republic of Vietnam.*

Finally, the fall of South Vietnam in 1975 created new waves of refugee migrations. From the time the North Vietnamese attacked Quang Tri to the final flight of the last Americans in 1975, widespread population dislocations occurred throughout South Vietnam. Between 1975 and 1985, more than 1,500,000 people fled Indochina,* with more than half of them settling in the United States.

Sources: Guenter Lewy, *America in Vietnam*, 1978; "No More Room for Refugees," *Time*, May 10, 1982; Barry Winn, *The Refused*, 1981; Gertrude Samuels, "Passage to Freedom," *National Geographic* 107 (June 1955), 858–74.

REGIMENT

A regiment is a basic military organizational unit in the United States Marine Corps,* and in the United States Army's* armored cavalry units. During the Vietnam War the 11th Armored Cavalry Regiment* was the only army regiment in the country. It consisted of three armored cavalry squadrons and an air cavalry troop. Three infantry battalions* constitute a marine regiment. Between 1965 and 1975, the marines used ten regiments in the Vietnam War: the 1st, 5th, and 7th regiments of the 1st Marine Division;* the 3rd, 4th and 9th regiments of the Third Marine Division* the 26th and 27th regiments of the 5th Marine Division;* and the 11th and 12th artillery regiments.

Source: Harry G. Summers, Jr., *Vietnam War Almanac*, 1985.

REGIONAL FORCES

The Regional Forces, part of the Territorial Forces* of the South Vietnamese Army, were paramilitary troops organized at the province level to protect villages, hamlets, and such fixed positions as bridges and ferries. The Regional Forces were first activated in 1955 under the control of the Interior Department of South Vietnam to protect critical positions in the Mekong Delta,* and by 1960 they were defending over nine thousand posts, more than half of which were in the Delta. At first they were called the Civil Guard. In 1960 the Regional Forces were transferred to the Defense Department and in 1964 to the South Vietnamese Army. Instead of being controlled by the province chief, they were under the command of the Joint General Staff.* The basic combat unit of the Regional Forces was the company,* and by 1973 the Regional Forces totaled more than 1,800 companies. Between 1965 and 1973, the Regional Forces and Popular Forces* lost more than eighty thousand dead.

Sources: Ngo Quang Truong, *Territorial Forces*, 1981; Harvey H. Smith, et al., *Area Handbook for South Vietnam*, 1967.

REINHARDT, GEORGE FREDERICK

G. Frederick Reinhardt was born on October 21, 1911, in Berkeley, California. After graduating from the University of California in 1933, he went on to Cornell University where he earned a master's degree in 1935. Reinhardt attended the Cesare Alfien Institute of Diplomacy in Florence, Italy, in 1937, and then received an appointment to the U.S. Foreign Service. During the 1930s Reinhardt had minor posts in Austria, Latvia, Estonia, and the Soviet Union,* and during World War II he was a staff aid with General Dwight Eisenhower.* Between 1945 and 1948 he served as first secretary and consul general in Moscow and then held a variety of positions with the State Department in Washington until 1955. Reinhardt became ambassador to the Republic of Vietnam* in 1955 and held the post until 1957. He later held ambassadorships to the United Arab Republic, Yemen, and Italy. Reinhardt retired from public life in 1968.

Source: John E. Findling, *Dictionary of American Diplomatic History*, 1980.

REPUBLIC OF KOREA   *See* Korea

REPUBLIC OF VIETNAM

The term "Republic of Vietnam"* was the name given to the government of South Vietnam. After the Geneva Accords* of 1954 had divided North from South Vietnam at the seventeenth parallel, Ngo Dinh Diem* became prime minister in a government headed by Emperor Bao Dai.* After consolidating his power, Diem called for a national referendum on October 23, 1955, to determine whether Bao Dai should remain emperor or whether the country should become a republic under Diem's leadership. Diem reported after the referendum that 98 percent of the people of South Vietnam wanted a republic. So on October 26, 1955, Diem proclaimed establishment of the Republic of Vietnam and named himself president. A new constitution was promulgated on October 26, 1956.

Source: Harvey Smith et al., *Area Handbook for South Vietnam*, 1967.

REVOLUTIONARY PERSONALIST LABOR PARTY   *See* Can Lao Nhan Vi Cach Mang Dang

REVOLUTIONARY YOUTH LEAGUE   *See* Thanh Nien Cach Menh Dong Chi Hoi

RHEAULT CONTROVERSY

In 1969 Colonel Robert Rheault, commander of the Fifth Special Forces Group,* was arrested for ordering the execution of Thai Khac Chuyen, a Special Forces employee Rheault discovered was a double agent for the Vietcong.* Because of the highly secret nature of the project Chuyen was working, the Central Intelligence Agency* refused to release classified information and the case against Rheault had to be dismissed. He resigned from the Special Forces in 1969.

Source: Charles M. Simpson III, *Inside the Green Berets: The First Thirty Years*, 1983.

RIVERINE ASSAULT FORCE (TASK FORCE 116)   *See* Mobile Riverine Force

RIVERINE PATROL FORCE (TASK FORCE 117)   *See* Mobile Riverine Force

"THE ROCKPILE"

On July 4, 1966, about ten miles from the southern boundary of the Demilitarized Zone* (DMZ) and sixteen miles west of Dong Ha, a small marine reconnaissance patrol made note of "a sort of toothpick-type mountain stuck out in the middle of an open area" with a "sheer cliff straight up and down." The 700-foot "Rockpile," often manned by a marine squad, became a key post from which to observe North Vietnamese Army* activity in the central and western sectors of northern I Corps.* Located at a fork in the Cam Lo River, the Rockpile was supplied by helicopter, and within a kilometer of Route 9 it dominated the landscape between Camp Carroll to the east and Khe Sanh* to its southwest. Marines launched numerous operations from the Rockpile area, and the peak was a familiar landmark for those fighting the DMZ war.

Sources: Jack Shulimson, *Marines in Vietnam: An Expanding War, 1966*, 1982; Edward Doyle and Samuel Lipsman, *The Vietnam Experience: America Takes Over, 1965–1967*, 1985.

Dudley Acker

ROGERS, WILLIAM PIERCE

William P. Rogers was born at Norfolk, New York, on June 23, 1913. He graduated from Colgate University in 1934, and in 1937 he earned a law degree at Cornell University, where he edited the law review. Rogers worked briefly with a Wall Street firm in 1937 before joining the staff of New York County District Attorney Thomas E. Dewey, who was about to launch his campaign against racketeers. While serving on Dewey's staff, Rogers gained extensive experience as a trial lawyer. He was an officer with the United States Naval Reserve in the Pacific during World War II. After the war Rogers returned to Dewey's staff briefly and then went to work as counsel to several congressional committees. During those years he came to know Congressman and later Senator Richard Nixon* and worked on the Alger Hiss case. In 1950 Rogers returned to private law practice and continued as a Nixon adviser. When Dwight D. Eisenhower* was elected president in 1952, Rogers became deputy attorney general. In October 1957 he became attorney general in the Eisenhower cabinet.

Between 1960 and 1968 Rogers practiced law, but when Nixon entered the White House in 1969, Rogers became secretary of state. But while naming Rogers to the State Department, Nixon also named Henry Kissinger* to the post of special White House assistant on foreign affairs. From the beginning, Kissinger's influence was dominant. Nixon tended to be suspicious and secretive, and he distrusted the "Ivy League types" at the State Department. Rogers was always upstaged by Kissinger. The making of foreign policy had definitely shifted to the White House. Thus, William Rogers was often put in the position of explaining and defending policies before Congress* and the nation which had been formulated by Nixon and Kissinger with little or no input from the State Department. This was especially true in the areas of Sino-Soviet and Vietnam policy. Rogers himself was often the subject of unkind chatter on the cocktail circuit. But he continued to serve until 1973, when he resigned to return to his private law practice. In 1986, he was chosen by the Reagan administration to head the investigation of the Challenger disaster.

Sources: *Current Biography*, 1969, pp. 372–75; Thomas G. Paterson, *American Foreign Policy*, 1983; *U.S. News and World Report*, February 24, 1986.

Joseph M. Rowe, Jr.

ROMAN CATHOLICISM

Roman Catholicism came to Vietnam in the sixteenth and seventeenth centuries with the arrival of Portuguese, French, and Spanish missionaries. Dominican priests from Portugal arrived in the Mekong Delta* in 1550 and in Quang Nam Province in central Vietnam in the 1580s. French Jesuits, the most prominent of whom was Alexandre de Rhodes, worked throughout Vietnam in the seventeenth century, and by 1700 there were nearly one million converts there. Perhaps 25 percent of them were in Tonkin* and the rest in Annam* and Cochin China.* During the eighteenth century Confucians and Buddhists throughout Vietnam campaigned against Catholicism as an alien religion tied closely to European imperial expansion. Persecution of Catholics was widespread.

With the French conquest of Vietnam in the nineteenth century, Catholicism was liberated from nationalist opposition, built a native clergy, and received great support from the French colonial bureaucracy. After 1954, when Ngo Dinh Diem* took control of the government of South Vietnam, Catholicism got an even stronger foothold in the country. The French had encouraged Catholicism as a counter to Buddhism,* and Diem filled his government with Roman Catholics. Diem's brother, Ngo Dinh Thuc,* was the archbishop of Hue* and leader of the Catholic clergy in Vietnam. Although the dominant position of Catholics in the government of South Vietnam declined after the assassination of Diem in 1963, they still exerted extraordinary influence because of their dominance of the officer corps of the South Vietnamese military, the higher levels of the government bureaucracy, and the professions. Roman Catholics were better educated and more prosperous than the rest of the country.

There were actually two Catholic communities in South Vietnam during the years of the Vietnam War. Of the 1.5 million Roman Catholics in the country, approximately 900,000 of them in the 1960s were refugees* from the Red River Delta area of North Vietnam. Led by Father Hoang Quynh, they were more anti-

Buddhist and anti-Communist than their southern counterparts. Father Hoang Quynh's lay organization, the Luc Luong Dai Doan Ket, or Greater Unity Force, was an activist organization in South Vietnam. Southern Catholics were led by Paul Nguyen Van Binh,* the archbishop of Saigon.* Southern Catholics were more sympathetic to Buddhist grievances, not nearly as militant as the northerners, and received less support from the Diem regime. As a whole, however, Catholics in Vietnam were pro-Western and anti-Communist, and wanted little compromise with the Vietminh* and later the Vietcong.* The northern Catholic refugees came into the South after the Geneva Accords* in 1954, and migrated in village units with their local priest. The government established 319 refugee villages for them. Nearly 400,000 refugees settled in villages in the Mekong Delta, 60,000 in the Central Lowlands, and 70,000 in the Central Highlands.* Others ended up in slums of Saigon or Cholon.* Northern Catholics were consequently more impoverished than southerners.

The northern refugees were for the most part poorly educated peasants who had lived in exclusively Roman Catholic villages in North Vietnam and who had rarely had contact with non-Catholics. Catholics born in South Vietnam lived mainly in cities and coastal areas of the northern provinces. In Saigon the Catholic community was upper middle-class and virtually controlled the military, civil service, and professions. South Vietnam by the 1960s was divided into 13 dioceses with 700 local parishes. In the late 1960s there were more than 1,700 priests, 4,000 nuns, and 625 seminarians in the country. The church enrolled 400,000 students in parochial schools, maintained a college at Dal Lat,* operated 26 hospitals, 7 leper sanitariums, and 55 orphanages.

Sources: Harvey Smith, *Area Handbook for South Vietnam*, 1967; Virginia Thompson, *French Indochina*, 1937; Joseph Buttinger, *Vietnam: A Dragon Embattled*, 2 vols., 1967; Pierro Gheddo, *The Cross and the Bo-Tree: Catholics and Buddhists in Vietnam*, 1970.

ROME PLOW

Manufactured by the Rome Caterpillar Company of Rome, Georgia, the Rome plow was used to clear jungle areas during the Vietnam War, especially potential ambush locations along supply routes. The huge tractor had a large, cutting blade more curved than most bulldozer blades and extending out at the bottom. The blade was sharp and powerful enough to cut easily through tree trunks up to 36 inches in diameter, and a spike at one edge of the blade could split even larger trees.

Source: John H. Hay, Jr., *Tactical and Materiel Innovations*, 1974.

ROMNEY, GEORGE

George Romney was born on July 8, 1907, in the Mormon colonies in Chihuahua, Mexico. He attended the University of Utah and George Washington University in the 1920s but never graduated. In 1929 Romney went to work as a tariff specialist for Senator David Walsh of Massachusetts, and in 1930 he became a lobbyist for the Aluminum Company of America (ALCOA). Romney spent the next twenty-three years working for ALCOA, and the Automobile Manufacturers Association, and in 1954 he became president of American Motors. In 1962 Romney ran on the Republican ticket and won the governorship of Michigan. He was reelected in 1964 and 1966. Romney had a reputation as a moderate to liberal Republican, and in 1968 he made a run for the Republican presidential nomination. At the time he was harboring serious reservations about the war in Vietnam, and after traveling there on a fact-finding mission, he returned to the United States and, during the New Hampshire presidential primary campaigning, claimed that the Pentagon had tried to "brainwash" him. Although subsequent events would prove he was correct, use of the term "brainwash" hurt him politically in New Hampshire; and Richard Nixon* won the primary, the Republican nomination, and the White House. In January 1969, Nixon named Romney to his cabinet as secretary of housing and urban development. Romney retired from public life in 1973.

Sources: Clark Mollenhoff, *George Romney, Mormon in Politics*, 1968; Theodore White, *The Making of the President, 1968*, 1969.

ROOSEVELT, FRANKLIN DELANO

Franklin D. Roosevelt, the thirty-second president of the United States, was born in Hyde Park, New York, on January 30, 1882. Raised amidst family wealth, he developed a paternalistic liberalism, graduated from Harvard in 1904, and studied law at Columbia University. He was admitted to the New York bar in 1907 and practiced law privately. After serving a term in the state legislature between 1911 and 1913, Roosevelt was appointed assistant secretary of the navy, a post he occupied until 1920. Roosevelt was James Cox's running mate in the presidential election of 1920, but they lost by a landslide to the Republican ticket of Warren G. Harding and Calvin Coolidge. After being attacked by polio in 1921, Roosevelt spent much of the rest of the decade trying to restore his health, and in 1928 he was elected governor of New York. He served in Albany until 1933, when he entered the White House as president of the United States. Roosevelt's presidency was one of the most important in U.S. history; his New Deal attempted to ease the Great Depression of the 1930s, and his leadership of the country during World War II made him a beloved figure until his death on April 12, 1945.

Midway through World War II, Roosevelt realized that colonialism was dead and that the United States would best be served by aligning itself with the forces of nationalism in the Third World. He had little faith in Charles de Gaulle and thought France* had badly mismanaged its affairs in Indochina.* By 1944 Roosevelt was advocating placing Indochina under an international trusteeship. Early in 1945, however, as the British contemplated returning to their former colonies in Asia, Roosevelt amended his point of view, and at the Yalta Conference in 1945 agreed to a proposal calling for trusteeships only with the approval of the mother country. The Yalta agreement killed any hope for a trusteeship over Indochina. After Roosevelt's death in 1945, Harry S. Truman* took over as president of the United States, and Truman shared none of Roosevelt's concerns about imperialism and colonialism, and American policy shifted strongly toward French policies in Indochina.

Sources: George Herring, *America's Longest War: The United States in Vietnam, 1950–1975*, 1986; Chester Bain, *Vietnam: The Roots of Conflict*, 1967; Frances FitzGerald, *Fire in the Lake: The Vietnamese and the Americans in Vietnam*, 1972.

ROSTOW, WALT WHITMAN

W. W. Rostow, an economist with extensive service in the federal government, began advising John F. Kennedy,* then a senator from Massachusetts, on foreign policy in 1958 and was active in Kennedy's successful 1960 presidential campaign. Kennedy appointed Rostow deputy special assistant to the president for foreign security affairs in the incoming administration, and as such Rostow participated throughout 1961 in the formulation of U.S. policy toward Laos* and Vietnam. He generally advocated a strong diplomatic and military role in opposing Communist insurgents operating in Asia. Later, Rostow moved to the State Department, where he was placed in charge of long-range analysis and planning in a broad range of foreign policy areas.

Beginning in June 1964 Rostow began to exert direct influence upon President Lyndon B. Johnson* by serving as one of his principal advisers on Southeast Asia. During this period W. W. Rostow developed his unique foreign policy perspective on Vietnam and like situations, which came to be called the "Rostow thesis." Essentially, he argued that externally supported insurgencies could be stopped only by military action against the source of external support. As a result, he urged a series of escalating military measures designed to impart the maximum possible psychological blow and thereby force a cessation of the external support. This policy approach flowed from Rostow's belief that modernization—expressed in his important 1960 study, *The Stages of Economic Growth*—created certain dislocations and discontents which, although transitional, could be used by Communists to gain support. He commented that it was necessary to hold off any Communist challenge until full modernization was achieved.

Consistent with this general approach to the problem in Southeast Asia, Rostow argued in June 1964 that the United States commit both military force and a strong public stance against North Vietnamese support for rebel forces in Laos and South Vietnam. Although not without critics, according to the Pentagon Papers,* "the outlook embodied in the 'Rostow thesis' came to dominate a good deal of Administration thinking on the question of pressures against the North in the months ahead."

Although Rostow had previously worked in the background, on March 31, 1966, President Johnson appointed him special assistant to the president for national security affairs, succeeding McGeorge Bundy.* In this post Rostow worked closely with Johnson for the remainder of the administration on virtually all foreign policy issues. One of these involved the bombing of the North Vietnamese industrial base. In May 1966, for instance, Rostow argued for the "systematic and sustained bombing" of petroleum-product facilities in North Vietnam. This goal was realized in the bombing* campaigns that followed in the Hanoi* and Haiphong areas.

Throughout the remainder of the Johnson administration Rostow continued to support the large-scale bombing program, although the president chose to limit aerial attacks during the latter months of his term. During this time, overtures were reportedly made in Rostow's behalf to MIT and several other leading universities to secure for him a teaching position after the administration's end. Eventually, he accepted a position as professor of economics and history at the University of Texas at Austin, where a Lyndon B. Johnson School of Public Affairs was planned. In the final hours of his presidency, Johnson awarded Rostow and nineteen others the Medal of Freedom, the country's highest civilian honor.

Sources: W. W. Rostow, *The Stages of Economic Growth: A Non-Communist Manifesto*, 1960; Seyom Brown, *The Faces of Power: Constancy and Change in United States Foreign Policy from Truman to Johnson*, 1968; Eric F. Goldman, *The Tragedy of Lyndon Johnson*, 1969; George C. Herring, *America's Longest War: The United States and Vietnam, 1950–1975*, 1986; W. W. Rostow, *The Diffusion of Power, 1957–1972*, 1972.

Roger D. Launius

ROWE, JAMES NICHOLAS

Special Forces* adviser and early prisoner of war in Vietnam, James N. Rowe was born in 1938 at McAllen, Texas. He graduated from the United States Military Academy in 1960, B.S., and was commissioned second lieutenant, United States Army. An early volunteer for the Special Forces* (Green Berets), Rowe was sent to Vietnam in 1963 as an adviser to an Army of the Republic of Vietnam* (ARVN) unit. On October 29, 1963, Lieutenant Rowe accompanied his ARVN unit on a raid of a Vietcong village in the Mekong Delta.* But the plan of attack went awry when the Vietcong (VC) declined to react in the prescribed manner. As a contingent of the ARVN unit surged through the village firing into the huts, the VC were expected to flee into the forest, where an ambush awaited them. But the VC moved in the opposite direction, regrouped and counterattacked. The ARVN unit soon found itself in desperate straits. When help failed to arrive from other units in the area, the ARVN was cut off and decimated. Lieutenant Rowe and two other Green Berets were among the survivors taken prisoner.

For the next five years, Rowe was held a captive in the field, forced to live the life and share the squalor and privation of his captors. Three attempts to escape failed, resulting in punishment and closer confinement for a while. Finally, on December 31, 1968, Lieutenant Rowe was able to break away from his captors in the confusion when American helicopter gunships* attacked the VC. Fortunately, a gunship crewman spotted him in a clearing, and he was rescued.

In 1971, Rowe (by then Major) published a detailed autobiographical account of his service and captivity in Vietnam. Reaction to his book reflected the intensity of the domestic discord over the Vietnam War. On the one hand, Rowe was hailed as a genuine hero and his book was commended for its "shattering impact," a revelation of the evils of communism. But other reviewers called it self-serving and parochial, a revelation of American attitudes of superiority and disdain for the Vietnamese people. One reviewer cast doubts on the author's integrity, questioning how Rowe could have recalled all the minute details of his service and captivity years after the fact. The details of his imprisonment were called "boring." The comments no doubt reflected the reviewer's attitude toward the war more than toward Rowe himself.

Rowe continued to serve in the army until 1974, when he resigned. In 1975, he ran on the Republican ticket for state office in Texas, but lost. He then turned his attention to writing as a career.

Sources: See James N. Rowe, *Five Years to Freedom*, 1971; *Contemporary Authors*, 1st rev., vols. 37–40, 1979, pp. 469–71.

Joseph M. Rowe, Jr.

RUBIN, JERRY

Jerry Rubin was born on July 14, 1938, in Cincinnati, Ohio. He graduated from the University of Cincinnati in 1961, and in 1964 he was active in Mario Savio's Free Speech Movement at the University of California at Berkeley. As the Free Speech Movement was transformed into an anti-Vietnam campaign, Rubin emerged as a radical leader and organizer of the Vietnam Day Committee (VDC), a prominent antiwar group. VDC demonstrations took on the image of radical insurgency in 1966 when they tried to block trains carrying Vietnam-bound soldiers to training and embarkation posts. Early in 1968, Rubin joined with Abbie Hoffman* in forming the Youth International party, or "Yippies," to promote counterculture ideas and oppose the war in Vietnam. The Yippies sponsored large and disruptive demonstrations in Chicago during the Democratic National Convention* in August 1968, and Rubin was arrested as one of the Chicago 7.* His behavior at the subsequent trial, where he was charged with conspiracy to riot, was outrageous and he was found guilty of contempt. Convicted of conspiracy, Rubin appealed and won in the federal appeals court in 1972. When the war ended in 1973, Rubin's public personality lost some of its attraction, and he disappeared from the public scene. By the early 1980s Jerry Rubin was a successful stockbroker on Wall Street, the ultimate symbol of the transformation of 1960s Yippies into 1980s Yuppies.

Sources: Jerry Rubin, *Growing Up at 37*, 1976; Thomas Powers, *Vietnam: The War at Home*, 1984; Nancy Zaroulis and Gerald Sullivan, *Who Spoke Up? American Protest Against the Vietnam War, 1963–1975*, 1984.

RUNG SAT SWAMP

The Rung Sat Swamp consisted of the swamp deltas of the Saigon and Dong Nai rivers. Vietcong* sappers harassed the flow of supplies to Saigon by placing mines in the deep ship lanes. The Rung Sat Swamp was the area from which the sappers operated.

Source: Harry G. Summers, Jr., *Vietnam War Almanac*, 1985.

RURAL DEVELOPMENT PROGRAM   *See* Rural Reconstruction

RURAL RECONSTRUCTION

By 1968, a "two pincers" strategy dominated the American war effort. The "violence" pincer consisted of attacking main force North Vietnamese Army* (NVA) and National Liberation Front (NLF; *see* Vietcong) units, pushing them into uninhabited regions, breaking their ties with local NLF guerrilla and political cadres, and eliminating local NLF infrastructures. Main force units would address the first three "violence" objectives, while local units and the Phoenix Program* would address the fourth. The second pincer would be Rural Reconstruction, a comprehensive pacification program developed by Colonel Nguyen Be. Rather than win people to the government's side, Rural Reconstruction was intended to put the government on the side of the people. The program failed for three basic reasons: (1) U.S.-GVN (*see* Republic of Vietnam) commitment to "conventional" military thinking; (2) inability to change the attitudes of civilian officials; and (3) the resulting corruption and misallocation of resources. The program's heart consisted of fifty-nine member Rural Reconstruction cadres trained largely by former Vietminh.* Cadres had the following assignments: (1) to live in villages cleared of NLF military units; (2) to gain villagers' trust and cooperation by hearing their grievances against the government; (3) to recommend or take action redressing those grievances; (4) to assist villagers in education, health, public works, and agricultural projects; and (5) to root out the NLF political and local guerrilla infrastructure. Gaining villagers' confidence was often difficult because of GVN corruption and memories of past pacification programs such as Strategic Hamlets.* Villagers often feared that cadres would force them to build new strategic hamlets or force them to do other work, such as erecting defensive positions for Regional Forces.*

Teams were created too rapidly. Many were inadequately trained. Many were assigned to inadequately secured villages only to be driven out or killed by the NLF. Adequate security was dependent upon ridding the area of main force units and training Popular Forces* to protect villages against local guerrilla attack. Such forces generally were poorly trained and poorly armed. In some instances local officials refused to arm them at all. Unable to defend themselves, much less their village, they often ran away at any perceived threat. This was a major failure since studies of the effectiveness of previous pacification programs indicated that an inability to establish adequate security precluded any meaningful decision on whether pacification programs could work (apparently overlooking the possibility that necessary security could not be established because the populace was unwilling to be "pacified"). Village chiefs and GVN officials often failed to cooperate with cadres by refusing to furnish necessary resources or to act on cadre recommendations. Complaints about corruption in particular went unheeded. Military considerations almost always took precedence over reconstruction priorities; sometimes the military destroyed reconstruction projects during their operations. Without cooperation of either villagers or GVN officials, cadres' morale plummeted. One-fourth deserted within their first year.

While the primary objective of the American effort in Vietnam officially was always pacification, the allocation of resources and the options considered indicated clearly that pacification programs were secondary to the military effort, demonstrating a curious Catch–22 logic. The United States insisted that the underlying problems were political and required a political solution. However, before a political solution could be found, stability and order had to be established. Consequently, political solutions had to be postponed until a military solution to the insurgency produced stability and order. At that point energies could be directed to development of political solutions which redressed the original causes of instability.

Ultimately, Rural Reconstruction evolved into military control with a few welfare programs. This is not because the military mentality dominated thinking on Vietnam. The military position dominated largely by default. American nonmilitary planning was woeful, and policymakers were ignorant of the history and culture of the Vietnamese people. Furthermore, the Vietnamese High Command and GVN officials themselves were virtually out of touch with their own people. French- or American-educated, living primarily in Saigon,* Vietnamese officials and commanders knew little about the people and conditions of the countryside. The NLF excelled because of its intimate knowledge of both. Rural Reconstruction was designed to copy the tactics of the NLF. The effort failed because Reconstruction cadres ultimately were dependent on Saigon and the United States, whereas NLF cadres were dependent on the people, a difference in dependency not lost on the Vietnamese peasant.

Sources: David Halberstam, *The Making of a Quagmire*, 1964; Frances FitzGerald, *Fire in the Lake: The Vietnamese and the Americans in Vietnam*, 1972; Larry E. Cable, *Conflict of Myths: The Development of American Counterinsurgency Doctrine and the Vietnam War*, 1986; Andrew F. Krepinevich, Jr., *The Army in Vietnam*, 1986.

Samuel Freeman

RUSK, DAVID DEAN

Dean Rusk was born on February 9, 1909, in Cherokee County, Georgia. He grew up barefooted and poor in rural Georgia, graduated from Davidson College in 1931, and then attended Oxford University as a Rhodes scholar. Rusk joined the United States Army during World War II, received a commission as an infantry officer, and saw combat as operations officer under General Joseph Stilwell in the China-Burma theater. Between 1946 and 1962 Rusk worked for the State Department as an assistant secretary of state for Far Eastern affairs, becoming a dedicated anti-Communist and advocate of the containment policy.* Rusk became head of the Rockefeller Foundation in 1952 and remained there until 1960, when president-elect John F. Kennedy* nominated him as his new secretary of state.

Known as "the Buddha,"Rusk rarely spoke up in general meetings and had a penchant for loyalty, giving it to his superiors and expecting it from his subordinates. At first Rusk hoped to leave Vietnam to the Department of Defense as essentially a military question, but by 1963 he had lost hope in the ability of Ngo Dinh Diem* to govern South Vietnam. Throughout 1963 Rusk became increasingly outspoken that Diem had to initiate serious reforms or be removed from office. In the process, Rusk became a more and more visible advocate of a hard-line approach to Vietnam, taking a Cold Warrior position.

During the years of the Johnson* administration, Rusk's reputation as a hawk became even more obvious. He opposed any negotiated settlement to the conflict, especially as long as the Vietcong* and North Vietnamese held any military advantages in the field, and he favored an aggressive bombing* campaign against North Vietnam. Unlike Secretary of Defense Robert S. McNamara* and his successor Clark Clifford,* Rusk never wavered in support of American policies in Vietnam, at least never publicly. Rusk refused to accept the growing conviction in 1967 that the Vietnam conflict was essentially an internal civil war originating in a nationalist rebellion, preferring instead to see it in Cold War terms as a clear case of Communist aggression, this time orchestrated by the People's Republic of China.* Rusk consistently supported military demands for increasing troop commitments to Vietnam, including the request after the Tet Offensive* for another 200,000 soldiers. He urged President Lyndon B. Johnson* to stay with the war despite the increasing strength of the antiwar movement* at home and the counsel of the "Wise Old Men"* that the United States disengage. Rusk was disappointed with the president's decision late in March 1968 not to seek reelection. Rusk became closely associated in the public mind with administration policy in Vietnam, perhaps paying a price of sorts upon leaving office in January 1969 when most prestigious universities refused to even consider him for a faculty appointment. Ultimately, Rusk accepted a teaching post at the University of Georgia.

Sources: David Halberstam, *The Best and the Brightest*, 1972; Arthur M. Schlesinger, Jr., *A Thousand Days: John F. Kennedy in the White House*, 1965; Richard J. Walton, *Cold War and Counterrevolution: The Foreign Policy of John F. Kennedy*, 1972; Doris Kearns, *Lyndon Johnson and the American Dream*, 1976; Warren Cohen, *Dean Rusk*, 1980.

Charles Dobbs

RUSSELL, RICHARD BREVARD

A native Georgian, Richard Russell was born on November 2, 1897, and received a law degree from the University of Georgia in 1918. He practiced law for three years and then was elected as a Democrat to the state legislature. Ten years later, at the age of thirty-three, he became the youngest governor in the history of Georgia. Russell won a seat in the U.S. Senate in the election of 1932, where he remained for the next thirty-eight years. He became a master of parliamentary maneuver and a formidable debater. Although he fought social welfare and civil rights legislation, Russell nevertheless kept great respect among liberal senators because of his ability and integrity. By 1952 Russell was a major figure in the Democratic party. He lost the presidential nomination to Adlai Stevenson that year, but as chairman of the Senate Armed Services Committee and of the military expenditures subcommittee of the Appropriations Committee, Russell wielded vast influence over military policy.

As early as 1954, Russell warned Dwight D. Eisenhower* against sending arms and technicians to bolster French forces in Indochina.* He once told John Foster Dulles* that he was "weary of seeing American soldiers being used as gladiators to be thrown into every arena around the world." When Eisenhower decided to make the commitment, Russell said that he would "support the flag," but that "it is going to be a long drawn-out affair costly in both blood and Treasure." Russell remained faithful to his word. As long as American forces were fighting in Vietnam, he supported the policies of successive presidents. But he regretted the intervention, calling it "one of the great tragedies of our history."

Throughout the summer and fall of 1970, Senator Richard Russell's health deteriorated. He had to enter Walter Reed Medical Center on December 8, 1970, and died there on January 21, 1971, at the age of seventy-three.

Sources: *Current Biography*, 1949, pp. 536–39; Obituary, *New York Times*, January 22, 1971.

Joseph M. Rowe, Jr.

RUSSO, ANTHONY J., JR.

Born in Suffolk, Virginia, on October 14, 1936, Anthony (Tony) Russo was codefendant with Daniel Ellsberg* in the Pentagon Papers Trial* of 1972–73. Russo attended the Virginia Polytechnic Institute where he received a B.S. in aeronautical engineering in 1960 and participated in the cooperative engineering program at NASA's Langley Space Laboratory. In 1961, he entered Princeton University and earned an M.S. in aeronautical engineering in 1963 and a master's of public affairs degree from the Woodrow Wilson School of Public and International Affairs in 1964. There he assisted Oskar Morgenstern in the Econometrics Research Program and studied foreign policy under Richard Falk, Edmundo Flores, George Kennan,* and Klaus Knorr. In June 1964, Russo joined the Rand Corporation.* He then spent twenty-four months in South Vietnam— between February 1966 and January 1968—where he interviewed prisoners for Rand's "Viet Cong Motivation and Morale" study for the U.S. Department of Defense. Russo also participated in a statistical assessment of the U.S.-sponsored crop destruction program. These research experiences led Russo to begin questioning U.S. policy in Vietnam. Independently, Russo also published a study to show that, contrary to some earlier research, local and peasant support for the National Liberation Front (*see* Vietcong) tended to be strongest in South Vietnam's poorest provinces and hamlets (see Russo, "Economic and Social Correlates of Government Control in South Vietnam," in Ivo K. Feierabend et al., eds., *Anger, Violence, and Politics*, 1972). Russo was dismissed by the Rand Corporation for "budgetary reasons" in July 1968, but was allowed to remain on staff to complete pending work. He left Rand in January 1969 to join the firm of Social Engineering Technology in Los Angeles, California. He also became involved in poverty and civil rights work in Los Angeles. In December 1970, he joined the Research and Information Systems Office of the Los Angeles County Probation Department. Russo and Daniel Ellsberg first met at the Rand villa in Saigon* in 1965 but did not become friends until 1968 when they occupied offices across the hall from each other at Rand's headquarters in Santa Monica, California. When Ellsberg sought a way to copy the Pentagon Papers* in 1969, Russo arranged for the rental of a Xerox machine at an advertising agency owned by his friend Lynda Sinay. Russo then assisted Ellsberg in photocopying the "secret" documents. He was first questioned by the Federal Bureau of Investigation (FBI) about his role in the publication of the Pentagon Papers on June 19, 1971, but refused to answer FBI questions. On June 23, he was subpoenaed to testify before a federal grand jury in Los Angeles. Despite a grant of immunity, Russo refused to testify unless his testimony could be made public. On August 16, he began serving a forty-seven-day jail term for contempt of court. During portions of his imprisonment, according to Russo, he was shackled and beaten, placed in solitary confinement, and abused for leading a twenty-one-day hunger strike in protest of government actions against prisoners in the Attica state prison in New York. On October 1, U.S. District Court Judge Warren J. Ferguson released Russo from prison and ordered the government to provide Russo with a transcript of any testimony he might be required to give to the grand jury. Assistant U.S. Attorney David R. Nissen held the order to be "unlawful" and refused to comply with it. Russo again declined to testify before the grand jury. On December 29, the grand jury issued a new indictment in the Pentagon Papers case, which added new charges against Ellsberg and also included criminal charges against Russo. The trial of Ellsberg and Russo opened in Los Angeles on July 10, 1972. In October 1972, during a stay in the trial, Russo testified at the third annual session of the Commission of Enquiry into U.S. War Crimes in Indochina, held in Copenhagen, Denmark. On May 11, 1973, U.S. District Court Judge William Matthew Byrne dismissed all charges against Ellsberg and Russo and declared a mistrial in their case because of "improper government conduct." After the trial, Russo continued his antiwar activity, sought to organize a nationwide campaign to impeach President Richard M. Nixon,* and ultimately returned to social work.

Sources: Mike Gravel, ed., *Pentagon Papers*, 1971; Peter Schrag, *Test of Loyalty*, 1974.

John Kincaid

• S •

SAIGON

Saigon was the capital city of South Vietnam during the Vietnam War. Originally settled by Cambodians, Saigon has for centuries been a major port city in Southeast Asia. It is located approximately 45 miles up the Ben Nghe River, or Saigon River, from the South China Sea. The French began using the name Saigon in 1861 when they moved into the city and prepared for their takeover of the rest of the country. By 1980 the city had a population of nearly two million people concentrated into 27 square miles, making it one of the most population-dense areas in the world. Right next to Saigon is the city of Cholon,* composed mostly of ethnic Chinese.* In 1956 Ngo Dinh Diem* named Saigon the capital city of South Vietnam. When North Vietnamese and Vietcong* forces overran Saigon in 1975, they renamed it Ho Chi Minh City.*

Sources: Virginia Thompson, *French Indochina*, 1968; Ellen J. Hammer, *Vietnam, Yesterday and Today*, 1966.

SALEM HOUSE   *See* Daniel Boone Operations

SALISBURY, HARRISON EVANS

Harrison Evans Salisbury was born on November 14, 1908, in Minneapolis, Minnesota. Between 1930 and 1948 Salisbury worked for the United Press and traveled widely in his assignments. He joined the staff of the *New York Times* in 1948. Salisbury was assigned as Moscow bureau chief for the *Times* and remained there until 1953. He became assistant managing editor of the *Times* in 1964. Late in 1966 Salisbury traveled to North Vietnam to report on the effects of American bombing.* His reports were controversial on two levels: first, he confirmed North Vietnamese claims that civilian casualties from American bombing were quite high; and second, he argued that the bombing efforts were only increasing the resolve of the North Vietnamese to continue the war effort. During the 1960s and 1970s Salisbury continued to write widely for the *Times*, and has become widely known as the patriarch of American journalism.

Sources: Harrison E. Salisbury, *Behind the Lines: Hanoi, December 23, 1966–January 7, 1967*, 1967; *Who's Who in America, 1976–1977*, 1977.

SAM

The acronym SAM described surface-to-air missiles employed by the North Vietnamese against United States Navy* and Air Force* bombers and fighter-bombers (*see* fighters). The standard SAM was the Soviet SA–2 Guideline, a two-stage missile equipped with a 285-pound warhead and a maximum range of 30 miles. The first SA–2 Guidelines were deployed in the summer of 1965, and by the end of the war more than 200 SA–2 sites were operational, most of them protecting Hanoi* and Haiphong. Because of the United States "Wild Weasel"* program and various other electronic jamming efforts, the North Vietnamese used 150 SA–2s for every American aircraft they destroyed.

Source: Anthony Robinson, "Air Forces in Vietnam," in John S. Bowman, ed., *The Vietnam War: An Almanac*, 1985.

SAN ANTONIO FORMULA

On September 29, 1967, in San Antonio, Texas, President Lyndon B. Johnson* delivered a speech in which he offered to stop the bombing* of North Vietnam if Ho Chi Minh* would agree to begin serious negotiations for a peaceful settlement of the conflict, and if he would promise not to use the bombing halt as an opportunity to increase their infiltration* of troops and supplies into South Vietnam. In diplomatic and journalistic circles, the president's offer became known as the San Antonio Formula. Hanoi never responded positively to the offer, even though Johnson reiterated it on March 31, 1968, after the Tet Offensive* and his own decision not to seek reelection. For six months Johnson unilaterally stopped all bombing of North Vietnam above the nineteenth parallel, but the North Vietnamese did not seriously consider a negotiated settlement at the time.

Sources: Guenter Lewy, *America in Vietnam*, 1978; *New York Times*, September 30, 1986.

SANCTUARIES

Throughout the war in Vietnam the North Vietnamese and Vietcong* would use "hit and run" tactics and often fled across the border into sanctuaries in neutral Laos* and Cambodia (*see* Kampuchea). Although the inability of a neutral nation to keep a belligerent from exploiting its territory allows, according to international law, the other belligerent to use force on neutral territory, the United States had a difficult time with the issue. Periodically regular American military units would cross the border in "hot pursuit,"* and Studies and Observation Groups* regularly operated in Cambodia and Laos, as did naval and air force units bombing infiltration* routes. But not until the Cambodian invasion of 1970 (*see* Operation Binh Tay) and the Laotian invasion of 1971 (*see* Lam Son 719) did the United States openly assault North Vietnamese and Vietcong strongholds across the border. Although those invasions posed serious threats to the integrity of the sanctuaries, the subsequent withdrawal of American and South Vietnamese forces allowed the North Vietnamese and Vietcong to return to their original positions.

Sources: Guenter Lewy, *America in Vietnam*, 1978; Harry G. Summers, Jr., *On Strategy: A Critical Analysis of the Vietnam War*, 1982; William Shawcross, *Sideshow: Kissinger, Nixon, and the Destruction of Cambodia*, 1979; Keith William Nolan, *Into Laos: The Story of Dewey Canyon II/Lam Son 719*, 1986.

"SANITIZE"

"Sanitize" was one of a number of euphemisms developed to refer to assassination. It became infamous in conjunction with the Central Intelligence Agency's* Phoenix Program* in which as many as 20,000 South Vietnamese were killed because of suspected ties to the National Liberation Front (*see* Vietcong). Still, the term was widely used before the Phoenix Program to describe political assassinations carried out by South Vietnamese and American personnel. Critics charged that use of the term was indicative of the war's degrading and dehumanizing nature. The act of killing people who may or may not have been "innocent" was masked by a sterile, antiseptic term which occluded its reality even from those actively involved in the deaths. Critics saw development of such terminology as insidious, part of what they perceived as the larger fabric of lies surrounding the war and of how its very nature served to debase and degrade both those who participated in it and the United States as a nation.

Sources: Loren Baritz, *Backfire*, 1985; Guenter Lewy, *America in Vietnam*, 1978.

Samuel Freeman

SCHLESINGER, ARTHUR MEIER, JR.

Arthur M. Schlesinger, Jr., was born in Columbus, Ohio, on October 15, 1917. The son of distinguished historian Arthur M. Schlesinger, he attended public schools, Phillips Exeter Academy, and Harvard. His senior thesis, a biography of Orestes A. Brownson, was published in 1939. Schlesinger joined the Harvard faculty that same year. He won the Pulitzer Prize for his book *The Age of Jackson* (1945). His trilogy *The Age of Roosevelt* in the late 1950s firmly established Schlesinger as one of America's most outstanding historians. In 1961, President John F. Kennedy* appointed Schlesinger as a special adviser, and he served until Kennedy's assassination in 1963. Schlesinger's book *A Thousand Days*, though essentially an apology, was nevertheless a cogent description of the "Age of Camelot."

Schlesinger, although a supporter of the antipoverty and civil rights thrusts of Lyndon B. Johnson's* Great Society,* broke with the administration over Vietnam. In 1966 Schlesinger wrote *The Bitter Heritage*, a history of American involvement in South Vietnam, and he accused American policymakers of confusing communism and nationalism, backing an essentially fascist dictator in the person of Ngo Dinh Diem,* and using conventional tactics in a futile guerrilla war (see Vietcong). Schlesinger denied the reality of the domino theory* and doubted that the Chinese (see People's Republic of China), traditionally the enemies of the Vietnamese, had any intention of intervening. After leaving the Kennedy administration, Schlesinger continued teaching and writing. He is currently a professor emeritus of history at the City University of New York.

Sources: Arthur M. Schlesinger, Jr., *The Bitter Heritage: Vietnam and American Democracy, 1941–1966*, 1966; *Directory of American Scholars, History*, 1984.

SCHLESINGER, JAMES RODNEY

James Schlesinger was born in New York City on February 15, 1929. He graduated from Harvard University in 1950 and then took the M.A. and Ph.D. there in economics in 1952 and 1956. Between 1955 and 1963 Schlesinger taught at the University of Virginia. He spent the next six years with the Rand Corporation.* During his years at Virginia and Rand, Schlesinger wrote two important books: *The Political Economy of National Security* (1960) and *Issues in Defense Economics* (1967). Schlesinger became assistant director of the Bureau of the Budget in 1969, chairman of the Atomic Energy Commission in 1971, head of the Central Intelligence Agency* in 1973, and secretary of defense later in 1973. He served in that position throughout the Watergate* crisis involving President Richard M. Nixon* and the fall of the Republic of Vietnam* in 1975. Schlesinger left the Pentagon in 1975, served for a time as a visiting scholar at Johns Hopkins University, and then became secretary of energy under President Jimmy Carter in 1977. Schlesinger left the Carter administration in 1979 and became a senior adviser to the Center for Strategic and International Studies at Georgetown University.

Source: *Who's Who in America, 1984–1985*, 1985.

SEABEES

Naval construction units, known as Seabees, were active in the Vietnam conflict from the very beginning of the American presence there. As early as 1954, the Amphibious Construction Battalion 1 was constructing refugee camps in South Vietnam, and between 1962 and 1965 they built camps for the Fifth Special Forces Group.* During that period they were also heavily engaged in civic action programs building airstrips, bridges, dams, roads, housing, and schools. Naval Mobile Construction Battalions, each staffed with 24 officers and 738 enlisted men, began arriving at Da Nang* in May 1965 as part of the 30th Naval Construction Regiment. The 3rd Naval Construction Brigade arrived in Vietnam on June 1, 1966. The 32nd Naval Construction Regiment was sent to Vietnam on August 1, 1967, to take care of construction needs in the Hue*– Phu Bai region. Most Seabee activities took place in I Corps,* where they constructed waterfront facilities, storage areas, ammunition dumps, roads, and bridges. The Seabees were based at Da Nang,* Chu Lai, Hue–Phu Bai, Dong

Tam, and Quang Tri. At their peak strength in 1968, Seabees totaled more than 10,000 men. The last Seabee unit to leave Vietnam was the 3rd Naval Construction Brigade, which departed on November 1, 1971.

Sources: Shelby L. Stanton, *Vietnam Order of Battle*, 1981; Richard Tregakis, *Southeast Asia: Building the Bases: The History of Construction in Southeast Asia*, 1975.

SEALORDS

SEALORDS was an acronym for South East Asian Lake Ocean River Delta Strategy. In February 1969, as part of the Vietnamization* program, the United States Navy* began handing over to South Vietnam a fleet of nearly 250 patrol craft and 500 motorized junks which had formerly been part of the Mobile Riverine Force* and Task Forces 116 and 117. The Army of the Republic of Vietnam,* assisted by U.S. naval advisers, took control of the patrol craft and the program was renamed SEALORDS. Virtually all of the craft fell into the hands of the Vietcong* and the North Vietnamese in 1975.

Sources: Edward J. Marolda and G. Wesley Pryce III, *A Short History of the United States Navy and the Southeast Asia Conflict, 1950–1975*, 1984; William B. Fulton, *Riverine Operations, 1966–1969*, 1973.

SEAL TEAMS

Early in 1961 teams of United States Special Forces* units began arriving in South Vietnam to train the Vietnamese in counterinsurgency.* The first Special Forces teams were army units, but the United States Navy* also established its own counterinsurgency groups, known as sea, air, and land (SEAL) teams. The first SEAL groups arrived in South Vietnam in 1966 and went into the swamps of the Mekong Delta.* They engaged in a variety of activities. SEAL teams infiltrated Vietcong* areas in small boats or as frogmen, parachuted in or landed by helicopters, conducted "hunter-killer" raids, worked with Studies and Observation Groups* intelligence teams, and operated from fast-moving airboats and Seawolf helicopters. The SEAL were supported by naval Task Force 116 (*see* Mobile Riverine Force).

Source: Edward J. Marolda and G. Wesley Pryce III, *A Short History of the United States Navy and the Southeast Asian Conflict, 1950–1973*, 1984.

SEARCH AND DESTROY STRATEGY

The term "search and destroy" was the euphemism for the strategy of attrition the United States employed in Vietnam between 1965 and 1968. Developed primarily by Generals William Westmoreland* and William Depuy, "search and destroy" relied on the naive assumption that superior American technology and firepower would eventually inflict casualties so severe that the Vietcong* and the North Vietnamese Army* (NVA) would be unable to sustain the war. Instead of the enclave strategy* which would confine the United States to a defensive posture, "search and destroy" meant seeking out the enemy and, with artillery, air power, and ground forces, destroying their base areas and personnel. Once the main NVA regiments had been eliminated, the United States hoped the South Vietnamese would be able to deal effectively with the Vietcong.

But the search and destroy strategy rested on a major assumption—that the United States would be able to inflict massive losses on the North Vietnamese without itself experiencing unacceptable casualty levels. That assumption, however, was contradicted by two basic facts in Vietnam: first, the Vietcong and North Vietnamese retained the strategic initiative and could pick and choose their battles, including the timing of attacks and the resource investment; and second, more than 200,000 young men reached draft age in North Vietnam each year, allowing them to resupply their military units. Both of these facts together guaranteed that the United States would at best only be able to fight them to a standstill. The irony, of course, was that the Vietcong and North Vietnamese were also banking on their ability to inflict unacceptable losses on the United States until the patience of the American public wore out and the troops were withdrawn. Their scenario proved to be the correct one. The Tet Offensive* of 1968 was a political disaster in the United States, forcing Lyndon B. Johnson's* decision not to seek reelection and convincing large numbers of Americans that the war in Vietnam was not worth the effort and that the United States might not be capable of "winning" by any means. The election of 1968* turned out to be the strategic watershed of the Vietnam War. Between 1969 and 1973 the United States pursued a policy of staged withdrawal rather than trying to "search and destroy" the enemy. The war of attrition* had failed.

Sources: Robert Shaplen, *The Road from War: Vietnam, 1965–1970*, 1970; George C. Herring, *America's Longest War: The United States in Vietnam 1950–1975*, 1986; W. Scott Thompson and Donaldson D. Frizzell, *The Lessons of Vietnam*, 1977; Harry G. Summers, Jr., *On Strategy: A Critical Analysis of the Vietnam War*, 1982.

SEARCH AND RESCUE OPERATIONS

During the course of the war the United States Air Force* (USAF) rescue service recovered several thousand American and allied fighting men who went down in the jungles, mountains, and waters of Southeast Asia. The first USAF rescue team, consisting of three officers and three airmen, arrived in South Vietnam on temporary duty on January 10, 1962. Based at Tan Son Nhut Air Base,* near Saigon,* this unit's mission was to organize a search and rescue (SAR) control center and network throughout the country. In April 1962 the six-man cadre was officially designated Detachment 3, Pacific Air Rescue Center, with overall responsibility for rescue operations within the theater. Its job was especially difficult at first, for the detachment had no aircraft and had to rely on American advisers to provide helicopter assistance for air rescue missions.

In addition to not having its own aircraft, the detachment lacked most of the basic equipment needed for an effective SAR system. For example, in the early days of its operations the SAR center sent requests for help to operational units by bicycle, a method faster and more reliable than trying to use the existing Vietnamese telephone network. Its reliance on the United States Army* and later the United States Marines* for helicopter support also created problems because they were not prepared for rescue missions and had other duties which they considered of higher priority.

Very quickly after the establishment of the rescue center in Vietnam, it became clear to air force officials that specialized aircraft and devices were needed to operate effectively over the jungle and mountainous terrain of Southeast Asia. As a result, in November 1963 the commander of the Air Rescue Service pressed for the acquisition of the CH–3 single rotor cargo amphibian helicopter for use in the theater. It had a forward speed of about 150 mph, ability to remain aloft more than four hours, and a range of approximately 500 miles. He reported that the Air Service was not equipped to do the job in Southeast Asia and that, by "utter default," air force combat crews were "made dependent upon ill-equipped and ill-trained . . . U.S. Army and Marine Corps helicopter resources diverted to accomplish our mission. . . . Their noble efforts have wrought confusion and even disaster when engaged in some attempts to prosecute Air Service missions."

In response, Headquarters USAF ordered a number of combat-modified CH–3s. But, pending their manufacture, the Air Force was forced to use existing HH–43s and HU–16s, decent helicopters but not as well suited to jungle operations as the CH–3. In March 1964 three USAF HH–43 units were transferred from the Philippines* and Okinawa to Southeast Asia. In June 1964 the first temporary-duty contingent—two HH–43s and thirty-six personnel—was sent to Nakhon Phanom, Thailand.* That same month the 31st Air Rescue Squadron at Clark Air Base, the Philippines, deployed two HU–16 amphibian helicopters to Da Nang,* South Vietnam, to provide rescue service for American airmen downed in the Gulf of Tonkin. Two HU–16s from the 33d Air Rescue Squadron also were deployed to Korat Air Base, Thailand, to support USAF operations there and in Laos.* By January 1, 1965, five helicopter detachments were operating in the theater: at Bien Hoa and Da Nang, South Vietnam, and at Udorn, Nakhon Phanom, Takhli, and Korat, Thailand.

Air rescue in Vietnam entered a new phase in January 1966 when the air force activated the 3rd Aerospace Rescue and Recovery Group at Tan Son Nhut Air Base to serve as the primary rescue agency in Southeast Asia. The group eventually directed the activities of four rescue squadrons and ten rescue detachments based throughout South Vietnam and Thailand. These units were solely responsible for the recovery of 3,883 flyers between 1964 and mid-August 1973. Of this number, 2,807 American—926 army, 680 navy, and 1,201 air force—aircrew members were rescued. The rescuemen also saved 555 allied military flyers, 476 civilians, and 45 other unidentified persons. During the course of the war in Vietnam, 71 American search and rescue men were killed and 45 aircraft destroyed while conducting recovery operations.

Source: Earl H. Tilford, Jr., *Search and Rescue in Southeast Asia, 1961–1975*, 1980.

Roger D. Launius

II CORPS

II Corps was the second allied combat tactical zone in South Vietnam. It included the Central Highlands* and contiguous central lowlands, and was known politically as the Central Vietnam Highlands, one of the four major administrative political units of South Vietnam in the 1960s and early 1970s. II Corps was also known as Military Region 2 (MR 2). The military and administrative headquarters of II Corps was in Pleiku,* and it consisted of the following provinces: Kontum, Binh Dinh, Pleiku, Phu Bon, Phu Yen, Darlac, Khanh Hoa, Quang Duc, Tuyen Duc, Ninh Thuan, Lam Dong, and Binh Thuan. The major ARVN (*see* Army of the Republic of Vietnam) units operating in II Corps were the 22nd and 23rd divisions.

Sources: Harvey Smith, et al., *Area Handbook for South Vietnam*, 1967; Shelby L. Stanton, *Vietnam Order of Battle*, 1981.

II FIELD FORCE VIETNAM

Headquartered at Bien Hoa, the II Field Force Vietnam was in the Republic of Vietnam* between March 1966 and May 1971, assisting ARVN forces (*see* Army of the Republic of Vietnam) in III* and IV Corps,* protecting Saigon,* controlling U.S. military operations in the Mekong Delta,* and directing the invasion of Cambodia (*see* Operation Binh Tay) in 1970. II Field Force Vietnam was a corps*-level military organization. The following individuals commanded II Field Force Vietnam: Major General Jonathan Seaman (March 1966–March 1967); Lt. General Bruce Palmer, Jr. (March 1967–July 1967); Lt. General Frederick C. Weyand* (July 1967–August 1968); Lt. General Walter Kerwin, Jr. (August 1968–April 1969); Lt. General Julian Ewell (April 1969–April 1970); and Lt. General Michael S. Davison (April 1970–May 1971).

Source: Shelby L. Stanton, *Vietnam Order of Battle*, 1981.

SECRETARY OF DEFENSE

In 1946 Congress passed the National Security Act, which coordinated the army, navy, and air force into a Department of Defense, with a secretary of defense enjoying cabinet status. The secretary of defense is in the direct chain of military command, between the president of the United States and the Joint Chiefs of Staff (*see* Chairman, JCS). During the course of direct American involvement in the Vietnam War, seven men served as secretary of defense. Neil H. McElroy was serving under Dwight Eisenhower* when the U.S. commitment began to escalate, and in December 1959 Thomas S. Gates, Jr., replaced him. When John F. Kennedy* took over the White House in 1961, Robert S. McNamara* became the new secretary of defense. He served under Kennedy and Lyndon B. Johnson* until Johnson let him go in March 1968, replacing him with Clark M. Clifford.* When Richard M. Nixon* took over the White House in January 1969, Clifford left the Pentagon and Melvin Laird* became the new secretary of defense. Laird resigned in January 1973 and Elliot Richardson took over. Richardson resigned in July 1973 and James Schlesinger* assumed the post and remained there until the war ended.

Sources: Guenter Lewy, *America in Vietnam*, 1978; Douglas Kinnard, *The Secretary of Defense*, 1980.

SECRETARY OF STATE

The secretary of state is a cabinet-level position and chief foreign policy officer for the United States. During the years of the war in Vietnam, five men served as secretary of state. John Foster Dulles* (1953–59) and Christian Herter (1959–61) served under President Dwight Eisenhower;* Dean Rusk* (1961–69) served under presidents John F. Kennedy* and Lyndon B. Johnson;* William P. Rogers* (1969–73) served under President Richard M. Nixon;* and Henry Kissinger* (1973–77) served under Presidents Nixon and Gerald Ford.*

Source: Guenter Lewy, *America in Vietnam*, 1978.

SENATE FOREIGN RELATIONS COMMITTEE

Long considered one of the most prestigious of Senate committees, the Foreign Relations Committee has traditionally been identified with bipartisan support of foreign policy. Its leadership has frequently cooperated closely with whatever administration has happened to be in power. J. William Fulbright,* the Arkansas Democrat who became chairman in 1959 and remained in that position through 1974, was floor manager for the Gulf of Tonkin Resolution* when it passed the Senate in 1964. However, by 1965 Fulbright and others on the committee were having strong second thoughts about Johnson* administration Vietnam policies. The committee became a focal point for the gradually emerging opposition in Washington. Early in 1966 the committee held nationally televised hearings on the war policy. Chairman Fulbright called both administration officials and outside experts to testify, and the hearings served as the first national forum on Vietnam.

As the committee continued to examine Vietnam policy, a confrontational attitude developed between it and the executive branch, and the committee became the stronghold of those favoring a more assertive congressional role in foreign policy. In 1967–68, the committee conducted an inquiry into the events leading up to the 1964 Gulf of Tonkin Resolution and raised many questions about the accounts provided by the Johnson administration. In March 1968, following the Tet Offensive* and at a pivotal political point, the committee again held highly publicized hearings on Johnson administration policies. When the Nixon* administration took office in 1969, the committee maintained its pressure for an end to American military involvement in Southeast Asia, and particularly opposed the 1970 incursion into Cambodia (*see* Operation Binh Tay) and the American bombing in Cambodia (*see* Operation Menu). Although the committee was a forum for vigorous discussion, and several of its members became leading dissenters from executive branch policies on Vietnam, the committee did not until 1973–74 begin to impose major legislative restrictions on U.S. activities in Southeast Asia.

Sources: Anthony Austin, *The President's War*, 1971; Thomas M. Franck and Edward Weisband, *Foreign Policy by Congress*, 1979; Haynes Johnson and Bernard Gwertzman,

Fulbright: The Dissenter, 1968; Edward P. Haley, *Congress and the Fall of South Vietnam and Cambodia*, 1982.

Hoyt Purvis

SEVENTEENTH PARALLEL   *See* Geneva Accords of 1954

SEVENTH AIR FORCE

The presence of the United States Air Force* (USAF) in Vietnam began in 1961 when the 4400th Combat Crew Training Squadron was deployed to Bien Hoa. Their activities were code-named Farmgate,* and using B–26 bombers, C–47* transports, T–28D Nomads, and A–1E Skyraiders* they trained Vietnamese pilots and provided close air support for ARVN operations (*see* Army of the Republic of Vietnam). Until April 1966, USAF operations in Vietnam were under the direction of the Second Air Division, but the massive buildup of 1965 required command reorganization; and on April 1, 1966, the Seventh Air Force, stationed at Tan Son Nhut Air Base* outside Saigon, took over. The Seventh Air Force had tactical fighter wings at Bien Hoa in III Corps,* Cam Ranh Bay* and Phan Rang in II Corps,* and Da Nang* in I Corps.* During the war seven individuals commanded the Seventh Air Force: Lt. General Joseph Moore (April–July 1966); General William Momyer* (July 1966–August 1968); General George S. Brown* (August 1968–September 1970); General Lucius Clay (September 1970–August 1971); General John Lavelle* (August 1971–April 1972); General John W. Vogt* (April 1972–October 1973); and Lt. General Timothy O'Keefe (October 1972–March 1973).

Source: Carl Berger, ed., *The United States Air Force in Southeast Asia, 1961–1973*, 1977.

SEVENTH FLEET

The Seventh Fleet was responsible for all U.S. naval operations in the Western Pacific in general and Southeast Asia in particular between 1965 and 1973. During the years of the Vietnam conflict, the Seventh Fleet was commanded by Vice Admiral Roy L. Johnson (June 1964–March 1965), Vice Admiral Paul P. Blackburn (March 1965–October 1965), Rear Admiral Joseph W. Williams (October 1965–December 1965), Vice Admiral John J. Hyland (December 1965–November 1967), Vice Admiral William F. Bringle (November 1967–March 1970), Vice Admiral Maurice F. Weisner (March 1970–June 1971), Vice Admiral William P. Mack (June 1971–May 1972), and Vice Admiral James Holloway (May 1972 to the end of the war). In the Seventh Fleet, Task Force 77 was the aircraft carrier* attack unit; Task Force 76 was the amphibious unit; Task Force 73 was the logistic support unit; Task Force 70.8 was the group of destroyers and cruisers responsible for shore bombardment; and Task Force 117 was the Riverine Assault Force (*see* Mobile Riverine Force).

Source: Edward J. Marolda and G. Wesley Pryce III, *A Short History of the United States Navy and the Southeast Asia Conflict, 1950–1975*, 1984.

SHANGHAI COMMUNIQUÉ OF 1972

Issued by Richard Nixon* during his precedent-breaking diplomatic mission to the People's Republic of China* in 1972, the Shanghai Communiqué promised that the United States would reduce its military presence on Taiwan as soon as diplomatic tensions began to ease. The promise encouraged the Chinese that the United States was finally preparing to recognize them as the legitimate representative of the Chinese people, but the North Vietnamese were extremely suspicious. The last thing they wanted was improved relations between the United States and China. Mao Zedong* had been pressing North Vietnam to consider a reduced military effort in South Vietnam, and the North Vietnamese interpreted the Shanghai Communiqué as part of a larger Chinese-American conspiracy to reduce their influence in Southeast Asia.

Source: Stanley Karnow, *Vietnam: A History*, 1983.

SHARP, ULYSSES S. GRANT

U. S. Grant Sharp was born on April 2, 1906, in Chinook, Montana. After graduating from the United States Naval Academy in 1927, Sharp rose through the officer ranks. He commanded a minesweeper during World War II and in June 1964 became commander in chief, Pacific Command* (CINCPAC), with its 400 ships, 3,500 aircraft, and 500,000 men and women spread out over 85 million square miles. Sharp oversaw the Vietnam buildup through the Tet Offensive* early in 1968. Sharp frequently advocated more intensive bombing* of North Vietnam, asserting that "toughness" was "the only policy that the Communists understand." He retired in July 1968, and his memoir, *Strategy for Defeat* (1978), gives his alternative to the military policy U.S. forces implemented in Vietnam as well as a general prescription for the future.

Sources: U. S. Grant Sharp, *Strategy for Defeat*, 1978; *Who's Who in America, 1964–1965*, 1965; Edward J. Marolda and G. Wesley Pryce III, *A Short History of the United States Navy and the Southeast Asian Conflict, 1950–1975*, 1984.

Dudley Acker

"SHORT-TIMER"

A "short-timer" was an individual who had a relatively short time remaining on his or her assignment to duty in Southeast Asia. Unlike previous wars, when troops had been in the service "for the duration," during the Vietnam War, troops were assigned to the Southeast Asia combat area for a limited period, either twelve months (U.S. Army)* or thirteen months (U.S. Marines).* When the soldier's 365 days in the combat zone ended, he was reassigned. As a result, each individual knew the precise date he would be eligible to leave the combat zone, and those with relatively little time left to serve in Southeast Asia were "short-timers." The term acquired an ethos and became the subject of countless hours of discussion. "Short-timers" became focal points of envy in every unit and manifested their high status by publicly demonstrating how soon they would be reassigned. Two common ways of showing how "short" an individual had were by calendars drawn on helmet covers and the "short-timer's stick," which was notched so that each day a knob could be removed until there were no knobs remaining.

Source: Al Santoli, *Everything We Had: An Oral History of the Vietnam War by Thirty-three American Soldiers Who Fought It*, 1981.

Stafford T. Thomas

THE SHORT-TIMERS

The Short-Timers is the title of Gustav Hasford's 1979 novel about the Vietnam War. An extraordinarily violent book, the novel focuses on William "Joker" Doolittle, marine combat reporter in Vietnam who refuses promotion to sergeant and insists on wearing a peace button. With his time running "short"—only 49 days remaining on his tour—Doolittle's insubordination rankles a superior officer and he finds himself reassigned to a vulnerable combat unit. Supposedly fighting for freedom, the soldiers appear more as prisoners of the Vietnam War themselves.

Sources: Gustav Hasford, *The Short-Timers*, 1979; Philip D. Beidler, *American Literature and the Experience of Vietnam*, 1982.

SHOUP, DAVID MONROE

An aspiring poet with the world's largest private collection of sake cups and bottles, Shoup became commandant of the Marine Corps* when President Eisenhower* elevated him over several senior generals in 1959. Born in Indiana in 1904, Shoup attended DePauw University on an academic scholarship and after receiving his commission in 1927 spent the prewar years at sea, in naval yards and China. After duty in Iceland in 1941, Shoup was wounded while serving as a division operations officer on Guadalcanal (1942) and earned a second Purple Heart, plus the Medal of Honor, while commanding the initial assault at Tarawa (1943).

Although Shoup missed service in Korea, top staff and command billets marked his rise to commandant, and once confirmed by the Senate he began issuing pithy, handwritten "Shoupisms" that challenged tradition and abolished "swagger sticks," "drumming out" marines convicted by courts-martial, gun salutes preceding his post inspections, and the custom allowing senior officers to select staffs that would follow them from post to post for years. Shoup also presided over the transition from pure amphibious doctrine to the vertical assault, participated in the Bay of Pigs and Cuban Missile Crisis decisions, and alone among the Joint Chiefs of Staff (*see* Chairman, JCS) favored the Nuclear Test Ban Treaty of 1963.

Shoup retired after the Kennedy assassination and held positions with an insurance firm and presidential commissions on amateur athletics and the Selective Service before emerging as a prominent Vietnam War critic in May 1966. "I don't think the whole of Southeast Asia, as related to the present and future safety and freedom of the people of this country," he told a Los Angeles college audience, "is worth the life or limb of a single American." Although often identified as an activist, Shoup published only one article, testified twice before Congress,* and gave a few short interviews to the press. In declining health, he loaned his name if not his skills to the peace movement and mostly confined his arguments to practical military concerns: "I was among the first," he said in a final interview in 1971, "to say we could not win because we were not permitted to go to the heart of the war—to North Vietnam. As soon as we get out, North Vietnam will be able to move right in and take over. After all that killing—it is frustrating, frustrating." Shoup died in 1983, less than eight years after the fall of Saigon.*

Source: Dudley Acker, Jr., "The World According to Shoup," unpublished manuscript, Northern Arizona University, April 1985.

Dudley Acker

SIGMA II

In 1963, as the political and military situation in South Vietnam was deteriorating, the Joint Chiefs of Staff (*see* Chairman, JCS) staged a series of war games carrying the code name Sigma I. The outcome confirmed some of their worst fears: that a military victory over the Vietcong* in South Vietnam would require more than 500,000 American combat troops. In September 1964, the Joint Chiefs of Staff conducted another war game scenario for South Vietnam, this time with national security adviser McGeorge Bundy* participating. Known as Sigma II, the games were designed to assess the impact of a major air offensive against North Vietnam. The results were no more encouraging than those of Sigma I. Indeed, it seemed, from the results of Sigma II at least, that the United States had little chance of stopping a Vietcong* victory. Nevertheless, political and diplomatic events during the next eight months pushed the United States closer and closer to military intervention on a large scale.

Source: Stanley Karnow, *Vietnam: A History*, 1983.

SIHANOUK, NORODOM

Born in 1922 in Cambodia (*see* Kampuchea), Norodom Sihanouk was crowned king of Cambodia by French officials in 1941. He functioned as a puppet ruler until 1954 when, after the French defeat at Dien Bien Phu,* Cambodia was given its independence. Between 1954 and 1970, Sihanouk tried to maintain Cambodian neutrality between the People's Republic of China* and the Vietnamese, and between the United States and the major Communist powers, but it proved to be an impossible task. When the American buildup in South Vietnam began in 1965, Sihanouk started leaning toward the Vietnamese, but that only lasted until North Vietnamese Army* (NVA) troops began exploiting his neutrality. In 1969 Sihanouk acquiesced to American requests for secret bombing of NVA installations in Cambodian territory, and in March 1970, while he was visiting the Soviet Union* and asking them to assist him in expelling the NVA troops, he was deposed by Lon Nol.* Sihanouk then moved to Peking, hoping but failing to get Chinese support in his attempt to regain power. Throughout the 1970s and 1980s Sihanouk periodically tried to regain his throne in Cambodia but failed.

Sources: *International Who's Who, 1971–1972*, 1972; William Shawcross, *Sideshow: Kissinger, Nixon, and the Destruction of Cambodia*, 1979; Ben Kiernan, "How Pol Pot Came to Power," Ph.D. diss., 1986.

SILENT MAJORITY SPEECH

President Richard Nixon's* November 3, 1969, "silent majority" speech was made in response to the massive antiwar protest of the Moratorium Day demonstration* of October 15 and in anticipation of the moratorium days set for mid-November. In this televised speech, Nixon both attacked the antiwar movement* as subversive of his administration's policies and outlined a plan of action for the future. He made a patriotic appeal to "the great silent majority" of Americans to support his search for a "just and lasting peace" as an alternative to immediate withdrawal which, he stated, would lead to "a collapse of confidence in American leadership, not only in Asia but throughout the world." Nixon outlined the history of American involvement in Vietnam since his inauguration, and stated that the previous administrations had "Americanized the war," but his administration would henceforth "Vietnamize the search for peace." To this end, he described a plan of withdrawal of American forces from Vietnam to correspond with the buildup and strengthening of South Vietnam's forces. He then attacked the antiwar movement as a "vocal minority" and stated that "North Vietnam cannot defeat or humiliate the United States. Only Americans can do that." Despite the White House claim of 80,000 letters and telegrams of support following the speech, the Moratorium Day demonstrations of mid-November exceeded their October counterparts. Nevertheless, Nixon's appeal to patriotism and his promise of Vietnamization* and the consequent return of American troops marked the beginning of the end of the massive antiwar demonstrations of the Vietnam era.

Sources: Richard Nixon, *RN: The Memoirs of Richard Nixon*, 1978; Nancy Zaroulis and Gerald L. Sullivan, *Who Spoke Up? American Protest Against the War in Vietnam, 1963–1975*, 1984.

Linda Alkana

SKYCRANE   *See* CH–54 Skycrane

SLAM

SLAM was the acronym for "seek, locate, annihilate, monitor," a concept developed by General William M. Momyer,* commander of the Seventh Air Force.* First introduced during Operation Neutralize* in September 1967 at the siege of Con Thien,* SLAM involved an overall coordination of B–52* air strikes, tactical air support, naval bombardment,* artillery assaults, and ground fire. B–52 Stratofortresses struck first and were followed by tactical air attacks, naval gunfire, and artillery barrages, all of them concentrated in small areas. For the next five years SLAM was the standard approach to concentrating American firepower.

Sources: Terrence Maitland and Peter McInerney, *The Vietnam Experience: A Contagion of War*, 1983; William W. Momyer, *Airpower in Three Wars*, 1978.

SLICK

The Vietnam War became a helicopter war for American forces, and a common way for an infantryman to go into action was by slick. "Slick" was the term used to refer to an assault helicopter used to place troops into combat during airmobile operations. The UH–1* became the premier helicopter for this. Troops could ride in the wide doors of the aircraft, normally in two rows on each side, and could exit quickly when landing in a "hot LZ"*—a landing zone under fire. Often a UH–1 would not touch down during slick operations; instead it would hover a couple of feet above the ground while troops evacuated the aircraft. Troops learned to feel the UH–1 "bounce" as it came in quickly and went into a hover, and would exit on the bounce, so that slicks spent very little time close to the ground.

Source: Jim Mesko, *Airmobile: The Helicopter War in Vietnam*, 1985.

Nolan J. Argyle

SMART BOMBS

Because of the increasingly devastating effectiveness of North Vietnamese antiaircraft defenses, the United States developed the so-called smart bombs, which could be dropped from safe distances and would then head toward their targets with the assistance of laser beams, television cameras, and computers. There were two types of smart bombs—laser-guided bombs and computer-directed, electro-optically guided bombs. The first laser-guided "Paveway" bomb was tested in 1966, and in 1967 the first electro-optically guided bomb, known as the "Walleye," was used over North Vietnam. The Walleye, a 2,000-pound bomb with a camera and computer attached to its front, could be dropped more than thirty miles from its target and could be carried by any combat jet. During the Christmas bombing of 1972 (*see* Operation Linebacker II), when the United States wanted to make sure that the North Vietnamese lived up to the agreement they had accepted in October, smart bombs were used extensively over North Vietnam, achieving an accuracy rate unknown earlier in the war.

Source: Edgar C. Doleman, Jr., *The Vietnam Experience: Tools of War*, 1984.

SMITH, WALTER BEDELL

Walter B. Smith was born in Indianapolis, Indiana, on October 5, 1895. After serving in the state national guard between 1910 and 1915, Smith made a career out of the United States Army,* seeing action in France during World War I and attaining the rank of lieutenant general during World War II. He was chief of staff to Dwight D. Eisenhower* during the North African campaign in 1942 and 1943. After the war, Smith served as ambassador to the Soviet Union* from 1946 to 1949, director of the Central Intelligence Agency* from 1950 to 1953, and under secretary of state during the Eisenhower administration. Smith headed the American delegation to the Geneva Conference (*see* Geneva Accords) on Vietnam in 1954, and then retired from government service to accept a vice chairmanship of the American Machine and Foundry Company. The author of two books (*My Three Years in Moscow*, 1950, and *Eisenhower's Six Great Decisions*, 1956), W. Bedell Smith died on August 9, 1961.

Sources: *Who Was Who in America*, 4:880; *New York Times*, August 10, 1961.

SOCIALIST REPUBLIC OF VIETNAM

Ho Chi Minh* had proclaimed establishment of the Democratic Republic of Vietnam* on January 14, 1950, when his Vietminh* forces were struggling for power with the French. At the Geneva Conference (*see* Geneva Accords) of 1954, North Vietnam became officially known as the Democratic Republic of Vietnam, while South Vietnam was designated the Republic of Vietnam.* But when North Vietnamese forces finally conquered South Vietnam in 1975, they changed the name of the entire country to the Socialist Republic of Vietnam, by which it is currently known.

Source: Stanley Karnow, *Vietnam: A History*, 1983.

SONG NGAN VALLEY   *See* Helicopter Valley

SON TAY RAID

In the summer of 1970 Secretary of Defense Melvin Laird* presented President Richard Nixon* a Pentagon plan for a daring raid to rescue over one hundred American prisoners from the Son Tay prison installation located 23 miles west of Hanoi.* Only a few months earlier, in April, the United States's invasion of Cambodia (*see* Kampuchea) had torn the nation apart. The one issue that still bound the American people was their growing concern for the prisoners of war* (POWs) and servicemen classified as missing in action. Nixon had been receiving reports that American POWs were dying from torture and ill-treatment. In Nixon's view the raid, if successful, would not only be humanitarian; it would also give him some clout at the Paris peace talks.* These were stalled, partly because of the POW issue. Therefore, he approved the raid.

Planning for the mission was headed by Army Brigadier General Donald D. Blackburn, the special assistant for counterinsurgency activities for the Joint Chiefs of Staff (*see* Chairman, JCS), and Army Colonel E. E. "Ed" Mayer, the head of Special Operations Division within SACSA (Special Assistant for Counterinsurgency and Special Activities). The plan they developed entailed a helicopter assault on the Son Tay prison compound by a fifty-six-man force. One helicopter would have to crash-land inside the compound to give the assault team enough time to eliminate the guards. The remaining helicopters would land outside the compound. Two would contain security forces to prevent the camp from being reinforced; they would also use satchel charges to breach the walls of the compound. The other helicopters would be empty to accommodate the seventy to one hundred expected POWs. To divert enemy attention away from Son Tay, U.S. Navy* and Air Force* planes would pretend to attack Haiphong Harbor. Although not in the original plan, F–105s* were to be used to escort the helicopters in and act as bait for North Vietnamese surface-to-air missiles. The raid would last no longer than thirty minutes because it had been determined that it would take that long for the North Vietnamese to respond with overwhelming force.

The man in overall command of the mission was Air Force Brigadier General Leroy J. Manor, and Army Colonel Arthur D. Simons would lead the actual raid on the prison compound. The fifty-six men who were to comprise the newly designated Joint Contingency Task Force Ivory were carefully selected Special Forces* and Ranger volunteers. The task force underwent six months of training and three months of rehearsal at Eglin Air Force Base in Florida. Intelligence for the mission relied heavily on photos from SR–71 high-altitude flyovers and low-altitude drones. Neither of these were able to confirm that POWs were still at Son Tay. Prior to the raid, in fact, intelligence was received from a Central Intelligence Agency* contact, Nguyen Van Hoang, a senior North Vietnamese official who dealt with POW interrogations, that the prisoners had been moved to a new camp called Dong Hoi 15 miles to the east. The move had been made on July 14, 1970, because of severe flooding. Although this intelligence was available, it was decided to proceed with the raid.

After a flight from Thailand* the raiders were above Son Tay prison camp at a little after 2:00 A.M. on November 21. The raid went off with only a few hitches. One mistake proved fortuitous, however. The helicopter containing Colonel Simons and the support group landed in the wrong compound. They had landed in what had been identified as a "secondary school" but in fact contained Russian or Chinese troops who were training North Vietnamese air defense technicians. Simons's group was able to eliminate the "primary external ground threat" to the Son Tay assault team. The Americans suffered no casualties, with the exception of one man slightly injured during the crash-landing. Although they found the camp empty of American POWs, General Manor praised the operation as "a complete success with the exception that no prisoners were rescued."

The raid did produce some positive results, however. Prisoners who had previously been scattered throughout the countryside were now concentrated in a prison in Hanoi called the "Hanoi Hilton."* This move had a positive effect on prisoner morale if not treatment. The raid also caused serious concern among the North Vietnamese and their allies because it showed their vulnerability to this type of raid.

Source: Benjamin F. Schemmer, *The Raid*, 1976.

Mike Dennis

SORTIES

The word "sortie" is a U.S. Air Force* term to describe one round-trip for cargo planes or one attack by gunships,* fighters,* fighter-bombers, and strategic bombers.

Source: Harry G. Summers, Jr., *Vietnam War Almanac*, 1985.

SOUTHEAST ASIA TREATY ORGANIZATION (SEATO)

Similar to the North Atlantic Treaty Organization (NATO) and the Central Treaty Organization (CENTO), SEATO was created in 1954 as part of the Manila Pact, a regional defense scheme for the South Pacific. Although SEATO calls for consultation in the event of military or political emergencies, it does not include a unified military command or joint forces so important to NATO. The Senate ratified the treaty by an 82 to 1 vote, and SEATO became an important link in U.S. global containment policy.* Along with the United States, SEATO contained Great Britain,* the Philippines,* France,* Australia,* New Zealand,* Pakistan, and Thailand.* Conspicuous by their absence from the organization were India, Burma, and Indonesia, each of which preferred a nonaligned status in the conflict between the United States and the Soviet Union.* Although President Lyndon Johnson* used SEATO membership to justify the American commitment in Vietnam, President Richard Nixon,* in the Nixon Doctrine,* denied that SEATO membership guaranteed the commitment of U.S. troops to Asian conflicts. Nevertheless, membership in SEATO greatly increased U.S. involvement in Asian politics. Under the pressure of the conflict in Vietnam, in which SEATO nations had originally supported the American struggle against the Vietcong* and North Vietnamese, strains appeared in SEATO, and the organization dissolved in 1977.

Source: Walter LaFeber, *America, Russia, and the Cold War, 1945–1975*, 1975.

Kim Younghaus

SOUTH KOREA   *See* Korea

SOUTH VIETNAM   *See* Republic of Vietnam

SOUTH VIETNAMESE ARMY   *See* Army of the Republic of Vietnam

SOUTH VIETNAMESE MARINE CORPS

The South Vietnamese Marine Corps, first organized in April 1965, consisted of one division divided up into the 147th, 258th, and 369th brigades and nine battalions. They worked closely with United States Marine Corps* units in I Corps* but suffered from many of the same liabilities as the Army of the Republic of Vietnam*—low morale, as well as corruption among the officer corps. By 1972 there were more than 13,000 troops in the South Vietnamese Marine Corps.

Source: Harry G. Summers, Jr., *Vietnam War Almanac*, 1985.

SOUTH VIETNAMESE NATIONAL POLICE

In addition to maintaining law and order and administering the criminal justice system, the National Police were directly charged with counterinsurgency efforts against the Vietcong.* Beginning in 1967, the United States decided that strengthening the National Police would help the pacification (*see* Rural Reconstruction) process by replacing military with civilian authority. Between 1965 and 1972 the size of the National Police increased from 52,000 to nearly 121,000 people. The National Police Field Forces and the Provincial Reconnaissance Units were offices of the National Police. Trained by American advisers, the police units were not above the use of terrorism themselves to deal with the Vietcong. Of all the organizations wielding political and military authority in South Vietnam, the National Police were probably the most corrupt and the least respected. Wages were extremely low, and because the South Vietnamese military units had conscription priority, the National Police had a difficult time recruiting or training effective leaders. The National Police were riddled with Vietcong infiltrators. Late in 1969 a reform movement of the National Police began, one which limited the brutal treatment of arrestees and provided for dismissal of corrupt officers, but it was too little and too late to change its reputation.

Source: Guenter Lewy, *America in Vietnam*, 1978.

SOUTH VIETNAMESE NAVY

At the beginning of the war, the South Vietnamese Navy consisted of approximately 500 small junks which had been plying the coast of the South China Sea since 1960. By 1969, after four years of large-scale American participation in the conflict, the South Vietnamese Navy had added 460 other ships, ranging from 640-ton PCEs to patrol the coast down to small riverine craft—LSTs and fiberglass and aluminum patrol boats. In 1969, when the Mobile Riverine Force* was discontinued, the South Vietnamese Navy received another 242 patrol craft. Finally, as part of Vietnamization* between 1969 and 1972, the United States Navy* handed over another 800 ships and craft to the South Vietnamese Navy—minesweepers, patrol craft, Coast Guard cutters, seaplane tenders, and destroyer escorts. By the time the United States withdrew from Vietnam late in 1972, the South Vietnamese Navy—with 1,500 ships, 40,000 officers and sailors, and 13,000 marines—was one of the largest in the world. It was not, however, one of the most powerful. Morale within the South Vietnamese military in general, including the navy, was poor, and the dumping of so many ships and so much sophisticated technology, without proper training, was more than the Vietnamese could handle. Efficiency was extremely low and the navy unable to seriously cripple the Vietcong* or North Vietnamese assault on the Republic of Vietnam.*

Sources: John S. Bowman, ed., *The Vietnam War Almanac*, 1985; Edward J. Marolda and G. Wesley Pryce III, *A Short History of the United States Navy and the Southeast Asia Conflict, 1950–1975*, 1984.

SOUVANNA PHOUMA

Prince Boun Khong fathered twenty children, among them Prince Souvanna Phouma (a middle child) and his half brother Prince Souphanouvong (the youngest), who were raised after Boun Khong's death by his oldest son, Prince Phetsart. All three were educated in France* as engineers—Phetsart as a mechanical engineer, Souvanna as a marine, electrical, and civil engineer, and Souphanouvong as a road and bridge engineer. For years they were the only engineers in Laos,* a primitive country of under three million ethnically diverse people. About half the population is Lao, and the remaining is composed of a variety of tribal groups including the Meo (Hmong)* who have clashed with the Lao historically.

Although each was a nationalist opponent of French colonialism, they pursued independence in different ways. Having acquired a taste for Western life, Souvanna Phouma favored a negotiated independence. Since there were no paved roads anywhere in Laos and the French were building neither roads nor bridges, Souphanouvong built roads in Vietnam where he witnessed the abominable living conditions on French-owned rubber plantations and labor camps. He developed contempt for French colonialism and ties with the Vietminh.* Phetsart took a middle position, working to maintain an alliance between his two brothers in the face of what became a determined American effort to split them apart.

In August 1945 Souphanouvong, with the support of his brothers, expelled the French and established an independent government with Phetsart and Souvanna Phouma as ministers. However, the French, after reasserting themselves in Vietnam and Cambodia (*see* Kampuchea), launched a three-pronged offensive, defeating Lao forces. While Souphanouvong organized Lao resistance groups in the countryside which cooperated with the Vietminh and participated at the siege of Dien Bien Phu,* Souvanna Phouma and Phetsart lived in exile in Thailand.* Eventually the French enticed him to return to Vientiane to form a provisional government. Phetsart remained in Thailand, refusing all French entreaties.

Souphanouvong's ties with the Vietminh made him a Communist to American officials, who conspired with the French to exclude him from the 1954 Geneva Conference. But the Geneva Accords* called for negotiations between all three factions in Laos—the French collaborator rightists under Phoumi Nosovan, Souvanna Phouma's neutralists, and Souphanouvong's Pathet Lao* (Land of the Lao). The brothers quickly reached agreement on a government of "national reconciliation"—something they would do repeatedly between 1954 and 1964. Phoumi Nosovan was uncooperative.

Unfortunately for Laos, the United States, while professing desire for a neutral government, was determined that it would be a pro-West neutralism. The Pathet Lao, in addition to being denied a voice in the government, were to be destroyed. Thus Souvanna Phouma and his brother could not be permitted to enter an alliance which unquestionably would control Laos. This prompted a secret war directed by the Central Intelligence Agency* (CIA) with the active assent of the State Department and the U.S. Army.* Between 1954 and 1960 the United States spent over $300 million in Laos (over $100 for every inhabitant, more than Laos's annual per capita income), with $239 million for military purposes and $7 million for economic development. In 1959 the United States paid $100 per vote in the National Assembly to bring down the coalition government, throwing Souvanna Phouma out of office.

The 1961 Laotian "crisis" resulted from a Souvanna Phouma and Souphanouvong attempt to defeat the mercenary army of the corrupt and incompetent Phoumi Nosovan. The 1962 Geneva Conference, convened to thwart the alliance, produced an agreement giving the Pathet Lao a minor voice in a new government headed by Souvanna Phouma and calling for neutrality, an end to American military activities, expulsion of all foreign military personnel, a prohibition against Laotian military alliances, and election of a National Assembly. This government was subverted by American intrigue, including the assassination of uncooperative political leaders.

While all parties violated the agreements, it is clear the United States never intended anything more than a pretense of compliance. The Pathet Lao utilized North Vietnamese Army* (NVA) advisers and protected the eastern border so North Vietnam could infiltrate men and supplies south. While only a trickle of southerners and small amounts of supplies moved down the trail between 1959 and 1964, main force NVA units and substantial amounts of materiel were moved through Laos after 1965. The U.S. "secret war" included 5,000 to 12,000 military and CIA personnel and 5,000 Tai soldiers illegally stationed in Laos to lead a mercenary army of Hmong tribesmen against the Pathet Lao, and another 1,000 military personnel running secret training bases in Thailand. Under the pretext of bombing NVA infiltration* routes, the United States began bombing Laos in 1964 before the Gulf of Tonkin incident.* The justification for this was that the Pathet Lao would threaten Thailand if they came to power, a weak claim for three reasons. First, there is no way a primitive society such as Laos could threaten a highly developed nation such as Thailand which had a population ten times larger. Second, even the Pathet Lao army, which was generally regarded as better disciplined and more effective than either the neutralist or rightist armies, was poorly trained, poorly equipped, and poorly disciplined. Laotians simply do not have much heart for war, which is one reason why the United States had to resort to building a Meo army. Finally, Laos has yet to threaten Thailand since the Pathet Lao came to power in 1975.

The result, lasting until 1975, was a de facto partitioning with an increasingly rightist government in Vientiane headed (most of the time) by Souvanna Phouma and Souphanouvong's Pathet Lao controlling two northern provinces, the northeastern border, and about one-third of the population. In February 1971, the South Vietnamese invaded southern Laos in a disastrous attempt to cut the Ho Chi Minh Trail.* The invasion, as well as the American withdrawal from Vietnam and the surging Khmer Rouge* strength in Cambodia, undermined the government of Souvanna Phouma, and in 1975 the Pathet Lao took over in all of Laos, deposing Souvanna Phouma.

424 SOVIET UNION

Sources: Roger Hilsman, *To Move a Nation*, 1967; Wilfred Burchett, *The Second Indochinese War: Cambodia and Laos*, 1970; Peter Poole, *Eight American Presidents and Indochina*, 1973; Arthur M. Schlesinger, Jr., *A Thousand Days: John F. Kennedy in the White House*, 1965; John Prados, *Presidents' Wars: CIA and Pentagon Covert Operations Since World War II*, 1986.

Samuel Freeman

SOVIET UNION

The origins of the Vietnam War reach back to the Cold War assumption on the part of the United States that the Soviet Union was expansionist and inspiring many of the anticolonial rebellions occurring throughout the world. The containment policy* was designed to deal with Soviet aggression, and it resulted in the Truman Doctrine, Marshall Plan, Berlin airlift, NATO, and the Korean War. The irony is that the Soviet Union was preoccupied with Europe after World War II, and Josef Stalin viewed Ho Chi Minh's* campaign in Vietnam as more nationalistic than communistic. The Soviet Union did not extend diplomatic recognition to the Democratic Republic of Vietnam* (DRV) until 1950; Vietnam was very much outside the Soviet area of interest. Therefore, Moscow provided rhetorical support but little else to the Vietminh.*

In 1954 the Soviet Union cochaired, along with Great Britain,* the Geneva Conference (*see* Geneva Accords) to settle the Vietnamese question. Actually, the Soviets pursued a pro-Western course at Geneva. At the time they were currying French opinion since French Communists had done well in recent elections. Also, they wanted to dissuade France* from joining the American-led European Defense Community with its plans for rearming West Germany.* Finally, the Russians were interested in reaching an accommodation, if possible, with the United States. For these reasons the Soviet Union worked for an armistice acceptable to the French and agreed to a partitioning of Vietnam between a Communist North and a non-Communist South. Later, when South Vietnam and the United States balked on holding the prescribed elections, the Soviet Union carefully sidestepped Ho Chi Minh's pleas for assistance.

Soviet interest in Indochina* intensified, however, as the independence of the People's Republic of China* increased in the 1950s. Vietnam became an important counterweight to expanding Chinese influence. Gradually the Soviet Union began to increase its shipment of military equipment, training personnel, and economic assistance to North Vietnam, and by the late 1960s Moscow was far and away the largest supplier of North Vietnam and the Vietcong.* The assistance exceeded $1 billion a year by 1970. At the same time, the Soviet Union hoped that the American preoccupation with Vietnam would distract her from European concerns.

North Vietnam was unusually astute in maintaining a diplomatic balance between the Soviet Union and China, neatly playing them off against each other in a diplomatic minuet. For the Soviets, North Vietnam was maddeningly independent, especially in 1968 when Ho Chi Minh condemned the invasion of

Czechoslovakia. Still, the DRV leaned more to Moscow than to Peking, not only because Moscow was a more reliable supplier of military equipment but because of ancient fears of Chinese expansion into Indochina. Also, the Cultural Revolution in the People's Republic of China left China too weak and internally preoccupied to be very reliable.

The United States never appreciated the independence of Vietnamese communism. Presidents Lyndon B. Johnson* and Richard Nixon* both sought to have the Soviet Union restrain North Vietnam, assuming that Moscow had direct influence in Hanoi.* What few understood was that Hanoi would pursue policies sanctioned neither by Moscow nor Peking, and in fact notoriously irritated the Russians throughout the war by taking their aid, expressing gratitude for it, but keeping them in the dark about DRV war plans.

As the war concluded in 1975, the Soviets were considered the diplomatic victors internationally. The border skirmishes between the Vietnamese and the Chinese increased Soviet influence, and they secured important military bases at Da Nang* and Cam Ranh Bay.* They could now challenge American military superiority in the Indian Ocean and the Western Pacific. Moreover, the Soviet line about the inevitable decline of American power received a major boost in the Vietnam defeat. Finally, the Soviets have appreciated the new "realism" in American foreign policy growing out of Vietnam, a development which they believe has given them a freer hand in Angola, Afghanistan, and Ethiopia. A war which began in order to staunch the tide of Soviet communism has had a different result.

Sources: George McT. Kahin, *Intervention. How America Became Involved in Vietnam*, 1986; Daniel S. Papp, *Vietnam: The View from Moscow, Peking, Washington,*, 1981; Robin Edmonds, *Soviet Foreign Policy, 1962–1973: The Paradox of a Superpower*, 1975; Leif Rosenberger, *The Soviet Union and Vietnam: An Uneasy Alliance*, 1986.

Gary M. Bell

SPECIAL FORCES

First organized in 1952 to establish guerrilla warfare capabilities behind enemy lines, the Special Forces eventually evolved into the military's primary counterinsurgency* unit. The 1st U.S. Army* Special Forces Group was established in Japan in June 1957, and they sent personnel to South Vietnam that year to train ARVN (*see* Army of the Republic of Vietnam) commandos at Nha Trang.* Later the 5th and 7th U.S. Army Special Forces Groups sent other training personnel into Vietnam. Fascinated with counterinsurgency tactics, President John F. Kennedy* authorized the Special Forces to wear the distinctive Green Beret. Kennedy also expanded the Special Forces from 2,500 to 10,000 men and gave them a counterinsurgency mission—organizing, training, and equipping Civilian Irregular Defense Group* (CIDG) forces. The Central Intelligence Agency* (CIA) had been organizing the Montagnard* tribes into CIDG troop programs, and by 1963, when there were 12,000 troops in 200 villages, the Special Forces took the program over from the CIA.

The Fifth Special Forces Group* arrived in Vietnam on October 1, 1964, and established headquarters at Nha Trang. The first CIDG border camp had been established at Ban Me Thuot* in 1961, but the Fifth Special Forces Group greatly expanded the program, eventually building the CIDG up to 42,000 troops and dozens of border camps. The camps were located along important supply and infiltration* routes. By 1966 the Special Forces were organizing Mobile Strike Forces* to attack Vietcong* and North Vietnamese Army* bases, reconnaissance teams for the Studies and Observation Groups,* and thousands of educational, welfare, and medical projects. The Special Forces left South Vietnam in March 1971.

Sources: Shelby L. Stanton, *Green Berets at War*, 1985; Andrew F. Krepinevich, Jr., *The Army and Vietnam*, 1986; Larry E. Cable, *Conflict of Myths: The Development of American Counterinsurgency Doctrine and the Vietnam War*, 1986; Francis J. Kelly, *U.S. Army Special Forces, 1961–1971*, 1973.

SPOCK, BENJAMIN McLANE

Born in New Haven, Connecticut, May 2, 1903, Benjamin Spock was a prominent figure in the antidraft and anti–Vietnam War movements of the 1960s. He received a B.A. from Yale University in 1925 and an M.D. from Columbia University in 1929. While on active duty as a psychiatrist in the U.S. Naval Reserve in 1944–46, he wrote *The Common Sense Book of Baby and Child Care* (1946) which, through subsequent editions, became one of the best-selling books in publishing history. In the early 1960s, Dr. Spock began to speak out against nuclear weapons testing. He supported a full-page advertisement in the *New York Times* in 1962 entitled "Dr. Spock is Worried." The ad warned of dangers of radioactive contamination of milk and other food from nuclear bomb tests. From 1963 to 1967, he served as co-chairman of the National Committee for a Sane Nuclear Policy (SANE). By 1963, he had also become a public opponent of U.S. military involvement in Vietnam. He supported President Lyndon B. Johnson* as the peace candidate in 1964, but when Johnson increased U.S. military operations in Vietnam in February 1965, Dr. Spock wrote to the president in protest and began to appear at many public demonstrations against the war. In 1967 he retired as supervising pediatrician of the Family Clinic at Case Western Reserve University to devote full time to anti–Vietnam War and antidraft activity. Dr. Spock joined a delegation that turned in 992 draft* cards to the U.S. Department of Justice in Washington, D.C., in October 1967; he was then arrested in December 1967 for an act of civil disobedience outside of the armed forces induction center on Whitehall Street in Manhattan. He also signed a nationally distributed "Call to Resist Illegitimate Authority." In 1968 he and four others— William Sloane Coffin, Jr.,* Michael Ferber, Mitchell Goodman, and Marcus Raskin—were indicted for conspiring to violate Selective Service laws. In July, Dr. Spock was found guilty, fined $5,000, and sentenced to two years in prison. The conviction, however, was overturned by the U.S. Court of Appeals for the First Circuit. At the end of the trial, Dr. Spock said: "There is no shred of legality or constitutionality to this war; it violates the United Nations Charter, the Geneva Accords,* and the United States' promise to obey the laws of international conduct. It is totally, abominably illegal.'' Dr. Spock continued to protest the Vietnam War and ran for president in 1972 on the People's party ticket. (He received 78,801 votes.) After the war, he continued to oppose nuclear arms and U.S. military involvement abroad, and remained an active and prominent member of SANE. On December 7, 1978, he was fined $200 and sentenced to two months in jail for participation in a protest against construction of the nuclear power plant at Seabrook, New Hampshire. On June 2, 1981, he and eleven others were arrested for refusing to leave the White House after a public tour, stopping instead to pray to protest budget cuts proposed by the Reagan administration.

Sources: Jessica Mitford, *The Trial of Dr. Spock*, 1969; Lynn Z. Bloom, *Doctor Spock: Biography of a Conservative Radical*, 1972.

John Kincaid

SPRING MOBILIZATION TO END THE WAR IN VIETNAM

The Spring Mobilization to End the War in Vietnam was organized on November 26, 1966, to sponsor antiwar* demonstrations in the spring of 1967. Veteran peace activist A. J. Muste* was chairman of the group, and its four vice chairmen were David Dellinger,*, editor of *Liberation*; Edward Keating, publisher of *Ramparts*; Sidney Peck, a professor at Case Western Reserve University; and Robert Greenblatt, a professor at Cornell University. In January 1967, they named the Reverend James Luther Bevel, a close associate of Martin Luther King, Jr.,* as director of the Spring Mobilization to End the War in Vietnam. During the next four months they prepared for mass demonstrations, one scheduled for New York City, and the other for San Francisco, and on April 15, 1967, the demonstrations occurred. More than 125,000 marched in New York City against the war—including Martin Luther King, Jr., James Luther Bevel, and Benjamin Spock*—and another 60,000 marched in San Francisco. Up to its time, the Spring Mobilization was the largest antiwar demonstration in U.S. history.

Sources: Thomas Powers, *Vietnam: The War at Home*, 1984; Clark Dougan and Steven Weiss, *The Vietnam Experience: A Nation Divided*, 1984; Nancy Zaroulis and Gerald Sullivan, *Who Spoke Up? American Protests Against the War in Vietnam, 1963–1975*, 1984.

SQUAD

A squad is a basic organizational institution in the United States Army* and Marine Corps.* A sergeant usually commands the squad, and the squad is composed of two teams of four men each. A tank and its crew is considered the squad for an armored unit, as is the howitzer or gun and its crew in an artillery unit.

Source: Harry G. Summers, Jr., *Vietnam War Almanac*, 1985.

SQUADRON

The term "squadron" refers to a cavalry unit of battalion* size in the United States Army.* Usually commanded by a lieutenant colonel, a squadron has approximately 1,000 officers and men, divided into three troops. The squadron is a basic organizational institution in the United States Air Force* and Navy* and consists of two or three groups of five aircraft each.

Source: Harry G. Summers, Jr., *Vietnam War Almanac*, 1985.

SRV   *See* Socialist Republic of Vietnam

STENNIS, JOHN CORNELIUS

John Cornelius Stennis was born on August 3, 1901, in Kemper County, Mississippi, and has served as a circuit judge (1937–47) and as a member of the U.S. Senate since 1947. Originally Stennis had severe reservations about the U.S. commitment in Vietnam. During the early 1950s Stennis voiced concern over U.S. support of the French and Ngo Dinh Diem* regime during the late 1950s. Stennis, however, became a hard-liner once the Gulf of Tonkin incident* occurred.

Although Stennis questioned from time to time the actions taken by the Johnson* administration in Vietnam, he recoiled from the notion of a U.S. pullout or military defeat. He echoed the sentiments of many Americans who believed that once involved in an overseas war the United States could accept nothing less than total victory. After Johnson's commitment of troops to Vietnam in 1965, Stennis is purported to have made a statement that "America's purpose [in Vietnam] is to win." Because of his hard-line view, Stennis even suggested that Johnson's Great Society* programs might have to be curtailed to win the Vietnam War.

Stennis's view of a military victory in Vietnam endeared him to the Pentagon with its vast assortment of senior officers. As a member of the Senate Armed Services Committee, he wielded much power, which he used to assist the Pentagon's prosecution of the Vietnam War. Beginning in the spring of 1967, Stennis began to criticize the Johnson administration's handling of the conflict. The hearings, which were held before Stennis and the Senate Armed Services Committee, revealed a lack of success in winning the Vietnamese conflict, although Robert McNamara* and other officials presented evidence of progress.

Stennis came away from the hearings determined that the Johnson administration had failed in Vietnam, not America's military officials. Hence he advocated more latitude for military commanders in the field. Lyndon Johnson, however, was not about to give up his constitutional powers as commander in chief. He privately ridiculed Stennis and others on the committee for trying to push him deeper into war. Johnson nonetheless avoided direct confrontation with the committee, because he realized public opinion polls indicated that a great many Americans favored tougher measures in Vietnam.

The Tet Offensive* of 1968 shattered Stennis's belief that the war could be won. When General William Westmoreland* suggested that more troops might be needed, Stennis and hard-line senators questioned the winnability of the war. Stennis and others warned Secretary of Defense Clark Clifford* that Congress* had serious doubts about the conduct of the war. Thereafter Stennis would support a pullout of American troops, although not without assisting the South Vietnamese in gaining the requisite skills to defend themselves.

Sources: *Who's Who in America*, 1984–85; Ernest R. May, *"Lessons" of the Past*, 1973; Stanley Karnow, *Vietnam: A History*, 1983.

John S. Leiby

STRATEGIC AIRLIFT

When the large-scale deployment of military forces to South Vietnam began in 1965, the United States Air Force's* Military Airlift Command* (MAC) found itself assigned the task of providing urgent transportation of personnel and certain supplies from the United States to Southeast Asia. American reliance on strategic airlift stemmed from the necessity of projecting forces over long distances within a relatively short period of time and from the inability of the United States Navy* and merchant transports to move personnel and supplies efficiently to the other side of the world. This requirement gave rise to the creation of an extensive strategic airlift operation between American West Coast bases and Southeast Asia.

The task of getting essential supplies, personnel, and units to Vietnam was a staggering one. Air force officials found that traffic to the Pacific grew from a monthly average of 33,779 passengers and 9,123 tons of cargo in fiscal 1965 to 65,350 passengers and 42,296 tons of cargo in fiscal 1967. During 1967, moreover, strategic airlift carried most of the cargo, while chartered commercial airliners carried most of the passengers. Not to be overlooked were the thousands of combat personnel flown by these aircraft to Honolulu and nine other cities in the Pacific area for rest and recuperation leaves (R & R). The R & R flights began in fiscal 1966 with 14,970 passengers. The numbers increased to 521,496 in 1967 and to 774,386 in fiscal 1968.

To expedite the flow of critically required cargo from aerial ports during the Vietnam buildup, the air force developed a series of intercontinental airlift routes, each with well-equipped and efficiently managed personnel and equipment-handling facilities. It also employed a series of priority designations: among them a "999," which identified the highest priority cargo, and the "Red Ball" (an airlift reference to the famous World War II truck express in Europe), which tagged priority United States Army* spare parts for inoperative combat equipment. The MAC began its Red Ball Express on December 8, 1965, guaranteeing shipment within 24 hours of receipt at the aerial port. The 1,000th Red Ball mission departed Travis Air Force Base, California, on May 1, 1967.

On several occasions during the war, the air force was called on to undertake the deployment of major army units under special conditions. The first of these, designated Operation Blue Light, came late in 1965 when strategic airlift transports moved the 3rd Brigade, 25th Infantry Division,* from Hawaii to Pleiku,* Vietnam, to offset a buildup of Communist forces in the area. These aircraft flew 231 sorties* over a 26-day period and moved 3,000 troops and 4,700 tons of equipment the 6,000 miles to Pleiku by January 23, 1966.

In mid–1969 emphasis shifted to the return of units to the United States in accordance with the president's policy of gradual American withdrawal from Vietnam, beginning with 25,000 troops before August 31. The MAC strategic airlift fleet carried out the redeployments through a series of operations called Keystone. In the first of these, C–141 transports airlifted 15,446 of the 25,000 troops plus 47.5 tons of materiel. As the president directed other incremental withdrawals over the next several years, these airlift managers responded accordingly.

As American participation in the war phased out, MAC devoted considerable strategic airlift capacity to equipment being delivered to South Vietnamese forces. Following the peace agreements in January 1973, the command turned its attention to the withdrawal of the remaining American military personnel and equipment from Vietnam. This task involved several thousand tons of equipment and more than 20,000 personnel.

Source: Carl Berger, *The United States Air Force in Southeast Asia, 1961–1973, An Illustrated Account*, 1984.

Roger D. Launius

STRATEGIC HAMLET PROGRAM

Launched in 1962, the Strategic Hamlet Program had high hopes for depriving the Vietcong* ''fish'' of the peasant ''sea.'' Designed by Sir Robert Thompson,* the architect of similar counterinsurgency* programs in Malaya and the Philippines,* the Strategic Hamlet Program would bring peasants in from scattered villages to hamlets surrounded by moats and fences and protected by well-trained military forces. In the strategic hamlets, peasants would be won over to the government of the Republic of Vietnam* by fair elections, land reform, good schools, and improved medical facilities. The Vietcong would then have nobody to exploit and no villages in which to hide; they would be forced to come out into the open where ARVN (*see* Army of the Republic of Vietnam) and American forces would destroy them.

The theoretical hopes of the Strategic Hamlet Program were dashed on the rocks of reality. By the end of 1962 the government claimed to have established more than 3,500 hamlets, but they were hardly secure from Vietcong attack or infiltration.* In the Mekong Delta* the program required massive relocation of peasants away from their ancestral homelands, which only further alienated them from the South Vietnamese government. Ngo Dinh Diem* never implemented the promised land reform, and large volumes of U.S. assistance money were diverted by corrupt government officials away from hamlet medical, educational, and welfare programs to their own pockets. The Vietcong were able, by simply massing their forces, to overrun any strategic hamlet at will. The program proved to be so unpopular that it may have actually increased the Vietcong appeal among peasants. After the assassination of Ngo Dinh Diem in November 1963, the program was abandoned.

Sources: Roger Hilsman, *To Move a Nation*, 1967; Larry E. Cable, *Conflict of Myths: The Development of American Counterinsurgency Doctrine and the Vietnam War*, 1986; Frances FitzGerald, *Fire in the Lake: The Vietnamese and the Americans in Vietnam*, 1972; Tran Dinh Tho, *Pacification*, 1980.

"STREET WITHOUT JOY"

Highway 1 is Vietnam's north-south highway. During both Indochina* wars, opposing forces tried to control it. Running south to north, Highway 1 went from Saigon* to Bien Hoa,* Phan Rang, Nha Trang,* Tuy Hoa, Qui Nhon,* Quang Ngai, Chu Lai,* Quang Nam, Da Nang,* Hue,* and Quang Tri,* and then across the Demilitarized Zone* to Dong Hoi, Vinh, Ninh Binh, and Hanoi.* The stretch from Hue north to Quang Tri City ran through major Vietminh* and later Vietcong* strongholds. French soldiers, used to costly and futile efforts to clear the road, referred to it sardonically as *la rue sans jolie*, "the street without joy." American soldiers easily understood that perspective.

Sources: Terrence Maitland and Steven Weiss, *The Vietnam Experience: Raising the Stakes*, 1982; Danny J. Whitfield, *Historical and Cultural Dictionary of Vietnam*, 1976; Bernard Fall, *Street Without Joy: Insurgency in Vietnam*, 1961.

Samuel Freeman

STUDENTS FOR A DEMOCRATIC SOCIETY

Students for a Democratic Society (SDS) was a leading, campus-based, antidraft and anti–Vietnam War organization of the mid–1960s. SDS was established in January 1960, primarily by students who had been affiliated with the Socialist party. After an organizing conference in May 1960 at the University of Michigan, SDS obtained a $10,000 grant from the United Auto Workers (UAW). SDS then opened an office in New York City, with Tom Hayden* serving as the first SDS field secretary. The primary purposes of SDS were to support the black civil rights movement and engage in community organizing in poor neighborhoods in northern cities. SDS began to gain strength and notoriety after its June 1962 conference at a UAW camp in Port Huron, Michigan. At that conference, SDS issued the first major manifesto of the New Left, the *Port Huron Statement*, which called for a more participatory democratic society and an end to the nuclear arms race. The statement also criticized other aspects of U.S. foreign policy associated with the Cold War. By 1964, especially after the Gulf of Tonkin incident* in August, elements within SDS began to organize campus demonstrations and teach-ins* against the Vietnam War and to circulate "We Won't Go" petitions among draft-age men. SDS organized a demonstration against the Vietnam War that brought more than 20,000 protesters to Washington, D.C., on April 17, 1965. Membership in SDS grew rapidly during 1965, to about 124 chapters by the end of the year. After endorsing the "black power" position of CORE and SNCC in June 1966, SDS, a mostly white student organization, turned its full attention to campus protests against the war, the draft,* and corporate capitalism. By December 1966, when it adopted a militant draft resistance position, SDS had about 250 chapters, approximately 25,000 chapter members, and some 6,000 national members. However, SDS was soon plagued by internal dissension, independent-minded local chapters, many members who were stimulated more by the new counterculture than by politics, a futile search for a new revolutionary working class, and a concerted attempt by the "Marxist-Maoist" Progressive Labor party to take over SDS. During 1967, antiwar and antidraft demonstrations on and off campuses became more frequent, increasingly militant, and occasionally violent. Students seized campus buildings; sought to drive recruiters for the military, Central Intelligence Agency,* and Dow Chemical Company off campuses; picketed or attacked military induction centers; rioted; and sometimes bombed buildings or set them aflame. During Stop the Draft Week in October 1967, Carl Davidson, a national SDS leader, said, "We must tear them [induction centers] down, burn them down if necessary." Nearly three-quarters of the nation's universities had experienced demonstrations by the end of the 1967–68 academic year, at which time SDS had about 300 chapters. The militance of protests escalated further during 1968. From March through May 1968, the SDS chapter at Columbia University,* led by Mark Rudd, initiated several seizures of campus buildings, which led to violent confrontations with New York City police and a campus-wide strike that shut down the university. Under SDS pressure, Columbia agreed to sever its ties to the Institute of Defense Analysis, abandon plans to build a gymnasium in Morningside Park, and drop charges against most of the student demonstrators. Nationally, SDS helped to organize a series of militant demonstrations held in parks and streets outside the Democratic National Convention* in Chicago in late August 1968. The National Commission on the Causes and Prevention of Violence later concluded that the violence associated with the Chicago demonstrations was caused by a "police riot," not by the demonstrators. The Chicago demonstrations helped to boost SDS membership, which apparently reached its peak in December 1968 when SDS may have had as many as 400 chapters. However, SDS's national convention, held in Ann Arbor, Michigan, on December 26, 1968, was split by factionalism and by a growing desire to adopt "revolutionary violence" as the means to end the draft and the Vietnam War. Seeing themselves allied with "Third World revolutionaries," sizable factions within the SDS leadership began to encourage or engage in violent protests. In March 1969, the SDS national "war council," meeting in Austin, Texas, resolved to promote "armed struggle as the only road to revolution" in "the heartland of a world-wide monster" (i.e., the United States). Out of this grew a violent group, the Weathermen, which brought 600 people to Chicago in October 1969 to engage in violent protests, called the "Days of Rage." By fall 1969, however, SDS was disintegrating rapidly, and the leadership for organizing massive protest demonstrations against the Vietnam War had already passed to other organizations, particularly the Moratorium and the New Mobilization Committee. The Weathermen, some local SDS chapters, and various SDS factions continued to function through the early 1970s, but SDS, which had never been a highly coherent national organization, ceased to exist as a coordinated nationwide entity by early 1970.

Source: Kirkpatrick Sale, *SDS: Ten Years Toward A Revolution*, 1973.

John Kincaid

STUDIES AND OBSERVATION GROUPS

In January 1964 the Military Assistance Command, Vietnam* organized the Studies and Observation Groups (SOG), supposedly to evaluate the success of the military adviser program but actually to perform clandestine operations throughout Southeast Asia. The SOG program was directed by the special assistant for counterinsurgency and special activities, who reported directly to the Joint Chiefs of Staff (*see* Chairman, JCS). By 1966 the SOG included more than 10,000 personnel, of which 2,000 were Americans and 8,000 were South Vietnamese and Montagnard* troops. They were divided into a number of different groups. The Psychological Studies Group, operating out of Hue* and Tay Ninh, made false radio broadcasts from powerful transmitters. The Air Studies Group—complete with UH–1F* and H–34 helicopters, a C–130* squadron, and a C–123 squadron—specialized in dropping and recovering special intelligence groups into Laos,* Cambodia (*see* Kampuchea), and North Vietnam. The Maritime Studies Group concentrated its efforts on commando raids along the North Vietnamese coast and the Mekong Delta.* The Gulf of Tonkin incident* in July and August 1964 was triggered by SOG operations. The Ground Studies Group carried out the greatest number of missions, including monitoring the location of American POWs,* assassinations, kidnapping, rescue of airmen downed in enemy territory, early long-range reconnaissance patrols,* and harassment and booby-trapping* of infiltration* routes. SOG operations were headquartered in Kontum, Ban Me Thuot,* and Da Nang.*

Sources: Larry E. Cable, *Conflict of Myths: The Development of American Counterinsurgency Doctrine and the Vietnam War*, 1986; Andrew F. Krepinevich, Jr., *The Army and Vietnam*, 1986.

• T •

TACTICAL AIRLIFT

One of the hallmarks of modern American warfare has been airmobility to, around, and from the battlefield. As a result of this basic means of waging war, the United States Air Force* early sent tactical airlift transports to Vietnam; four C–47s* arrived at Bien Hoa* Air Base, near Saigon,* on November 16, 1961, as part of the first air force detachment. These C–47 airlifters performed diverse missions—supporting flights by other air force aircraft, airdrops of Vietnamese paratroops, and night flareship operations. Their most demanding task, however, was to resupply United States Army Special Forces* detachments at remote locations throughout South Vietnam.

In 1963 the number of C–47s in Vietnam was increased to six, but airlift tasks gradually shifted to large, twin-engine C–123 Providers. Although the C–123 had been tagged as "obsolescent" as early as 1955, sixteen were deployed to Vietnam in December 1961 as part of Project Mule Train to provide "tactical airlift support of South Vietnamese armed forces." The first four ships reached Tan Son Nhut Air Base* on January 2, 1962, with the remaining aircraft following during the next two years. All were assigned to the 315th Air Commando Wing. Until 1965 these aircraft were the principal airlift element in South Vietnam.

Beginning in 1965 the C–130 Hercules began to dominate Vietnam tactical airlift activities. Equipped with four turboprop engines, the C–130 could move a fifteen-ton payload, about three times that of the C–123. Although used to transport personnel and materiel between bases in the Western Pacific and the Asian mainland before 1965, C–130 in-country missions from South Vietnamese bases became routine in April 1965. At first beginning with a handful of C–130 aircraft and a small mission assignment, by December 1965 the in-country force had grown to thirty-two ships and by February 1968 it stood at ninety-six C–130s.

Also used for tactical airlift in Vietnam during this period were six squadrons of C–7A Caribou transports (*see* Caribou aircraft). These aircraft were initially flown by the United States Army,* and several had been deployed to Vietnam since the spring of 1962. By 1966 the force had expanded to six companies and operated under the scheduling and mission control of specified army corps and divisions. In April 1966 the two services agreed to transfer the Caribous to the air force in keeping with a decision to centralize all land-based fixed-wing aircraft under the control of the air force.

Aerial transport aircraft played key roles in virtually all operations of the Vietnam conflict. One example of the key role played by air transport was seen in the operations of the 1st Brigade, 101st Airborne Division,* during the spring and summer of 1966. The 1st Brigade made five successive moves, each requiring more than 200 C–130 missions and each operation largely sustained by aerial resupply. The C–130s first airlifted the brigade from Tuy Hoa to Phan Thiet early in April, next to the highlands airstrip at Nhon Co later that month, then north to Dak To* soon after, and finally back to Tuy Hoa in July.

Perhaps the greatest test of tactical airlift capability came during the 1968 Tet Offensive.* The early attacks at Tan Son Nhut Air Base and many of the upcountry airstrips temporarily dislocated the airlift system. However, transport crews managed to fly numerous emergency troop and supply missions on behalf of hard-pressed garrisons. By February 3, the fourth day of the offensive, the tactical airlift force had regained its prerogative, and resupply operations played a critical role in the defeat of the Communist offensive. For instance, at the critical siege of Khe Sanh,* tactical airlift ensured that the defense of the fire base was successful.

Over the years between 1962 and 1973, the Air Force's tactical airlift forces delivered more than 7 million tons of passengers and cargo within South Vietnam. By comparison, American and British transports carried slightly more than 2 million tons during the Berlin airlift and about 750,000 tons during the Korean War. The air force lost 53 C–130s in the Southeast Asia war, more than half of them in 1967 and 1968. C–123 losses also totaled 53, and C–7 losses numbered 20. Of these 126 aircraft, enemy action accounted for 61, including 17 destroyed by sapper or shelling attacks. The other 65 were lost from accidents mainly associated with the difficult conditions at forward airstrips. All but 10 of the losses occurred in South Vietnam.

Source: Ray L. Bowers, *The U.S. Air Force in Southeast Asia: Tactical Airlift*, 1983.

Roger D. Launius

TACTICAL AREA OF RESPONSIBILITY

"TAOR" is a military acronym referring to "Tactical Area of Responsibility." It refers to a specific area of land where responsibility for security and military operations is assigned to a commander. The TAOR is used as a measure of control for assigning forces, coordinating support, and evaluating progress.

Source: Edward Doyle and Samuel Lipsman, *The Vietnam Experience: America Takes Over, 1965–1967*, 1985.

TA'I

The Ta'i were a Laotian ethnic minority living in the region surrounding Dien Bien Phu* in Tonkin.* They made a living raising rice and trading for opium with the Hmong.* The Ta'i were frequently recruited to assist first the French and later the Americans in resisting the North Vietnamese and Vietcong* during the struggle for power in Indochina* after World War II.

Sources: Edgar O'Ballance, *The Indochina War 1945–1954: A Study in Guerrilla Warfare*, 1964; Charles A. Stevenson, *The End of Nowhere: American Policy Toward Laos Since 1954*, 1973.

TAIWAN   *See* Chiang Kai-shek

TANG PHUC

Tang phuc are the white mourning clothes worn by the Vietnamese after the death of a relative.

Source: Ann Crawford, *Customs and Culture of Vietnam*, 1966.

TAN SON NHUT AIR BASE

Located just on the fringe of Saigon,* Tan Son Nhut handled the bulk of South Vietnamese commercial and military air traffic throughout the war. Tan Son Nhut was the headquarters of the South Vietnamese Air Force* and after 1962, headquarters for the U.S. Second Air Division. It was in charge of all American air operations in South Vietnam. Between 1966 and 1973, the Seventh Air Force* assumed control of those operations. Tan Son Nhut was also known as "Pentagon East" because the headquarters of the U.S. Military Assistance Command, Vietnam* (MACV) was located there. On April 29, 1975, after the evacuation of several thousand Americans and Vietnamese, military demolition teams destroyed MACV Headquarters. The airport there was later rebuilt by North Vietnamese and Soviet engineers to serve the commercial and military needs of Ho Chi Minh City,* formerly Saigon.

Sources: Harvey Smith et al., *Area Handbook for South Vietnam*, 1967; Thomas G. Tobin, *Last Flight from Siagon*, 1978.

TASK FORCE 116   *See* Mobile Riverine Force

TASK FORCE 117   *See* Mobile Riverine Force

TASK FORCE OREGON   *See* 23rd Infantry Division

TAYLOR, MAXWELL DAVENPORT

Maxwell D. Taylor was born on August 26, 1901, in Keysteville, Missouri, and graduated from West Point in 1922. He taught at West Point between 1927 and 1932, and during World War II was generally credited with playing a major role in the development of airborne warfare. He was with the 82nd Airborne Division in North Africa and Sicily and commanded the 101st Airborne Division at the Normandy invasion. After the war Taylor spent four years, between 1945 and 1949, as commandant of West Point. He commanded the Eighth Army in Korea, and became commander in chief of the Far East Command in 1955. In June 1955 Taylor became chief of staff of the United States Army* and served there until 1959. During the late 1950s, afraid that the army would be eclipsed by the nuclear powers of the United States Air Force,* Taylor began advocating the "flexible response" theory, which argued that a deterrence policy based exclusively on nuclear weapons would leave the United States unable to deal with conventional crises around the world. Taylor wrote *The Uncertain Trumpet* in 1959 calling for a diversified military capability and counterinsurgency* work.

President John F. Kennedy* read the book, and on July 1, 1961, Taylor became the president's military adviser. Kennedy sent Taylor and W. W. Rostow* to Vietnam in October 1961 on a fact-finding mission, and their report advocated the commitment of several thousand combat troops to assist the government of Ngo Dinh Diem* in stopping the Vietcong.* Between 1962 and 1964 Taylor served as chairman of the Joint Chiefs of Staff (*see* Chairman, JCS), and then spent a year as ambassador to South Vietnam. He worked desperately in 1964 and 1965 to return South Vietnam to civilian rule after the assassination of Diem, and late in 1965 he became a special adviser to President Lyndon B. Johnson.* Johnson made Taylor a member of the Senior Advisory Group studying the Vietnam problem in 1968, and Taylor became a strong advocate of a continued American military presence in the country. Taylor left government service in 1969 to serve as chairman of the Foreign Intelligence Advisory Board. He died April 19, 1987.

Sources: Maxwell D. Taylor, *The Uncertain Trumpet*, 1959, and *Swords and Plowshares*, 1972; *Who's Who in America, 1976–1977*, 1977; David Halberstam, *The Best and the Brightest*, 1972; *New York Times*, April 20, 1987.

Gloria Collins

TAYLOR-ROSTOW MISSION OF 1961

In October 1961, President John F. Kennedy* sent an investigative team, led by General Maxwell D. Taylor* and his deputy Walt W. Rostow,* to survey the military and political situation in South Vietnam. They found very poor morale there and the government of Ngo Dinh Diem* weak and losing support among peasants in the countryside. Taylor and Rostow recommended an increase in military aid, larger numbers of military advisers, and the placement of an 8,000-man logistical task force to serve as soldiers and/or economic and political workers. Both men felt the increase in the American commitment would not lead to concomitant increases in Communist strength because they assumed that North Vietnam was too vulnerable to American air power. The Kennedy administration accepted their recommendations, and the Taylor-Rostow Mission played an important role in the early escalation of the conflict.

Sources: Maxwell D. Taylor, *Swords and Plowshares*, 1972; Paul Y. Hammond, *Cold War and Detente*, 1975; Walt W. Rostow, *The Diffusion of Power, 1957–1972*, 1972.

TAY SON REBELLION

By the late eighteenth century, peasant resentment about high taxes, poverty, and the struggle for power between the Trinh* family in the North and the Nguyen* dynasty in the South had dramatically increased. In 1773 the three Tay Son brothers—Ho Nhac, Ho Lu, and Ho Hue—led a rebellion against the Nguyen dynasty and captured Saigon.* At the same time, the Trinh used the Nguyen defeat to take control of Hue.* But in 1786, Ho Hue Tay Son turned on the north and seized control of the Trinh capital of Hanoi.* After repulsing an invading Chinese army in 1788, the Tay Son were rulers of all of Vietnam. They quickly replaced Chinese with Vietnamese as the language of government and tried to break Chinese commercial influence. Their promises of redistribution of property to peasants, however, were never fulfilled. The three Tay Son brothers all died early in the 1790s and left behind no stable group to rule the country. Gia Long,* the surviving member of the Nguyen clan, then led a resistance movement against Tay Son rule which succeeded in 1802.

Source: Joseph Buttinger, *The Smaller Dragon: A Political History of Vietnam*, 1958.

TCHEPONE   *See* Lam Son 719

TEACH-INS

In early February 1965, when the United States began to bomb North Vietnam, a group of faculty members at the University of Michigan wrote to President Lyndon B. Johnson* protesting the escalation of the conflict. When Johnson ordered three thousand marines into Da Nang* on March 10, they organized a teach-in for 8:00 P.M. on March 24, 1965. Three thousand Michigan students attended the first teach-in, where faculty members discussed the nature of the conflict. The major speaker at the teach-in was Arthur Waskow of the Institute for Policy Studies in Washington. In the six weeks after the teach-in at the University of Michigan, faculty members across the country were holding similar meetings as forums for opposing the escalation of the war. Those teach-ins continued on college campuses throughout the war. A national teach-in was held on May 15, 1965, on 122 campuses throughout the country. Tom Hayden* and Jane Fonda* adapted the teach-in program to reach soldiers in the "Free the Army" (FTA) campaign with more informal teach-ins being for military personnel at coffeehouses and other places near military posts.

Sources: Thomas Powers, *Vietnam: The War at Home*, 1984; Nancy Zaroulis and Gerald Sullivan, *Who Spoke Up?*, 1984; Larry Waterhouse and Mariann Wizard, *Turning the Guns Around*, 1971.

Samuel Freeman

TELEVISION

Between 1964 and 1975, the war in Vietnam was broadcast nightly in two- and three-minute segments on American television. It was the first war to be significantly "covered" by television, the first war in which television, as opposed to the print media, was the primary means of informing the public about the course and the nature of the conflict. Critics charged that television telescoped events, selected film for its dramatic quality, and had a built-in liberal bias. They also believed that commercial television's message was aimed at the viewers' emotions rather than their intellect. The result, they insisted, was inaccurate coverage, distortion, and ultimately propaganda. Military and political leaders in particular used the arguments of television critics to suggest that television "lost" the war in Vietnam.

Defenders of television maintained that television's coverage of the war was accurate and even-handed. To be sure, it was not perfect; mistakes were made, inaccurate reports were issued. But defenders argued that the print media was just as prone to make mistakes, and that often the mistakes originated with military- and government-issued reports. Investigative journalism, whether done by the print or the television media, always lags behind the day's top stories.

The two most controversial aspects of television coverage of the war involved the battle of Khe Sanh* and the Tet Offensive.* Television, as well as the print media, reported the engagement of Khe Sanh as if it were another Dien Bien Phu.* "The parallels are there for all to see," reported Walter Cronkite.* The "historical ghost" of the French disaster was "casting a long shadow," echoed Marvin Kalb. The comparison was indeed inaccurate, and it did obscure the actual nature of the conflict. General William Westmoreland* was especially critical of the coverage. Nevertheless, Walt Rostow* and other government officials were also guilty of the unjustified comparison.

Westmoreland and his supporters also claimed that television, and to a lesser extent the print media, transformed the Communist failure in the Tet Offensive into a "psychological victory" for the North Vietnamese. Peter Braestrup made the same charge in his book *Big Story*, noting that "crisis journalism" had seldom "veered so widely from reality" as in the coverage of the Tet Offensive. Defenders of television, however, have claimed that while mistakes were made during Tet, television was not instrumental in leading the American public against the continuation of the war. In fact, public opinion surveys indicated that public support of the war had started to decline two years before Tet.

When the Vietnam War finally came to an end in April 1975, with North Vietnamese soldiers storming into Saigon,* television fittingly played its final role in the conflict, broadcasting the near riot on the roof of the U.S. embassy as panic-stricken South Vietnamese tried to get on evacuation helicopters before the North Vietnamese Army* got into the compound. Tens of millions of Americans, sitting in their living rooms, actually saw the war end.

Sources: Peter Braestrup, *Big Story: How the American Press and Television Reported and Interpreted the Crisis of Tet 1968 in Vietnam and Washington*, 1983; Michael Arlen, *Living Room War*, 1969; Jorge Lewinski, *The Camera at War*, 1978.

Randy Roberts

"TERMINATE WITH EXTREME PREJUDICE"

"Terminate with extreme prejudice" was a Central Intelligence Agency* euphemism used to refer to killing people, especially civilians suspected of belonging to or supporting the National Liberation Front (*see* Vietcong). Critics said such terminology was part of a government propaganda effort by the United States to manipulate the general population into supporting an unjust and immoral war by hiding its grisly nature. Although others disagreed, one needs only to watch any number of documentaries on the war and listen to the mangled speech of government officials defending U.S. policy in Vietnam to get the feeling that obfuscation was intentional.

Sources: WGBH Educational Foundation, "Vietnam, A Television History," 1983; CBS, "1984 Revisited with Walter Cronkite," 1984.

Samuel Freeman

TERRITORIAL FORCES

The South Vietnamese Territorial Forces, including the Regional Forces* and Popular Forces,* were responsible for local population security in villages throughout the Republic of Vietnam.* Territorial Forces were first organized after the Geneva Accords,* and they expanded in size from 102,000 people in 1955 to 532,000 in 1972. By that time they represented just over half of South Vietnam's military force.

Sources: Ngo Quang Truong, *Territorial Forces*, 1981; Andrew F. Krepinevich, Jr., *The Army in Vietnam*, 1986.

TET

Tet is the most important Vietnamese festival and celebrates the lunar new year. In the belief that the first week of the new year will determine family fortunes for the rest of the year, Vietnamese paint their houses for Tet and buy new clothes. The holiday is characterized by family visits to pagodas, churches, and cemeteries, sacrifices to deceased family members, firecrackers, drums, gongs, and family visitations.

Source: Anne Crawford, *Customs and Culture of Vietnam*, 1967.

TET OFFENSIVE

On January 30, 1968, Vietcong* units launched attacks throughout I* and II Corps,* and by January 31, 1968, Vietcong and North Vietnamese soldiers were assaulting American and South Vietnamese forces throughout the country. In addition to attacking thirty-six of forty-four provincial capitals and five of six major cities, the Vietcong attacked the U.S. embassy in Saigon,* Tan Son Nhut Air Base,* the presidential palace, and South Vietnam general staff headquarters. In the summer of 1967, the North Vietnamese commenced planning for the January 1968 offensive. They decided to launch diversionary raids in the Central Highlands* and northern border areas, the most famous of which was the months-long siege of United States Marines* at Khe Sanh.* The purpose of the raids was to deceive American intelligence, because during the campaigns in the highlands and northern provinces, Vietcong were slowly moving into the provincial capitals and major cities to prepare for the Tet attacks. While all this was going both the North Vietnamese and the National Liberation Front (*see* Vietcong) called for a cease-fire during the Tet* holiday celebrations. By the time of the holiday they had moved 100,000 soldiers and vast amounts of supplies undetected into the cities.

On two levels, the Tet Offensive was a tactical disaster for the Vietcong and North Vietnamese. The offensive had failed in that the South Vietnamese army had held and American troops, airlifted into the critical areas, quickly regained control, except in Hue* where the fighting continued for weeks. Nor had the South Vietnamese risen up in mass and rallied to the "Vietcong liberators." Finally, the Vietcong and North Vietnamese may have suffered as many as 40,000 battlefield deaths, compared to 1,100 for the United States and 2,300 for the South Vietnamese. The Vietcong were so decimated by the fighting that they never regained their strength, and after the Tet Offensive the war in Vietnam was largely a struggle between mainline U.S., ARVN (*see* Army of the Republic of Vietnam), and North Vietnamese regulars.

But if the Tet Offensive was a tactical defeat for the Vietcong and North Vietnamese, it was also a colossal strategic victory. Throughout 1966 and 1967 American military and political leaders had been talking of the progress in the war, how the enemy would not long be able to sustain such enormous losses, how there was a "light at the end of the tunnel,"* how the war would soon be over. The Tet Offensive, by exposing the determination of the Vietcong and North Vietnamese, as well as their continuing vitality, demoralized American public opinion. Television reporters broadcast home the incredible sight of General William Westmoreland,* standing beside several dead Vietcong *inside* the U.S. embassy compound, describing the American victory. The Tet Offensive led quickly to the defeat of President Lyndon B. Johnson* in the New Hampshire Democratic primary and his withdrawal from the race in March 1968. After Tet, American policy toward Vietnam had little to do with winning the war, only with finding an "honorable" way out.

Sources: Don Oberdorfer, *Tet! The Turning Point*, 1983; Robert Pisor, *The End of the Line: The Siege of Khe Sanh*, 1982; Pham Van Son and Le Van Duong, eds., *The Viet Cong Tet Offensive 1968*, 1969.

Charles Dobbs

THAI HOANG VAN

Thai Hoang Van was born in 1906 in Thai Binh Province. He studied at the Hoang Pho Military Academy and joined the Communist party in 1930, becoming a founding member of the Vietminh* in 1945. He was promoted to brigadier general in the Vietminh in 1946, and to major general in the People's Army of Vietnam, North Vietnam, in 1959. Thai Hoang Van served as deputy minister of national defense in 1961, and became commander of Military Region 5 in 1965, which was the northern region of South Vietnam. During the 1960s and early 1970s Thai Hoang Van was a member of the Central Committee of the Lao Dong party* and the Central Military Party Committee.

Source: Borys Lewytzkyj and Juliuz Stroynowski, *Who's Who in the Socialist Countries*, 1978.

THAILAND

Thailand, with 198,115 square miles and a population of more than 52 million, is drained by the Menam River Valley, and has a southern arm extending down the Malay Peninsula. Eastern Thailand is drained by the Mekong River, which is the boundary between much of Thailand and Laos.* Originally, Thailand was a buffer state between British interests in Burma and French interests in Indochina.* Although 94 percent of the Thais are Buddhist, including the four million ethnic Chinese,* the Malay minority along the southern extension are Moslem.

More than 60 percent of Thailand is forested, especially the northern and eastern regions. From these forests come such valuable woods as teak, ebony, boxwood, and rosewood. Traditional agricultural is handicapped by elevation, slope, soil leaching, and winter drought. The major breadbasket of Thailand is along the Menam River Valley. The central alluvial plains of the Menam are capable of producing two crops a year of rice, tobacco, and peanuts. Rice cultivation is found on 90 percent of the farmland and is the major export. Unlike most Asian nations, Thailand produces a rice surplus each year. The Thais usually supplement their diet with fish. Bangkok, located in the delta on the lower Chao Phraya, has a population of 2.4 million and is the commercial, financial, and political center of the country.

During the war in Vietnam, Thailand was a close American ally. Although the Thais had traditionally gotten along with the Vietnamese, they were suspicious of Communist intentions, feared the fall of Cambodia (*see* Kampuchea) and Laos to guerrillas, and wanted above all else to preserve their independence. By 1969 the Thais had a total of nearly 12,000 combat troops in Vietnam, including the elite Queen's Cobras* and the Black Panther Division of the Royal Thai Army Volunteer Force. The United States 46th Special Forces* Company assisted Thai forces in resisting Communist guerrilla activity along the Laotian border and in the south on the Malay Peninsula. The last of the Thai troops left Vietnam in April 1972.

The United States also had a strong military presence in Thailand, including the 8th, 355th, 366th, and 388th Tactical Fighter Wings and the 307th Strategic Wing. Strategic bombing operations over North and South Vietnam often originated in Thailand.

Sources: Stanley Robert Larsen and James Lawton Collins, Jr., *Allied Participation in Vietnam*, 1975; Shelby L. Stanton, *Vietnam Order of Battle*, 1981.

THANH NIEN CACH MENH DONG CHI HOI

Known as the Revolutionary Youth League, the Thanh Nien Cach Menh Dong Chi Hoi was organized by Ho Chi Minh* shortly after his arrival in China in 1924. Ho organized students in southern China into small cell groups to agitate for revolution through writing and speeches. The group ceased to function after Ho fled to Moscow in 1927.

Source: William J. Duiker, *The Rise of Nationalism in Vietnam, 1900–1941*, 1976.

THICH NU THANH QUANG

A native of South Vietnam, Thich Nu Thanh Quang was born in 1911 and entered a Buddhist monastery to become a nun. She gained international attention on May 28, 1966, when she committed suicide in front of the Dieu De Pagoda in Hue.* After dousing herself with five gallons of gasoline, Quang ignited herself and remained motionless in a kneeling position for nine seconds before collapsing. Before her death, she drafted a letter to President Lyndon Johnson* calling for the United States to abandon its support for the political regime of Nguyen Cao Ky.* Her death triggered a series of mass Buddhist protests throughout the country.

Source: *New York Times*, May 29, 1966.

THICH QUANG DUC

Thich Quang Duc was a 66-year-old Buddhist monk whose self-immolation on June 11, 1963, profoundly affected the attitude of the Kennedy* administration toward Ngo Dinh Diem* and dramatically signified the Buddhist-government crisis in South Vietnam. Quang Duc burned himself to death at a busy Saigon* intersection in full view not only of passersby but also the media, which the Buddhists* had alerted before the incident. The result was maximum exposure, especially in the United States. While self-immolation is a traditional form of protest in many parts of Asia, the event violated the sensibilities of the policymakers in Washington and was a critical factor in convincing them that Diem was incapable of governing the Republic of Vietnam.* Thus, the incident also reflected the sophistication of the Buddhist anti-Diem movement in understanding the importance of the press as a convenient method of expressing its position. Quang Duc's action also reflected the increasing inability of the Diem government to deal with the pervasive pluralism that characterized South Vietnam in this period. With his mandarin mentality, Diem responded to dissatisfaction with his regime by more repression. The result of this escalation was a growing stubbornness by Diem and more self-immolations by Buddhist monks, as well as other anti-Diem demonstrations. Thus, Thich Quang Duc's suicide marked the beginning of the end of the Diem regime.

Sources: Stanley Karnow, *Vietnam: A History*, 1983; *New York Times*, June 12–13, 1963.

Stafford T. Thomas

THICH TRI QUANG

Historically, Vietnamese Buddhist monks have taken part in public affairs *only* during crises when they have claimed with some legitimacy to speak for the Vietnamese people. At those times, they have demonstrated formidable abilities to organize and mobilize mass protests against those they hold responsible for the crisis. Thich Tri Quang, a charismatic Buddhist monk born in 1922, mobilized Buddhists* three times in the 1960s. Profound nationalists, the Buddhists objected to foreign dominance and foreign influence in Vietnam. Therefore, they opposed the American presence almost as much as they opposed communism. Although Tri Quang worked with the Vietminh* in the struggle against France,* he broke with them because they claimed to represent all Vietnamese with an alien ideology when only the Buddhists could truly represent them. Tri Quang advocated a "middle way" based on traditional values between the foreign-influence doctrines of Catholicism* and communism.

Tri Quang organized Buddhist opposition to Ngo Dinh Diem,* a Catholic. Animosity between Catholics* and Buddhists stemmed from their theological differences and from French favoritism of Catholics and persecution of Buddhists. When some 900,000 northern Catholics moved south after the 1954 Geneva Conference (*see* Geneva Accords) and Diem became president, relations worsened. In May 1963, Tri Quang moved against Diem. Monks took to the streets demanding Diem's resignation, a return to traditional ways, and an end to Catholic domination of the government. They applied pressure until Diem was overthrown.

Recognizing Tri Quang's power, Ambassador Henry Cabot Lodge* recommended he hold office in the post-Diem government. It was not to be. In the convoluted politics of General Nguyen Khanh's* tenuous rule, Tri Quang mobilized Buddhists first to force his resignation and then to bring him back. After 1964 the Buddhists were relatively quiet until 1966 when Nguyen Cao Ky* fired I Corps* commander General Thi, who had developed a close relationship with Tri Quang. Buddhists protests paralyzed the government and forced Ky to call elections. Determined U.S. support enabled Ky to survive and break the monk's power. Tri Quang, placed under house arrest, began a long fast and almost died. Distrusted by the North Vietnamese, Tri Quang was exiled to a monastery in 1975.

Sources: Frances FitzGerald, *Fire in the Lake: The Vietnamese and the Americans in Vietnam*, 1972; Stanley Karnow, *Vietnam; A History*, 1983; George McTurnan Kahin and John W. Lewis, *The United States in Viet Nam*, 1967.

Samuel Freeman

III CORPS

III Corps was the third allied combat tactical zone in South Vietnam. During the 1960s and early 1970s, the country was divided into four major administrative and military regions, and III Corps extended from the northern Mekong Delta* to the southern Central Highlands. It was also known as Military Region 3 (MR 3). III Corps had its headquarters in Saigon,* and consisted of the following provinces: Tay Ninh, Binh Long, Phuoc Long, Phuoc Tuy, Long An, Binh Duong, Long Khanh, Binh Tuy, Gia Dinh, Hau Nghia, and Bien Hoa. The 18th and 25th Divisions of ARVN (*see* Army of the Republic of Vietnam) played prominent roles in the military defense of III Corps, as did the 2nd Armored Cavalry and the 81st Airborne Rangers.

Sources: Harvey Smith et al., *Area Handbook for South Vietnam*, 1967; Shelby L. Stanton, *Vietnam Order of Battle*, 1981.

THIRD MARINE AMPHIBIOUS BRIGADE

When the Third Marine Amphibious Force* departed Da Nang* in April 1971, the Third Marine Amphibious Brigade (3rd MAB) took its place at headquarters under Major General Alan J. Armstrong. The brigade began planning on March 1 with a target date for beginning operations set at April 14. Assuming responsibility for over 13,600 marines who remained in Vietnam, 3rd MAB included a marine regiment, fixed-wing and helicopter gunships,* and the remainder of a force logistics command. Remnants of the marine civic action program deactivated shortly, and 3rd MAB formally ceased to exist and was out of Vietnam by June 26, leaving behind a scattering of naval gunfire teams along the Demilitarized Zone,* a marine advisory unit, a few officers at the Military Assistance Command, Vietnam,* and guards for the U.S. embassy in Saigon*— in a "transitional-support" group of some 500 marines.

Source: Edwin H. Simmons, "Marine Corps Operations in Vietnam, 1969–1972," in *The Marines in Vietnam, 1954–1973*, 1983.

Dudley Acker

III MARINE AMPHIBIOUS FORCE

A corps headquarters established at Da Nang* in May 1965, III Marine Amphibious Force (MAF) replaced the 9th Marine Expeditionary Brigade* (MEB) and grew by 1968 to include two reinforced marine divisions, one air wing, a United States Army* corps, plus several Republic of Vietnam* and South Korean* units. With tactical responsibility for the five northern provinces of South Vietnam, I Corp's* seven marine commanders often disagreed with Military Assistance Command, Vietnam* (MACV) strategy, and this strain characterized the relationship until the army's XXIV Corps* took over command of the region in March 1970.

III MAF's role in Vietnam reflected but another of the war's ironies—trained and equipped for rapid deployment as shock troops, marines were wedded to earlier contingency plans calling for a force that could be supplied over a beach and once committed were held in relatively static defensive positions around coastal enclaves* and later along the Demilitarized Zone* (DMZ). Meanwhile, MACV ordered an army division retrained for Mobile Riverine Force* operations in the Mekong Delta,* an area perhaps more suitable to the marines' traditional purpose.

III MAF's tactical area of responsibility* (TAOR) thus became a 30- to 70-mile-wide zone that stretched from the DMZ south some 225 miles to Sa Huynh at a spur in the Annamite Mountain chain. In 1965 an estimated 2.6 million (85 percent ethnic Vietnamese) lived in the 10,000-square-mile TAOR, mostly fishermen and farmers clustered in hamlets along the flat coastal plains or in small alluvial valleys lying inland between steep mountain slopes. These inhabitants were culturally and historically different from those, say, in Saigon* and also included Montagnard* tribesmen in the hills and business-oriented Chinese,* Indians, and a few remaining French in Da Nang, Hue,* and other urban areas.

At first assigned to defend the Da Nang airfield and a nearby ridgeline, III MAF believed that no more than 2,000 Vietcong* operated in the densely populated agricultural area of Quang Nam Province (150,000 civilians within 81mm mortar range of the marines) and thus stressed pacification (see Rural Reconstruction) in its contribution to MACV planning. Although never completely rejecting General William Westmoreland's* decision to "search and destroy"*— III MAF's early operations were labeled "clear and hold"*—marine staffs objected to the drift toward a "big unit" war and won support from Fleet Marine Force, Pacific Command* (FMFPAC) in Hawaii and the commandant in Washington, both prevailing upon the commander in chief, Pacific Command* (CINC-PAC) and the Joint Chiefs of Staff (see Chairman, JCS) to slightly but never substantially alter MACV's reliance on increased firepower. Indeed, by 1966 the marine effort became two distinct wars—one in the south stressing pacification, another at the southern boundary of the DMZ seeking to stop North Vietnamese Army* infiltration* and find and destroy large units.

III MAF never quarreled with the lack of a pacification effort in the sparsely populated northern area of its TAOR, but it did object strenuously to Secretary of Defense Robert McNamara's* 1966 concept of an unmanned barbed-wire and electronic sensor barrier along the DMZ (see Project Practice Nine). ("Hell," remarked a grunt in rare agreement with staff officers, "they'll just walk around it.") Although the project began in the Gio Linh–Con Thien* sector, III MAF eventually prevailed and ordered construction of what it argued was a more feasible "mobile defense/conventional barrier," and by 1967 completed most of the strong points that dotted the northern tier of Quang Tri Province until abandoned in favor of a "mobile mode" after the 1968 siege of Khe Sanh.*

Meanwhile, III MAF's war with MACV intensified. While marines retook Hue and defended Khe Sanh* in the wake of the Tet Offensive,* General Westmoreland reexamined the command structure in I Corps and briefly in February-March 1968 installed an interim headquarters, MACV(Fwd), at Phu Bai under General Creighton Abrams* to coordinate with III MAF the conduct of all operations in I Corps's two northern provinces. Bemoaning throughout the war what it described as "fluctuating command direction" from Saigon, III MAF became particularly incensed with another 1968 decision by MACV, approved by CINCPAC, to end the marines' relative autonomy over air-ground operations and give the Seventh Air Force* "mission direction" over the 1st Marine Aircraft Wing based at Da Nang.

During Vietnamization* the marine presence in I Corps dwindled more rapidly than the army's, and after XXIV Corps assumed command of all operations in 1970, III MAF confined its concern to seven operations in Quang Nam Province and ten special landing forays to the south of Da Nang. Just short of six years in country, III MAF headquarters yielded its command to the Third Marine Amphibious Brigade* and left Da Nang on April 14, 1971.

Between 1965 and 1971, III MAF was commanded by six individuals: Major General William R. Collins (May 1965–June 1965); Major and then Lt. General Lewis W. Walt* (June 1965–February 1966 and March 1966–June 1967); Major and then Lt. General Keith B. McCutcheon (February 1966–March 1966 and March 1970–December 1970); Lt. General Robert E. Cushman, Jr.* (June 1967–March 1969); Lt. General Herman Nickerson, Jr. (March 1969–March 1970); Lt. General Donn J. Robertson (December 1970–April 1971).

Sources: *The Marines in Vietnam, 1954–1973*, 1983; Lewis W. Walt, *Strange War, Strange Strategy*, 1976; Victor H. Krulak, *First to Fight: An Inside View of the U.S. Marine Corps Story*, 1982; Shelby L. Stanton, *Vietnam Order of Battle*, 1981; Allan R. Millett, *Semper Fidelis: The History of the United States Marine Corps*, 1980; J. Robert Moskin, *The U.S. Marine Corps Story*, 1982.

Dudley Acker

THIRD MARINE DIVISION

The March 1965 deployment of two battalions from the Third Marine Division on Okinawa to guard the Da Nang* air base marked the first overt commitment of U.S. combat forces to South Vietnam's defense. Composed eventually of the 3d, 4th, and 9th Marine Regiments, plus the 5th Marine Division's* 26th Marines, the division's headquarters moved north to the Hue* area in October 1966, to Quang Tri eighteen months later, then finally to Dong Ha* in June 1968.

Medals of Honor were awarded to twenty-nine marines and one corpsman who served with the division. Units from the Third Marine Division became chiefly responsible for setting up a defensive barrier along the Demilitarized Zone* (DMZ) and fought and operated out of Gio Linh and Con Thien,* both within five kilometers of the DMZ and together with Dong Ha and Cam Lo forming "Leatherneck Square"; Camp Carroll, the Rockpile,* and Ca Lu along Route 9; and successfully defended Khe Sanh* in the spring of 1968.

The division, which had not seen action since landing on Bougainville, Guam, and Iwo Jima during World War II, received a Presidential Unit Citation and Vietnamese Cross of Gallantry with Palm, redeployed to Okinawa in late November 1969, and in 1975 provided troops involved in the Pnom Penh, Da Nang, and Saigon* evacuations as well as the units which attacked Koh Tang island during the *Mayaguez** affair.

Sources: *The Marines in Vietnam, 1954–1973*, 1983; R. Robert Moskin, *The U.S. Marine Corps Story*, 1982; Allan R. Millett, *Semper Fidelis: The History of the United States Marine Corps*, 1980; William Turner Huggett, *Body Count*, 1973.

Dudley Acker

THOMPSON, ROBERT

Born in England on April 16, 1916, Robert Thompson served in a variety of positions in Malaysia during the 1930s and then spent six years in the Royal Air Force during World War II. He returned to Malaya after the war and served as deputy and later secretary of defense between 1957 and 1961. During his years in Malaya Thompson became a recognized expert in counterinsurgency* against Communist guerrillas. At the request of the United States, Thompson was brought to South Vietnam in 1961 as head of the British mission there, and he remained there until 1965, playing an important role in advising American military and political officials on how to deal with the Vietcong.* Thompson tried to apply the lessons the English had learned in Malaya to Vietnam, urging the United States to establish the Strategic Hamlet Program* and win the "hearts and minds"* of the people. He warned the United States about relying too heavily on a military solution to the problem in Vietnam, but his advice was not really heeded. Also, Thompson placed too much faith in the government of the Republic of Vietnam.* The British had succeeded with their counterinsurgency in Malaya in part because they were the government of a colony, but the United States had to deal with a native South Vietnamese government, one run by the likes of Ngo Dinh Nhu* and Nguyen Khanh.* Extraordinary corruption and lack of vision doomed the counterinsurgency effort. Early in the 1970s Thompson spent some time as a consultant to the Nixon* administration and approved of the concept of Vietnamization.*

Sources: Robert Thompson, *Revolutionary War in World Strategy, 1945–1949*, 1970, and *Peace is Not at Hand*, 1974; Larry E. Cable, *Conflict of Myths: The Development of American Counterinsurgency Doctrine and the Vietnam War*, 1986.

365 DAYS

365 Days is the title of Ronald J. Glasser's 1971 book on the Vietnam War. A medical officer in Japan* treating wounded American soldiers in Japan, Glasser picks his title from each of the wounded men's preoccupation with the number

365—the number of days in a Vietnam tour of duty. The book deals primarily with the unbelievable sense of futility expressed by dying and wounded teenagers.

Sources: Ronald J. Glasser, *365 Days*, 1971; Philip D. Beidler, *American Literature and the Experience of Vietnam*, 1982.

THURMOND, STROM

Strom Thurmond, a Republican senator from South Carolina throughout the Vietnam era, had long been in the political arena. After having served as both state senator and circuit court judge, in 1946 Thurmond was elected governor of South Carolina on the Democratic ticket. In 1948, after the Democratic National Conventional adopted a civil rights plank for its platform, the breakaway States Rights party, sometimes referred to as the Dixiecrats, selected Thurmond as its presidential candidate. Unsuccessful in this bid, Thurmond was able to enter the Senate in 1954. Ten years later he transferred his allegiance to the Republican party, so that he could work openly for the candidacy of conservative Barry M. Goldwater,* the Republican senator from Arizona, during the presidential election of 1964.

Although best known for his conservative southern stand in opposition to antidiscrimination measures and civil rights legislation, Thurmond also favored a militantly anti-Communist foreign policy and large defense appropriations. Indeed, the South Carolina senator was one of the few to associate himself with the causes of ideological right-wing organizations like the John Birch Society and the Young Americans for Freedom in the early 1960s. During the presidency of Lyndon Johnson,* Thurmond was among the five leading Republican supporters of a tough anti-Communist foreign policy in the Senate.

To offset what he regarded as unrelenting Communist expansionism, Thurmond favored the unrestrained use of military force in Vietnam. He charged in August 1966, as one example, that the administration was following a ''no-win'' policy in Southeast Asia and urged the use of increased force to ensure the continued existence of South Vietnam. The following April he criticized an East-West treaty governing the peaceful exploration and use of outer space as ''another step in the artificial and unrealistic atmosphere of détente with Communism.''

In 1968 Thurmond backed Richard M. Nixon* for the Republican presidential nomination and was credited with convincing most Southern Republican delegates to the party's national convention to support Nixon instead of another candidate. As a result, Thurmond wielded considerable influence in the White House during the Nixon administration. Harry Dent, his former aide, was a political adviser to the president, and about twenty other friends and associates of the senator received significant administrative jobs. He supported President Nixon's efforts to conclude the conflict in Southeast Asia through a negotiated peace but has continued to urge the constant opposition to Communist activity throughout the world.

Sources: Seyom Brown, *The Faces of Power: Constancy and Change in United States Foreign Policy from Truman to Johnson*, 1968; Eric F. Goldman, *The Tragedy of Lyndon*

Johnson, 1969; George C. Herring, *America's Longest War: The United States and Vietnam, 1950–1975*, 1979.

Roger D. Launius

TICONDEROGA   *See* USS *Ticonderoga*

TIGER CAGES

"Tiger cages" were small stone compartments used by the South Vietnamese to confine prisoners of war* (POWs) in the Con Son Correction Center on Con Son Island (*see* Poulo Condore). The cages measured 5 feet by 9 feet and had bars on top. According to official releases of the Saigon* government, prisoners were humanely treated and confined only temporarily in the tiger cages, and all were obstinate troublemakers. But in July 1970 the Red Cross reported that the prisoners were abused and that South Vietnam was violating the Geneva Convention. Chained to walls day and night, denied adequate food, water, and exercise, the prisoners often died or lost the use of their legs. While South Vietnam claimed prisoners were common criminals, the Red Cross disagreed, saying the prisoners were mostly North Vietnamese POWs or Buddhist dissidents. On July 7, 1970, Congressmen Augustus Hawkins and William Anderson condemned the prison after touring it. In February 1971, the U.S. mission in Saigon announced that the State Department would provide $400,000 to construct 288 isolation cells to replace the notorious tiger cages and that all POWs would be removed from the facility.

Source: Edward W. Knappman, ed., *South Vietnam: U.S.–Communist Confrontation in Southeast Asia*, vols. 6 & 7, 1973.

Linda Casci

TIGER DIVISION

The Tiger Division was the Capital Division* of the Republic of Korea* Army. The Tiger Division was first deployed to South Vietnam in September 1965, and spent most of the war fighting in II Corps.* They were headquartered at Qui Nhon.* The Tiger Division's primary activity involved protecting the major American installations along the coast in II Corps and keeping transportation lanes open between those installations and the U.S. air bases at Phu Cat and Phan Rang.

Sources: Shelby L. Stanton, *The Rise and Fall of an American Army. U.S. Ground Troops in Vietnam, 1965–1973*, 1985; Harry G. Summers, Jr., *Vietnam War Almanac*, 1985; Shelby L. Stanton, *Vietnam Order of Battle*, 1981.

TO HUU

Originally known as Nguyen Kim Thanh, To Huu was born in Thua Thien Province in 1920 and educated in Hue.* He became a devoted Communist as a student and eventually was known as the poet laureate of North Vietnam. Huu has held a variety of positions in the government of the Democratic Republic of Vietnam,* including minister of culture.

Source: Danny J. Whitfield, *Historical and Cultural Dictionary of Vietnam*, 1976.

TON DUC THANG

Ton Duc Thang, also known as Ton That Thien, was a native of South Vietnam born in 1889. While attending school in Saigon* in 1910, Thang met Ho Chi Minh* and became a dedicated anti-French, Vietnamese nationalist. For political activities against the empire, the French placed Thang in the notorious prison at Poulo Condore* between 1929 and 1945. After World War II he immediately began working with the Vietminh* and served in various leadership positions in the Lao Dong party.* After Ho Chi Minh's death in 1969, Thang moved up from vice president of the Democratic Republic of Vietnam* to president, but it was only a figurehead position he filled until his death.

Sources: "Meet Uncle Tom," *Newsweek*, 74 (October 6, 1969), 92; "North Viet Nam," *Time*, 94 (October 3, 1969), 26; William J. Duiker, *The Rise of Nationalism in Vietnam, 1900–1941*, 1976.

TONKIN

Geographers generally divide Vietnam into three major regions: Tonkin* in the north, Annam* in the center, and Cochin China* in the south. Anciently, the ancestors of the Vietnamese migrated out of southern China (*see* People's Republic of China) and settled first in Tonkin and later in Annam. Not until the nineteenth century did they displace Cambodians from Cochin China in the south. Drained primarily by the Red River, much of Tonkin is a fertile delta capable of supporting a dense population. In addition to the Red River, the Clear, Black, and Thai Binh rivers cut through Tonkin, depositing a rich loam soil. The major city of Tonkin is Hanoi,* a commercial and manufacturing center, and the port city of Haiphong is connected to the Thai Binh River. The Red River Delta is a huge rice field. Because the Red River regularly floods, Tonkin is covered with an elaborate system of dikes* and canals. During the Vietnam War, the United States considered but never used air strikes to attack the canals and dikes, primarily because it would have destroyed a civilian food supply and constituted a war crime according to international law. Inland from the Red River Delta, Tonkin becomes a series of hills and then mountains at the Chinese and Laotian borders. In those mountains, tribes of Montagnards* ("mountain people") are widely scattered. Those mountain areas are rich in such ore deposits as iron, zinc, tin, and coal.

Sources: Pierre Gourour, *The Peasants of the Tonkin Delta*, 1955; Edward Doyle and Samuel Lipsman, *The Vietnam Experience: Setting the Stage*, 1981.

TON THAT DINH

Born a southerner in 1930, Ton That Dinh rose to power in the Republic of Vietnam* because of his close personal relationship with Ngo Dinh Diem.* Diem viewed Dinh with trust and paternalism, and in 1961 he had made Dinh the youngest general in the Army of the Republic of Vietnam* (ARVN). Dinh converted to Roman Catholicism* early in the 1960s and was an active member of Ngo Dinh Nhu's* Personalist Labor party. Ambitious for a prominent political position in Ngo Dinh Diem's cabinet, Dinh turned to plotters against the regime after Diem refused. In November 1963 he played a leading role in the coup d'état which toppled and assassinated Diem. Suspected of still being loyal to the Diem faction, Dinh was arrested by General Nguyen Khanh,* but was held only temporarily. When Nguyen Cao Ky* took control of the government, Dinh was again in command of an ARVN corps, but he lost favor during the Buddhist crisis of 1966 when he resented the tactics Ky used to crush the protest. In the summer of 1966 Dinh lost command of his corps and was exiled from the Republic of Vietnam.

Sources: Joseph Buttinger, *Vietnam: A Dragon Embattled*, 2 vols., 1967; Frances FitzGerald, *Fire in the Lake: The Vietnamese and the Americans in Vietnam*, 1972.

THE TRAITORS

The Traitors is the title of John Briley's 1969 Vietnam War novel. It centers on an American patrol ambushed and captured by the Vietcong.* At a detention camp an American defector tries to brainwash them, eventually convincing two of the captives to participate in a harebrained scheme to free an imprisoned Buddhist from a political prison in South Vietnam on the naive hope that he will be able to end the war.

Sources: John Briley, *The Traitors*, 1969; Philip D. Beidler, *American Literature and the Experience of Vietnam*, 1969.

TRAN BUU KIEM

Tran Buu Kiem was born in 1921 in Can Tho and took a law degree at Hanoi University. A fervent anti-French nationalist, Kiem organized student protest movements against the French Empire and became active as a leader on the central committee of the National Liberation Front (*see* Vietcong) in the 1950s and 1960s. Kiem served on the delegation to the Paris peace talks* in 1968 and was minister to the president of the Provisional Revolutionary Government of South Vietnam.*

Source: *International Who's Who, 1982–1983*, 1983.

TRAN DO

Born in North Vietnam in 1922, Tran Do served as deputy commander of North Vietnamese and Vietcong* forces in South Vietnam during the 1960s and early 1970s. Do lived with his troops in underground bunkers and jungle camps, established no headquarters, and always kept on the move, confusing and frustrating American forces trying to capture him. Although the South Vietnamese resented the leadership of northerners in their campaign against the governments of Ngo Dinh Diem,* Nguyen Cao Ky,* and Nguyen Van Thieu,* Do managed to prevent factionalism from seriously hindering the war effort. Tran Do planned and executed the Tet Offensive* in 1968 which, although resulting in tens of thousands of casualties for the Vietcong and North Vietnamese, was a political deathblow to the American war effort.

Source: John S. Bowman, ed., *The Vietnam War Almanac*, 1985.

TRAN KIM TUYEN

A native of North Vietnam, Tuyen attended medical school, practiced medicine for a time in Hanoi,* and then fled to South Vietnam in 1954 as part of the large-scale Catholic relocation across the Demilitarized Zone.* In South Vietnam, Tuyen became head of the feared Office of Political and Social Studies, a Central Intelligence Agency*–established secret police force loyal to Ngo Dinh Diem.* He became disaffected from Diem late in the 1950s, primarily because he believed Diem's weak and corrupt government would guarantee a Communist takeover. In 1962 and 1963 Tuyen began plotting the overthrow of the Diem government, but when Diem found out, he exiled Tuyen, naming him diplomatic counsel to Egypt. Tuyen never reached Egypt but ended up in Hong Kong where he continued to oppose Diem. After the fall of the Diem government Tuyen returned to South Vietnam but played no prominent political role. He fled to Great Britain* just before the fall of Saigon* in 1975.

Source: Stanley Karnow, *Vietnam: A History*, 1983.

TRAN THIEN KHIEM

Tran Thien Khiem, South Vietnamese diplomat and ambassador to the United States, was born on December 15, 1925. Khiem joined the Vietnamese army as a young man, and rose quickly through the ranks. In 1960, after stopping an attempted coup against Ngo Dinh Diem,* Khiem became army chief of staff and a powerful figure in South Vietnamese politics. Three years later, however, Khiem was a leading figure in the successful coup d'état and assassination of Ngo Dinh Diem. The next year Khiem joined with General Nguyen Khanh* in deposing General Duong Van Minh.* Khiem was then named defense minister and commander in chief of the new government. The Khanh government was soon shaky, and Khiem was plotting against it. For a brief time in 1964 Khiem joined Khanh and Duong Van Minh in a triumvirate government until the forces of air force general Nguyen Cao Ky* took over. Khiem was then sent into honorable exile, first as ambassador to the People's Republic of China* between October of 1964 and October of 1965, and then from 1965 to 1968 as ambassador to the United States.

Khiem returned to Saigon* in 1968 as minister of the interior, and for five months in 1969 he served as deputy prime minister. He became prime minister in 1969 and remained in that post until 1975. General Khiem was considered a leading figure in the lucrative South Vietnamese heroin traffic, a trade which included most other prominent officials in the government. In April 1975, as North Vietnamese and Vietcong* forces were moving into Saigon, Khiem escaped to Taiwan.

Sources: *The International Who's Who, 1976–1977*, 1976; Stanley Karnow, *Vietnam: A History*, 1983.

TRAN VAN CHUONG

Tran Van Chuong was born in 1898 and educated at the University of Paris. He set up a law practice in Hanoi* in 1925 and became a prominent member of the French-Vietnamese establishment. His daughter, Tran Le Xuan, married Ngo Dinh Nhu* (*see* Ngo Dinh Nhu, Madame), and in 1954 Tran Van Chuong became minister of state for the Republic of Vietnam.* He then served as ambassador to the United States between 1954 and 1963. He resigned in protest in August 1963 when Ngo Dinh Diem* began his attacks on the Buddhists, and in the fall of 1963 Tran Van Chuong followed his daughter around the United States contradicting her statements of support for the Diem government. After the assassination of Diem, Tran Van Chuong remained in the United States, living in Washington, D.C.

Sources: *Who's Who in the Far East and Australasia, 1974–1975*, 1975; Stanley Karnow, *Vietnam: A History*, 1983.

TRAN VAN DO

Tran Van Do was minister of foreign affairs in Ngo Dinh Diem's* first cabinet in 1954. A physician and a man of distinguished reputation in Vietnam, Do was head of the State of Vietnam's delegation to the Geneva Conference at the time of the completion of the Geneva Accords* in 1954. He made a determined but futile effort to prevent the partitioning of Vietnam at Geneva and, in the name of his government, denounced the final accords.

Do had been a longtime and close associate of Ngo Dinh Diem. His brother, Tran Van Chuong,* was the father of Madame Ngo Dinh Nhu* and became Diem's ambassador to the United States. Do split with Diem in the spring of 1955, however, because he objected to Diem's unwillingness to broaden his government beyond the Ngo family circle. Do was one of the signers of the "Caravelle" petition in 1960 that urged Diem to initiate political reforms. After Diem's death, Do served once again as foreign minister in the cabinet of Prime Minister Phan Huy Quat.*

Source: Bernard B. Fall, *Viet-Nam Witness, 1953–66*, 1966.

David L. Anderson

TRAN VAN DON

General Tran Van Don was one of the leaders of the South Vietnamese Army who helped Ngo Dinh Diem* secure power and who later helped remove Diem from office. Although he lived most of his life in Vietnam, Don was born in France* in 1917 while his father was attending medical school. As a French citizen, he found himself in the French Army during World War II, and largely through circumstance, he became a career military officer. When the French decided during their war with the Vietminh* to create a Vietnamese National

Army* (VNA), Don, who was then a colonel, became chief of staff for General Nguyen Van Hinh,* whom the French placed in command of the VNA. It was with the support of such key officers as Colonel Don that Ngo Dinh Diem was able to secure VNA support in 1955 in subduing the private and sectarian military forces in South Vietnam.

Under Diem, Don became a general and rose to command of the First Corps with headquarters at Hue.* Like other military officers, however, he became increasingly disillusioned with Diem and the entire Ngo family. In 1963, Don was one of the principal conspirators in the coup that ended with Diem's assassination. With the rise to power in 1965 of younger military officers such as Nguyen Cao Ky* and Nguyen Van Thieu,* Don was among the senior officers forced to retire. Elected to the South Vietnamese Senate in 1967, Don remained an influential figure in South Vietnam. On April 29, 1975, the day before North Vietnam's seizure of Saigon,* he chose to seek exile in the United States.

Source: Tran Van Don, *Our Endless War: Inside Vietnam*, 1978.

David L. Anderson

TRAN VAN HUONG

Tran Van Huong was born on December 1, 1903. He worked as a schoolteacher before joining the Vietminh* resistance movement against the French. Huong served as mayor of Saigon* in 1954 and again in 1964, until he became prime minister of South Vietnam in a civilian government orchestrated by General Nguyen Khanh.* Huong encountered bitter opposition from various Buddhist factions and was in office only three months. After the Tet Offensive* in 1968, General Nguyen Van Thieu* appointed Huong prime minister again. He lasted there until 1969. In 1971, Huong became vice president of South Vietnam and remained in that position until April 21, 1975, when Thieu abdicated. Huong was president of South Vietnam for nine days until he surrendered authority to General Duong Van Minh* on the eve of the North Vietnamese victory.

Sources: George C. Herring, *America's Longest War: The United States in Vietnam, 1950–1975*, 1986; *The International Who's Who, 1976–1977*, 1976.

TRAN VAN LAM

Tran Van Lam was born on July 30, 1913, in Cholon.* He was educated at Hanoi University as a pharmacist and spent his career in Saigon.* Lam was elected to the Saigon city council in 1952 and served in the national assembly between 1956 and 1961. Between 1961 and 1964 Tran Van Lam was the ambassador to Australia* and New Zealand* for the Republic of Vietnam.* He returned to South Vietnam in 1964, and in 1968 was appointed minister of foreign affairs, where he served until 1973 when he became speaker of the Senate. He remained in that position until the collapse of South Vietnam in 1975.

Source: *Who's Who in the Far East and Australasia*, 1974.

TRAN VAN TRA

Tran Van Tra was born in Quang Ngai in central Vietnam in 1918. He worked on the railroads until the end of World War II when he joined the Vietminh* to oppose the return of the French Empire. Successful at politics, Tra became a senior officer, received political and military training in the Soviet Union* and People's Republic of China,* and in 1963 assumed command of Vietcong* forces in South Vietnam. He led the attack on Saigon* during the Tet Offensive* of 1968. Tra joined the armistice commission after the January 1973 cease-fire, but two months later he was back in Hanoi* planning the final assault on the South. He then was transferred to Loc Ninh, a command post about 75 miles north of Saigon, and planned the assault. In 1975 Tra was a leader of the conquest of Saigon when ARVN forces (*see* Army of the Republic of Vietnam) collapsed. When he published in 1982 a critical account of internal dissension among Communist leaders during the Vietnam conflict, Tran Van Tra was purged from the Communist party.

Source: John S. Bowman, ed., *The Vietnam War Almanac*, 1985.

TRINH

The Trinh were the family dynasty in control of Tonkin* in the northern portion of Vietnam. By the 1590s Trinh Kiem was the power behind the throne of the Le dynasty in Tonkin, and the Trinh ruled Tonkin until 1786, when leaders of the Tay Son Rebellion* invaded and seized Hanoi.* When the Tay Son government collapsed in 1802, the Trinh were unable to return to power in Hanoi because the Nguyen* dynasty, under Gia Long,* had unified Cochin China,* Annam,* and Tonkin* under one rule.

Source: Joseph Buttinger, *The Smaller Dragon: A Political History of Vietnam*, 1958.

TROOP

The term "troop" usually refers to a cavalry unit of company* size. Usually commanded by a captain, a troop is made up of two or more platoons.* During the war in Vietnam, there were also reconnaissance troops, armored cavalry troops, and air cavalry troops.

Source: Harry G. Summers, Jr., *Vietnam War Almanac*, 1985.

TRUMAN, HARRY S

Harry S Truman, the thirty-third president of the United States, was born on May 8, 1884, in Lamar, Missouri. After graduating from high school he worked the family farm near Independence, Missouri, and joined the army in 1917. Truman saw combat with the 129th Field Artillery of the 35th Division at St. Miniel and the Meuse-Argonne offensives. After the war he operated a clothing store and studied law in night school. Active in the politics of Tom Pendergast's Kansas City machine, Truman became a Jackson County judge in 1922, served as presiding judge between 1926 and 1934, and won election to the U.S. Senate in 1934. Truman was reelected in 1940 but served in obscurity until he chaired the Senate Committee to Investigate the National Defense Program. Franklin D. Roosevelt* selected Truman as his running mate to replace Henry A. Wallace in 1944, and when Roosevelt died of a stroke on April 12, 1945, Truman became president of the United States.

Unlike Roosevelt, however, Truman had no philosophical opposition to colonialism nor any real interest in Indochina.* Truman was content to let France* return to control of her colonial empire. So instead of pursuing Roosevelt's plan to establish intermediary "trusteeship" status on former European colonies, Truman wanted the European powers to resume their imperial positions as a way of fighting Communist expansion in the world. Truman also had a distinct distrust for Ho Chi Minh* because of his ties to Moscow, and instead of viewing Ho as a legitimate nationalist, Truman could only see him as a Communist. Although the United States adopted a position of pro-French neutrality toward the war in Indochina during the late 1940s and early 1950s, the president provided for covert economic and military assistance to the French. Hundreds of millions of dollars of Marshall Plan assistance to France were also diverted to the colonial enterprises in Indochina and Africa. When Harry S. Truman left office in January 1953, the United States was clearly a French supporter in the Indochina war. Fear of communism had replaced opposition to imperialism as the main focus of American Third World policy.

Sources: Alfred Steinberg, *The Man from Missouri: The Life and Times of Harry S. Truman*, 1962; George C. Herring, *America's Longest War: The United States and Vietnam, 1950–1975*, 1986.

TRUONG CHINH

Truong Chinh was born in 1907 in Nam Dinh. He joined the Revolutionary League of Vietnamese Youth in 1927 and was expelled from the Nam Dinh School for anti-French, revolutionary activities. Chinh joined the Communist party in 1930 and was imprisoned by the French. After his release in 1936, Chinh worked as a journalist until 1939 when the French imprisoned him again. He escaped prison and fled to Yenan late in 1939 and returned to Vietnam in 1941. Between 1941 and 1945 Chinh was the secretary-general of the Central Committee of the Communist party of Indochina (*see* Lao Dong party). During the 1950s he was active in the Labor party of Vietnam and was appointed deputy prime minister of North Vietnam in 1958. Chinh's relationship with Ho Chi Minh* was a close one, with him acting as Ho's chief Marxist theorist. Chinh was viewed, however, as a moderate and an advocate of negotiation whenever possible. After the fall of South Vietnam in 1975, Chinh rose to more power in the Socialist Republic of Vietnam,* eventually becoming the second most powerful individual in the country. He resigned as party chief and president in December 1986 after severe economic problems in the Socialist Republic of Vietnam eroded his political base.

Sources: *Who's Who in the Socialist Countries*, 1978; Frances FitzGerald, *Fire in the Lake: The Vietnamese and the Americans in Vietnam*, 1972; *Washington Post*, December 18, 1986.

TRUONG DINH DZU

In 1967 an obscure Buddhist lawyer ran an unexpectedly strong second to the presidential ticket of Nguyen Van Thieu* and Nguyen Cao Ky.* Dzu took 17 percent of the vote in a field of ten candidates to Thieu's 35 percent, an unheard-of result in the quagmire of South Vietnamese politics. Candidates who were "pro-Communist," "neutralist," or allied with "militant Buddhists" were excluded from the election, and Truong Dinh Dzu had kept his platform relatively secret. But he was allowed to run because he had Central Intelligence Agency* contacts and because he advocated a bombing* "pause" rather than a "halt" in North Vietnam and because he initially opposed negotiations with the National Liberation Front (see Vietcong). Nevertheless, Truong Dinh Dzu, in the absence of stronger peace candidates, became the token peace candidate, and his 17 percent electoral finish was an embarrassment to the government. In a country where the "will of heaven" determines political authority, the election weakened Thieu's legitimacy. In response he jailed and later exiled Truong Dinh Dzu.

Sources: Frances FitzGerald, *Fire in the Lake: The Vietnamese and the Americans in Vietnam*, 1972; Stanley Karnow, *Vietnam: A History*, 1983; Edward Herman and Frank Brohead, *Demonstration Elections*, 1984.

Samuel Freeman

TRUONG NHU TANG

Truong Nhu Tang was born in 1923 in the Saigon* suburb of Cholon.* Educated at the University of Paris, he became a successful banker in South Vietnam, directing the Viet-Nam Bank for Industry and Commerce and the Viet-Nam Sugar Company in Saigon. During the late stages of the government of Ngo Dinh Diem* in the early 1960s, Tang became disenchanted with the corruption and American involvement. In 1964 he became a director of the People's Movement for Self-Determination, and in 1966 president of the Viet-Nam Youth Union. He was imprisoned in 1967 and 1968 for advocating peace with the Vietcong,* and in 1968 Tang joined the National Liberation Front (see Vietcong). In 1969 he was named minister of justice for the Provisional Revolutionary Government of South Vietnam,* and remained in that position until the fall of South Vietnam in 1975. He then became the minister of justice for the southern part of the new Socialist Republic of Vietnam.*

Source: *The International Who's Who 1976–77*, 1976.

TUNNEL RATS

The term "tunnel rats" was a slang term describing American soldiers specially trained to attack Vietcong* and North Vietnamese Army* underground positions. In South Vietnam there were hundreds of miles of tunnels the Vietcong used to protect living areas, storage depots, ordnance factories, hospitals, and supplies from American air and artillery strikes. The most elaborate tunnels, first constructed by the Vietminh* in the 1940s, were located around Cu Chi, approximately 25 miles northeast of Saigon* on Highway 1 (see "Street Without

Joy''). The area around Cu Chi became the most bombed, gassed, defoliated, and devastated area in the history of combat because of the American attempts to destroy the tunnel network.

Source: Tom Mangold and John Penycate, *The Tunnels of Cu Chi*, 1985.

20TH ENGINEER BRIGADE

The 20th Engineer Brigade served in South Vietnam between August 1967 and September 1971. It consisted of eighteen battalions* in the 34th and 79th Engineer Groups and was stationed at Bien Hoa.* The 20th Engineer Brigade confined its construction work to III* and IV Corps* operations.

Source: Shelby L. Stanton, *Vietnam Order of Battle*, 1981.

25TH INFANTRY DIVISION

Nicknamed the ''Tropic Lightning'' Division, the 25th Infantry Division served in the southwest Pacific during World War II and in Korea* from 1951 to 1953. The division's 3rd Brigade deployed to Vietnam from Hawaii in December 1965, with the rest of the division following in January and April 1966. (The original components of the 3rd Brigade were transferred to the 4th Infantry Division* in August 1967. In return, the 25th Infantry Division received the 3rd Brigade of the 4th Infantry Division. The original 3rd Brigade of the 25th Infantry Division was reunited with the division following the withdrawal from Vietnam in 1970.)

During most of its time in Vietnam, the 25th Infantry Division served in the Saigon* vicinity and along the Cambodian border of III Corps.* Until August 1967, the division's 3rd Brigade served in the western highlands around Pleiku.* In August this brigade became part of the 4th Infantry Division. The rest of the division participated in operations intended to clear the Iron Triangle* in early 1967, and returned to that area with several other American units as a part of Operation Junction City.* During the Tet Offensive* of 1968 the division assisted in the defense of Saigon, and was engaged in bitter fighting while protecting Tan Son Nhut Air Base.* During most of late 1968 and 1969 the division was responsible for the security of the area around Cu Chi, and elements of the division were often involved in hard fighting in defense of base areas. In 1970 the division participated in the invasion of Cambodia (*see* Operation Binh Tay) before turning over responsibility for the security of its area to the Army of the Republic of Vietnam.* Most of the 25th Infantry Division left Vietnam in December 1970. The division's 2nd Brigade remained in Vietnam until April 1971. During the course of the Vietnam War, the 25th Infantry Division suffered 34,500 casualties, twice the number it suffered in World War II and Korea combined.

Sources: Shelby Stanton, *Vietnam Order of Battle*, 1981, and *The Rise and Fall of an American Army. U.S. Ground Troops in Vietnam, 1965–1973*, 1985.

Samuel Freeman and Robert S. Browning III

XXIV CORPS

Headquartered at Phu Bai in I Corps,* the XXIV Corps was first activated in Vietnam after the Tet Offensive* in 1968. Until 1970, when the Third Marine

Division* left Vietnam, XXIV Corps was subordinate to the III Marine Amphibious Force.* In March 1970 the headquarters of the XXIV Corps was shifted to Da Nang,* and the XXIV Corps then assumed control of marine and South Vietnamese military operations in I Corps. The XXIV Corps was deactivated at the end of June 1972. During its nearly four years in I Corps, the XXIV Corps had responsibility at various times for all or parts of the following units: the 1st Cavalry Division,* the 82nd* and 101st* Airborne Divisions, the Fifth Infantry Division,* the 108th Artillery Group, and the III Marine Amphibious Force.* The following lieutenant generals commanded XXIV Corps: William B. Rosson (February–July 1968); Richard Stilwell (July 1968–June 1969); Melvin Zais (June 1969–June 1970); James W. Sutherland (June 1970–June 1971); and Welborn G. Dolvin (June 1971–June 1972).

Source: Shelby L. Stanton, *Vietnam Order of Battle*, 1981.

23RD INFANTRY DIVISION

In February 1967, in order to support U.S. Marine* operations along the Demilitarized Zone,* the U.S. Army formed an ad hoc division-sized unit known as Task Force Oregon. Support troops were provided by various units, and the combat units consisted of one brigade from each of the two divisions already in Vietnam (101st Airborne Division* and the 25th Infantry Division)* plus the independent 196th Light Infantry Brigade.* In September 1967, the "borrowed" brigades were returned to their parent divisions and replaced by the 11th Infantry Brigade and the 198th Infantry Brigade. At that time the Task Force was renamed the Americal Division (resurrecting a name first used in World War II when the army formed a new division on New Caledonia). Officially the Americal Division was known as the 23rd Infantry Division, but the American high command preferred to use the designation Americal Division, calling it the only named division on active service.

The Americal Division's area of responsibility consisted of the three southern provinces in I Corps.* From November 1967 to November 1968 the division conducted numerous sweeps and patrols through this region as part of a yearlong operation code-named Wheeler/Wallowa.* Also during this period units of the 11th Infantry Brigade committed a series of atrocities while conducting operations in Quang Ngai Province. The worst of these incidents occurred on March 16, 1968, at the hamlet of My Lai* in Son My village where some 200 South Vietnamese civilians were killed by American soldiers.

The division continued to patrol its region during 1969 and 1970, fighting numerous small unit engagements. The Americal Division was deactivated in November 1971, and the 196th Infantry Brigade returned to independent status. During its period of service the Americal Division suffered over 17,500 casualties.

Sources: Shelby Stanton, *Vietnam Order of Battle*, 1981, and *The Rise and Fall of an American Army. U.S. Ground Troops in Vietnam, 1965–1973*, 1985; Willard Pearson, *The War in the Northern Provinces, 1966–1968*, 1975.

Robert S. Browning III

· U ·

UH–1

The Bell UH–1 helicopter is one of aviation's true success stories. Thousands of the aircraft have been made in a number of variations, serving a multitude of roles. Called the Iroquois by the United States Army,* the aircraft is much better known by its nickname of "Huey," derived from its initial designation of HU–1. In its multitude of roles in Vietnam, the Huey became a familiar sight on the television screens of America. Hardly a night passed without the evening news showing Hueys in dustoff,* slick,* or other missions.

Bell was chosen in 1955 to provide the army with a utility helicopter capable of serving as a front-line medical evacuation (*see* medevac) aircraft, a general utility aircraft, and an instrument training aircraft. Deliveries to the U.S. Army began in 1959. In 1961 a more powerful version, the UH–1B, was introduced. In 1967, starting with the UH–1D series, the airframe length was increased, giving the Huey a much roomier passenger-cargo compartment capable of carrying more troops or supplies. In 1968 Bell developed a specialized version of the aircraft with a stronger airframe and more powerful engine. The "Huey tug," as it was nicknamed, was capable of lifting loads of up to three tons, nearly double that of a conventional Huey.

The UH–1 carried out a variety of missions in Vietnam, and it carried them all out well. As a troop transport, the Huey could carry from eleven to fourteen fully equipped combat troops. As a medical evacuation helicopter, the Huey carried six litters and a medical attendant. Conventional Hueys could carry 3,880 pounds of supplies, either internally or in a sling under the fuselage. As a gunship,* the Huey could carry a variety of armaments, including rocket packs on each side of the fuselage, a nose-mounted M–5 40mm grenade launcher capable of firing 220 rounds per minute, or two side-mounted XM–140 30mm cannon.

Powered by a 1,400 SHP Avco Lycoming engine, the Huey had a cruising speed of 127 mph and a range of 318 miles. Fast and highly maneuverable, the Huey proved far superior to the CH–21* or CH–34* as an assault helicopter. Combat troops normally rode in the wide doors on each side of the aircraft, and could exit quickly, greatly reducing the time the helicopter was on the ground. Often troops jumped from a Huey just above the ground as it "bounced" in ground effect and then left, with the entire ground time reduced to a matter of seconds.

The Huey continues to serve a major role in military organizations throughout the non-Communist world. The U.S. Army plans to retain at least 2,700 improved UH–1H models beyond the year 2000 to serve in a variety of roles, including resupply, troop transport, command, electronic warfare, and medical evacuation.

Sources: *Jane's All the World's Aircraft: 1970–71*, 1971; *Jane's All the World's Aircraft: 1985–86*, 1986.

Nolan J. Argyle

UNCOMMON VALOR

One of the many POW-genre films of the early 1980s, *Uncommon Valor* was released in 1983 and starred Gene Hackman as Colonel Jason Rhodes and Robert Stack as a Texas multi-millionaire, both of whom are intent on financing and carrying out a mission to rescue their sons, whom both believe are still prisoners of war* in Vietnam. Hackman recruits several of their sons' former comrades and they stage a rescue. The film tells the story of the recruitment and training of the rescue squad and the successful mission.

UNITED STATES AGENCY FOR INTERNATIONAL DEVELOPMENT

In the Foreign Assistance Act of September 4, 1961, Congress* recommended that the United States adopt programs assisting foreign countries in economic development and external and internal security, and two months later President John F. Kennedy* established the Agency for International Development (AID) by executive order. New York lawyer Fowler Hamilton became the first AID administrator, and he was succeeded in 1962 by economist David E. Bell. During the 1960s AID represented a shift in American foreign aid away from Europe and toward the Third World. In addition to loans and grants, AID assigned American specialists abroad. By the end of 1962 AID had more than 5,000 employees abroad, and they were training another 8,000 foreign nationals. By 1965 AID was spending more than $2 billion a year, and loans were beginning to replace grants as a major form of assistance. AID missions were established in seventy foreign countries, and most workers were assigned to projects in agriculture, education, and public health. By that time AID employees had reached more than 15,000 people.

During the early years of the Vietnam buildup AID became increasingly involved in anti-Communist programs—public safety, civic action, and rural and community development. Its 1967 budget earmarked more than $550 million for Vietnam. AID workers tried unsuccessfully to establish farming cooperatives, self-help projects, and village elections. As the war became more and more controversial at home, the public image of AID deteriorated, especially as revelations of Central Intelligence Agency* involvement in AID appeared. Between 1968 and 1975, AID personnel strength dropped from 18,000 people to less than 6,000. In addition to continuing its development activities, AID began running refugee assistance programs around the world. It also conducted Operation Babylift* in 1975 when thousands of refugees* were removed from Vietnam. After new legislation passed through Congress in 1973, AID programs shifted away from industrially oriented capital expenditures to popular participation programs in public health, education, and agriculture.

Sources: Rober E. Asher, *Development Assistance in the Seventies: Alternatives for the United States*, 1970; Paul G. Clark, *American Aid for Development*, 1972; John Prados, *Presidents' Secret Wars: CIA and Pentagon Covert Operations Since World War II*, 1986.

UNITED STATES AIR FORCE   *See* Air Force, United States

UNITED STATES ARMY VIETNAM

The United States Army Vietnam was a logistical command headquarters between July 1965 and March 1973. It functioned at Saigon* and later Long Binh.* The deputy commander of the Military Assistance Command, Vietnam* supervised the United States Army Vietnam.

Source: Harry G. Summers, Jr., *Vietnam War Almanac*, 1985.

USS *C. TURNER JOY* (DD–951)

The *C. Turner Joy* is a *Forrest Sherman* class destroyer of 4,200 tons and a crew of 360 people. She has three 5-inch guns, two 3-inch guns, six torpedoes, and depth charges. Commissioned on August 3, 1959, the *C. Turner Joy* completed two Western Pacific deployments and was in the midst of her third in August 1964 when she went to the assistance of the USS *Maddox*,* another destroyer under attack by North Vietnamese torpedo boats. After firing, along with the carrier USS *Ticonderoga*,* on the boats and destroying one of them, the *C. Turner Joy* retired to an area 100 miles off the North Vietnamese coast and continued patrolling. On August 4, 1964, both destroyers picked up on radar what they believed to be small surface craft approaching at extreme range in poor weather. Gunfire from the destroyers and aircraft from the *Ticonderoga* sank two of the boats and damaged two others, although the attacking boats were never positively identified. In retaliation of this "Gulf of Tonkin Incident,"* President Lyndon B. Johnson* ordered air strikes against four torpedo houses and supporting facilities. Congress* passed the Gulf of Tonkin Resolution,* which legally cleared the way for direct U.S. involvement in the Vietnam War. Throughout the rest of the Vietnam War the *C. Turner Joy* conducted shore bombardment (*see* naval bombardment) and screening patrols in the South China Sea.

Sources: *Jane's Fighting Ships 1976–77*, 1978; Tom Carhart, *Battles and Campaigns in Vietnam*, 1984.

Charles Angel

USS *MADDOX* (DD-731)

Commissioned on June 2, 1944, the USS *Maddox* was an *Allen M. Sumner* class destroyer that carried six 5-inch guns and ten 21-inch torpedoes. The USS *Maddox* was assigned to the Third Pacific Fleet and supported the Luzon invasion in late 1944 and early 1945, as well as the Okinawa and Japanese home islands campaigns in the summer of 1945. As part of the Seventh Fleet* in the South China Sea in the summer of 1964, the USS *Maddox* came under attack by three North Vietnamese patrol boats. With help from the destroyer *C. Turner Joy** and the carrier *Ticonderoga*,* the *Maddox* destroyed one of the patrol boats and damaged two others. Two days later, on August 4, 1964, the *Maddox* picked up radar information of five attacking patrol boats, and the same three vessels engaged them for more than two hours. The Gulf of Tonkin incident* was used by President Lyndon Johnson* to begin air strikes against North Vietnam and to justify a major escalation of the war. The *Maddox* completed two additional tours in Vietnamese waters in 1965 and 1966, supporting carriers and bombarding the shore. In 1969 the USS *Maddox* was decommissioned.

Sources: U.S. Navy Department, *Dictionary of American Naval Fighting Ships*, 4:189–90, 1969; Tom Carhart, *Battles and Campaigns in Vietnam*, 1984.

Charles Angel

USS *PUEBLO*

Early in the morning of January 23, 1968, forces from the North Korean navy seized the USS *Pueblo*, a highly sophisticated American intelligence ship. The seizure reportedly occurred 15 miles off the North Korean coast, well beyond the 12-mile territorial limit, and there were eighty-three Americans aboard. One was killed in the attack and four wounded. North Korea claimed that the ship was seized in waters seven miles off the coast, in what was a violation of their territorial sovereignty. Even if the territorial violation had been accurate, the North Korean action was a severe reaction, since American and Soviet intelligence vessels regularly worked the Asian coasts and occasionally wandered off course. Such occurrences usually warranted only orders to leave. Although the United States immediately ordered 350 aircraft to air bases in South Korea as a show of force, the crew of the *Pueblo* spent eleven months in captivity and were beaten, tortured, and forced to sign false confessions. Because the diplomatic controversy over the *Pueblo* lasted throughout 1968—along with the Tet Offensive,* election of 1968,* My Lai,* and the assassinations of Martin Luther King, Jr.,* and Robert Kennedy*—American energies were distracted, and a more vigorous response, one which held out at least the possibility of military action against Korea,* was out of the question. The quagmire in Vietnam had limited the American capacity to deal with other crises in the world.

Source: F. Carl Schumacher and George C. Wilson, *Bridge of No Return*, 1971.

Sally Smith

USS *TICONDEROGA*

The *Ticonderoga* was an *Essex* class aircraft carrier commissioned on May 8, 1944. After participating in the Pacific campaigns against Japan in 1945, the *Ticonderoga* spent two years bringing American servicemen home from Japan* and was decommissioned on January 9, 1947. She was converted for jet operations and recommissioned on September 11, 1954. On August 1, 1964, while operating in international waters in the Gulf of Tonkin, the *Ticonderoga* received reports from the destroyer *Maddox** of attacks by three torpedo boats. The carrier deployed four aircraft to attack the boats. Two days later the *Ticonderoga* assisted the destroyer *C. Turner Joy** when it was being attacked by torpedo boats. The Gulf of Tonkin incident* led to the Gulf of Tonkin Resolution* by Congress* authorizing air strikes against North Vietnam, and along with the USS *Constellation*, the *Ticonderoga* flew sixty sorties* against four bases and oil storage facilities, destroying twenty-five torpedo boats and causing severe damage. Between November 1965 and August 1969, the *Ticonderoga* completed five combat tours in the Far East and its aircraft flew over 35,000 sorties* against North and South Vietnamese targets. The *Ticonderoga* was decommissioned on September 1, 1973, and sold for scrap.

Sources: Tom Carhart, *Battles and Campaigns in Vietnam*, 1984; U.S. Navy Department, *Dictionary of American Naval Fighting Ships*, Vol. 3, 1978.

Charles Angel

U THANT

U Thant was born in Burma in 1909 and became secretary of the Ministry of Information in 1949, where he served until 1957. In 1957 Thant received appointment as the Burmese ambassador to the United Nations (UN). During the next four years he proved himself as a strong neutralist with great diplomatic skills. In 1961 Thant became secretary-general of the UN. Thant presided over the General Assembly during the most intense years of the Vietnam War, and he frequently urged a negotiated settlement of the conflict and occasionally played a direct role in negotiating such a settlement. His major attempt came in 1964 when he tried to work with Premier Nikita Khrushchev* in bringing the North Vietnamese to the negotiating table. His efforts were stillborn until 1968, when he helped in working out some of the detail of the Paris peace talks.* U Thant resigned as secretary-general of the UN in 1971 and died in 1974.

Sources: *Webster's New Biographical Dictionary*, 1983, p. 1979; Stanley Karnow, *Vietnam: A History*, 1983.

• V •

VANCE, CYRUS ROBERTS

Cyrus Vance was born on March 27, 1917, in Clarksburg, West Virginia, and received an undergraduate and a law degree from Yale in 1939 and 1942 respectively. After service in the navy during World War II, Vance began practicing law in New York City, and became general counsel for the Department of Defense in 1961. In 1962 President John Kennedy* named Vance secretary of the army. Vance was a close friend of Lyndon B. Johnson,* and he became deputy secretary of defense in 1964. He toured Vietnam in 1966 and publicly defended administration policy, and from 1968 to 1969 Vance served on the negotiating team at the Paris peace talks* on Vietnam. When Richard Nixon* entered the White House in 1969, Vance's role in foreign policy faded, except for periodic consultation assignments with Secretary of State Henry Kissinger,* but in 1977 the new president, Jimmy Carter, named Vance secretary of state. Then Vance advocated diplomatic recognition and restoration of relations with the government of Vietnam. He resigned as secretary of state after the abortive American attempt to rescue the Iranian hostages in 1980. Cyrus Vance is a member of the Council on Foreign Relations.

Sources: *Current Biography*, 1977, pp. 405–11; *Who's Who in America*, 1976–1977, p. 3210.

VAN TIEN DUNG

Van Tien Dung, the protégé of General Vo Nguyen Giap,* who led the final assault on South Vietnam in 1975, was born on May 1, 1917, in Ha Deng Province, Tonkin,* of peasant ancestry. Dung joined the revolutionary movement in the mid–1930s, fought against the French before and during World War II, as well as against the Japanese occupation forces of Indochina* after 1940. Vo Nguyen Giap took notice of the peasant soldier and moved him up through the army ranks, appointing him chief of staff in 1953 and giving him logistical command of the assault against French forces at Dien Bien Phu* in 1954. Dung was second in command to Giap throughout the 1960s, and early in the 1970s became the youngest member of the politburo in North Vietnam. Giap named Dung commander of the campaign against South Vietnam in 1975. Dung's book *Our Great Spring Victory* describes the assault on and collapse of the South Vietnam government. Dung replaced Giap as minister of national defense in February 1980.

Sources: Van Tien Dung, *Our Great Spring Victory*, 1976; U.S., Central Intelligence Agency, *Who's Who in North Vietnam*, 1969; Stanley Karnow, *Vietnam: A History*, 1983.

VIETCONG

In 1954, after the Geneva Conference (*see* Geneva Accords) on Indochina,* Ho Chi Minh,* just as he had promised, ordered his forces to withdraw back into North Vietnam, where he would wait for the results of the promised elections to reunite the country in 1956. Included in the withdrawing troops were those Vietminh* originally from southern Vietnam. Some of them undoubtedly stayed in the south, but they were few in number and restrained by Hanoi.* But five years later, with the government of Ngo Dinh Diem* firmly in control of the Republic of Vietnam* and the elections cancelled, Ho Chi Minh decided to rejoin the battle in the south. He permitted southern Communists to return home, recruit new supporters, and prepare for the "revolutionary struggle." Southern Communists engaged in a frenzy of assassination and terrorism to destabilize the Saigon* regime. On December 20, 1960, Ho Chi Minh organized the National Liberation Front (NLF) of South Vietnam, with Nguyen Huu Tho* serving as chairman. The purpose of the NLF was to foment a general uprising in the Republic of Vietnam to bring about a Communist revolution which would unite the south with the north. It remains arguable how firmly southern Communists controlled the NLF and how firmly Hanoi controlled the southern Communists.

During the Kennedy* administration, the southern insurgents became stronger. South Vietnamese President Ngo Dinh Diem, seeking to deride the insurgency, called the guerrillas the Vietcong (short for Vietnamese communists). American troops later called them VC, or "Charlie." But the VC soon appeared more than a match for Diem's government forces. At the Battle of Ap Bac,* for example, in January 1963, the Vietcong were outnumbered ten to one but managed to inflict a humiliating defeat on ARVN forces (*see* Army of the Republic of Vietnam). By late 1963 American intelligence analyses found that the Vietcong controlled more villages in the south than did the Saigon government.

The Vietcong high-water mark came in 1963–64. In 1965 President Lyndon B. Johnson* began committing the first of what became more than a half million troops and a vast array of weaponry. Hanoi responded with its own buildup of North Vietnamese regular troops. The Vietcong were battered by American forces and taken over gradually by North Vietnamese Army* cadres. The Tet Offensive* in January and February 1968, although a political disaster for the United States, was a death stroke for the independence of the Vietcong. By the end of 1968, the Vietcong had suffered deep and disastrous losses, and North Vietnamese troops were largely responsible for the war effort in South Vietnam. In 1969 the Provisional Revolutionary Government of South Vietnam* superseded the Vietcong-NLF.

Sources: Douglas Pike, *Viet Cong: The Organization and Techniques of the National Liberation of South Vietnam*, 1966, and *History of the Vietnamese Communist Party*, 1978; Truong Nhu Tang, *A Viet Cong Memoir*, 1985.

Charles Dobbs

VIETMINH

Vietminh is the shortened and most commomly used name for the Viet Nam Doc Lap Dong Minh Hoi, or League for the Independence of Vietnam. The Vietminh was a patriotic front organization created at the Eighth Plenum of the Indochinese Communist party (ICP; *see* Lao Dong party) in May 1941. Under the direct guidance of Ho Chi Minh,* the front provided the vehicle for the party to mobilize the anti-French and anti-Japanese nationalism of the Vietnamese people. At the same time, the party made a conscious decision to de-emphasize ideology and class war until national independence was achieved.

The creation of the Vietminh also represented a shift in military strategy by the ICP to guerrilla (*see* Vietcong) warfare, and it was largely through rural insurgency that the Vietminh led the resistance first against the Japanese and then against the French. The anticolonial war of the Vietminh gained its most spectacular success with the surrender of the French garrison at Dien Bien Phu* in May 1954. It was with representatives of the Vietminh that the French negotiated the Geneva Accords* of 1954 that led to de facto recognition of Ho Chi Minh's government in Hanoi* and to the eventual military withdrawal of the French from Vietnam.

Long before Dien Bien Phu and Geneva, the Communist identity of the Vietminh leadership was clearly apparent in Vietnam. In 1951, in an effort to maintain and attract broad support for the liberation struggle, the Communist party dropped the name Vietminh and adopted the name Lien Viet Front. Despite this move, Vietminh remained during the 1950s the designation most commonly used in South Vietnam for the Communists. Around the time of the creation of the National Liberation Front (*see* Vietcong) in South Vietnam in 1960, the name Vietcong replaced Vietminh as the term used outside of North Vietnam for the Vietnamese Communists.

Source: William J. Duiker, *The Communist Road to Power in Vietnam*, 1981.

David L. Anderson

VIET NAM CACH MENH DONG MINH HOI (Vietnam Revolutionary League)

The Vietminh's* origins can be traced to an anti-Communist Chinese nationalist warlord, Chang Fa-kwei, who had jailed Nguyen Ai-Quoc (Nguyen the Patriot) for Communist activities. The Chinese had had designs on Vietnam for centuries, and the end of World War II presented new opportunities. Chang and two other warlords, Lu-Han and Lung-Yun, wanted control over Tonkin.* The Viet Nam Quoc Dan Dang* (VNQDD), a pro-Chinese Vietnamese nationalist organization formed by Chiang Kai-shek,* and other non-Communist nationalist organizations, were weak, with aging leadership, and in no position to serve Chinese interests. Nguyen Ai-Quoc led the well-organized Indochinese Communist party (ICP; see Lao Dong party). Ai-Quoc's willingness to set aside ideological differences with Chang and collaborate in forming the Viet Nam Cach Menh Dong Minh Hoi (a coalition of Vietnamese nationalist organizations which became known more simply as the Vietminh), typified his willingness to compromise Communist principles in order to strengthen his organization.

Chang released Ai-Quoc from prison and funded the new coalition. Ai-Quoc promptly changed his name to Ho Chi Minh* (He Who Enlightens) because he was too well-known as a Communist. Since the ICP comprised a small minority of the Vietnam Revolutionary League, Chang mistakenly believed he could prevent Ho from dominating the organization. Ho returned to Vietnam and, with Vo Nguyen Giap,* organized Vietnamese resistance to Japan. They established ties with the United States OSS (Office for Strategic Services), rescued downed Allied pilots, collected intelligence, harassed Japanese forces, and planned to seize control of Vietnam before the Allies could execute plans to accept the Japanese surrender in Indochina.*

Though much more numerous, the non-Communist members of the Revolutionary League were no match for Ho's leadership. On September 2, 1945, with American military personnel on the reviewing stand and warplanes flying overhead in salute, Ho Chi Minh proclaimed the independence of Vietnam under the governance of the Vietminh.

Sources: Bernard Fall, *The Two Viet-Nams: A Political and Military Analysis*, 1963; William J. Duiker, *The Rise of Nationalism in Vietnam, 1900–1941*, 1976.

Samuel Freeman

VIET NAM DOC LAP DONG MINH HOI   *See* Vietminh

VIETNAMESE AIR FORCE
In 1951 the French established a small unit in the Army Air Corps which formed the beginning nucleus of the South Vietnamese Air Force. Primarily engaged in observation, liaison, and small cargo transport, the Vietnamese Air Force used Morane Saulnier MS500 Criquets. The Vietnamese Air Force became an independent military unit in 1955 after the withdrawal of the French from Indochina.* At that time its equipment included Grumman F8F Bearcat fighters, Cessna L–19 aircraft for reconnaissance, and C–47 and AAC–1 Toucan aircraft for transport. Beginning in 1960 the United States began supplying the Vietnamese Air Force with A–1 Skyraiders* and T–28Ds. The United States Air Force* began training Vietnamese pilots on jet aircraft—primarily Northrop F–5As (*see* F–5) in 1966, and early in 1967 established the 522nd squadron at

Bien Hoa.* Eight Vietnamese Air Force squadrons were eventually established using F–5As or F–5Es. They also used A–37 Dragonflys. The A–1s were replaced by A–37s between 1967 and 1969.

Between 1969 and 1973 the Vietnamese Air Force was greatly expanded as part of Richard Nixon's* Vietnamization* process. By December 1972 there were 42,000 men and 49 squadrons in the Vietnamese Air Force. It had nearly 2,100 aircraft—primarily A–37 and F–5 squadrons; AC–47 and AC–119 gunships;* O–1 FAC aircraft; C–7, C–119, C–123, and C–130* transports; and UH–1* and CH–47* helicopters. The real weaknesses in the Vietnamese Air Force were lack of trained maintenance personnel, shortages of spare parts, and serious problems of morale.

Sources: Dong Van Kuyen, *The RVNAF*, 1980; Carl Berger, ed., *The United States Air Force in Southeast Asia, 1961–1973*, 1977; John S. Bowman, ed., *The Vietnam War Almanac*, 1985.

VIETNAMESE NATIONAL ARMY

During the late 1940s and early 1950s, the Truman* administration urged the French to establish a Vietnamese army to assist them in fighting the Vietminh.* The French were reluctant to do so, but finally decided in 1950 to go ahead with the idea. Although they had a goal of 115,000 troops for the Vietnamese National Army (VNA), it totaled only 38,000 soldiers by the end of 1951. But the army was poorly trained and deeply infiltrated by the Vietminh. The Navarre Plan* of 1953 called for increasing the size of the VNA and improving its training, but the defeat at Dien Bien Phu* in 1954 ended those plans. In 1955 the new leader of the Republic of Vietnam,* Ngo Dinh Diem,* took over the VNA, and it became the nucleus of the Army of the Republic of Vietnam.*

Sources: George Herring, *America's Longest War: The United States and Vietnam, 1950–1975*, 1986; Bernard Fall, *The Two Viet-Nams: A Political and Military Analysis*, 1963.

VIETNAMESE NATIONALIST PARTY   *See* Viet Nam Quoc Dan Dang

VIETNAMIZATION

In 1969 the new president, Richard Nixon,* wanted to extricate the nation from the Vietnam quagmire. When Hanoi* appeared unwilling to negotiate and when military analysts convinced him that there were few immediate levers to move the North Vietnamese to the peace table, Nixon turned a three-prong policy: American troop withdrawal, consequently lowered draft* calls permitting creation of a lottery system, and—the key to the entire process—turning the ground fighting over to the Army of the Republic of Vietnam,* so-called Vietnamization, which became the basis for the Nixon Doctrine,* that Asians, not Americans, should fight Asian wars.

The policy was not new. In the 1950s the French had their policy of turning fighting over to native units, *jaunissement*, or yellowing. And certainly the rationale for commitment of U.S. forces in 1965–68 had been, eventually, to use the breathing space to build an effective South Vietnamese Army and to turn the ground burden over to it.

Still, the U.S. government pursued Vietnamization with great vigor, and by the end of 1970 the South Vietnamese Army was among the largest and best equipped in the world. In those cases where officers were competent and brave, the units were excellent and capable of holding the line. But the record was mixed. A larger army meant larger draft calls and severe dislocations in the Vietnamese economy. Desertion rates remained high. And the quality of officers remained uneven, sometimes excellent, all too often mediocre.

Vietnamization had three major tests. In 1971 Nixon ordered a hastily planned South Vietnamese invasion of Laos (*see* Lam Son 719); it went badly. In 1972 North Vietnam launched a strong offensive that crushed and routed many South Vietnamese units; massive application of U.S. air power managed to restore the balance. Then in March 1975 the North Vietnamese attacked with nearly twenty divisions and within two months crushed the south.

Sources: Stanley Karnow, *Vietnam: A History*, 1983; George C. Herring, *America's Longest War: The United States in Vietnam, 1950–1975*, 1986; Nguyen Duy Hinh, *Vietnamization and Cease-Fire*, 1985.

Charles Dobbs

VIETNAM LOBBY   *See* American Friends of Vietnam

VIETNAM INDEPENDENCE LEAGUE   *See* Vietminh

VIET NAM QUOC DAN DANG

The Viet Nam Quoc Dan Dang, or Vietnamese Nationalist party, was established in Canton, China, in 1925 to oppose Ho Chi Minh's* forces in Vietnam. In 1927 Nguyen Thai Hoc, a schoolteacher, secretly established a branch of the party in Hanoi.* Patterned after the Kuomintang in China, the Vietnamese Nationalist party wanted to modernize Vietnam and expel the French. An unsuccessful uprising at Yen Bay, northwest of Hanoi, in 1930 severely hurt the party and many of its members fled to Yunnan in southwest China. Although the Vietnamese Nationalist party was generally inactive during the Ngo Dinh Diem* years, its leader then, Nguyen Tuong Tam, opposed Diem and called for the end of Buddhist suppression. He committed suicide in 1963. After the fall of Diem, the Vietnamese Nationalist party became a major force in South Vietnam, opposing communism and calling for democratic socialism and an end of discrimination against Buddhists.* By the late 1960s, there were four major factions in the Vietnamese Nationalist party. The largest faction was centered in the Mekong Delta* and had 95,000 members. Most of them were Buddhists led by Nguyen Hoa Hiep and Tran Van Tuyen. A second group of 50,000 was based in Quang Ngai Province as well as in the provinces of Quang Nam and Quang Tin. It was led by Nguyen Dinh Bach and Bui Hoanh, who was the political administrator of Quang Ngai Province. Buddhist militant Thich Tri Quang* was influential in this faction. A third group, numbering about 10,000 people, consisted of Roman Catholic refugees* from North Vietnam and was led by Le Hung. Another group had only 1,000 members, also influential among Roman Catholic refugees.

Sources: William J. Duiker, *The Rise of Nationalism in Vietnam, 1900–1941*, 1976; Harvey H. Smith et al., *Area Handbook for South Vietnam*, 1967.

VIETNAM REVOLUTIONARY LEAGUE   *See* Viet Nam Cach Menh Dong Minh Hoi

VIETNAM VETERANS AGAINST THE WAR

Vietnam Veterans Against the War (VVAW) was founded in 1967 after six veterans who marched together in an antiwar* demonstration decided veterans needed their own antiwar organization. Its membership ultimately included several thousand veterans and a few government infiltrators. The VVAW participated in most major antiwar activities, including the 1968 Democratic National Convention* in Chicago. Government officials saw VVAW from its inception as a special threat because Vietnam veterans had a unique credibility. Furthermore, officials feared their capacity for violence although VVAW demonstrations were always among the most peaceful and orderly. With Jane Fonda's* financial assistance, VVAW conducted the Detroit "Winter Soldier Investigation"* (February 1971) where numerous veterans testified about "war crimes" they either witnessed or perpetrated. Selected testimonies were published in *The Winter Soldier Investigation* (1972). Speaking at the hearings, prompted in part by VVAW outrage over the assertion that the My Lai* massacre was an aberration resulting from soldiers having "gone berserk," executive secretary Al Hubbard stated: "The crimes against humanity, the war itself, might not have occurred if we, all of us, had not been brought up in a country permeated with racism, obsessed with communism, and convinced beyond a shadow of a doubt that we are good and most other countries are inherently evil." The government and its supporters denounced the proceedings and made several attempts to discredit testimony given.

On April 19, 1971, the VVAW began "Dewey Canyon III." (Dewey Canyon* I and II were military operations in Laos.*) It included over 1,000 veterans, led by men in wheelchairs and mothers of men killed in combat, who held a memorial service at the Tomb of the Unknown Soldier, and then were refused permission to lay wreaths on graves of fallen comrades at Arlington Cemetery (although after much haggling 200 were permitted in to lay wreaths the next day). They camped on the mall in defiance of a court order which was rescinded after it was realized that it would be poor public relations to arrest peaceful combat veterans. On April 23, 1971, more than 1,000 veterans threw medals they had won in Vietnam over police barricades on the Capitol steps.

Subsequent activities included several protests in December 1971 of the heaviest bombing of North Vietnam since 1968 and at the 1972 Republican convention in Miami, for which eight members (and two sympathizers) were tried on contrived criminal conspiracy charges. In July 1974 about 2,000 members demonstrated in Washington demanding universal amnesty for draft* resisters and deserters, implementation of the Paris peace treaty, ending aid to Nguyen Van Thieu* and Lon Nol,* Richard Nixon's* impeachment, and a universal discharge with benefits for all Vietnam veterans.

In all its activities, the VVAW had an overriding goal: to make the nation realize, in the words of cofounder Jan Barry, "the moral agony of America's Viet Nam war generation"—whether "to kill on military orders and be a criminal, or to refuse to kill and be a criminal."

Sources: Myra MacPherson, *Long Time Passing: Vietnam and the Haunted Generation*, 1984; Nancy Zaroulis and Gerald Sullivan, *Who Spoke Up? American Protest Against the War in Vietnam, 1963–1975*, 1985.

Samuel Freeman

VIETNAM WAR MEMORIAL

After watching the film *The Deer Hunter** in 1979, Vietnam veteran Jan C. Scruggs first conceived of the idea for a Vietnam War Memorial. Scruggs had little success promoting the idea until "CBS Evening News" did a prime-time spot on the campaign. Robert Doubek and John Wheeler, two attorneys in Washington, D.C., who were both veterans, heard the spot and soon organized the Vietnam Veterans Memorial Fund to raise money and construct the memorial. With the assistance of Senator Charles Mathias, Jr., of Maryland, they formed a National Sponsoring Committee which included Bob Hope, former president Gerald Ford,* Rosalynn Carter, Senator George McGovern,* and General William Westmoreland.* On April 30, 1980, the Senate unanimously approved a bill setting aside two acres on the mall near the Lincoln Memorial. The House approved the measure more than a month later, and on July 1, 1980, President Jimmy Carter signed the bill into law.

A national competition for memorial designs received 1,421 entries by the deadline of March 31, 1981, and the winner was Maya Lin, a Yale architecture student. Her proposal for a black granite sculpture, rising out of the ground and then descending back again in angular form, with the names of more than 58,000 dead or missing American soldiers inscribed on it, soon raised a storm of protest. Some Vietnam veterans resented the fact that an Asian-American woman had designed it, while others thought it memorialized the shame of the war. Still, by January 4, 1982, more than 650,000 people had donated more than $5 million, and Secretary of the Interior James Watt issued a building permit after a compromise agreement to include a sculpture of three soldiers by Frederick Hart. Hart's sculpture was finished on September 20, 1982, and the entire memorial was dedicated on November 13, 1982. At that time a total of 58,022 names were on the memorial. In 1986, another 108 names were added, 95 servicemen killed on combat missions outside the formal war zone and 13 others who died of wounds after leaving the war zone.

Sources: Joel L. Swerdlow, "To Heal a Nation," *National Geographic* 167 (May 1985), 555–73; Jan C. Scruggs and Joel L. Swerdlow, *To Heal a Nation: The Vietnam Veterans Memorial*, 1985.

Robert L. Shadle

VOGT, JOHN W., JR.

John Vogt was born on March 19, 1920, in Elizabeth, New Jersey. He was an Army Air Corps pilot during World War II. Vogt rose through the ranks of the United States Air Force* officer corps during the 1950s, and between 1965 and 1968 served as deputy for plans and operations at the Pacific Air Force headquarters in Honolulu. Vogt took command of the Seventh Air Force* in 1972. As part of the American withdrawal from Vietnam, Vogt moved the Seventh Air Force out of Tan Son Nhut Air Base* to Thailand* in March 1973. Vogt stepped down as commander of the Seventh Air Force in October 1973 to become commander in chief of the Pacific Air Force. He retired from the air force in 1975 after a stint as commander in chief of the United States Air Force in Europe.

Source: Harry G. Summers, Jr., *Vietnam War Almanac*, 1985.

VO NGUYEN GIAP

Vo Nguyen Giap was born in 1912 in Quang Binh Province and studied in Hanoi* at the Lycée Albert Sarraut and the University of Hanoi Law School. As a teenager he was politically active in the Revolutionary party of New Vietnam, and in 1933 he joined the Indochinese Communist party (*see* Lao Dong party). In 1939 he was forced into exile for anti-French activities, and his wife died in 1941 in a French jail. By that time Giap was thoroughly familiar with the interests of Ho Chi Minh,* and in 1941 he helped Ho organize the Vietminh.* Between 1941 and 1945 Giap was active in the mountains of northern Tonkin* and southern China* putting together an army and harassing French and Japanese units. Ho Chi Minh promoted Giap to general and commander in chief of the Democratic Republic of Vietnam* in 1946.

As military leader of the Vietminh, Giap put together an army of nearly 300,000 revolutionary troops and militia, and in 1953 he launched a drive into Laos,* having already gained control of most of central and northern Vietnam outside the coastal lowland areas. The new French commander, Henri Navarre (*see* Navarre Plan), reversed himself and chose to commit 10,000 troops to an isolated plateau, Dien Bien Phu,* in northwest Vietnam, astride Giap's line of communications. Giap then reversed course, cut off the French, secretly brought artillery up into the surrounding mountains (a tactic the French considered impossible), massed 50,000 troops of his own, and established a siege of Dien Bien Phu. The French surrendered on May 7, 1954, and gave up their Indochinese Empire.

Giap also led the military campaign against the United States and South Vietnam during the 1960s and 1970s. A believer in direct military confrontation as opposed to guerrilla action, Giap frequently orchestrated frontal attacks on U.S. positions, with disastrous results. The Tet Offensive* all but destroyed the Vietcong* and forced North Vietnamese Army* troops to carry the burden of the war. Still, Tet had been a strategic victory even if a tactical defeat. In 1972, Giap planned and tried to implement the Eastertide Offensive,* assuming that with the United States all but out of South Vietnam, the country was ripe for attack. Throughout most of the country ARVN (see Army of the Republic of Vietnam) held its positions, and buttressed with massive B–52* strikes from the United States, they were able to regain all that they had lost in the initial stages of the offensive. The North Vietnamese suffered more than 100,000 casualties, and in the wake of the defeat Giap was replaced by his chief of staff, Van Tien Dung.* Dung led the final assault on South Vietnam in 1975. In 1980, Giap retired as minister of defense of the Socialist Republic of Vietnam.*

Sources: Vo Nguyen Giap, *Dien Bien Phu*, 1962; *Big Victory, Big Task*, 1967; and *Unforgettable Days*, 1978; G. H. Turley, *The Eastertide Offensive: Vietnam 1972*, 1985; *Who's Who in the Socialist Countries*, 1978.

Charles Dobbs

VUNG TAU

Vung Tau, the fifth largest city in South Vietnam, with nearly 40,000 people, was also the southernmost, major port facility in the country. Located in Phuc Tuy Province in III Corps,* Vung Tau was more than 400 miles south of Hue.* It was formerly known as Saint Jacques. The port at Vung Tau was the main support center for the southern area of South Vietnam, and was situated at the entrance to the Mekong River system leading into Saigon.* Vung Tau was also the support area for the Mobile Riverine Force.*

Sources: Harvey H. Smith et al., *Area Handbook for South Vietnam*, 1967; Carroll H. Dunn, *Base Development in South Vietnam, 1965–1970*, 1972.

VU VAN MAU

Vu Van Mau was born in Hanoi* on July 25, 1914. He attended law school at Hanoi University and the University of Paris and began practicing law in Hanoi in 1949. He became a professor of law at Hanoi University in 1950 and dean of the law school in 1954. After the division of Indochina* in 1954, Mau moved to the south and became minister of foreign affairs in the government of Ngo Dinh Diem.* In 1963 Vu Van Mau resigned in protest when Diem's police forces began attacking Buddhist strongholds. He even shaved his head in the fashion of Buddhist monks to protest the discrimination and persecution. After the fall of the Diem government Mau returned to private law practice.

Source: *Asia Who's Who*, 1960.

· W ·

"WALK IN THE SUN"

"Walk in the Sun" was a phrase soldiers used to denote some type of ground troop movement free of the risk of combat. These were rare, cherished events when troops could move freely without having to be constantly alert for ambush or booby traps.* The need to be constantly alert to every detail of the environment, to any aberration in the nature of the terrain or vegetation, to smells in the air, to any changes in the noise of the jungle—to a sudden quiet or the sound of startled animals or birds—had a grinding and exhausting effect on the men who stalked the jungles. All of their senses were finely honed so that reaction came instinctively. But such a high level of alert consumed enormous amounts of nervous energy. A "walk in the sun" provided a tremendous if temporary sense of relief from the omnipresent burden of intense vigilance.

Sources: Shelby L. Stanton, *Vietnam Order of Battle*, 1981; Al Santoli, *Everything We Had: An Oral History of the Vietnam War by Thirty-three American Soldiers Who Fought It*, 1981.

Samuel Freeman

WALT, LEWIS

Lewis Walt was born on February 16, 1913, in Wabaunsee County, Kansas. He graduated from the Colorado School of Mines in 1936 and that summer accepted a commission as a lieutenant in the Marine Corps. Walt saw combat in Tulagi, Guadalcanal, New Britain, and Peleliu during World War II, and he served with the Fifth Marines during Korea. He took command of the Third Marine Division* in 1965 and the III Marine Amphibious Force* in Vietnam. In 1967 Walt returned to the United States, and after a stint as assistant commandant of the United States Marine Corps,* he retired in 1971.

Sources: Lewis W. Walt, *Strange War, Strange Strategy*, 1976; Edwin H. Simmons, "Marine Corps Operations in Vietnam: 1965–66, 1967, 1968, 1969–72," in *The Marines in Vietnam, 1954–1972*, 1974.

WARNKE, PAUL CULLITON

A native of Webster, Massachusetts, Paul Warnke was born on January 31, 1920, and graduated from Yale in 1941 and the Columbia University Law School in 1948. He practiced law in Washington, D.C., until 1966, when he was named general counsel for the Department of Defense. Between 1967 and 1969, Warnke served as assistant secretary of defense for international security affairs. During those years Warnke came to be a vigorous opponent, within the Defense Department, of the Vietnam War. Warnke was convinced that it was the wrong war in the wrong place, and that the United States would be unable to prevail. Warnke had great influence over Secretary of Defense Clark Clifford,* and General William Westmoreland* would later blame Warnke for converting Clifford from a hawk to a dove about Vietnam. Later Warnke became one of Clifford's law partners. When Richard Nixon* won the election of 1968, Warnke found himself exiled with the rest of the Democrats; so he returned to private practice and continued to work on antiwar programs for the Democratic National Committee. Warnke returned to government service in 1977 during the Carter administration as director of the Arms Control and Disarmament Agency and chief negotiator of the second Strategic Arms Limitation Treaty (SALT II). Warnke's appointment was quite controversial because of his open opposition to the Vietnam War and because he opposed deployment of the B–1 bomber and the Trident nuclear submarine. Although Warnke had no illusions about Soviet benevolence, he did believe that both countries had the capacity to destroy one another many times over and that weapons reduction was essential to world peace. Warnke continued to work on the SALT II treaty until his resignation in October 1978. Since then he has been a member of the Council on Foreign Relations.

Sources: *Current Biography*, 1977, 427–30; Stanley Karnow, *Vietnam: A History*, 1983; Paul Warnke, "Apes on a Treadmill," *Foreign Policy* 18 (1975), 12–30.

WAR OF ATTRITION

The primary, indeed the only strategy the U.S. military pursued in Vietnam was "attrition," the wearing away of enemy forces to the point where they were either unable or unwilling to continue fighting. At that point victory would be achieved. Given this strategy, the goal was to find the most economical tactics— "economical" in maximizing enemy losses while minimizing allied losses. In pursuing this, a number of substrategies were tried and retried, giving rise to tactics like "enclaves,"* "oil spots," "search and destroy,"* "search and clear," "strategic hamlets,"* "new life hamlets,"* and "really new life hamlets." Pacification (*see* Rural Reconstruction) was only given lip service by the United States as evidenced by miniscule resources allocated for pacification compared to the resources allocated for military combat operations. General William Westmoreland* believed in attrition, pronouncing in 1967 that the "crossover" point had been reached—that the Vietcong* and North Vietnamese were now losing personnel faster than they could replace them. The Tet Offensive* of 1968 proved Westmoreland wrong but gave him a new basis for justification—Tet enemy losses were so great that the United States now had a stranglehold on enemy troop strength. He soon learned that such a stranglehold did not really exist.

Eventually the strategy of attrition suffered from at least two serious flaws. First, U.S. military planners had not forseen the enormous casualties which the North Vietnamese were willing to accept. American forces were highly effective in their mission of inflicting losses upon the enemy, but attrition alone was not sufficient to destroy North Vietnam's will to wage war. Second, the American military failed to take into consideration American public opinion. American casualties proved to be unacceptable to the public. In retrospect, it can be argued that the most strategically decisive attrition figures were American rather than North Vietnamese. North Vietnam was able and willing to absorb extremely heavy military losses in pursuit of its objectives. American casualties, although a smaller percentage than North Vietnamese Army* losses, were nevertheless sufficient to cause the American public to question the wisdom of a distant war in an alien land.

Sources: Stanley Karnow, *Vietnam: A History*, 1983; John E. Mueller, "The Search for the 'Breaking Point' in Vietnam: The Statistics of a Deadly Quarrel," *International Studies Quarterly* 4 (December 1980), 497–519; Russell F. Weigley, *The American Way of War*, 1973; Harry G. Summers, Jrs., *On Strategy: A Critical Analysis of the Vietnam War*, 1982; Andrew F. Krepinevich, Jr., *The Army and Vietnam*, 1986.

Samuel Freeman and Sean A. Kelleher

WAR POWERS RESOLUTION (1973)

By 1973, congressional reaction began to sharpen to the cumulative effect of having been ignored and deceived by the executive branch on the question of the Vietnam-Indochina* War. By midsummer, there was ample evidence that the Nixon* administration had consistently and deliberately falsified statistics, data, and reports to Congress* to hide the extent of questionable activity in Vietnam, Cambodia (*see* Kampuchea), and Laos.* Such revelations spurred Congress into belated action, and in July the House and Senate finally agreed on passage of a War Powers Resolution to restrain the president and reassert the authority of Congress over the war-making power, despite the opposition of administration loyalists in Congress and the threat of a presidential veto.

The measure did not apply to the Indochina war, since the president and the Congress had already agreed to a date for cutoff of funds there. But in the future, the bill required that the president must report to Congress within 48 hours if (a) he committed American forces to a foreign conflict, or (b) he "substantially" increased the number of combat troops in a foreign country. Unless Congress approved the president's action within 60 days, the commitment would have to be terminated. However, at the insistence of the Senate, a loophole was inserted allowing the deadline to be extended another 30 days if the president certified that more time was necessary to complete the safe evacuation of American forces. Congress could also order an immediate withdrawal within the 60- or 90-day period by passing a concurrent resolution, which was veto-proof.

President Richard M. Nixon* vetoed the War Powers Resolution, but after nine attempts both House and Senate voted to override the veto on November 7, 1973, and the measure became law.

Sources: *Facts on File*, 1973, pp. 624–625, 928; *United States Code: Congressional and Administrative News*, 93rd Congress, 1st Session, 1973, pp. 2346–2366; *United States Statutes at Large, 1973*, Vol. 87, 1974, pp. 555–559.

Joseph M. Rowe, Jr.

WAR RESISTERS LEAGUE

The War Resisters League (WRL) headquartered at 339 Lafayette Street, New York City, is "a secular pacifist organization that advocates Gandhian nonviolence to create a democratic society without war, racism, sexism and exploitation." Members pledge that "War is a crime against humanity. I therefore am determined not to support any kind of war, international or civil, and to strive for the removal of all the causes of war." WRL publishes a magazine called *The Nonviolent Activist*. WRL is also linked to a wider organization, War Resisters International. Founded in 1923 by Jessie Wallace Hughan as a secular counterpart to the Fellowship of Reconciliation, WRL played an important role in the antidraft, antiwar tax, and anti–Vietnam War protests of the 1960s and 1970s. As early as Lincoln's birthday in 1947, WRL had helped to sponsor demonstrations around the United States in which some 400–500 men destroyed their draft cards or mailed them to President Harry Truman.* Dwight Macdonald spoke on behalf of WRL at the New York rally at which 63 men burned their draft cards. Under attack during the McCarthy era, WRL was supported by such notable figures as Albert Einstein, who wrote in 1953: "The War Resisters League is important because. . . . The existence of such a moral elite is indispensable for the preparation of a fundamental change in public opinion, a change that, under present day circumstances, is absolutely necessary if humanity is to survive." In the late 1950s and early 1960s, WRL actively supported ban-the-bomb demonstrations, civil disobedience against civil defense drills, and black civil rights protests. By 1963, under the leadership of Dave Dellinger* and David McReynolds, WRL focused its protests on the escalation of the Vietnam War and the rise in Selective Service inductions. Dave Dellinger and A. J. Muste* edited *Liberation*, an influential radical magazine initially supported by WRL and published from 1956 to 1975. On May 16, 1964, WRL cosponsored a demonstration in New York City at which twelve men burned their draft* cards. In December 1964, WRL cosponsored the first nationwide demonstration against the Vietnam War. According to WRL, its membership grew from 3,000 to 15,000 between 1964 and 1973. From 1965 through 1983, WRL's Workshop in Nonviolence published a widely read "movement" magazine called *WIN*. WRL was the major organizer of Stop the Draft Week in late 1967 as well as a cosponsor or endorser of many "teach-ins"* and demonstrations, including the May Day demonstrations of 1971. WRL organized draft counseling networks to assist young men who wished to obtain conscientious objector status, refuse registration or induction, or flee into exile. WRL also spearheaded a major campaign to promote refusal of payment of income taxes and of a federal tax on telephone charges levied to raise revenue for the Vietnam War. On April 18, 1974, the Internal Revenue Service (IRS) seized $2,537.43 in taxes not paid by WRL employees during 1969–71. Similar IRS seizures have occurred periodically since then. After the Vietnam War, WRL experienced membership attrition, slipped largely from public view, and turned its attention to such issues as disarmament, amnesty for draft resisters, and U.S. policies in the Middle East and Central America. WRL announced disapproval of the Soviet invasion of Afghanistan in 1979–80 and strongly protested the Israeli invasion of Lebanon in 1982. David McReynolds continues to be the principal figure in WRL.

Sources: Thomas Powers, *Vietnam: The War at Home*, 1984; Pauline Maier, *The Old Revolutionaries*, 1980; Nancy Zaroulis and Gerald Sullivan, *Who Spoke Up? American Protest Against the War in Vietnam 1963–1975*, 1984.

John Kincaid

WARS OF NATIONAL LIBERATION

On January 6, 1961, Soviet Premier Nikita Khrushschev* delivered a speech in Moscow in which he predicted that the world was moving toward socialism and that "wars of national liberation" were the primary vehicle of that movement. Furthermore, he pledged Soviet support for indigenous rebellions to overthrow fascists and capitalists. President John F. Kennedy* interpreted the speech as a formal statement of the Soviet Union's* intention to use surrogate forces to promote its interests rather than direct engagements with the United States. Kennedy saw the Communist movements in Latin America, Africa, and Southeast Asia as part of that large Soviet strategy, and he devised new counterinsurgency* strategies to oppose them. Vietnam became the test case for Kennedy's counterinsurgency program to thwart a war of national liberation.

Sources: Bruce Miroff, *Pragmatic Illusions: The Presidential Politics of John F. Kennedy*, 1976; Bower J. Bell, *The Myth of the Guerrilla*, 1971.

WAR ZONE C

The term "War Zone C" was used by the United States Army* to describe a region near the Cambodian border in III Corps* where Vietcong* activity was particularly strong. War Zone C included portions of Tay Ninh Province, Binh Long Province, and Binh Duong Province.

Sources: Bernard William Rogers, *Cedar Falls–Junction City: A Turning Point*, 1974; Andrew F. Krepinevich, Jr., *The Army and Vietnam*, 1986.

WAR ZONE D   *See* Iron Triangle

"WASTED"

Many people, especially combat soldiers, came to see the entire U.S. effort and the resulting loss of life in Vietnam as a waste. "Wasted," which referred to killing people, evolved from this sentiment. A soldier who killed an enemy soldier in combat might describe the incident in colorful, profane language by saying he "wasted the ————"* (expletive deleted) with his M–16* or M–79.* "Wasted" might also be used to describe the mercy killing of a wounded soldier, either enemy or allied, who was obviously mortally wounded, or the summary execution of a prisoner of war.* However, the term is most frequently associated with what is considered to be an unnecessary killing—the accidental or intentional killing of civilian noncombatants or the killing of another soldier.

Sources: Thomas D. Boettcher, *Vietnam: The Valor and the Sorrow*, 1985; Vietnam Veterans Against the War, *The Winter Soldier Investigation: An Inquiry into American War Crimes*, 1972.

Samuel Freeman

WATER BUFFALO

The water buffalo was the most important domesticated animal in the Vietnamese economy. Throughout all of Vietnam there were more than two million water buffalos, most of which were used as draft animals by Vietnamese farmers.

Source: Danny J. Whitfield, *Historical and Cultural Dictionary of Vietnam*, 1976.

WATERGATE

On June 22, 1972, Washington, D.C., police caught several men attempting to wiretap Democratic Party National Headquarters in the Watergate Building. At their arraignment the next morning, one of the burglars, James McCord, revealed he had worked for the Central Intelligence Agency* and was working for the Richard Nixon* reelection campaign. Under the impact of extraordinary investigative reporting by people like Bob Woodward and Carl Bernstein of the *Washington Post* and Seymour Hersh of the *New York Times* during 1973 and early 1974, as well as a Senate investigating committee, it became clear that the highest officials in the Nixon administration had orchestrated a series of illegal and unethical campaign programs, and that the president himself had ordered a cover-up of the entire affair. Eventually the House Judiciary Committee voted two articles of impeachment against Richard Nixon, on charges of obstructing justice and abuse of power, and the Supreme Court voted 8 to 0 that Nixon turn over key tapes to the Watergate Special Prosecutor, Leon Jaworski. Richard Nixon resigned the presidency on August 9, 1974. The revelations over Watergate totally eliminated the president's credibility as well as his capacity to act directly in matters of foreign policy. United States troops were all out of South Vietnam by the time the Watergate crisis erupted, but the Nixon administration was politically unable to marshal any resources to sustain the Republic of Vietnam* against North Vietnamese attack.

Source: Henry Kissinger, *White House Years*, 1979; Theodore H. White, *Breach of Faith*, 1976.

Charles Dobbs

WEST GERMANY

West Germany, long conceded to be America's strongest ally in Europe next only to Great Britain,* had little to do with Vietnam. Officially, West Germany supported the anti-Communist policy in South Vietnam, but privately German leaders had serious reservations about the American commitment there. More important is the question of the impact of Vietnam on West Germany. American preoccupation with Vietnam drew attention away from Europe, and, by default, West Germany assumed a much more significant role in NATO. There is some evidence that Soviet restraint in Vietnam was tacitly bought by U.S. assurances of keeping West Germany from joint nuclear control over weapons stationed on her soil. The denouement of the war contributed to a decline in American prestige in Europe and to a more independent stance by West European nations. West Germany's increasing trade and political contacts with eastern bloc countries attests to her new independence.

Sources: Viola Herms Drath, ed., *Germany in World Politics*, 1979; Wolfram Hanreider, *The Stable Crisis: Two Decades of German Foreign Policy*, 1970; Terence Prittie, *Willy Brandt: Portrait of a Statesman*, 1974.

Gary M. Bell

WESTMORELAND, WILLIAM CHILDS

William Westmoreland was born on March 26, 1914, in Spartanburg County, South Carolina, to a distinguished family. He entered the United States Military Academy in 1932 and graduated in 1936 as First Captain (the senior cadet in the corps). During World War II Westmoreland served in North Africa, Sicily, France, and Germany, and during the Korean War he commanded the 187th Airborne Infantry Regimental Combat Team. Before his appointment in 1964 as Military Assistance Command, Vietnam* (MACV) commander, Westmoreland had commanded the 101st Airborne Division* and served a stint as superintendent of West Point. He decided to seek a holding action combined with spoiling attacks to prevent a major enemy offensive while the United States constructed the necessary logistical infrastructure to support a larger military force in the south. Later, as that force became larger, Westmoreland turned to a strategy of attrition. He sent United States and ARVN (*see* Army of the Republic of Vietnam) forces on "search and destroy"* missions, sometimes with success, sometimes without, seeking to kill, wound, capture, or cause to desert more enemy troops than the enemy could resupply. With the enormous firepower of the American military, Westmoreland thought his war of attrition* was succeeding by the end of 1967.

The Communist Tet Offensive* of 1968 proved to be Westmoreland's downfall. The massive attack on South Vietnam's urban areas seemingly belied Westmoreland's claims of approaching victory. Although American and ARVN forces
all but annihilated the Vietcong,* the Tet Offensive was a strategic victory for
the Communists because the American public, forced to choose between Westmoreland's positive analysis of the outcome and the media's view of the strength
of the attack, moved decidedly against the war. Creighton Abrams* replaced
Westmoreland as MACV commander in July 1968. After serving as army chief
of staff during the Nixon* administration, Westmoreland retired from active duty
in 1972. He flirted with South Carolina and national politics in the late 1970s,
but the Vietnam War proved to be too much of an albatross.

Westmoreland came back into the American headlines in 1982 when the CBS
News documentary "The Uncounted Enemy: A Vietnam Deception" accused
him of manipulating data on enemy troop strength in 1967 to paint a brighter
picture of the military situation in South Vietnam. In response Westmoreland
filed a libel suit against CBS, but an out-of-court settlement in 1985 ended the
issue without any payments by either party.

Sources: William Westmoreland, *A Soldier Reports*, 1976; David Halberstam, *The
Best and the Brightest*, 1972; Andrew F. Krepinevich, Jr., *The Army in Vietnam*, 1986;
Larry E. Cable, *Conflict of Myths: The Development of American Counterinsurgency
Doctrine and the Vietnam War*, 1986.

                                                                                    Charles Dobbs

WEYAND, FREDERICK CARLTON

Frederick C. Weyand was born on September 15, 1916, in Arbuckle, California. He graduated from the University of California at Berkeley in 1939 and
joined the army, serving in the Burma area during World War II and as an
infantry officer in Korea. In 1966 Weyand took command of the 25th Infantry
Division,* and early in 1967 he became head of II Field Force Vietnam.* Weyand
left Vietnam in 1968, spent some time as a military adviser to the Paris peace
negotiations in 1969, and in 1970 returned to Vietnam as Military Assistance
Command, Vietnam* (MACV) deputy commander. In June 1972 he replaced
General Crieghton Abrams* as MACV commander and presided over the American withdrawal from South Vietnam. Weyand became army chief of staff in
1974 and retired from active duty in 1976.

Sources: Frederick Weyand, "Vietnam Myths and American Military Realities," *Commanders Call*, July/August, 1976; Clark Dougan and David Fulghum, *The Vietnam
Experience: The Fall of the South*, 1985.

WHEELER, EARLE GILMORE

A former chairman of the Joint Chiefs of Staff (*see* Chairman, JCS), Earle
Wheeler was born on January 13, 1908, and after high school decided to attend
West Point, where he graduated in 1932. Between 1932 and 1936 he was the
company officer with the 29th Infantry. He then saw service in Tientsin, China,
from 1937 through 1938. During the first half of World War II, Wheeler trained

new divisions which eventually saw action in the European theater. In 1944 he was reassigned in Europe, where he saw service in logistics. After World War II he was posted to the National War College, and by 1962 was a full general. In that same year he became deputy chief of the U.S. European Command and then army chief of staff. In 1964 Earle Wheeler was appointed chairman of the Joint Chiefs of Staff.

After U.S. warships were attacked in the Gulf of Tonkin in 1964, Wheeler began to press President Lyndon Johnson* for drastic measures. Wheeler was particularly alarmed at the deterioration of the Saigon* regime after Ngo Dinh Diem's* ouster and subsequent assassination. The chairman received reports, from Pentagon and Central Intelligence Agency* officials, which indicated that the collapse of the South Vietnamese regime might result in a complete takeover of Southeast Asia—the domino theory.* By 1965, along with other administration officials, Wheeler was urging direct U.S. intervention in South Vietnam. As the U.S. presence grew in Vietnam, he supported U.S. ground forces engaging the enemy in the field. The chairman had good relations with Congress,* especially Senators John Stennis* and Henry Jackson.

By early 1967, the U.S. commitment to Vietnam had grown to massive proportions. The American public began to sour on the war as casualties mounted. The U.S. media televised in gruesome and realistic detail the ferocity of the war. Congress also began to reassess its commitment to the war, and members of Johnson's administration also questioned their rationale for the continuing involvement in Vietnam. In the summer of 1967, President Johnson held a special meeting to assess the Vietnam War. In that meeting Johnson asked Wheeler when would the United States succeed and what would be the ultimate troop commitment to achieve victory. To both questions Wheeler asked for additional manpower and a call-up of the reserves. Johnson and his White House aides were shocked. While William Westmoreland* portrayed optimism, General Wheeler had presented them with a protracted war with no end in sight. President Johnson decided not to run for reelection and offered overtures for de-escalation.

President Richard Nixon* came into office in 1969 pledged to "peace with honor" in Vietnam. Melvin Laird* with Wheeler began the process of Vietnamization.* General Wheeler, however, believed in slow disengagement to give the South Vietnamese armed forces enough time to adjust to the transition. In 1970 Wheeler successfully lobbied Nixon for incursions of U.S. combat forces into Cambodia (see Kampuchea; Operation Binh Tay) to destroy North Vietnamese sanctuaries.* He told Nixon that if these actions were successful, the South Vietnamese would be able to take over the war faster. In 1970 Wheeler retired and then died in December 1975.

Sources: *Current Biography*, November 1965; Stanley Karnow, *Vietnam: A History*, 1983; *New York Times*, December 19, 1975.

John S. Leiby

WHITE HORSE DIVISION

Throughout the Vietnamese conflict, the South Koreans maintained a substantial commitment in support of the U.S. military effort. The "White Horse

Division'' was the nickname of the Republic of Korea's Ninth Infantry Division. The Ninth was in Vietnam between September 27, 1966, and March 16, 1973, and was headquartered in Ninh Hoa.

Source: Shelby L. Stanton, *Vietnam Order of Battle*, 1981.

WHITE STAR MOBILE TRAINING TEAM

In July 1959, President Dwight D. Eisenhower* authorized the use of United States Special Forces* groups, known as White Star Mobile Training Teams, to help train the Laotian army. Between 1959 and 1962, when they were withdrawn after the negotiated settlement with the Pathet Lao,* they worked with both the Laotian army and Hmong* tribal groups in Laos,* trying to assist them in resisting the guerrilla tactics of the Pathet Lao. At its peak in 1962, the program had more than five hundred American soldiers working in Laos.

Sources: Charles A. Stevenson, *The End of Nowhere: American Policy Toward Laos Since 1954*, 1973; John Prados, *Presidents' Secret Wars: CIA and Pentagon Covert Operations Since World War II*, 1986.

WHY ARE WE IN VIETNAM?

Why Are We in Vietnam? is the title of Norman Mailer's 1967 novel. Although the novel's setting is Texas, New York City, and the Brooks Range of Alaska, it is an antiwar story without ever being directly in Vietnam. A cast of characters—D. J. Jellicoe, Rusty Jellicoe, Alice Lee Jellicoe, Medium Asshole Pete, Medium Asshole Bill, and Tex Hude—end up in the Brooks Range of Alaska on a hunting trip. There, in a pristine and naturally savage environment, they use all the hunting technology they can muster and literally slaughter wolves, caribou, bighorn sheep, and bears. The carnage is extraordinary and, in Norman Mailer's mind, symbolic of what American military technology was doing to the life and habitat of Southeast Asia.

Sources: Norman Mailer, *Why Are We in Vietnam?* 1967; Philip D. Beidler, *American Literature and the Experience of Vietnam*, 1982.

WILD WEASEL

The term "Wild Weasel" referred to a new weapons system for tactical fighter aircraft. "Weasel" was used to describe the system's ability to ferret out and destroy enemy surface-to-air missiles (SAM)* and antiaircraft installations. Usually the "Weasel" was an F–105* equipped with electronic devices capable of tuning in on SAM radar beams. While other aircraft attacked the designated enemy targets, the Wild Weasels went after the SAM and antiaircraft installations.

Sources: Dewey Waddell and Norm Wood, eds., *Air Power-Vietnam*, 1978; William Momyer, *Airpower in Three Wars*, 1978.

WILLIAMS, SAMUEL T.

Lieutenant General Samuel T. Williams was chief of the United States Army Military Assistance and Advisory Group* (MAAG), Vietnam, from October

1955 to August 1960. He enlisted in the Texas National Guard as a private in 1916 and was commissioned a second lieutenant, infantry, in 1917. He served as a platoon and company commander in World War I and was decorated several times for valor. In World War II he commanded an infantry regiment and was an assistant division commander in the Normandy invasion. During the Korean War he commanded the 25th Infantry Division and was deputy commander of a Korean Army Corps. He was commanding general of the Fourth Army at the time of his selection as chief of MAAG, Vietnam.

Known within the Army as "Hanging Sam," Williams was a sharp-tongued commander who demanded strict discipline and maximum effort from his subordinates. His no-nonsense style appealed to Ngo Dinh Diem,* and Williams established a good relationship with the South Vietnamese president. Like most American officers of his generation, he thought in terms of conventional, not guerrilla, warfare. He organized and equipped the South Vietnamese Army to protect the South from invasion from the North and to provide internal security against essentially conventional tactics. Even when Diem's government began to experience increasing attacks by guerrilla forces in 1960, Williams tended to view this insurgency as a diversionary move by the regime's enemies in Hanoi.* He retired in 1960 after forty-three years of active service and lives in San Antonio, Texas, where he continues to speak and write on military topics.

Source: Ronald H. Spector, *Advice and Support: The Early Years, 1941–1960*, 1983.

David L. Anderson

WING

"Wing" is a term describing a unit of up to 500 aircraft in the United States Marine Corps.* It is commanded by a major general. In the United States Air Force* and Navy,* a wing is a smaller organizational institution. A naval air wing is commanded by a captain and consists of approximately seventy-five aircraft, usually in the form of two fighter squadrons,* four attack squadrons, and reconaissance aircraft. An air force wing is under the command of a colonel and consists of three squadrons of twenty-five aircraft each, as well as a wing headquarters and supply and engineering squadrons.

Source: Harry G. Summers, Jr., *Vietnam War Almanac*, 1985.

WINTER SOLDIER INVESTIGATION

Late in 1969, as the revelation of the My Lai* atrocities caused intense public debate over the nature of the war in Vietnam, the Vietnam Veterans Against the War* wanted to make it clear that My Lai was by no means the only example of war crimes. The American public had been conditioned by the brutality of the Nazis and the Japanese during World War II, and the "brainwashing" of the North Koreans, to assume that only other countries committed war crimes. Between January 31 and February 2, 1971, the Vietnam Veterans Against the War convened the "Winter Soldier Investigation" in Detroit, Michigan. For three days 116 veterans testified of war crimes they had either committed or witnessed. There were also panel discussions on weaponry, medical care, prisoners, racism, the ecological devastation of Vietnam, and the psychological effects of the war on American soldiers.

Source: Vietnam Veterans Against the War, *The Winter Soldier Investigation*, 1972.

"WISE OLD MEN"

The term "Wise Old Men" was used in the last days of the Lyndon B. Johnson* administration to describe a group of experienced American diplomats and former public officials who advised the president on the Vietnam War. The group included W. Averell Harriman,* Dean Acheson,* Paul Nitze,* George Kennan,* John McCloy, Robert Lovett, and Charles Bohlen, all of whom had a lifetime of experience in European affairs but knew little about Vietnam. Among some antiwar liberals, the term "Wise Old Men," or "WOMs," was a derisive name for establishment liberals who had caused the war. But early in 1968 they began to turn against the war, and in a dramatic meeting on March 25, 1968, they advised Johnson to end the war. Less than a week later Johnson announced his decision not to seek reelection.

Source: Walter Isaacson and Evan Thomas, *The Wise Men: Six Friends and the World They Made*, 1986.

WITHDRAWAL

In April 1969, just three months after Richard Nixon* took office as president, U.S. troop strength in Vietnam reached its peak of 543,000. He had promised a disengagement from South Vietnam when he was campaigning for president in 1968, and during a visit to Vietnam in July 1969 he ordered General Creighton Abrams,* commander of American military forces, to reduce U.S. casualties and initiate Vietnamization*—turning the war over to South Vietnamese military forces. Abrams then developed a fourteen-stage withdrawal process, designed to begin in August 1969 and end in November 1972. By January 1970 troop strength had dropped to 473,00 as Abrams saw to the removal of U.S. Marines* first and some of the army infantry divisions. Troop levels steadily declined to 404,000 in July 1970, 336,000 in January 1971, 225,000 in July 1971, 133,200 in January 1972, and 45,600 in July 1972. The last of the combat troops, the Third Battalion of the 21st Infantry, left South Vietnam in August 1972. The final withdrawal of all American troops took place in March 1973, except for a handful of soldiers left with the Defense Attaché Office.*

Sources: Shelby L. Stanton, *Vietnam Order of Battle*, 1981; Guenter Lewy, *America in Vietnam*, 1978.

WOMEN, UNITED STATES

More than 7,500 women saw military service in Vietnam between 1965 and 1973. Most of them were army nurses* and medical technicians. One woman was killed in action in Vietnam—army nurse Sharon Lanz, who died in a rocket attack in 1969.

Source: June A. Willenz, *Women Veterans: America's Forgotten Heroines*, 1984.

· X ·

XUAN LOC, BATTLE OF (1975)

By mid-April 1975 nine North Vietnamese Army* (NVA) divisions were bearing down on Saigon* from three directions—from Tay Ninh in the northwest, south along Highway 4, and east along Highway 1 (*see* "Street Without Joy"). Xuan Loc was located 35 miles northeast of Saigon on the road to Bien Hoa* air base. The 341st NVA Division led the attack on Xuan Loc, which was defended by the 18th ARVN Division (*see* Army of the Republic of Vietnam). The fighting was bitter and intense, and the ARVN troops fought well, holding up the assault on Saigon for two weeks. Xuan Loc was reduced to rubble in the struggle, and its population fled in a mass exodus. The North Vietnamese broke through Xuan Loc with Soviet T54 tanks and headed straight toward Bien Hoa, and from there made the southern turn into Saigon at the end of the month. Although defeated at Xuan Loc, ARVN troops in the 18th Division had fought well—the only contingent of ARVN troops to perform well during the 1975 campaign.

Source: Clark Dougan and David Fulghum, *The Vietnam Experience: The Fall of the South*, 1985.

XUAN THUY

Xuan Thuy, a veteran North Vietnamese diplomat, was born in 1912. He was among the earliest of the Vietnamese nationalists, resisting the French Empire through the Vietminh,* being imprisoned and tortured by French officials, but surviving to become the foreign minister of North Vietnam between 1963 and 1965. Between 1968 and 1970, Xuan Thuy headed the North Vietnamese delegation at the Paris peace talks,* always insisting with uncompromising firmness on a unilateral American withdrawal from South Vietnam, recognition of the National Liberation Front (*see* Vietcong) as the legitimate government of South Vietnam, and dissolution of the South Vietnamese government. In 1970 North

Vietnam dispatched Le Duc Tho* to Paris to continue the negotiations with Henry Kissinger,* and Xuan Thuy served as Tho's chief deputy. Xuan Thuy participated in the signing of the peace treaty between the United States and North Vietnam in January 1973. He died on June 18, 1985, in Hanoi.*

Sources: *New York Times*, June 19, 1985; U.S., Central Intelligence Agency, *Who's Who in North Vietnam*, 1969.

• Y •

YANKEE STATION

"Yankee Station" was the place name for the United States Seventh Fleet's* staging area in the South China Sea. After 1966, Task Force 77, the carrier strike group in the Seventh Fleet, used Yankee Station as the reference point for its operations. Yankee Station was located at 17°30′N 108°30′E in the South China Sea.

Source: Harry G. Summers, Jr., *Vietnam War Almanac*, 1985.

YEAR ZERO   *See* Pol Pot

· Z ·

ZHOU ENLAI

A leading figure in the development of the People's Republic of China,* Zhou Enlai was born in China in 1896. He joined the Chinese Communist party in 1921 when he was a student in France, and in 1924 he returned to China and joined Sun Yat-sen's Kuomintang. In 1927 he was appointed director of the military department of the Chinese Communist Central Committee, and later that year he escaped Chiang Kai-shek's* purge of Communists in the Kuomintang. A close associate of Mao Tse-tung,* Enlai became a leading figure in the Chinese Revolution of 1949. Between 1949 and 1958 he served as foreign minister of the People's Republic of China, and between 1949 and his death in 1976 Enlai was also premier. He was a skilled negotiator.

In his approach to the war in Vietnam, Enlai was suspicious about a united Vietnam. For two thousand years China and Vietnam had been engaged in a struggle for power, and Zhou Enlai preferred a Southeast Asia divided into a number of nation-states instead of one dominated by the Vietnamese, whom he considered imperialistic and aggressive. Enlai therefore supported a negotiated settlement of the conflict, even though the Chinese provided military supplies to the Vietminh,* the Vietcong,* and the North Vietnamese Army.* Enlai also wanted to improve Chinese relations with the United States as a way of gaining leverage with the Soviet Union,* and the war in Vietnam complicated that endeavor. When Richard Nixon* began normalizing American relations with China in 1971 and 1972, the North Vietnamese were convinced that the Chinese were out to betray them. Although massive Chinese assistance and a Chinese invasion of North and South Vietnam to fight the United States was an American fear in the 1960s, such a development was unthinkable to Zhou Enlai. He was not that ideologically locked into the Cold War to respond in such rigid ways.

Sources: Henry Kissinger, *White House Years*, 1979; Stanley Karnow, *Vietnam: A History*, 1983; *Webster's New Biographical Dictionary*, 1983; Douglas S. Papp, *Vietnam: The View from Moscow, Peking, Washington*, 1981.

"ZIPPO WAR"

The zippo has long been the lighter of choice for outdoorsmen because of its dependable flame, even under windy conditions, and it was popular for similar reasons among American troops in Vietnam. During search and destroy* missions, soldiers often used their zippo lighters to burn the homes of people in Vietcong*-controlled areas. Television and magazine photographs of American soldiers torching peasant homes with the lighters gave rise to the term "zippo war." On the other hand, the Vietcong frequently booby-trapped zippos by filling them with explosives and leaving them conspicuously in bars or other places frequented by American troops. Thinking another GI had forgotten it, a soldier would pick it up, only to have it explode in his hand when he tried to light it. The term "zippo" was also used to describe a flamethrower, especially the M2A17 portable flamethrower.

Sources: Shelby L. Stanton, *Vietnam Order of Battle*, 1981; Edgar C. Doleman, Jr., *The Vietnam Experience: Tools of War, 1984*.

Samuel Freeman

Appendix A
The Population and Provinces of South Vietnam, 1971

Province	Corps Zone	Area*	Population	Capital City
An Giang	IV	734	605,497	Long Xuyen
An Xuyen	IV	1,941	279,113	Quan Long
Bac Lieu	IV	988	352,230	Bac Lieu City
Ba Xuyen	IV	997	436,668	Khanh Hung
Bien Hoa	III	929	496,638	Bien Hoa City
Binh Dinh	II	3,640	754,150	Qui Nhon
Binh Duong	III	784	257,900	Phu Cuong
Binh Long	III	1,010	42,000	An Loc
Binh Thuan	II	1,930	284,929	Phan Thiet
Binh Tuy	III	1,427	74,315	Ham Tan
Cam Ranh**	II		104,666	
Chau Doc	IV	801	576,818	Chau Doc City
Chuong Thien	IV	884	285,517	Vi Thanh
Danang**	I		437,668	
Dinh Tuong	IV	598	478,586	My Tho
Darlac	II	6,552	244,772	Ban Me Thuot
Gia Dinh	III	552	1,345,425	Gia Dinh City
Go Cong	IV	196	198,088	Go Cong City
Hau Nghia	III	496	234,756	Khiem Cuong

Appendix A: Continued

Province	Corps Zone	Area*	Population	Capital City
Hue**	I		199,893	
Khanh Hoa	II	2,292	250,000	Nha Trang
Kien Giang	IV	2,000	386,094	Rach Gia
Kien Hoa	IV	804	618,870	Truc Giang
Kien Phong	IV	923	497,729	Cao Lanh
Kien Tuong	IV	1,720	519,000	Muc Hoa
Kontum	II	3,930	117,046	Kontum City
Lam Dong	II	2,125	89,106	Bao Loc
Long An	III	632	381,861	Tan An
Long Khanh	III	1,723	161,605	Xuan Loc
My Tho**	IV		100,000	
Nha Trang**	II		194,969	
Ninh Thuan	II	1,324	203,404	Phan Rang
Phong Dinh	IV	616	337,159	Can Tho
Phu Bon	II	1,847	69,765	Cheo Reo
Phuoc Long	III	2,045	47,210	Phuoc Long City
Phuoc Tuy	III	850	124,844	Phuoc Tuy City
Phu Yen	II	2,020	334,184	Tuy Hoa
Pleiku	II	3,260	214,912	Pleiku City
Quang Duc	II	2,300	38,305	Gia Nghia
Quang Nam	I	2,527	575,686	Hoi An
Quang Ngai	I	2,207	731,471	Quang Ngai City
Quang Tin	I	1,876	405,421	Tam Ky
Quang Tri	I	1,583	310,000	Quang Tri City
Qui Nhon**	II		188,717	
Sa Dec	IV	315	316,877	Sa Dec City
Saigon**	III		1,804,880	
Tay Ninh	III	1,515	386,738	Tay Ninh City
Thua Thien	I	1,919	555,514	Hue
Tuyen Duc	II	1,898	116,205	Tung Nghia
Vinh Binh	IV	873	411,190	Phu Vinh
Vinh Long	IV	658	563,282	Vinh Long City
Vung Tau**	III		86,636	

Source: Judith Banister, The Population of Vietnam (Washington, D. C., 1985);
          Danny J. Whitfield, Historical and Cultural Dictionary of Vietnam
          (Metuchen, N. J., 1976); Encyclopedia of the Third World (New York, 1982),
          Volume III: 1929.

*Area in Square Miles.

**Independent Municipality.

Appendix B
The Minority Groups of
South Vietnam, 1970

Group	Culture	Population	Primary Residence
Chinese	Chinese	1,100,000	Cholon and the major cities
Khmer	Cambodian	700,000	Mekong Delta
Jarai	Montagnard	150,000	Pleiku and Phu Bon
Rhade	Montagnard	100,000	Darlac, Phu Bon, Tuyen Duc, and Khanh Hoa
Koho	Montagnard	100,000	Lam Dong and Tuyen Duc
Hre	Montagnard	100,000	Quang Ngai
Bahnar	Montagnard	75,000	Kontum, Pleiku, and Binh Dinh
Roglai	Montagnard	57,000	Khanh Hoa, Ninh Thuan, Binh Thuan, and Binh Tuy
Bru	Montagnard	40,000	Quang Tri
Katu	Montagnard	40,000	Quang Nam and Quang Tin
M'Nong	Montagnard	40,000	Quang Duc
Sedang	Montagnard	40,000	Kontum
Cham	Indian	40,000	Thua Thien
Stieng	Montagnard	30,000	Phuoc Long and Binh Long
Cua	Montagnard	20,000	Quang Ngai and Quang Nam
Chru	Montagnard	15,000	Tuyen Duc
Chrau	Montagnard	15,000	Long Khanh, Binh Tuy, Phuoc Tuy, and Bien Hoa
Pacoh	Montagnard	15,000	Thua Thien
Rengao	Montagnard	15,000	Kontum
Halang	Montagnard	10,000	Kontum
Jeh	Montagnard	10,000	Quang Nam, Quang Tin, and Kontum
Hroy	Montagnard	10,000	Phu Yen and Phu Bon
Duan	Montagnard	3,500	Kontum
Takua	Montagnard	3,000	Quang Nam and Quang Tin
Monom	Montagnard	2,000	Kontum
Strieng	Montagnard	1,000	Kontum

Source: Gerald C. Hickey, Free in the Forest: An Ethnohistory of the Central Highlands, 1954 to 1976, (New Haven, 1982); Minority Rights Group, The Montagnards of South Vietnam (New York, 1973).

Appendix C
Vietnam War Acronyms
and Slang Expressions

AAA: antiaircraft artillery

Abn: airborne (paratrooper or parachutist-qualified)

ACAV: armored cavalry assault vehicle

Admin: administration

Advance Guard Youth: a Vietnamese student organization that became a nationalistic group by World War II

AF: Air Force

AFB: Air Force base

AFLC: Air Force Logistics Command

AFL-CIO: American Federation of Labor and Congress of Industrial Organizations

AG: Adjutant General

Agency: Central Intelligence Agency

Agitprop: agitation propaganda designed to indoctrinate Vietnamese civilians, Vietcong, and NVA with anti-Communist values

AHC: an assault helicopter company

AID: Agency for International Development

Airborne: people or materiel dropped by parachute

Air cav: air cavalry, referring to helicopter-borne infantry

Air mattress: an affectionate nickname for the 3rd Brigade of the 82nd Airborne Division

Airmobile: people or materiel delivered by helicopter

AK: an AK–47 rifle

ALCOA: Aluminum Company of America

All-Afro: another nickname for the 3rd Brigade of the 82nd Airborne Division. The nickname was taken from the AA (officially meaning ''All American'') on the division's shoulder patch

Alpha bravo: slag expression for ambush, taken from the initials AB

AM or AMBL: airmobile

Americal: 23rd Infantry Division

Amtrack: an amphibious vehicle, equipped with armor, used primarily by United States Marines to transport troops and materiel

A-O: area of operations

Ao Dai: long dress worn over black or white baggy pants by Vietnamese women. The Ao Dai is split at the hips, creating a front and back panel. Among men the Ao Dai reaches only the knees, instead of the ankles as it does for women.

Ap: Vietnamese word meaning hamlet

APC: an armored personnel carrier

Ap Doi Moi: ''New Life'' hamlet

ARA: aerial rocket artillery

Arm: armored

Article 15: a nonjudicial punishment handed out by an officer to enlisted personnel

Arty: artillery

ARVN: (Arvin) the South Vietnamese Army (Army of the Republic of Vietnam)

ASAP: (A-sap) as soon as possible; a request for extreme urgency in a military assignment

ASH: assault support helicopter

ATC: air traffic control

A Teams: 12-man Green Beret units

ATFV or ATFG: Australian Task Force, Vietnam

AWC: an aerial weapons company

AWOL: absent without leave

Banh Chunq: a traditional Vietnamese dish prepared for the Tet holidays. It is a cake made from rice, soybeans, and pork, wrapped in banana leaves, and steamed for several hours.

Banh Da: a traditional Vietnamese cookie made from rice paste and sesame seeds. It is either dried or toasted until very crisp.

Banh Duc: a traditional Vietnamese dish of rice flour mixed with a small amount of limestone powder and water. It is a jelled rice after cooling.

Banh Giay: a traditional Vietnamese rice cake usually served on ceremonial occasions

BAR: a Browning automatic rifle

Base area: an area of installations, defensive fortifications, or other physical structures used by the enemy

Baseball: a baseball-shaped grenade about 2 1/2" in diameter

Base Camp: a semipermanent field headquarters and center for a given unit usually within that unit's tactical areas responsibility . A unit may operate in or away from its base camp. Base camps usually contain all or part of a given unit's support elements.

Battalion days in the field: days when battalions were patrolling in the field. It was used to measure a battalion's efficiency.

BC: body count; the number of enemy dead on a given battlefield

BCD: bad conduct discharge

Bde: brigade

Beans: a meal; chow

Beehive: antipersonnel artillery rounds filled with thousands of small metal darts

Believer: a dead soldier, usually the enemy

Berm, berm line: hedgerow or foliated built-up area which divided rice paddies; also, a rise in the ground such as dikes or a dirt parapet around fortifications

Betel nut: a nut Vietnamese chew with lime and tobacco. It has a numbing effect, sometimes causing drool. The chewer frequently spits out a red juice.

B–5 Front: Communist military command operating in Quang Tri and Thua Thien provinces in I Corps

B–40 rocket: a shoulder-held RPG launcher

Big shotgun: a 106mm recoilless rifle using antipersonnel canister ammunition

Big stuff: artillery fire support on air force ordnance

Binh tram: an NVA logistical unit responsible for defense and maintenance for a section of the Ho Chi Minh Trail

Bird: any aircraft, usually helicopters

Bird dog: a light fixed-wing observation aircraft, but in particular the army O–1A or E planes

BK amputee: below-the-knee amputation of the leg

Black Hats: an affectionate term for Pathfinders

Black Magic: nickname for the M16A1 rifle

Bladder: a heavy-duty, rubberized collapsible petroleum drum ranging from 2,000 to 50,000 gallons

Bladder Bird: a C–123 or C–130 aircraft equipped with rubberized collapsible drum and 350-GPM pumps; also called "Cow" or "Flying Cow"

Blade time: used when referring to available helicopter support. Units were generally allocated a specific amount of "blade time" daily for command and control and logistical support.

Blanket Division: an affectionate nickname for the 1st Cavalry Division. The name came from its large shoulder patch.

Blivet: a 250- or 500-gallon rubberized fabric collapsible drum (*see* bladder)

Bloody One: a nickname for the 1st Infantry Division. It came from the red numeral "1" on the division shoulder patch. Also known as the "Big Dead One."

BLT: battalion landing team

Bluper: an M–79 grenade launcher

Bn: battalion

Boat People: refugees fleeing Vietnam by boat after 1975

Bo doi: a uniformed NVA soldier

Body bags: plastic bags used for retrieval of bodies on the battlefield

Booby trap: an explosive charge hidden in a harmless object which explodes on contact

Boondocks, boonies, bush: expressions for the jungle, or any remote area away from a base camp or city; sometimes used to refer to any area in Vietnam

Bring smoke: to direct intense artillery fire or air force ordnance on an enemy position

BS: border surveillance

Bubble: the two-man OH–13 "Sioux" helicopter

Buddy system: placing South Vietnamese units under U.S. sponsorship for training. Also used when an American soldier recently arrived in Vietnam was paired up with an experienced soldier.

Bush: an infantry term for the field or the "boonies"

Bushmasters: any elite unit skilled in jungle operations

bust caps: marine term for rapid firing of an M–16 rifle

Butcher brigade: a derogatory nickname given the 11th Infantry Brigade after the My Lai massacre

C–4: a very stable plastic explosive carried by infantry soldiers

CAG: Combined Action Groups; pacification teams organized by the communists as a base camp. Usually contained fortifications, supply depots, hospitals, and training facilities.

Cambodian Liberation Army: also called Khmer Liberation Army. Communist armed forces of National United Front of Kampuchea (FUNK).

C and C: command and control helicopter used by reconnaissance or unit commanders

C and S: cordon and search. An operation to seal off and search an area or village.

CAP: Capital Division (Republic of Korea). Also, Combined Action Platoons.

Capital Military Zone: Saigon and the immediate surrounding area

Caribou: the CV–2 twin-engine cargo airplane used by the army until turned over to the air force in December 1966

CAS: (Cass) Saigon office of the Central Intelligence Agency

Cat: caterpillar tractor

Caterpillar: an administrative or logistical convoy on a normally secure road

Cav: a nickname for air cavalry

Cbt: combat

CBU: cluster bomb unit

CENTO: Central Treaty Organization

CG: commanding general

Cha Gio: Vietnamese dish of pork, noodles, vegetables, and crab, wrapped in rice paper and deep fried.

Charlie, Charles, Chuck: Vietcong, short for the phonetic representation Victor Charlie.

Charlie rats: army combat rations (C-rations). The term "Charlie" was both the phonetic alphabetization of the "C" in C-rations and signified the enemy or enemy activity.

Cha Tom: Vietnamese dish of sugar cane sticks grilled in a shrimp paste

Che: a sweet dish sold by street vendors in Vietnam. Che is a dessert pudding of beans, noodles, and coconut.

Checkerboard sweep: a specific technique employed dividing a fixed area into blocks, into one of which a ground element is inserted while mechanized/armor elements operate around the periphery to saturate the area and prevent an enemy escape.

Checkmate: a security roadblock

Chem: chemical

Cherry: a new troop replacement

Chicom: (Cheye-com) a term describing a Chinese Communist or weapons manufactured in China

Chickenplate: bulletproof breastplate

Chieu Hoi: (Choo Hoy) "Open arms." Program under which GVN offered amnesty to VC defectors.

Chinh huan: North Vietnamese indoctrination sessions for all Communist party members.

Chinook: the CH–47 cargo helicopter; also called "Shithook" or "Hook"

Chogie, cut, a chogie: to move out quickly. Term brought to Vietnam by soldiers who had served in Korea.

Chopper: helicopter

Chops: chief of operations

CIA: Central Intelligence Agency or simply "The Agency" or "The Company"

CIC: Combat Information Center

CIB: Combat Infantry Badge for actual time in combat

CIDG: (Sidgee) Civilian Irregular Defense Group

CINCPAC: Commander in Chief, Pacific

CIO: Congress of Industrial Organizations

CIP: Counterinsurgency Plan. A 1961 plan calling for additional U.S. aid to support a 20,000-man increase in the ARVN and to train, equip, and supply a 32,000-man addition to South Vietnam's Civil Guard.

Civic action: a combination of MEDCAPS (medical civic action programs), ICAPS (intelligence civic action programs), and other civil affairs activities

Claymore: a popular fan-shaped antipersonnel land mine

CLCV: Clergy and Laity Concerned About Vietnam

Clearance: permission from military and political authorities to engage the enemy in a particular area

Clear and hold: an American military tactic in which U.S. troops captured and then attempted to permanently hold an area

Close air support: air strikes against enemy targets that are close to friendly forces, requiring detailed integration of each air mission with the fire and movement of those forces

Cloverleaf: a patrol technique in which subordinate elements move out from a central area and "loop" back toward the main advance unit's direction starting point. It was used as a technique of advance by units in unknown terrain.

Clutch belt: an ammunition cartridge belt worn by marines

CO: commanding officer

Co: company

Cobra: the AH–1G attack helicopter

Code of Conduct: military rules for U.S. soldiers taken prisoner

Combat sky spot: radar-controlled air strike

Comm: communications

Commo: communications of signal capacity, personnel, or equipment

Concertina barbed wire: coiled barbed wire used as infantry obstacles

Cong: short for Vietcong

Connex: a large metal box used for shipping and storage

Contact: slang expression to describe firing on the NVA or Vietcong or being fired upon by them

CONUS: continental United States

CORDS: Civil Operations and Rural Development Support

CORE: Congress of Racial Equality

Corps: two or more divisions, responsible for the defense of a Military Region

COSMUSMACV: Commander, U.S. Military Assistance Command, Vietnam

COSVN: Central Office of South Vietnam

Cow: C–123 or C–130 aircraft equipped with a rubberized collapsible drum and 350-GPM pumps. Also called "Bladder Bird," "Flying Cow."

COWIN: Conduct of the War in Vietnam. A report commissioned in 1971 by the U.S. Army Deputy Chief of Staff for Military Operations.

CP: command post

C-ration: box of canned food used in military operations

CRB: Cam Ranh Bay

CRID: (Crid) Republic of Korea Capitol Infantry Division. Americans called it the "Tiger" Division.

Crispie critter: enemy soldier killed through burning to death

Crunchies: infantrymen; also, "Ground Pounders" and "Grunts"

CS: Composite Service. Also riot control gas agent, such as a CS-grenade, used widely to clear out enemy tunnel works. Also a type of tear gas.

C's: C-rations or combat rations; canned army meals for field use

CTZ: Corps Tactical Zones (*see* I, II, III, and IV Corps)

Cu Chi National Guard: nickname of the 25th Infantry Division. Its division headquarters and most of its troops were stationed at Cu Chi throughout the war.

CWC: civilian war casualties

Cyclo: a motorized three-wheel passenger vehicle

Daisy Cutter: a 15,000-pound bomb designed to clear helicopter landing zones in heavy jungle areas

DAO: Defense Attaché Office. Part of the U.S. Embassy to South Vietnam, it replaced the Military Assistance Command, Vietnam.

Dead space: an area which cannot be covered by fire or observation due to the nature of the terrain

Deep serious: the worst possible position, such as being nearly overrun

Defcon: defensive contact artillery fire. Usually plotted at night by artillery forward observers "ringing the perimeter with steel."

Delta Tango: phonetic alphabetization of DT, meaning defensive targets

DePuy foxhole: defensive position ensuring interlocking defensive fire named after Major General William E. DePuy, commanding the 1st Infantry Division in Vietnam in 1966

DEROS: (Dee-ros) date eligible for return from overseas; the date a person's tour in Vietnam was estimated to end.

DeSoto: destroyer naval patrols in the South China Sea

Det-cord: detonating cord used for explosives

DIA: Defense Intelligence Agency

Di di mau: move quickly

Dink: a racist reference to enemy forces or Vietnamese civilians

Diome nickel: a 105mm howitzer

Div: division

DMS boot: direct molded-sole jungle boot

DMZ: demilitarized zone

DNG: Da Nang

Doc: affectionate title for enlisted medical aidman

DOD: Department of Defense

Dong: Vietnamese monetary unit; one piaster

Double force: buddy operations combining U.S. and ARVN forces

Doubtfuls: indigenous personnel who cannot be categorized as either Vietcong or civil offenders. It also can mean suspect personnel spotted from ground or aircraft.

Doughnut dollies: Red Cross girls

Doughnut six: chief of Red Cross girls. Six was the customary military number of a commander on any level when using the radio.

Dozer-infantry: team of tank-dozers, bulldozers, Rome plows, and infantry which use jungle-busting techniques in difficult terrain

DRAC: Delta Regional Assistance Command

The Drag: squad behind the main maneuver element to ensure rear safety

Dragon Ship: AC–47 aircraft fitted out with Gatling-type machine guns. Also called "Puff," "Puff the Magic Dragon," and "Spooky."

Drum: metal container for fuel

DRV: Democratic Republic of Vietnam

Dua Dam: Vietnamese funeral procession—complete with altar, horse-drawn hearse and coffin, and marchers bearing wreaths, banners, and flags

Dud: any explosive that fails to detonate when activated

Duster: a nickname for the M42 tracked vehicle mounting twin 40mm antiaircraft guns used as ground support

Dustoff: a nickname for a medical evacuation helicopter or mission

DX: direct exchange of equipment for repair and replacement

DZ: drop zone in airborne operations

Eagle flights: large air assault of helicopters

ECM: electronic countermeasures, such as jamming and deception

EDT: Eastern Daylight Time

Electric Strawberry: a nickname for the 25th Infantry Division because of the division's shoulder patch representation of "Tropic Lightning"

Elephant grass: tall, sharp-edged grass found in the highlands of Vietnam

EM: enlisted man

En: engineer

ENGR CMD/COM: Engineer Command

ENI: enemy-initiated incident

E-Nine, E–9: a sergeant major, the highest enlisted rank

Errand boy: daily scheduled courier flight; also called Pony Express

Escort: armed helicopter escort

ETS: date of departure from overseas duty station

Extraction: voluntary or involuntary withdrawal by air of troops from any operational area via helicopter

FAC: (Fack) Forward air controller

FAE: fuel air explosive

FAL-FAR: pro-U.S. Royal Armed Forces of Laos

FANK: Forces Armées Nationales Khmeres

fatigues: standard combat uniform, green in color

Fatikees: nickname for jungle fatigues

FBI: Federal Bureau of Investigation

FEC: French Expeditionary Corps

FFV: Field Force, Vietnam

Field of fire: area that a weapon or group of weapons can cover effectively with fire from a given position

Fireballing: concentration of large amounts of artillery fire in an area

Fire base: temporary artillery firing position often secured by infantry

Firefight: exchange of small arms fire between opposing units

Firefly: helicopter team consisting of one helicopter equipped with a searchlight or arc lamps and two gunships

Fire support base: a semifixed artillery base established to increase fire coverage of an area and provide security for the firing unit

I Corps: northernmost military region in South Vietnam

Flack jacket: heavy fiberglass-filled vest worn for protection from shrapnel

Flare: illumination projectile; hand-fired or shot from artillery, mortars, or air

Flare ship: any aircraft used primarily to drop illumination flares

Flower power: nickname for the 9th Infantry Division. It came from the Octofoil design on the division shoulder patch.

Flying Cow: C–123 or C–130 aircraft equipped with rubberized collapsible drum and 350-GPM pump. Also called Cow, Bladder Bird.

Flying Crane: the CH–54 heavy helicopter

FMFPAC: Fleet Marine Force, Pacific Command

FNG: most common name for newly arrived person in Vietnam. It was literally translated as a ''Fuckin' new guy.''

FOB: forward operating base. A combined command post and logistical base established in the field, usually by a battalion but also widely used by Special Forces.

Foo-gas: *see* Phougas

FOR: Fellowship of Reconciliation

Forest penetrator: device lowered and raised by cable from a helicopter and used for extracting a person from heavy jungle

Forward support area: a fixed or semifixed area utilized as a forward logistical base.

Four Corners: the town of Di An, where the 1st Infantry Division was stationed. It also came to mean any small town near a U.S. military base.

IV Corps: the southernmost military region in South Vietnam, located in the Mekong Delta

FPJMC: four-party joint military commission

FPJMT: four-party joint military team

Frag: to kill or attempt to kill one's own officers or sergeants, usually with a fragmentation grenade; also the common term for any grenade

Freak: short term used for radio frequency

Free fire zone: any area in which permission was not required prior to firing on targets

FRI: (Fry) friendly initiated incident

FSB: fire support base. Semipermanent base established to provide artillery support for allied units operating within range of the base.

FTA: Free the Army

FULRO: United Front for the Struggle of Oppressed Races; resistance organization in the highlands of Vietnam made up of Montagnards, Cham, and ethnic Khmer. FULRO continues to fight against the Communist government.

FUNK: National United Front of Kampuchea. Popular front established in 1970 and nominally headed by Prince Norodom Sihanouk, dedicated to the overthrow of the Lon Nol government in Phnom Penh.

Funky Fourth: a nickname of the 4th Infantry Division

FWMAF: Free World Military Assistant Forces. The term referred to allies of South Vietnam.

GAO: General Accounting Office

Ghost: take off; take it easy in a unit; do nothing; being absent; shirking duty

Ghost time: free time off duty

Go-go ship: an armed CH–47 helicopter

Gom dan: ''gathering'' or ''herding in.'' Term used by Vietnamese Communists to describe resettlement of rural villagers in cities and GVN-sponsored refugee camps.

Gooks: slang expression brought to Vietnam by Korean War veterans. The term refers to anyone of Asian origin.

Gooney bird: nickname for the C–47 aircraft

GOP: Grand Old Party (Republican)

GPM: gallons per minute

Gravel: type of mine

Green: used to signify "safe," such as a Green LZ (safe landing zone)

Green Berets: members of Special Forces of the U.S. Army. They were awarded the green beret headgear as a mark of distinction.

Ground Pounder: infantryman

Grunt: a popular nickname for an infantryman in Vietnam; supposedly derived from sound one made when lifting up his rucksack

Guerrilla: soldiers of a resistance movement who are organized on a military or paramilitary basis.

Guerrilla warfare: military operations conducted in enemy-held or hostile territory by irregular, predominantly indigenous forces

Gung ho: very enthusiastic and committed

Gun jeep or truck: armored vehicle equipped with machine guns.

Gunney: marine gunnery sergeant

Gunship: an armed helicopter or adapted fixed-wing aircraft

GVN: Government of South Vietnam

Gypsy operation: frequent displacement of small unit bases

Ha: HAWK missile

Hamlet: a small rural village

Hammer and anvil: an infantry tactic of surrounding an enemy base area, then sending in other units to drive the enemy out of hiding

Hanoi Hilton: nickname American prisoners of war used to describe the Hoa Loa Prison in Hanoi

Hardspot: ambush by a tank element

Hasty defense: defense normally organized while in contact with the enemy

Hawks: nickname for the battalion reconnaissance platoon

HE: high explosive, such as HE artillery rounds

He: Hercules missile

Heavy arty: B–52 bombing strikes

Heavy gun team: three armed helicopters operating together

Heavy stuff: heavy artillery such as 8-inch or 175mm cannon, but also meaning fire support from the battleship *New Jersey*

Hedgehogs: isolated outposts in which the French high command concentrated troops

Heliborne: aloft in a helicopter

Helix: air force spotter

The Herd: nickname of the 173rd Airborne Brigade, the first major combat unit sent into Vietnam

Herringbone: tactical formation for mechanized and armor units during halts (or during ambush), when the unit is moving in column. The armored vehicles turn alternately to the sides of the road to orient their main armament and heaviest armor obliquely to the flanks.

HES: Hamlet Evaluation System

HH: heavy helicopter

H & I: harassing and interdictory fire by artillery

High angle hell: mortar fire

High points: CIA and MACV term for brief periods (usually about three days) of intense enemy activity, such as attacks against population centers or military posts

HJ: Honest John missile

Hmong: a dominant Laotian hill tribe. Most of them opposed the North Vietnamese and Pathet Lao.

Hog flight: helicopter(s) mounting the 40mm cannon M5 nose-mounted armament for direct-fire weapon support

Hoi Chanh: one who joined the Chieu Hoi program

Honcho: individual in charge; also meaning to supervise

Hook: nickname for the CH–47 Chinook helicopter

Hootch: house or living quarters or a native hut

Hop Tac: Vietnamese for "cooperation." Name of unsuccessful pacification program begun in 1964, concentrated in one seven-province area around Saigon.

Horse pill: the antimalaria tablet taken weekly by U.S. personnel in Vietnam

Hot: dangerous, such as Hot LZ (where aircraft are receiving enemy fire)

Hotel Alpha: phonetic alphabetization of HA meaning "haul ass," move out immediately

Hotel Echo: phonetic alphabetization of HE, high-explosive artillery or mortar rounds

Hot Pursuit: policy allowing American military to chase Vietcong and NVA soldiers across the border into Cambodia

HP: horsepower

HQ: headquarters

Huey: nickname for the UH-series helicopters

Hug: close with the enemy or to be pinned down in close quarters with the enemy

Hump: rotation of 25 percent or more of a unit within a thirty-day period; also called "rotational hump." It also meant to carry or march.

ICC: International Control Commission

ICCS: International Commission of Control and Supervision

ICP: Indochinese Communist Party

ICSC: International Commission for Supervision and Control

IDA: Institute for Defense Analysis

Illum: to illuminate, as with flares or searchlights

Incoming: receiving enemy mortar or rocket fire

in country: Vietnam

Indirect fire: bombardment by mortars or artillery in which shells travel to an unseen target

Infusion: program for transfer of personnel within or between commands to reduce rotational hump

In, Inf: infantry

Insertion: secret helicopter placement of combat troops in an operational area

Intelligence & Interdiction (I & I): night artillery to disturb enemy sleep, curtail their movement, and weaken their morale

In the field: any forward combat area or any area outside of a town or base camp

Irregulars: armed individuals and groups not members of the regular armed forces, police, or other internal security forces

IRS: Internal Revenue Service
ITR: Infantry Training Regiment

Jacob's Ladder: a rope ladder dropped by a Chinook helicopter and used to climb down through difficult foilage or onto rough terrain
JCS: Joint Chiefs of Staff
JGS: Joint General Staff, South Vietnamese counterpart of the JCS
JMC: Joint Military Commission. Consisted of representatives of the DRV, the PRG, the U.S., and the RVN. It was to ensure that the concerned parties implemented and abided by the Paris agreement.
JMT: four-party Joint Military Team. Established in 1973; consisted of representatives of the DRV, the PRG (Provisional Government of South Vietnam), the U.S., and the RVN. It was to account for prisoners and MIAs on all sides.
Jolly Green Giant: heavily armed air force C–47 aircraft supporting troops or an air force HH–53 heavy rescue helicopter
Jumping Junkies: derogatory nickname for paratroopers or parachutist-qualified troops
Jungle-busting: use of a tank or armored vehicle to cut trails through the jungle or other heavy vegetation
JUSPAO: Joint United States Public Affairs Office

Kalishnikov: AK–47 rifle
K-bar: combat knife
Keystone, Keystoning: Operation Keystone was the code word for the incremental process in which the United States Army withdrew from Vietnam. These were divided into Keystone Eagle, Cardinal, Bluejay, Robin, Oriole, Mallard, Owl, etc., and spanned the period July 1969–November 1972.
K-Fifty: Chinese Communist 7.62mm submachine gun
KHA: Killed in Hostile Action. Since the United States was not engaged in a "declared war," the use of the official term "KIA (Killed in Action)" was not authorized by Department of Defense. KIA came to mean enemy dead
Khmer Rouge: "Red Khmers." The forces of the Cambodian Communist party
KIA: killed in action
Killer team: marine mobile ambush team
Kit Carson Scout: an ex-VC/NVA soldier employed by U.S. units as a scout
KKK: Khmer Kampuchea Kron, a pro-U.S. Cambodian exile group
Klick: short for kilometer
KP: kitchen police
KPNLF: Khmer People's National Liberation Front; the major non-Communist Cambodian political and resistance organization fighting against Vietnamese occupation forces

Laager: positioning of helicopters in a secure forward area so that weapons systems may be used in defense. Also, all-around night-defensive position established by mechanized vehicles
Land tail: that part of an air-transported unit not committed to combat by air but which joins the unit via land movement
Lao Dong party: Vietnam Worker's party, Marxist-Leninist party of North Vietnam
LAPE: low altitude parachute extraction
LAW: (Law) M72 light antitank weapon. A shoulder-fired, 66mm rocket with a one-time disposable fiberglass launcher.

LBJ Ranch: (L-B-J) the Long Binh Stockade. The last word was changed to make a pun on the initials of President Lyndon Baines Johnson.

LCM: mechanized landing craft used in harbors and inland waterways

Lifer: career soldier

Lift: a single helicopter trip carrying cargo from a loading area to a landing zone

Light at the End of the Tunnel: term describing the imminent demise of the Vietcong and North Vietnamese

Lightning bug: helicopter equipped with searchlights; also called ''firefly''

Limited conventional war: U.S. Department of Defense designation for conflict involving American units larger than four thousand men. Used by Pentagon to reclassify Vietnam War from a guerrilla war.

The Line: being on duty with an infantry unit in the field

Line Haul: long-distance military truck convoys; also called Long Haul

Little Appalachia: nickname for the headquarters of the 1st Infantry Division; derived from the poor living conditions in some parts of the Appalachian Mountains in the United States

LJ: Little John missile

Local force: Vietcong combat unit subordinate to a district or province headquarters

Log bird: logistical resupply helicopter

Log run: aerial logistical resupply mission

LOH: (Loach) light observation helicopter, notably the OH–6A

Long green line: column of infantry advancing through jungle terrain

LORAPL: Long Range Planning Task Group. Created in July 1968 by General Abrams to review U.S. strategy in Vietnam over the previous four years and recommend changes. Headed by Lieutenant Colonel Dr. Donald S. Marshall.

LP: listening post forward off a defensive perimeter

LRP or LRRP: (Lurp) long-range reconnaissance patrol

LST: troop-landing ship

Lt.: Lieutenant

LTG: Lieutenant General

Luc Luong Dac Biet: (LLDB) South Vietnamese Special Forces

Lurps: long-range reconnaissance patrol members. Also, an experimental lightweight food packet consisting of a dehydrated meal and named after the soldiers it was most often issued to.

LZ: landing zone

MAAG: Military Assistance and Advisory Group

MAB: Marine Amphibious Brigade

MAC: Military Airlift Command

MACOI: MACV Office of Information

MAC-SOG: Military Assistance Command Studies and Observation Group

MACV: (Mac-vee) Military Assistance Command, Vietnam

Mad minute: concentrated fire of all weapons for a brief period of time at maximum rate; also called ''Mike-mike''

MAF: Marine Amphibious Force

Main Force: Vietcong and North Vietnamese military units

Maj.: Major

Mama-san: mature Vietnamese woman

marching fire: fire delivered by infantry in an assault, especially with automatic rifles and machine guns fired from the hip or rapidly firing rifles from the shoulder while advancing

MAT: Mobile Advisory Team. Usually a six-member team of two U.S. Army officers, three enlisted men, and an interpreter responsible for training territorial forces (RF and PF).

Mat Tran: the National Liberation Front

Maverick: a government vehicle stolen

MASH: Mobile Army Surgical Hospital

MCRD: Marine Corps Recruit Depots

MEB: Marine Expeditionary Brigade

Mech: mechanized infantry

MEDCAP: (Med-cap) Medical Civil Action Program

Medevac: medical evacuation by helicopter; also called ''Dustoff''

Meeting engagement: collision between two advancing forces, neither of which is fully deployed for battle

M–14: rifle used in early portion of Vietnam conflict

MG: machine gun

MGF: mobile guerrilla force, composed of highly trained indigenous personnel commanded by U.S. Special Forces, who operated as a guerrilla force in Vietcong-controlled areas.

MIA: Missing in Action

MiG: Soviet fighter plane

Mighty Mite: blower used to force smoke and tear gas throughout tunnel systems

Mike Force, MSF: Special Forces Mobile Strike Force; composed of indigenous personnel and used as a reaction or reinforcing unit

Mission: an operational flight by several aircraft; also the embassy or legation

Mission Council: organized by U.S. Ambassador Maxwell Taylor, it met weekly to coordinate activities among all U.S. agencies in Vietnam. After Henry Cabot Lodge replaced Taylor, OCO (later CORDS) oversaw the Mission Council.

Mission ready: any equipment, but especially helicopters, completely capable of performing assigned missions

MIT: Massachusetts Institute of Technology

M–1: World War I–vintage American rifle

Moonshine: a flare-carrying aircraft

Mort: mortar

MP: Military Police

Mpc: military pay certificates, used instead of American currency in war zones to discourage black marketeering

mph: miles per hour

MR: Military Region

MSFC: Mobile Strike Force Command

M–16: the standard American rifle used in Vietnam after 1966

M–60: American-made machine gun

M–79: single-barreled grenade launcher used by infantry

MSU Advisory Group: Michigan State University team

Mxd: mixed artillery of 105mm/155mm types

Napalm: incendiary used in Vietnam by French and Americans both as defoliant and
    antipersonnel weapon

Nap-of-the-earth: flight as close to the earth's surface as terrain will permit

NASA: National Aeronautics and Space Administration

National Council of Reconciliation and Concord: institution provided for by the Paris
    agreement to promote implementation of the agreement, ensure democratic liberties,
    and organize elections

National Revolutionary Movement: Diem's followers, dominated by his brothers Nhu and
    Can

Native sport: hunting for Vietcong

NATO: North Atlantic Treaty Organization

NCC: National Coordinating Committee to End the War in Vietnam

NCO: noncommissioned officer, usually a squad leader or platoon sergeant

NDP: night defensive position

Nem: traditional Vietnamese dish in which ground pork is mixed with powdered rice and
    packed as a sausage into banana leaves

Neutralize: to render an enemy force, installation, or operation ineffective by military
    action

New Mobe: the New Mobilization Committee to End the War

Next: soldier due for rotation to United States in a few days; also "Short"

NG: National Guard

NH: Nike-Hercules missile

NLF: National Liberation Front, officially the National Front for the Liberation of the
    South

No-doze mission: airborne broadcast of psychological operations tapes of appeals, music,
    and propaganda during the hours of darkness

No Fire Zone: an area in which any use of military fire must be cleared by the appropriate
    authority

Non: the ubiquitous conical hat worn by men and women in Vietnam. Usually it is made
    from latania leaves.

NORS: (Nors) not operationally ready—reason, support

No sweat: with little effort or no trouble

NSA: National Security Agency. An intelligence-gathering agency established in 1952,
    NSA is responsible to the executive branch and specializes in code breaking and
    electronic surveillance.

NSC: National Security Council. Responsible for developing defense strategies for the
    United States. Situated in the White House, it exerts general direction over the CIA.

Number One: the best, prime

Number Sixty: the M60 machine gun

Number Ten: the worst. "Number ten-thou" meant the very worst.

Nungs: Chinese tribal troops from the Highlands of North Vietnam. They provided special
    troops to the U.S. Special Forces.

Nuoc-mam: a pungent Vietnamese concentrated fish-sauce used to flavor rice

NVA: North Vietnamese Army

NZ: New Zealand

OCO: Office of Civilian Operations. Created to have command responsibility over all
    civilian agencies operating in Vietnam, forming in effect a pacification high com-

mand, under jurisdiction of the U.S. Embassy. Transformed into CORDS in 1967. (*See also* CORDS.)

OCS: Officers' Candidate School

One-buck: code designation for units held in readiness in the United States for deployment in Vietnam on 48-hour notice

One-oh-worst: derisive nickname for the 101st Airborne Division (Airmobile) based on its numerical designation

On station: armed helicopter flight in position to support a ground commander

Ontos vehicle: lightly armored tracked vehicle equipped with six mounted 106mm recoilless rifles. In the Vietnam War it was used primarily to support infantry.

OPLAN: Operations Plan

Option IV: U.S. military plan for helicopter evacuation from Saigon

Ord: ordnance

OSS: Office of Strategic Services. Created in 1942, the OSS was an intelligence-gathering operation which became a forerunner of the CIA.

Out-country: the Southeast Asian conflict outside South Vietnam (i.e., Laos and North Vietnam, sometimes Thailand, Cambodia, and China)

PACAP: Pacific Air Force

P's: piasters, the Vietnamese monetary unit

P–38: can opener for canned C-rations

Pacification: several programs of the South Vietnamese and U.S. governments to destroy the Vietcong in the villages, gain civilian support for the GVN, and stabilize the countryside

PACOM: Pacific Command

Pathet Lao: the Laotian Communists, who from their inception have been under the control of the Vietnamese Communist party

PAVN: (Pavin) People's Army of Vietnam. The North Vietnamese Army; also known as the NVA

PE: Pershing missile

Peers Inquiry: *Report of the Department of the Army Review of the Preliminary Investigation into the My Lai Incident*, May 14, 1970. The inquiry was directed by Lt. Gen. W. R. Peers.

Penny nickel nickel: a 155mm howitzer

Pentagon East: the Military Assistance Command, Vietnam headquarters complex at Tan Son Nhut Air Base

Perim: perimeter surrounding a fire base or position or even base camp

PF: Popular Forces

PFC: Private First Class

Phougas: drums of jellied gasoline fired defensively as a fixed-fire weapon; also spelled ''foo-gas''

Piaster: South Vietnamese currency

Piss tube: a mortar

PLA: People's Liberation Army

Platoon: approximately forty-five men belonging to a company

Pods: rubberized 500-gallon containers

Point man: lead soldier in a unit cutting a path through dense vegetation if needed and constantly exposed to the danger of tripping bobby traps or being the first in contact with the enemy

Poison Ivy: nickname for the 4th Infantry Division. The name came from the design of its shoulder patch and its official designation as the Ivy Division.

poncho liner: nylon insert to the military rain poncho, used as a blanket

Pony Soldiers: members of a long range-patrol or any soldier in the 1st Cavalry Division

POW: prisoner of war

Prep: preparation or prestrike by air force, artillery, or armed helicopter fire placed on an LZ or objective prior to attack or landing

PRGVN: Provisional Revolutionary Government of South Vietnam

Prick: nickname for the PRC–25 lightweight infantry field radio

Province chief: governor of a state-sized administrative territory in South Vietnam, usually a high-ranking military officer

PRP: People's Revolutionary party; Communist party that dominated the NLF. Founded on January 15, 1962, as the successor to the Lao Dong party in South Vietnam.

PSDF: People's Self-Defense Fund

Psychedelic Cookie: nickname for the 9th Infantry Division derived from the Octofoil design of its shoulder patch

Psyops: psychological operations; planned use of propaganda to influence enemy thinking

Psywar: psychological warfare

PTSD: post-traumatic stress disorder

Puff the Magic Dragon, Puff: a C–47 up-gunned air force support aircraft; also called "dragon ship"

Puking Buzzards: derisive term for the 101st Airborne Division gleaned from the design of the screaming eagle on its shoulder patch

Punji stake: razor-sharp bamboo stake sometimes coated with poison or feces and usually hidden under water, along trails, at ambush sites, or in deep pits

Purple-out zone: emergency evacuation

PX: post exchange

PZ: pickup zone for helicopter loading, troop assembly, and troop extraction

QM: Quartermaster

QNH: Qui Nhon

quad–60: four 60-caliber machine guns mounted as one unit

Rabbits: white American soldiers, according to black vernacular

Rallier: an individual who voluntarily surrenders to the South Vietnamese

Ramp alert: fully armed aircraft on the ground at a base or forward strip ready for takeoff in about fifteen mintues

R & R: rest-and-recreation vacation taken during a one-year duty tour in Vietnam. Out-of-country R & R was at Bangkok, Hawaii, Tokyo, Australia, Hong Kong, Manila, Penang, Taipei, Kuala Lampur, or Singapore. In-country R & R locations were at Vung Tau or China Beach.

RD: Revolutionary Development

RD cadres: Revolutionary Development cadres; South Vietnamese who were trained to use Vietcong political tactics to carry out GVN pacification

React: for one unit to come to the aid of another under enemy fire

Recon: reconnaissance

Recon-by-fire: a method of reconnaissance in which fire is placed on suspected enemy positions to cause the enemy to disclose his presence by movement or return fire

Red haze: reconnaissance flight to detect heat emissions from the ground

Redleg: nickname for an artilleryman

Red LZ: landing zone under hostile fire. *See also* Hot.

Reeducation camps: political prisons and labor camps of varying degrees of severity throughout Vietnam

Rehab: rehabilitate or recuperate

REMF: Rear Area Mother Fucker. Nickname given to men serving in the rear by front-line soldiers.

Retrograde: any movement, voluntary or involuntary, to the rear

Rev-dev: troop nickname for revolutionary development programs

RF/PF: Regional and Popular Forces of South Vietnam; also known as "Ruff-Puffs"

RLT: regimental landing team

Roadrunner: road-clearing operation with mission of catching local guerrillas by surprise; also, a Special Forces trail-watch team

Rock 'n' roll: to put an M16A1 rifle on full automatic fire

Rocket belt: encircling zone around friendly locality from which enemy large-caliber (122mm, 140mm, etc.) rocket attacks could be launched

ROKs: (Rocks) Republic of Korea soldiers and marines

Rome plow: specially mounted bulldozer blade used in forest or jungle clearing and heavy-duty land clearing

RON: (Ron) Remain overnight position. Known also as "NL" for night location.

Rotate: to return to the United States at the end of a tour of duty in Vietnam

ROTC: Reserve Officers' Training Corps

Round Eye: slang term used by American soldiers to describe another American or an individual of European descent

RPG: Russian-manufactured antitank grenade launcher: also, rocket-propelled grenade.

RR: either recoilless rifle or radio relay

RTO: radio telephone operator who carried the "lightweight" infantry field radio

Ruck, Rucksack: backpack issued to infantry in Vietnam

Ruff-Puffs: South Vietnamese Regional Forces and Popular Forces (RF/PF); paramilitary forces usually of squad or platoon size recruited and utilized within a hamlet, village, or district

RVN: Republic of Vietnam (South Vietnam)

RVNAF: Republic of Vietnam Armed Forces

SAC: Strategic Air Command

Saigon tea: an "alcoholic" beverage consisting primarily of Coca-Cola

Saigon warrior: derisive term for troops stationed in Saigon

SALT: Strategic Arms Limitation Treaty

Salty dog: a "battle loss item" lost as a result of enemy action.

SAM: Soviet-made surface-to-air missile

Sampan: a Vietnamese peasant's boat

SANE: Committee for a Sane Nuclear Policy. Moderate American disarmament group active in the 1960s.

sanitize: a euphemism for assassination which became widely used in conjunction with the CIA's Phoenix Program.

Sappers: North Vietnamese Army or Vietcong demolition commandos

SAR: search and rescue

SAS: Students Afro-American Society

SA–2: a Russian-built surface-to-air missile with an effective altitude of 59,000 feet and a speed of Mach 2.5

Scared Horse: nickname for the 11th Armored Cavalry Regiment, derived from the design on its shoulder patch displaying a rearing horse

Science Fiction: nickname for the U.S. Army Special Forces

Scoutships: OH–13 or OH–23 helicopters used for surveillance or reconnaissance

Screaming Chickens: nickname for the 101st Airborne Division derived from the eagle emblem of the divisional shoulder patch as well as a disparagement of the division motto ''Screaming Eagles''

SDS: Students for a Democratic Society. Founded in 1962, SDS became the largest radical student organization in the country, focusing its energies on community organization of the poor and opposition to the Vietnam War.

Seabees: naval construction engineers. Derived from C.B.—navy construction battalion.

SEAIR: Southeast Asian Airlift

SEAL: navy special-warfare force members

Seal bins: 500-gallon rubberized containers

SEALORDS: South East Asian Lake Ocean River Delta Strategy

Search and clear: offensive military operations to sweep through areas to locate and attack the enemy

Search and destroy: offensive operations designed to find and destroy enemy forces rather than establish permanent government control; also called ''Zippo missions.''

SEATO: Southeast Asia Treaty Organization

II Corps: Central Highlands military region in South Vietnam

Seventeenth parallel: temporary division line between North and South Vietnam established by the Geneva Accords of 1954

70th Corps: NVA military command activated in 1970 to control defense of base areas in Laos

SF: U.S. Army Special Forces; also called ''Green Berets''

SHP: shaft horsepower

SG: Sergeant missile

Shadow: AC–119 with three miniguns used for aerial fire support

Shake 'n' bake: sergeant who earned his rank quickly through NCO schools or other means with less than the normal amount of time in service

Shit burning: the sanitization of latrines by kerosene incineration of excrement

Short, short-time: individual with little time remaining in Vietnam

Short rounds: rounds of ammunition or bombs falling short of the target. Also the inadvertent or accidental delivery of ordnance to friendly forces or civilians.

Shotgun, shotgunner: armed guard on or in a vehicle who watches for enemy activity and returns fire if attacked. Also a door gunner on a helicopter.

Skycrane: huge double-engine helicopter used for lifting and transporting heavy equipment

Slapflare: a cylindrical, hand-held flare

Slick: helicopter used to lift troops or cargo with only protective armaments systems

Smokey Bear: C–47 aircraft used to drop illuminating flares or a helicopter-mounted smoke generator

SNCC: Student Non-Violent Coordinating Committee

Sneaky Petes: U.S. Army Special Forces or Rangers

Snoop 'n' poop: marine search and destroy offensive mission

SOG: Studies and Observations Group

Sortie: one aircraft making one takeoff and landing to conduct the mission for which it was scheduled

Spec. 4: Specialist 4th Class, army rank similar to corporal

Special Forces: U.S. soldiers, popularly known as Green Berets, trained in techniques of guerrilla warfare

Special operations: military operations requiring specialized or elite forces

Spectre: AC–130 equipped with Vulcan machine guns and 105mm howitzer

Sperm: marine light observation helicopter

Spider hole: Vietcong guerrilla foxhole

Spook: civilian intelligence agent

Spooky: AC–47 aircraft with Gatling guns and illumination flares

SP pack: cellophane packet containing toiletries and cigarettes issued to soldiers in the field

Spray: to open fire, usually on automatic

SRV: Socialist Republic of Vietnam

Stand-down: period of rest and refitting in which all operational activity, except for security, is stopped

Starlight: night reconnaissance or surveillance mission employing a light-intensifier scope

Starlight scope: an image intensifier using reflected light from the stars or moon to identify targets

State: U.S. Department of State

Stopper: support fire immediately available to impede enemy movement across a defensive line or area

Strac: ready in the best possible condition. Derived from STRAC (Strategic Army Command, where units were kept at peak readiness in the United States itself).

Strip alert: fully armed aircraft at a base or forward strip ready to take off within five minutes

Sugar reports: mail from home or specifically from a girlfriend

Surv: surveillance aircraft

TAC: Tactical Air Command

Tac air: tactical air support

Tail-end Charlie: the last man in a given file

Talk-quick: a secure voice communications system

Talon Vise: original name of the military contingency for the U.S. evacuation of Saigon; *see* Operation Frequent Wind

Tank farm: group of storage tanks

TAOR: tactical area of operational responsibility

Terminate with Extreme Prejudice: a CIA euphemism for assassination

Tet: Vietnamese Lunar New Year holiday period

III Corps: military region between Saigon and the Highlands

III MAF: III Marine Amphibious Force

Thump-gun: nickname for the M–79 40mm grenade launcher, a popular squad weapon

Thunder run: movement of armored columns up and down a road or trail with the vehicles firing alternately to each side

Tiger cages: term describing cells at the Con Son Correction Center on Con Son Island

Tigers: battalion patrol and ambush element

Tiger suits: striped camouflage jungle fatigues

Tonkin: northern section of Vietnam

Top: First Sergeant of a company; also known as the First Shirt

TOT: time on target; an artillery term meaning artillery rounds from different batteries dropped onto a target simultaneously

Track: slang expression for an APC

Tri-Thien Front: North Vietnamese military region comprising Quang Tri and Thua Thien provinces. Unlike other Communist military districts in South Vietnam, it was controlled directly by North Vietnam and not indirectly through COSVN.

Truong Son Corridor: supply lines paralleling the Ho Chi Minh Trail but located within South Vietnam

Tunnel rat: a U.S. soldier who searched enemy tunnel systems with a flashlight

Turtle: a replacement, so named because it seemed like forever until he arrived

XXIV Corps: U.S. Army command activated in 1968 to operate in I Corps Tactical Zone

UCLA: University of California at Los Angeles

USAF: U.S. Air Force

USAID: U.S. Agency for International Development

USARMYFMR: U.S. Army Forces Military Region

USARPAC: U.S. Army, Pacific

USARV: U.S. Army, Vietnam

USIA: U.S. Information Agency. Established in 1953 with the purpose of international dissemination of information about the United States Overseas, the agency was referred to as the USIS

USMC: U.S. Marine Corps

USO: United Service Organizations

Utilities: marine slang for their combat fatigues

VA: Veterans Administration

VC: Vietcong

VIC: Vietcong infrastructure

VDC: Vietnam Day Committee

Victor Charlie: phonetic alphabetization of VC, the popular name for the Vietcong

Vietcong: Communist forces fighting the South Vietnamese government

Vietminh: Viet Nam Doc Lap Dong Minh Hoi, or the Vietnamese Independence League

Vietnamization: President Nixon's program to gradually turn the war over to the South Vietnamese while phasing out American troops

VMS: Vietnam Moratorium Committee

VNA: Vietnam National Army

VNAF: Vietnamese Air Force (South)

VNMC: South Vietnamese Marine Corps

VNN: South Vietnamese Navy

VNSF: South Vietnamese Special Forces

VNQDD: Viet Nam Quoc Dan Dang, or Nationalist party of Vietnam

VVA: Vietnam Veterans of America

VVAW: Vietnamese Veterans Against the War

WAAPM: wide area antipersonnel munition
Walk in the sun: ground troop movement free of the risk of combat
Waste: to kill or destroy
Web gear: canvas belt and shoulder straps used for packing equipment and ammunition on infantry operations
Wheel jockeys: truck drivers on convoy or line-haul operations
Whiskey Papa, Willie Peter, W-P: phonetic alphabetization for white phosphorus mortar or artillery rounds and grenades
Whistler: artillery fuse deliberately set to scare troops up front
White Mice: South Vietnamese police. The nickname came from their uniform white helmets and gloves.
WIA: wounded in action
Widow-maker: nickname for the M–16 rifle
Wild Weasel: new weapons system for tactical fighter aircraft allowing for the detection and destruction of enemy surface-to-air missiles and antiaircraft installations
Willie Peter: popular nickname for white phosphorus mortar or artillery rounds or grenades
WOMs: Wise Old Men
The world: the United States
WRL: War Resisters League
W-P: white phosphorus mortar/artillery rounds or grenades

XO: executive officer second in command to the senior officer

Yards: Montagnard soldiers

Zap: to shoot at and hit, wound, kill, or destroy
Zippo: flamethrower
Zippo mission: search-and destroy mission

SOURCES

Dougan, Clark et al. *The Vietnam Experience: Nineteen Sixty-Eight*, 1983.
———. *The Vietnam Experience: The Fall of the South*, 1985.
Doyle, Edward et al. *The Vietnam Experience: America Takes Over, 1965–67*, 1982.
———. *The Vietnam Experience: Passing the Torch*, 1981.
Fulghum, David et al. *The Vietnam Experience: South Vietnam on Trial*, 1984.
Lewy, Guenter. *America in Vietnam*, 1978.
Lipsman, Samuel et al. *The Vietnam Experience: Fighting for Time*, 1983.
Maitland, Terrence et al. *The Vietnam Experience: A Contagion of War*, 1983.
———. *The Vietnam Experience: Raising the Stakes*, 1982.
Santoli, Al. *To Bear Any Burden: The Vietnam War and Its Aftermath in the Words of Americans and Southeast Asians*, 1985.
———. *Everything We Had: An Oral History of the Vietnam War by Thirty-Three American Soldiers Who Fought It*, 1981.
Stanton, Shelby L. *Vietnam Order of Battle*, 1981.
Terry, Wallace. *Bloods: An Oral History of the Vietnam War by Black Veterans*, 1984.
Whitfield, Danny J. *Historical and Cultural Dictionary of Vietnam*, 1976.

Appendix D
Selected Bibliography of the Vietnam War

AIR WAR

Ballard, Jack S. *The United States Air Force in Southeast Asia: Development and Employment of Fixed Wing Gunships, 1962–1972*, 1982.

Berger, Carl, ed. *The United States Air Force in Southeast Asia, 1961–1973, An Illustrated Account*, 1977.

Bowers, Ray L. *The U.S. Air Force in Southeast Asia: Tactical Airlift*. 1983.

Buchanan, Albert R. *The Navy's Air War: A Mission Completed*. 1946.

Buckingham, William A., Jr. *Operation Ranch Hand: The United States Air Force and Herbicides in Southeast Asia. 1961–1971*. 1982.

Burbage, Paul, et al. *The Battle for the Skies Over North Vietnam, 1964–1972*. 1976.

Corum, Delbert, et al. *The Tale of Two Bridges*. 1976.

Dong Van Khuyen. *The RVNAF*. 1980.

Drendel, Lou. *Air War over Southeast Asia*. 1984.

———. *B–52 Stratofortress in Action*. 1984.

———. *Huey*. 1983.

Eastman, James N., Jr., Walter Hanak, and Lawrence J. Paszek, eds. *Aces and Aerial Victories: The United States Air Force in Southeast Asia, 1965–1973*. 1976.

Fox, Roger P. *Air Base Defense in the Republic of Vietnam, 1961–1973*. 1979.

Futrell, R. Frank, et al. *Aces and Aerial Victories: The United States Air Force in Southeast Asia, 1965–1973*. 1976.

Futrell, Robert F. *The United States Air Force: The Advisory Years, 1961 to 1965*. 1981.

Gropman, Alan L. *Airpower and the Airlift Evacuation of Kham Duc*. 1979.

Harvey, Frank. *Air War—Vietnam*. 1967.

Jane's All the World's Aircraft, 1964–1965. 1965.

Lavalle, A.J.C., ed. *Airpower and the 1972 Spring Invasion*. 1976.

———. *The Battle for the Skies Over North Vietnam*. 1976.

———. *Last Flight from Saigon*. 1978.

Littauer, Raphael, and Norman Uphoff, eds. *The Air War in Indochina*. 1972.

McCarthy, James R., and Allison McCarthy. *George B. Linebacker: A View from the Rock*. 1986.

McDonald, Charles, and A.J.C. Lavalle, eds. *The Vietnamese Air Force 1951–1975: An Analysis of Its Role in Combat*. 1976.
Mason, Robert C. *Chickenhawk*. 1983.
Mersky, Peter, and Norman Polmar. *The Naval Air War in Vietnam: 1965–1975*. 1981.
Mesko, Jim. *Airmobile: The Helicopter War in Vietnam*. 1985.
Mikesh, Robert C. *B–57 Seven Canberra at War: 1964–1972*. 1980.
Momyer, William W. *Airpower in Three Wars*. 1978.
Momyer, William W., and Louis L. Wilson, Jr. *The Vietnamese Air Force, 1951–1975: An Analysis of Its Role in Combat*. 1986.
Morrocco, John. *The Vietnam Experience. Rain of Fire: Air War, 1969–1973*. 1984.
———. *The Vietnam Experience. Thunder From Above: Air War, 1941–1968*. 1984.
Nalty, Bernard C. *Air Power and the Fight for Khe Sanh*. 1973.
———. *An Illustrated Guide to the Air War over Vietnam*. 1981.
Nalty, Bernard C., George M. Watson, and Jacob Neufield. *The Air War over Vietnam*. 1971.
Osborne, Arthur M. "Air Defense for the Mining of Haiphong." *U.S. Naval Institute Proceedings*, Series 100 September 1974.
Prados, John. *The Sky Would Fall: Operation Vulture; The U.S. Bombing Mission in Indochina, 1954*. 1983.
Rausa, Rosario. *Skyraider: The Douglas A–1 "Flying Dump Truck."* 1982.
Robbins, Christopher. *Air America*. 1979.
Schneider, Donald K. *Air Force Heroes in Vietnam*. 1986.
Smith, Myron J., Jr. *Air War Southeast Asia, Nineteen Sixty-One to Nineteen Seventy-Three: An Annotated Bibliography and 16mm Film Guide*. 1979.
Thompson, James Clay. *Rolling Thunder: Understanding Policy and Program Failure*. 1980.
Tilford, Earl H., Jr. *Search and Rescue in Southeast Asia, 1961–1975*. 1980.
Tobin, Thomas G., et al. *Last Flight from Saigon*. 1978.
Tolson, John J. *Airmobility, 1961–1971*. 1973.
Warbirds Illustrated. Vol. 2, *Air War over Vietnam*. 1982.
Windchy, Eugene C. *Tonkin Gulf*. 1971.

ANTIWAR MOVEMENT

Anson, Robert Sam. *McGovern: A Biography*. 1972.
Bannan, John F., and Rosemary S. Bannan. *Law, Morality, and Vietnam: The Peace Militants and the Courts*. 1978.
Baskir, Lawrence M. and William A. Strauss. *Chance and Circumstance: The Draft, the War, and the Vietnam Generation*. 1978.
Bender, David L., ed. *The Vietnam War: Opposing Viewpoints*. 1984.
Bloom, Lynn Z. *Doctor Spock: Biography of a Conservative Radical*. 1972.
Chatfield, Charles, ed. *Peace Movements in America*. 1973.
Chomsky, Noam. *American Power and the New Mandarins*. 1969.
———. *At War with Asia*. 1970.
Cohen, Mitchell, and Dennis Hale, eds. *The New Student Left: An Anthology*. 1966.
Cortright, David. *Soldiers in Revolt*. 1976.
Critchfield, Richard. *The Long Charade: Political Subversion in the Vietnam War*. 1968.
Dellinger, David. *Revolutionary Non-Violence*. 1970.

Destler, I. M., Leslie H. Gelb, and Anthony Lake. *Our Own Worse Enemy*. 1984.

Doan Van, Taoi and David Chanoff. *The Vietnam Gulag*. 1986.

Dougan, Clark, and Samuel Lipsman. *The Vietnam Experience: A Nation Divided*. 1984.

Ellsberg, Daniel. *Papers on the War*. 1972.

Friedman, Leon, and Burt Neuborne. *Unquestioning Obedience to the President: The ACLU Case Against the Legality of the War in Vietnam*. 1972.

Johnson, James Turner. *Just War Tradition and the Restraint of War*. 1981.

King, Martin Luther, Jr. *Where Do We Go from Here: Chaos or Community?* 1967.

Larner, Jeremy. *Nobody Knows: Reflections on the McCarthy Campaign of 1968*. 1970.

McCarthy, Eugene. *The Year of the People*. 1969.

Meconis, Charles A. *With Clumsy Grace: The American Catholic Left, 1961–1975*. 1979.

Menashe, Louis, and Ronald Radosh. *Teach-ins: U.S.A.* 1967.

Meyer, Ernest L. *Hey Yellowbacks; The War Diary of a Conscientious Objector*. 1972.

Michener, James. *Kent State: What Happened and Why*. 1971.

Peterson, Richard E., and John Bilorsky. *May 1970: The Campus Aftermath of Cambodia and Kent State*. 1971.

Polenberg, Richard. *One Nation Divisible*. 1980.

Powers, Thomas. *The War at Home: Vietnam and the American People*. 1973.

———. *Vietnam, the War at Home: The Antiwar Movement, 1964–1968*. 1984.

Prugh, George S. *Law at War: Vietnam, 1964–1973*. 1975.

Quigley, Thomas E., ed. *American Catholics and Vietnam*. 1968.

Rosenberg, Milton J., Sidney Verba, and Philip E. Converse. *Vietnam and the Silent Majority*. 1970.

Sale, Kirkpatrick. *SDS*. 1973.

Schandler, Herbert Y. *The Unmaking of a President: Lyndon Johnson and Vietnam*. 1977.

Skolnick, Jerome H., et al. *The Politics of Protest*. 1969.

Staff of the Columbia *Daily Spectator*. *Up Against the Ivy Wall: A History of the Columbia Crisis*. 1969.

Surrey, Davis S. *Choice of Conscience: Vietnam Era Military and Draft Resisters in Canada*. 1982.

Thomas, Norman M. *Is Conscience a Crime?* 1972.

Walzer, Michael. *Just and Unjust Wars: A Moral Argument with Historical Illustrations*. 1977.

Zaroulis, Nancy, and Gerald Sullivan. *Who Spoke Up? American Protest Against the War in Vietnam, 1963–1975*. 1984.

BIOGRAPHIES

Ambrose, Stephen E. *Eisenhower*. Vol. 2, *President and Elder Statesman, 1952–1969*. 1984.

Blakey, Scott. *Prisoner at War: The Survival of Commander Richard A. Strattan*. 1978.

Cohen, Warren. *Dean Rusk*. 1980.

Eisele, Albert. *Almost to the Presidency: A Biography of Two American Politicians*. 1972.

Evans, Rowland, and Robert Novak. *Lyndon B. Johnson: The Exercise of Power*. 1966.

Fenn, Charles. *Ho Chi Minh: A Biographical Introduction*. 1973.

Geyelin, Philip. *Lyndon B. Johnson and the World*. 1969.

Goldman, Eric. *The Tragedy of Lyndon Johnson*. 1969.

Halberstam, David. *Ho*. 1971.
————. *The Unfinished Odyssey of Robert Kennedy*. 1968.
Hammer, Richard. *The Court-Martial of Lieutenant William Calley*. 1971.
Hersh, Seymour. *The Price of Power: Kissinger in the Nixon White House*. 1983.
Hoopes, Townsend. *The Devil and John Foster Dulles*. 1973.
Kalb, Bernard, and Marvin Kalb. *Kissinger*. 1974.
Kearns, Doris. *Lyndon Johnson and the American Dream*. 1976.
Johnson, Haynes, and Bernard Gwertzman. *Fulbright: The Dissenter*. 1968.
Lacouture, Jean. *Ho Chi Minh: A Political Biography*. 1968.
Lewis, David. *King: A Critical Biography*. 1970.
McGovern, James R. *Black Eagle: General Daniel "Chappie" James, Jr., USAF*. 1985.
Mazlish, Bruce. *Kissinger: The European Mind in American Policy*. 1976.
Miller, Merle. *Lyndon: An Oral Biography*. 1980.
O'Neill, Robert J. *General Giap: Politician and Strategist*. 1969.
Powell, Lee J. *William Fulbright and America's Lost Crusade: Fulbright's Opposition
      to the Vietnam War*. 1984.
Pruessen, Ronald W. *John Foster Dulles: The Road to Peace*. 1982.
Rust, William J. *Kennedy In Vietnam*. 1985.
Schlesinger, Arthur M., Jr. *A Thousand Days: John F. Kennedy in the White House*.
      1965.
————. *Robert Kennedy and His Times*. 1978.
Sorenson, Theodore C. *Kennedy*. 1965.
Steele, Ronald. *Walter Lippmann and the American Century*. 1980.
Warner, Denis. *The Last Confucian*. 1963.
Wills, Garry. *The Kennedy Imprisonment: A Meditation on Power*. 1982.

CAMBODIA AND LAOS

Ablin, David A., and Marlowe Hood, eds. *The Cambodian Agony*. 1986.
Barron, John, and Paul Anthony. *Murder of a Gentle Land*. 1977.
Branfman, Fred. "Presidential War in Laos, 1964–1970." In N. Adams and A. McCoy,
      eds. *Laos: War and Revolution*. 1970.
Briggs, Lawrence P. *Ancient Khmer Empire*. 1951.
Brown, MacAlister, and Joseph J. Zasloff. *Apprentice Revolutionaries: The Communist
      Movement in Laos, 1930–1985*. 1986.
Burchett, Wilfred. *The China-Cambodia-Vietnam Triangle*. 1982.
Burns, Richard D., and Milton Leitenberg. *The Wars in Vietnam, Cambodia, and Laos,
      1945–1982: A Bibliographic Guide*. 1984.
Caldwell, Malcolm, and Tan Lek. *Cambodia in the Southeast Asian War*. 1973.
Chandler, David P. *A History of Cambodia*. 1983.
Chandler, David P., and Ben Kiernan, eds. *Revolution and Its Aftermath in Kampuchea:
      Eight Essays*. 1983.
Chang, Pao-Min. *Kampuchea between China and Vietnam*. 1985.
Charny, Joel, and John Spragens, Jr. *Obstacles to Recovery in Vietnam and Kampuchea*.
      1984.
Dommen, Arthur J. *Laos: The Keystone of Indochina*. 1985.
Etcheson, Craig. *The Rise and Demise of Democratic Kampuchea*. 1984.
Goldstein, Martin E. *American Policy Toward Laos*. 1973.

Haley, P. Edward. *Congress and the Fall of South Vietnam and Cambodia*. 1982.

Hersh, Seymour. *Cover-Up*. 1972.

Hildebrand, George, and Gareth Porter. *Cambodia: Starvation and Revolution*. 1976.

Isaacs, Arnold R. *Without Honor: Defeat in Vietnam and Cambodia*. 1983.

Kiernan, Ben. "How Pol Pot Came to Power." Ph.D. diss., 1986.

Langer, Paul F., and Joseph J. Zasloff. *North Vietnam and the Pathet Lao: Partners in the Struggle for Laos*. 1970.

Leifer, Michael. *Cambodia: The Search for Security*. 1967.

Marshall, S.L.A. *West to Cambodia*. 1983.

Nguyen Duy, Hinh. *Lam Son 719*. 1981.

Osborne, Milton. *Before Kampuchea: Preludes to Tragedy*. 1985.

———. *Politics and Power in Cambodia*. 1973.

Ponchaud, François. *Cambodia: Year Zero*. 1978.

Poole, Peter A. *The Expansion of the Vietnam War Into Cambodia: Action and Response by the Governments of North Vietnam, South Vietnam, Cambodia and the United States*. 1985.

Porter, Gareth, and George C. Hildebrand. *Cambodia: Starvation and Revolution*. 1976.

Ratnam, Perala. *Laos and the Super Powers*. 1980.

Rowan, Roy. *The Four Days of Mayaguez*. 1975.

Sananikone, Gudone. *The Royal Lao Government and U.S. Army Advice and Support*. 1981.

Shaplen, Robert. *Bitter Victory*. 1986.

Shawcross, William. *Sideshow: Kissinger, Nixon, and the Destruction of Cambodia*. 1979.

———. *The Quality of Mercy: Cambodia, Holocaust, and the Modern Conscience*. 1984.

Simon, Sheldon W. *War and Politics in Cambodia: A Communications Analysis*. 1974.

Stevenson, Charles A. *The End of Nowhere: American Policy Toward Laos Since 1954*. 1973.

Sutsakhan, Sak. *The Khmer Republic at War and the Final Collapse*. 1980.

Tran Dinh Tho. *The Cambodian Incursion*. 1979.

Vickery, Michael. *Cambodia, 1975–1982*. 1984.

Vongsavanh, Solitchay. *RLA Military Operations and Activities in the Laotian Panhandle*. 1981.

DIPLOMACY

Albinski, Henry. *Politics and Foreign Policy in Australia*. 1970.

Ball, George W. *Diplomacy in a Crowded World*. 1976.

Baral, Jaya K. *The Pentagon and the Making of U.S. Foreign Policy: A Case Study of Vietnam, 1960–1968*. 1978.

Bator, Victor. *Drawing the Line: The Origin of the American Containment Policy in East Asia*, 1982.

———. *Vietnam, a Diplomatic Tragedy: Origins of U.S. Involvement*. 1965.

Betts, Richard K. *Soldiers, Statesmen and Cold War Crises*. 1977.

Blum, Robert. *Drawing the Line: The Origin of the American Containment Policy in East Asia*. 1982.

Brown, William A. *The Soviet Role in Asia*. 1983.

Chayes, Abram, et al. *Vietnamese Settlement: Why 1973 Not 1969?* 1973.

Chen, King C. *Vietnam and China, 1938–1954*. 1969.

Cole, Allen, ed. *Conflict in Indochina and Its International Repercussions*. 1956.

Dacy, Douglas. *Foreign Aid, War and Economic and Development: South Vietnam, 1955–1975*. 1988.

Dillard, Walter Scott. *Sixty Days to Peace*. 1982.

Donovan, John C. *The Cold Warriors: A Policy-Making Elite*. 1974.

Drachman, Edward R. *United States Policy Toward Vietnam, 1940–1945*. 1970.

Edmonds, Robin. *Soviet Foreign Policy, 1962–1973: The Paradox of a Superpower*. 1975.

Franck, Thomas M., and Edward Weisband. *Foreign Policy by Congress*. 1980.

Fulbright, J. William. *The Arrogance of Power*. 1967.

———. *The Crippled Giant*. 1962.

Goodman, Allan E. *The Lost Peace: America's Search for a Negotiated Settlement of the Vietnam War*. 1978.

Herrington, Stuart A. *Peace with Honor?* 1983.

Honey, P. J. *Communism in North Vietnam: Its Role in the Sino-Soviet Dispute*. 1963.

Hsiao, Gene T., ed. *The Role of External Powers in the Indochina Crisis*. 1973.

Jordan, Amos A. and William J. Taylor, Jr. *American National Security: Policy and Process*. 1981.

Kraslow, David, and Stuart Lorry. *The Secret Search for Peace in Vietnam*. 1968.

Larsen, Stanley Robert, and James Lawton Collins, Jr. *Allied Participaton in Vietnam*. 1975.

Lawson, Eugene K. *The Sino-Vietnamese Conflict*. 1984.

Morganthau, Hans. *Vietnam and the United States*. 1973.

Papp, Daniel S. *Vietnam: The View from Moscow, Peking, Washington*. 1981.

Porter, Gareth. *A Peace Denied*. 1975.

Ray, Hemen. *China's Vietnam War*. 1983.

Rosenberger, Leif. *The Soviet Union and Vietnam: An Uneasy Alliance*. 1986.

Rosie, George. *The British in Vietnam: How the Twenty-five Years War Began*. 1970.

Ross, Douglas A. *In the Interests of Peace: Canada and Vietnam, 1954–1973*. 1984.

Sutter, Robert G. *Chinese Foreign Policy after the Cultural Revolution: 1966–1977*. 1978.

Szulc, Tad. *The Illusion of Peace: Foreign Policy in the Nixon Years*. 1978.

Taylor, Charles. *Snow Job: Canada, the United States and Vietnam (1954–1973)*. 1974.

Thakur, Ramesh. *Peacekeeping in Vietnam: Canada, India, Poland, and the International Commission*. 1984.

Thies, Wallace. *When Governments Collide: Coercion and Diplomacy in the Vietnam Conflict, 1964–1968*. 1980.

FALL OF THE SOUTH

Butler, David. *The Fall of Saigon*. 1985.

Cao Van Vien. *The Final Collapse*. 1983.

Dawson, Alan. *55 Days: The Fall of South Vietnam*. 1977.

Dougan, Clark, and David Fulghum. *The Vietnam Experience: The Fall of the South*. 1985.

Fulghum, David, and Terrence Maitland. *The Vietnam Experience. South Vietnam on Trial*. 1984.

Haley, Edward P. *Congress and the Fall of South Vietnam and Cambodia*. 1982.

Hosmer, Stephen, et al. *The Fall of South Vietnam*. 1978.

Nguyen Long, with Harry Kendall. *After Saigon Fell*. 1981.

Pilger, John. *The Last Day*. 1975.

Porter, Gareth. *A Peace Denied: The United States, Vietnam, and the Paris Agreement*. 1975.

Snepp, Frank. *Decent Interval*. 1977.

Tobin, Thomas G., et al. *Last Flight from Saigon*. 1978.

Van Tien Dung. *Our Great Spring Victory*. 1977.

Warner, Denis. *Certain Victory: How Hanoi Won the War*. 1977.

FIRST INDOCHINA WAR

Bodard, Lucien. *The Quicksand War: Prelude to Vietnam*. 1967.

Devillers, Philippe, and Jean Lacouture. *End of a War: Indochina, 1954*. 1969.

Fall, Bernard. *Hell in a Very Small Place: The Siege of Dien Bien Phu*. 1966.

———. *Street Without Joy: Insurgency in Vietnam, 1946–1963*. 1961.

———. *The Viet Minh Regime*. 1956.

Gurtov, Melvin. *The First Vietnam Crisis: Chinese Communist Strategy and United States Involvement, 1953–54*. 1967.

Halberstam, David. *The Making of a Quagmire*. 1964.

Hammer, Ellen. *The Struggle for Indochina*. 1954.

Lancaster, Donald. *The Emancipation of French Indochina*. 1961.

Langlais, Pierre. *Dien Bien Phu*. 1963.

O'Ballance, Edgar. *The Indochina War 1945–1954: A Study in Guerrilla Warfare*. 1964.

Patti, Archimedes L. A. *Why Vietnam? Prelude to America's Albatross*. 1980.

Rose, Lisle Abbott. *Roads of Tragedy: The United States and the Struggle for Asia, 1945–1953*. 1976.

Roy, Jules. *The Battle of Dien Bien Phu*. 1965.

Werth, Alexander. *France 1940–1955*. 1956.

FRENCH EMPIRE

Cady, John. *The Roots of French Imperialism in Indochina*. 1954.

Doyle, Edward, and Samuel Lipsman. *The Vietnam Experience: Setting the Stage*. 1981.

Ennis, Thomas. *French Policy and Developments in Indochina*. 1956.

Long, Ngo Vinh. *Before the Revolution: The Vietnamese Peasants Under the French*. 1973.

Marr, David G. *Vietnamese Anticolonialism, 1885–1925*. 1981.

Osborne, Milton E. *The French Presence in Cochinchina and Cambodia: Rule and Response (1859–1905)*. 1969.

Taylor, Keith Weller. *The Birth of Vietnam*. 1983.

Thompson, Virginia. *French Indochina*. 1937.

GENERAL HISTORIES

Austin, Anthony. *The President's War*. 1971.

Berman, Larry. *Planning a Tragedy: The Americanization of the War in Vietnam*. 1982.

Boettcher, Thomas D. *Vietnam: The Valor and the Sorrow*. 1985.

Bonds, Ray, ed. *The Vietnam War*. 1979.

———. *The Vietnam War: The Illustrated History of the Conflict in Southeast Asia.* 1983.

Bowman, John S., ed. *The Vietnam War: An Almanac*. 1985.

Braestrup, Peter, ed. *Vietnam As History*. 1984.

Buttinger, Joseph. *Vietnam: The Unforgettable Tragedy*. 1977.

Cairns, James Ford. *The Eagle and the Lotus: Western Intervention in Vietnam, 1847– 1968*. 1969.

Charlton, Michael, and Anthony Moncrief. *Many Reasons Why: The American Involvement in Vietnam*. 1978.

Chester, Lewis, Godfrey Hodgson, and Bruce Page. *An American Melodrama*. 1969.

Cooper, Chester L. *The Lost Crusade: America in Vietnam*. 1970.

Doyle, Edward, and Samuel Lipsman. *The Vietnam Experience: Passing the Torch*. 1981.

Fall, Bernard. *The Two Vietnams: A Political and Military Analysis*. 1967.

Fishel, Wesley R., ed. *Vietnam: Anatomy of a Conflict*. 1968.

FitzGerald, Frances. *Fire in the Lake: The Vietnamese and the Americans in Vietnam*. 1972.

Gallucci, Robert L. *Neither Peace Nor Honor: The Politics of American Military Policy in Vietnam*. 1975.

Gettleman, Marvin E., et al., eds. *Vietnam and America: A Documented History*. 1985.

Halberstam, David. *The Best and the Brightest*. 1972.

Hammer, Ellen Joy. *Vietnam, Yesterday and Today*. 1966.

Hammond, William Michael. *The Vietnam War*. 1979.

Harriman, W. Averell, and Elie Abel. *Special Envoy to Churchill and Stalin, 1941–1946*. 1975.

Harrison, James P. *The Endless War: Fifty Years of Struggle in Vietnam*. 1982.

Herring, George C. *America's Longest War: The United States in Vietnam, 1950–1975*. 1986.

Higgins, Marguerite. *Our Vietnam Nightmare*. 1965.

Kahin, George McTurnan, and John W. Lewis. *The United States in Vietnam: An Analysis in Depth of the History of American Involvement in Vietnam*. 1967.

Kalb, Marvin, and Elie Abel. *Roots of Involvement: The U.S. in Asia, 1784–1971*. 1971.

Karnow, Stanley. *Vietnam: A History*. 1983.

Kattenburg, Paul L. *The Vietnam Trauma in American Foreign Policy, 1945–1975*. 1980.

Kendrick, Alexander. *The Wound Within: America in the Vietnam Years, 1945–1974*. 1974.

Kenny, Henry J. *The American Role in Vietnam and East Asia*. n.d.

LeGro, William E. *Vietnam: From Cease-fire to Capitulation*. 1981.

Lewy, Guenter. *America in Vietnam*. 1978.

Maclear, Michael. *The Ten Thousand Day War: Vietnam, 1945–1975*. 1981.

O'Ballance, Edgar. *The Wars in Vietnam: 1954–1973*. 1975.

———. *The Wars in Vietnam: 1954–80*. 1981.

Palmer, Bruce, Jr. *The 25-Year War: America's Military Role in Vietnam*. 1984.

Palmer, David R. *Summons of the Trumpet: U.S.-Vietnam in Perspective*. 1978.

Patti, Archimedes. *Why Vietnam? Prelude to America's Albatross*. 1981.

Raskin, Marcus G., and Bernard Fall, eds. *The Viet-Nam Reader: Articles and Documents on American Foreign Policy and the Viet-Nam Crisis*. 1965.

Scigliano, Robert. *South Viet-Nam: Nation Under Stress*. 1964.
Shaplen, Robert. *The Lost Revolution: The U.S. in Vietnam, 1946–1966*. 1966.
———. *The Road from War: 1965–1970*. 1970.
Smith, Harvey H., et al. *Area Handbook for North Vietnam*. 1967.
———. *Area Handbook for South Vietnam*. 1967.
Smith, R. B. *An International History of the Vietnam War: Revolution Versus Containment, 1955–61*. 1983.
Sobel, Lester A., ed. *South Vietnam: US-Communist Confrontation in Southeast Asia*. Seven volumes. 1966–1973.
Stavins, Ralph, Richard J. Barnet, and Marcus G. Raskin. *Washington Plans an Aggressive War*. 1971.
Summers, Harry G., Jr. *Vietnam War Almanac*. 1985.
Turley, William S. *The Second Indochina*. 1986.
Whitfield, Danny J. *Historical and Cultural Dictionary of Vietnam*. 1976.
Zasloff, Joseph J., and Allan E. Goodman, eds. *Indochina in Conflict: A Political Assessment*. 1972.

INSURGENCY AND COUNTERINSURGENCY

Andrews, William R. *The Village War: Vietnamese Communist Revolutionary Activities in Dinh Tuong Province, 1960–1964*. 1973.
Beckwith, Charles, and Donald Knox. *Delta Force*. 1983.
Bell, J. Bower. *The Myth of the Guerrilla: Revolutionary Theory and Malpractice*. 1971.
Blaufarb, Douglas S. *The Counterinsurgency Era: U.S. Doctrine and Performance 1950 to Present*. 1977.
Cable, Larry E. *Conflict of Myths: The Development of American Counterinsurgency Doctrine and the Vietnam War*. 1986.
Cao Van Vien. *The U.S. Adviser*. 1980.
da Silva, Peer. *Sub Rosa: The CIA and the Uses of Intelligence*. 1978.
Duiker, William. *The Communist Road to Power*. 1981.
Fall, Bernard. *Street Without Joy: Insurgency in Vietnam, 1946–1963*. 1961.
———. *The Viet Minh Regime*. 1956.
Goodman, Allen E. *The Making of a Quagmire*. 1964.
Greene, Graham. *The Quiet American*. 1956.
Henderson, William. *Why the Vietcong Fought: A Study of Motivation and Control in a Modern Army in Combat*. 1979.
Herrington, Stuart A. *Silence Was a Weapon: The Vietnam War in the Villages*. 1982.
Hosmer, Stephen T. *Viet Cong Repression and Its Implications for the Future*. 1970.
Johnson, Chalmers. *Autopsy on People's War*. 1973.
Kelly, Francis J. *U.S. Army Special Force, 1961–1971*. 1973.
Komer, Robert W. *Bureaucracy Does Its Thing: Institutional Constraints on US-GVN Performance*. 1972.
McGarvey, Patrick J. *Visions of Victory: Selected Vietnamese Communist Military Writings, 1964–1968*. 1969.
Mecklin, John. *Mission in Torment*. 1965.
Mus, Paul, and John T. McAlister, Jr. *The Vietnamese and Their Revolution*. 1970.
Nighswonger, William A. *Rural Pacification in Vietnam*. 1966.

O'Meara, Andrew P. *Infrastructure and the Marxist Power Seizure: An Analysis of the Communist Model of Revolution*. 1973.

Osborne, Milton E. *Strategic Hamlets in South Vietnam: A Survey and a Comparison*. 1965.

Pike, Douglas. *Viet Cong: The Organization and Techniques of the National Liberation Front of South Vietnam*. 1966.

———. *The Viet Cong Strategy of Terror*. 1970.

———. *War, Peace, and the Viet Cong*. 1969.

Popkin, Samuel L. *The Rational Peasant: The Political Economy of Rural Society in Vietnam*. 1979.

Prados, John. *Presidents' Secret Wars*. *CIA and Pentagon Covert Operations Since World War II*. 1986.

Race, Jeffrey. *War Comes to Long An: Revolutionary Conflict in a Vietnamese Village*. 1972.

Sansom, Robert L. *The Economics of Insurgency in the Mekong Delta*. 1970.

Shackleton, Ronald A. *Village Defense: Initial Special Forces Operations in Vietnam*. 1975.

Smith, R. Harris. *OSS: The Secret History of America's First CIA*. 1972.

Stimpson, Charles M. III. *Inside the Green Berets: The First Thirty Years*. 1983.

Stanton, Shelby L. *Green Berets at War*. 1985.

Stolfi, Russell H. *U.S. Marine Corps Civil Action Efforts in Vietnam, March 1965–March 1966*. 1968.

Tanham, George Kilpatrick. *Communist Revolutionary Warfare: From the Vietminh to the Viet Cong*. 1967.

Thompson, Robert. *Defeating Communist Insurgency*. 1966.

———. *Peace Is Not at Hand*. 1974.

———. *Revolutionary War in World Strategy, 1945–1949*. 1970.

Tran Dinh Tho. *Pacification*. 1979.

Tran Van Don. *Our Endless War: Inside Vietnam*. 1978.

Tran Van Tra. *Ending the 30 Years War*. 1982.

Trullinger, James Walker, Jr. *Village at War: An Account of Revolution in Vietnam*. 1980.

Truong Chinh. *Primer for Revolt: The Communist Takeover in Vietnam*. 1963.

Turner, Robert F. *Vietnamese Communism: Its Origins and Developments*. 1975.

West, Francis J. *The Village*. 1972.

LAND WAR

Albright, John, John A. Cash, and Allan W. Sandstrum. *Seven Firefights in Vietnam*. 1970.

Anderson, Charles R. *The Grunts*. 1976.

Candlin, A.H.S. "The Spring Offensive in Vietnam." *Army Quarterly and Defense Journal*. July 1972.

Carhart, Tom. *Battles and Campaigns in Vietnam*. 1984.

Cincinnaus. *Self-Destruction: The Disintegration and Decay of the United States Army During the Vietnam Era*. 1978.

Collins, James Lawton, Jr. *The Development and Training of the South Vietnamese Army, 1950–1972*. 1975.

Cook, John L. *The Advisor*. 1973.

Dickson, Paul. *The Electronic Battlefield*. 1976.

Doleman, Edgar C., Jr. *The Vietnam Experience: The Tools of War*. 1984.

Dunn, Carroll H. *Base Development in South Vietnam, 1965–1970*. 1972.

Dunstan, Simon. *Vietnam Tracks: Armor in Battle, 1945–1975*. 1982.

Ezell, Edward Clinton. *The Great Rifle Controversy*. 1984.

First Air Cavalry Division in Vietnam. 1967.

The First Air Cavalry Division: Vietnam, August 1965 to December 1969. 1970.

The First Marine Division and Its Regiments. 1981.

Garland, Albert N., ed. *A Distant Challenge: The U.S. Infantryman in Vietnam, 1967–1972*. 1983.

———. *Infantry in Vietnam: Small Unit Actions in the Early Days 1965–66*. 1982.

Gershen, Martin. *Destroy or Die: The True Story of My Lai*. 1971.

Hay, John H., Jr. *Tactical and Material Innovations*. 1975.

Heiser, Joseph M., Jr. *Logistic Support*. 1974.

Hymoff, Edward. *The First Cavalry Division*. 1985.

The Infantry Brigade in Combat: First Brigade, 25th Infantry Division ("Tropic Lightning") in the Third Viet Cong–North Vietnamese Army Offensive, August 1968. 1984.

Johnson, Harold K. "The Enclave Concept: A "License to Hunt.' " *Army*. April 1968.

Krepinevich, Andrew F., Jr. *The Army and Vietnam*. 1986.

Krulak, Victor H. *First to Fight: An Inside View of the U.S. Marine Corps*. 1984.

Mahler, Michael D. *Ringed in Steel: Armored Cavalry. Vietnam, 1967–68*. 1986.

Mangold, Tom, and John Penycate. *The Tunnels of Cu Chi*. 1985.

The Marines in Vietnam, 1954–1973. 1974.

Marshall, S.L.A. *Ambush: The Battle of Dau Tieng, Also Called The Battle of Dong Ming Chau, War Zone C, Operation Attleboro, and Other Deadfalls in South Vietnam*. 1969.

———. *Battles in the Monsoon: Campaigning in the Central Highlands, South Vietnam, Summer 1966*. 1966.

———. *Bird: The Christmastide Battle*. 1968.

———. *The Fields of Bamboo: Dong Tre, Trung Luong, and Hoa Hoi: Three Battles Just Beyond the China Sea*. 1971.

———. *Vietnam: Three Battles*. 1982.

Mertel, Kenneth D. *Year of the Horse—Vietnam: First Air Cavalry in the Highlands*. 1968.

Meyerson, Harvey. *Vinh Long*. 1970.

Miller, Kenneth E. *Tiger, The LURP Dog*. 1983.

Millet, Allan R. *Semper Fidelis: The History of the United States Marine Corps*. 1980.

Neel, Spurgeon. *Vietnam Studies: Medical Support of the U.S. Army in Vietnam, 1965–1970*. 1973.

Ngo Quang Truong. *The Easter Offensive of 1972*. 1980.

———. *Territorial Forces*. 1981.

Nolan, Keith William. *The Battle for Hue: Tet, 1968*. 1983.

Ott, David Ewing. *Field Artillery, 1954–1973*. 1975.

Parker, William D. *U.S. Marine Corps Civil Affairs in I Corps, Republic of Vietnam, April 1966–April 1967*. 1970.

Pearson, Willard. *The War in the Northern Provinces, 1966–1968*. 1975.

Peers, W. R. *The My Lai Inquiry*. 1979.

Pimlott, John, ed. *Vietnam: The History and the Tactics*. 1982.

Pisor, Robert. *The End of the Line: The Siege of Khe Sanh*. 1982.

Ploger, Robert R. *U.S. Army Engineers, 1965–1970*. 1974.

Rienzi, Thomas M. *Vietnam Studies: Communications-Electronics, 1962–1970*. 1972.

Robinson, Anthony, ed. *The Weapons of the Vietnam War*. 1983.

Rogers, Bernard William. *Cedar Falls–Junction City: A Turning Point*. 1974.

Schell, Jonathan. *The Village of Ben Suc*. 1967.

Shore, Moyers S. II. *The Battle for Khe Sanh*. 1969.

Shulimson, Jack. *U.S. Marines in Vietnam: An Expanding War 1966*. 1982.

Shulimson, Jack, and Charles M. Johnson. *U.S. Marines in Vietnam: The Landing and the Buildup 1965*. 1978.

Spector, Ronald H. *United States Army in Vietnam: Advice and Support: The Early Years, 1965–1973*. 1985.

Staff of the *Infantry* Magazine, ed. *A Distant Challenge: The U.S. Infantryman in Vietnam, 1967–1970*. 1971.

Stanton, Shelby L. *The Rise and Fall of an American Army: U.S. Ground Forces in Vietnam, 1965–1973*. 1985.

————. *Vietnam Order of Battle*. 1981.

Starry, Donn A. *Mounted Combat in Vietnam*. 1979.

Stolfi, Russell H. *U.S. Marine Corps Civil Action Efforts in Vietnam, March 1965–March 1966*. 1968.

Stuckey, John D., and Joseph H. Pistorius. *Mobilization of the Army National Guard and Army Reserve: Historical Perspective and the Vietnam War*. 1984.

The Third Marine Division and Its Regiments. 1983.

Tolson, John J. *Airmobility, 1961–1971*. 1973.

Tregakis, Richard. *Southeast Asia: Building the Bases; The History of Construction in Southeast Asia*. 1975.

Turley, G. H. *The Easter Offensive: Vietnam 1972*. 1985.

West, Francis J. *Small Unit Action in Vietnam, Summer 1966*. 1967.

Whitlow, Robert H. *U.S. Marines in Vietnam: The Advisory and Combat Assistance Era, 1954–1964*. 1977.

LEGACY OF VIETNAM

Alley, Rewi. *Refugees from Viet Nam in China*. 1980.

Chanda, Nayan. *Brother Enemy. The War After the War: A History of Indochina Since the Fall of Saigon*. 1986.

Duiker, William J. *Vietnam Since the Fall of Saigon*. 1980.

Elliott, David W. P., ed. *The Third Indochina Conflict*. 1981.

Gelb, Leslie, and Richard Betts. *The Irony of Vietnam: The System Worked*. 1979.

Grant, Bruce. *The Boat People*. 1979.

Isaacs, Arnold R. *Without Honor: Defeat in Vietnam and Cambodia*. 1983.

Lake, Anthony, ed. *The Legacy of Vietnam*. 1976.

Nguyen Long. *After Saigon Fell*. 1981.

Nguyen Van Canh, with Earle Cooper. *Vietnam Under Communism, 1975–1982*. 1983.

Palmer, Dave R. *Summons of the Trumpet: U.S.-Vietnam in Perspective*. 1984.

Podhoretz, Norman. *Why We Were in Vietnam*. 1982.

Sagan, Ginette, and Stephen Denney. *Violations of Human Rights in the Socialist Republic of Vietnam*. 1983.

Salisbury, Harrison E., ed. *Vietnam Reconsidered: Lessons from a War*. 1984.

Schultz, Richard H., Jr., and Richard A. Hunt. *Lessons from an Unconventional War*. 1982.

Thompson, W. Scott, and Donaldson Fuzell, eds. *The Lessons of Vietnam*. 1977.

Vietnam: 10 Years Later. 1984.

Wheeler, John. *Touched with Fire: The Future of the Vietnam Generation*. 1984.

LITERATURE AND FILM

Adair, Gilbert. *Hollywood's Vietnam*. 1983.

———. *Vietnam on Film*. 1981.

Baber, Asa. *The Land of a Million Elephants*. 1970.

Balaban, John. *After Our War*. 1974.

Balk, H. Wesley. *The Dramatization of 365 Days*. 1972.

Beidler, Philip D. *American Literature and the Experience of Vietnam*. 1982.

Berry, D. C. *Saigon Cemetery*. 1972.

Berry, Jan, and W. D. Ehrhart, eds. *Demilitarized Zones: Veterans after Vietnam*. 1976.

Blacker, Irwin R. *Search and Destroy*. 1966.

Briley, John. *The Traitors*. 1969.

Bryan, C.D.B. *Friendly Fire*. 1976.

Bunting, Josiah. *The Lionheads*. 1972.

Casey, Michael. *Obscenities*. 1972.

Cassidy, John. *A Station in the Delta*. 1979.

Clark, Alan. *The Lion Heart*. 1969.

Coe, Charles. *Young Man in Vietnam*. 1968.

Coleman, Charles. *Sergeant Back Again*. 1980.

Coonts, Stephen. *Flight of the Intruder*. 1986.

Corson, William R. *The Betrayal*. 1968.

Crumley, James. *One to Count Cadence*. 1969.

Duncan, David Douglas. *War Without Heroes*. 1970.

Duncan, Donald. *The New Legions*. 1967.

Durden, Charles. *No Bugles, No Drums*. 1976.

Eastlake, William. *The Bamboo Bed*. 1969.

Ehrhart, W. D., ed. *Carrying the Darkness: American Poetry of the Vietnam War*. 1985.

Emerson, Gloria. *Winners and Losers*. 1976.

Ford, Daniel. *Incident at Muc Wa*. 1967.

Glasser, Ronald J. *365 Days*. 1971.

Groom, Winston. *Better Times Than These*. 1978.

Hasford, Gustav. *The Short-Timers*. 1979.

Heath, G. Louis, ed. *Mutiny Does Not Happen Lightly: The Literature of the American Resistance to the Vietnam War*. 1976.

Heinemann, Larry. *Close Quarters*. 1977.

Herr, Michael. *Dispatches*. 1977.

Hollenbeck, Peter, et al. *Vietnam Literature Anthology*. 1985.

Hughes, Larry. *You Can See a Lot Standing under a Flare in the Republic of Vietnam*. 1969.

Huggett, William Turner. *Body Count*. 1973.
Just, Ward. *Military Men*. 1970.
———. *To What End*. 1968.
Karlin, Wayne, Basil T. Paquet, and Larry Rottman, eds. *Free Fire Zone*. 1973.
Kolpacoff, Victor. *The Prisoners of Quai Dong*. 1967.
Kopit, Arthur. *Indians*. 1969.
Kovic, Ron. *Born on the Fourth of July*. 1976.
Kowet, Don. *A Matter of Honor*. 1984.
Kozloff, Max, ed. *Artists and Writers Protests Against the War in Vietnam: Anthology of 18 Authors*. 1967.
Lifton, Robert Jay. *Home from the War*. 1973.
Lomperis, Timothy J. *Reading the Wind: The Literature of the Vietnam War*. 1986.
Lowenfels, Walter, ed. *Where Is Vietnam?* 1967.
Lowry, Timothy S. *And Brave Men, Too*. 1985.
McCarthy, Gerald. *War Story: Vietnam War Poems by an Ex-Marine*. 1977.
McCarthy, Mary. *The Seventeenth Degree*. 1974.
Mailer, Norman. *Why Are We in Vietnam?* 1967.
Maiman, Joan M., et al. *Vietnam Heroes: A Tribute: An Anthology of Poems by Veterans and Their Friends*. 1982.
Mayer, Tom. *Weary Falcon*. 1971.
Moore, Gene D. *The Killing at Ngo Tho*. 1967.
Moore, Robin. *The Green Berets*. 1965.
Morrison, C. T. *The Flame in the Icebox*. 1968.
O'Brien, Tim. *Going after Cacciato*. 1978.
———. *If I Die in a Combat Zone*. 1973.
Parks, David. *G.I. Diary*. 1965.
Pelfrey, William . *The Big V*. 1972.
Rabe, David. *The Basic Training of Pavlo Hummel and Sticks and Bones*. 1973.
———. *Streamers*. 1977.
Roth, Robert. *Sand in the Wind*. 1973.
Rottmann, Larry, ed. *Winning Hearts and Minds: Poems by Vietnam Veterans*. 1972.
Rowe, John. *Count Your Dead*. 1968.
Russ, Martin. *Happy Hunting Ground*. 1968.
Sack, John. *M*. 1967.
Schulze, Gene. *Third Face of War*. 1969.
Sloan, James Park. *War Games*. 1971.
Stone, Robert. *Dog Soldiers*. 1974.
Tiede, Tom. *Coward*. 1968.
Tegaskis, Richard. *Vietnam Diary*. 1963.
Topham, J., ed. *Poems of the Vietnam War*. 1985.
Vance, Samuel. *The Courageous and the Proud*. 1970.
Webb, James. *Fields of Fire*. 1978.
Weigel, Bruce. *A Romance*. 1979.
Wilson, James C. *Vietnam in Prose and Film*. 1982.
Woods, William Crawford. *The Killing Zone*. 1970.

MEMOIRS AND FIRST-PERSON ACCOUNTS

Anderson, Charles B. *The Grunts*. 1976.
Baer, Gordon, and Nancy Howell-Koehler. *Vietnam: The Battle Comes Home*. 1984.

Baker, Mark. *Nam: The Vietnam War in the Words of the Men and Women Who Fought There*. 1981.

Ball, George W. *The Past Has Another Pattern*. 1982.

Bernard, Edward. *Going Home*. 1973.

Bleier, Rocky, and Terry O'Neill. *Fighting Back*. 1980.

Brant, Toby L. *Journal of a Combat Tanker Vietnam, 1969*. 1986.

Brennan, Matthew. *Brennan's War: Vietnam, 1965–1969*. 1986.

Bridwell, Ric. *Manchu Delta*. 1986.

Briscoe, Edward G. *Diary of a Short-Timer in Vietnam*. 1970.

Broughton, Jack. *Thud Ridge*. 1969.

Brown, John M. *Rice Paddy Grunt: Unfading Memories of the Vietnam Generation*. 1986.

Browne, Malcom. *The New Face of War*. 1986.

Burchett, Wilfred G. *Vietnam: Inside Story of the Guerrilla War*. 1965.

Cao Van Vien and Dong Van Khuyen. *Reflections of the Vietnam War*. 1980.

Caputo, Philip. *A Rumor of War*. 1977.

Carter, Jimmy. *Keeping Faith*. 1982.

Cassidy, John. *A Station in the Delta*. 1982.

Chanoff, David, and Doan Van Toai. *Portrait of the Enemy*. 1986.

Clark, Johnnie M. *Guns Up!* 1986.

Cleland, Max. *Strong at the Broken Places*. 1980.

Colby, William E., and Peter Forbath. *Honorable Men: My Life in the CIA*. 1978.

Collins, James Lawton, Jr. *The Development and Training of the South Vietnamese Army, 1950–1972*. 1975.

Cook, John L. *The Advisor*. 1973.

Currey, Richard. *Crossing Over: A Vietnam Journal*. 1980.

Dengler, Dieter. *Escape from Laos*. 1979.

Denton, Jeremiah A. *When Hell Was in Session*. 1976.

Donovan, D. *Once a Warrior King: Memories of an Officer in Vietnam*. 1985.

Downs, Frederick. *The Killing Zone: My Life in the Vietnam War*. 1978.

Drury, Richard S. *My Secret War*. 1979.

Ehrhart, W. D. *Vietnam-Perkasie: A Combat Marine Memoir*. 1983.

Ehrhart, William. *Marking Time*. 1986.

Eisenhower, Dwight D. *White House Years*. 1963.

Ellsberg, Daniel. *Papers on the War*. 1972.

Enthoven, Alain C., and K. Wayne Smith. *How Much is Enough? Shaping the Defense Program, 1961–1969*. 1971.

The Eyewitness History of the Vietnam War: 1961–1975. 1983.

Fall, Bernard, ed. *Ho Chi Minh on Revolution*. 1968.

Garrett, Richard. *P.O.W.* 1981.

Giap, Vo Nguyen. *Big Victory, Big Task*. 1967.

————. *Dien Bien Phu*. 1962.

————. *Unforgettable Days*. 1978.

Goldman, Peter, and Tony Fuller. *Charlie Company: What Vietnam Did to Us*. 1983.

Grauwin, Paul. *Doctor at Dienbienphu*. 1955.

Hakes, Thomas L. *A Soldier's Diary of Thoughts, Memories and Letters*. 1987.

Haldeman, Joe. *War Year*. 1972.

Halstead, Fred. *Out Now! A Participant's Account of the American Movement Against the Vietnam War*. 1978.

Harriman, W. Averell. *America and Russia in a Changing World: A Half Century of Personal Observation.* 1971.

Harriman, W. Averell, and Elie Abel. *Special Envoy to Churchill and Stalin, 1941–1946.* 1975.

Herbert, Anthony B. *Soldier.* 1973.

Herr, Michael. *Dispatches.* 1984.

Herrington, Stuart A. *Peace with Honor? An American Reports on Vietnam, 1973–1975.* 1983.

Hilsman, Roger. *To Move a Nation: The Politics of Foreign Policy in the Administration of John F. Kennedy.* 1967.

Ho Chi Minh. *Prison Diary.* 1966.

Hoopes, Townsend. *The Limits of Intervention.* 1969.

Hosmer, Stephen T., ed. *The Fall of South Vietnam: Statements by Vietnamese Military and Civilian Leaders.* 1978.

Hubbell, John G., et al. *POW.* 1976.

Javits, Jacob. *Who Makes War? The President Versus Congress.* 1973.

Johnson, Lyndon Baines. *The Vantage Point: Perspectives of the Presidency, 1963–1969.* 1971.

Jones, James. *Viet Journal.* 1973.

Joyner, William, et al. *Vietnam Heroes: That We Have Peace.* 1983.

Kamazi, I. *Nam Book.* 1981.

Kauffman, Joel. *The Weight.* 1980.

Ketwig, John. *And a Hard Rain Fell: A Soldier's True Story of His Stay in Vietnam.* 1985.

Kirban, Salem. *Goodbye, Mr. President.* 1974.

Kirk, Donald. *Tell It to the Dead: Memories of a War.* 1975.

Kissinger, Henry. *White House Years.* 1979.

———. *Years of Upheaval.* 1982.

Klein, Joe. *Payback: Five Marines after Vietnam.* 1984.

Lansdale, Edward Geary. *In the Midst of Wars: An American's Mission to Southeast Asia.* 1972.

Lee, Larry. *American Eagle: The Story of a Navajo Vietnam Veteran.* 1977.

Lewis, Lloyd B. *The Tainted War: Culture and Identity in Vietnam War Narratives.* 1985.

Linedecker, Clifford. *Kerry: Agent Orange and an American Family.* 1982.

Lodge, Henry Cabot. *The Storm Has Many Eyes: A Personal Narrative.* 1973.

McCarthy, Eugene. *The Year of the People.* 1969.

McCauley, Anna K. *Miles from Home.* 1984.

McDonough, James R. *Platoon Leader.* 1985.

Marshall, Samuel L. *Ambush.* 1982.

———. *Bird: The Christmastide Battle.* 1968.

———. *Campaigning in the Central Highlands, Vietnam, Summer 1966.* 1984.

Mason, Robert C. *Chickenhawk.* 1984.

Mecklin, John. *Mission in Torment.* 1965.

———. *Selected Works.* Vols. 1–4. 1966–67.

Mulligan, James A. *The Hanoi Commitment.* 1981.

Nasmyth, Virginia, and Spike Nasmyth. *Hanoi Release John Nasmyth.* 1984.

Nguyen Cao Ky. *Twenty Years and Twenty Days.* 1976.

Nguyen Ngoc, Ngan. *The Will of Heaven*. 1981.

Nixon, Richard M. *No More Vietnams*. 1985.

———. *RN: The Memoirs of Richard Nixon*. 1978.

Noel, Chris, et al. *Matter of Survival*. 1987.

O'Brien, Tim. *If I Die in a Combat Zone*. 1979.

Page, Tim. *Tim Page's Nam*. 1983.

Palmer, Dave R. *Summons of the Trumpet*. 1984.

Parrish, John A. *Twelve, Twenty & Five: A Doctor's Year in Vietnam*. 1986.

Porter, Gareth, ed. *Vietnam: The Definitive Documentation of Human Decisions*. 1979.

Regan, David J. *Mourning Glory: The Making of a Marine*. 1980.

Ridgway, Matthew B. *Soldier: The Memoirs of Matthew B. Ridgway*. 1956.

Risner, Robinson. *The Passing of the Night: My Seven Years as a Prisoner of the North Vietnamese*. 1974.

Roche, John P. *Sentenced to Life: Reflections on Politics, Education, and Law*. 1974.

Roskey, William. *Muffled Shots: A Year on the DMZ*. 1987.

Rostow, W. W. *The Diffusion of Power, 1957–1972*. 1972.

Rowan, Stephen A. *They Wouldn't Let Us Die: The Prisoners of War Tell Their Story*. 1975.

Rowe, James N. *Five Years to Freedom*. 1971.

Rubin, Jerry. *Do It!* 1970.

———. *Growing (Up) at 37*. 1976.

Sack, John. *Lieutenant Calley: His Own Story*. 1971.

Salinger, Pierre. *With Kennedy*. 1966.

Salisbury, Harrison. *Behind the Lines: Hanoi, December 23, 1966–January 7, 1967*. 1967.

Santoli, Al. *Everything We Had: An Oral History of the Vietnam War by Thirty-Three American Soldiers Who Fought It*. 1981.

———. *To Bear Any Burden: The Vietnam War and Its Aftermath in the Words of Americans and Southeast Asians*. 1985.

Schanberg, Sydney. *Death and Life Dith Pran*. 1985.

Scholl-Latour, Peter. *Death in the Rice Fields: An Eyewitness Account of Vietnam's Three Wars, 1945–1979*. 1985.

Sharp, U.S.G. *Strategy for Defeat: Vietnam in Retrospect*. 1978.

Sharp, U.S.G. and William Westmoreland. *Report on the War in Vietnam*. 1968.

Simpson, Charles M. III. *Inside the Green Berets: The First Thirty Years*. 1983.

Snepp, Frank. *Decent Interval: An Insider's Account of Saigon's Indecent End*. 1977.

Sorenson, Theodore C. *Kennedy*. 1965.

Stockdale, Jim, and Sybil Stockdale. *In Love and War: The Story of a Family's Ordeal and Sacrifice During the Vietnam Years*. 1984.

Taylor, Maxwell D. *Swords and Plowshares*. 1972.

———. *The Uncertain Trumpet*. 1959.

Terry, Wallace. *Bloods: An Oral History of the Vietnam War by Black Veterans*. 1984.

Thompson, Robert. *No Exit from Vietnam*. 1970.

———. *Peace Is Not at Hand*. 1974.

Tran Van Dinh. *This Nation and Socialism Are One: Selected Writings of Le Duan*. 1977.

Triotti, John. *Phantom over Vietnam: Fighter Pilot, USMC*. 1984.

Truong Nhu Tang, with David Chanoff and Doan Van Toai. *A Viet Cong Memoir*. 1985.

Vance, Cyrus. *Hard Choices*. 1983.

Vance, Samuel. *Courageous and the Proud*. 1970.
Van Devanter, Lynda, and Christopher Morgan. *Home Before Morning: The Story of an Army Nurse in Vietnam*. 1983.
Walter, Keith. *A Piece of My Heart: Stories of Twenty-Six American Women Who Served in Vietnam*. 1986.
Webb, Kate, *On the Other Side: 23 Days with the Viet Cong*. 1972.
Westmoreland, William C. *A Soldier Reports*. 1976.
Whittington, Ruben B. *Moonspinners, Vietnam 65–66*. 1986.
Williams, William Appleman, et al., eds. *America in Vietnam: A Documentary History*. 1985.
Willwerth, James. *Eye in the Last Storm*. 1972.
Zalin, Grant. *Survivors: American POWs in Vietnam*. 1985.
Zumwalt, Elmo, et al. *My Father, My Son*. 1986.
Zumwalt, Elmo R., Jr. *On Watch*. 1976.

MIAs/POWs

Calvin, Rodney. *First Heroes: American MIAs-POWs Left Behind in Vietnam*. 1987.
Clarke, Douglas L. *The Missing Man, Politics and the MIA*. 1979.
Grooth, Winston, and Duncan Spencer. *Conversations with the Enemy*. 1983.
Hubbell, John G. *P.O.W.: A Definitive History of the American Prisoner-of-War Experience in Vietnam, 1964–1973*. 1976.
Kim, Samuel. *The American POWs*. 1978.
O'Daniel, Larry J. *Missing in Action*. 1979.
Reader's Digest. *POW: A Definitive History of the American Prisoner of War Experience in Vietnam, 1964–1973*. 1976.
Schlemmer, Benajmin. *The Raid*. 1976.
Zalin, Grant. *Survivors: American POWs in Vietnam*. 1985.

MINORITIES

Binkin, Martin, et al. *Blacks in the Military*. 1982.
Byrd, Barthy. *Home Front: Women and Viet Nam*. 1986.
Goff, Stanley, and Robert Sandfors. *Brothers: Black Soldiers in the Nam*. 1982.
Holm, Jeanne. *Women in the Military*. 1982.
Mullen, Robert W. *Blacks and Vietnam*. 1981.
Taylor, Clyde, ed. *Vietnam and Black America: An Anthology of Protest and Resistance*. 1973.
Terry, Wallace. *Bloods: An Oral History of the Vietnam War by Black Veterans*. 1984.
Vance, Samuel. *Courageous and the Proud*. 1970.
Willenz, June A. *Women Veterans: America's Forgotten Heroines*. 1984.

NAVAL WAR

Butler, James. *River of Death—Song Vam Sat*. 1979.
Croizat, Victor. *The Brown Water Navy: The River and Coastal War in Indo-China and Vietnam, 1948–1972*. 1984.

Fulton, William B. *Riverine Operations, 1966–1969*. 1973.

Galloway, John. *The Gulf of Tonkin Resolution*. 1970.

Goulden, Joseph C. *Truth Is the First Casualty*. 1969.

Hooper, Edwin B. *Mobility, Support, Endurance: A Story of Naval Operational Logistics in the Vietnam War, 1965–1968*. 1972.

Hooper, Edwin B., Dean C. Allard, and Oscar P. Fitzgerald. *The United States Navy and the Vietnam Conflict: The Setting of the Stage to 1959*. 1976.

Luckow, Ulrik. "Victory Over Ignorance and Fear: The U.S. Minelaying Attack on North Vietnam." *Naval War College Review*. January-February 1982.

Marolda, Edward J., and G. Wesley Pryce III. *A Short History of the United States Navy and the Southeast Asian Conflict, 1950–1975*. 1984.

Mersky, Peter, and Norman Polmar. *The Naval Air War in Vietnam: 1965–1975*. 1981.

Naval Facilities and Engineering Command. *Southeast Asia: Building the Bases. The History of Construction in Southeast Asia*. 1975.

Riverine Warfare: The U.S. Navy's Operations on Inland Waterways. 1968.

Triotti, John. *Phantom over Vietnam: Fighter Pilot, USMC*. 1984.

Tulich, Eugene. *The United States Coast Guard in Southeast Asia During the Vietnam Conflict*. 1975.

Van Vleet. *Naval Aviation in Viet Nam*. 1985.

Windchy, Eugene C. *Tonkin Gulf*. 1971.

PRESS/MEDIA

Arlen, Michael. *Living Room War*. 1969.

Bailey, George A. "Intepretive Reporting of the Vietnam War by Anchormen." *Journalism Quarterly* 53, no. 2 (Summer 1976).

———. "Television War: Trends in Network Coverage of Vietnam 1965–1970." *Journal of Broadcasting*, 20 (Spring 1976).

Bailey, George A., and Lawrence W. Lichty. "Rough Justice on a Saigon Street: A Gatekeeper Study of NBC's Tet Execution Film." *Journalism Quarterly* 49, no. 2 (Summer 1972).

Barnouw, Erik. *The Image Empire*. 1970.

Braestrup, Peter. *Battle Lines: Report of the Twentieth Century Fund Task Force on the Military and the Media*. 1985.

———. *Big Story: How the American Press and Television Reported and Interpreted the Crisis of Tet 1968 in Vietnam and Washington*. 1983.

Brewin, Bob, and Sydney Shaw. *Vietnam on Trial: Westmoreland vs. CBS*. 1986.

Gitlin, Todd. *The Whole World Is Watching*. 1980.

Goulden, Joseph C. *Truth Is the First Casualty*. 1968.

Gravel, Mike, ed. *The Pentagon Papers*. 1971.

Hallin, Daniel C. *The Uncensored War: The Media and Vietnam*. 1986.

Herz, Martin F., and Leslie Rider. *The Prestige Press and the Christmas Bombing, 1972: Images and Reality in Vietnam*. 1985.

Lunn, Hugh. *Vietnam: A Reporter's War*. 1986.

Mills, Nick. *The Vietnam Experience: Combat Photographer*. 1983.

Mueller, John E. *War, Presidents, and Public Opinion*. 1973.

Turner, Kathleen J. *Lyndon Johnson's Dual War: Vietnam and the Press*. 1985.

STRATEGY AND WAR MANAGEMENT

Baldwin, Hanson W. *Strategy for Tomorrow*. 1970.
Baral, Jaya. *The Pentagon and the Making of U.S. Foreign Policy*. 1978.
BDM Corporation. *A Study of Strategic Lessons Learned in Vietnam*. 1980.
Berman, Larry. *Planning a Tragedy: The Americanization of the War in Vietnam*. 1982.
Collins, John M. *U.S. Defense Planning: A Critique*. 1982.
Eckhart, George S. *Command and Control, 1950–1969*. 1974.
Fallows, James. *National Defense*. 1981.
Gabriel, Richard, and Paul Savage. *Crisis in Command*. 1978.
Hoang Ngoc Long. *Strategy and Tactics*. 1980.
Kinnard, Douglas. *The Secretary of Defense*. 1980.
———. *The War Managers*. 1977.
Korb, Lawrence J. *The Joint Chiefs of Staff: The First Twenty-Five Years*. 1976.
Luttwack, Edward N. *The Pentagon and the Art of War*. 1985.
Mueller, John E. "The Search for the 'Breaking Point' in Vietnam: The Statistics of a
     Deadly Quarrel." *International Studies Quarterly* 4 (December 1980).
O'Brien, William V. *The Conduct of Just and Limited War*. 1981.
O'Neill, Robert J. *The Strategy of General Giap Since 1964*. 1969.
Palmer, Gregory. *The McNamara Strategy and the Vietnam War: Program Budgeting in
     the Pentagon, 1960–1968*. 1978.
Pettit, Clyde Edwin. *The Experts*. 1975.
Pimlott, John, ed. *Vietnam: The History and the Tactics*. 1982.
Summers, Harry G., Jr. *On Srategy: A Critical Analysis of the Vietnam War*. 1982.
Van Dyke, Jon M. *North Vietnam's Strategy for Survival*. 1972.
Walt, Lewis W. *Strange War, Strange Strategy*. 1976.

TET OFFENSIVE

Brodie, Bernard. *The Tet Offensive*. 1976.
Dougan, Clark, and Steven Weiss. *The Vietnam Experience: Nineteen Sixty-Eight*. 1983.
Nolan, Keith W. *Battle for Hue: Tet, 1968*. 1983.
Oberdorfer, Don. *Tet!* 1971.
———. *TET: The Turning Point of the Vietnam War*. 1983.
Pham Von Son and Le Van Duong, eds. *The Viet Cong Tet Offensive 1968*. 1969.

VETERANS AND SOLDIERS

Baskir, Lawrence M., and William A. Strauss. *Chance and Circumstance: The Draft,
     the War, and the Vietnam Generation*. 1978.
Boyle, Richard. *Flower of the Dragon: The Breakdown of the U.S. Army in Vietnam*.
     1972.
Brandon, Heather. *Casualties: Death in Vietnam, Anguish and Survival in America*.
     1984.
Card, Josephina J. *Lives After Vietnam*. 1983.
Cohen, Eliot A. *Citizens and Soldiers: The Dilemmas of Military Service*. 1985.

Cortright, David. *Soldiers in Revolt.* 1976.
Goldstein, Joseph, Burke Marshall, and Jack Schwartz, eds. *The My Lai Massacre and Its Cover-up: Beyond the Reach of the Law?* 1978.
Hanser, William L. *America's Army in Crisis.* 1973.
Hendin, Herbert, and Ann P. Haas. *Wounds of War.* 1984.
Hersh, Seymour. *My Lai 4.* 1970.
King, Edward. *The Death of the Army.* 1972.
Klein, Robert. *Wounded Men, Broken Promises.* 1981.
Kubey, Craig, et al. *The Viet Vet Survival Guide: How to Cut Through the Bureaucracy and Get What You Need and Are Entitled To.* 1985.
Lifton, Robert Jay. *Home from the War.* 1973.
MacPherson, Myra. *Long Time Passing: Vietnam and the Haunted Generation.* 1984.
Moskos, Charles. *The American Enlisted Man.* 1970.
Peers, W. R. *The My Lai Inquiry.* 1979.
Sonnenberg, Stephen M., et al., eds. *The Trauma of War: Stress and Recovery in Viet Nam Veterans.* 1985.
Starr, Paul. *The Discarded Army.* 1973.
Whiteside, Thomas. *The Withering Rain.* 1971.
Wilcox, Fred A. *Waiting for an Army to Die: The Tragedy of Agent Orange.* 1983.

VIETNAMESE CULTURE AND ETHNICITY

Crawford, Ann (Caddel). *Customs and Culture of Vietnam.* 1966.
Dumoutier, Gustave. *Annamese Religions.* 1955.
Dutt, Sukumar. *Buddhism in East Asia.* 1966.
Embree, John F. *Ethnic Groups of Northern Southeast Asia.* 1950.
Gheddo, Pierro. *The Cross and the Bo-Tree: Catholics and Buddhists in Vietnam.* 1970.
Gregerson, Marilyn J. "The Ethnic Minorities of Vietnam," *Southeast Asia: An International Quarterly* 20. Winter 1972.
Groslier, Bernard Philippe. *The Art of Indochina.* 1962.
Hickey, Gerald Cannon. *Free in the Forest: An Ethnohistory of the Vietnamese Central Highlands, 1954–1976.* 1982.
———. *The Highland People of South Vietnam: Social and Economic Development.* 1967.
———. *Sons of the Mountains: Ethnohistory of the Vietnamese Central Highlands to 1954.* 1982.
———. *Village in Vietnam.* 1964.
Hoskins, Marilyn W., and Eleanor Shepherd. *Life in a Vietnamese Urban Quarter.* 1971.
Iredell, F. Raymond. *Vietnam: The Country and the People.* 1966.
Karnow, Stanley. *Life, Southeast Asia.* 1962.
McAlister, John T. *Southeast Asian Tribes, Minorities and Nations.* 1967.
Mole, Robert L. *The Montagnards of South Vietnam: A Study of Nine Tribes.* 1970.
Nguyen Dinh-Hoa, ed. *Some Aspects of Vietnamese Culture.* 1972.
Oliver, Victor L. *Cao Dai Spiritualism: A Study of Religion in Vietnamese Society.* 1976.
Rawson, Philip. *The Art of Southeast Asia.* 1967.
Schrock, Joan L., et al. *Minority Groups in the Republic of Vietnam.* 1967.

VIETNAMESE HISTORY

Bain, Chester. *Vietnam: The Roots of Conflict.* 1967.

Bastin, John Sturgis. *The Emergence of Modern Southeast Asia.* 1967.

Bone, Robert C. *Contemporary Southeast Asia.* 1962.

Buttinger, Joseph. *The Smaller Dragon: A Political History of Vietnam.* 1958.

————. *Vietnam: A Dragon Embattled.* 2 vols. 1967.

————. *Vietnam: A Political History.* 1968.

Cady, John Frank. *Southeast Asia: Its Historical Development.* 1958.

Chen, King C. *Vietnam and China, 1938–1954.* 1969.

Chesneaux, Jean. *The Vietnamese Nation: Contribution to a History.* 1966.

Coedes, George. *The Indianized States of Southeast Asia.* 1968.

————. *The Making of Southeast Asia.* 1966.

Cotter, Michael G. "Towards a Social History of the Vietnamese Southward Movement." *Journal of Southeast Asian History* 9 (March 1968), 12–24.

Donnell, John C., and Charles A. Joiner, eds. *Electoral Politics in South Vietnam.* 1974.

Duncanson, Dennis J. *Government and Revolution in Vietnam.* 1968.

Duiker, William J. *The Rise of Nationalism in Vietnam, 1900–1941.* 1976.

Goodman, Allen E. *Politics in War: The Bases of Political Community in South Vietnam.* 1973.

Hall, Daniel. *A History of Southeast Asia.* 1955.

Hall, D.B.E. *A History of Southeast Asia.* 1968.

Hammer, Ellen Joy. *Vietnam, Yesterday and Today.* 1966.

Harrison, Brian. *Southeast Asia, A Short History.* 1954.

Hawthorne, Lesleyanne, ed. *Refugee: The Vietnamese Experience.* 1982.

Joiner, Charles A. *The Politics of Massacre: Political Processes in South Vietnam.* 1974.

Lacouture, Jean. *Vietnam: Between Two Truces.* 1966.

McAlister, John T., Jr. *Vietnam: The Origins of Revolution.* 1970.

————. *The Vietnamese and Their Revolution.* 1970.

McAlister, John T., Jr., and Paul Mus. *The Vietnamese and Their Revolution.* 1970.

McAleavy, Henry. *Black Flags in Vietnam: The Story of the Chinese Intervention.* 1968.

Marr, David G. *Vietnamese Anticolonialism, 1885–1925.* 1971.

Ngo Vinh Long. *Before the Revolution: The Vietnamese Peasant Under the French.* 1973.

Nguyen Phuc-Tan. *A Modern History of Vietnam, 1802–1954.* 1964.

Pike, Douglas. *History of the Vietnamese Communist Party.* 1978.

Samuels, Gertrude. "Passage to Freedom in Vietnam." *National Geographic* 107 (June 1955), 858–74.

Scigliano, Robert. *South Viet-Nam: Nation Under Stress.* 1963.

————. *South Viet-Nam Since Independence.* 1963.

Steinberg, David J., ed. *In Search of Southeast Asia.* 1971.

Thai, Van-Kiem. *Viet Nam Past and Present.* 1956.

Turner, Robert F. *Vietnamese Communism: Its Origins and Developments.* 1975.

Warner, Denis. *The Last Confucian.* 1963.

Appendix E
A Chronology of the Vietnam War, 1945–1975

1945

Sept. 02   Ho Chi Minh proclaims the Democratic Republic of Vietnam.
26   A. Peter Dewey, head of the OSS mission in Saigon, is shot by Vietminh troops, becoming the first American to die in the Vietnam War.

1946

Mar. 06   Franco-Vietnamese Accords signed.
June 01   The Fontainebleau Conference convenes.
Dec. 19   The Vietminh attack French forces in Tonkin, formally beginning the First Indochina War.

1948

June 05   The French name Bao Dai head of state of Vietnam.

1949

Mar. 08   Élysée Agreement signed.
Oct. 01   Mao Zedong proclaims the People's Republic of China.

1950

Jan. 14   Ho Chi Minh again proclaims establishment of the Democratic Republic of Vietnam.
June 27   President Harry S. Truman announces increased U.S. military assistance to Vietnam.
Aug. 03   United States Military Assistance and Advisory Group arrives in Saigon.
Dec. 30   United States signs a Mutual Defense Assistance Agreement with France, Vietnam, Cambodia, and Laos.

1952

Nov. 04   Dwight D. Eisenhower is elected president.

1953

July 27   Korean War armistice is signed.

1954

Mar. 13	Vietminh attack the French fortress at Dien Bien Phu.
20	Admiral Arthur Radford proposes Operation Vulture to assist the French in defending Dien Bien Phu.
Apr. 07	President Dwight D. Eisenhower uses the domino analogy to explain the political significance of Indochina.
25	Winston Churchill and the British refuse to participate in Operation Vulture.
29	President Eisenhower announces that the United States will not provide air support to the French garrison at Dien Bien Phu.
May 07	The Vietminh conquer Dien Bien Phu.
08	The Geneva Conference opens.
July 20	France signs a cease-fire ending hostilities in Indochina.
Aug. 01	The first of nearly one million refugees from North Vietnam cross into South Vietnam.
Sept. 08	United States signs the Manila Treaty forming the Southeast Asia Treaty Organization.

1955

Mar. 28	Ngo Dinh Diem attacks the Binh Xuyen.
June 05	Ngo Dinh Diem attacks the Hoa Hao.
July 06	Ngo Dinh Diem repudiates the Geneva Agreements and refuses to plan for open elections throughout the country.
Oct. 26	Ngo Dinh Diem proclaims the Republic of Vietnam with himself as president.

1957

May 5–19	Ngo Dinh Diem visits the United States.

1959

Apr. 04	President Eisenhower makes his first commitment to maintain South Vietnam as a separate nation.
22	Christian A. Herter replaces John Foster Dulles as secretary of state.
July 01	General Lyman Lemnitzer replaces General Maxwell Taylor as chief of staff, U.S. Army.
08	First American servicemen (Major Dale Bius and Master Sergeant Chester Ovnard) killed by Vietcong attack at Bien Hoa.
Dec. 01	Thomas S. Gates, Jr., replaces Neil H. McElroy as secretary of defense.
31	Approximately 760 U.S. military personnel in Vietnam.

1960

Oct. 01	General George Decker replaces General Lyman Lemnitzer as chief of staff, U.S. Army.
Dec. 20	National Liberation Front established.
31	Approximately 900 U.S. military personnel in Vietnam.

1961

Jan. 21	John F. Kennedy succeeds Dwight D. Eisenhower as president. Dean Rusk succeeds Christian A. Herter as secretary of state. Robert S. McNamara succeeds Thomas S. Gates, Jr., as secretary of defense. McGeorge Bundy succeeds Gordon Gray as national security adviser.
28	Kennedy approves a Vietnam counterinsurgency plan.
Mar. 23	Kennedy insists that a Laotian cease-fire must precede negotiations to establish a neutral Laos.
May 9–15	Vice President Lyndon Johnson visits South Vietnam and recommends a strong American commitment there. Geneva Conference on Laos opens.
June 09	President Ngo Dinh Diem asks for U.S. military advisers to train the South Vietnamese Army.
July 01	General Maxwell Taylor is appointed military adviser to president John F. Kennedy.
Oct. 01	Ngo Dinh Diem requests a bilateral defense treaty with the United States.
Nov. 03	General Maxwell Taylor concludes that U.S. military, financial, and political aid will bring victory without a U.S. takeover of the war. He advises Kennedy to send 8,000 U.S. combat troops to Vietnam.
Dec. 15	Kennedy restates U.S. commitment to an independent South Vietnam.
31	U.S. military personnel in Vietnam now number 3,205.

1962

Feb. 06	MACV (U.S. Military Assistance Command, Vietnam) established in Saigon under the command of General Paul Harkins. The major buildup of American forces begins.
14	Kennedy authorizes U.S. military advisers in Vietnam to return fire if fired upon.
Mar. 22	United States launches the Strategic Hamlet (rural pacification) Program.
May 15	United States sends 5,000 marines and 50 jet fighters to Thailand to resist Communist aggression in Laos.
July 23	Geneva Accords on Laos signed.
Oct. 01	General Earle Wheeler replaces General George Decker as chief of staff, U.S. Army. General Maxwell Taylor replaces General Lyman Lemnitzer as chairman, Joint Chiefs of Staff.
Dec. 31	U.S. military personnel now in Vietnam number 11,300.

1963

Aug. 21	South Vietnam troops attack Buddhist pagodas.
22	Henry Cabot Lodge replaces Frederick Nolting as U.S. ambassador to Vietnam.
24	State Department instructs Henry Cabot Lodge to eliminate the influence of Ngo Dinh Nhu in the South Vietnamese government.
Nov. 01	Military coup overthrows the government of President Ngo Dinh Diem.
02	Diem and his brother Ngo Dinh Nhu assassinated.
22	President John F. Kennedy assassinated.
Dec. 31	U.S. military personnel in Vietnam now number 16,300.

1964

Feb. 07	Johnson removes American dependents from South Vietnam.
June 20	General William Westmoreland replaces General Paul Harkins as head of MACV.
23	General Maxwell Taylor replaces Henry Cabot Lodge as U.S. ambassador to South Vietnam.
30	Admiral Ulysses S. Grant Sharp replaces Admiral Harry D. Felt as CINCPAC.
July 03	General Harold Johnson replaces General Earle Wheeler as chief of staff, U.S. Army.
Aug. 02	U.S. destroyer *Maddox* allegedly attacked by North Vietnamese patrol boats in the Gulf of Tonkin.
04	U.S. destroyer *Turner Joy* claims attack by North Vietnamese patrol boats.
07	U.S. Congress passes Gulf of Tonkin Resolution.
Oct. 01	U.S. Army Fifth Special Forces Group arrives in Vietnam.
Nov. 01	Vietcong attack Bien Hoa Air Base. Six U.S. B–57 bombers destroyed; five American service personnel killed.
02	Johnson defeats Senator Barry Goldwater in presidential election.
Dec. 24	Vietcong kill two U.S. soldiers in an attack on the Brinks Hotel in Saigon.
31	U.S. military personnel in Vietnam now number 23,300.

1965

Feb. 07	Vietcong launch a widespread attack on American military installations in South Vietnam.
Mar. 02	Operation Rolling Thunder begins.
08	First American combat troops (U.S. Third Marine regiment) arrive in Vietnam to defend Da Nang.
24	First teach-in held at the University of Michigan.
Apr. 06	Johnson permits U.S. ground combat troops to conduct offensive operations in South Vietnam.
17	Students for a Democratic Society hold antiwar rally in Washington, D.C.
May 15	National Teach-In held throughout the country.
June 08	State Department reports that Johnson has authorized the use of U.S. troops in direct combat if the South Vietnamese Army requests assistance.
18	Arc Light Operations begin.
July 08	Henry Cabot Lodge succeeds Maxwell Taylor as U.S. ambassador to South Vietnam.
Aug. 18	Operation Starlight begins.
21	Operation Starlight ends.
Oct. 15–16	Antiwar protests in forty American cities.
23	Operation Silver Bayonet begins.
Nov. 14–16	Battle of the Ia Drang Valley.
20	Operation Silver Bayonet ends.

Dec. 25 Johnson suspends bombing of North Vietnam (Operation Rolling Thunder) and invites North Vietnam to negotiate.
31 U.S. military personnel in Vietnam now number 184,300; 636 U.S. military personnel killed in action to date; 22,420 Allied troops in Vietnam.

1966

Jan. 19 Operation Van Buren begins.
24 Operation Masher/White Wing/ Thank Phong II begins.
31 Bombing of North Vietnam (Operation Rolling Thunder) resumes.
Feb. 04 Senate Foreign Relations Committee opens televised hearings on the Vietnam War.
06 President Lyndon Johnson convenes the Honolulu Conference.
21 Operation Van Buren ends.
Mar. 01 Senate refuses to repeal the Gulf of Tonkin Resolution.
04 Operation Utah/Lien Ket 26 begins.
06 Operation Masher/White Wing/Thang Phong II ends.
08 Operation Utah/Lien Ket 26 begins.
20 Operation Texas/Lien Ket 28 begins.
    President Lyndon Johnson convenes the Guam Conference.
24 Operation Texas/Lien Ket 28 ends.
Apr. 01 Walt Rostow replaces McGeorge Bundy as national security adviser.
07 President Lyndon Johnson offers the Johns Hopkins Speech.
May 01 U.S. forces bombard Vietcong targets in Cambodia.
10 Operation Paul Revere/Than Phong 14 begins.
June 02 Operation Hawthorne/Dan Tang 61 begins.
    Operation El Paso II begins.
21 Operation Hawthorne/Dan Tang 61 ends.
29 United States bombs oil facilities in Haiphong and Hanoi.
July 04 Operation Macon begins.
07 Operation Hastings/Deckhouse II begins.
13 Operation El Paso II ends.
30 Operation Paul Revere/Than Phong 14 ends.
Aug. 01 Operation Paul Revere II begins.
03 Operation Hasting/Deckhouse II ends.
    Operation Prairie begins.
06 Operation Colorado/Lien Ket 52 begins.
21 Operation Colorado/Lien Ket 52 ends.
25 Operation Paul Revere II ends.
26 Operation Byrd begins.
Sept. 14 Operation Attleboro begins.
23 Operation Maeng Ho 6 (South Korean Capital Division) begins.
Oct. 02 Operation Irving begins.
18 Operation Paul Revere IV begins.
24 Operation Irving ends.
25 Operation Thayer II begins.
26 Johnson visits U.S. troops in Vietnam.

	27	Operation Macon ends.
Nov.	09	Operation Maeng Ho 6 ends.
	24	Operation Attleboro ends.
	30	Operation Fairfax begins.
Dec.	30	Operation Paul Revere IV ends.
	31	U.S. military personnel now in Vietnam number 385,300; 6,644 U.S. military personnel killed in action to date; 52,500 Allied military personnel in Vietnam.

1967

Jan.	01	Operation Sam Houston begins.
	06	Operation Palm Beach begins.
	08	Operation Cedar Falls begins.
	26	Operation Cedar Falls ends.
	31	Operation Prairie ends.
Feb.	01	Operation Prairie II begins.
	11	Operation Pershing begins.
	12	Operation Thayer II ends.
	13	Operation Enterprise begins.
	17	Operation Lien Ket 81 begins.
	22	Operation Lien Ket 81 ends.
		Operation Junction City begins.
Mar.	07	Operation Oh Jac Kyo I (South Korean) begins.
	18	Operation Prairie II ends.
Apr.	05	Operation Sam Houston ends.
		Operation Francis Marion begins.
	15	One hundred thousand antiwar protesters rally in New York.
	18	Operation Oh Jac Kyo I ends.
	21	Operation Union begins.
May	01	Ellsworth Bunker replaces Henry Cabot Lodge as U.S. ambassador to South Vietnam.
	09	Robert Komer appointed deputy to the MACV commander.
	14	Operation Junction City ends.
		Operation Kole Kole begins.
	17	Operation Union ends.
	19	U.S. planes bomb a power plant in Hanoi.
	25	Operation Union II begins.
	31	Operation Palm Beach ends.
June	05	Operation Union II ends.
July	02	Operation Buffalo begins.
	07	Congressional Joint Economic committee estimates the war will cost $4 to $6 billion more in 1967 than the $20.3 billion requested by Johnson.
	14	Operation Buffalo ends.
	16	Operation Kingfisher begins.
Sept.	03	Nguyen Van Thieu elected president of South Vietnam.
	04	Operation Swift begins.
	05	Operation Dragon Fire begins.
	15	Operation Swift ends.

19	Operation Bolling begins.
27	Operation Shenandoah II begins.
29	Johnson offers to stop bombing of North Vietnam if they will immediately come to the negotiating table (San Antonio Formula).
Oct. 12	Operation Francis Marion ends.
	Operation MacArthur begins.
21	Fifty thousand antiwar activists protest at the Pentagon.
30	Operation Dragon Fire ends.
31	Operation Kingfisher ends.
Nov. 01	Operation Scotland begins.
11	Operation Wheeler/Wallowa begins.
19	Operation Shenandoah II ends.
Dec. 07	Operation Kole Kole ends.
08	Operation Yellowstone begins.
14	Operation Fairfax ends.
17	Operation Uniontown begins.
	Operation Maeng Ho 9 begins.
19	Operation Muscatine begins.
31	U.S. military personnel now in Vietnam number 485,600; 16,021 U.S. military personnel killed in action to date.

1968

Jan. 03	Senator Eugene McCarthy announces his decision to seek the Democratic presidential nomination.
19	Operation Pershing ends.
20	Operation McLain begins.
	Operation Byrd ends.
21	Operation Lancaster II begins.
	Operation Nicaragua begins.
	NVA siege of Khe Sanh begins.
22	Operation Pershing II begins.
	Operation Jeb Stuart begins.
30	Operation Maeng Ho 9 ends.
	Tet Offensive begins.
31	Vietcong and NVA capture Hue.
	General Leonard F. Chapman replaces General Wallace M. Greene as Marine Corps commandant.
Feb. 01	Richard M. Nixon announces his candidacy for the presidency.
05	Operation Tran Hung Dao begins.
16	Operation Maeng Ho 10 begins.
17	Operation Tran Hung Dao ends.
	Operation Tran Hung Dao II begins.
24	Operation Yellowstone ends.
25	ARVN and U.S. troops reconquer Hue.
26	Operation Houston begins.
27	Westmoreland requests 206,000 more troops.
	CBS anchorman Walter Cronkite predicts over the evening news that the war cannot be won.

29	Operation Pershing II ends.
	Operation Napoleon/Saline begins.
Mar. 01	Operation Maeng Ho 10 ends.
08	Operation Uniontown ends.
	Operation Tran Hung Dao ends.
11	Operation Enterprise ends.
	Operation Saratoga ends.
	Operation Quyet Thang begins.
12	Eugene McCarthy wins the New Hampshire Democratic presidential primary.
16	Senator Robert Kennedy annouonces his decision to seek the Democratic presidential nomination.
	My Lai massacre takes place.
17	Operation Duong Cua Dan begins.
25–26	Senior Advisory Group on Vietnam recommends deescalation of the American commitment in Vietnam.
30	Operation Cochise Green begins.
31	Operation Scotland ends.
	Operation Jeb Stuart ends.
	Lyndon Johnson announces his decision not to run for reelection.
Apr. 01	Operation Pegasus/Lam Son 207 begins.
	Operation Carentan II begins.
07	Operation Quyet Thang ends.
08	Operation Toan Thang begins.
	Operation Burlington Trail begins.
15	Operation Pegasus/Lam Son 207 ends.
	Operation Scotland II begins.
19	Operation Delaware/Lam Son 216 begins.
23	Columbia University demonstrations begin.
26	Two hundred thousand people in NYC demonstrate against the war.
27	Vice President Hubert Humphrey announces his decision to seek the Democratic presidential nomination.
May 03	Johnson announces that formal peace talks will take place in Paris.
04	Operation Allen Brook begins.
12	Vietnam peace talks open in Paris.
17	Operation Carentan II ends.
	Operation Delaware/Lam Son 216 ends.
	Operation Jeb Stuart III begins.
	Operation Nevada Eagle begins.
18	Operation Mameluke Thrust begins.
31	Operation Toan Thang ends.
June 06	Robert Kennedy is assassinated.
10	Operation Muscatine ends.
July 01	General Creighton Abrams replaces General William Westmoreland as head of MACV.
03	General William Westmoreland replaces General Harold Johnson as chief of staff, U.S. Army.
17	Operation Quyet Chien begins.

30	Operation Truong Cong Dinh ends.
	Operation Duong Cua Dan ends.
31	Admiral John McCain replaces Admiral U.S. Grant Sharp as CINCPAC.
Aug. 02	Operation Lam Son 245 begins.
24	Operation Allen Brook ends.
	Operation Tien Bo begins.
28	Antiwar protests and riots in Chicago during the Democratic National Convention.
Sept. 09	Operation Tien Bo ends.
11	Operation Lam Son 261 begins.
12	Operation Houston ends.
Oct. 16	Operation Lam Son 271 begins.
23	Operation Mameluke Thrust ends.
24	Operation Henderson Hill begins.
31	Johnson announces end of bombing of North Vietnam.
	Operation Rolling Thunder ends.
Nov. 03	Operation Jeb Stuart III ends.
05	Richard Nixon defeats Hubert Humphrey in the 1968 presidential election.
11	Operation Wheeler/Wallowa ends.
	Operation Burlington Trail ends.
23	Operation Lancaster II ends.
Dec. 01	Operation Speedy Express begins.
06	Operation Henderson Hill ends.
	Operation Taylor Common begins.
08	Operation Le Loi I begins.
09	Operation Napoleon/Saline ends.
31	U.S. military personnel in Vietnam now number 536,000; 30,610 U.S. military personnel killed in action to date; 65,600 Allied troops in Vietnam.

1969

Jan. 01	Operation Quyet Thang begins.
	Operation Rice Farmer begins.
22	Operation Dewey Canyon begins.
	Richard Nixon inaugurated as president.
	William Rogers becomes secretary of state.
	Melvin Laird becomes secretary of defense.
	Henry Kissinger becomes national security adviser.
31	Operation Bolling ends.
	Operation MacArthur ends.
	Operation McLain ends.
	Operation Cochise Green ends.
Feb. 10	Operation Le Loi I ends.
24	Operation Quyet Thang 22 begins.
27	Operation Quang Nam begins.
28	Operation Kentucky ends.
	Operation Scotland II ends.

		Operation Nevada Eagle ends.
Mar.	01	Operation Oklahoma Hills begins.
		Operation Wayne Grey begins.
	04	Operation Quyet Chien ends.
	07	Operation Taylor Common ends.
	10	Operation Quyet Thang 22 ends.
	18	Operation Dewey Canyon ends.
		Operation Menu begins.
	20	Operation Quyet Thang 25 begins.
	26	Women Strike for Peace demonstration in Washington, D.C.
	31	Operation Quyet Thang 25 ends.
Apr.	14	Operation Wayne Grey ends.
	15	Operation Washington Green begins.
	18	Operation Dan Thang 69 begins.
	22	Operation Lam Son 277 begins.
		Operation Putnam Tiger begins.
	24	Operations Lam Son 245, 261, and 271 end.
	30	The number of U.S. military personnel in Vietnam reaches 543,300.
May	01	Operation Virginia Ridge begins.
	10	Operation Apache Snow begins.
	14	Nixon proposes peace plan for Vietnam involving mutual troop withdrawal.
	15	Operation Dan Quyen 38-A begins.
	16	Lamar Plain begins.
	29	Operation Oklahoma Hills ends.
	31	Operation Speedy Express ends.
June	07	Operation Apache Snow ends.
		Operation Dan Quyen 38-A ends.
	08	Nixon announces the removal of 25,000 troops from Vietnam.
	20	Operation Quang Nam ends.
		Operation Lam Son 277 ends.
July	16	Operation Virginia Ridge ends.
	21	Operation Idaho Canyon begins.
	25	Richard Nixon proclaims the Nixon Doctrine.
Aug.	13	Operation Lamar Plain ends.
	25	Operation Lien Ket 414 begins.
	26	Operation Lien Ket 531 begins.
	27	U.S. Ninth Infantry Division withdraws from Vietnam.
	31	Operation Rice Farmer ends.
Sept.	03	Ho Chi Minh dies.
	22	Operation Putnam Tiger ends.
	25	Operation Idaho Canyon ends.
	29	Operation Quyet Thang 21/38 begins.
Oct.	15	National Moratorium antiwar demonstrations staged throughout the United States.
Nov.	01	Operation Dan Tien 33D begins.
	12	Operation Dan Tien 40 begins.

15   The New Mobilization Committee to End the War in Vietnam sponsors a demonstration of 250,000 in Washington, D.C.
16   My Lai massacre described in the press.
30   U.S. Third Division withdraws from Vietnam.
Dec. 07   Operation Randolph Glen begins.
11   U.S. Third Brigade, 82nd Airborne Division, withdraws from Vietnam.
28   Operation Dan Tien 33D ends.
      Operation Dan Tien 40 ends.
31   Operation Quyet Thang ends.
      Operation Dan Thang 69 ends.
      Operation Lien Ket 414 ends.
      Operation Lien Ket 531 ends.
      Operation Quyet Thang 21/38 ends.
      U.S. military personnel strength in Vietnam declines to 475,200; 40,024 U.S. military personnel killed in action to date. Allied personnel in Vietnam totals 70,300.

1970

Feb. 20   Henry Kissinger opens secret peace negotiations in Paris.
Mar. 18   Prince Norodom Sihanouk of Cambodia deposed by General Lon Nol.
31   Operation Randolph Glen ends.
Apr. 01   Operation Texas Star begins.
15   U.S. 1st Infantry Division withdraws from Vietnam.
29   Operations in Cambodia begin.
30   United States invades Cambodia.
May 04   National Guard troops kill four students at Kent State University during demonstrations against the Cambodian invasion.
June 30   Operations in Cambodia end.
Sept. 05   Operation Texas Star ends.
      Operation Jefferson Glenn/Op ORD 13–70 begins.
Oct. 11   U.S. Third Brigade, Ninth Infantry Division, leaves Vietnam.
Nov. 21   Unsuccessful raid on the Son Tay Prison in North Vietnam.
Dec. 07   U.S. 4th Infantry Division leaves Vietnam.
08   U.S. 25th Infantry Division withdraws from Vietnam.
22   U.S. Congress prohibits U.S. combat forces or advisers in Cambodia and Laos.
31   U.S. military personnel strength in Vietnam reaches 334,600; 44,245 U.S. military presonnel killed in action to date. Allied military personnel declines to 67,700.

1971

Jan. 01   Operation Washington Green ends.
30   Operation Lam Son 719 begins.
      Operation Dewey Canyon II begins.
31   Winter Soldier Investigation begins in Detroit.
Feb. 07   Operation Dewey Canyon II ends.
Mar. 03   U.S. Fifth Special Forces Group leaves Vietnam.
05   U.S. 11th Armored Cavalry Regiment withdraws from Vietnam.

29	Lt. William L. Calley, Jr., found guilty of murder.
Apr. 06	Operation Lam Son 719 ends.
14	U.S. III Marine Amphibious Force withdraws from Vietnam.
20	Demonstrators in Washington, D.C., and San Francisco call for an end the war.
29	U.S. 1st Cavalry Division withdraws from Vietnam.
30	U.S. Second Brigade, 25th Infantry Division, withdraws from Vietnam.
May 3–5	People's Coalition for Peace and Justice demonstrates against the war in Washington, D.C.
June 13	*New York Times* starts publishing the Pentagon Papers.
30	Supreme Court allows publication of the Pentagon Papers.
Aug. 25	U.S. 173rd Airborne Brigade withdraws from Vietnam.
27	U.S. First Brigade, Fifth Infantry Division, withdraws from Vietnam.
31	Royal Thai Army withdraws from Vietnam.
Oct. 08	Operation Jefferson Glenn/OP ORD 13–70 ends.
Nov. 12	Nixon confines U.S. ground forces to a defensive role.
29	Americal Division divided into individual units.
Dec. 26	Nixon orders resumption of bombing of North Vietnam.
31	U.S. military strength declines to 156,800; 45,626 U.S. military personnel killed in action to date. Allied military personnel in Vietnam declines to 53,900.

1972

Feb. 21	Nixon seeks détente with the People's Republic of China by visiting Beijing.
Mar. 10	U.S. 101st Airborne Division leaves Vietnam.
23	United States suspends Paris peace talks until North Vietnam and the NLF enter into "serious discussions."
30	Eastertide Offensive begins.
Apr. 07	Battle of An Loc begins.
15	U.S. bombing of Hanoi begins again.
15–20	Widespread antiwar demonstrations across the United States.
27	Paris peace talks resume.
May 01	North Vietnamese conquer Quang Tri.
04	United States suspends the Paris peace talks.
08	U.S. Navy mines North Vietnamese ports.
June 18	NVA forces an end to the battle of An Loc.
22	Watergate break-in and arrests.
26	U.S. Third Brigade, 1st Cavalry Division, withdraws from Vietnam.
29	U.S. 196th Infantry Brigade withdraws from Vietnam.
July 01	General Bruce Palmer, Jr., becomes acting chief of staff, U.S. Army.
13	Paris peace talks resume after ten weeks.
Aug. 23	U.S. Third Battalion, 21st Infantry, withdraws from Vietnam.
Sept. 15	ARVN forces recapture Quang Tri.
26–27	Henry Kissinger conducts secret talks with North Vietnamese diplomats in Paris.
Oct. 16	General Creighton Abrams becomes chief of staff, U.S. Army.
17	Peace talks begin in Laos.

19–20	Kissinger meets with President Nguyen Van Thieu in Saigon to secure South Vietnamese support for the pending Paris Peace Accords.
Nov. 07	Nixon is reelected president in a landslide over Senator George McGovern.
20–21	Kissinger and Le Duc Tho put finishing touches on the Paris Peace Accords.
Dec. 13	Paris peace talks stall.
18–29	Operation Linebacker II conducted.
31	U.S. military strength declines to 24,000; 45,926 U.S. military personnel killed in action to date. Allied personnel drops to 35,500.
	SVNAF personnel killed in action to date numbers 195,847.

1973

Jan. 8–12	Kissinger and Le Duc Tho convene more private negotiations.
15	Nixon halts all U.S. offensive action against North Vietnam
27	Peace pact signed in Paris by the United States, South Vietnam, North Vietnam, and the National Liberation Front.
30	Elliot L. Richardson becomes secretary of defense.
Feb. 12	First of American POWs released by North Vietnam.
21	Peace agreement signed in Laos.
Mar. 16	ROK Capital Division and Ninth Infantary Division withdraw from Vietnam.
29	MACV headquarters removed.
	Last of American POWs released by North Vietnam.
June 13	Implementation accord signed in Paris by the United States, South Vietnam, North Vietnam, and the National Liberation Front.
24	Graham Martin becomes U.S. ambassador to South Vietnam.
	Congress prohibits all bombing in Cambodia after August 15.
July 02	James Schlesinger becomes secretary of defense.
Aug. 14	Arc Light Operations end.
	All direct American military operations end in all of Indochina.
Sept. 22	Henry Kissinger becomes secretary of state.
Nov. 07	War Powers Resolution becomes laws despite a presidential veto.
Dec. 31	American military personnel in South Vietnam drops to 50. To date, 46,163 U.S. military personnel killed in action. No Allied military personnel remain in Vietnam.

1974

Aug. 09	Nixon resigns the presidency.
	Gerald Ford is inaugurated as president of the United States.
20	Congress reduces aid to South Vietnam from $1 billion to $700 million.
Sept. 04	General Creighton Abrams dies.
16	Ford offers clemency to draft evaders and military deserters.
Oct. 03	General Frederick Weyand becomes chief of staff, U.S. Army.
Dec. 13	Combat between NVA and ARVN is conducted in Phuoc Long Province.
31	U.S. military strength in Vietnam remains at 50.

1975

Jan. 06	NVA troops take control of Phuoc Long Province.
08	North Vietnam decides on a massive invasion of South Vietnam.
Mar. 10	NVA captures Ban Me Thuot.
14	President Nguyen Van Thieu withdraws ARVN forces from Central Highlands.
19	NVA captures Quang Tri Province.
26	Hue falls to the NVA.
30	Da Nang falls to the NVA.
Apr. 01	Cambodian President Lon Nol flees Cambodia in face of Khmer Rouge invasion.
	South Vietnam abandons the northern half of the country to North Vietnam.
8–20	Battle of Xuan Loc.
11–13	Operation Eagle Pull removes U.S. embassy personnel from Phnom Penh, Cambodia.
12	President Nguyen Van Thieu resigns.
14	Operation Babylift ends.
17	Cambodia falls to Khmer Rouge troops.
29–30	Operation Frequent Wind evacuates all American personnel and some South Vietnamese from Vietnam.
	NVA captures Saigon.
30	Vietnam war ends.
May 12	*Mayaquez* seized in Kampuchean waters.

Appendix F
Maps of the Republic of Vietnam, 1975

Map prepared by Gerald Holder.

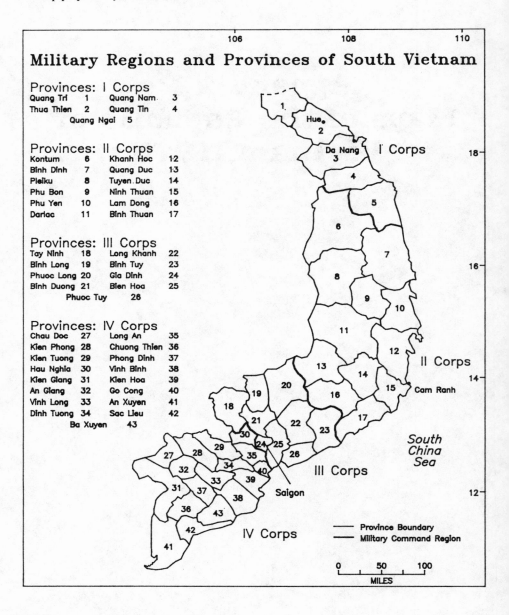

Military Regions and Provinces of South Vietnam

Provinces: I Corps

Quang Tri	1	Quang Nam	3
Thua Thien	2	Quang Tin	4
	Quang Ngai	5	

Provinces: II Corps

Kontum	6	Khanh Hoc	12
Binh Dinh	7	Quang Duc	13
Pleiku	8	Tuyen Duc	14
Phu Bon	9	Ninh Thuan	15
Phu Yen	10	Lam Dong	16
Darlac	11	Binh Thuan	17

Provinces: III Corps

Tay Ninh	18	Long Khanh	22
Binh Long	19	Binh Tuy	23
Phuoc Long	20	Gia Dinh	24
Binh Duong	21	Bien Hoa	25
	Phuoc Tuy	26	

Provinces: IV Corps

Chau Doc	27	Long An	35
Kien Phong	28	Chuong Thien	36
Kien Tuong	29	Phong Dinh	37
Hau Nghia	30	Vinh Binh	38
Kien Giang	31	Kien Hoa	39
An Giang	32	Go Cong	40
Vinh Long	33	An Xuyen	41
Dinh Tuong	34	Sac Lieu	42
	Ba Xuyen	43	

Map prepared by Gerald Holder.

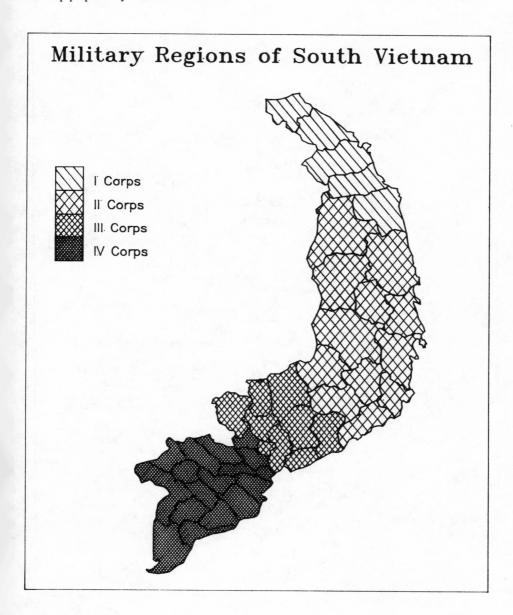

Military Regions of South Vietnam

I Corps

II Corps

III. Corps

IV Corps

Map prepared by Gerald Holder.

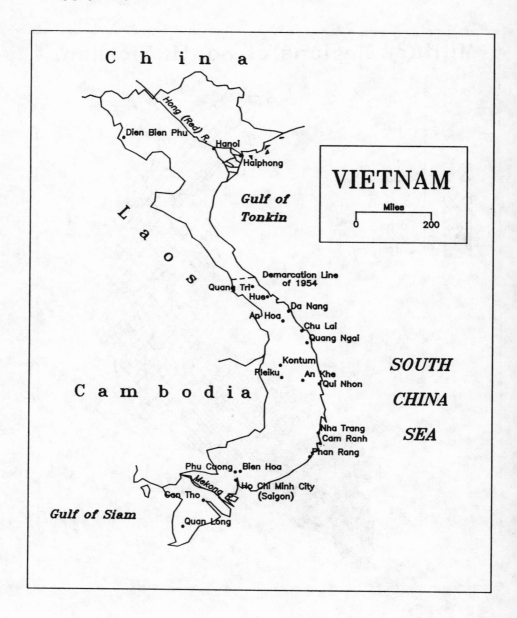

Index

About the Editor and Contributors

G. DUDLEY ACKER, JR. is currently working on a Ph.D. in history and teaching at Northern Arizona University in Flagstaff.

LINDA K. ALKANA is currently a lecturer in the Department of History at California State University at Long Beach.

CHARLES ANGEL teaches history at North Harris Junior College.

NOLAN J. ARGYLE is an Associate Professor at Valdosta State College in Valdosta, Georgia. In addition to a number of articles in professional journals, he is the author of *The Bridge at Kilometer 575* and *Tax Expenditure Analysis: A Concept Whose Time Has Come*.

GARY M. BELL is an Associate Professor of History at Sam Houston State University, Huntsville, Texas.

DAVID BERNSTEIN teaches in the Department of History at California State University, Long Beach.

LINDA CASCI teaches at McCulloch High School in The Woodlands, Texas.

GLORIA COLLINS teaches at Aldine High School in Houston, Texas.

JOANNA D. COWDEN is currently the Chair of the Department of History at California State University at Chico. She is the author of a number of articles in professional journals, and editor, with Richard O. Curry, of *Slavery in America: Theodore Weld's American Slavery As It Is*.

CHARLES M. DOBBS is Professor of History at Metropolitan State College in Denver, Colorado.

SAMUEL FREEMAN teaches political science at Pan American University in Edinburgh, Texas.

FRANCES FRENZEL teaches at Madisonville High School, Madisonville, Texas.

JAMES HINDMAN is the Dean of Liberal Arts and Professor of History at Eastern New Mexico University.

GERALD HOLDER teaches in the geography department of Sam Houston State University.

SEAN A. KELLEHER is an Associate Professor of political science at the University of Texas of the Permian Basin.

JOHN KINCAID is a Professor of Political Science at North Texas State University. He is the author of a number of books and articles, including *Covenant, Polity, and Constitutionalism* and *The Covenant Connection: Federal Theology and the Origins of Modern Politics*.

ROGER D. LAUNIUS is Deputy, Office of History, Headquarters Air Force Systems Command, Andrews Air Force Base, Washington, D.C.

JOHN S. LEIBY teaches economics and history in the Maricopa Community College District. He is the author of *Report to the King: Colonel Juan Camargo y Cavallero's Historical Account of New Spain, 1815* and *Colonial Bureaucrats and the Mexican Economy: Growth of a Patrimonial State, 1763–1821*.

TERRY MARTIN teaches at Willis High School in Willis, Texas.

JAMES S. OLSON teaches at Sam Houston State University in Huntsville, Texas. He is the author of many books on recent American history, including *The Ethnic Dimension in American History* and *Saving Capitalism: The Reconstruction Finance Corporation and the New Deal, 1933–1940*.

HOYT HUGHES PURVIS is serving as Director of the Fulbright Institute of International Relations at the University of Arkansas, following a distinguished career in journalism.

JOHN A. RICKS III is an Associate Professor of history at Valdosta State College in Valdosta, Georgia.

JOSEPH M. ROWE, JR. teaches history at Sam Houston State University, Huntsville, Texas.

ROBERT W. SELLEN is Professor of History at Georgia State University, Atlanta, and the author of many articles in professional journals.

SALLY SMITH teaches history at McCullogh High School in The Woodlands, Texas.

STAFFORD T. THOMAS is Assistant Professor of Political Science at California State University, Chico, and the author of *The United States Intelligence Community*.

JOHN E. WILSON teaches history at Conroe High School in Conroe, Texas.

KIM YOUNGHAUS is a graduate student at Sam Houston State University.